Official CompTIA Study Guide for Server+ (Exam SK0-004)

CompTIA.

Acknowledgements

CompTIA. **Official CompTIA Study Guide for Server+ (SK0-004)**

PROJECT TEAM

Thomas Reilly, Vice President Learning
Katie Hoenicke, Director of Product Management
James Chesterfield, Manager, Learning Content and Design
Becky Mann, Senior Manager, Product Development
James Pengelly, Courseware Manager
Rob Winchester, Senior Manager, Technical Operations

This page left blank intentionally.

Table of Contents

About This Course

This course is designed to prepare you to take the CompTIA Server+ SK0-004 exam. CompTIA Server+ is a foundation-level certificate for IT professionals with 18-24 months of experience, and whose job role is focused on server infrastructure.

> *This exam will certify that the successful candidate has the knowledge and skills required to build, maintain, troubleshoot, secure, and support server hardware and software technologies, including virtualization. The successful candidate will be able to identify environmental issues, understand and comply with disaster recovery and general security procedures, be familiar with industry terminology and concepts, and understand server roles and their interaction in a dynamic computing environment.*
>
> *CompTIA Server+ Exam Objectives Blueprint*

This course focuses on server hardware technologies and operating systems plus related storage and network systems and support procedures.

Course Outcomes

This course will teach you advanced-level technical competency of server issues and technology, including installation, configuration, upgrading, maintenance, environment, troubleshooting, and disaster recovery. It will prepare you to take the CompTIA Server+ SK0-004 exam by providing 100% coverage of the objectives and content examples listed on the syllabus.

On course completion, you will be able to:

- Install and upgrade server-class hardware.
- Install and configure server NOS and applications software.
- Configure RAID arrays.
- Use management and monitoring tools.
- Create disaster recovery plans.
- Troubleshoot hardware, storage, networking, and software issues.

Target Audience and Course Prerequisites

CompTIA Server+ certification is aimed at IT professionals with (or seeking) job roles such as Server Support Technician, Server Administrator, Application Server Administrator, and Storage Administrator.

It is recommended that you have the following skills and knowledge before starting this course:

- Taken and passed both CompTIA A+ Certification exams or have equivalent knowledge and experience.
- Six months to one year of post-A+ Certification support experience.
- Extensive experience of supporting end-users and PC-based systems.

About the Course Material

The CompTIA Server+ exams contain questions based on objectives and example content listed in the exam blueprint, published by CompTIA. The objectives for the SK00-004 exam are divided into seven **domains**, as listed below. Each domain has a **weighting**, indicating its relative importance in terms of questions in the exam:

CompTIA Server+ SK0-004 Domain Areas	Weighting
1.0 Server Architecture	12%
2.0 Server Administration	24%
3.0 Storage	12%
4.0 Security	13%
5.0 Networking	10%
6.0 Disaster Recovery	9%
7.0 Troubleshooting	20%

This course is divided into five **modules**, each covering a different subject area. Each module is organized into several **units**, containing related topics for study.

- Module 1 / Server Setup
- Module 2 / Server Networking
- Module 3 / Server Applications
- Module 4 / Server Maintenance
- Module 5 / Server Security

The modules in the course do not correspond directly to domains in the exam. Doing so would involve quite a lot of jumping around between different technologies. Instead, we try to cover topics in the most straightforward order for candidates at a foundation level to understand, starting with an overview of server installation followed by networking technology and application / service roles and then finishing with maintenance, troubleshooting, security, and disaster recovery. Each module starts with a list of the CompTIA domain objectives and content examples that will be covered in each unit.

Each unit in a module is focused on explaining the exam objectives and content examples. Each unit has a set of **review questions** designed to test your knowledge of the topics covered in the unit. Answers to the review questions are provided on the course support website. At the back of the book there is an **index** to help you look up key terms and concepts from the course and a **glossary** of terms and concepts used.

The following symbols are used to indicate different features in the course book:

Icon	Meaning
	A tip or warning about a feature or topic.
	A reference to another unit, where more information on a topic can be found.
	Review questions to help test what you have learned.

Making a Study Plan

If you are completing this course as self-study, you need to plan your study habits. The best way to approach the course initially is to *read through* the whole thing quite quickly. On this first reading, do not worry if you cannot recall facts, get two similar technologies mixed up, or do not completely understand some of the topics. The idea is to get an overview of everything you are going to need to know. The first reading shouldn't take you too long - a few hours is plenty of time. You don't have to do it at one sitting, but try to complete the read through within about a week.

When you have completed your first read through, you should make a **study plan**. For your study plan, keep in mind the following things:

- How much you know about server technologies *already*.
- How much *time* you have to study each day or each week.
- *When* you want to (or have to) become CompTIA Server+ Certified.

In your study plan, you'll identify how much time you want to spend on each unit and when you're going to sit down and do that study. We recommend that you study no more than one or two units per day. Studying a unit means reading it closely, making notes about things that come to mind as you read, using the glossary to look up terms you do not understand, then using the review questions to test and reinforce what you have learned.

Only you can decide how long you need to study for in total. Server+ Certification is supposed to represent the knowledge and skills of someone with 18-24 months of practical server support experience. If you cannot get that experience, you will need to do a corresponding amount of study to make up.

You also need to think about *where* you are going to study. You need to find somewhere comfortable and where you are not subject to interruptions or distractions. You will also need a computer or tablet with an Internet connection for the review and practical activities.

Preparing for the Exams

When you've completed reading the units in detail, you can start to prepare for the exam. The "Taking the Exams" chapter contains tips on booking the test, the format of the exam, and what to expect.

About CompTIA Certifications

It is CompTIA's policy to update the exam regularly with new test items to deter fraud and for compliance with ISO standards. The exam objectives may therefore describe the current "Edition" of the exam with a date different to that above. Please note that this training material remains valid for the stated exam code, regardless of the exam edition. For more information, please check the FAQs on CompTIA's website (support.comptia.org).

CompTIA Exam Vouchers

When you are ready to take your CompTIA A+ exam, visit comptiastore.com and purchase an exam voucher for CompTIA A+ exam.

Visit CompTIA online - www.comptia.org - to learn more about getting CompTIA certified. Contact CompTIA - call 866-835-8020 ext. 5 or email questions@comptia.org.

CompTIA Career Pathway

CompTIA offers a number of credentials that form a foundation for your career in technology and allow you to pursue specific areas of concentration. Depending on the path you choose to take, CompTIA certifications help you build upon your skills and knowledge, supporting learning throughout your entire career.

Study of the course can also help to prepare you for vendor-specific technical support qualifications and act as groundwork for more advanced training. Other qualifications available include:

- **CompTIA Network+** - a foundation-level certification of competency in network installation and configuration.

- **CompTIA Security+** - validates knowledge of communication security, infrastructure security, cryptography, operational security, and general security concepts.
- **Microsoft Certified Solutions Expert (MCSE)** - Windows-specific qualifications covering support and design of client and server infrastructure, as well as other Microsoft technologies. **Cisco Certified Network Associate (CCNA)** - a foundation-level certification of competency in Cisco networking appliance installation and configuration.

Module 1 / Server Setup

CompTIA Server+ SK0-004 Domain Areas	Weighting
1.0 Server Architecture	12%
2.0 Server Administration	24%
3.0 Storage	12%
4.0 Security	13%
5.0 Networking	10%
6.0 Disaster Recovery	9%
7.0 Troubleshooting	20%

The following table lists the CompTIA Server+ domain objectives and content examples covered in the units in this module:

Refer To	Domain Objectives/Examples
Unit 1.1 / Servers and Racks	**1.1 Explain the purpose and function of server form factors** *Rack mount (Dimensions [1U, 2U, 4U], Cable management arms, Rail kits) • Tower • Blade technology (Blade enclosure [Backplane / Midplane, Power supply sockets, Network modules / switches, Management modules], Blade server)*
	4.6 Given a scenario, implement proper environmental controls and techniques *Safety (Proper lifting techniques, Rack stability, Floor load limitations, Sharp edges and pinch points)*
Unit 1.2 / Storage Devices	**3.1 Given a scenario, install and deploy primary storage devices based on given specifications and interfaces** *Disk specifications (RPM, Dimensions / form factor, Capacity, Bus width, IOPS, Seek time and latency, Hot-swap vs. non-hot-swap components) • Interfaces (SAS, SATA, SCSI, USB) • Hard drive vs. SSD*
Unit 1.3 / RAID	**3.2 Given a scenario, configure RAID using best practices** *RAID levels and performance considerations (0, 1, 5, 6, 10) • Software vs. hardware RAID (Performance considerations) • Configuration specifications (Capacity, Bus types, Drive RPM) • Hot-swap support and ramifications • Hot spare vs. cold spare • Array controller (Memory, Battery backed cache, Redundant controller)*
Unit 1.4 / System Setup	**1.2 Given a scenario, install, configure and maintain server components** *BIOS / UEFI (CMOS battery) • Firmware*
	2.1 Install and configure server operating systems *Update firmware • BIOS / UEFI configuration (Boot order) • Disk preparation (RAID setup, Partitioning, Formatting, File system type [ext 2, 3, 4, NTFS, FAT32, ReiserFS, UFS, VMFS, ZFS], Swap)*

Refer To	Domain Objectives/Examples
Unit 1.5 / Server Operating Systems	**2.1 Install and configure server operating systems** *Determine server role / purpose • Configure host name • Local account setup • Connect to network • Install drivers • Performance baseline (Swap or pagefile optimization) • Unattended / remote installations (Deploying images and cloning, Scripted installs [PXE boot, TFTP])*
Unit 1.6 / Troubleshooting Procedures	**7.1 Explain troubleshooting theory and methodologies** *Identify the problem and determine the scope (Question users / stakeholders and identify changes to the server / environment, Collect additional documentation / logs, If possible, replicate the problem as appropriate, If possible, perform backups before making changes) • Establish a theory of probable cause / question the obvious (Determine whether there is a common element of symptom causing multiple problems) • Test the theory to determine cause (Once theory is confirmed, determine next steps to resolve problem, If theory is not confirmed, establish new theory or escalate) • Establish a plan of action to resolve the problem and notify impacted users • Implement the solution or escalate as appropriate (Make one change at a time and test / confirm the change has resolved the problem, If the problem is not resolved, reverse the change if appropriate and implement new change) • Verify full system functionality and if applicable implement preventive measures • Perform a root cause analysis • Document findings, actions and outcomes throughout the process*

Module 1 / Unit 1

Servers and Racks

Objectives

On completion of this unit, you will be able to:

- Distinguish between servers and desktops and workstations and know what is meant by fault tolerance, availability, scalability, and load balancing.
- Describe the features, advantages, and disadvantages of tower, rack, and blade servers.
- Describe the features and installation requirements of rack-mounted equipment.

Server Hardware and Software

A **server** is any computer providing services to other computers, but usually the term server implies a powerful computer that supports a number of users *simultaneously* (in a computer **network**).

The term "server" also means a software application that provides services to client applications. You will learn about examples of server applications later in the course.

Servers and Desktops

There is a distinction between server-class hardware and computers used as desktop PCs ("desktops") and workstations. A **desktop** PC is a low or medium spec machine provided to an end-user. "Desktop" in this sense doesn't refer to the desktop form factor case. Most home and office computers come in tower cases but can still be referred to as desktops.

Any desktop PC can act as a server, but when a computer is *designed* to act as a **server computer**, it will have a number of features that distinguish it from a desktop computer.

Some of the major manufacturers of PC servers include Hewlett-Packard (HP), Dell, Lenovo, IBM, Sun Microsystems, Fujitsu-Siemens, and Apple.

At the entry-level, server computers are not that much more expensive than desktops. Most businesses would require enterprise-class features however and these quickly increase the required budget. Some of the features that distinguish server-class hardware from regular desktop PCs are listed below.

High Availability and Fault Tolerance

It is a well-known maxim that time costs money. Any time that an organization's staff spend in the workplace without access to the computer system (**downtime**) is likely to be time wasted, and therefore a significant cost. If you calculate this cost based on the amount of time lost multiplied by employees' salaries, you can provide a cost-justification for upgrading server infrastructure to improve reliability.

Availability is not restricted to catastrophic crashes or complete system failures. A system that is slow is also costing time (and probably contributing to stress and low morale in the workplace).

Availability is also critical when providing an interface for customers. If a web server crashes or responds slowly, it makes the company look inefficient at best; at worst it makes the company invisible (a customer can switch to a competitor's site with a couple of mouse clicks).

Fault tolerance refers to a server's ability to keep serving even if something goes wrong.

Availability is provided through the robustness of computer components and by providing for **redundancy** in the system (additional components that take over in the event of failure or extra capacity that can be utilized in high load conditions). Where redundancy is provided, the component is said to be **n+1**, where *n* is the number of components in use and 1 is a spare to be used in the event of failure.

Another important feature is that as many configuration, maintenance, and repair operations as possible can take place without interrupting services (**hot-swappable** components for instance).

Load Balancing

Load balancing refers to distributing requests between multiple components. From the point-of-view of the client, there is only one resource.

In some configurations, having multiple components can provide load balancing *and* redundancy. If one of the components fails, the others can continue to provide the service, albeit at a reduced level of performance. Other load balancing configurations do not provide redundancy; if one component fails, the whole system goes down.

Scalability

Scalability means the ability to improve the performance of a server without diminishing its usefulness or increasing its cost disproportionately. A well-designed server is able to expand to meet the increased needs of its users. For example, if a company doubles its staff, it is likely to require about twice as much capacity from its server.

If components such as an additional processor and more memory and disk drives can be added to the existing server then the server could be said to be scalable. The system is no more difficult to manage than before and performing the upgrade will have entailed a minimum of downtime.

Contrast this with the circumstance in which a company had to buy a new server or an additional server. These solutions cannot be said to be scalable as they involve greater expense and complexity of administration.

Workstations

A **workstation** is a high-spec machine provided to "power users", such as designers or developers. A workstation may have some of the features associated with servers, such as multiple processors and redundant disks (RAID). A workstation may also be able to function productively as a server in a small workgroup (up to about 10 users). Workstations can also be provided through server-like infrastructure. For example, HP produce blade workstations accessed remotely via client PCs. The main difference between such a workstation and a server is that the workstation is likely to have a high-performance graphics adapter. Servers only require basic graphics functionality while workstations used in design and creative industries need to be able to handle 3D and texture processing.

Server Roles

While "server" can refer to the computer hardware, the term also refers to software. Server software can broadly be divided into Network Operating System server platform and server applications software.

Server Platform

The **server platform** is the underlying Network Operating System (NOS). This will usually be a version of Windows Server or some "flavor" of Linux.

The server platform is likely to include a number of basic roles enabling the server to provide local and remote user authentication, network services (routing, DHCP, and DNS), file and printer sharing, and web, FTP, and email.

The current trend is for virtualized server platforms. This means that a single hardware server, installed with a virtual machine manager or hypervisor, hosts multiple OS platforms. These multiple instances or VMs could all be running similar services (web servers for instance) or different types of application.

Web Hosting

Running web services is one of the most common server roles. As mentioned above, any server platform can host a basic website but web services are very often provisioned on a larger scale.

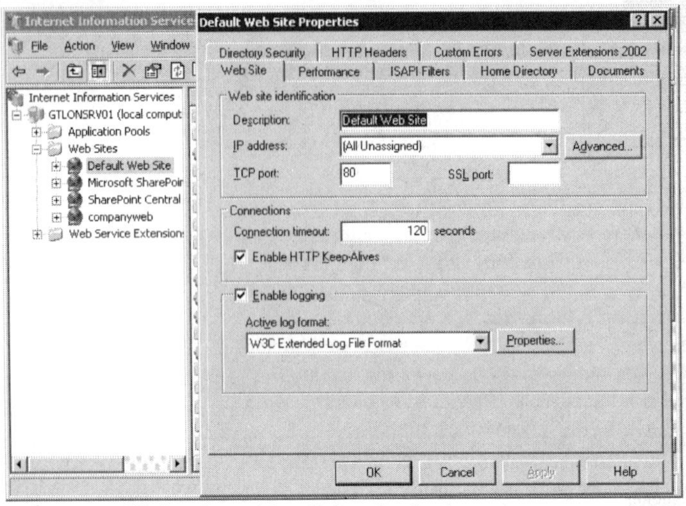

Windows Server Internet Information Services web server

Internet Service Providers (ISPs) operate huge web server farms to provide web hosting services to subscribers. Enterprise websites are also backed up by multiple servers for load balancing and availability.

Messaging, Groupware, and Collaboration

Messaging servers provide services such as email, Voice over IP (VoIP), Instant Messaging (IM), and web conferencing. The same machines may also run "groupware" services, allowing users to arrange meetings and collaborate on projects and documents.

Media / Streaming

Servers designed to serve audio and video files to large numbers of users are often provisioned as dedicated hardware, separated from the web server(s) to improve performance and availability.

Application, Database, and Middleware

A client-server application can be designed for any sort of business function (Customer Relationship Management [CRM] and accounting are typical examples). These applications often feature split front- and back-end servers. The front-end servers host the user interface while the back-end servers host the database. There may also be "middle" tiers supporting functions such as business logic and data queries.

Small Business

Enterprise networks run multiple server applications on multiple server machines, physical and virtual. Small and Medium Size Enterprises (SME) may use "one-box" solutions where, as well as the underlying OS platform, the same server provides network services such as DHCP and DNS, messaging and calendaring, and routing, remote access, and firewall services.

Server Form Factors

A server's **form factor** is the type of case it uses.

Tower Servers

A **tower** server uses the same sort of case as a PC. Often the case is substantially larger and the design gives more thought to providing airflow through the case, improving cooling. The tower form factor allows flexibility in terms of placement and is the cheapest option.

Tower servers are available in a wide range of models, allowing for different budgets and requirements. They are also usually the easiest machines to customize and upgrade.

HP full tower server

A tower server is a good option if only a few servers need to be stored. However, when the server equipment needs to be integrated with network equipment or where an organization needs to be able to grow processing power rapidly and effectively, a rack-mounted solution is required.

Rack-mounted Servers

Rack servers are designed to bolt into racks. They are built to fit within a standard width (19" / 48.26cm) and height. The height of the case will be a multiple of 1.75" / 4.45cm called a U. Typically, servers are one of 1U, 2U, or 4U in height.

Rack servers look somewhat similar to the old desktop form factor PCs, but are *not* designed to be placed free-standing on a desk.

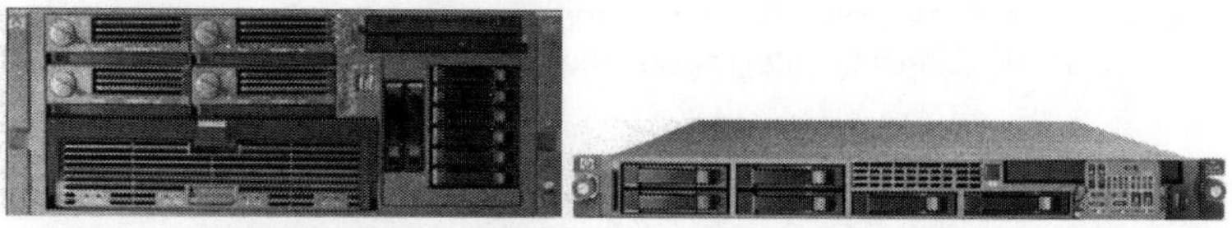

HP Proliant 4U (left) and 1U (right) rack-mounted servers

Rack servers can be far more compact than tower servers, but contain the same components. Each server has its own cooling solution.

The cost of buying rack equipment makes rack-mounted servers seem a more expensive option than tower servers, but these costs can be offset by the greater security and manageability of rack-mounted equipment. Rack-mounted equipment also allows the server array to grow more easily.

Racks are said to offer density, as units can be stacked vertically as well as horizontally.

Blade Servers

A **blade server** is a space-saving variation of a rack server. The power and cooling systems are not incorporated within the server unit. Instead, servers are housed in thin cases installed together in an **enclosure**, like books in a book case. Each enclosure shares a common power and cooling system and also I/O and network ports.

HP Proliant blade server (front view) and enclosure (back view)

Blade servers offer the best density of any server form factor. A rack that can fit 42 1U servers could fit 60 blade servers. The individual server units are usually fairly low cost (though not as cheap as similarly specified 1U rack servers), allowing the organization to grow capacity organically.

An extra consideration is the overall power consumption of the rack, especially as energy prices are likely to continue to rise. With shared power and cooling, blade servers are typically more efficient than ordinary rack-mounted servers. Also, cable management is significantly easier.

One problem with blade servers is the lack of standards. Machines from different manufacturers (IBM, HP, and Dell) cannot be integrated in the same chassis.

The management software offered with the solution also needs to be evaluated carefully, as it has a strong impact on the usability of the server array. Blade servers are ideal for supporting server clusters. Often servers can be hot-swapped out of the array, allowing for fault tolerance and redundancy.

Organizations considering a solution would need to make a careful comparison of the costs and benefits of blade servers versus the 1U equivalent.

Blade Enclosures

Modern blade enclosures are designed to incorporate modules other than servers. They are designed to integrate servers closely with networking, storage, and power functions. In these designs, the internal wiring and components that connect the individual blades are usually split between two separate circuit boards or "planes":

- **Midplane** - supports the interconnections that connect server blades to networking and shared storage functions. The midplane provides a number of lanes to each interconnect module, with each lane comprising a number of wires (or traces). The lanes facilitate point-to-point links between device bays and interconnect modules or between device bays directly. The midplane will support very high bandwidths. For example, HP's c7000 enclosure system has a midplane capable of 7 terabits per second throughput.
- **Backplane** - shares the power available from the redundant power supply modules installed in the enclosure between the blades. Separating the power circuitry from the interconnect circuitry improves performance and reliability. The backplane will also host the **power supply sockets** to connect to an electrical supply circuit. This allows the power supply modules to be hot-swappable. For redundancy, the backplane might be connected to two (or more) separate supply circuits.

As mentioned, the type of blades used is not restricted to server appliances:

- **Network modules / switches** - interconnects supporting different I/O, networking, and Storage Area Network (SAN) technologies, such as PCI Express, Serial Attached SCSI (SAS), Ethernet, Fibre Channel, and iSCSI. The midplane circuitry is "passive"; that is, it has no signal-processing logic. The hard-wired traces on the interconnect and device bay connectors can be mapped to different I/O, network, and storage ports on the blade device.
- **I/O modules** - blade servers do not have room for expansion cards. Instead, expansion adapters are installed as separate blades then linked to servers over the midplane crosslinks.
- **Management modules** - most enclosures will come with an integrated module for configuring, managing, monitoring. Additional blade modules might be used for redundancy, for Keyboard, Video, Mouse (KVM) connectivity, or for devices such as Uninterruptible Power Supplies (UPS).
- **Power supply modules** - multiple power supplies are critical for ensuring that the blades have sufficient overall power and that there is redundancy in the case of power failure. As mentioned above, the supplies plug into a backplane that distributes power to the blade devices.
- **Fan modules** - as with any computer system, cooling is essential so that the components within the enclosure do not suffer errors or damage due to overheating.

The slots in the enclosure may be designed to take a mixture of full and half-height blade modules, giving the system designer a great deal of choice in selecting appropriate components.

Rack Systems

A **rack** is a specially configured steel shelving system for server and network equipment. Using a rack allows equipment to be stored more securely and compactly than ordinary desks or shelving would allow for.

Rack Specifications

HP rack for blade server enclosures

Rack server or blade enclosures and network equipment are EIA standard width (19" / 48.26cm), allowing them to be screwed into the rack directly. Non-standard components, such as a tower server or monitor, can be installed on shelves.

Racks can be purchased with varying depths (from 30-40" / 76.2-101.6cm) and heights. Rack height is measured in EIA units of 1.75" / 4.45cm called U. Racks are sold in heights from 8U to 48U. Rack-compatible equipment is designed with a vertical height quoted in U so you can plan exactly how much vertical space you require.

Racks have a maximum overall weight capacity. Rack accessories such as shelves will also have a maximum weight capacity.

Most racks are designed to be free-standing, though smaller wall-mounted cabinet units are also available. Free-standing racks can be bolted together in rows.

It is possible to obtain racks that are dust and water-resistant, which can be useful for highly-sensitive equipment or where there is the risk of flood (though such racks are water-resistant, not water-proof).

Racks can be purchased direct from the major server vendors or from third parties. Third-party racks are sometimes designed for a specific vendor's equipment. Many vendors have online specification tools which you can use to build a complete network solution (including the important question of what color it should be).

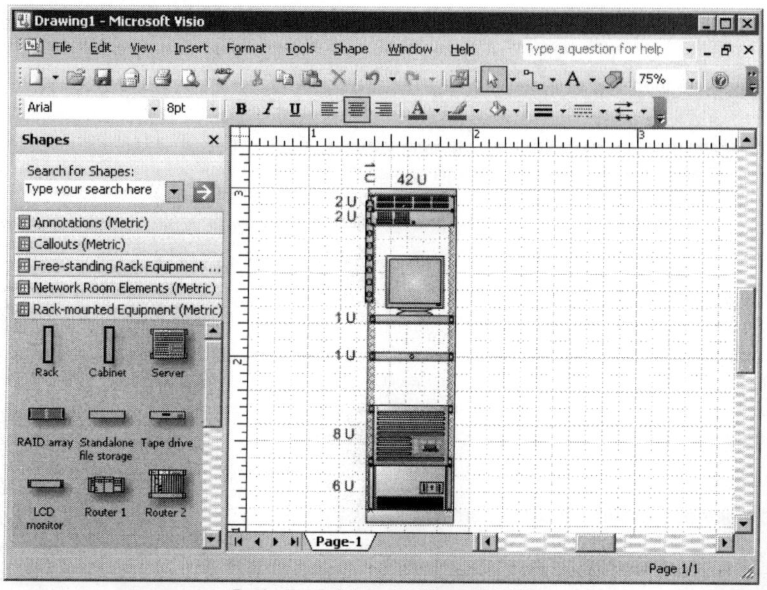

Designing rack layout in Microsoft Visio

Rack Accessories

A number of accessories are available to make the basic rack configuration fit different requirements.

Shelving and Rails

If there is little need to remove it for upgrades or maintenance, an appliance can be screwed directly into the rack. Devices are often mounted on rail kits however so that they can be slid out of the rack for configuration. Other equipment can be mounted on shelves, sliding or otherwise.

Doors and Panels

Side panels and banking plates (to cover unused slots) are used to improve airflow. Lockable doors (front and rear) obviously help to prevent access to the equipment.

Server cooling works on the basis of cold air through the front and warm air out the back. Energy is wasted if the warm air is allowed to contaminate the cool air. See Unit 4.2 for more information about environment and cooling.

Stabilizers

Some racks can be wheel mounted; others require stabilization or leveling. It is also possible to add ballast; weight to balance a rack where the weight of devices in the rack cannot be distributed evenly.

Cable Management

Keep cables tidy within the rack using arm brackets and ties, taking care not to pinch the cabling too tightly. Do not allow cables to hang in front of devices; make sure the cabling is led to one side of the rack. **Cable trays** can be used to channel cabling from and between racks. A cable tray is usually made of metal, with holes for ventilation. They provide easier access to cables than conduits.

Rack Installation and Safety

The first step is to place the racks in the correct location in the server room. Multiple rows should be placed back-to-back not front-to-back to maximize cooling and there should be about 3 feet (1 meter) clearance (for service access and airflow).

If necessary, bolt the racks together and check that they are stable, adjusting leveling bolts if necessary.

Generally speaking, large and heavy items should be placed lower in the rack. Weight distribution is probably the main factor in determining where an item should be placed in the rack, but also consider the following:

- Try not to place backup tape drives and network cabling near UPS, which can generate EMI (though the risk of data corruption is low, except with the most powerful UPS). Electromagnetic Interference (EMI) is interference in one electromagnetic device caused by the radiation generated by another.
- A KVM (Keyboard, Video, Mouse) console will obviously need to be positioned at standing height.

Use a numbering system to identify the servers to KVM port switch buttons and position the servers in number order (top-to-bottom and left-to-right). Incorporate the number into the server's desktop wallpaper so that it is easy to see which server is being controlled at any one time.

- Check cable lengths and plan ahead for any devices that need to be connected, as removing and re-inserting equipment is time-consuming. Keep cables tidy using brackets and ties. Do not allow cables to hang in front of devices.

- Check that equipment on pull-out rails does not cause the rack to tip. If there is any sign of instability, add ballast to compensate. Also check that pulling the tray out does not dislodge any connectors. Leave enough slack in the cable for an item to be pulled out along the length of its rail.

Never pull out more than one item at a time.

Personal Safety and Lifting Techniques

A **trip hazard** is caused by putting any object in pathways where people walk. When installing equipment, ensure that cabling is secured, using cable ties or **cable management** products if necessary.

Be careful about moving heavy or bulky equipment. To lift a heavy object safely, plant your feet around the object with one foot slightly toward the direction in which you are going to move. Bend your knees to reach the object while keeping your back as straight as is possible and comfortable and your chin up. Find a firm grip on the object then lift smoothly by straightening your legs - do not jerk the object up.

Carry the object while keeping your back straight. To lower an object, reverse the lifting process; keep your chin up and bend at the knees. Beware of **pinch points** - take care not to trap your fingers or to lower the object onto your feet. Also ensure you are placing the object where it cannot fall or topple.

If you cannot lift an object because it is too awkward or heavy, get help. It may be necessary to use special equipment, such as a jack or lift, to raise a heavy object to the required height (for insertion at a particular point in rack for instance). If you need to carry an object for some distance, make sure that the route is unobstructed and that the pathway (including stairs or doorways) is wide and tall enough.

Lifting a heavy object in the wrong way can damage your back, but lifting and manual handling risks are not limited to particularly heavy objects. An object that is large or awkward to carry could cause you to trip over or walk into something else. An object that has sharp or rough edges or contains a hot or corrosive liquid could cause you to cut or hurt yourself. If necessary, you should obtain protective clothing (gloves and possibly goggles).

Floor Load Limitations

As well as the weight distribution and stability of each individual rack, you also need to consider the overall weight of the rack installation and whether the total load can be supported by the floor. Most data centers do not use solid flooring but have raised tiles under which there will be conduit for cabling and ventilation systems. You need to calculate the maximum load for both the floor substrate and the raised floor tiles. Load is calculated in pounds (lbs) or kilos per square foot. You cannot risk exceeding the maximum floor load limitation; you would need to sacrifice some density to spread the load over a larger area.

Review Questions / Module 1 / Unit 1 / Servers and Racks

Answer these questions to test what you have learned in this unit.

1) Apart from fault tolerance and scalability, what general feature distinguishes server-class systems from desktop PCs?
2) What is the advantage of rack-mounted or blade servers over the tower form factor?
3) Which circuit board supports data interconnections between modules in a blade enclosure?
4) What is the minimum height of a server designed to fit into a standard rack system?
5) When installing equipment into racks, what general guidelines should you try to follow?
6) While putting a heavy object down, you are being careful not to put stress on your back. What two other factors should you be thinking about?

Module 1 / Unit 2

Storage Devices

Objectives

On completion of this unit, you will be able to:

- Describe the features and performance characteristics of server-class hard disks and solid state drives.
- Describe features of the SCSI interface and know how to configure devices correctly.
- Describe features of the SATA and SAS interfaces and know how to configure devices correctly.

Mass Storage Drives

Like a desktop PC, a server will be configured with one or more mass storage devices to store the operating system and applications software. Disk space may also be provided on a file server as a shared resource for network users.

Unlike most desktop PCs however, server disks will typically be faster for higher performance and add resilience features such as RAID - the ability for multiple hard disks to work together to increase access speed to files or provide redundancy in case one of the drives fails.

All new servers use disk interfaces based on either Serial Attached SCSI (SAS) or Serial Advanced Technology Attachment (SATA). Some older servers may be configured with parallel SCSI interfaces.

Drives are available in several sizes. Most hard drives are 3.5" or 2.5" width (the width refers to the size of the drive bay rather than the disk unit). 2.5" now dominates the market, with 3.5" drives gradually being phased out. Internal optical and tape drive units often use the larger 5.25" form factor. There is also a distinction between half height and low profile units.

Hard Disk Drives (HDD)

Most hard disks are of the mechanical type (HDD). Data is stored on a number of metal or glass platters coated with a magnetic substance. The top and bottom of each platter is accessed by its own read/write head, moved by an actuator mechanism.

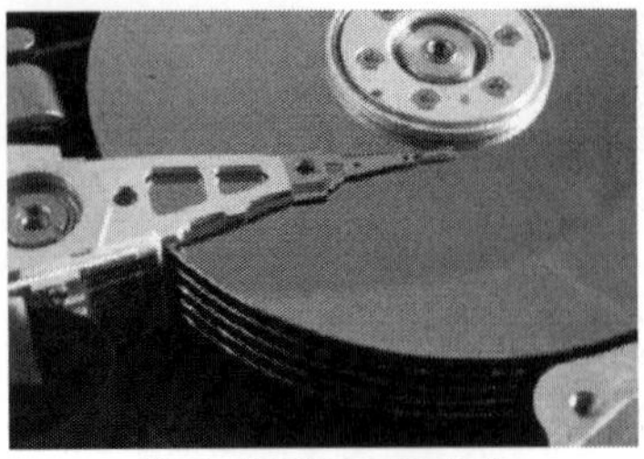
Stack of platters on spindle

The heads do not actually touch the surface of the platters. The platters are mounted on a spindle and spun at high speed and the heads "float" above them at a distance of less than a millionth of an inch. The disk unit is kept sealed to maintain a constant air pressure (important for keeping the drive heads at the correct distance from the platters) and to prevent the entry of dust.

Each side of each platter is divided into circular **tracks** and each track contains a number of **sectors**, each with a capacity of 512 bytes. The collection of tracks in the same place on each platter is called a **cylinder**. This low-level formatting is also referred to as the drive *geometry*.

As hard drive sizes have increased, some disk models now use ***Advanced Format****, with 4 kilobyte (4K) sector sizes. If supported by the OS and PC firmware, these can be used in native mode; if not, the drive controller will usually present the disk in 512 emulated (512e) mode.*

The performance of a hard disk is a measure of how fast it can read and write data. There are a number of factors that determine overall hard disk performance. One factor is the speed at which the disks can spin (measured in **Revolutions Per Minute [rpm]**). The higher the rpm, the faster the drive is. High performance drives are rated at 15,000 or 10,000 rpm; average performance is 7200 or 5400 rpm.

RPM is one factor determining **access time** (measured in milliseconds), which is the delay that occurs as the read/write head locates a particular track position (**seek time**) and sector location (**rotational latency**) on the drive. A high performance drive will have an access time below 3 ms; a typical drive might have an access time of around 6 ms.

The **internal transfer rate** (or data or disk transfer rate) of a drive is a measure of how fast read/write operations are performed on the disk platters. A 15K drive should support an internal transfer rate of up to about 180 MBps while 7.2K drives will be around 110 MBps. The **external transfer rate** (often simply described as the transfer rate) measures how fast data can be transferred to the CPU across the bus. Cache memory can help to sustain better transfer rates. A high performance disk may feature an 8 MB or better cache.

The last, but by no means least, characteristic of a hard drive is its capacity. Advances in hard disk technology have enabled disks of up to 8 terabytes (8000 GB) to be produced but often smaller capacities are used because they offer better reliability and redundancy (as part of an array).

Enclosures and Backplanes

A drive is housed in an enclosure or caddy. The drive may then be connected to the host bus adapter via a cable but on enterprise-class servers it is more usual for the enclosures to be connected via a **backplane**. Rather than using cabled connectors, the drives plug (or "mate") into a combined data and power port on the enclosure. This means that drives can be easily added and removed from the front of the case without having to open the chassis.

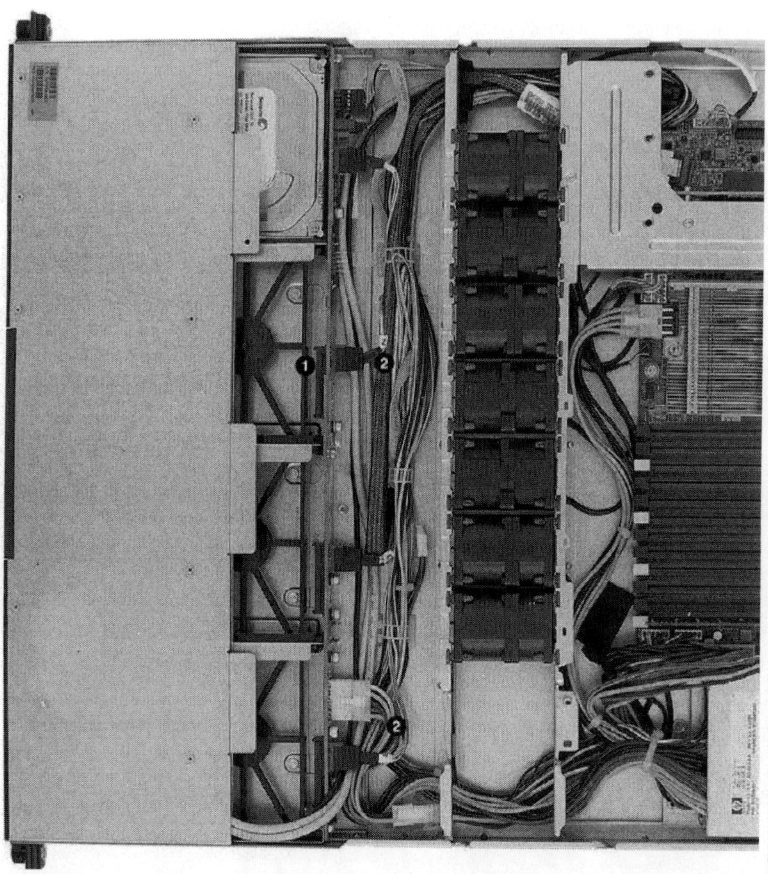

Enclosure and backplane on an HP server - 1) The drive mates with the port on the backplane card; 2) Data and power cables on the other side of the backplane card connect to the drive port and PSU

The drives are secured and released from the server using a latch. Many server drives are hot-swappable, meaning that they can be added or removed without powering down the server.

The SCSI Interface

The **Small Computer System Interface (SCSI)** has been in use as an expansion bus interface since the 1980s. There have been many revisions to the standard. Originally a parallel interface, SCSI is now used for serial connections for disk drives (Serial Attached SCSI) and peripheral devices (Firewire or IEEE 1394).

More information about SCSI can be located on the T10 Committee website (www.t10.org) and from the SCSI Trade Association (www.scsita.org).

Parallel SCSI Standards

The original iterations of the SCSI standards defined a parallel bus, originally 8 bits wide but later updated to 16 bits (wide SCSI). As a parallel interface, SCSI is more-or-less obsolete but the main iterations are listed below:

Interface	Devices (Excluding Host Adapter)	Rate	Max Cable Length (m)			Connector
			SE	LVD	HVD	
SCSI-1	7	5 MBps	6	-	25	50-pin
Fast SCSI	7	10 MBps	3	-	25	50-pin
Fast-Wide SCSI	15	20 MBps	3	-	25	68-pin
Ultra SCSI	7	20 MBps	1.5	-	25	50-pin
Wide Ultra SCSI	15	40 MBps	-	-	25	68-pin
Ultra2 SCSI	7	40 MBps	-	12	25	50-pin
Wide Ultra2 SCSI	15	80 MBps	-	12	25	68-pin / 80-pin
Ultra3 SCSI (Ultra160 SCSI)	15	160 MBps	-	12	-	68-pin / 80-pin
Ultra320 SCSI	15	320 MBps	-	12	-	68-pin / 80-pin
Ultra640 SCSI	15	640 MBps	-	12	-	68-pin / 80-pin

The number of devices listed in the table excludes *the host adapter. So for example, narrow SCSI supports 8 devices including the host adapter and wide SCSI supports 16.*

Parallel SCSI Configuration Issues

Given the number of different versions of the standard, SCSI configuration is relatively complex.

- **Host adapter** - the SCSI host adapter must be installed and recognized by the system for devices to be attached and detected. A third-party driver might have to be installed for the host adapter to be recognized.

- **Bus width** - SCSI originally supported 8 devices (the host adapter counts as a device). Wide SCSI supports up to 16 devices.

- **Signaling** - SCSI specifies three signaling methods. Most buses and devices now use LVD (Low Voltage Differential). SE (Single Ended) devices can be added to a LVD bus, but it reduces the performance of the whole bus. H(igh)VD is incompatible with the other two and must not be mixed.

- **Termination** - a SCSI bus must be terminated at both ends, usually by enabling termination on the first and last devices in the chain. Termination may either be enabled internally on the device by setting a switch or by physically connecting a terminator pack to a device or the host adapter. There are passive and active terminators. Passive terminators are generally used with older devices (pre-Ultra SCSI). When installing a terminator pack, the terminator must match the signaling type (SE, LVD, HVD, or SE/LVD). Termination is also made more complex if there is a mix of narrow (8-bit) and wide (16-bit) devices on the bus.

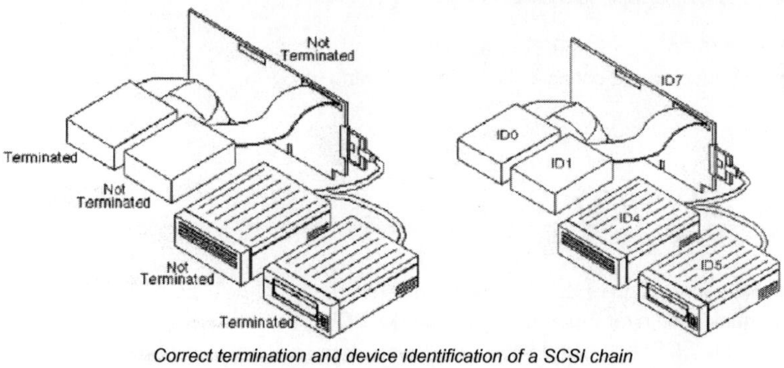

Correct termination and device identification of a SCSI chain

- **ID** - each SCSI device must be allocated a unique ID, from 0 to 7 (or 15 for wide SCSI). IDs may be allocated automatically or by setting a jumper or click-wheel on the device itself. The order of SCSI ID priorities (from highest to lowest) is 7 through to 0 then 15 through to 8.

The host adapter is usually set to 7 or 15. A bootable hard disk is usually allocated ID 0.

- **Logical Unit Number (LUN)** - some parallel SCSI devices can perform more than one function (an auto-loading tape drive for instance). In this case, each function must be allocated a **Logical Unit Number (LUN)** from 0 to 7 or 0 to 15. This is normally assigned by the manufacturer.

Longer (64-bit) LUNs are also used in Storage Area Networks (SAN) based on Fiber Channel or iSCSI. See Unit 3.2 for more information about SANs.

Parallel SCSI Connectors

A SCSI port is denoted by the following symbol: . There are numerous SCSI connectors. The most common are:

- IDC50 - a 50-pin internal connector used with early SCSI devices (SCSI-1).
- CN50 - a 50-pin Centronics-style connector used for external connections in early SCSI devices.
- HD68 - 68-pin connectors used for internal and external ports. 68-pin adapters support Wide SCSI.

Internal (left) and external male HD connectors

- Single Connector Attachment (SCA) - an 80-pin connector that incorporates both a power connector and configuration wires, allowing for hot swappable drives.

Serial Attached SCSI (SAS)

Serial Attached SCSI is the next generation of SCSI interface. It uses a serial interface with full-duplex communication over 2-pair wiring (much like PCI Express) but retains support for the SCSI command set.

SAS components can be rated at 3 Gbps (SAS-1), 6 Gbps (SAS-2), or 12 Gbps (SAS-3).

A significant feature of SAS is support for *thousands* of devices (up to 16,384), using an Ethernet switch-like device called an **expander**. Each device is identified by a unique, manufacturer-coded ID, so there is no manual configuration to be performed. Also, SAS does not require termination, removing another complex configuration issue.

SAS also goes some way to uniting the SATA and SCSI standards. It provides both hardware support (the same connectors and cable) and software support (through the SATA Tunneling Protocol) for SATA drives. This offers the opportunity to mix low-cost SATA drives with high-cost, high-performance SAS drives in an integrated storage solution.

Serial Attached SCSI Installation

SAS devices feature a combined 7-pin data port and 15-pin power port (though some drives may also have a legacy 4-pin Molex power port too). In fact, on most SAS devices there are two data connectors (for redundancy). This is referred to as "dual-port". Obviously the backplane or cable must also support a redundant connection for this to work.

SAS connections are typically either single-lane (a simple adapter to device connection) or multi-lane (a single port on the adapter is connected to four devices).

Ports can either be "straight-through" or flush / surface mounted with right-angle connectors. Flush-mounted fittings are used in blade servers and other systems with restricted space. SAS backplane connectors are designed to "blind-mate", which means that a connection is made reliably when a drive caddy is inserted into a backplane. The design of the pins also reduces the chance of damage through ESD or a power spike (the full power pins connect after the other pins).

Hot-pluggable drives are not screwed into the chassis but slot into a drive cage. The cables for the devices connect to the drive cage (backplane) rather than the drive units.

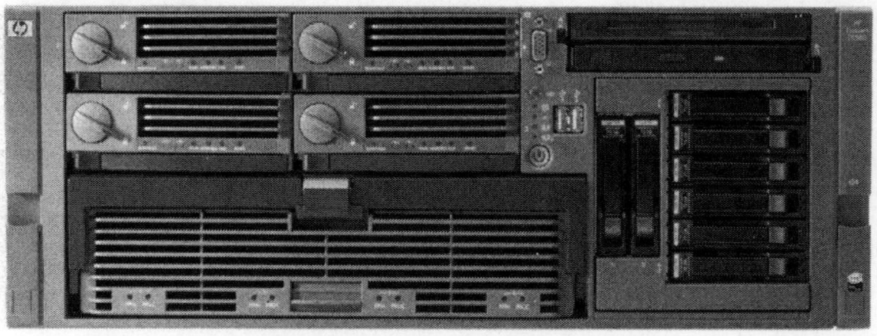

Hot-pluggable drives on HP Proliant server

When removing a drive, you will probably need to use a utility or the OS to stop the device. This completes any cached write operations and prevents the NOS from trying to write data to the device while it is being removed. You also need to power down the device, either using software or a switch on the drive bay. Indicators on the drive bay should show when a drive is safe to remove. The drives are physically released and inserted using a lever or latch mechanism.

Unused drive slots should be filled with blanks to maintain the correct airflow and cooling within the chassis.

Serial Attached SCSI Connectors

A number of connectors are associated with the use of SAS host adapters and drives:

- SFF 8087 - internal mini connector for both adapter card ("host") and drive or backplane ports ("target").
- SFF 8088 - external mini connector for both adapter card and drive enclosures.
- SFF 8484 ("Multilane") - legacy 32-pin internal or external HD connector (host) supporting four 7-pin lanes (target). The remaining pins are used for "sideband" signals (LEDs and status monitoring).
- SFF 8470 ("Infiniband") - legacy jackscrew connector for both internal and external use.
- SFF 8482 - internal connector compatible with both SAS and SATA drives. This type of connector would be used principally to attach SATA devices (such as DVD drives) to an SAS bus.

The Serial ATA Interface

Serial ATA (SATA) was developed to address the limitations of the now obsolete parallel ATA or IDE interface. SATA would be used on low-end server hardware as a cheaper option than SAS.

4 SATA motherboard ports in front of an IDE port on an Intel motherboard

As the name suggests, SATA transfers data in *serial* format. This allows for thinner, longer, more flexible cables (up to 1m [39"]) with smaller, 7-pin data connectors. Each port supports a single device.

SATA cable for HP workstations

The first commercially available SATA standard supports speeds of up to 1.5 Gbps. This standard was quickly augmented by SATA revision 2 (3 Gbps) and then SATA revision 3 (6 Gbps). Another key advantage of SATA over PATA is that SATA is a **hot swappable** interface. This means that a compatible drive can be connected or disconnected while the system is running.

Other additions in SATA revision 2 include the use of port multipliers, which allow up to 15 drives to be connected to a single SATA adapter, and **Native Command Queuing (NCQ)**, which enables the drive to analyze read/write operations and perform them in the most efficient manner, depending on the location of data on the disk

SATA revision 3 adds some extensions to NCQ to support isochronous data transfer (prioritizing real time data such as video to ensure smooth playback). SATA revisions 3.1 and 3.2 add better support for Solid State Drives (SSD).

More information on SATA standards can be obtained from www.sata-io.org.

Hot Swapping

One of the major advantages of SATA over PATA is the support for hot swapping and consequently better compatibility with RAID configurations. Serial ATA 15-pin power connectors have been redesigned to provide support for both hot plugging and a 3.3V power supply in addition to the usual 5V and 12V.

Many drives retain a 4-pin Molex port for compatibility with legacy power supplies). Molex-SATA conversion adapters are also available.

SATA power connector

SATA and SAS

As mentioned earlier, SAS includes hardware and software support for SATA devices. The reverse is not true however; SAS devices *cannot* be plugged into a SATA bus.

Solid State Drives (SSD)

Recently, flash memory based drives (**Solid State Drives [SSD]**) have been introduced to the market.

There are broadly two types of SSD: Single Layer Cell (SLC) and Multi Layer Cell (MLC). SLC stores 1 bit per cell while MLC stores 4 or more bits per cell, yielding higher capacities at lower cost. MLC can be slower however as it requires substantial error correction processing. It is also perceived as not reliable enough for enterprise server applications as it supports fewer write cycles, though improvements in the technology (enterprise-grade eMLC technology for instance) may change that perception over time.

HP SSD with SATA interface (Image © 2014 Hewlett-Packard Development Company)

The advantages of flash memory-based SSDs are that the lack of moving parts makes them quieter, more power efficient, and less prone to catastrophic failure or damage due to shock (dropping or moving a device rapidly for instance). Read times are better because seek time and consequently the effect of file fragmentation is eliminated. They are also less susceptible to data loss in the event of power failure. Most drives still feature DRAM-based write cache to improve performance. In the event of a power failure, unwritten cache would be lost. However, the DRAM cache may be backed up by a battery to cover this eventuality.

The main disadvantage is the high cost; a *64 GB* SSD costs a bit more than a *2 TB* HDD (a 1 TB SSD can cost the same as a top-end server).

SSD Interfaces

An SSD might be installed as the server's only internal drive. The SSD would normally be used to install the OS and software applications while a disk array or other shared storage would be used for data files.

An SSD might be installed to an SAS or SATA port as with a mechanical HDD. SSDs are now often provided as PCIe adapter Add In Cards (AIC) though, taking advantage of the higher bandwidths available from a native PCIe interface. Where SAS uses SCSI and SATA uses the **Advanced Host Controller Interface (AHCI)** to communicate with the bus, PCIe-based SSDs use the **Non-Volatile Memory Host Controller Interface Specification (NVMHCI)** or **NVM Express (NVMe)** for short. One of the big advantages of NVMe over SCSI and AHCI is support for much longer command queues (64,000 versus 64 in SCSI).

An SSD can also be packaged as a 2.5" drive and connect to an NVMe controller via a SFF 8639 / U.2 port.

SSD Performance

SSDs normally outperform HDDs but there are situations where they can perform worse than HDDs, when serving large (GB) files for example.

When making a detailed comparison between different types of storage technology, you need to compare performance against different types of data transfer. For example, read and write performance are not equivalent. There are also differences between sequential access (reading data from the same "block" as might happen when transferring a large file) and random access (reading data from different locations on the drive or transferring lots of small files for instance). Along with the data throughput (measured in Mbps) and latency / access time, you may need to consider the number of **Input / Output Operations per Second (IOPS)** that can be achieved by a device for different kinds of data transfer operation.

Flash chips are also susceptible to their own type of degradation over the course of many write operations, so the drive firmware and operating system must use **wear leveling** routines to prevent any single storage location from being overused and optimize the life of the device.

Review Questions / Module 1 / Unit 2 / Storage Devices

Answer these questions to test what you have learned in this unit.

1) True or false? LFF and SFF represent two different fixed drive technologies?

2) What two mechanical factors affect hard disk access times?

3) How would you expect hot-pluggable drives to be attached to a server?

4) What type of SCSI hard disk subsystem would you expect to be provisioned on a new server - SAS or Ultra320?

5) What are the main issues to consider when configuring a parallel SCSI bus?

6) True or false? SATA and SAS use compatible connectors.

7) What is the principal factor reducing the operational life of SSDs and what process is used to mitigate it?

8) You need to configure servers to cache files for a content delivery network. What type of storage technology is best suited to this task?

Module 1 / Unit 3

RAID

Objectives

On completion of this unit, you will be able to:

- Select an appropriate RAID level for a given storage solution.
- Configure a RAID array using software or hardware.

Drive Arrays (RAID)

With **RAID** (**Redundant Array of Independent Disks**), multiple physical disks can be grouped into a single logical volume. Usually, this is done to improve **fault tolerance**; if a physical drive fails, the logical volume is protected by the data stored on the other physical drives in the array.

RAID can also be said to stand for "Redundant Array of Inexpensive Disks" and the "D" can also stand for "devices".

The RAID advisory board defines RAID levels. The most common levels are numbered from 0 to 6, where each level corresponds to a specific type of fault tolerance. There are also proprietary RAID solutions.

RAID Level	Fault Tolerance
Level 0	Striping without parity (*no* fault tolerance)
Level 1	Mirroring / duplexing
Level 2	Striping with ECC (Error Correction Code)
Level 3	Striping with a dedicated parity disk
Level 4	Independent data disks with shared parity disk
Level 5	Independent data disks with distributed parity blocks (striping with parity)
Level 6	Second parity

In addition to these primary levels, it is also possible to "nest" one RAID solution within another (for example, you could mirror two stripe sets to boost performance without sacrificing fault tolerance).

RAID Performance

To choose an optimum RAID solution, you need to balance the server role with factors such as cost, performance, and security. Higher RAID levels usually require more costly controllers.

Security is a measure of the number of drive failures that an array can support. Performance involves a number of different factors but the most important to assess are probably the balance between read and write operations and between transactional and sequential Input / Output (I/O):

- Read / write balance - depending on the server role, disk activity may be predominantly reads or writes (for example, 80% reads and 20% writes). Some RAID levels have better read performance and some have better write performance.
- Sequential versus transactional (or random) I/O - this refers to how data on the volume is typically accessed. Sequential I/O means reading or writing data at the same physical location; transactional (or random) I/O means the controller has to scan different areas of the disk or array to retrieve or write the data. In terms of database applications, transactional I/O is associated with adding and updating records while sequential I/O is more typical of querying data for reports or serving large files. The OS and user file access is also typically transactional but a media server would use predominantly sequential I/O.

RAID 0 (Striping Without Parity)

Disk striping is a technique where data is divided into blocks and spread in a fixed order among all the disks in the array. The block **stripe size** is often 64K but can be configured to an optimum value between 2K and 512K based on the size of the array and the type of data served (in much the same way as a cluster size can be chosen for a volume file system).

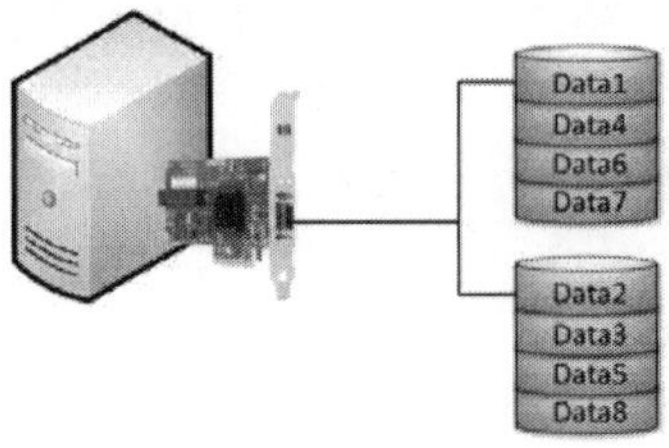

RAID 0 (striping) - data is spread across the array

RAID 0 requires at least two disks. Its principal advantage is to improve performance by spreading disk I/O over multiple drives. As disk reads and writes can take place on multiple disks simultaneously, the effects of seek time and latency are reduced. The number of physical disks used in the array sets the **stripe width**; using more disks (greater width) should benefit performance. Also, the best performance is obtained when each disk has its own controller.

The logical volume size is the combined total of all the disks in the array, limited by the capacity of the smallest disk. When building a RAID array, all the disks should normally be identical in terms of capacity, and ideally in terms of type and performance, though this is not mandatory. If disks are different size, the size of the smallest disk in the array determines the maximum amount of space that can be used on the larger drives. RAID 0 adds no storage overhead and is a means of obtaining a large logical volume from multiple, low capacity disks.

However, because it provides *no redundancy*, this method cannot be said to be a true RAID implementation. If *any* physical disk in the array fails, the *whole logical volume* will fail, causing the server to crash and requiring data to be recovered using disk recovery tools (and as the data on the failed physical disk may not be recoverable, this can be very difficult, if not impossible). Note that the chance of failure increases with the number of drives used in the array (stripe width).

Consequently, RAID 0 would never be used for live data storage. It has specialist applications for hosting read-only or relatively static data (in a front-end web server or media server to serve files that are backed up elsewhere for instance) where speed is more important than data security.

As well as data security, RAID 0 risks availability, as the failure of one disk causes the whole array, and therefore the server, to fail. You could compensate for this by duplicating servers (clustering) but only at considerable expense.

RAID Mirroring and Parity

RAID level 1 provides redundancy through mirroring while RAID levels 5 and 6 use parity information.

RAID 1 (Mirroring/Duplexing)

Mirroring requires two hard disks and a single disk controller. The mirror disk is a duplicate of the data disk. Each write operation is duplicated on the second disk in the set, introducing a small performance overhead. A read operation can use either disk, boosting performance somewhat.

Performance is difficult to quantify but RAID 1 is generally seen as performing worse than a single drive but better than higher RAID levels at writes and better than a single drive but worse than other RAID levels at reads.

Mirroring is the simplest way of protecting a single disk against failure. If one disk fails (**degrading** the array), the other takes over. There is little impact on performance during this time (obviously the boost of having two drives available for read operations is lost), so availability remains good, but the failed disk should be replaced as quickly as possible as there is no longer any redundancy. When the disk is replaced, it must be populated with data from the other disk (**rebuilding**). Performance while rebuilding is reduced, though RAID 1 is better than other levels in that respect and the rebuilding process is generally shorter than parity-based RAID.

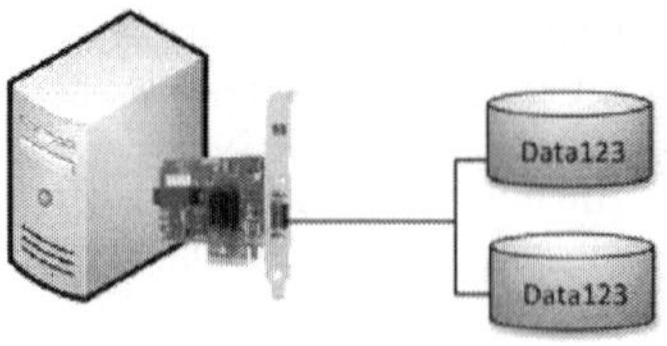

RAID 1 (Mirroring) - data is written to both disks simultaneously

In terms of cost per gigabyte, disk mirroring is more expensive than other forms of fault tolerance because disk space utilization is only 50 percent. Also the total volume size cannot exceed the available capacity of the physical disks. However, for peer-to-peer and modest server-based LANs or for enterprise workstations, disk mirroring usually has a lower entry cost because it requires only two disks and a relatively cheap RAID controller. RAID 1 is also a good choice for servers where fault tolerant write performance is paramount.

Duplexing is a mirrored pair with an additional disk controller on the second drive. This reduces channel traffic and potentially improves performance. Duplexing is intended to protect against controller failures as well as media failures.

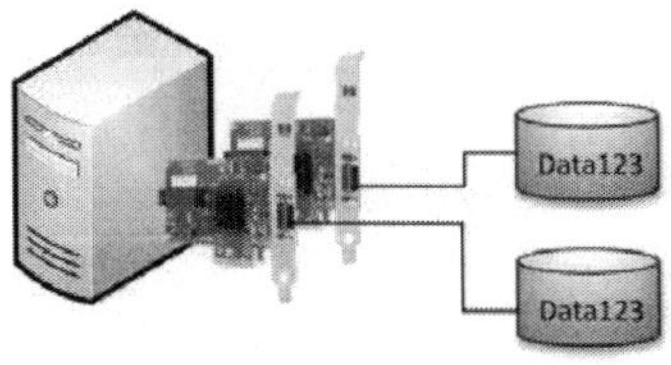

RAID 1 (Duplex mirror) - an extra controller provides redundancy

RAID 5 (Striping with Distributed Parity)

Striping with parity (RAID 5) is a popular strategy for fault tolerant designs. RAID 5 writes parity information across all the disks in the array. The data and parity information are managed so that the two are always on different disks. If a single disk fails, enough information is spread across the remaining disks to allow the data to be completely reconstructed. Only one disk failure can be tolerated however and performance while the array is degraded can be poor. Rebuilding is also lengthy.

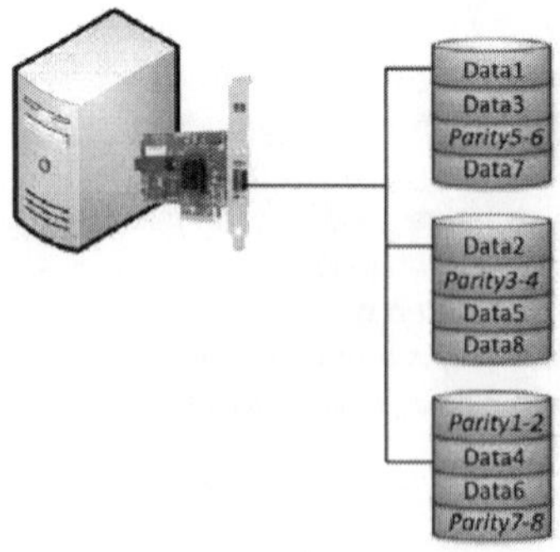

RAID 5 (Striping with Parity)

Read performance is good, especially for transactional (or random) I/O. Write performance is worse than RAID 1. RAID 5 requires a minimum of three drives but can be configured with more. This allows more flexibility in determining the overall capacity of the array than is possible with RAID 1. A "hard" maximum number of devices is set by the controller or OS support but the number of drives used is more likely to be determined by practicalities such as cost and risk (remember that adding more disks increases the chance of failure).

If the controller supports it, the risk of disk failure can be offset by configuring a hot spare (see "Enterprise RAID Configurations") below.

RAID 6 (Second Parity)

RAID 6 is like RAID 5 but with two sets of parity information, meaning that the array can support the simultaneous loss of *two* disks before it fails. This improves fault tolerance and availability at the expense of write performance. Rebuilding the array is still slow but the backup of a second parity set means that the operation can be delayed more safely to a convenient time than is the case with RAID 5. RAID 6 requires a minimum of 4 disks. RAID 6 is not that widely deployed however as RAID 5 with a hot spare or nested RAID are generally seen as providing more effective solutions.

Nested RAID

Nested RAID means configuring an array of arrays (or a spanned array) to combine the benefits of redundancy and performance. Nested RAID also allows for larger logical volumes while preserving fault tolerance.

RAID 1+0 (RAID 10)

As described above, RAID 0 is striping with no parity (that is, no fault tolerance is provided). This provides high throughput, but leaves the data at risk. RAID 1 provides mirroring; the highest achievable disk fault tolerance. RAID 1+0 (or RAID 10) is a stripe of mirrors. This configuration offers better fault tolerance as one disk in each mirror can fail and the array will still function.

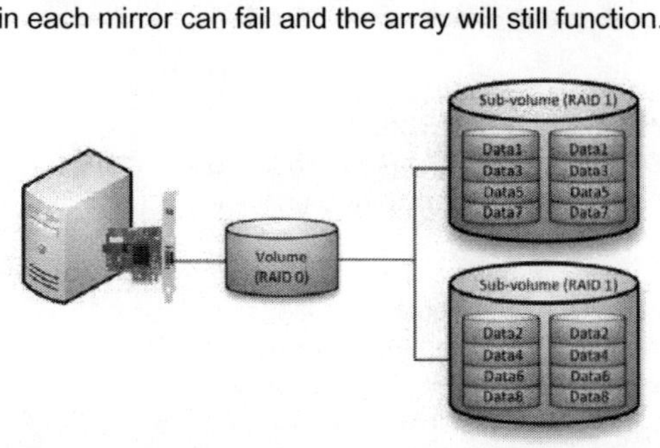

RAID 10 - either disk in each of the sub-volumes can fail without bringing down the main volume

RAID 10 allows for large logical volumes (an array may support up to 128 disks for instance) and high performance. The main drawback is the 50% disk space utilization.

RAID 5+0 (RAID 50)

RAID 5 provides for fault tolerance across a stripe set. It allows for moderate write performance, good read performance, and acceptable fault tolerance. RAID 0 gives higher throughput but no fault tolerance.

RAID 5+0 (or RAID 50) is RAID 5 sets striped across a RAID 0 set. This provides better performance and fault tolerance. Each of the RAID 5 stripes can sustain a single disk failure, so in essence, your single RAID 5+0 array can support multiple disk failures.

RAID 5+1

RAID 5+1 (or RAID 51) is mirroring RAID 5 arrays. This provides outstanding fault tolerance and availability, but is complex to implement and expensive; as well as the cost of the controller, the array is likely to have below 50% storage efficiency.

Hardware and Software RAID

A RAID array should be composed of identical or near-identical disks. If a mixture of disks with different capacities or performance characteristics (such as RPM) are used, the array will be limited by the lowest capacity or worst performing device.

It is possible to implement RAID using either hardware or software.

Hardware Solutions (Array Controllers)

A hardware solution means that creating volumes from an array of physical disks is an operation supported by a plug-in controller card or by the motherboard, independently of the installed operating system. Two controllers could be provided for redundancy.

Hardware solutions are principally differentiated by their support for RAID levels. Entry-level controllers might support only RAID 0 or RAID 1, mid-level controllers might add support for RAID 5, RAID 6, and RAID 1+0, while the top-end would add support for RAID 5+0 and RAID 5+1. Vendors may also define proprietary RAID levels and solutions.

In addition, some hardware implementations allow you to replace a failed drive without shutting down the system. Another advantage of hardware-based RAID is that the operating system sees the array as one volume. This allows you to install the operating system onto an array, which isn't always possible when using software arrays.

The disadvantages of a hardware implementation are that they can be more expensive than software solutions and may lock you into a single vendor solution. Hardware RAID can only use disks attached to the same bus, so you could not (for instance) mix SCSI and SATA devices within the same array.

A RAID controller may have the following performance-boosting components:

- **Processor** - a true RAID controller card comes with a CPU to handle the I/O and parity calculations, reducing the load on the server's main CPU.

  Zero Channel RAID is a low cost card for use where the motherboard has its own SCSI channels. This reduces the cost and size of the adapter card. RAIDIOS (RAID Input/Output Steering) is an Intel standard for ZCR motherboard and card design.

- **Cache** - memory in which to store read/write operations that cannot be processed quickly enough. This improves the throughput of the RAID controller. However, using write cache reduces fault tolerance because in the event of a power failure, data in the cache will be lost.

  High-end RAID controllers feature an on-board **battery** (which can supply power for between 24 and 72 hours) to mitigate this risk. Otherwise, the write cache can be disabled via the management program or the card's firmware setup program.

  The cache can usually be allocated flexibly between read and write operations to reflect the server role. This will usually be set to 50/50 by default but could be changed using the array configuration software to 80/20 for instance or to 100/0 or 0/100 to completely disable write or read cache respectively.

HP RAID controller card with battery-backed cache

Array Configuration Utilities

Having installed the controller and connected the drives, the next step in configuring a hardware array would be to boot the server and access the low-level **RAID Array Configuration Utility** stored on the controller's firmware. This is usually accessed by a key combo such as **Ctrl+A**, **Ctrl+C**, or **F8**. This utility will allow you to choose which drives to use as part of an array and in what configuration (RAID 0, RAID 1, RAID 5, or RAID 10 for instance).

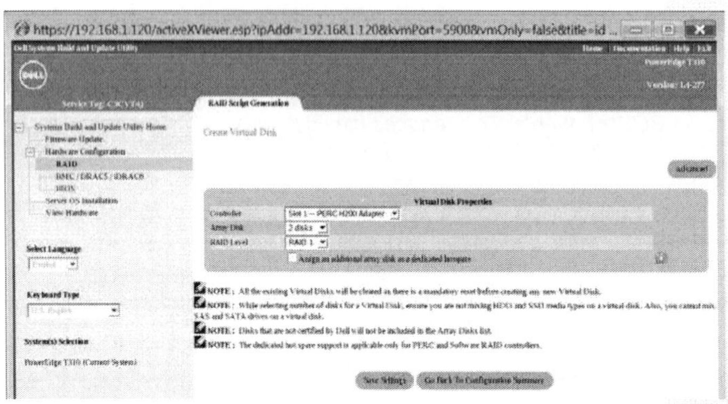

Configuring RAID on a Dell server

Some utilities might be set to apply a default configuration automatically - for example if there are two drives it selects RAID 1 and if there are three or more it selects RAID 5.

Having configured the array, the next step would be to use the operating system setup software to configure formatted partitions or volumes on the array and install the OS.

File systems and disk utilities are covered in *Unit 1.4* *and* *Unit 3.3**.*

When the OS is installed, you can install the graphical RAID management software. This will allow you to monitor the health of the array, add or remove disks, rebuild a degraded array, configure the cache, and so on. High-end controllers and management software may support additional functions (see "Enterprise RAID Configurations" below).

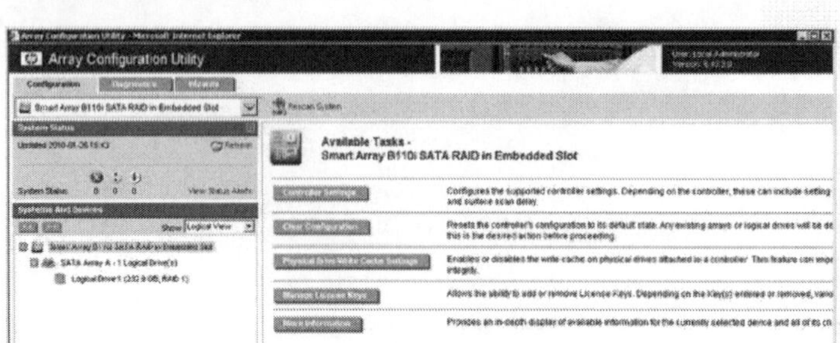

HP RAID configuration utility

Software Solutions

Many operating systems provide the option to configure disk arrays into logical volumes using standard disks and controllers.

The following tools are used to manage software RAID volumes:

- Windows volumes are created and managed using **`diskpart`** or the **Disk Management** snap-in. RAID volumes use the **Dynamic Disks** feature. Server 2012 also allows the use of **Storage Spaces** to create drive pools with RAID-like functionality.
- In Linux the **md** driver provides kernel-level RAID functionality and is managed using the **`mdadm`** tool. The Logical Volume Manager (LVM) tools can also be used to implement RAID-like mirroring and striping with parity.
- The ZFS file system provides native RAID support and is managed using a number of **`zfs`** and **`zpool`** subcommands.

The following table lists the general level of support for software RAID in Windows, Linux, and in the ZFS file system:

RAID Level	OS Support
Level 0	Windows / Linux / ZFS
Level 1	Windows / Linux / ZFS
Level 5	Windows / Linux / ZFS (RAID-Z)
Level 6	Linux / ZFS (RAID-Z2)
Level 1+0	Linux / ZFS

A software solution is considerably cheaper, as RAID controller cards can be very expensive. The capacity of multi-core CPUs means that a software solution may be able to compete on performance with hardware RAID solutions (especially with budget hardware RAID). A software solution could combine devices on different bus types within the array.

Some motherboard RAID solutions are "fake RAID"; that is, they are advertised as a RAID controller but actually only provide multiple disk channels and offload all the processing to the main CPU. Fake RAID controllers do not support battery-backed cache (though not all controllers without battery-backed cache are "fake").

Another feature of operating systems is the ability to create logical volumes that **span** multiple physical disks. This is referred to as **Just a Bunch of Disks (JBOD)**. *Unlike* RAID 0, data in a spanned volume is usually written to each disk sequentially rather than striped across all the disks in the set, so there are no performance benefits. However, *like* RAID 0, if any disk underpinning the volume fails, the whole volume will fail. Consequently, this is not a configuration that is used too often. One possible use is to "rescue" an OS that has run out of disk space. It should only be seen as a stopgap measure though.

Calculating Usable Storage

The following table shows how to calculate the amount of disk space available when using commonly implemented RAID configurations.

If the disks are different sizes, the size used is that of the smallest disk. Extra disk space on larger drives is wasted.

RAID Level	Usable Disk Space
Level 0	Total space of all disks in stripe set. For example, 3 disks each 80 GB in size would result in a 240 GB volume.
Level 1	Half of the disk space on the disks is available. One disk is a copy of the other. Therefore, if you implement RAID 1 with two 80 GB disks, you end up with 80 GB of storage available.
Level 5 Level 6	(# Drives - 1) * Drive Size for RAID 5 or (# Drives - 2) * Drive Size for RAID 6. The level of fault tolerance and available disk space are inverse. As you add disks to the set, fault tolerance decreases but usable disk space increases. If you configure a RAID 5 set using 3 disks, ⅓ of each disk is set aside for parity; if four are used, ¼ is reserved on each disk. Using a three 80 GB disk configuration would create a 160 GB usable volume.
Level 1+0	This is the same as for RAID 1: (Drive Size * # Drives) / 2 (or half)

Remember that a RAID 5 array can only sustain a single drive failure; RAID 6 can sustain two drive failures. The more drives there are in a set, the higher the risk is that one will fail.

Enterprise RAID Configurations

Most hardware vendors, such as Dell and HP, provide server configurations for small businesses which include a RAID controller and a basic disk configuration which allows the installer to configure RAID - implementing RAID 1 with 2 disks or RAID 5 across 3 disks being fairly typical approaches. The operating system, of course, sees only a single hard disk, and the vendor will provide software tools to monitor and configure the RAID controller.

In addition, because hardware RAID has been implemented, the administrator will be able to hot swap the damaged disk (replace the failed unit without shutting down the OS), thereby keeping the system operational all the time. When the new disk is installed, the RAID controller transparently synchronizes it with the remaining disks in the set.

At a lower entry-level, an administrator could implement RAID using software provided by the vendor. The advantage is slightly reduced cost, but because the OS is responsible for distributing data across the set, it involves workload, which has a performance impact on the server. In addition, if a disk fails, the server would need to be shut down for the disk to be replaced, and that defeats the object of fault tolerance.

These two scenarios deal with small business solutions - buying an off-the-shelf RAID controller and a minimal number of disks. Both these solutions present the network administrator with a potential problem in the future - expansion.

All these configurations suffer from the same problem; space cannot be added. Once a mirror or stripe set (with or without parity) has been configured, the volume created remains fixed in size. The only way to extend the volume is to back up the data, remove the volume, add a new disk to add space, then create a new volume - restoring the data to the new, bigger volume. A mirror can be "broken" without the need to backup and restore. However, the disk that makes up the mirror will still need to be made bigger, which means a new disk.

Enterprise systems utilize more advanced and flexible schemes for disk configuration. Some of these schemes allow for the expansion of sets with total transparency to the user, and no downtime for the server. For example:

- **Hot swapping** - the ability to add or remove disks while the server is operational.

- **Hot spare** - this is one or more drives that are installed in the server but not actively used as part of the array. If the controller detects a drive failure, it switches a hot spare into the array automatically and starts to rebuild it. While expensive in terms of provisioning, this reduces risk in situations where it would be difficult for a technician to physically add a new drive within an acceptable time frame.

Conversely, a cold spare is one that must be physically installed in the server before it can be used.

- **Online Capacity Extension** - OCE allows an administrator to extend the volume without needing to start over. The administrator can add one, or more, disks to a RAID configuration at any time, increasing the available usable disk space.

- **Online RAID Level Migration** - ORLM allows an administrator to change the RAID level (from RAID 1 to RAID 5 for instance).

  Consider the benefits in this scenario. Your server was installed with an off-the-shelf RAID 5 configuration, utilizing three disks, and has performed reasonably well. However, the nature of RAID 5 is that disk writes are fairly slow. You need to improve the throughput. By adding a single new disk, while the system is online (hot swap), you can configure a RAID 10 volume (ORLM), improving the volume's write throughput.

Other enterprise class RAID features include:

- **Drive Roaming** - the ability to move disks from one server to another without downing that server. The array system keeps track of where the disk is. This might be useful in situations where large volumes of data need to be shifted from server to server.

- **Controller spanning** - allows an array to encompass disks that are attached to multiple controllers. There are practical limits to the number of devices a single controller can support. Supporting multiple controllers extends these limits.

- **n-way mirroring** - this allow for a mirror to contain more than 2 copies - in fact, it contains *n* copies. This provides for very high fault tolerance at the expense of extremely low storage efficiency.

- **Array splitting** - this feature allows an administrator to remove (without impacting function of the server) any of the disks in the array.

Installing Drives in a RAID Array

It is best (and may be required, especially for a proprietary hardware RAID solution) for all drives in an array to be the same size and model.

When replacing a failed drive in a RAID array, take extreme caution to remove the correct drive. The consequences of removing a working drive if the array supports only one drive failure should be obvious. The failed drive should be made obvious through a red LED.

If adding drives to the array, verify that the controller supports additions.

Once a drive has been added or replaced, reboot to check that the drive has been recognized. The management software may rebuild the array automatically or you may need to start the process manually.

If upgrading the RAID **controller**, make sure you backup data first and research the manufacturer's instructions thoroughly. It may be possible to migrate the existing configuration and data from one controller to another, but you cannot depend on this being the case and so must plan to have to rebuild the array and restore data from backup. As well as installing the controller adapter card, you may need to update the firmware on the controller. The firmware level of the controller is displayed at boot time during the POST sequence or will be reported to management software.

In some cases, you may want also want to update the firmware on the hard drives themselves. Firmware updates might fix performance or reliability issues, especially if the disks belong to a new model or use a relatively new technology, such as SSDs.

Most vendors now provide software tools for updating the firmware on disks and controllers, making the process much simpler than before.

?

Review Questions / Module 1 / Unit 3 / RAID

Answer these questions to test what you have learned in this unit.

1) What four principal factors should you take into account when measuring different IOPS performance characteristics?
2) What type of fault tolerant RAID is most likely to be provided on low-end controllers?
3) What is a degraded RAID volume?
4) What feature of a RAID controller card mitigates the risk of incomplete disk writes being lost because of power failure?
5) What distinguishes JBOD from RAID?
6) If each drive is 120 GB, what is the capacity of a RAID 6 array consisting of 7 drives?

Module 1 / Unit 4
System Setup

Objectives

On completion of this unit, you will be able to:

- Understand the differences between BIOS and UEFI system firmware.
- Use the system setup program to configure basic settings.
- Identify appropriate partition formats and file systems for installing a given operating system.

BIOS and UEFI Configuration

The **BIOS (Basic Input / Output System)** provides industry standard program code that operates the essential components of a computer and ensures that the design of each manufacturer's motherboard is PC compatible. The BIOS is often described as **firmware** as it consists of both the physical chip (hardware) and the programs coded into it (software).

Newer motherboards may use a different kind of firmware called **UEFI (Unified Extensible Firmware Interface)**. UEFI provides support for 64-bit CPU operation at boot, a full GUI and mouse operation at boot, and better boot security. A server with UEFI may also support booting in a legacy BIOS mode.

System Firmware Setup Program

System settings can be configured via the system firmware setup program. This may also be referred to as CMOS setup, BIOS setup, or UEFI setup.

The term "CMOS Setup" is still widely used, even though CMOS RAM is obsolete.

You can normally access the system setup program with a keystroke during the power-on (boot) process. The key combination used will vary from system to system; typical examples are `Esc`, `Del`, `F1`, `F2`, or `F10`. The server's documentation will explain how to access the setup program; often a message with the required key is displayed when you boot the server.

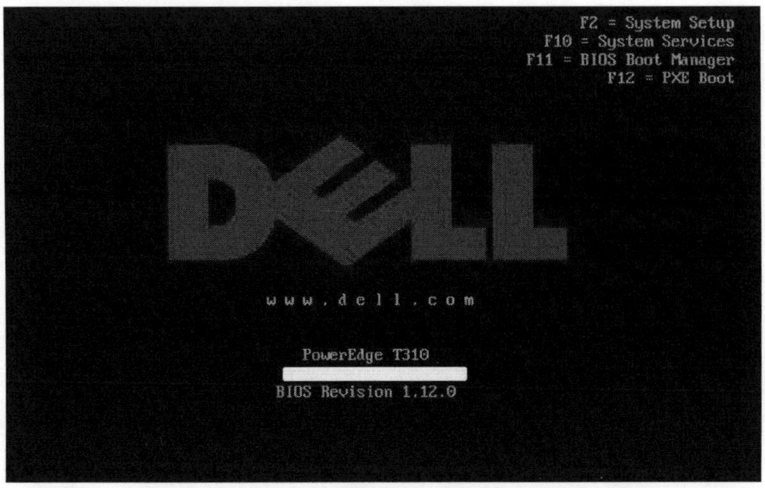

Press the key to enter setup before or during the memory count

Navigating the System Setup Program

You navigate a legacy BIOS setup program using the keyboard arrow keys. Pressing **Esc** generally returns to the previous screen. When closing setup, there will be an option to exit and discard changes or exit and save changes. Sometimes this is done with a key (**Esc** versus **F10** for instance) and but more often there is a prompt.

There will also be an option to reload the default settings, in case you want to discard any customizations you have made.

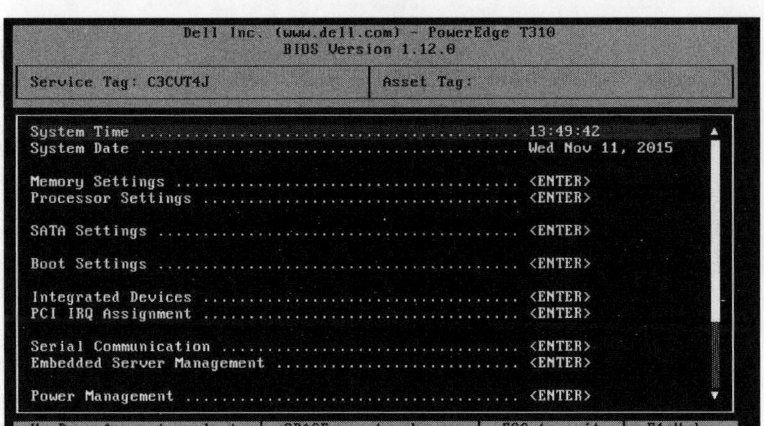

System firmware BIOS setup program

A UEFI setup program may feature a graphical interface with mouse support.

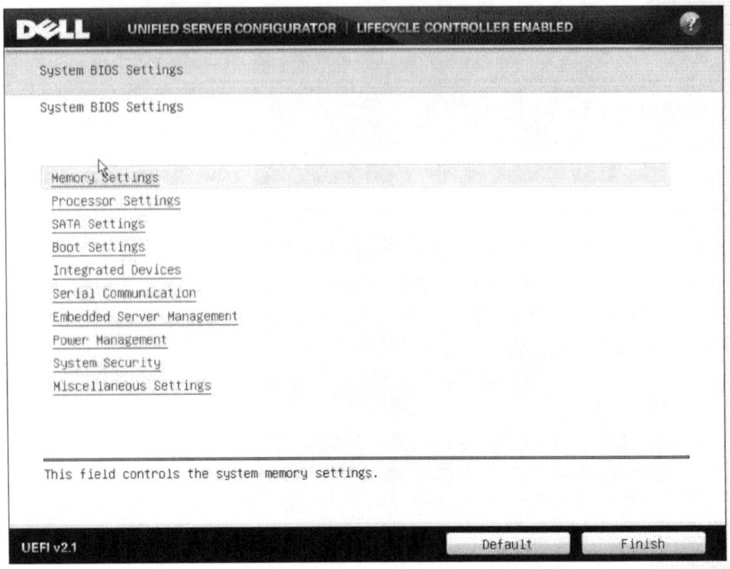

UEFI system setup software with a full GUI and mouse support

Configuring Devices and Boot Properties

A server with UEFI will usually also support booting in a legacy BIOS mode. This might be labeled as a **Compatibility Support Module (CSM)**. This allows the installation of operating systems that do not support the UEFI boot process.

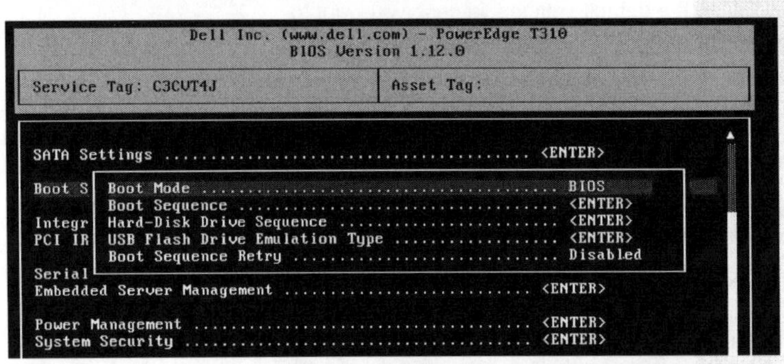

Configuring boot parameters - one choice here is between legacy BIOS boot mode and UEFI boot mode

Secure Boot

You may also need to use the UEFI setup program to disable **Secure Boot** mode. Secure Boot prevents the installation of untrusted operating systems. It is designed to prevent a computer from being hijacked by malware. Under secure boot, UEFI is configured with a secure digital certificate from valid OS vendors. The system firmware checks the operating system boot loader using the stored certificate to ensure that it has been digitally signed by the OS vendor. This prevents a boot loader that has been modified by malware (or an OS installed without authorization) from being used.

Certificates from vendors such as Microsoft (Windows 8 and Windows Server 2012) and Linux distributions (Fedora, openSUSE, and Ubuntu) will be pre-loaded. Additional certificates for other boot loaders can be installed (or the pre-loaded ones removed) via the system setup software.

Boot Order

Another important parameter in system setup is the **boot sequence** or **boot device priority**. This defines the sequence in which the system firmware searches devices for a boot loader. You will usually be able to set 3 or 4 options in priority order. The typical choices are:

- Hard drive - an SATA boot disk should generally be connected to the lowest numbered port but it is usually possible to select the hard drive sequence if multiple fixed drives are installed. If the system is configured with a RAID controller, there will be an option to boot from the virtual disk.
- Optical drive (CD/DVD/Blu-ray) - if you are performing a repair install, you might need to make this device highest priority.
- USB - most modern systems can boot from USB drives.
- Network / PXE - uses the network adapter to obtain boot settings from a specially configured server.

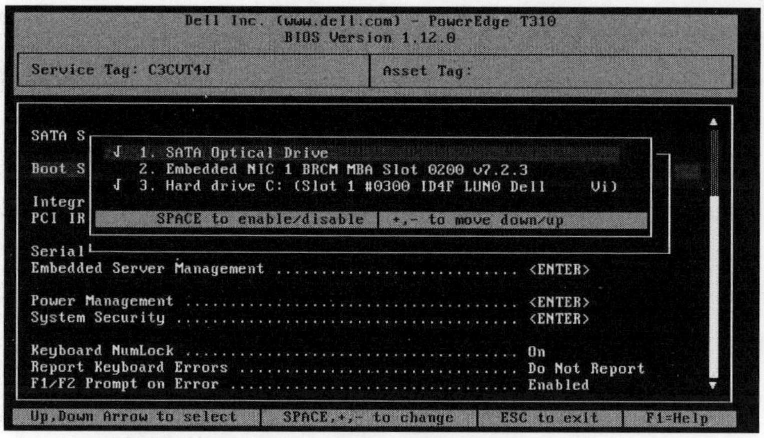

Enabling and disabling boot devices and changing boot priority order

There is also usually an option to disable particular boot methods. This is a useful security feature.

Upgrading Firmware

System vendors and motherboard manufacturers may regularly update their firmware in order to fix bugs, solve incompatibilities with operating systems or to add new features. You should visit the relevant support website regularly to check whether upgrades are available. As upgrading the firmware is relatively risky (a failed motherboard update can leave the server unbootable for instance), it is only worth doing if the update fixes a specific problem that you are encountering or if it is regarded as a **critical** update.

Before you start, record any custom system setup settings, as updating the firmware may reset the system configuration to the default. You will need to change the system settings back after the update.

To perform a server firmware upgrade, download the upgrade program from the website to your computer (if the files are in a zip archive, extract them). If there is an option to back up the existing firmware configuration, use it. As a security feature, a jumper on the motherboard may have to be adjusted in order to allow system firmware upgrades to take place.

Also ensure that you have an up-to-date data and system backup in case the firmware upgrade goes wrong. When performing a firmware upgrade, ensure the power supply is reliable by (ideally) using an Uninterruptible Power Supply.

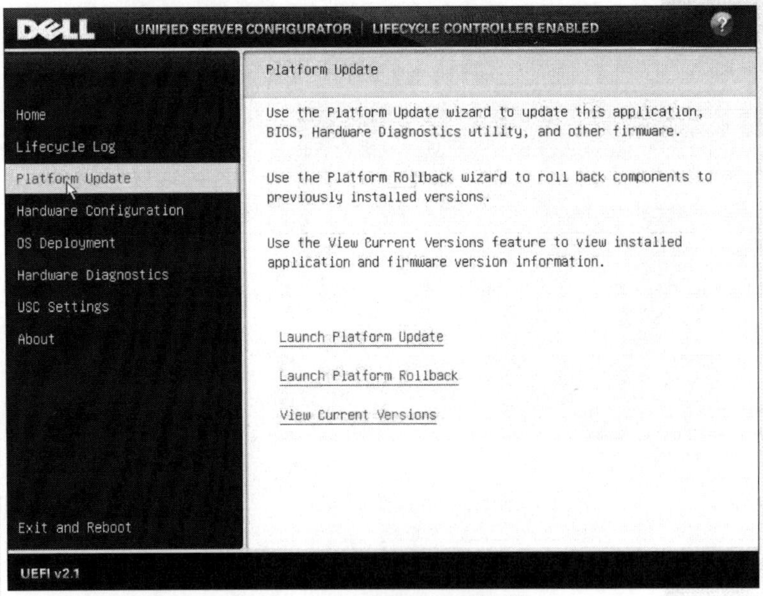

Running a system firmware update utility

There will usually be two or three options for running the firmware update:

- Start the system setup utility and look for the option to update the system firmware. You can then navigate to the folder where you saved the update and run it or you may need to copy the file to a USB stick and run it from there.

- Run the update utility from Windows. Using a Windows utility is relatively risky. Before running it, close all other software programs and disable anti-virus scanners. You must minimize the risk of another process causing a lockup during the firmware update.

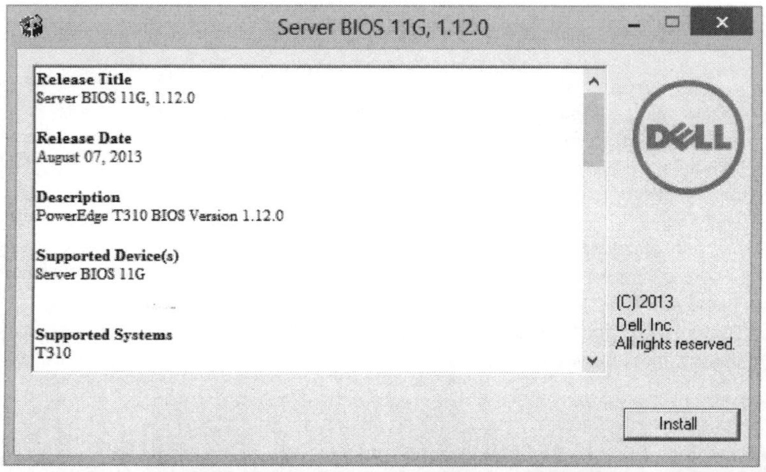

Updating a Dell PC's firmware using a Windows flash utility

If a firmware update goes wrong (for example if there is a power cut during the flashing process), you may be able to re-install the old firmware from a backup. However, it is equally likely that the component will be unusable. If this is the case, you will have to contact the manufacturer for help or buy a new one.

In the case of failed motherboard updates, the motherboard may feature a recovery mode jumper. You may also need to remove the RTC battery.

The recovery mode jumper is to the left of the battery

MBR and GPT Partitions

When you install an NOS to a server, you will first use the RAID management tool to create a **virtual disk**. If the server does not support RAID, you can install the NOS directly to a hard disk but as this does not provide any sort of fault tolerance it is not a common configuration. The virtual disk must be **partitioned** and **formatted** with an appropriate **file system** before it can be used with an operating system.

Partitions

Partitioning the disk is the act of dividing it into logically separate storage areas, often referred to as "drives". You must create at least one partition on the disk before performing a high-level format to create a **file system**. Typically, this is done through NOS setup program.

Information about partitions is usually stored in a **Master Boot Record (MBR)**, which is located in the first 512 byte sector on the disk. The **GUI (Globally Unique Identifier) Partition Table (GPT)** provides a more up-to-date scheme to address some of the limitations of MBR and most new server hardware will now be using GPT-style partitioning, if the server firmware is UEFI.

Volume (or drive) is a term used at the OS level to refer to a contiguous storage area formatted with a single file system. This could mean a partition on a hard disk, a CD-ROM, a floppy disk, or a RAID partition spanning multiple hard disks. The term partition is more specific than volume - it refers to an area on a hard disk recorded in the disk's MBR.

MBR-style Partitioning

With basic storage and MBR-style partitions, a given disk can contain up to four **primary** partitions, any one of which can be marked as **active**, and therefore made bootable. This allows for four different "drives" on the same disk and for multiple operating systems (a **multiboot** system). Each drive can be formatted with a different **file system**.

If for some reason, four drives are insufficient, then *three* primary partitions can be created and the remaining disk space allocated to an **extended** partition, which itself can be divided into as many **logical** drives as needed.

Each primary partition contains a boot sector (or Partition Boot Record [PBR] or Volume Boot Record [VBR]) at the start of the partition. When a partition is marked as active, its boot sector is populated with a record that points to the OS boot loader (c:\Windows\System32\winload.exe for example). This active partition is also referred to as the **system partition** or **system reserved partition**. Extended partitions do not have boot sectors and cannot be made active.

The drive containing the operating system files (the system root) is referred to as the **boot partition**. This *can* be on a logical drive in an extended partition and does not have to be the same as the system drive. The typical installation options for Windows create a "hidden" system reserved partition (with no drive letter) and label the boot partition as drive c:.

GPT-style Partitioning

The **GUID (Globally Unique ID) Partition Table (GPT)** is not subject to the restrictions on number and size of partitions that limit MBR; there are still limits but not ones that are likely to be reached in practice. With the GPT boot scheme, the boot information is not restricted to a single sector but still serves the same basic purpose of identifying partitions and boot loaders.

GPT often uses a "protective" MBR to prevent disk tools from overwriting the GPT.

GPT is associated with UEFI firmware but can also be used by most legacy BIOS firmware if supported by the OS.

Boot Process

When a computer starts, the firmware runs a **Power On Self Test (POST)** to verify that the system components are present and functioning correctly. It then identifies a boot device and passes control to the operating system's boot loader process.

With a legacy BIOS, the firmware scans the disk identified as the boot device and reads the **Master Boot Record (MBR)** in the first sector of the disk. The MBR identifies the **boot sector** or **Volume Boot Record (VBR)** for the partition marked as active. The VBR loads the boot manager.

With an EFI boot, the initial part of the boot process is different. Following POST, the firmware reads the **GUID Partition Table (GPT)** on the boot device. The GPT identifies the EFI System Partition. The EFI System Partition contains the boot manager information for each OS installed on the computer. The main boot managers are:

- **bootmgr.exe** - used by Windows Server with MBR-style partitioning. The boot manager reads information from the **Boot Configuration Data (BCD)** file.
- **bootmgfw.efi** - used by Windows Server with a UEFI computer. Each Windows installation has a subfolder under \EFI\Microsoft\ on the EFI system partition containing a BCD and bootmgfw.efi
- **GRUB (Grand Unified Bootloader)** - used by most types of Linux.
- **LILO (Linux Loader)** - alternative bootloader for Linux servers.

If there is more than one OS installation, the boot manager shows a boot menu allowing the user to select the installation to boot.

The boot manager may present boot options (if more than one OS is installed) but its main function is to start the OS by running its **boot loader**. For example, for Windows, the boot manager loads the Windows boot loader **winload.exe** in the system root folder. winload then continues the Windows boot process by loading the kernel (ntoskrnl.exe), the Hardware Abstraction Layer (hal.dll), and boot device drivers. Control is then passed to the kernel, which initializes and starts loading the required processes. When complete, the winlogon process waits for the user to authenticate.

File System Choices

In order for the NOS to read and write data to a partition, it must be formatted with a **file system**. The choice of file system depends on the NOS being installed and client-access compatibility.

You might be able to use the array management tool to partition and format the disk but it is more usual to use the tools provided in the NOS setup program.

Windows NTFS

Under Windows, partitions ("drives") are identified by letters (C through Z, with A and B being reserved for floppy drives). Directories, subdirectories, and files are browsed from the root directory of each partition.

It is possible to assign A or B to data drives but most administrators would avoid doing so.

Disks and partitions / volumes are managed using the **Disk Management** console or the `diskpart` command-line tool.

In Windows, the partition marked active that contains the boot manager is referred to as the **system partition**. As noted above, this might be a System Reserved partition (on an MBR-style partition scheme) or the EFI System Partition. The drive containing the operating system files (the system root) is referred to as the **boot partition**. This is usually a different partition to the system partition. The boot partition must be formatted using NTFS.

The **New Technology File System (NTFS)** provides a 64-bit disk addressing scheme, allowing for very large partitions (16 exabytes). Also, it includes extended attribute space so allowing for file security, encryption, compression and quota management. The key NTFS features are:

- **Journaling** - NTFS utilizes sector sparing and transaction tracking to provide reliable data transfer. When data is written to an NTFS volume, the data is re-read and verified. In the event of a problem, the sector concerned is marked as bad and the data relocated. The transaction tracking logs all disk and file system activity, making recovery after power outage a faster and more reliable process
- **Security** - NTFS can record Access Control Lists for files and folders, enabling local file security and access audit trails.
- **Compression** - NTFS allows file- or folder-level compression.
- **Quota Management** - it is possible to limit the amount of disk space allocated to each user on a given volume.
- **Encryption** - the **Encrypting File System (EFS)** included in NTFS allows users to make files and folders of data confidential by encrypting them. Only the user that encrypted the file can read it. This protects the data even if the disk is removed from the server.
- **Dynamic Disks** - this is a disk management feature allowing space on multiple physical disks to be combined into volumes (software support for RAID 0, RAID 1, and RAID 5).
- **Volume Shadow Copy Service (VSS)** - can create a snapshot copy of data on a volume. This serves two purposes - it allows backup software to backup open files and it allows for the recovery of previous versions of a changed or deleted file.
- **Mount points** - NTFS allows other file systems to be mounted within an NTFS directory rather than accessed via a drive letter (in a manner similar to *nix file systems).

The main drawback of NTFS is that other operating systems cannot use it directly. NTFS drivers are available for Linux but they can be problematic, especially when attempting to write data. There are not many circumstances in which you would want a Linux server to be able to access the NTFS disks of a Windows Server directly however. There are simple ways of sharing files between them over a network.

FAT / FAT32

The **File Allocation Table (FAT)** file system is compatible with all Microsoft operating systems and many non-MS OSs, but the maximum partition and file size is 2 GB. FAT32 is an enhanced and extended version of FAT. It supports a maximum partition size of 2 terabytes but the maximum size of a single file is limited to 4 GB. FAT32 is used to format an EFI System Partition and might be used to format removable drives, as it has the best compatibility between different operating systems.

*nix File Systems

Before discussing formatting disk partitions under *nix , it is important to understand that *everything* available to the OS is represented as a file in the file system, including devices. This is referred to as the **unified file system**. Also, unlike Windows, drive letters like C: or D: are not used. The file system starts at the **root**, represented by **/**. Directories and subdirectories can be created from the root to store files.

*Note that *nix uses the forward slash (/) to delimit directory names while Windows uses a back slash (\).*

Linux File Systems (ext, ReiserFS, and swap)

Most Linux distributions use some version of the **ext** file system to format partitions on mass storage devices. **ext3** is a 64-bit file system with support for journaling, which means that the file system tracks changes, giving better reliability and less chance of file corruption in the event of crashes or power outages. Support for journaling is the main difference between ext3 and its predecessor (**ext2**). **ext4** delivers significantly better performance than ext3 and would usually represent the best choice for new systems.

The **ReiserFS** introduced support for journaling some time before ext3 was developed. It remains an option but most distributions prefer to use ext3 or ext4 by default. Linux can also support FAT / FAT32, though it is designated as **VFAT**.

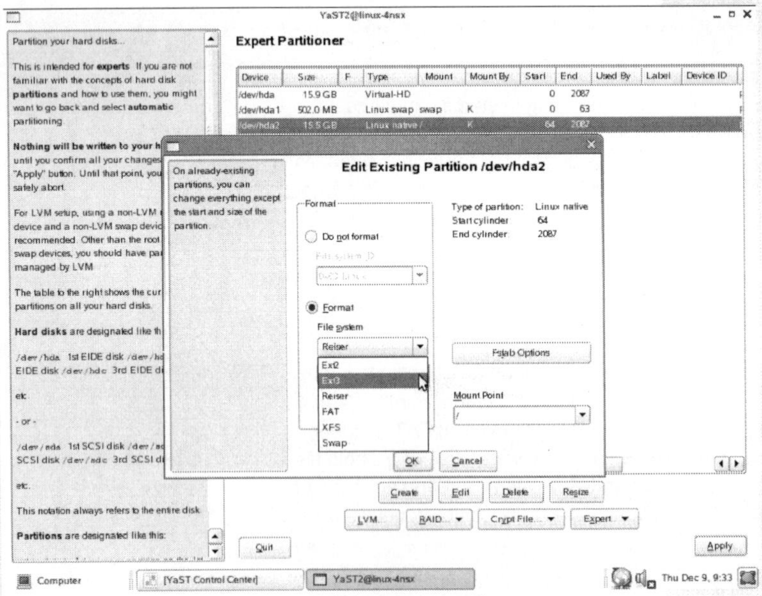

Using YaST to format a partition

Most Linux distros provide GUI tools for managing disks and file systems, but the following represent the main command-line options:

- **fdisk** - used to manage partitions on a hard disk. For disks over 2 TB or for GPT-style partitioning, you can use **parted** or **gdisk**.
- **mkfs** - used to format a partition.
- **fsck** - check a partition for errors.
- **df** and **du** - check free space and report usage by directories and files.

Standard Linux setup will also create a "swap" partition for use as virtual memory (a pagefile in Windows terms). "swap" is not a file system as such but marks the swap area.

UFS (UNIX File System)

The **UNIX File System (UFS)** is regarded as the "default" choice for many types of UNIX. Different UNIX implementations may add proprietary extensions. UFS2 supports 64-bit addressing.

ZFS

Sun's Solaris version of UNIX can use a file system called **ZFS**. Sun and consequently Solaris are now owned by Oracle. The source code for ZFS is available as open source software but Sun use a different type of open source license so it has not been widely adopted by Linux distributions. ZFS is a 128-bit file system that provides numerous fault tolerance and high integrity features. ZFS also supports software RAID; striping (RAID 0) and mirroring (RAID 1), striping with parity (RAID-Z, which provides features similar to RAID 5 and RAID 6), and hot spares.

Virtual Machine File System (VMFS)

VMware's ESX Server is a bare metal hypervisor. This means ESX Server is installed as the underlying OS and then additional Windows or *nix virtual machines are installed "within" ESX.

See Unit 2.5 for more information about hypervisors and virtualization.

The **Virtual Machine File System (VMFS)** is the preferred option for storing VM images managed by ESX servers. The VMFS could be a partition on a local disk / array or a volume on a Storage Area Network (SAN). VMFS is optimized to allow multiple ESX servers to access the disk media concurrently while also preventing more than one ESX server from controlling any VM in use by another ESX server. It also allows for making snapshots of images for backup.

Review Questions / Module 1 / Unit 4 / System Setup

Answer these questions to test what you have learned in this unit.

1) What do BIOS and UEFI stand for?
2) What might you need to do to install a 32-bit OS on a UEFI platform?
3) If you have just installed a RAID controller and configured a volume using the controller firmware, how would you ensure that the volume can be used to boot the server?
4) You have made a record of custom System Setup settings before a planned firmware upgrade. What precaution should you take before proceeding to install the update?
5) You are planning a storage server that will have to host partitions larger than 2 TB. What server feature should you look for?
6) What program(s) might you expect to be used to bootstrap Linux?
7) Which *nix file system supports snapshots?

Module 1 / Unit 5
Server Operating Systems

Objectives

On completion of this unit, you will be able to:

- Identify different types and versions of Network Operating System and evaluate hardware requirements.
- Identify different methods for performing software installations.
- Perform post-setup tasks such as installing additional drivers and configuring virtual memory.

Server Pre-installation Planning

Planning for the installation of a new server requires three main tasks:

- Establish what specification is required. How powerful does the server need to be? What components are to be installed?
- Establish how the server will be integrated with existing hardware, software, and network resources.
- Create an ongoing management plan. Who will be responsible for maintaining the server? Is there current expertise within the organization to support the chosen NOS or applications software? Will users require retraining or will operations management procedures require updating?

Specifying the Server

The first job in specifying a new server is to know as far as possible what it is going to do, both now and in the future. Purchasing decisions should be business-led, arising from a specific business need and offering demonstrable benefits (such as a percentage increase in sales or call throughput). Given that, it is also true to say that spending the least amount of money possible for a minimum spec machine is not necessarily cost-effective. Installing a new server is not a completely straightforward task, and upgrading one can be even more complex, so future-proofing is likely to make sense economically, but this benefit needs to be quantified to justify the additional up-front cost.

If the requirements and objectives are clearly specified and related to concrete business benefits, the budget is far more likely to be approved.

In terms of selecting components, remember that reliability, security, and availability of technical support should be given greater consideration than pure performance. New and unproven technologies are significant risk factors. You should read up on the components used in the server, looking for reviews, white papers and technical tips on the Internet. You also need to evaluate the vendor carefully: what customer support is offered and how good is their customer service?

From a performance point-of-view, the two main factors will be the applications that the server will run and the number of users.

Applications have very different hardware requirements. In particular, email and database applications have high processing and storage requirements. Also consider that if a server is configured to perform multiple roles or support multiple software server instances (virtualization), it will have to be that much more powerful, so that one application does not impact too much on the performance of another.

For users, the main tasks are to identify average and peak simultaneous access (the number of clients using an application at the same time) and storage requirements.

The main factors determining performance are the processor, system memory, speed of the disk subsystem, and network bandwidth.

Other specification decisions that may need to be made include:

- Provision for fault tolerance (storage, power, and network connectivity).
- Provision for data backup.

The timing of the installation project also needs to be considered with reference to wider business factors. Obviously the company needs to be doing well enough to afford the budget but you also need to be alert to other projects running in the business (product rollouts, recruitment drives, or training initiatives for instance) that could impact your project or which your new server project could affect (adversely).

Integrating the Server

One of the first decisions to make about a new server is where to put it. Some of the issues to consider here are:

- Environment - the server needs to be in a secure and climate-controlled environment. As a bare minimum, the server needs enough space and an adequate power supply.
- Network access - the server needs to be as physically close as possible to the network that it serves. This could be a local network (intra-site) or WAN (inter-site) link. Network cabling imposes restrictions on how far apart equipment can be placed.

You should prepare plans indicating how the server will be located physically in the building and logically on the network. Diagramming applications such as Microsoft Visio can be used to create such plans. The next point is to work out how the server will integrate with the rest of the network. Interoperability will largely be determined by the operating system selected for the server. By far the simplest solution is to use a single operating system for all servers on the network, but this is not always possible. The two most important factors are:

- Support for protocols - this means that the server is able to exchange data with other computers on the network.
- Support for clients - this means that software is available for client workstations to use applications running on the server directly.

If machines are not directly interoperable, it may be possible to configure another machine to act as a gateway. However, this will add complexity to the network design and decrease performance.

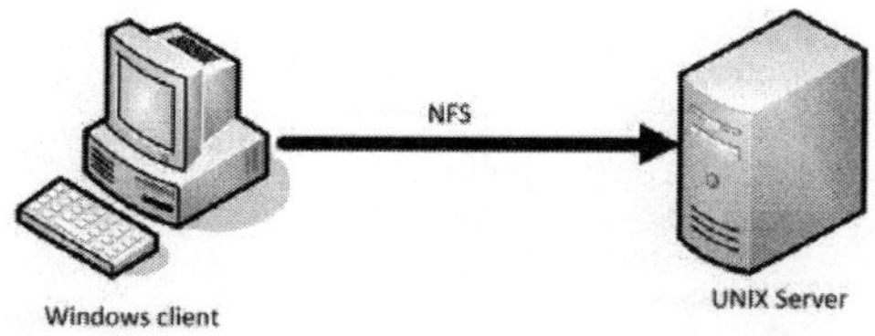

Connecting a Windows client to a UNIX server using a client-based service

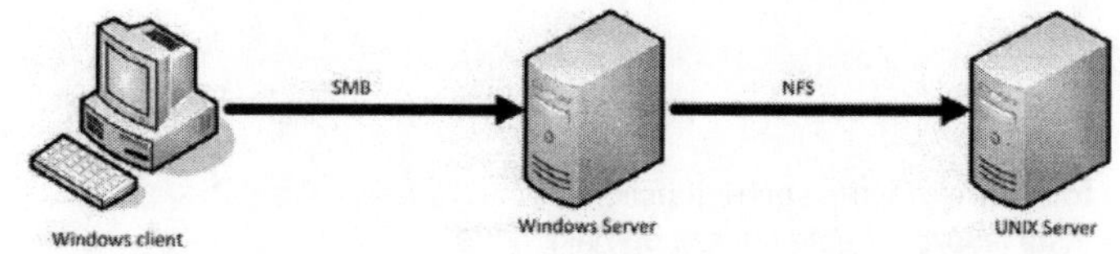

Connecting a Windows client to a UNIX server using a server gateway

The server will also need to be configured for the network. The information required usually consists of:

- Network protocol (including addressing and other configuration parameters). More than one protocol can be installed if necessary but this can degrade performance and make the system less secure. Many Windows systems run NetBIOS over TCP/IP to support pre-Windows 2000 hosts (and some features of Windows networking where NetBIOS still performs some functions).
- Network name (domain suffix).
- Computer (host) name.

As the computer name needs to be unique, there may be some convention in place for adding new computers. Some companies use character names from books or films but putting a structured, descriptive naming scheme in place can greatly assist configuration and troubleshooting. A structured naming scheme might use fixed length codes identifying key attributes of the machine:

- Physical Location.
- Client or Server / OS.
- Department.
- Server Role or main user's Job Role.
- Unique ID.

One drawback is that it can assist attempts to infiltrate (hack) the network as host names become quite easy to guess. The naming scheme could also give an attacker quite a lot of information about how the network is structured. It is important not to use the user name as the computer name.

Ongoing Management

Most management issues center on having personnel expert in the configuration of the operating system and applications software installed on the server, though some hardware systems may require specially trained staff. As well as providing staff that can administer the server, it also important to incorporate it into backup and other security procedures.

See Unit 4.2 for more information about routine maintenance.

Pilot Program

A pilot program is a test program to ensure that the server functions as expected. In the case of a server installation, it would consist of making the new server available to a number of selected users (test group) who would then perform a number of representative tasks, during which the server is closely monitored to evaluate performance and identify faults.

Another type of testing involves using software to simulate heavy user access, allowing load testing of the server under extreme conditions.

Pilot programs are quite complex to set up, but may be considered necessary for any component or software upgrade, especially if the upgrade is taking place on a mission-critical system.

Installation Procedures

Performing a server NOS installation will generally involve the following steps:

1) Check system performance and hardware components are compatible with the software.
2) Configure a volume on which to install the NOS.
3) Choose an installation method to connect to the NOS setup files and install the software.
4) Check the installation and configure basic options.

Network Operating Systems

The principal choice between PC server operating systems is between Microsoft Windows, UNIX, and Linux. Within each of these groups, there are various versions, editions, and distributions to consider however.

Microsoft Windows Server

Windows Server is the basis of most SME networks and many enterprise networks. It has been in development since the 1980s (Windows NT). The current version is Windows Server 2012 R2 with Windows Server 2016 due to be released soon (at the time of writing) .

Windows Server is produced in a number of editions, designed for different markets. Windows Server 2008 R2 and later are only available as 64-bit software.

The following list represents the editions in the Server 2012 range:

- The **Standard** edition is the mainstream server platform for enterprise networks.
- The **Datacenter** edition is a different licensing mode that allows unlimited use of virtualized instances compared to the Standard edition.
- The **Foundation** and **Essentials** editions are designed for smaller networks of up to 15 and 25 users respectively.

Windows Server has too many features to list here but you should be aware of two important operating modes:

- Server Core - a minimal installation operated only by a command prompt.
- Hyper-V - Microsoft's virtualization platform. Hyper-V can be installed as one role among others on a Windows Server or installed as a stand-alone Hyper-V Server product.

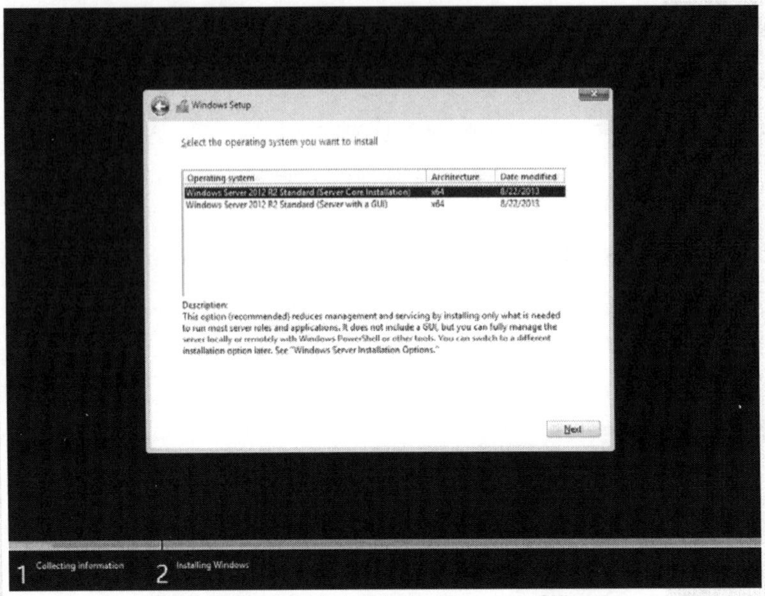

Windows Server can be installed in either core or GUI mode

*nix

*nix refers to various operating systems based to a greater or lesser extent on UNIX.

UNIX itself has been in development for just over 40 years. UNIX is available from a variety of vendors and is also available freely as open source software. Some of the main implementations of UNIX are:

- System V - developed by AT&T and then sold to Novell, who then sold the rights on again. It has spawned Sun Solaris and SCO's OpenServer and UnixWare.
- BSD (including NetBSD, OpenBSD, and FreeBSD) - based on the version of UNIX developed at the University of California at Berkley. Apple have based OS X on BSD UNIX.

UNIX is widely used on academic networks and also supports high performance server computing applications in major enterprises.

Linux, initially developed in the 1990s by Linus Torvalds, is a fully open source version of UNIX. Linux is packaged in distributions or "distros". The Linux **kernel** is common to all distributions; what distinguishes them is the packages included, the method of distribution, the frequency of updates, availability of support, and so on. There are too many distributions to list fully but some of the best known are:

- Red Hat (Fedora) - the most commercially successful distribution.

- SUSE - originally developed in Germany from a distribution called Slackware, SUSE was adopted by Novell as a means of porting the successful elements of its Netware NOS to an ongoing server platform.

- Debian - established as a non-commercial, volunteer-oriented project. One of the derivatives of Debian is Ubuntu, promoted by the company Canonical. Ubuntu is provided in desktop and server versions. Knoppix is another popular Debian derivative.

There are more GUI tools available for most distributions of Linux than there are for UNIX but most configuration tasks are still better performed at the command line or by editing configuration files directly.

Linux is probably most widely deployed as a web application server. A **Linux, Apache, MySQL, PHP (LAMP)** server provides the NOS (Linux), web server (Apache), database (MySQL), and programming language (PHP) required to host a typical ecommerce, training, or social networking web application. Linux is also very widely used as an embedded file server in Network Attached Storage (NAS) devices. Linux is being increasingly widely deployed in local network server roles as companies, schools, and government departments try to reduce the licensing costs associated with running services on Windows.

OS X

As noted above, Apple OS X is based on BSD UNIX, with the Apple Mac GUI running on top. The distinctive point about OS X is that it can only be installed to Apple's range of computers. Consequently it is restricted to a specialist market only, especially as far as the server edition is concerned.

Hardware Compatibility List (HCL)

The first step in specifying or upgrading server hardware is to confirm that it will support the NOS and applications software that you want to install on it.

Each version of Windows Server and the main distributions of Linux are accompanied by **Hardware Compatibility Lists (HCL)** containing all the components known to work with the NOS. This will include expansion cards and peripheral devices.

You also need to verify **processor and memory compatibility**. There are two things to consider here. The system requirements are the absolute minimum spec (without which the NOS will not install). There is not much point in provisioning a server that barely meets the minimum specification however as it is unlikely to deliver acceptable performance if configured as anything other than a very basic file or web server.

The other consideration, if you are provisioning servers for a really high performance role, is the **system limitations** - that is, the *maximum* number of CPUs and system memory supported. Windows Server comes in different editions with different limits. For example, the Essentials edition of Server 2012 supports up to 64 GB RAM while the Standard and Datacenter editions support up to 4 TB. The various distributions of Linux may have different system limits, though these are usually determined by the kernel version rather than being distribution-specific.

64-bit platforms support more processors and system memory than 32-bit platforms.

When upgrading a server, you need to consider many other compatibility issues (such as matching expansion cards to available slot types). Hardware upgrades are covered in Unit 4.1.

Vendor Standards for Hardware

Software vendors often develop standards for hardware vendors to certify their products against. This allows the hardware vendor to use the software vendor's logo to market their products. For example, Microsoft operate a **Windows Logo** testing program. A server or hardware device / driver can be tested at a number of levels. A "Certified for Windows Server 2012 R2" logo represents a product that has passed more stringent tests than one with a "Works with Windows Server 2012 R2" logo for instance. Driver software that has passed Windows Logo testing can be published to Windows Update.

Information for hardware developers is published at www.microsoft.com/whdc. A catalogue of Windows Logo products for Windows Server is published at www.windowsservercatalog.com.

Similarly, some of the commercial Linux vendors, such as Red Hat and Novell (YES Certified SUSE), operate their own hardware testing logo programs.

Installation and Deployment Methods

The NOS installation method refers to the way in which the server computer accesses the setup files.

Using a particular type of installation method depends on the server supporting that type of boot media and being configured to allow booting from that type of device. See Unit 1.4 for more information selecting boot devices.

Local Media

The simplest sort of installation is via local media. The most common local installation method is **optical media** (CD or DVD). In this situation, the installer simply inserts the product disc and boots the computer from the disc.

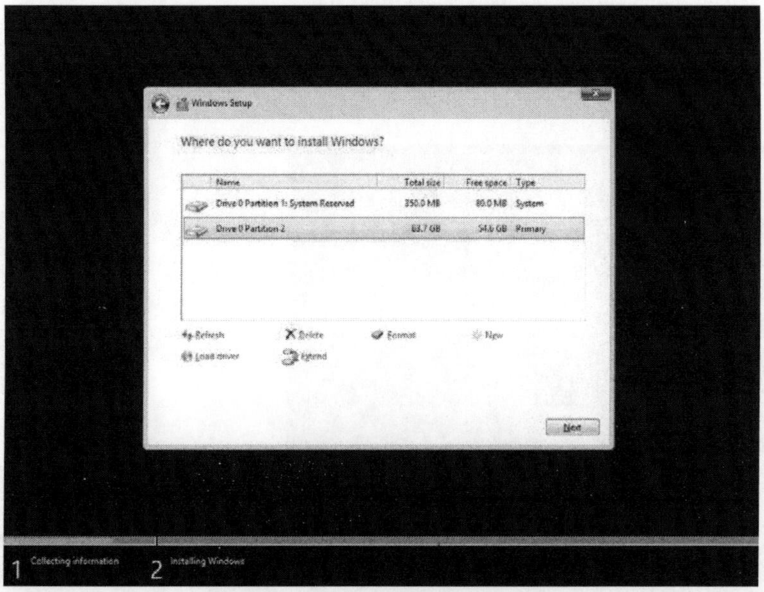

Configuring the disk using Windows Setup

The setup process will prompt the installer to configure partitions and file systems on the disk and then choose installation options, such as network settings and default users.

Another local media option is to put the setup files on **USB media** (such as a USB thumb drive or a USB-connected hard drive). This is a useful method if the setup files you use change often. For example, you could slipstream product updates or service packs into the master setup files, avoiding the need to install them all post-setup.

Most NOSs will also provide a means of performing an **unattended installation.** This means that rather than having an installer key in the setup options, they are provided as part of an answer file or script and used by the setup program automatically.

The answer file has to be made available to the setup program somehow. With older software, it used to be placed on a floppy disk. Another option is to add it to the setup media.

Local installation is not a very practical method in most enterprise network environments, which are far more likely to use some sort of cross-network deployment.

Cross-network Installation

If the installer has several machines to install, a **network share** containing the necessary installation files can be created on a file server. The server then needs some method of connecting to the network share when it boots. This could be accomplished using a network boot disk but that might involve the installer having to go to the server. A server equipped with a PXE-enabled network adapter can boot from the network card, obtain an IP configuration, and start the setup process from the network share using the **Trivial File Transfer Protocol (TFTP)**.

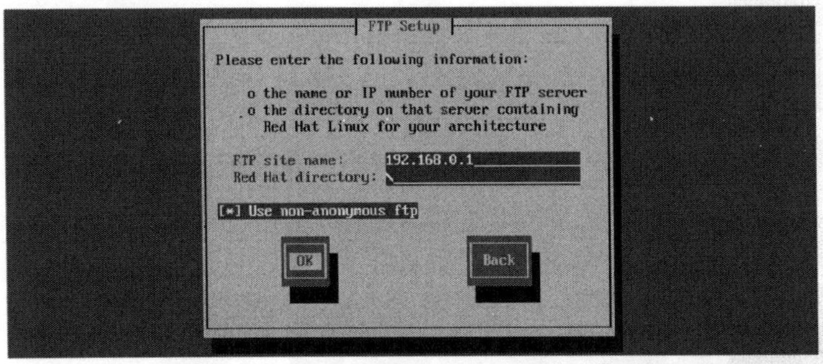

Connecting to a remote installation share when installing Linux

Alternatively, a server equipped with a "Lights Out" management card could be booted remotely.

See Unit 4.5 for more information about management tools.

Once again, an answer file, stored on the source server, could be created to automate the deployment.

Image-based Installation

Installing from setup media only installs the underlying NOS with very basic configuration options (such as video options or the means of obtaining a network address). The setup media might be slipstreamed to include the latest product updates but that is about the limit of what can be customized.

An enterprise network may involve several application servers each of which needs to be configured in the same way. In this case, it can save a lot of time to take an existing system installation - the NOS, plus server applications, and custom configuration options - and **clone** it. To clone an installation on a physical server, you use software to make an image of the boot volume, using imaging software. This image can then be deployed to a new, blank volume in another server.

Cloning a virtual machine is easier as the machine is run from an image anyway - you just need to copy the image file. See Unit 2.5 for more information about server virtualization.

Windows System Image Manager

The **Windows System Image Manager** is used to configure **answer files**. An answer file contains the information input during setup, such as disk partitions and file systems, product key, computer name, language and network settings, and so on. This file is accessed automatically during setup, meaning that an installer does not have to be present. The System Image Manager is packaged with the **Windows Assessment and Deployment Kit (ADK)**, formerly the **Windows Automated Installation Kit (WAIK)**, available from Microsoft's site.

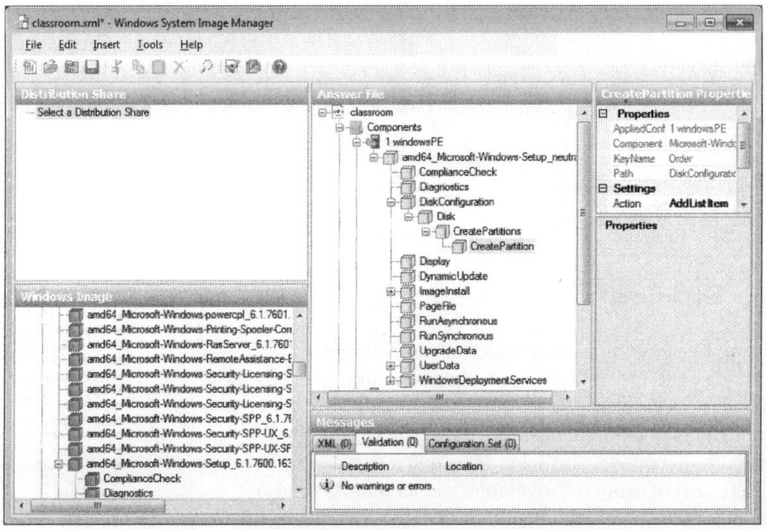

Windows System Image Manager

Another option is the Microsoft Deployment Toolkit (MDT), which provides a more user-friendly interface to the tools in the WAIK and gives more options for deploying applications and drivers.

Drive Cloning and Sysprep

If Windows is to be deployed to multiple machines with similar hardware specifications, the most common method of deployment is to use disk imaging software to clone an installation from one PC (the reference machine) to the rest. This has the advantage that a full system can be built, including applications, service packs and patches, and default user settings.

You need different images for 32- and 64-bit platforms.

Microsoft's ImageX tool (part of the WAIK) or third-party disk imaging software, such as Symantec's Ghost, is used to duplicate the disk contents. However, duplicating the disk exactly can cause problems, as it repeats the SID (a unique identifier for each machine) and assumes that the machines have exactly the same hardware configuration, which may not be the case.

Microsoft's **System Preparation Tool (Sysprep)** utility should be run *before* imaging the disk to side-step these problems.

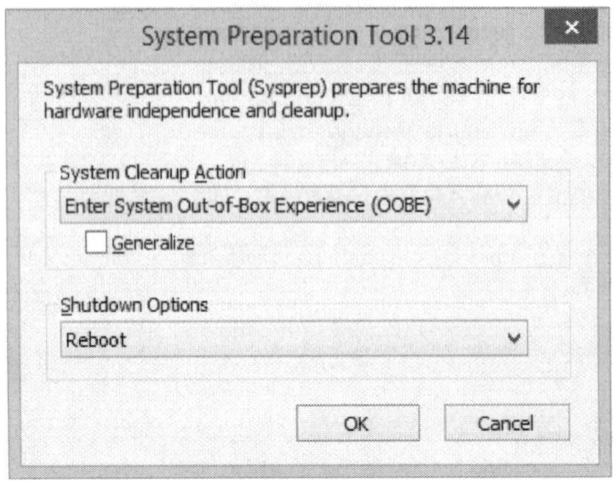

Resealing your computer using sysprep

Windows Deployment Services

A basic network installation can be setup by putting the installation files in a network share, booting the machine to the network, then accessing the installation program from the share. **Windows Deployment Services** is a Windows Server component used to implement network installs more effectively. This works with image-based installs, using Microsoft's **Windows Imaging Format (WIM)**. To support network deployments, clients must have a PXE compatible firmware and network adapter.

Enterprise networks are also likely to use the OS Deployment (OSD) feature in Microsoft's System Center Configuration Manager (SCCM). One of the principal advantages of SCCM is that it can perform Zero Touch Installation (ZTI), where the technician does not have to press a key (F12) to start the install from PXE. Unlike WAIK and MDT however, SCCM licences must be paid for.

Commented [MNS1]: Please check. Chunks of text have been highlighted throughout this study guide.

Ghost / Altiris

Symantec Ghost and Altiris Deployment Services are two separate imaging products, though both are now owned by Symantec. The main reason to use these tools would be to support non-Windows servers (or client workstations). Support departments might also be used to using one tool over another and prefer not to have to train in the use of something else.

Configuring the NOS

When setup is complete, you should log in to the OS to complete some basic configuration tasks. When those are complete, you can configure network and security (firewall) settings and then you will be ready to configure a server role (install and configure applications).

Driver Installation

Drivers are required to provide an interface between a device, such as an expansion card or peripheral, and the OS. When you install the OS, the setup media contains drivers for compatible devices at the time the disc was manufactured. If a driver is not available on the setup disc, the device will not be installed. You can install drivers manually by obtaining them from the server vendor's support site or directly from the device vendor's support site. For Windows, you can also obtain new or updated drivers from Windows Update.

32-bit and 64-bit drivers are not compatible. If you have a 64-bit OS installed, you must obtain 64-bit driver software.

Some drivers are installed by running the vendor's setup software. This installs the driver to a system location that the OS checks automatically when detecting new hardware. Sometimes a driver will just be supplied in a compressed archive, in which case you need to extract the files from the archive then point the OS to the driver file location when prompted.

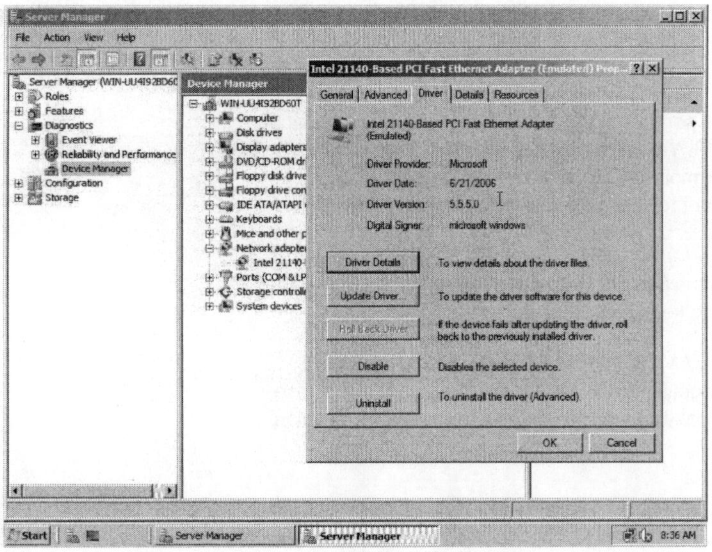

Device Manager in Windows Server 2008

In Windows, you manage devices via the **Device Manager** console. You can use the shortcut menus here to scan for new hardware, update device drivers, roll a driver back to a previous version, disable a device, or remove it from the system completely.

Bad driver software could be used to infect a computer with malware or could cause system instability. Microsoft created a driver signing policy for Windows that can prevent the installation of unsigned drivers (those that have not received a digital certificate from Microsoft). In earlier versions of Windows, you can disable driver signing if you prefer to take the risk, but in the x64 versions driver signing is mandatory and cannot be disabled.

In Linux, device drivers are usually provided as loadable kernel modules. The **modprobe** command is used to load a module (if the kernel has not done so automatically) while **lsmod** gives a list of currently loaded modules.

Virtual Memory

All operating systems support **virtual memory**, sometimes known as a **swap file** or **pagefile**. Virtual memory is used when the operating system requires access to more memory than is physically installed in the computer. Rather than generate an error message, or worse, abend (Abnormal End of Task - a crash), the use of the swap file allows the operating system to satisfy the memory request.

As RAM gets filled up, pages of memory are moved to disk, on the designated swap file, freeing those pages in RAM for system use. Since disk access is slow compared with RAM, it is generally desirable to minimize paging, or swapping (by installing more system RAM), although you should always ensure you have the recommended amount of swap file space allocated for your OS.

Paging in Windows

By default, Windows creates a pagefile in the boot drive (generally the root of drive C) called PAGEFILE.SYS. You might want to tune the pagefile size based on the server role, the amount of system memory, and the disk subsystem. You might also want to configure a pagefile on other physical disks, to improve performance.

The pagefile is configured via the System Properties dialog. When tuning the pagefile the following should be kept in mind:

- Use the equation System RAM * 1.5 to calculate the initial (minimum) pagefile. The maximum pagefile size is configured to prevent disk space being exhausted. The typical value for maximum is twice the initial value.

  *1.5 * System RAM is the typical advice but on a 64-bit server with a large amount of system RAM or on a server where disk space is tight you may want to "tune" the pagefile size to reflect actual usage. You can use the Performance Monitor tool to check pagefile usage. Microsoft recommend setting the pagefile to the highest value shown by Page File Bytes Peak * 0.7. Keep monitoring pagefile usage to ensure it does not exceed 70%.*

- It can boost performance to allocate a fast, dedicated disk to house the main pagefile. You could also create a pagefile on each physical disk - Windows will use the fastest one available. You should *not* configure multiple pagefiles in different partitions of the same physical disk however. The partition storing the pagefile should be formatted with NTFS.

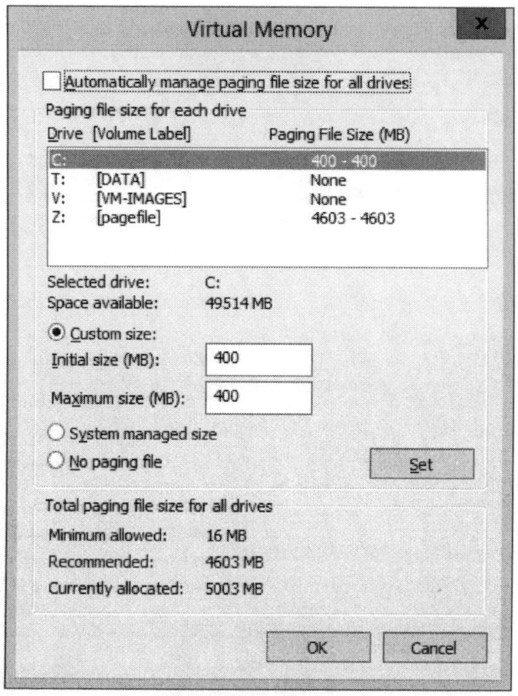

Paging file configuration

If you move the pagefile from the system root to another volume, you will not be able to collect data following a system crash into a memory debug file. It is a good idea to configure a small pagefile on the boot volume for redundancy.

- The pagefile does not have to use contiguous disk space - although performance is further enhanced if it does. Disk defragmentation is a process whereby the contents of a disk are moved around to optimize disk access times. The components of a file (known as clusters) are placed adjacent on the disk surface (they are said to be contiguous). To ensure that the pagefile uses contiguous space you will need to defragment the drive then ensure that the maximum and minimum sizes of the pagefile are the same.

- It is possible that secure information will be paged. If security is a concern, then the paging file content can be deleted during shut down by configuring the registry or local security settings.

Virtual Memory in Linux

In Linux, virtual memory can be configured either as a **swap file** or as a **swap partition**. Swap partitions are more efficient but more difficult to manage (it is easier to change the size of a swap file). The setup program will normally create a swap file or partition by default but in SUSE Linux (for example), you can use the YaST control center program, and select the **Expert Partitioner** manager, and create additional swap files.

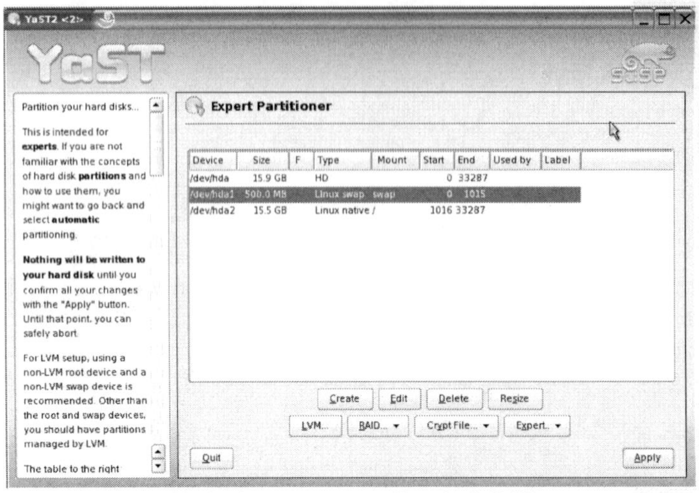

Viewing the current swap configuration in YaST

Assuming you have an area of free and un-partitioned space on a disk attached to your Linux system, use the same utility to create a swap partition.

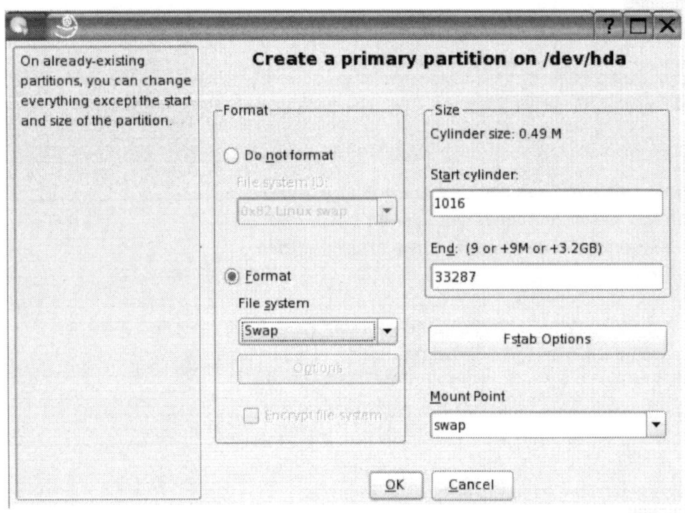

Adding a swap partition in SUSE Linux

At the command line, the **mkswap** command is used to configure a swap partition while the **swapon** and **swapoff** commands activate or deactivate it. A swap file is created using the **dd** command and then activated with **swapon**.

Other Environmental Settings

Virtual memory is probably the most important environmental setting, but you should also check that the system is configured with the correct date and time. You should also verify that the installation options have left the server configured with the appropriate regional settings (date and currency format, keyboard layout, time zone, and so on).

Review Questions / Module 1 / Unit 5 / Server Operating Systems

Answer these questions to test what you have learned in this unit.

1) What three main stages would you consider when planning for a new server installation?
2) What is a pilot program?
3) What two main alternatives to a GUI-based Windows Server are offered by Microsoft?
4) What is a "LAMP" server?
5) What does a logo testing program demonstrate?
6) What would you need to put in place to allow an automated installation of a server across the network?
7) What additional step do you usually need to take if deploying a new NOS from an existing system image?
8) True or false? Virtual memory performance can be improved by configuring a pagefile on each partition of a single disk or virtual disk.

Module 1 / Unit 6

Troubleshooting Procedures

Objectives

On completion of this unit, you will be able to:

- Identify the steps in the CompTIA Server+ troubleshooting model.
- Use troubleshooting procedures to diagnose and resolve issues methodically.

Troubleshooting Procedures

When you encounter a problem, you must try to get it resolved as quickly as you reasonably can. However, you must also take enough time to determine what has caused the problem, so that you can avoid a recurrence. You should make sure you familiarize yourself with the order of the steps in the CompTIA Server+ troubleshooting model:

1) Identify the problem and determine the scope
    - Question users / stakeholders and identify changes to the server / environment
    - Collect additional documentation / logs
    - If possible, replicate the problem as appropriate
    - If possible, perform backups before making changes
2) Establish a theory of probable cause / question the obvious
    - Determine whether there is a common element of symptom causing multiple problems
3) Test the theory to determine cause
    - Once theory is confirmed determine next steps to resolve problem
    - If theory is not confirmed, establish new theory or escalate
4) Establish a plan of action to resolve the problem and notify impacted users
5) Implement the solution or escalate as necessary
    - Make one change at a time and test / confirm the change has resolved the problem
    - If the problem is not resolved, reverse the change if appropriate and implement new change

6) Verify full system functionality and if applicable implement preventive measures

7) Perform a root cause analysis

8) Document findings, actions, and outcomes throughout the process

These steps are explained in more detail in the following topics.

Identifying the Problem

The first step in the troubleshooting process is to establish what the best sources of information about the problem may be.

Determining the Scope and Gathering Information

At the outset, define the scope of the problem (that is, the area affected). This is helpful in two ways - firstly, if it's a single backup FTP server then it's not as urgent as the other outstanding call you have. But if it's the multiple virtual server instances affecting hundreds of users, then it's more urgent. In addition, the fact that the problem affects a wider area means that it is unlikely to be a problem with one particular server configuration. Knowing the scope of the problem can help to identify its source and also prioritize the issue in relation to other incidents. As well as the information gathering techniques discussed below, consider what indirect sources of information there may be:

- If the system is available, check the event logs for system, application, or security errors. You might also have a management server to collect logs from remote machines, though if the problem server has failed it might not be transmitting its logs.
- Check the system documentation (such as installation or maintenance logs) for useful information.
- Check recent job logs or consult any other technicians that might have worked on the system recently or might be working at the moment on some related issue.
- Use vendor support sites (knowledge bases) and forums.

Question Users and Stakeholders

The first report of a problem will typically come from a user or another technician and they will be one of the best sources of information, if you can ask the right questions. You might also need to question stakeholders, such as the business managers who rely on the service provided by that server or the application developers who built the service. Remember that as well as solving a technical problem (fixing the server) you also need to provide business solutions (letting users get on with their work as soon as possible).

The basis of getting troubleshooting information from users is asking good *questions*.

Questions are commonly divided into two types:

- Open questions invite someone to explain in their own words. Examples are, "What is the problem?" or "What happens when you try to switch the computer on?" Open questions are good to start with as they help to avoid making your own assumptions about what is wrong and encourage the user to give you all the information they are able to.
- Closed questions invite a Yes/No answer or a fixed response. Examples include, "Can you see any text on the screen?" or "What does the error message say?" Closed questions can be used to "drill down" into the nature of the problem and guide a user towards giving you information that is useful.

Information gathering is the first step in troubleshooting

Identify Symptoms and Replicate the Problem

Of course, you cannot always rely on the user to let you know everything that has happened. To diagnose a problem, you may also need to use the following techniques:

- Make a physical inspection; look for something out of the ordinary.
- Replicate the problem on the user's system (if appropriate) or a test system. Issues that are transitory or difficult to reproduce are often the hardest to troubleshoot. You need to consider whether replicating the problem is an appropriate action to take - could you cause more damage by doing so?
- Check system logs or diagnostic software for information.

Determine If Anything Has Changed

There are two key questions to ask when trying to identify the cause of a problem:

- **Did it ever work?** Hopefully your users will answer the question truthfully, because the correct answer is important. If the system worked before 9 am, you must ask what happened at 9 am. If the system never worked, then you are not looking for something that stopped working, but for something which was never done in the first place. Two different approaches required.

- **What has changed since it was last working?** The change that caused the problem may be nothing obvious. Maybe the window cleaners were in the building, and one of them tripped over a cable and now the user can't login. Maybe a technician has moved a server from one rack to another and plugged a cable into the wrong port.

Perform Backups

Consider the importance of data stored on the server when performing troubleshooting or maintenance. Check when a backup was last made. If a backup has not been made, perform one before changing the system configuration, if at all possible. The simplest way of making a backup before troubleshooting is to use disk imaging software.

Establishing a Probable Cause

If you obtain accurate answers to your initial questions, you will have determined the severity of the problem (how many are affected), a rough idea of where to look (workstation or server end), and whether to look for a recent change or an oversight in configuration.

You diagnose a problem by identifying the **symptoms**. From knowing what causes such symptoms, you can test each **possible cause** until you find the right one. Sometimes symptoms derive from more than one cause; while this type of problem is rarer, it is much harder to troubleshoot.

A network system comprises a number of components. Fault finding needs to identify which component is faulty. For difficult problems, be prepared to consider multiple approaches. If one approach does not identify the problem, use a different one. For example, you could consider two different styles of approaching troubleshooting:

- Question the obvious - step through what *should* happen and identify the point at which there is a failure or error. This approach can quickly identify obvious oversights, such as a network cable not being plugged in.

- Methodically prove the functionality of each component in sequence. This approach is more time consuming but may be necessary for a difficult problem.

Approaching Multiple Problems

When you start to investigate symptoms, you might discover symptoms of more than one problem. Perhaps a user has reported that a machine has lost Internet connectivity and you discover that it has also not been receiving maintenance updates. The issues could be related or one might be incidental to the other.

If the problems do not seem to be related, treat each issue as a separate case. If they seem to be related, check for outstanding support or maintenance tickets that might indicate existing problems.

It may also be the case that a user reports two different problems at the same time (often preceded by "While you're on the line…" sort of statements). Treat each problem as a separate case. In most cases you should advise the user to raise a separate support ticket.

Test a Probable Cause and Escalate a Problem

Hopefully you will have gathered sufficient data to come to an initial theory about the probable cause. Remember that you might be wrong! Without jumping to conclusions, set out to prove or disprove your suspicions by using your troubleshooting skills and toolkit.

If you can prove the cause of the problem, you can start to investigate the most appropriate solution. If you cannot prove the cause of the problem, you will need either to develop and test a new theory or decide to **escalate** the problem. **Escalation** means referring the problem to a senior technician, manager, or third-party. You may need to escalate a problem for any of these reasons:

- The problem is beyond your knowledge or ability to troubleshoot.
- The problem falls under a system warranty and would be better dealt with by the supplier.
- The scope of the problem is very large and / or the solution requires some major reconfiguration of services.
- A customer becomes difficult or abusive or demands help on an unsupported item.

Some of the alternatives for escalation include:

- Senior staff / Knowledge Experts / Subject Matter Experts / technical staff / developers / programmers / administrators within your company.
- Suppliers and manufacturers.
- Other support contractors / consultants.

When you escalate a problem, you should have established the basic facts, such as the scope of the problem and its likely cause and be able to communicate these clearly to the person to whom you are referring the incident.

Establishing a Plan of Action

Assuming you choose not to escalate the issue, the next step in the troubleshooting process is to establish an **action plan**. An action plan sets out the steps you will take to solve the problem. There are typically three solutions to any problem:

- **Repair** - you need to determine whether the cost of repair / time taken to reconfigure something makes this the best option.
- **Replace** - often more expensive and may be time-consuming if a part is not available. There may also be an opportunity to **upgrade** the device or software.

  A basic technique when troubleshooting a cable, connector, or device is to have a "known good" duplicate to hand (that is, another copy of the same cable or device that you know works) and to test by substitution.

- **Ignore** - as any software developer will tell you, not all problems are critical. If neither repair nor replace is cost-effective, it may be best either to find a workaround or just to document the issue and move on.

When you consider solutions you have to assess the cost and time required. Another consideration is potential effects on the rest of the system. A typical example is applying a software patch, which might fix a given problem but cause other programs not to work. This is where an effective configuration management system comes into play as it should help you to understand how different systems are interconnected and cause you to seek the proper authorization for your plan.

Implement the Solution

If you do not have authorization to implement a solution, you will need to escalate the problem to more senior personnel. If applying the solution is disruptive to the wider network, you also need to consider the most appropriate time to schedule the reconfiguration work and plan how to notify impacted users.

When you make a change to the system as part of implementing a solution, test after each change. If the change does not fix the problem, reverse it then try something else. If you make a series of changes without recording what you have done, you could find yourself in a tricky position.

Verify Full System Functionality and Implement Preventive Measures

When you apply a solution, test that it fixes the reported problem *and* that the system as a whole continues to function normally (that is, identify the results and effects of the solution). Ensure that you were right and that the problem is resolved. Can the user now login properly? Is there any way you can induce the problem again?

Before you can consider a problem closed, you should both be satisfied in your own mind that you have resolved it *and* get the customer's acceptance that it has been fixed. Restate what the problem was and how it was resolved then confirm with the customer that the incident log can be closed.

To fully solve a problem, you should try to eliminate any factors that may cause the problem to reoccur. For example, if a technician plugs a server into the wrong network jack, ensure that the jacks are clearly labeled to help other technicians in the future. If a faulty server induces hours of network downtime, consider implementing failover services to minimize the impact of the next incident.

Perform a Root Cause Analysis

Identifying the underlying cause of symptoms is called **root cause analysis**. There are several models to help with root cause analysis (such as the 5 Whys model or the Ishiwaka / Fishbone Diagram). For example, in the 5 Whys model, you ask a series of "why" questions aimed at illuminating cause and effect. You may not use precisely 5 Whys; the idea is to ensure that the process deals with relevant symptoms and gets to a conclusion:

- Why have several new servers been displaying blue screens?
- *Because there is a hard disk error.* Why is there an error?
- *Because sectors on the hard drive are corrupt.* Why is that?
- *Because the drives are degraded.* But why would a number of new drives fail at the same time?
- *Because there was a manufacturing defect.* Why did the vendor not inform me?
- *Because I didn't register the servers to obtain useful information and alerts such as this.*

If you don't get to an actual root cause, work back up the series of questions, look for a different answer, and see what new questions that answer raises.

Document Findings, Actions, and Outcomes

Most troubleshooting takes place within the context of a ticket system. This shows who is responsible for any particular problem and what its status is. This gives you the opportunity to add a complete description of the problem and its solution (findings, actions, and outcomes).

This is massively useful for future troubleshooting, as problems fitting into the same category can be reviewed to see if the same solution applies. It also helps to analyze IT infrastructure by gathering statistics on what type of problems occur and how frequently.

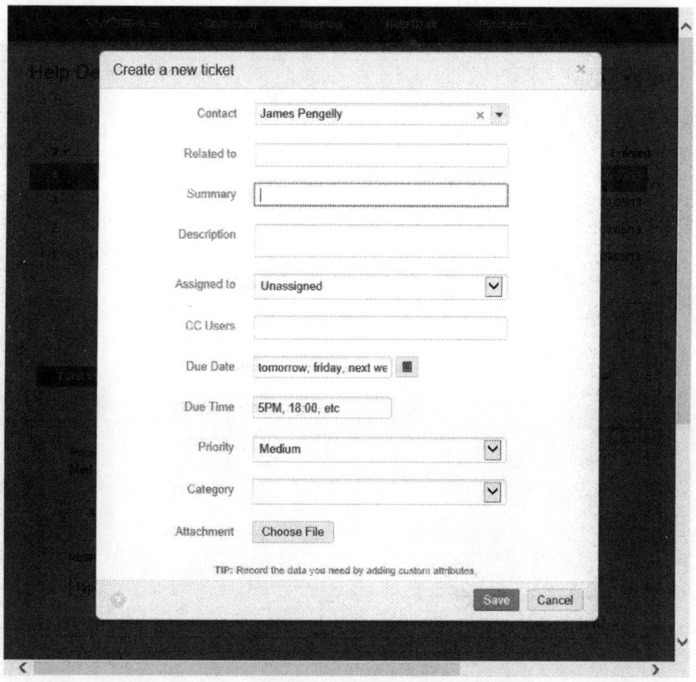

Creating a ticket in the Spiceworks IT Support management tool

When you complete a problem log, remember that people other than you may come to rely on it. Also, logs may be presented to customers as proof of troubleshooting activity. Write clearly and concisely, checking for spelling and grammar errors.

Review Questions / Module 1 / Unit 6 / Troubleshooting Procedures

Answer these questions to test what you have learned in this unit.

1) What step follows verifying system functionality in the Server+ troubleshooting model?
2) What are the five main information gathering activities involved in identifying the problem?
3) What approach might you take if no other methods have identified the cause of a problem?
4) What is the point of completing root cause analysis?

Module 1 / Summary
Server Setup

You learned about server-class hardware form factors and storage solutions along with installation and configuration management best practices and how to select and install a Network Operating System (NOS).

Module 1 / Unit 1 / Servers and Racks

- Make sure you can distinguish the features that characterize servers, desktops, and workstations and know what is meant by fault tolerance, availability, scalability, and load balancing.
- The server hardware and OS are provisioned to perform different functions and roles, such as network administration or web and email servers.
- Make sure you know the features, advantages, and disadvantages of tower, rack, and blade server form factors.
- Learn the features of rack-mounted equipment and understand how to install appliances, peripherals, and accessories into racks with regard to safe working practices.

Module 1 / Unit 2 / Storage Devices

- Make sure you can identify the features and performance characteristics of server-class hard disks and solid state drives.
- Know the features and performance characteristics of the SCSI, SATA, and SAS interfaces and how to install and configure devices on each type of bus.

Module 1 / Unit 3 / RAID

- RAID levels offer different cost, performance, redundancy options for a given storage solution. Make sure you know the number of disk failures a given RAID level can tolerate and how to calculate the capacity of an array.
- A RAID array can be configured using hardware or OS utilities. Make sure you know the features, advantages, and disadvantages of hardware versus software solutions.

Module 1 / Unit 4 / System Setup

- The system firmware can be either BIOS or UEFI. You should be able to use the system setup tools to configure low-level hardware settings and boot options.
- Make sure you can create and format hard disk partitions using an appropriate file system for the target NOS.

Module 1 / Unit 5 / Server Operating Systems

- Server deployment should be guided by an installation plan setting out the server role, the hardware, network, and backup requirements plus options for ongoing management and performance monitoring.
- You should be able to identify different types and versions of Network Operating System and evaluate hardware requirements.
- Make sure you can perform OS setup using local media or network-based unattended installations.
- Post-setup tasks include installing additional drivers, configuring virtual memory, and performing system updates.

Module 1 / Unit 6 / Troubleshooting Procedures

- Make sure you know the steps in the CompTIA Server+ troubleshooting model and can put them into the correct sequence.
- Learn the troubleshooting procedures to use to diagnose and resolve issues methodically.

Module 2 / Server Networking

CompTIA Server+ SK0-004 Domain Areas	Weighting
1.0 Server Architecture	12%
2.0 Server Administration	24%
3.0 Storage	12%
4.0 Security	13%
5.0 Networking	10%
6.0 Disaster Recovery	9%
7.0 Troubleshooting	20%

The following table lists the CompTIA Server+ domain objectives and content examples covered in the units in this module:

Refer To	Domain Objectives/Examples
Unit 2.1 / Ethernet	**5.1 Given a scenario, configure servers to use IP addressing and network infrastructure services** *MAC addresses • Network Interface Card configuration (NIC teaming, Duplexing [Full, Half, Auto], Speeds [10 / 100 / 1000 Mbps, 10 Gbps])*
	5.3 Given a scenario, install cables and implement proper cable management procedures *Copper (Patch cables [Crossover, Straight through, Rollover], CAT5, CAT5e, CAT6) • Fiber (Single-mode, Multi-mode) • Connectors (ST, LC, SC, SFP, RJ-45, RJ-11) • Cable placement and routing (Cable channels, Cable management trays [Vertical, Horizontal]) • Labeling • Bend radius • Cable ties*
	7.4 Given a scenario, effectively diagnose network problems, selecting the appropriate tools and methods *Causes of common problems (Component failure, Bad cables, Mis-configured NIC)*
Unit 2.2 / Internet Protocol	**5.1 Given a scenario, configure servers to use IP addressing and network infrastructure services** *IPv4 vs. IPv6 • Default gateway • CIDR notation and subnetting • Public and private IP addressing • Static IP assignment vs. DHCP*
	7.4 Given a scenario, effectively diagnose network problems, selecting the appropriate tools and methods *Common problems (DHCP server mis-configured, non-functional or unreachable, Destination host unreachable) • Causes of common problems (Improper IP configuration, IPv4 vs. IPv6 misconfigurations) • Networking tools (ping, ipconfig / ifconfig)*
Unit 2.3 / Routers and Firewalls	**4.3 Explain basic network security systems and protocols** *Firewall (Network-based, Host-based) • Router access list • VLAN • Security zones (DMZ, Public and private, Intranet and extranet)*
	5.1 Given a scenario, configure servers to use IP addressing and network infrastructure services *NAT / PAT*

Refer To	Domain Objectives/Examples
Unit 2.3 / Routers and Firewalls	**5.2 Compare and contrast various ports and protocols** *TCP vs. UDP • SNMP - 161 • SMTP - 25 • FTP - 20 / 21 • SFTP - 22 • SSH - 22 • SCP - 22 • NTP - 123 • HTTP - 80 • HTTPS - 443 • TELNET - 23 • IMAP - 143 • POP3 - 110 • RDP - 3389 • FTPS - 989 / 990 • LDAP - 389/3268 • DNS - 53 • DHCP – 68*
	7.4 Given a scenario, effectively diagnose network problems, selecting the appropriate tools and methods *Common problems (Internet connectivity failure, Default gateway mis-configured, Failure of service provider) • Causes of common problems (Improper IP configuration, VLAN configuration, Port security, Improper subnetting, Incorrect OS route tables, Firewall [mis-configuration, hardware failure, software failure], Routing / switch issues) • Networking tools (ping, tracert / traceroute, route, netstat)*
Unit 2.4 / Network Services	**2.2 Compare and contrast server roles and requirements for each** *Network services server (DHCP, DNS / WINS, NTP)*
	5.1 Given a scenario, configure servers to use IP addressing and network infrastructure services *DNS (FQDN, Default domain suffix / search domain) • WINS • NetBIOS*
	7.4 Given a scenario, effectively diagnose network problems, selecting the appropriate tools and methods *Common problems (Unknown host, Cannot reach by host name / FQDN) • Causes of common problems (DNS and/or DHCP failure, Mis-configured hosts file) • Networking tools (nslookup, nbtstat, netstat)*
Unit 2.5 / Virtualization Services	**2.6 Explain the purpose and operation of virtualization components** *Hosts and guests • Management interface for virtual machines • Hypervisor (Type I, Type II, Hybrid) • Hardware compatibility list (BIOS / UEFI compatibility and support, CPU compatibility support, AMD-V / Intel VT) • Resource allocation between Guest and Host (CPU, Storage, Memory, Network connectivity [Direct Access (Bridging) vs. NAT, Virtual NICs, Virtual switches], Video)*

Module 2 / Unit 1

Ethernet

Objectives

On completion of this unit, you will be able to:

- Describe the cable types and connectors that support Ethernet networking standards.
- Configure the properties of server-class network adapters.

Twisted Pair Cabling and Connectors

Most cabled LANs use a type of copper wire called **twisted pair** as transmission media.

Unshielded Twisted Pair Cable

The unshielded type of twisted pair cabling (UTP) used for computer networking comprises four copper conductor "pairs". Each conductor has an insulating sheath. Each pair of conductors is twisted, which reduces interference between the wires (crosstalk) and from other electromagnetic sources (Electromagnetic Interference [EMI]). The pairs are also twisted at **different rates** to further reduce interference. The signals sent over each pair are **balanced**; that is, each wire carries an equal but opposite signal to its pair. This is another factor helping to identify the signal against interference.

The four pairs are covered by a protective outer jacket. The insulation sheaths and jacket are usually made of **PVC (Polyvinyl Chloride)**.

UTP cable

The number of twists is one factor in determining the bandwidth of the cable. UTP cable is rated for different Ethernet applications according to "cat" specifications, defined in the **TIA/EIA-568-C Commercial Building Telecommunications Cabling Standards**.

Cat	Frequency	Capacity	Max. Distance	Network Application
5	100 MHz	100 Mbps	100m (328ft)	100BASE-TX
5e	100 MHz	1 Gbps	100m (328ft)	1000BASE-T
6	250 MHz	1 Gbps	100m (328ft)	1000BASE-T
		10 Gbps	55m (180ft)	10GBASE-T
6A	500 MHz	10 Gbps	100m (328ft)	10GBASE-T

Cat 5 cable is no longer available. Cat 5e is tested at 100MHz (like Cat 5 was) but to higher overall specifications for attenuation and crosstalk, meaning that the cable is rated to handle Gigabit Ethernet throughput. Cat 5e would still be an acceptable choice for providing network links for workstations. Cat 6 can support 10 Gbps but over shorter distances. Cat 6A is an improved specification cable with the ability to support 10 Gbps over 100m. It is mostly deployed in data centers or as backbone cabling between servers and network appliances.

Cabling is not the only part of the wiring system that must be rated to the appropriate category. For faster network applications (Gigabit Ethernet and better) the performance of connectors becomes increasingly critical. For example, if you are installing Cat 6A wiring, you must also install Cat 6A patch panels, wall plates, and connectors.

Network and Modem Ports

RJ-45 (left), RJ-11 (middle), and BT (right) connectors

RJ-45 (left) and RJ-11 ports

RJ-45 connectors are used with 4-pair (8-wire) cables. The connectors are also referred to as 8P8C, standing for 8-position / 8-contact. This means that all eight "potential" wire positions are supplied with contacts, so that they can all carry signals if needed. RJ-45 is by far the most common type in use for Ethernet network data cabling.

The smaller **RJ-11** connectors are used with 2- or 3-pair UTP or with flat ribbon "silver satin" phone cables. Typically only one pair carries the dial tone and voice circuit (also called the Tip and Ring wires after the way older phono plugs were wired). The other pair is usually unused but can be deployed for a secondary circuit. RJ-11 connectors are used for telephone systems (for example, to connect a modem to a phone jack). Note that an RJ-11 connector only has two contacts (6P2C); to use more pairs an RJ-14 (6P4C) connector is required. This is physically the same size as RJ-11 but has more wired contacts.

Patch Panels and Structured Cabling

An Ethernet link using twisted pair cabling can be up to 100m (328 feet). This means there must be no more than 100m of cabling between the switch and the computer. There is also a distinction between **solid** and **stranded** cabling.

Solid cabling uses a single thick wire for each conductor. Solid cable is used for "permanent" links, such as cable run through walls. This cable links the RJ-45 port on a wall plate with a **patch panel**. The solid cable terminates in **Insulation Displacement Connectors (IDC)** at the back of the wall plate and patch panel as shown below:

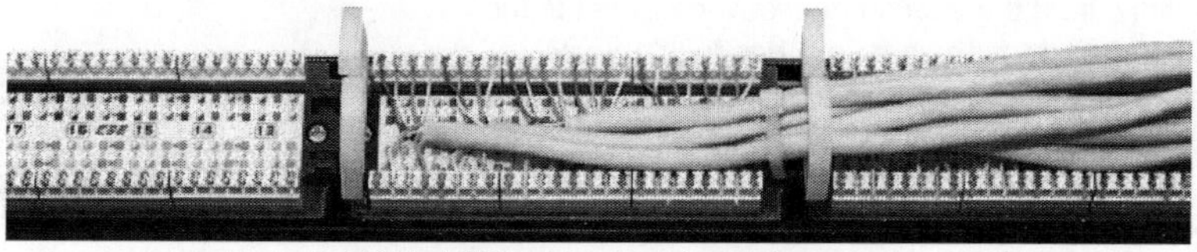

110 block IDCs at the rear of a patch panel

The other side of the patch panel has pre-wired RJ-45 ports. A patch cord, made using stranded cable with multiple thin wires wrapped around one another, is used to connect a port on the patch panel to a port on the switch. A patch cord is not supposed to be longer than 5m.

Siemon patch panel (Image © 2015 Siemon [www.siemon.com])

A second patch cord is used between the computer's network adapter and the wall port. This use of patch cords, permanent links, and patch panels is referred to as a structured cabling system:

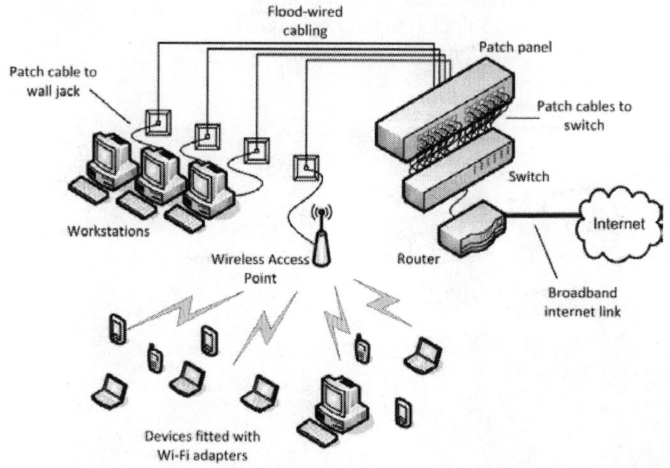

Typical larger office network - clients connect via cabled links (with solid cable in wall conduits and stranded patch cords at wall ports and the patch panel) or wireless access point to a switch while a router and broadband link provide Internet access

Installing Network Cables

A typical cabled network involves solid-core UTP run from a wall port to a distribution frame (patch panel). Both ends are terminated by **Insulation Displacement Connectors (IDC)**. At the PC end, a stranded-core UTP patch cable (with RJ-45 connectors) connects the computer's network adapter to the wall port. At the distribution frame end, a patch cable is used to connect the patch panel port to a port on the switch.

Installing fixed cable from a bulk spool is referred to as "pulling cable" because the cable has to pulled, carefully, from the telecommunications closet to the work area. Cable is normally routed through channels, conduits, or wall spaces, avoiding excessive bends and proximity to electrical power cables and fittings (such as fluorescent lights) as these could cause interference.

The main fixed cable run can be up to 90m (295 feet); stranded-wire patch cords (between the PC and wall port) and jumpers (a stranded-wire cable without connectors used on cross-connects) can be up to 5m each (16 feet) and no more than 10m (33 feet) in overall length. This is because the attenuation of stranded cable is higher than solid cable.

Starting at the patch panel, label the end of the cable with the appropriate jack ID then run it through to the work area. This is also referred to as a "drop" as in most cases you will be dropping the cable from the ceiling space through a wall cavity. If several cables are going to roughly the same place, you can bundle them and pull them together. There are various tools and techniques for pulling cable through difficult to reach areas, such as ceiling spaces. Leaving enough slack at both ends (a service loop) to make the connection, cut the cable, and label the other end with the appropriate ID. Electrician's scissors (**snips**) are designed for cutting copper wire and stripping insulation and cable jackets. Alternatively there are dedicated **wire stripper** tools that have replaceable blades for different data cable types. Cable cutting blades should be rounded to preserve the wire geometry. Stripping tools should have the correct diameter to score a cable jacket without damaging the insulation wires. Heavy duty cutters are required for armored cable.

Siemon equipment rack and cable management showing cable management brackets carrying patch cable to sides of rack and overhead cable trays routing cables to racks (Image © 2015 Siemon [www.siemon.com])

Keep cables tidy within the rack using brackets and cable ties, taking care not to pinch the cabling too tightly. Do not allow cables to hang in front of devices; make sure the cabling is led to one side of the rack. **Cable trays** can be used to channel cabling from and between racks. A cable tray is usually made of metal, with holes for ventilation. They provide easier access to cables than conduits. A vertical tray can channel cabling running up the side of a rack while a horizontal one can channel cabling between racks.

Labeling

The **ANSI/TIA/EIA 606 Administration Standard for Commercial Telecommunications Infrastructure** sets out a basic scheme for documenting a typical office network installation. It includes suggested identifiers for different subsystems and elements of the installation, including cables, distribution frames / patch panels, ports, circuits, and systems (appliances or computers).

A typical type of port **naming convention** is for alphanumeric identifiers for the campus (for multi-campus networks), building (for campus networks), telecommunications space, and port. For example CB01-01A-D01 could refer to a cable terminating at Main Campus Building (CB01), telecommunications space A on floor 1 (01A), data port 1 (D01). Structured cable and patch cords should be labelled at both ends to fully identify the circuit. A similar convention can be adopted for infrastructure and systems, such as distribution frames, patch panels, switches, routers, access points, and servers. It can be more complex to use location-based identifiers as hardware may get moved around during its service life, requiring the tag to be changed. The naming convention might also try to encode other information, such as the type and function of a device or its service/warranty support code. It is also helpful to use color-coding for cable types. One suggested scheme is as follows:

Color	Usage
Orange	Demarc / access provider
Green	Demarc / CPE
Purple	Router / PBX links
Red	Work area telephone links
White	MDF / 1st level backbone
Gray	IDF / 2nd level backbone
Brown	Campus backbone
Blue	Work area data links
Yellow	Other (alarm systems)

As well as identifying and labeling local network circuits, you should also ensure that WAN links to the Internet or to remote offices are clearly labeled and documented. The WAN provider will assign a circuit ID and you will need to quote this if raising any sort of support issue.

Patch Cable Types

Each conductor in 4-pair Ethernet cable is color-coded. Each pair is assigned a color (Blue, Orange, Green, or Brown). The first conductor in each pair has a predominantly white insulator with strips of the color; the second conductor has an insulator with the solid color.

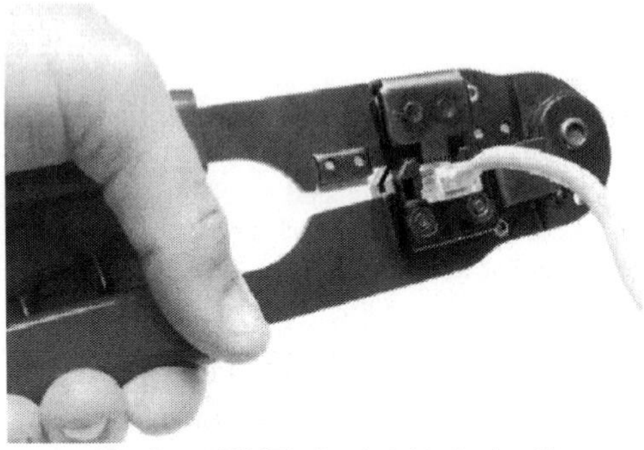

Crimping an RJ-45 jack onto twisted-pair cable

The ANSI/TIA/EIA 568 standard defines *two* methods for terminating RJ-45 connectors: T568A and T568B. The wiring for T568B is shown below. In T568A, pin 1 is wired to Green / White, pin 2 is wired to Green, pin 3 is wired to Orange / White, and pin 6 is wired to Orange or, put another way, the orange and green pairs are swapped over.

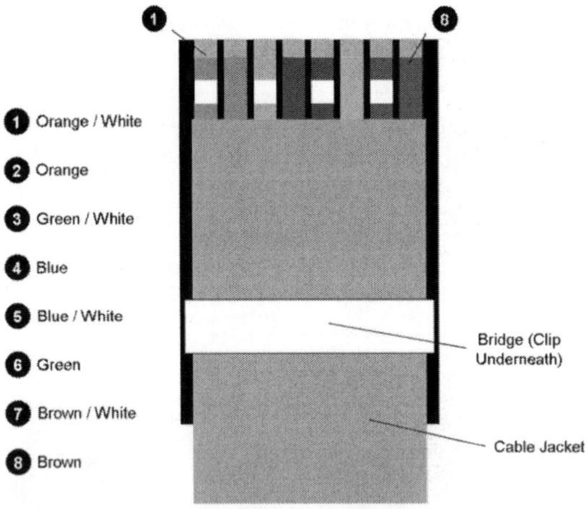

T568B wiring diagram

A regular "straight through" Ethernet cable is wired with the same type of termination at both ends. Using T568A at one end and T568B at the other creates a **crossover cable**. Crossover cables were once used to connect computers directly, but Gigabit Ethernet interfaces can perform the crossover automatically, even if standard cable is used. Organizations should try to avoid using a mixture of the two standards. It is difficult to say whether one is more prevalent than the other. T568A is mandated for US government premises and by the residential cabling standard (TIA 570).

Serial Cable and Console Cable

All network technologies transfer data in serial, but "serial cable" generally refers to the original asynchronous serial transmission standard; one of the oldest and simplest in computing. Asynchronous means there are no timing signals. Each byte of data is identified by start and stop signals. It was used on PCs to connect peripheral devices and the same technique is used by analog dial-up modems. It can also be deployed as a rudimentary type of network connecting two hosts. Devices with serial ports are defined in two categories:

- **DTE (Data Terminal Equipment)** - a PC is classed as DTE equipment, as are most data terminals and other devices that interact with users.
- **DCE (Data Circuit-terminating Equipment)** - DCE equipment is defined as those items that provide an interface between DTE equipment and other communication systems or networks (for example, modems).

DTE equipment is connected to DCE equipment with a **straight-through** wired cable (pin 1 on one end of a cable joins to pin 1 on the other end, pin 2 to pin 2, and so on.). This cabling works because DTE equipment uses pin 2 (TD) to transmit data and DCE equipment uses pin 2 (RD) to receive data.

The PC serial port is obsolete but the use of a serial connection remains current in networking as a means of establishing an "out-of-band" connection to the **console port** of a network appliance (a switch or router for instance). On older devices, the console port may be labeled the "management" or "admin" port. The console port connection on the appliance can use either a DB9 / DB25 port or a standard RJ-45 jack (but wired in a different way to Ethernet). In this latter scenario, a **rollover** or **console** cable featuring an RJ-45 plug on one end and a 9-pin serial connector on the other is used for connection to the terminal (PC).

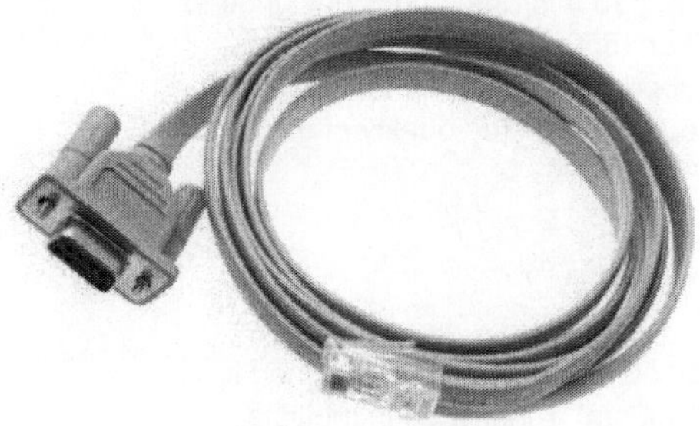

Rollover / console cable

One additional complication here is that most engineers would prefer to use laptops for this sort of task and very few laptops feature serial ports anymore. In this scenario, a serial-USB converter can be used. On newer network appliances, a USB console port is likely to be available anyway.

You may also need to configure the link speed, parity, and flow control settings. Usually these are 9,600 bps (baud), 8 data bits / 1 stop bit, and no parity or flow control.

Fiber Optic Cabling and Connectors

Copper wire carries electrical signals, which are subject to **interference** and **attenuation** (the reduction of signal quality over distance). Light signals are not susceptible to interference, cannot easily be intercepted (eavesdropped), and suffer less from attenuation. Consequently, fiber optic cabling can support much higher bandwidth (multiple gigabits per second) and longer cable runs (measured in kilometers rather than meters).

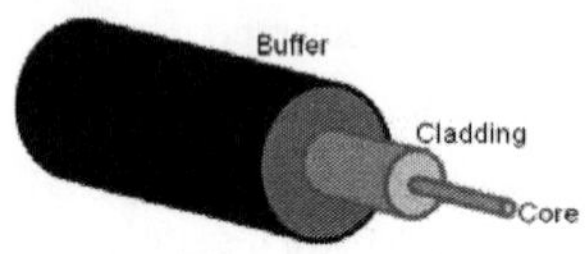

Fiber optic strand

An optical fiber consists of an ultra-fine core of glass to carry the light signals surrounded by glass or plastic cladding, which guides the light pulses along the core (a process called Total Internal Reflection), and a protective coating called the buffer. A fiber optic cable usually consists of two fibers (one for upstream and the other for downstream) contained in a protective jacket and terminated by a connector.

Fiber optic cables are specified using the mode, composition (glass/plastic), and core/cladding size. For example, 8.3 micron core/125 microcladding single-mode glass or 62.5 micron core/125 microcladding multi-mode plastic. Fiber optic cables fall into two broad categories: single-mode and multi-mode.

Single-mode (SMF)

Single-Mode Fiber (SMF) has a small core (8 - 10 microns) and is designed to carry a long wavelength, near infrared (1310 or 1550nm) light signal, generated by a laser. Single-mode cables support data rates up to 10 Gbps or better and cable runs of many kilometers, depending on the quality of the cable and optics.

Multi-mode (MMF)

Multi-mode (MMF) has a larger core (62.5 or 50 microns) and is designed to carry a shorter wavelength light (850nm or 1300nm) transmitted in multiple waves of varying length. MMF uses less expensive *optics* and consequently is less expensive to deploy than SMF. However, it does not support such high signaling speeds or long distances as single-mode and so is more suitable for LANs than WANs.

MMF is graded by **Optical Multi-mode (OM)** categories. 62.5 micron cable is OM1 while early 50 micron cable is OM2. OM1 and OM2 are mainly rated for applications up to 1 Gbps and use LED transmitters. OM1 and OM2 can run 10GBASE-SR but only over distances of 33m and 82m respectively. OM3 is also 50 micron cable but is manufactured differently, designed for use with 850nm Vertical-Cavity Surface-Emitting Lasers (VCSEL). It supports 10 Gbps at up to 300m range. OM4 supports 10G at 400m range or 100 Gbps at up to 150m.

Bend Radius Limitations

Bending a fiber optic cable too tightly can damage the fiber, leading to signal loss or degradation. There are two separate limits on the **bend radius**, known as the short term limit and the long term limit. The short term limit is applicable during cable installation and determines how tightly the cable can be bent during the installation process. The long term limit determines how tightly it can be bent when in its permanent location. The long term limit is actually smaller, meaning that the cable can be left in tighter curves when in place than during installation. Check the cable documentation for these limits. If none are explicitly stated, then assume that the short term limit is twenty times the cable diameter and the long term limit is ten times the cable diameter. Inspect the cable run for any tight turns that exceed the long term limit, as these may indicate possible damage to the cable.

Fiber Optic Connectors

A number of connectors have been designed for use with fiber optic cabling. Some types are more popular for multi-mode and some for single-mode; also some types support duplex operation. Connectors for MMF are usually color-coded beige while those for SMF are blue. The core of each connector is a ceramic or plastic ferrule that ensures continuous reception of the light signals.

- **ST (Straight Tip)** - a bayonet-style connector that uses a push-and-twist locking mechanism; used mostly for multi-mode networks.
- **SC (Subscriber Connector)** - this push / pull design allows for simpler insertion and removal than FC. There are simplex and duplex versions, though the duplex version is just two connectors clipped together. It can be used for single- or multi-mode.
- **LC (Lucent or Local Connector)** - a small form factor connector with a tabbed push / pull design. LC is similar to SC but the smaller size allows for higher port density.

From left-to-right: ST, SC, and duplex LC fiber optic connectors

Patch cords for fiber optic can come with the same connector on each end (ST-ST for instance) or a mix of connectors (ST-SC for instance). Fiber optic connectors are quite easy to damage and should not be repeatedly plugged and unplugged.

To protect your eyesight, do not look directly into a fiber optic port.

Interface Converters

Enterprise switches and routers are available with modular, hot-swappable transceivers for different types of fiber optic patch cord connections. Historically these were based on the **Gigabit Interface Converter (GBIC)** form factor but this has largely been replaced by **Small Form Factor Pluggable (SFP)**, also known as mini-GBIC. SFP+ is an updated specification to support Ethernet 10G.

Switch with hot-pluggable fiber transceivers (right)

Ethernet Standards

A typical office network will consist of a wired **Ethernet** network connecting all the client computers and servers. Ethernet is also sometimes referred to as **IEEE 802.3** (the IEEE [Institute of Electrical and Electronics Engineers] maintains the standard). Ethernet is also used as the network fabric in data centers.

Ethernet packages data from higher level protocols in a unit called a **frame**. A frame contains a number of **fields**, expressing start and end information, source and destination addresses, information about the length of the frame, and the data (payload) itself (between 46 and 1500 bytes).

The source and destination addresses are represented as 48-bit values matching the unique hardware address (or **MAC address**) of a network adapter.

There are a number of different types of Ethernet, specifying different media and speeds.

Fast Ethernet

The original type of Ethernet supported speeds of 10 Mbps. This was updated by the **802.3u** specification, which is known as **Fast Ethernet**, to support speeds of up to 100 Mbps. Fast Ethernet is designed to be backwards-compatible with the older standard, allowing devices supporting either standard to communicate on the same network.

Fast Ethernet can use Cat 5 twisted pair (referred to as 100BASE-T) and fiber optic cable (100BASE-FX).

An interconnection device must usually be used to join the nodes of the network. Fast Ethernet supports the use of either a hub or a switch.

- A **hub** is a multiport repeater - it takes the incoming signal from one port and repeats it on all other ports. Connected devices discard any communications that are not addressed with their MAC address (unless they are broadcast communications sent to all nodes). Nodes connected to a hub are described as being in the same **collision domain**. Collisions (when two nodes attempt to transmit frames at the same time) can slow down the network as devices have to wait for the network media to clear before they can send anything.
- A **switch** creates a virtual communications path between the devices identified as the source and destination addresses. No other devices on the network receive the communications and the performance reduction of collisions is eliminated.

While both are *supported*, in practical terms though, hubs are obsolete and only switches are used. Fast Ethernet itself is no longer widely deployed, having been largely replaced by its successor, Gigabit Ethernet.

Gigabit Ethernet

Gigabit Ethernet builds on the standards defined for Ethernet and Fast Ethernet. The bit rate is 10 times faster than with Fast Ethernet. The Gigabit Ethernet standard over fiber (LX and SX) is documented in IEEE 802.3z. The various fiber standards are collectively known as **1000BASE-X**. The IEEE also approved 1000BASE-T, a standard utilizing Cat 5e or Cat 6 copper wiring. This is defined in IEEE 802.3ab.

Specification	Cable	Maximum Distance
1000BASE-T	UTP (Cat 5e or Cat 6)	100m (328 feet)
1000BASE-SX	MMF (62.5/125) / 850nm MMF (50/125) / 850nm	220m (721 feet) 550m (1640 feet)
1000BASE-LX	SMF (9/125) / 1310nm MMF (62.5/125 or 50/125) / 1300nm	5km (3.1 miles) 550m (1800 feet)

For 1000BASE-T, Cat 5 is also acceptable (if properly installed) but Cat 5 cable is no longer available commercially. Unlike Ethernet and Fast Ethernet, Gigabit Ethernet uses all four pairs for transmission and so is much more sensitive to crosstalk.

In terms of network design, Gigabit Ethernet is implemented using switches. Gigabit Ethernet would be the mainstream choice for most new network installations. The main decision would be whether to use copper or fiber cable. Fiber cable would give better upgrade potential in the future while copper cable would be cheaper to install.

10G(igabit) Ethernet

10G Ethernet multiplies the nominal speed of Gigabit Ethernet by a factor of 10. 10G is not deployed in many office networks however as the cost of 10G network adapters and switches is high. The major applications of 10G Ethernet are:

- Increasing bandwidth for server interconnections and network backbones, especially in data centers and for Storage Area Networks (SAN).
- Replacing existing switched public data networks based on proprietary technologies with simpler Ethernet switches (Metro Ethernet).

10G Ethernet is standardized under a number of publications with letter designations (starting with 802.3ae), which are periodically collated (the current one being IEEE 802.3-2012).

Specification	Cable	Max Distance
10GBASE-T	Twisted Pair (Cat 6 or Cat 6A)	55 and 100m
10GBASE-SR	MMF / 850nm	300-400m
10GBASE-LR	SMF (9/125) / 1310nm	10km (6.2 miles)
10GBASE-ER	SMF (9/125) / 1550nm	40km (25 miles)

10G works only with switches in full-duplex mode.

HP transceivers (network ports) for 10GBASE-SR / ER / LR (fiber optic) links

A server that needs a lot of bandwidth could either use a 10G link or bonded Gigabit links (aggregating multiple links to achieve more bandwidth). Bonded Gigabit requires more cable but the price of 10G adapters can make it a cost-effective solution.

Network Adapter Cards

Network adapter cards, also known as **Network Interface Cards (NICs)**, move data between the computer and the network. The card packages data for sending into the frame format required for the network (or conversely extracts data from frames and checks that they are valid using a **Cyclical Redundancy Check [CRC]**). The adapter constantly "listens" to the network, detecting when it is clear to send frames and processing frames addressed to its hardware identifier (**MAC address**). A MAC address is a 48-bit number, expressed in 12 digits (for example, 00-01-E6-50-97-21). The first half is the ID of the adapter's manufacturer. The second half is a unique serial number assigned by the manufacturer.

The card's **transceiver** generates the appropriate signals to send over the network media (or conversely translates received signals into binary data). The adapter also has a memory **buffer** to store data until it is ready to transmit or receive.

Selecting a NIC

When purchasing a network card, ensure that the bus type is correct (for example, PCI-X or PCIe).

Broadcom PCIe Gigabit Ethernet adapter

The majority of adapters are designed for Ethernet over twisted pair and so have an RJ-45 port. Server-class cards are often dual-port (one card supports two network links). Each port has its own MAC address. Cards for fiber optic cabling are also available but you must ensure that the card you obtain supports the correct fiber optic connector type (ST / SC / LC).

You must also ensure that the adapter supports the network signaling rate. Adapters on the market now will all support Gigabit Ethernet (and can usually support slower speeds too).

PXE Cards

Pre-boot Execution Environment (PXE) means that a computer can boot from a server rather from disk. The network adapter and computer firmware must support PXE (Network will appear as a boot option in the computer's CMOS setup program).

PXE also supports **Wake-on-LAN**, which enables a remote administrator to switch on the server via the network. There must be motherboard support as well as a compatible NIC.

Configuring a Network Card

Network cards use system resources, such as interrupts, I/O ports and memory, in order to interact with the processor. Most adapters are configured automatically using Plug-and-Play. Most adapters will also auto-negotiate network settings such as signaling speed (10 / 100 / 1000 Mbps) and half- or full-duplex operation.

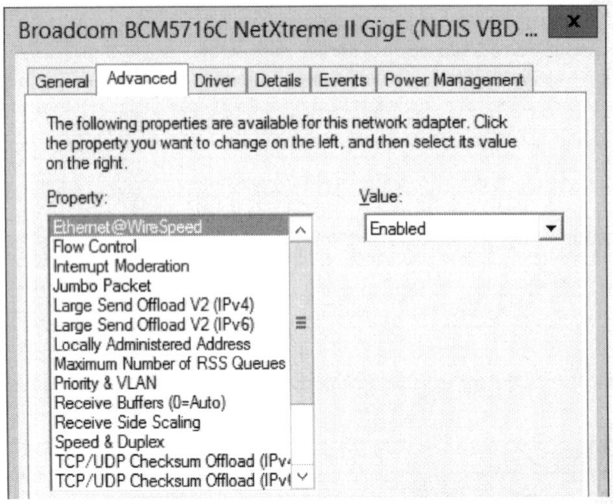

Network adapter properties in Device Manager

If these settings do need to be configured manually, in Windows, locate the adapter in **Device Manager**, alt-click and select **Properties**, then update settings using the card's driver software. You must also configure the card with the appropriate network client software and protocol, including addressing information relevant to the protocol.

Adapter Teaming and Port Bonding

Port bonding refers to aggregating multiple links into a single high-speed connection. For example, a single network adapter and cable segment might support 1 Gbps; bonding this with another adapter and cable segment gives a link of 2 Gbps (**adapter teaming**). Bonding can also provide **redundancy**; if one link is broken the connection is still maintained by the other (**fail over**). It is also often cost-effective; a 4-port Gigabit Ethernet card might not match the bandwidth of a 10G port (4 Gbps compared to 10 Gbps) but will cost less.

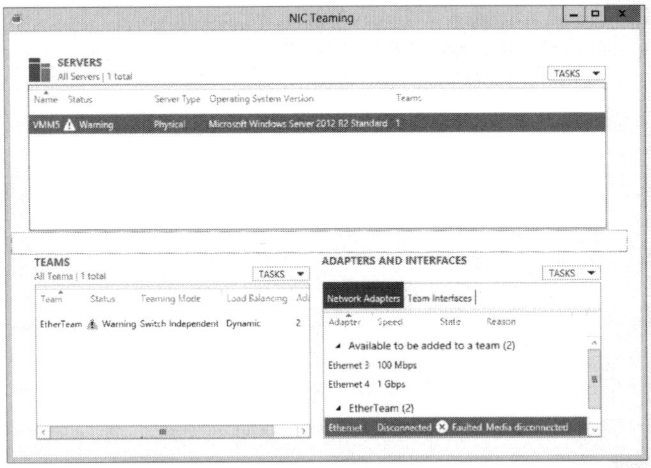

Configuring adapter teaming

In addition, adapter teaming can distribute network traffic across the various ports that make up the team. This will improve throughput to the server.

There are proprietary port bonding mechanisms but it has been standardized as **IEEE 802.3ad / 802.1ax**. 802.3ad bonded interfaces are described as a **Link Aggregation Group (LAG)**. 802.3ad also defines the **Link Aggregation Control Protocol (LACP)**, which can be used to detect configuration errors and recover from the failure of one of the physical links.

Troubleshooting Cabling

The **International Organization for Standardization (ISO)** developed the **Open Systems Interconnection (OSI)** reference model in 1977. It was designed to aid understanding of how a network system functions in terms of both the hardware and software components by separating the function of such components to discrete layers. Each layer performs a different group of tasks required for network communication. Although not all network systems implement layers using this *structure*, they all implement each *task* in some way. The OSI model is not a standard or a specification; it serves as a functional guideline for designing network protocols, software, and appliances and for troubleshooting networks

Troubleshooting network components can be approached by testing at each OSI model layer in turn. There are many components which go to make up a network:

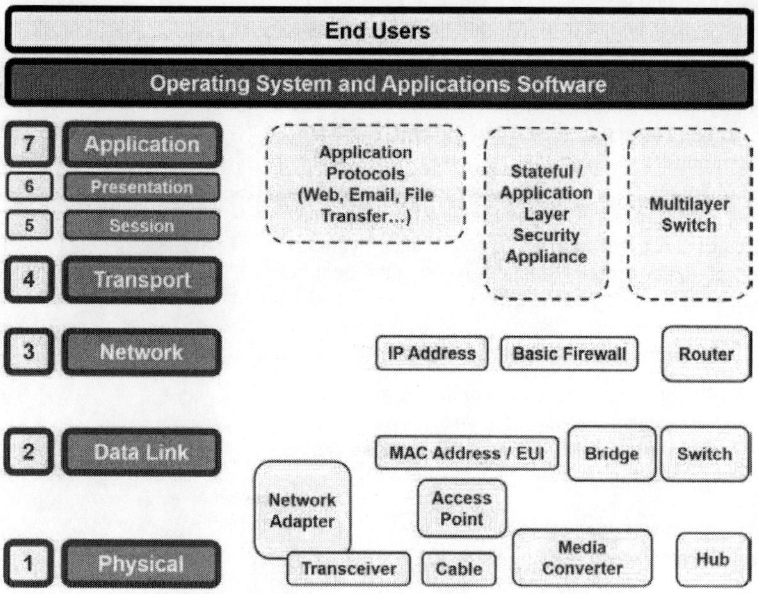

Troubleshooting top-to-bottom or bottom-to-top using the OSI model

Some, or several, of these components may be at fault when a problem is reported to you. It is important that you tackle the problem logically and methodically. Unless a problem is trivial, break the troubleshooting process into compartments or categories, using the OSI model as a guide and starting from either the top or bottom and only moving up or down when you have discounted a particular layer as the source of the problem. For example, when troubleshooting a server you might work as follows:

1) Decide whether the problem is hardware or software related (Hardware).

2) Decide which hardware subsystem is affected (NIC or cable).

3) Decide whether the problem is in the NIC adapter or connectors and cabling (cabling).

4) Test your theory (replace the cable with a "known good" one).

Network component failures could occur in the network adapter, the cable, the switch, or the router. You should ask if the problem follows some sort of maintenance work, which would probably indicate a misconfiguration. Spontaneous failures in these components are relatively uncommon, so while the physical and data link layers are at the bottom of the OSI model, it is worth discounting other causes first.

If you think there is a hardware problem, the first thing to do is to check the link LEDs on the NIC and the switch. Use these to determine if the link is operational and whether there might be a speed or duplex mismatch. A speed mismatch will cause the link to fail while a duplex mismatch will slow the link down (it will cause high packet loss and late collisions). Generally speaking both NIC driver and switch port should be set to autonegotiate these settings. Consider updating or reinstalling the driver if the NIC does not seem to be working properly.

If both NIC and switch seem to be operational, check that the patch cord is connected to the correct switch port. Make sure that the port is assigned to the correct VLAN, if VLANs are configured on the switch. Check that the switch hasn't been reset to its factory configuration or default settings or something similar. Check that the port is not configured with some sort of security (such as MAC address filtering or port authentication) that is preventing the host from connecting.

Remember that if several servers have the same problem, the issue is probably at the switch or router. If a single server loses connectivity, the problem is likely to be isolated to that server's components.

Try substituting patch cables with known good ones; if this doesn't resolve the problem, you will need to test the permanent link (the cable running between the wall port and the patch panel). Consider any devices that might be causing Electromagnetic Interference (EMI) in copper cabling (fluorescent lights, dynamos, power cabling, and so on). Eventually, through the process of substituting working components for suspect components, you should resolve a cable or component problem.

Review Questions / Module 2 / Unit 1 / Ethernet

Answer these questions to test what you have learned in this unit.

1) What networking product is defined by 1000BASE-T?
2) True or false? Cat5e cabling can be used for Gigabit Ethernet.
3) What is the difference between RJ-45 and RJ-11 connectors?
4) What features of fiber optic cable make it more suitable for WANs than copper cabling?
5) What is a MAC address?
6) What feature(s) should you check when ordering an Ethernet network card?
7) What alternative could you propose to provisioning expensive Ethernet 10G NICs and switches?
8) How could you identify a problem with a patch cable without cable testing tools?

Module 2 / Unit 2

Internet Protocol

Objectives

On completion of this unit, you will be able to:

- Describe the properties and characteristics of Internet Protocol (IP) addressing.
- Configure appropriate settings for an IP host.
- Troubleshoot IP configuration issues using command-line tools.

The TCP/IP Suite

Protocols are procedures or rules used by networked computers to communicate. For communication to take place, the two computers must have a protocol in common. Often, several protocols used for networking are designed to work together. This collection of protocols is known as a **protocol suite**. A number of protocol suites have been used for LAN and WAN communications over the years. However, the overwhelming majority of networks have now converged on the use of the **TCP/IP (Transmission Control Protocol/Internet Protocol)** suite. Most network implementations you will be required to undertake will depend on the use of TCP/IP.

The main protocols in the suite provide addressing and transport services:

- **IP (Internet Protocol)** - provides packet addressing and routing. It provides best effort delivery of an unreliable and connectionless nature (a packet might be lost, delivered out of sequence, duplicated, or delayed).
- **ARP (Address Resolution Protocol)** - when TCP/IP is being used with a physical / data link specification such as Ethernet or Wi-FI, there must be a mechanism to deliver messages from IP at the Network layer to computers addressed at the Data Link layer. ARP finds the MAC (network adapter) address associated with an IP address.
- **ICMP (Internet Control Message Protocol)** - delivers status and error messages and is used by diagnostic utilities such as ping and tracert.
- **TCP (Transmission Control Protocol)** - guarantees orderly transmission of packets. This is used by most TCP/IP application protocols as lost or out-of-order packets can cause serious data errors.
- **UDP (User Datagram Protocol)** - provides unreliable, non-guaranteed transfer of packets. This is faster and more efficient and is used in time-sensitive applications, such as speech or video, where a few missing or out-of-order packets can be tolerated.

- **Application protocols** - there are numerous protocols used for network configuration, management, and services. Application protocols use a TCP or UDP **port** to connect the client and server.

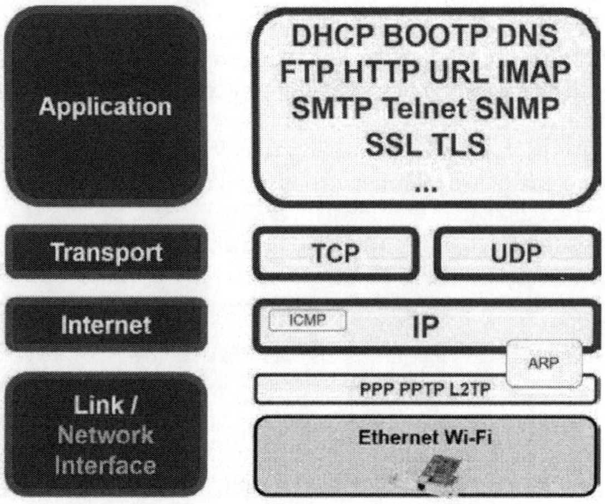

TCP/IP model

Internet Protocol and IP Addressing

The core protocol in TCP/IP is the **Internet Protocol (IP)**, which provides network identification and host addressing. An **IP address** is used to identify each device (host) at the network layer. The IP address provides two pieces of information:

- The network number (network ID) - this number is common to all hosts on the same IP network.
- The host number (host ID) - this unique number identifies a host on a particular IP network.

IP Address Format

An IP address is used within an IP packet to define the source and destination of the packet. An IP address is 32 bits long. In its raw form it appears as: 11000110001010010001000000001001

The 32 bits are subdivided into four groups of 8 bits (1 byte) known as **octets**. The above IP address could therefore be rearranged as:
11000110 00101001 00010000 00001001

This representation of an IP address makes human memorizing of the number almost impossible (much less entering it correctly into configuration dialogs). To make IP addresses easier to use, they are usually displayed in **dotted decimal notation**. This notation requires each octet to be converted to a decimal value. The decimal numbers are separated using a period. Converting the above number to this notation gives: 198.41.16.9.

Converting Between Binary and Decimal Format

The following examples demonstrate the process of converting between binary and decimal notation. The **base** of any number system tells us two things: how many different values any given digit can have and the factor by which the value of a digit increases as we move from right to left in a number. Thus, in base 10 (or **decimal**) numbers, a digit can take any one of ten different values (0 through 9), and the values of the different place positions within a number, moving from right to left, are units (ones), tens, hundreds, thousands, and so on. In base 2 (**binary**), digits can only take one of two different values (0 and 1). The place values are powers of 2 (2^1=2, 2^2=4, 2^3=8, 2^4=16, and so on). Consider the octet "11101101" represented in base 2: The table below shows the place value of each digit in the octet:

128	64	32	16	8	4	2	1
1	1	1	0	1	1	0	1
128 x 1	64 x 1	32 x 1	16 x 0	8 x 1	4 x 1	2 x 0	1 x 1

Therefore, the decimal equivalent is: 128 + 64 + 32 + 0 + 8 + 4 + 0 +1 = 237.

You can use the same sort of method to convert from decimal to binary. For example, the number 199 can be converted as follows:
199 = 128 + 64 + 0 + 0 + 0 + 0 + 4 + 2+ 1

128	64	32	16	8	4	2	1
128 x 1	64 x 1	32 x 0	16 x 0	8 x 0	4 x 1	2 x 1	1 x 1
1	1	0	0	0	1	1	1

If all the bits in an octet are set to 1, the number obtained is 255 (the maximum possible value). Similarly, if all the bits are set to 0, the number obtained is 0 (the minimum possible value). Therefore, theoretically an IPv4 address may be any value between 0.0.0.0 and 255.255.255.255. However, some addresses are not permitted or are reserved for special use.

Subnet Masks

An IP address represents both a **Network ID** and a **Host ID**. A **subnet mask** (or **netmask**) is used to distinguish these two components within the single IP address. It is used to "mask" the host ID portion of the IP address and thereby reveal the network ID portion. Where there is a binary 1 in the mask, the corresponding binary digit in the IP address is part of the network ID. The relative sizes of the network and host portions determines the number of networks and hosts per network a particular addressing scheme can support.

The 1s in the mask are always contiguous. For example, a mask 11111111 11110000 00000000 00000000 is valid but 11111111 00000000 11110000 00000000 is not.

Although you enter the mask in decimal, the computer "thinks" in binary terms. Until you are totally comfortable working with subnet masks, try to think in binary terms, switching the number to decimal only at the last moment to enter into the configuration dialog.

Masking an IP Address (ANDing)

The network ID portion of an IP address is revealed by "ANDing" the subnet mask to the IP address. The rules for a logical AND are shown in the table:

1	AND	1	=	**1**
1	AND	0	=	**0**
0	AND	1	=	**0**
0	AND	0	=	**0**

This table shows that when two ones are ANDed together, the result is a 1. Any other combination produces a 0.

For example, to determine the network ID of the IP address "172.30.15.12" with a subnet mask of "255.255.0.0", the dotted decimal notation of the IP address and subnet mask must first be converted to binary notation. The next step is to AND the two binary numbers. The result can be converted back to dotted decimal notation to provide the network ID.

IP address (172.30.15.12)	10101100	00011110	00001111	00001100
Mask (255.255.0.0)	11111111	11111111	00000000	00000000
Network ID (172.30.0.0)	10101100	00011110	00000000	00000000

Routing Decision

When two computers attempt to communicate via IPv4, the protocol compares the source and destination address in each packet against a subnet mask. If the masked portions of the source and destination IP addresses *match*, then the destination interface is assumed to be on the same IP network. For example:

Source IP (**172.30**.15.12)	**10101100**	**00011110**	00001111	00001100
Mask (**255.255**.0.0)	**11111111**	**11111111**	00000000	00000000
Destination IP (**172.30**.16.101)	**10101100**	**00011110**	00010000	01100101

In the example above, IP concludes the destination IPv4 address is on the same IP network and would try to deliver the packet locally. If the masked portion *does not* match, IP assumes the packet must be routed to another IP network. For example:

Source IP (**172.*30***.15.12)	**10101100**	**0001111*0***	00001111	00001100
Mask (**255.255**.0.0)	**11111111**	**11111111**	00000000	00000000
Destination IP (**172.*31***.16.101)	**10101100**	**0001111*1***	00010000	01100101

In this case, IP concludes the destination IPv4 address is on a different IP network and would forward the packet to a router rather than trying to deliver it locally.

IP Class

Under the system of **classful addressing**, *whole octets* in the subnet mask are set to all 1s or all 0s, allowing for three possible masks (255.0.0.0, 255.255.0.0, and 255.255.255.0). These masks are used with ranges of IP addresses, divided into three classes (A, B, and C) based on the value of the first octet in the IP address.

Class	First Octet	Default Mask	Network Prefix
A	1-126	255.0.0.0	/8
B	128-191	255.255.0.0	/16
C	192-223	255.255.255.0	/24

So, using our example IP address of 172.30.15.12 you should be able to see that it is a Class B address and would be used with the subnet mask 255.255.0.0. This means that the network ID is "172.30" and the host ID portion is "15.12". With a Class B address, half of the IP address (16 bits) is allocated to the network ID and half to the host ID. The length of the mask in bits can also be described as a network prefix (/16 for Class B for instance), discussed in more detail below.

A Class A address allows far more hosts per network (the network portion is 8 bits and the host portion 24 bits) while Class C networks allow fewer hosts but more networks.

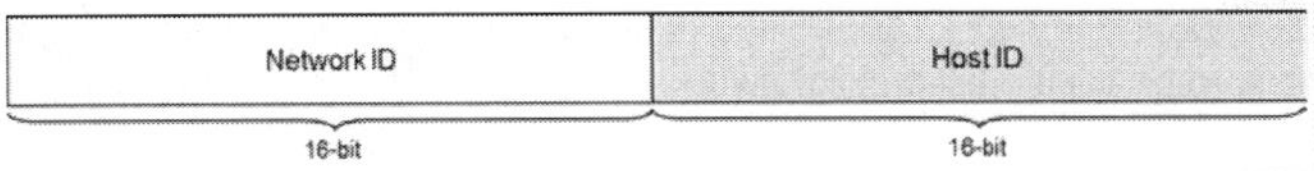

Network and host IDs in a Class B address

This describes **unicast addressing***, where a single host is addressed. An address where the host bits are all "1"s is the* **broadcast address** *for a network. A message sent to a broadcast address is received by all hosts on the network. The broadcast address of the example above would be 172.30.255.255.*

A host can communicate with any other host that has the same network ID. Communications with a host with a different network ID must be sent via a router.

Configuring IP

To use TCP/IP, you must bind the protocol to the network adapter (Windows automatically installs TCP/IP so there should be no need to do this manually) and then configure the IP address properties. This must be done carefully as if there is a mistake in the configuration the machine will not be able to communicate on the network.

IP Address and Subnet Mask

An **IP address** and **subnet mask** can be set manually (static address). The IP addresses for servers and the management interfaces of switches and routers are often configured statically. The IP address is entered in dotted decimal notation. The IP address identifies both the network to which the interface is attached and also its unique identity on that network. An interface *must* be configured with an IP address. The subnet mask is used in conjunction with the IP address to determine whether another interface is located on a local or remote network. An interface *must* be configured with a subnet mask.

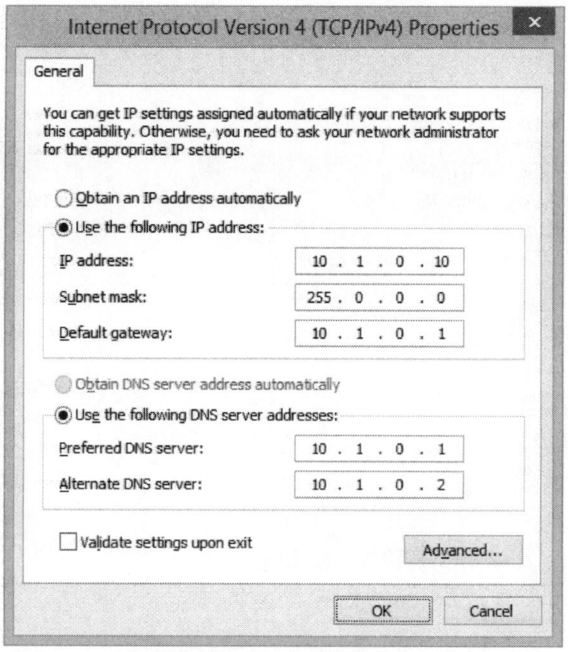

Defining a static IP address configuration

Default Gateway

The **default gateway** parameter is the IP address of a router to which packets destined for a remote network should be sent by default. This setting is not compulsory but failure to enter a gateway would limit the interface to communication on the local network only.

Client-side DNS

Another important part of IP configuration is specifying the IP address of one or more **Domain Name System (DNS)** servers. These servers provide resolution of host and domain names to their IP addresses and are essential for locating resources on the Internet and on Windows networks. Typically the DNS server would be the gateway address, though this may not be the case on all networks. On an enterprise network, each host would normally be configured with a default **domain suffix**. The domain suffix can be appended to the host name to resolve a **Fully Qualified Domain Name (FQDN)**. For example, if a client configured with the primary search suffix "classroom.local" searched for the host "sales", the query would normally try to resolve "sales.classroom.local." A host can be configured with multiple suffixes, in which case each is used in order.

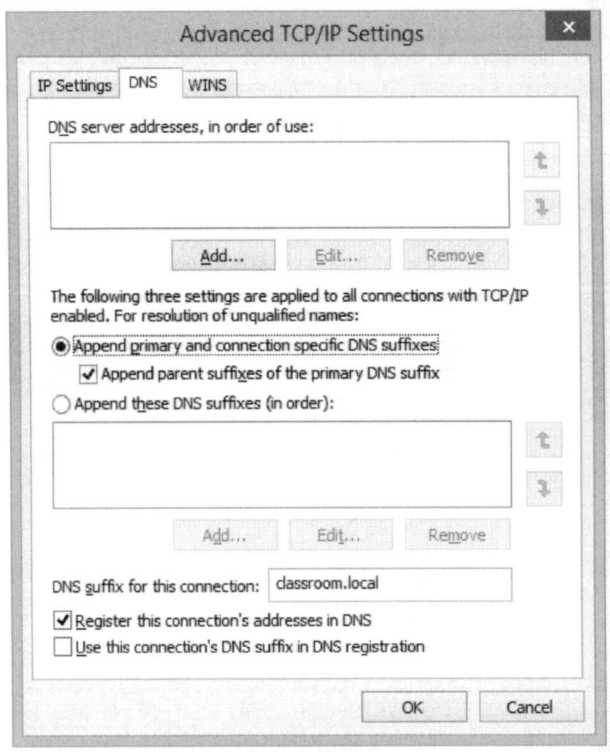

Configuring DNS suffixes

Client-side WINS

The **Windows Internet Name Service (WINS)** was used for name services on very early Windows networks. You might configure a WINS server to support legacy clients or applications.

Name resolution, DNS, and WINS are covered in more detail in Unit 2.4.

DHCP and APIPA

When an interface is given a static configuration, the installer may make a mistake with the address information (perhaps duplicating an existing IP address or entering the wrong subnet mask) or the configuration of the network may change, requiring the host to be manually configured with a new static address. To avoid these problems, a **DHCP (Dynamic Host Configuration Protocol)** server can be used to allocate an IP address and subnet mask (plus other settings) *dynamically*. The computer contacts the DHCP server as it starts up and is allocated a **lease** for an IP address.

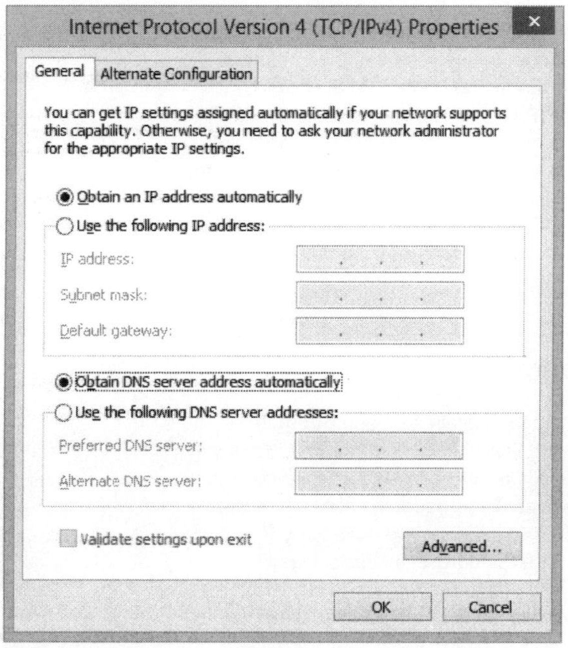

Configuring a network adapter to obtain an address automatically (use DHCP)

It is usually advantageous for a server or network device such as a printer or VoIP handset to use the same IP address. It is possible to do this with DHCP by creating a **reservation**, so that the device is always allocated the same address by the DHCP server. This combines the benefits of having a "known" IP while not losing the advantages of centralized administration offered by DHCP. Settings such as default gateway and DNS server addresses may be passed to the device at the same time. If the address information needs to change, this can be done on the DHCP server and clients will update themselves automatically when they seek a new lease (or a new lease can be requested manually).

Using DHCP reservations carries risks however. A server might not receive the correct IP address if the DHCP service fails. Another risk is that an attacker might try to deploy a "rogue" DHCP service. Consequently, it is usually considered best practice to use static addressing for critical servers (notably those that run authentication services and network services, such as DNS and DHCP) plus the management interfaces of network appliances such as switches and routers.

When using static assignments, it is critical to document these properly. Use a defined range of IP addresses for static allocation and ensure that they do not overlap with any DHCP scopes that have been configured.

One option is to configure the static assignment on the device but also duplicate the assignment as a DHCP reservation. This provides documentation of the assignment and a fallback mechanism in case the device is inadvertently set to use automatic addressing at a later date. Configuring a DHCP server is discussed in *Unit 2.4*.

Hosts also have a "fallback" mechanism for when the computer is configured to use a DHCP server but cannot contact one. In this scenario, the computer selects an address at random from the range 169.254.*x*.*y*. This is called **Automatic Private IP Addressing (APIPA)**. When a host is using an APIPA address, it can communicate with other hosts on the local segment that are using APIPA, but cannot reach other networks (or communicate with hosts that have managed to obtain a valid DHCP lease).

An APIPA address is sometimes described as link-local.

Public and Private Addressing

To communicate on the Internet, a host must obtain a unique **public IP address**. Typically this is allocated by an Internet Service Provider. Relatively few companies can obtain sufficient public IP addresses for all their computers to communicate over the Internet however. The IP address scheme defines certain ranges as **private addresses**. These ranges are defined by RFC 1918 and are sometimes referred to as RFC 1918 addresses. Hosts with IP addresses from these ranges are not allowed to route traffic over the Internet. Use of the addresses is confined to private LANs. Each address class has its own private range:

- 10.0.0.0 to 10.255.255.255 (Class A private address range).
- 172.16.0.0 to 172.31.255.255 (Class B private address range).
- 192.168.0.0 to 192.168.255.255 (Class C private address range).
- 169.254.0.0 to 169.254.255.255 (APIPA / link-local autoconfiguration). As discussed above, this range is used by hosts for autoconfiguration (selecting a link-local address).

Internet access can be facilitated for hosts using the private addressing scheme in two ways:

- Through a router configured with a single or block of valid public addresses; the router translates between the private and public addresses (Network Address Translation [NAT]).
- A proxy server that fulfills requests for Internet resources on behalf of clients.

Classless Addressing

In a **classless** scheme, the network ID does not depend on the class of the IP address number but on the number of bits set to 1 in an associated **network prefix**. The idea that the netmask should align along a particular octet boundary has been discarded completely.

For example, when expressed in binary, the subnet mask 255.255.240.0 contains 20 ones followed by 12 zeroes. Therefore, the network prefix, expressed in **slash notation**, is 172.30.0.0/20. This is also described as **Classless Interdomain Routing (CIDR) notation**.

Most configuration dialogs require you to input a subnet mask in dotted decimal format. Some may require you to enter the network address and prefix in slash notation however.

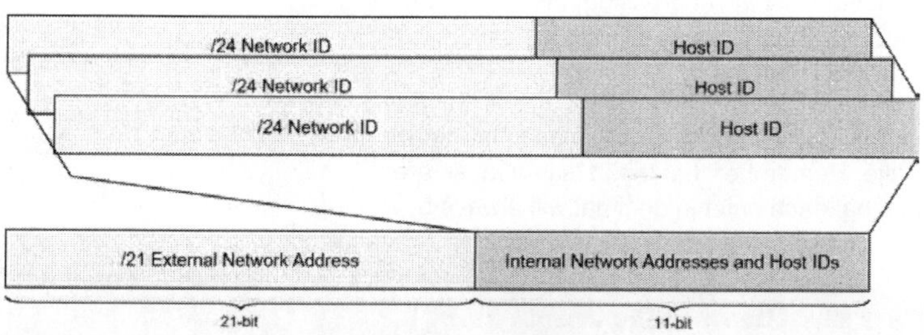

Classless Interdomain Routing (CIDR)

For example, rather than allocate a class B (or /16) network address to a company, several contiguous class C (or /24) addresses could be assigned. Eight /24 network addresses gives 2032 hosts. However, this would mean complicated routing with many entries in the route tables, because there are now eight IP networks. CIDR is used to collapse these routing entries into single entry.

If the network addresses assigned to a company were 192.32.168.0 through to 192.32.175.0 and we wished to view this as one network, we would only consider the first 21 bits of the address.

Net ID	Binary
192.32.168.0	**11000000.00100000.10101** *000*.00000000
192.32.169.0	**11000000.00100000.10101** *001*.00000000
192.32.170.0	**11000000.00100000.10101** *010*.00000000
192.32.171.0	**11000000.00100000.10101** *011*.00000000
192.32.172.0	**11000000.00100000.10101** *100*.00000000
192.32.173.0	**11000000.00100000.10101** *101*.00000000
192.32.174.0	**11000000.00100000.10101** *110*.00000000
192.32.175.0	**11000000.00100000.10101** *111*.00000000

The network address could also be expressed in classless notation as 192.32.168.0/21, meaning that the network prefix contains 21 bits.

As with subnetting, an ANDing process is used to determine whether to route or not. If the ANDed result reveals the same network ID as the destination address, then it is the same network. In the table below, the first two IP addresses belong to the same network (the second is the broadcast address for the network) but the third is in a different one:

Address	Binary
Mask: 255.255.248.0	**11111111.11111111.11111**000.00000001
IP: 192.32.168.1	11000000.00100000.1010**1**000.00000001
IP: 192.32.175.255	11000000.00100000.1010**1**111.11111111
IP: 192.32.176.1	11000000.00100000.1011**0**000.00000001

While routers have performed classless routing for years, the class terminology is still very widely used. Even under classless addressing, the old classes are often used as names for the default subnet masks; a Class A network is /8, a Class B network is /16, and a Class C network is /24.

To work out the subnet mask from classless notation, it helps to memorize the values that a mask octet can take. Remember that the "1"s in a mask are always contiguous. This means that each octet in decimal will always be one of the following:

Number of Mask Bits	Decimal Equivalent
1 (10000000)	128
2 (11000000)	192
3 (11100000)	224
4 (11110000)	240
5 (11111000)	248
6 (11111100)	252
7 (11111110)	254
8 (11111111)	255

Planning an IPv4 Addressing Scheme

A network designer will need to plan the IP network addressing scheme carefully. Before choosing a scheme, consider the following factors:

- Whether you need a public or private addressing scheme.
- How many IP networks and subnetworks you need.
- How many hosts per subnet.

There are some additional constraints to consider when planning an addressing scheme:

- Network ID cannot be 127 - this address is reserved for loopback testing.
- Network and / or host IDs cannot be all 1s in binary - this is reserved for broadcasts.
- Network and / or host ID cannot be all zeroes in binary - 0 means "This Network".
- Host ID must be unique on the IP network or subnet.
- Network ID must be unique on the Internet (if using a public addressing scheme) or on your internal system of networks (if using a private addressing scheme).

When performing subnet calculations, it helps to remember that each power of two is double the previous one:

2^2	2^3	2^4	2^5	2^6	2^7	2^8
4	8	16	32	64	128	256

The process of designing the scheme is as follows:

1) Work out how many subnets are required (remembering to allow for future growth) then round this number up to the nearest power of 2. For example, if you need 12 subnets, the next nearest power of 2 is 16. The exponent is the number of bits you will need to add to your default mask. For example, 16 is 2^4 (two to the power of four), so you will need to add 4 bits to the default network prefix. In dotted decimal, the mask is 255.255.240.0.

2) Next work out how many hosts each subnet must support and whether there is enough space left in the scheme to accommodate them. For example, if your network address (172.30.0.0 for instance) is in the /16 range and you use 4 bits for subnetting, you have 32 - (16+4) = 12 bits for hosts in each subnet. The number of hosts per subnet can be expressed using the formula 2^n-2, where *n* is the number of bits you have allocated for the host ID. 12 bits is enough for 4094 hosts in each subnet.

Remember that we subtract 2 because each subnet's network address and broadcast address cannot be assigned to hosts.

3) Now work out the subnets. The easiest way to find the first subnet ID is to deduct the least significant octet in the mask (240 in the example) from 256. This gives the first subnet ID, which, in full, is 172.30.16.0/20.

4) The subsequent subnet IDs are all the lowest subnet ID higher than the one before - 32, 48, 64 and so on.

5) Work out the host ranges for each subnet. Take the subnet address and add a binary 1 to it for the first host. Take the next subnet ID and deduct two binary digits from it. In our case, this is 172.30.16.1 and 172.30.31.254 respectively. Repeat for all subnets.

Troubleshooting IP

There are a number of command-line tools for testing and troubleshooting IP links.

Viewing IP Configuration (ipconfig)

In Windows, IP configuration information is displayed through the adapter's status dialog but can also be viewed at a command-line using the **`ipconfig`** tool. Used without switches, **`ipconfig`** displays the IP address, subnet mask, and default gateway (router) for all network adapters to which TCP/IP is bound. Typical **`ipconfig`** arguments are:

- **`ipconfig /all`** - display detailed configuration, including DHCP, DNS, and WINS servers, MAC address, and NetBIOS status.
- **`ipconfig /release`** ***`AdapterName`*** - releases the IP address obtained from a DHCP Server, so that the network adapter(s) will no longer have an IP address.
- **`ipconfig /renew`** ***`AdapterName`*** - forces a DHCP client to renew the lease it has for an IP address.
- **`ipconfig /displaydns`** - displays the DNS resolver cache. This contains host and domain names that have been queried recently. Caching the name:IP mappings reduces network traffic.
- **`ipconfig /flushdns`** - clears the DNS resolver cache.

Omitting the *AdapterName* argument releases or renews **all** adapters. If *AdapterName* contains spaces, use quotes around it (for example, **`ipconfig /renew "Local Area Connection"`**).

You would use **`ipconfig`** to determine whether the adapter has been correctly configured. **`ipconfig`** can resolve the following questions:

- Is the adapter configured with a static address? Are the parameters (IP address, subnet mask, default gateway, and DNS server correct)?
- Is the adapter configured by DHCP? If so:
    - An address in the range 169.254.x.y indicates that the client could not contact a DHCP server and is using **Automatic Private IP Addressing (APIPA)**. If this is the case, Windows will display a yellow alert icon and a notification that the adapter has only **Limited connectivity** .
    - A DHCP lease can be static (always assigns the same IP address to the computer) or dynamic (assigns an IP address from a pool) - has the computer obtained a suitable address and subnet mask?
    - Are other parameters assigned by DHCP correct (default gateway, DNS Server, and so on)?

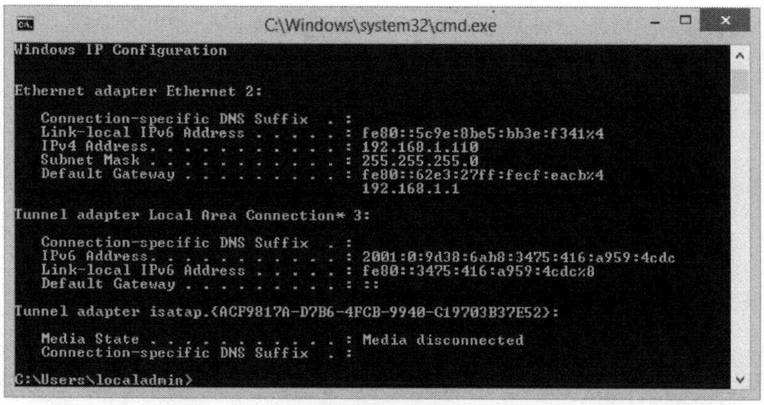

Using ipconfig

If any of these results are negative, you should investigate either communications between the client and the DHCP server, the configuration of the DHCP server (is the address pool exhausted?), or whether multiple DHCP servers are running on the network (and the client has obtained the wrong configuration from one).

ifconfig

UNIX and Linux hosts use a command called **`ifconfig`**, which provides similar output to Windows' **`ipconfig`** program. Note some differences between the Windows and Linux commands:

- **`ifconfig`** can be used to bind an address to an adapter interface, set up communication parameters, and enable or disable the adapter.
- The Windows switches for configuring the adapter with DHCP and DNS are not supported by **`ifconfig`**.
- The **`ifconfig`** command output does not show the default gateway (use **`route`** instead). It does show traffic statistics though.

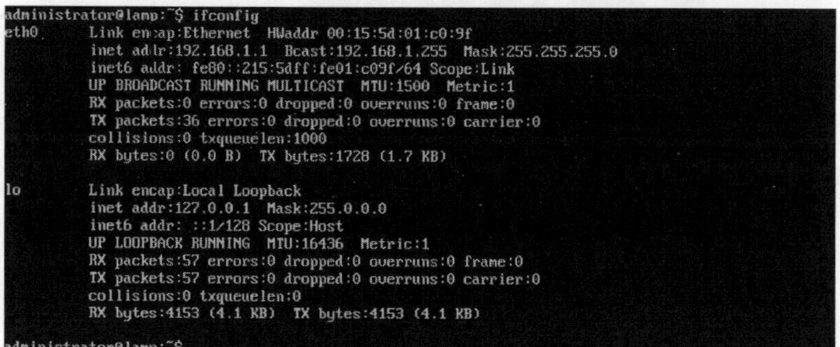

Using ifconfig

ping

The **ping** utility is a command-line diagnostic tool used to test whether a host can communicate with another host on the same network or on a remote network. It is the basic tool to use to establish that a link is working. **ping** uses the **Internet Control Message Protocol (ICMP)** to request status messages from hosts. The following steps outline the procedures for verifying a computer's configuration and for testing router connections:

1) Ping the loopback address to verify TCP/IP is installed and loaded correctly (**ping 127.0.0.1**) - the loopback address is a reserved IP address used for testing purposes.

2) Ping the IP address of the local host to verify it was added correctly and to check for possible duplicate IP addresses.

3) Ping the IP address of the default gateway to verify it is up and running and that you can communicate with a host on the local network.

4) Ping the IP address of a remote host to verify you can communicate through the router.

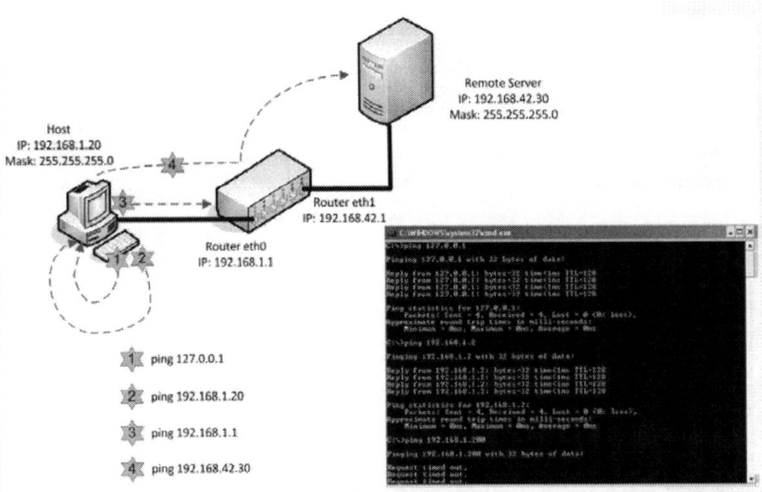

Troubleshooting with ping

If ping is successful, it responds with the message **Reply from IP Address** and the time it takes for the server's response to arrive. The millisecond measures of **Round Trip Time (RTT)** can be used to diagnose latency problems on a link.

If ping is unsuccessful, one of two messages are commonly received:

- **Destination host unreachable** - there is no routing information (that is, the local computer or an intermediate router does not know how to get to that IP address). If the host is on the same network, check the TCP/IP configuration. If the host is on another network, check the TCP/IP configuration and router.

- **No reply (Request timed out)** - the host is unavailable or cannot route a reply back to your computer. Check physical cabling and infrastructure devices such as the switch. If the host is on a remote network, try using **`tracert`**.

Be aware that ICMP traffic is often blocked by firewalls, making a response such as request timed out or destination unreachable inevitable. As well as network firewalls, consider that a host firewall, such as Windows Firewall, might be blocking ICMP.

Troubleshooting Connectivity Issues

The trick with ping is understanding the messages that you receive when there is a problem.

- If you cannot ping the loopback address, the protocol is not correctly installed on the local system.
- If a local host cannot be pinged, then verify the sending host's IP configuration - IP address, subnet mask, and so on. If you can discount any configuration error then there may be a hardware problem.
- If the previous tests are successful, but a remote IP address cannot be contacted, check the default gateway parameter on the local host and check whether the router responds to pings. If these tests do not identify the problem, utilize the **`tracert`** program to investigate the route being taken.
- If you can successfully perform all tests, but cannot ping by computer name, then this suggests a name resolution problem (see below).

You can also ping DNS names (**`ping gtslearning.com`** for example) or FQDNs (**`ping sales.gtslearning.com`** for instance). This will not work if a DNS server is not available. Use the **`-a`** switch to perform a reverse lookup on an IP address to try to get the host name. For example, **`ping -a 192.168.1.1`** should return the message "Pinging *HostName* [192.168.1.1]".

Commented [MNS2]: Please check if gtslearning in this context is okay.

Ping can be used with a number of switches. You can adjust the TTL (**`-i`**) and timeout (**`-w`**) and force the use of IPv4 (**`-4`**) or IPv6 (**`-6`**) when pinging by host name. With IPv4, you can also use loose (**`-j`**) or strict (**`-k`**) source routing (sending packets via a predetermined route). Also, **`-t`** continues to ping host until interrupted (**`Ctrl+C`**).

Two other switches are used to test the MTU path between two hosts. Each host and any intermediate routers and network segments are configured with a maximum packet size (Message Transfer Unit [MTU]). Normally, when a router receives a packet that is too big, it responds with an error message. Some routers may not respond correctly or a firewall may block the error message, and so packets sent via that route are lost.

You can use ping with the `-f` and `-l nn` switches to simulate packets with a given MTU and therefore work out the maximum permissible packet size. The `-f` switch prevents routers from fragmenting the packets (breaking them into smaller chunks) and the `-l` switch sets the size of the packet in bytes. When working out the size to send, you need to know the smallest MTU used along the network path. For Ethernet, this is 1500 bytes but on a WAN it may be less. You then need to subtract 28 bytes from that number as this is the size of the ICMP packet itself. Therefore, to test an Ethernet path, you would enter: **`ping x.x.x.x -f -l 1472`**.

Troubleshooting an IP Conflict

Two systems could end up with the same IP address because of a configuration error; perhaps both addresses were statically assigned or one was assigned an address that was part of a DHCP scope by mistake. If Windows detects a duplicate IP address, it will display a warning and disable IP. If there are two systems with duplicate IPs, a sort of "race condition" will determine which receives traffic. Obviously this is not a good way for the network to be configured and you should identify the machines and set them to use unique addresses.

IP Version 6

The addressing scheme discussed above is for IP version 4. Because it is feared the global supply of IP addresses will run out, a new version of IP addressing (version 6) has been developed. An IPv6 address is a 128-bit number (contrast with the 32-bit number used in v4).

Binary and Hexadecimal Notation

As you know, network addresses are represented as binary values when processed by the computer but because binary has only two values for each position and the values are typically very large, this would require a long string of characters to write out. This is difficult enough to read but even harder to type accurately into configuration dialogs.

Binary values are converted to decimal for IPv4 addresses but as IPv6 addresses are so much longer, hexadecimal notation is used. Hexadecimal has 16 characters (0...9 plus A, B, C, D, E, F). Therefore it only takes 1 hexadecimal character to represent 4 binary characters. The following table summarizes the equivalent representations of decimal values from 0-15 in binary and hex.

Decimal	Hexadecimal	Binary	Decimal	Hexadecimal	Binary
0	0	0000	8	8	1000
1	1	0001	9	9	1001
2	2	0010	10	A	1010
3	3	0011	11	B	1011
4	4	0100	12	C	1100
5	5	0101	13	D	1101
6	6	0110	14	E	1110
7	7	0111	15	F	1111

IPv6 Address Notation

A 128-bit IPv6 address is expressed in hexadecimal notation. The binary address is divided into 8 double-byte (16-bit) values delimited by colons. For example:

```
2001:0db8:0000:0000:0abc:0000:def0:1234
```

Even this is quite cumbersome, so where a double-byte contains leading zeros, they can be ignored. In addition, *one* contiguous series of zeroes can be replaced by a double colon place marker. Thus the address above would become:

```
2001:db8::abc:0:def0:1234
```

IPv6 Addressing Schemes

An IPv6 address is divided into two main parts: the first 64 bits are used as a network ID while the second 64 bits designate a specific interface.

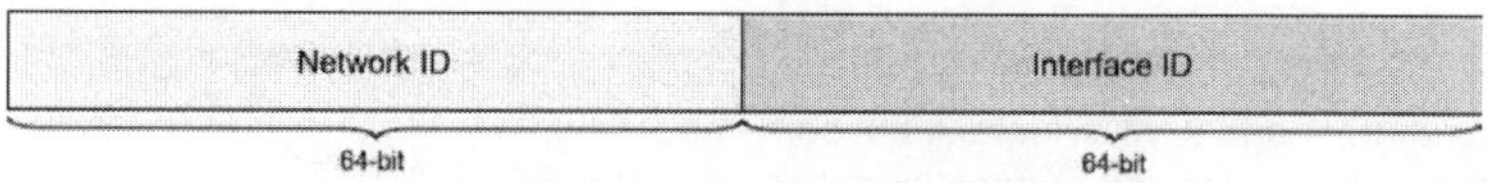

In IPv6, the interface identifier is always the last 64 bits; the first 64 bits are used for network addressing

As the network and host portions are fixed size, there is no need for a subnet mask. Network addresses are written using CIDR notation, where */nn* is the length of the routing prefix in bits. Within the 64-bit network ID, as with CIDR, the length of any given network prefix is used to determine whether two addresses belong to the same IP network.

As with IPv4, a **unicast address** identifies a single network interface. The main types of unicast addressing are global and link-local. A **global** address is one that is unique on the Internet (equivalent to public addresses in IPv4). Global unicast addresses have the following format:

IPv6 global unicast address format

- The first 3 bits indicate that the address is within the global scope. In hex notation, a global unicast address will start with either "2" or "3".
- The next 45 bits are allocated in a hierarchical manner to regional registries and from them to ISPs and end users.
- The next 16 bits identity site-specific subnet addresses.
- The final 64 bits are the interface ID. The interface ID is either generated from the adapter's MAC address (padded with extra bits to make it 64 bits in length) or is randomly generated. Windows now defaults to using randomly generated interface IDs though can be configured to use the MAC method.

Link-local addresses are used by IPv6 for network housekeeping traffic. Link-local addresses span a single subnet (they are not forwarded by routers). Nodes on the same link are referred to as **neighbors**. In hex notation, link-local addresses start with **fe80::**.

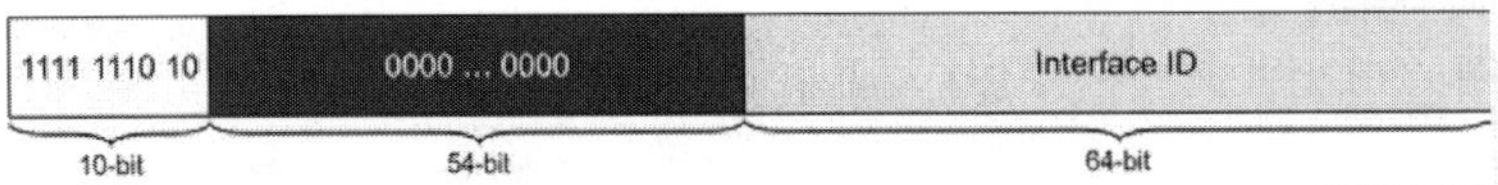

IPv6 link-local unicast address format

The equivalent in IPv4 is Automatic Private IP Addressing (APIPA) and its 169.254.0.0 addresses. However, unlike IPv4, an IPv6 host is *always* configured with link-local addresses (one for each link), even if it also has a globally unique address.

IPv4 versus IPv6 Misconfiguration

IPv6 is subject to much the same misconfiguration issues as IPv4, with duplicate addresses or incorrect network prefixes the most likely issues. It is also important to note the impact of running both protocols together. Most hosts are configured to use both IPv4 and IPv6 by default but some networks might consider one or the other as an unneeded protocol and disable it. A host running only IPv4 will not be able to contact a host running only IPv6 and vice versa, unless some sort of tunneling mechanism has been configured.

Review Questions / Module 2 / Unit 2 / Internet Protocol

Answer these questions to test what you have learned in this unit.

1) What is meant by dotted decimal notation?
2) If a host is configured with the subnet mask 255.255.255.0, what address class could that be related to?
3) A host is configured with the IP address 172.29.0.101. What is significant about this address?
4) True or false? The default gateway address is the IP address of a router on a remote network.
5) What is the purpose of a DHCP server?
6) True or false? Classful addressing is a feature of IP version 6.
7) You have restarted the DHCP server following a network problem. What command would you use to refresh the IP configuration on client workstations?
8) What command can you use on a Linux computer to report the IP configuration?
9) A single server on a network cannot connect to the Internet. Where would you start troubleshooting?
10) If a host has a firewall configured to block outgoing ICMP traffic, what result would you expect from pinging the host (assuming that the path to the host is otherwise OK)?

Module 2 / Unit 3

Routers and Firewalls

Objectives

On completion of this unit, you will be able to:

- Understand the basics of IP routing and use of tracert to troubleshoot.
- Explain the functions of TCP and UDP ports and use netstat to identify open ports.
- Implement secure network topologies using zones, NAT, firewalls, and VLANs.

IP Routing Basics

The subnet mask or network prefix is used by IP to identify whether the source and destination addresses in a packet are on the same IP network or subnetwork. If the destination address has a different network ID, the packet must be sent via one or more **routers**. The **default gateway** is the IP address of a router on the same IP network as the host. Messages destined for other IP networks are sent to the default gateway address by the source host.

Routing Decisions

When a message is sent using IP, the following steps occur:

1) IP will identify the network addresses of the source and destination hosts:
    - The subnet mask of the host is applied to the source IP address to determine the network address of the source host.
    - The subnet mask of the host is applied to the destination IP address to determine the network address of the destination host.
2) The destination network address is compared with that of the source:
    - If the two hosts are on the same IP network, IP uses ARP messaging to locate the destination interface. The response to this broadcast includes the hardware (MAC) address of the destination interface and the message can then be sent.
    - If the two machines are on different IP networks, IP uses ARP messaging to locate the default gateway (router). This machine responds with its MAC address and the message is then sent to the gateway.

3) IP then sends the packet. A data link protocol (such as Ethernet) encapsulates this into one or more frames and transmits them over the network.

4) If the packet has been routed, at the gateway, the Time to Live (TTL) is decreased by at least one. This could be greater if the router is congested. When the TTL is zero, the packet will not be forwarded to another router. This prevents badly addressed packets from permanently circulating the network.

5) The router then determines what to do with the packet by repeating these steps. If the message is destined for yet another network, the process is repeated to take it to the next stage and so on.

Routes to other IP networks can be manually configured or learned by a **routing protocol**. Discovered routes are held in a **routing table**. The more sophisticated routers can share information about known networks and possible paths to them. This information allows them to choose the best routes to any given destination and select alternate routes if one of these is unavailable.

Routers

At the data link layer, switches connect nodes on the basis of local or hardware (MAC) addresses. Everything connected to a basic switch is part of the same physical and logical network. The network layer transfers information between networks by examining the destination network layer address or logical network address, and routing the packet through the internetwork using intermediate systems (**routers**).

Selection of the path or route to the destination network address is determined **dynamically** or **statically**. The packet moves, hop by hop, through the internetwork to the target network. Once it has reached the destination network, the hardware address can be used to move the packet to the target node. This process requires each logically separate network to have a unique network address.

A router can connect networks that are based on different types of network technology or that are logically distinct by routing packets from one network to another. In such an internetwork each network is identified by a unique **network address**.

HP ProCurve router with different types of Ethernet and WAN interfaces (Image © 2014 Hewlett-Packard Development Company)

A router has two main functions:

- Divide a single physical network into multiple logical networks - this is useful for security and performance reasons.
- Join a network using one type of media with a network using different media. A typical example is to join a LAN to a WAN, such as the Internet.

Network Address Translation

Most hosts on private networks are not configured with IP addresses that can communicate directly to the Internet. Instead, clients on the local network connect via a router. The router converts the client's private IP address into a valid public address using **Network Address Translation (NAT)**. As well as making IP configuration easier, this protects the clients in the local network from direct access across the Internet. All traffic has to be channeled through the router, which will also usually incorporate a firewall to block unwanted communications.

A NAT address pool supports multiple simultaneous connections but is still limited by the number of available public IP addresses. Smaller companies may only be allocated a single or small block of addresses by their ISP. In this case, a means for multiple private IP addresses to be mapped onto a single public address would be useful, and this is exactly what is provided by **Network Address Port Translation (NAPT)**, which is also referred to as **PAT (Port Address Translation)** or as **NAT overloading**.

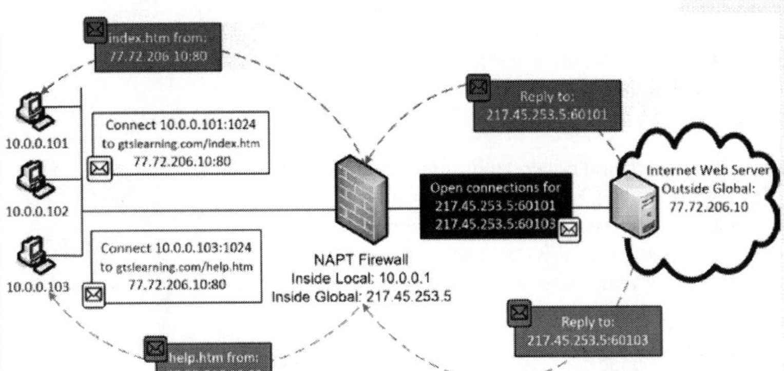

NAT overloading

NAPT works by allocating each new connection a high level TCP or UDP port. For example, say two hosts (10.0.0.101 and 10.0.0.103) initiate a web connection at the same time, requesting responses on the client (or source) port 1024. The NAPT service creates two new client port mappings for these requests (10.0.0.101:60101 and 10.0.0.103:60103). It then substitutes the private source IPs for a single public source IP (217.45.253.5) and forwards the requests to the public Internet. It performs a reverse mapping on any traffic returned to those client ports, inserting the original private IP address and client port number, and forwarding the packets to the internal hosts.

Troubleshooting Routing Issues

When users report problems, the description is usually unhelpful; "server unavailable", "Internet down", or "email not working" for instance. As with a local network, when troubleshooting suspected routing issues, you should try to connect to the server hosting the resource via IP first.

- If the IP link works, there may be a problem with a name resolution service, a firewall or security configuration, or some sort of application level problem with the server software (perhaps the email service has crashed or the server has run out of disk space). The fact that a basic connection exists prompts you to go and investigate the services running on top of the link.
- If the IP link doesn't work, there could be a routing or firewall / security problem, there could be a cable or component problem, or the server could have crashed completely or been switched off.

Improper Subnetting

As described above, if the source and destination network addresses are different, IP will attempt to use a router to forward the packet. If one or both hosts have an **improper subnetting** configuration, they may be unable to communicate. You may come across the situation where sent packets arrive at a host successfully but the reply packets are lost. For example, because it is configured with the wrong subnet mask value, a receiving host might incorrectly behave as though the sending host is local to it and attempt to locate it via ARP messaging. Another scenario is that a host may try to route replies to hosts that are actually local to it. These communications may succeed, depending on how the router is configured, but will be a drag on network performance.

Default Gateway and Routing Tables

If you can verify that both source and destination hosts have correctly configured IP addresses and subnet masks / network prefixes, next check whether the default gateway (router) address is misconfigured. Verify that you can ping the router itself; if not, investigate why the router is not responding (remember, if the router is down then multiple hosts / users will be experiencing connectivity problems).

If there is no problem with router availability, investigate the local host's OS route table - you can use the `route` command or `netstat -r` to do this. Assuming that the server is not a router, there should be a fairly simple set of entries - for example:

- Default route (0.0.0.0).
- Loopback address.
- Host's subnet address.

- Host's own address.
- Multicast address.
- Broadcast address.

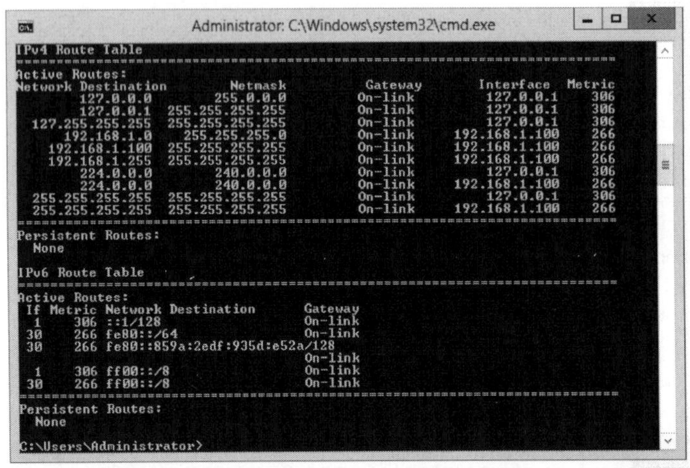

Default routing table for a Windows host

If a static route has been configured for some reason, that might be the cause of the problem. You can use the **route** command to add or delete routes to try to troubleshoot the issue.

Using tracert and traceroute

In a complex routed environment, use **tracert** (Windows) or **traceroute** (Linux) to test the route to the remote host you are trying to contact. These utilities probe each router on the path taken by a packet as it "hops" to the destination host on a remote network.

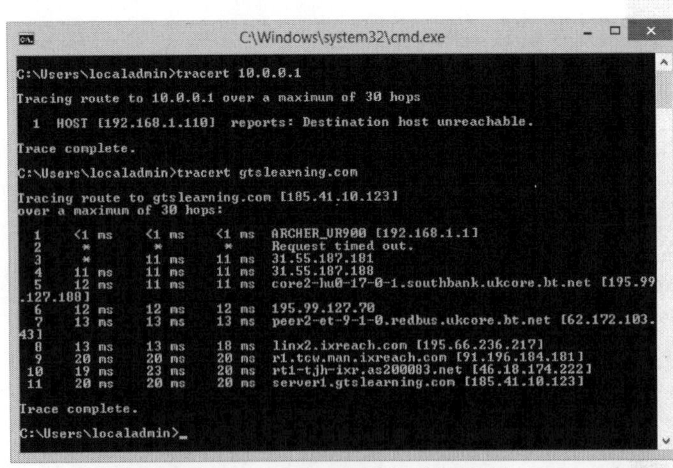

Using tracert - the first trace to a local private network has failed but the trace over the Internet to gtslearning.com's web server has succeeded, passing first through the SOHO router then through the routers belonging to the user's ISP then the routers belonging to the web host

If the host cannot be located, the command will eventually timeout but it will return every router that was attempted. The output shows the number of hops (when a packet is transferred from one router to another), the ingress interface of the router or host (that is, the interface from which the router receives the ICMP packet), and the time taken to respond to each probe in milliseconds (ms).

You can use the `-d` switch to suppress name resolution, `-h` to specify the maximum number of hops (the default is 30), and `-w` to specify a timeout in ms (the default is 4000). The `-j` option allows you to specify preferred routers (loose source routing).

It could be that one router somewhere along the line is down or there could be some sort of issue with a routing protocol, in which case it's probably time to escalate the problem to a specialist team.

Troubleshooting Service Provider Issues

It is worth bearing in mind that any issues that could affect your network could also affect your service providers' networks. An Internet connectivity failure may be nothing to do with your routers but be caused by an issue with your ISP's routers.

Make sure you can identify when a problem's cause lies with an external network and ensure you have the technical support information allowing you to escalate the problem and get it resolved quickly.

TCP and UDP Ports

Ethernet is primarily concerned with moving frames between nodes on a local network segment. IP provides addressing and routing functionality for a network of networks (or internetwork). Protocols at the **transport** layer (in OSI model terms) are concerned with effective delivery. At the transport layer (also known as the end-to-end or host-to-host layer) the *content* of the packets starts to become significant.

Any given host on a network will be communicating with many other hosts using many different types of application data. One of critical functions of the transport layer is to identify each type of network application by assigning it a **port number** between 0 and 65535. For example, data from the HTTP web browsing application can be identified as port 80 while data from an email application can be identified as port 143. At the transport layer, on the sending host, data from the upper layers is packaged as a series of **segments** and each segment is tagged with the application's port number. The segment is then passed to the network layer for delivery. The host could be transmitting multiple HTTP and email segments at the same time. These are **multiplexed** using the port numbers onto the same network link.

In fact, each host assigns two port numbers. On the client, the destination port number is mapped to the service that the client is requesting (HTTP on port 80 for instance). The client also assigns a random source port number (47747 for instance). The server uses this client-assigned port number (47747) as the destination port number for its replies and its application port number (80 for HTTP) as its source port. This allows the hosts to track multiple "conversations" for the same application protocol.

At the network and data link layers, the port number is not significant - it becomes part of the data payload and is "invisible" to routers and switches working at the network and data link layers. At the receiving host, each segment is extracted from its frame and then identified by its port number and passed up to the relevant handler at the upper session and application layers. Put another way, the traffic stream is de-multiplexed.

TCP versus UDP

The transport layer is also responsible for ensuring *reliable* data delivery so that packets arrive error-free and without loss. The transport layer can overcome any lack of reliability in the lower level protocols. This reliability is achieved by the **Transport Control Protocol (TCP)** using **acknowledgement** messages that inform the sender the data was successfully received. The kinds of problems that may occur during the delivery of the data are non-delivery and delivery in a damaged state. In the first case, the lack of acknowledgement results in the retransmission of the data and, in the second case, a **Negative Acknowledgement (NACK)** forces retransmission. TCP is described as connection-oriented, because it ensures the reliability and sequencing of messages passing over the connection.

On the other hand, sometimes it is more important that communications be faster than they are reliable. The acknowledgements process of TCP adds a lot of overhead in the form of message headers added to each data packet. The **User Datagram Protocol (UDP)** is a connectionless, non-guaranteed method of communication with no sequencing or flow control (the application layer controls delivery reliability). There is no guarantee regarding the delivery of messages or the sequence in which packets are received. UDP is suitable for applications that send small amounts of data and do not require acknowledgement of receipt. It may also be used for applications that transfer time-sensitive data but do not require complete reliability, such as voice or video. The reduced overhead means that delivery is faster.

Well Known Ports

Any application or process that uses TCP or UDP for its transport (such as HTTP for web services or IMAP for email) is assigned a unique identification number called a port. The server and client applications each use *different* ports. For example, a client may contact an HTTP server at IP address 77.72.206.10 on port 80 (77.72.206.10:80). The HTTP server would respond to the client on a temporary (or **ephemeral**) port number that the client has opened for that purpose (47747 for instance).

Server port numbers are assigned by the **Internet Assigned Numbers Authority (IANA)**. Some of the "well-known" port numbers are listed below:

#	TCP / UDP	Process	Description
20	TCP	ftp-data	File Transfer Protocol - Data
21	TCP	ftp	File Transfer Protocol - Control
22	TCP	ssh / sftp / scp	Secure Shell / Secure FTP / Secure Copy
23	TCP	telnet	Telnet
25	TCP	smtp	Simple Mail Transfer Protocol
53	TCP / UDP	domain	Domain Name System
67	UDP	bootps	BOOTP / DHCP Server
68	UDP	bootpc	BOOTP / DHCP Client
69	UDP	tftp	Trivial File Transfer Protocol
80	TCP	http	HTTP
110	TCP	pop3	Post Office Protocol
123	UDP	ntp	Network Time Protocol
143	TCP	imap	Internet Mail Access Protocol
161	UDP	snmp	Simple Network Management Protocol
162	UDP	snmp-trap	Simple Network Management Protocol Trap
443	TCP	https	HTTP Secure
445	TCP	smb	Server Message Block
989	TCP	ftps-data	FTP/S Data
990	TCP	ftps	FTP/S (FTP over SSL Implicit Mode)
3389	TCP	rdp	Remote Desktop Protocol

Enabling and disabling ports is an important part of configuring a **firewall**, to ensure that only valid application protocols are allowed.

netstat

netstat can be used to investigate open ports and connections on the local host. These connections are established by checking for ports that are active or merely listening for connection attempts.

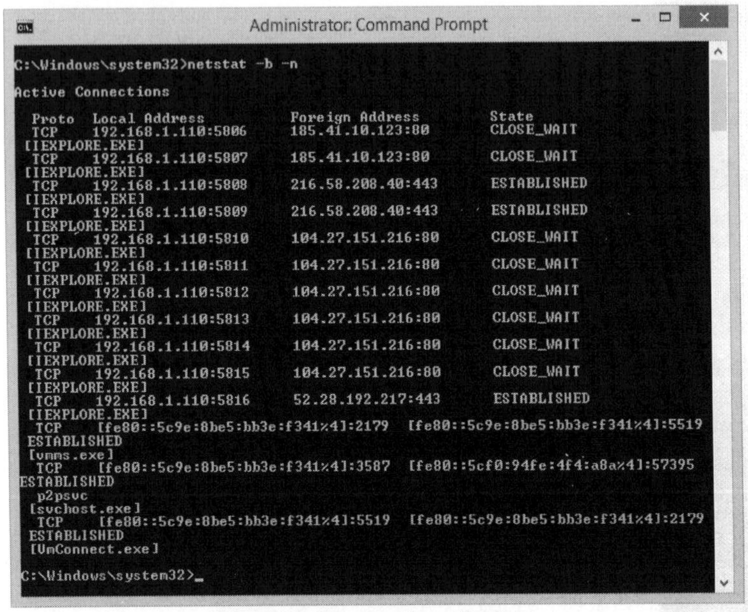

Displaying open connections with netstat

The following switches can be used:

- **-a** displays all the connections and listening ports.
- **-b** shows the process that has opened the port.
- **-e** displays Ethernet statistics.
- **-n** displays ports and addresses in numerical format. Skipping name resolution speeds up each query.
- **-s** shows per protocol statistics.
- **-p** ***proto*** displays connections by protocol (TCP or UDP or TCPv6 / UDPv6). When used with **-s**, this switch can also filter the statistics shown by IP, IPv6, ICMP, and ICMPv6.
- **-r** shows the routing table.

The utility can also be set to run in the background by entering **netstat** ***nn***, where *nn* is the refresh interval in seconds (press **Ctrl+C** to stop).

Linux supports a similar utility with slightly different switches. You can also use the **lsof** command to query open connections and running processes.

Zones and Access Control Lists (ACL)

Network segmentation is the process of determining which bits of the network are accessible to other bits. A highly secure network or single host computer may have to be physically separated from any other network. This is also referred to as an **air gap**. Air gapping creates many management issues however and so is only done rarely.

The technologies that can be used to enforce network segmentation include Virtual LANs (VLAN), subnets, VPNs, and virtualization. All these types of system enforce network segmentation by deploying **access controls** of different types. The networks are not physically separate but they are logically separate. For example, when a host is assigned to a VLAN, the switch restricts it to seeing packets designated for that VLAN. To communicate outside the VLAN, the host must use a router and a router equipped with a **firewall** can apply additional rules to what it allows in and out.

The main unit of a logically segmented network is a **zone**. A zone is an area of the network (or of a connected network) where the security configuration is the same for all hosts within it. Network traffic between zones is strictly controlled, using a security device - typically a **firewall**. A firewall is software or hardware that filters traffic passing into and out of the network. The firewall bases its decisions on a set of rules called an **Access Control List (ACL)**. For example, a basic router firewall can allow or deny a host access based on its IP address or by the port it is requesting or a combination of both. Different types of firewall (and other filtering devices) can apply different - often more sophisticated - criteria in their ACLs.

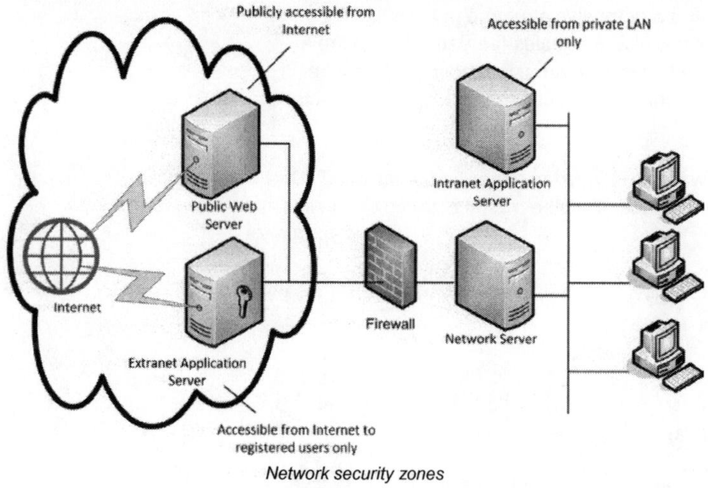

Network security zones

One of the most important reasons for segmenting networks is to separate public and private networks. The main private and public zones are as follows:

- **Private network (intranet)** - this is a network of trusted hosts owned and controlled by the organization.

Hosts are trusted in the sense that they are under your administrative control and subject to the security mechanisms (such as anti-virus software, user rights, software updating, and so on) that you have set up to defend the network.

- **Extranet** - this is a network of semi-trusted hosts, typically representing business partners, suppliers, or customers. Hosts must **authenticate** to join the extranet.
- **Internet** - this is a public zone permitting **anonymous** access (or perhaps a mix of anonymous and authenticated access) by untrusted hosts over the Internet.

Demilitarized Zones (DMZ)

One important distinction between different security zones is whether a host is Internet-facing. An Internet-facing host accepts **inbound** connections from the Internet. These Internet-facing hosts are placed in a **Demilitarized Zone (DMZ)**. A DMZ is also referred to as a perimeter network. The idea of a DMZ is that traffic cannot pass *through* it directly. Everything behind the DMZ is invisible to the outside network.

Servers that provide extranet or public access services should be placed in a DMZ. These would typically include web servers, mail and other communications servers, proxy servers, and remote access servers. The hosts in the DMZ are not fully trusted by the internal network because of the possibility that they could be compromised from the Internet. They are referred to as **Bastion Hosts**. A bastion is a defensive structure in a castle. The bastion protrudes from the castle wall and enables the defenders to fire at attackers that have moved close to the wall. A bastion host would not be configured with any services that run on the local network, such as directory services.

In a screened subnet, two firewalls are placed at either end of the DMZ. One restricts traffic on the external interface; the other restricts traffic on the internal interface.

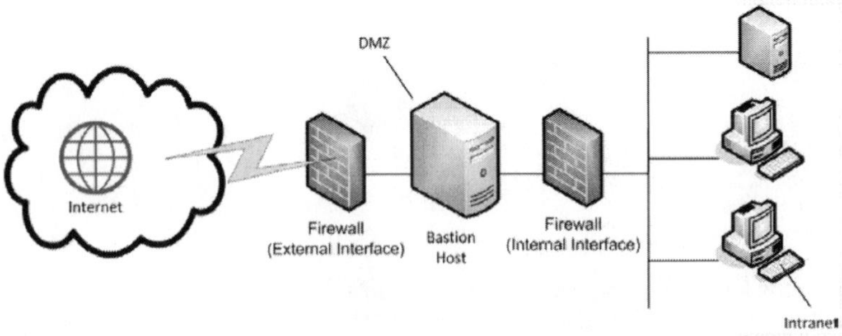

Screened subnet

A three-legged (or triple-homed) firewall is one with three network ports: he external interface, the DMZ port, and the internal interface.

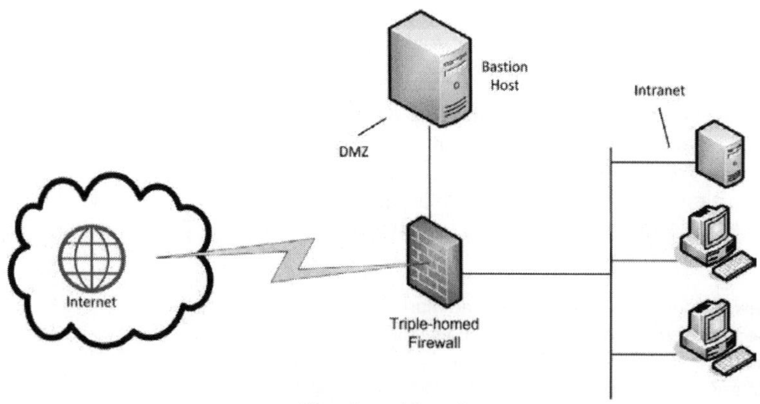

Three-legged firewall

This is more complex to configure than a screened subnet. Also, the firewall represents a single point of failure and is easier to compromise. However, this configuration does save on costs.

Internal Network Firewalls

There is no single way of designing a network. Rather, a network will reflect the business needs of the organization. You may want to define your own security zones to suit business needs. For example, simply deploying firewalls to protect perimeter security ignores the threat of internal malicious users. Consequently, it is also necessary to secure the links between internal systems and you might accomplish this by placing firewalls on the internal network as well as on the external / DMZ interface. Some examples could include:

- A zone containing untrusted or semi-trusted hosts on the local network (for example, computers that are publicly accessible).
- Zones representing departmental functions.

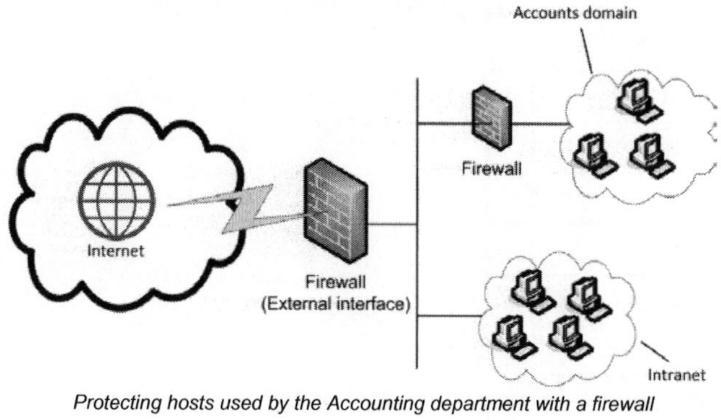

Protecting hosts used by the Accounting department with a firewall

Basic Firewalls

The basic function of a network-based firewall is **traffic filtering**. A firewall resembles a quality inspector on a production line; any bad units are knocked off the line and go no farther. The firewall processes traffic according to **rules**; traffic that does not conform to a rule that allows it access is blocked. Firewalls are the devices principally used to implement security zones, such as intranet, DMZ, and Internet.

There are many types of firewall and many ways of implementing a firewall. One distinction can be made between firewalls that protect a whole network (placed inline in the network and inspecting all traffic that passes through) and firewalls that protect a single host only (installed on the host and only inspect traffic destined for that host). Another distinction is on what parts of a packet a firewall can inspect and operate.

Packet Filtering Firewall

Packet filtering describes the earliest types of firewall. All firewalls can still perform this basic function. A packet filtering firewall can inspect the **headers** of IP packets. This means that rules can be based on the information found in those headers:

- IP filtering - accepting or blocking traffic on the basis of its source and / or destination IP address.
- Protocol ID / type (TCP, UDP, ICMP, routing protocols, and so on).
- Port filtering / security - accepting or blocking traffic on the basis of source and destination port numbers (TCP or UDP application type).

There may be additional functionality in some products, such as the ability to block some types of ICMP (ping) traffic but not others or the ability to filter by hardware (MAC) address. Packet filtering works mainly at Layer 3 (Network) of the OSI model.

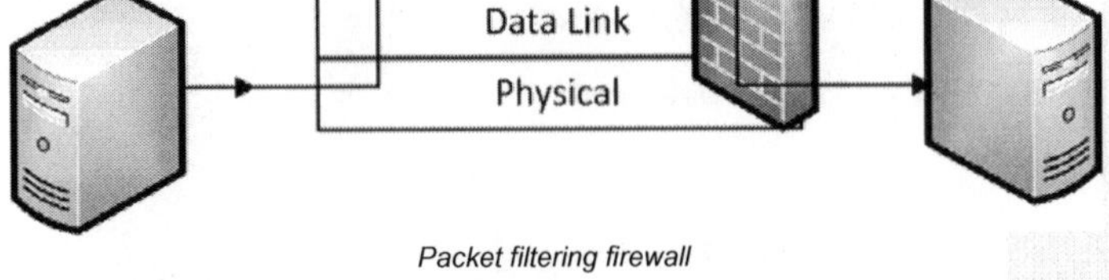

Packet filtering firewall

Another distinction that can be made is whether the firewall can control only inbound traffic or both inbound and outbound traffic. This is also often referred to as "ingress" and "egress" traffic or filtering. Controlling outbound traffic is useful because it can block applications that have not been authorized to run on the network and defeat malware such as backdoors.

A packet filtering firewall is configured by specifying a number of rules, called an **Access Control List (ACL)**. An ACL is a list of rules, each of which defines a specific type of data packet and the appropriate action to take when packet matches the rule.

Actions can be either **block** (drop the packet, and optionally log an event) or **allow** (let the packet pass through the firewall). There are separate rulesets covering **inbound** and **outbound** traffic.

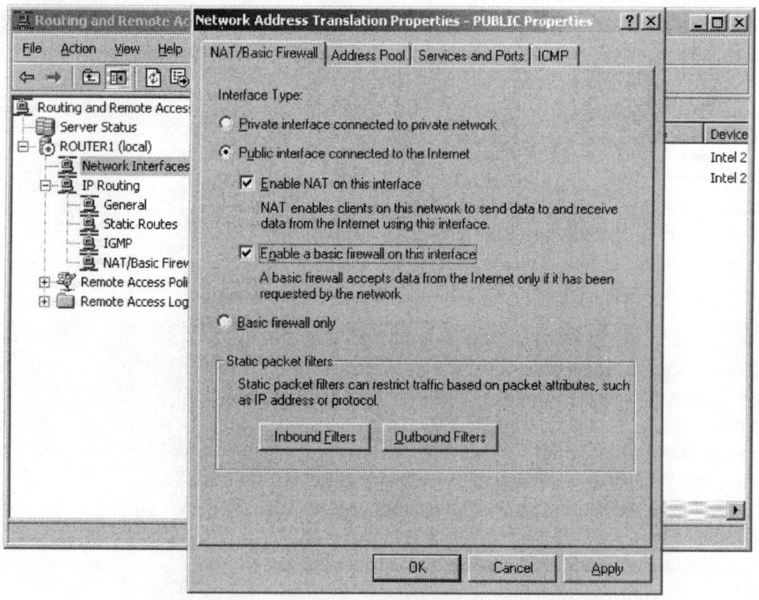

Configuring a packet filtering firewall under Windows Server

Troubleshooting Misconfigured Firewalls / ACLs

Firewall rules are configured on the principle of **least access**. This is the same as the principle of least privilege; only allow the minimum amount of traffic required for the operation of valid network services and no more.

The rules in a firewall's ACL are processed top-to-bottom. If traffic matches one of the rules then it is allowed to pass; consequently the most important and specific rules are placed at the top. The final default rule is typically to block any traffic that has not matched a rule (**implicit deny**).

Each rule can specify whether to block or allow traffic based on a number of parameters, often referred to as **tuples** (if you think of each rule being like a row in a database, the tuples are the columns). For example, in the screenshot, the tuples include "Program", "Local Address", "Remote Address", "Protocol", "Local Port", "Remote Port", "Authorized Users", and so on.

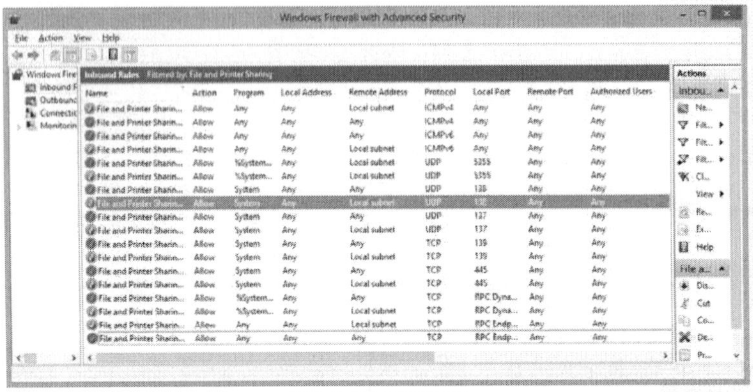

Sample firewall rule set

Even the simplest packet filtering firewall can be complex to configure securely. It is essential to create a written policy describing what the firewall should do and to test the firewall configuration as far as possible to ensure that the ACLs you have set up work as intended. Also test and document changes made to ACLs.

One type of firewall or ACL misconfiguration blocks packets that are supposed to be allowed through. This will cause an application or protocol to fail to function correctly. This type of error will usually be easy to identify, as users will report incidents connected with the failure of the data traffic. With such incidents, firewall configuration will always be a likely cause, so will be high on the list to investigate. Diagnosis can be confirmed by trying to establish the connection from both inside and outside the firewall. If it connects from outside the firewall but not from inside, this would confirm the firewall to be the cause of the issue. You can also inspect the firewall's log files to discover what rules have been applied to block traffic at a particular time.

The other possible outcome of a badly configured firewall is that packets may be allowed through that should be blocked. This is a more serious outcome because the result is to open the system to security vulnerabilities. It is also not necessarily so easily detected, as it does not typically cause anything to stop functioning. As no incidents usually arise from this outcome (except in the case that a vulnerability is exploited), it is not a scenario that is subject to troubleshooting. Rather, it underlines the need for regular firewall audits and thorough change control processes to deal with firewall change requests.

Also remember that the firewall represents a link in a chain of connectivity and if the hardware or software supporting the firewall fails, the link will be broken and network connectivity disrupted.

Host-based Firewalls

A network-based firewall is typically one running on a network device such as a router or a dedicated security appliance. Firewalls can also be implemented as software running alongside other services under an OS such as Windows or Linux however.

NOS Firewall

A **Network Operating System (NOS) firewall** is a software-based firewall running under a network server OS, such as Windows or Linux. The server would function as a gateway or proxy for a network segment.

Application Firewall

An **application firewall** is software designed to run on a server to protect a particular application only (a web server firewall for instance or a firewall designed to protect an SQL Server database). This is a type of host-based firewall and would typically be deployed in addition to a network firewall.

Personal Firewall

A **personal firewall** is implemented as a software application running on a single host. While they can perform basic packet filtering, personal firewalls tend to be program- or process-based; that is, when a program tries to initiate (in the case of outbound) or accept (inbound) a TCP/IP network connection, the firewall prompts the user to block, allow once, or allow always.

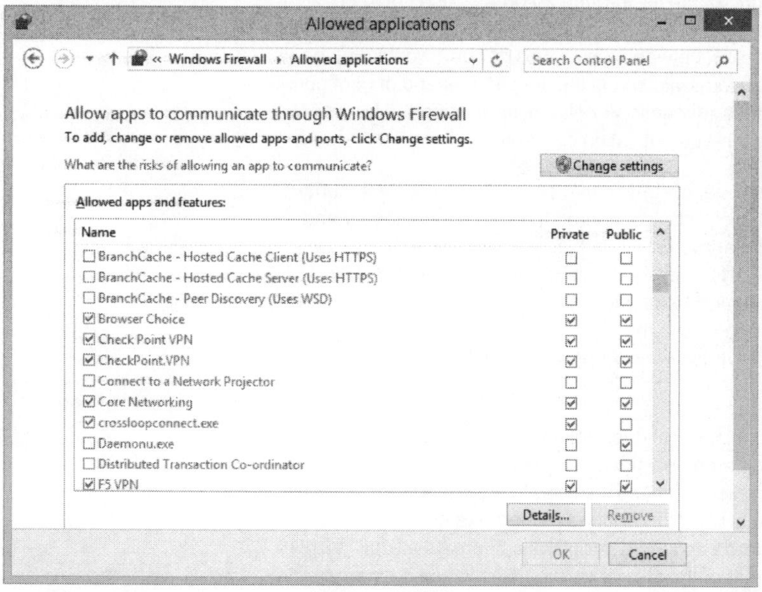

Windows Firewall

When using a personal firewall on an enterprise network, some thought needs to be given as to how it will interact with network border firewalls. The use of personal firewalls can make troubleshooting network applications more complex.

VLAN Configuration

Virtual LANs (VLAN) is a feature of most Ethernet switches whereby computers connected by the *same* cabling and switch appliances can appear to be in *different* local networks (or broadcast domains).

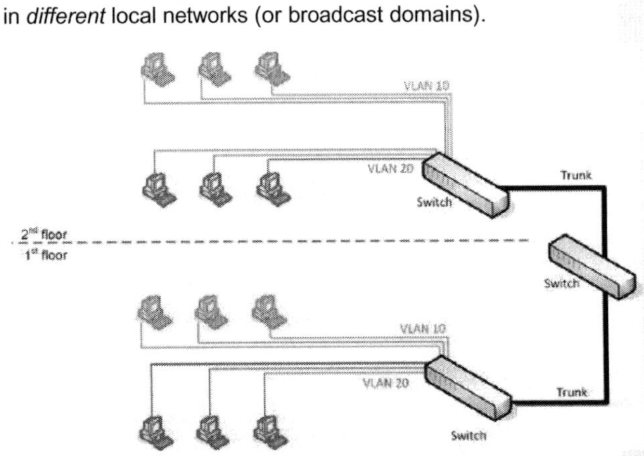

VLANs

For example, ports 1 through 10 and 11 through 20 on a switch could be configured as two separate VLANs, typically each with their own IP network or subnet address. Communication between the groups of ports would only be possible via a router. Port-based switching is the simplest means of configuring a VLAN (static VLANs). Others (dynamic VLANs) include using the host's MAC address, protocol type, or even authentication credentials.

From a security point-of-view, each VLAN can represent a separate security zone. These zones would typically be configured to protect the integrity and confidentiality of different departments within the organization. Any communication between VLANs needs to be channeled via a router. This means that in the event of a successful attack the scope of the attack can be limited to the single VLAN rather than the whole network. VLANs may also help to contain the spread of viruses and worms to a smaller group of computers.

As well as representing organizational departments and/or overcoming physical barriers between different locations, it is common practice to isolate server-to-server traffic from client-server traffic and to isolate administration / management traffic; channels used for inbound management of appliances and servers. Another standard configuration option is to create a "null" VLAN that is non-routable to the rest of the network. This VLAN is used for any ports that do not have authorized connected equipment.

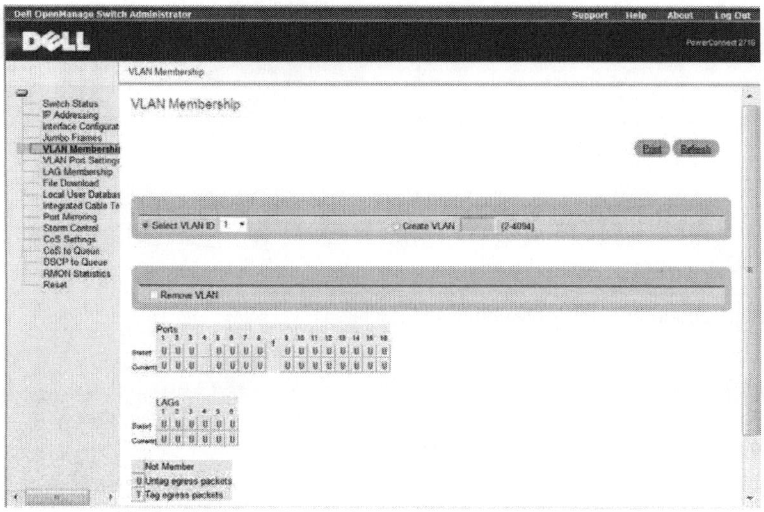

Viewing VLANs on a Dell switch using the web management interface

From a troubleshooting point-of-view, you need to be sure that clients within a particular VLAN can access the services they expect (such as DHCP, DNS, and so on). When you run into a connectivity problem that does not seem to have any sort of hardware or cable cause and the hosts' IP configurations seem correct, check whether the correct VLAN assignment has been made on the switch and that routing between VLANs is working as it should.

Review Questions / Module 2 / Unit 3 / Routers and Firewalls

Answer these questions to test what you have learned in this unit.

1) What is a routing table?

2) What is the function of NAT?

3) What tool is used to test the end-to-end path between two IP hosts on different IP networks?

4) What could you conclude if pings time out?

5) True or false? A transport protocol establishes a link between a port on the server AND a port on the client.

6) If a network application cannot tolerate a missing packet, what type of transport protocol should it use?

7) True or false? Protocols that stream video and audio over the Internet are likely to be based on UDP rather than TCP.

8) What port is used for FTP connection control (by default)?

9) How can a DMZ be implemented?

10) A server is configured to obtain an address automatically but isn't able to contact a DHCP server connected to the same switch. What might be a likely cause?

11) What is a null VLAN and why might it be used?

Module 2 / Unit 4

Network Services

Objectives

On completion of this unit, you will be able to:

- Understand the process of name resolution using HOSTS, DNS, and WINS.
- Identify basic configuration parameters for a DNS server.
- Use nslookup and nbtstat to verify and troubleshoot name resolution.
- Install and configure DHCP and NTP servers.

Network Services Servers

Many servers are configured to provide addressing information on a network, running TCP/IP services such as DHCP, DNS, and NTP. They may also be configured to provide more secure access to the Internet, functioning as a firewall or proxy server.

A server can also be configured to provide remote access to resources on the server. With remote access, a user connects to the server using a modem or through the Internet (a Virtual Private Network).

Host Names and FQDNs

The Internet Protocol uses the binary IP address for locating hosts on an internetwork. The dotted decimal (IPv4) or hex (IPv6) representation of this IP address is used for configuration purposes but is not particularly intuitive for people to remember. For this reason, a unique "friendly" name is also typically assigned to each host. There are two types of names: host names and Fully Qualified Domain Names (FQDN).

Host Names

A **host name** is assigned to a computer by the administrator. The host name can consist of letters, numbers, and hyphens, though it cannot be all numbers and cannot start with a hyphen. Host names are almost never treated as case-sensitive. Punctuation characters such as period (.) or forward slash (/) are not allowed.

Fully Qualified Domain Name

To avoid the possibility of duplicate host names on the Internet, a **Fully Qualified Domain Name (FQDN)** is used to provide a unique identity for the host belonging to a particular network. An example of a FQDN might be:

```
mole.riverbank.com.
```

An FQDN is usually made up of the **host name** and one or more **domain names** (a **domain suffix**). In the example, the host name is "mole" and the domain suffix is "riverbank.com.". This domain suffix consists of the domain name "riverbank" within the **top level domain** ".com". The domain suffix is appended to the host name to define the location of the host and ensure the uniqueness of the host name.

The domain suffix can also contain **subdomains** between the host and domain name. The trailing dot or period represents the root of the hierarchy.

Domain names must be registered with a central body to ensure they are unique within a top level domain. Once a domain name has been registered, it cannot be used by another organization. The same domain name may be registered within different top level domains however (**riverbank.com.** and **riverbank.co.uk.** are distinct domains for instance).

Numerous hosts may exist within a single domain. For example: **mole**, **ratty**, and **toad** might all be hosts within the **riverbank.com.** domain. Given that, FQDNs must follow certain rules:

- The host name must be unique within the domain. A DNS host name can contain letter, digit, and hyphen characters only. A label cannot begin or end with a hyphen. A label could consist of a single letter or number. Other domain labels can also contain underscores.
- The total length of an FQDN cannot exceed 253 characters, with each label (part of the name defined by a period) no more than 63 characters (excluding the periods).
- FQDNs are not case sensitive.

When configuring name records, an FQDN must include the trailing period to represent the root but this can be omitted in most other use cases.

Additionally, Internet registries may have their own restrictions.

Domain Name System (DNS)

To make use of these friendly names, there has to be a system for resolving a host name or FQDN to its IP address and also ensuring the names are unique.

Modern networks and the Internet use a system called the **Domain Name System** but before DNS was available, a **HOSTS file** was used.

Name Resolution Using the HOSTS File

The first method for resolving host names to IP addresses involved the InterNIC central authority maintaining a text file of host name to IP address mappings. This file was called **HOSTS**. Whenever a site wanted to add a new host to the Internet, the site administrator sent an email to InterNIC giving the new host name to IP address mapping. This information was manually entered into the file.

An example HOSTS file is shown below.

```
# Sample
128.103.100.1     toad
178.143.216.47    ratty
12.11.97.104      mole      # server
```

Any text preceded by the **#** symbol in a HOSTS file is a comment and will not be processed.

Network administrators were required to download a copy of the latest HOSTS file at regular intervals and install this on each host at their site. Each host could then perform name resolution by looking up a host name in the local copy of the HOSTS file and locating the corresponding IP address. The default location under Windows is **%SystemRoot%\system32\drivers\etc** while under Linux it is usually placed in the **/etc** directory.

The HOSTS file approach to naming became impractical as the number of hosts connected to the Internet grew - maintaining completeness and accuracy of the file became too difficult. Therefore, in the mid-1980s, the **Domain Name System (DNS)** was developed.

Domain Name System

The **Domain Name System (DNS)** is a hierarchical system of distributed **name server** databases that contain information on domains and hosts within those domains. The distributed nature of the system has the twin advantages that maintenance of the system is delegated and loss of one DNS server does not necessarily prevent name resolution from being performed.

At the top of the DNS hierarchy is the **root**, which is often represented by a **period** (.). There are 13 root level servers (A to M). Immediately below the root lie the **Top Level Domains (TLD)**. There are several types of top level domain, but the most prevalent are generic (.com, .org, .net, .info, .biz), sponsored (.gov, .edu), and country code (.uk, .ca, .de).

The domain name system is operated by ICANN (www.icann.org), who also manage the generic top level domains. Country codes are generally managed by an organization appointed by the relevant government. Each domain name has to be registered with a Domain Name Registry for the appropriate top-level domain.

Information about a domain is found by tracing records from the root down through the hierarchy. The root servers have complete information about the top-level domain servers. In turn, these servers have information relating to servers for the second level domains.

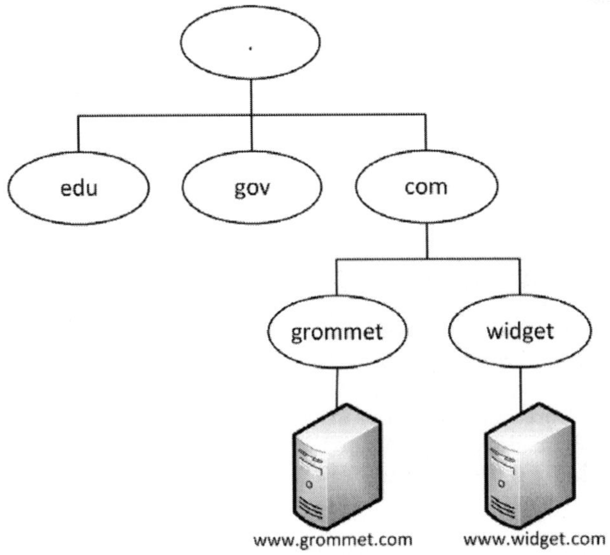

DNS hierarchy

No name server has complete information about all domains. Records within the DNS tell them where the missing information is found.

FQDNs reflect the hierarchy, from most specific (the host) to least specific (the top level domain followed by the root). For example: **www.widget.com.**

Name Resolution using DNS

The signal for the name resolution process to commence occurs when a user presents a FQDN (often as a URL) to an application program (such as a web browser). The DNS client (referred to as a **resolver**) sends a query to the local DNS server address (configured in TCP/IP) and requests that the name server translate the FQDN into an IP address. The resolution process then takes place as follows:

1) The client (resolver) in **grommet.co.uk** queries its local name server for the IP address of the host **www.widget.com**.

2) The name server checks its own zone database for the record.

3) It is not authoritative for the domain, so the name server queries a root server for the required IP address.

4) The root server checks its zone, finds that it is not authoritative for the requested record, and passes the name server in **grommet.co.uk** the IP address of a name server in the **.com** domain.

5) The originating name server queries the designated name server in **.com**, which doesn't have the required information.

6) However, it does have the IP addresses of name servers in the **widget.com** domain. It passes these to the originating name server.

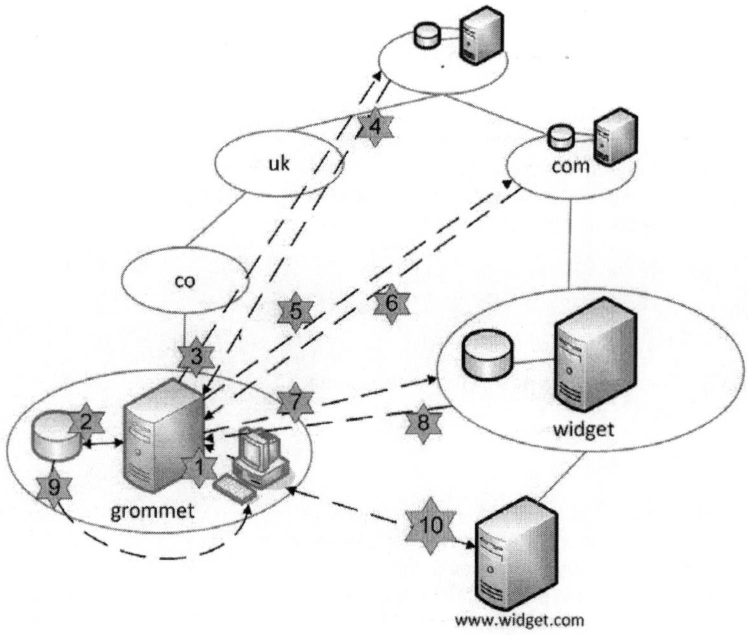

Resolving a name

7) The **grommet.co.uk** name server queries the name server in **widget.com**.

8) Because the name server is authoritative, it passes the required record back to the originating server.

9) The server caches the result and passes the requested IP address to the client.

10) The client establishes a session with the **www.widget.com** host.

Configuring DNS Servers

The **Domain Name System (DNS)** provides name resolution services (mapping a host name or FQDN to an IP address). DNS is essential to the function of the Internet. Windows Active Directory networks also require a DNS service to be running and correctly configured.

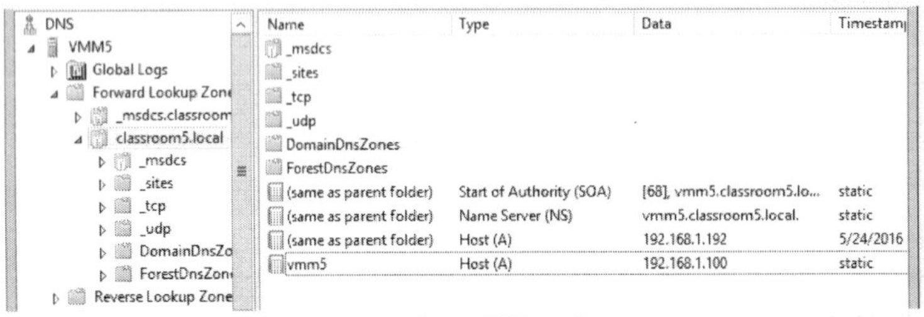

Windows Server DNS service

DNS Service Port

A **DNS server** is usually configured to listen for queries on **UDP port 53**. Some DNS servers are also configured to allow connections over **TCP port 53**, as this allows larger record transfers (over 512 bytes). Larger transfers might be required if IPv6 is deployed on the network or if the DNS servers are using a security protocol (DNSSEC).

Zones

Name servers maintain the DNS namespace in **zones**. A name server can maintain primary and secondary zones:

- **Primary** means that the zone can be edited.
- **Secondary** means a read-only copy of the zone. This is maintained through a process of replication known as a **zone transfer** from the zone master (usually a primary zone). A secondary zone would typically be provided on two or more separate servers to provide fault tolerance and load balancing.

Servers that don't *maintain* a zone (primary or secondary) are referred to as **cache-only** servers. They often rely on forwarding to resolve queries for client resolvers.

Iterative and Recursive Queries

Name servers can be configured to provide **forwarding**. Most queries *between* name servers are **iterative**; a name server responds to a query with whatever information it has. In the example above, at steps 4 and 5, the root server and .com name server simply pass the querying server the address of an authoritative name server. They do not take on the task of resolving the original query for www.widget.com.

A **recursive** query means that if the queried server is not authoritative, it *does* take on the task of referring to other name servers. This is typically used by a DNS server on a private network to contact the ISP's DNS server(s) to resolve Internet domain requests. This is the type of querying performed by the grommet.co.uk name server in the previous example.

Resource Records

A zone will contain **resource records**, which allow computers and services to be resolved into IP addresses. There are many different resource records, but the main ones are:

Record	Name	Description
SOA	**Start Of Authority**	Identifies the primary name server that is authoritative for the zone plus contact information and a serial number (for version control).
A	**Address**	A host name mapped to an IPv4 address.
AAAA	**Address**	A host name mapped to an IPv6 address. IPv6 is now enabled on the Internet root DNS servers.
NS	**Name Server**	Identifies an authoritative name server for the zone. Two or more records may be supplied for redundancy.
PTR	**Pointer**	An IP address mapped to a host name. This is used for reverse lookups, which are a useful security feature. Reverse name resolution uses a special domain called **in-addr.arpa**. The name server would hold a zone mapped to the first three octets of the IP address in reverse order; the final octet is a PTR record in this subdomain. For example, the reverse lookup FQDN for gtslearning.com is 15.202.72.77.in-addr.arpa, resolving to the IP address 77.72.202.15. IPv6 uses the **ip6.arpa** domain; each of the 32 hex characters in the IPv6 address is expressed in reverse order as a subdomain. For example, 2001:0db8:0000:0000:0bcd:abcd:ef12:1234 becomes 4.3.2.1.2.1.f.e.d.c.b.a.d.c.b.0.0.0.0.0.0.0.0.0.8.b.d.0.1.0.0.2.ip6.arpa
CNAME	**Canonical Name**	Defines an alias for a particular host. For example, the true name of a web server could be masked as the alias **www**.
MX	**Mail eXchanger**	Identifies a mail server for the domain. Multiple servers are often provided for redundancy. Each server is given a preference value. The lowest numbered server is preferred.
SRV	**Service**	Identifies the server hosting a particular service, such as VoIP or media server or a Windows Server Domain Controller. As with MX, records can be configured with a priority value.

Commented [MNS3]: Please check this.

Secure Configurations

As well as making sure that resource records for the managed domain(s) are accurate, administrators should ensure that DNS services are **fault tolerant** and **secure** (to prevent DNS spoofing, where an attacker is able to supply false name resolutions to clients).

Dynamic DNS

In modern networks, DNS is used not only to resolve the IP addresses of hosts on the Internet, but also those on the local intranet. This presents a challenge, as IP addresses on the LAN are typically assigned by DHCP, so the IP address of any given host cannot be guaranteed to remain the same from one day to the next. Dynamic DNS solves this problem by allowing either individual clients or the DHCP server to notify the DNS server of any IP address changes. In Windows this can be triggered manually using the **`ipconfig /registerdns`** command. The DNS server updates its A and PTR records based on the information provided, ensuring that the host name will resolve to the new IP address.

Dynamic DNS is also used by SOHO Internet routers. If the ISP does not provide a static IP address, the user can sign up with a Dynamic DNS (DDNS) service then configure the DDNS host and credentials on the SOHO router. Whenever the router IP is changed by the ISP, it will update the records at the DDNS provider so that the router remains addressable by FQDN on the Internet.

nslookup and nbtstat

If computers are experiencing DNS problems, symptoms will include an inability to connect to a web server by name when using the IP address works fine. Likewise, FTP sessions established by IP address work, but fail by name. Note that you may still be able to establish sessions using the Net Use or Map Network Drive features of Windows, because these features can also utilize NetBIOS.

To verify a name resolution problem, edit the **HOSTS** file and place the correct name or FQDN and IP address record in the file for the test host. The default location under Windows is **%SystemRoot%\system32\drivers\etc\hosts** while under Linux it is usually placed in **/etc/hosts**. When you ping, if that is successful, it suggests a name resolution problem.

Also verify that HOSTS does not contain erroneous or malicious name mappings. HOSTS is a target for malware attempting to perform spoofing attacks.

If there is a problem with a name resolution service, first check that the client is configured with the correct name resolution server addresses. Next check that you can ping the name servers.

If the correct name servers are available, they could be misconfigured.

nslookup

You can troubleshoot DNS server records with the **nslookup** command, either interactively or from the command prompt.

nslookup -*Option Host Server*

Host can be either a host name / FQDN or an IP address. ***Server*** is the DNS server to query; the default DNS server is used if this argument is omitted. ***-Option*** specifies an nslookup subcommand. For example, the following command queries Google's public DNS servers (8.8.8.8) for information about gtslearning.com's mail records:

nslookup -type=mx gtslearning.com 8.8.8.8

Commented [AB4]: Unsure if these can be deleted.

If **nslookup** is run without any arguments (or with just the argument - ***Server***), the tool is started in interactive mode. You can perform specific query types and output the result to a text file for analysis. When in interactive mode, keep the following points in mind:

- To interrupt interactive commands at any time, press **Ctrl+C**.
- To view subcommands, type **help** or **?**
- By default, host name (A) records will be returned; use the **set type=xx** command to display different records (for example, **set type=mx** returns mail server records for the domain).
- The command line length must be less than 256 characters.
- An unrecognized command is interpreted as a host name. To treat a built-in command as a host name, precede it with the escape character (\).

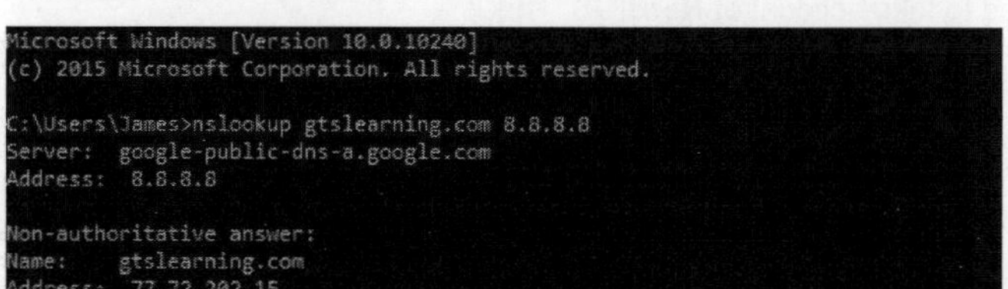

Using nslookup to resolve the gtslearning.com's domain name to an IP address using Google's public DNS servers (8.8.8.8)

*The **dig** utility is often used as a more up-to-date and flexible alternative to **nslookup**. **dig** allows you to query a name server directly and retrieve any of the information known about the domain name. It is helpful in determining if the server is running correctly and if the domain record is properly configured*

Having determined DNS as the cause, there are a number of possible reasons for the problem, which include:

- The client has been configured either with no DNS server address or the wrong DNS server address - reconfigure the DNS server address.
- The client has the incorrect DNS suffix - verify the DNS domain that the client is supposed to be in and check the settings actually configured match.
- The DNS server is offline - check and restart if necessary.
- If some DNS queries work from the client and others don't, then the problem is more complex - check the DNS service configuration itself, using the **`nslookup`** tool.

Bear in mind that in the first two situations, DHCP might be configuring these settings wrongly. Therefore, check the DHCP configuration at the DHCP server as well.

Linux and Windows networks both rely on DNS for name resolution and service discovery. In the absence of DNS servers, network client machines will be unable to logon or connect to services or servers.

Remember that if you have a DNS server problem, many users will be suffering rather than just one. The symptoms will appear quite quickly as the name cache of clients is defined in DNS and is usually just 1 hour.

Reconfiguration of DNS should be planned and implemented carefully, as the service is such a cornerstone of any network that its absence, or malconfiguration, will doubtless cause major problems.

NetBIOS and nbtstat

Windows networks may also need to take account of **NetBIOS**. This is a legacy Application Programming Interface (API) designed to provide programmers with an easy means of accessing and utilizing network resources over a Windows network, which originally ran on **NetBEUI (NetBIOS Extended User Interface)**. NetBIOS is still used for some Windows services and applications in legacy environments. To support these services, NetBIOS can be run over TCP/IP. NetBIOS over TCP/IP uses UDP port 137 for name services, UDP port 138 for datagram (connectionless) services, and TCP port 139 for session services. The **`nbtstat`** utility (NetBIOS over TCP/IP Statistics) is used to query NetBIOS status information. For example:

- **`nbtstat -n`** displays locally registered NetBIOS names.
- **`nbtstat -r`** displays how names are being resolved (broadcast or WINS). A **Windows Internet Name Service (WINS)** server performs the same sort of function for NetBIOS names as DNS does for host and domain names.
- **`nbtstat -c`** displays NetBIOS name-to-IP mappings in the local cache.

- **`nbtstat -R`** purges the NetBIOS name cache and loads #PRE tagged items from an LMHOSTS file. LMHOSTS provides the same sort of function for NetBIOS as HOSTS does for DNS. LMHOSTS is also stored in **%SystemRoot%\system32\drivers\etc**.

- **`nbtstat -s`** lists current sessions with destination computers represented by NetBIOS names. The **`-S`** switch shows sessions by IP address rather than name.

- **`nbtstat -a`** ***`RemoteName`*** lists a remote machine's NetBIOS name table. The **`-A`** switch can take an IP address for the remote host instead of a name.

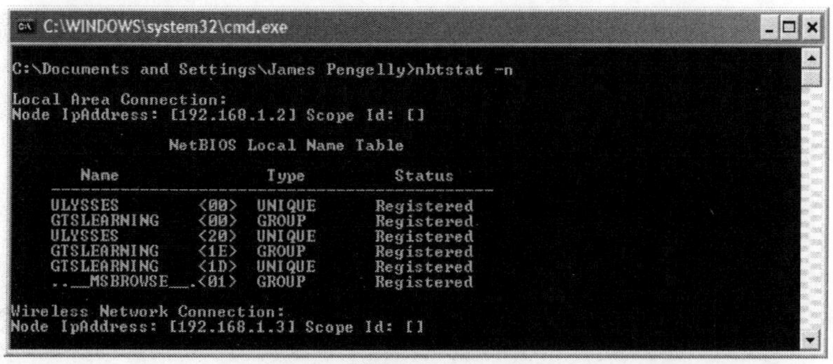

Using nbtstat

NetBIOS uses only 15 character computer names, which must be unique within the network. There is no concept of domain suffixes.

If you are experiencing name resolution problems, then a good test is to create an LMHOSTS file in the appropriate folder with the appropriate entries and then enter the **`nbtstat -R`** command to purge items from the cache, and load any **#PRE** tagged entries from the LMHOSTS straight into cache.

Assuming your clients have a WINS name resolution problem, possible reasons why include:

- The WINS server is offline - check the status of the server, and restart if required.

- There is a WINS database corruption - if you have been backing up WINS, you might want to restore the database. WINS does not backup by default.

- The client computer has either no WINS address configured or the wrong WINS address - try reconfiguring for a different WINS server. Ensure the server you use can be pinged. If the machine is obtaining an IP configuration via DHCP, ensure that DHCP has the option configured to allocate a WINS server address to the client.

- If a name server, such as WINS, is unavailable, in the absence of replica servers, clients will start (quickly) to lose the ability to connect to services. The clients most affected will be Windows NT and older systems (Windows 2000 and higher utilize DNS predominantly).

- Windows systems cache NetBIOS names for 10 minutes and after this period need to contact a WINS server for updated name to IP mappings. In the total absence of WINS, clients will resort to broadcast name registration, release, and discovery. This is limited to the local subnet. Therefore, obvious symptoms of missing WINS servers will be legacy systems can only connect to servers in their own subnet.

Configuring DHCP

The **Dynamic Host Configuration Protocol (DHCP)** provides an automatic method for allocating IP addresses, subnet masks and optional parameters, such as the default gateway, or domain name server (DNS) address. This avoids the configuration errors that can occur if addresses are specified manually. All the major operating systems provide support for DHCP clients and servers. DHCP servers are also embedded in many SOHO router / modems.

DHCP Servers

A DHCP server must be allocated a static IP address and configured with the following information:

- A range of IP addresses and subnet mask to allocate (its scope).
- A lease period plus renewal (T1) and rebinding (T2) timers.
- Other optional information to allocate, such as default gateway and DNS server address(es).

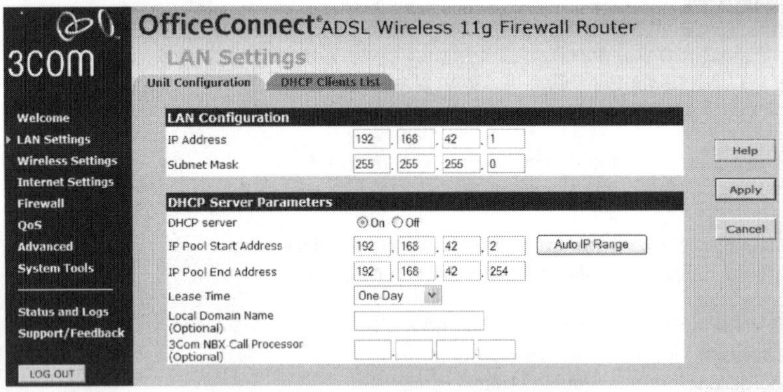

Configuring DHCP on a multifunction Wi-Fi DSL router

Note that not all DHCP servers support the same capabilities. The multifunction device shown above only supports a single IP address range while the Windows DHCP service supports far more options, including creating static and dynamic address reservations.

DHCP Scopes

A **scope** is a range of IP addresses that a DHCP server can allocate to clients. To define a scope, you must provide the start and end IP addresses, along with a subnet mask. The subnet mask given must be such that the entire range of addresses is contained within a single subnet. The DHCP server will then allocate the scope to this subnet.

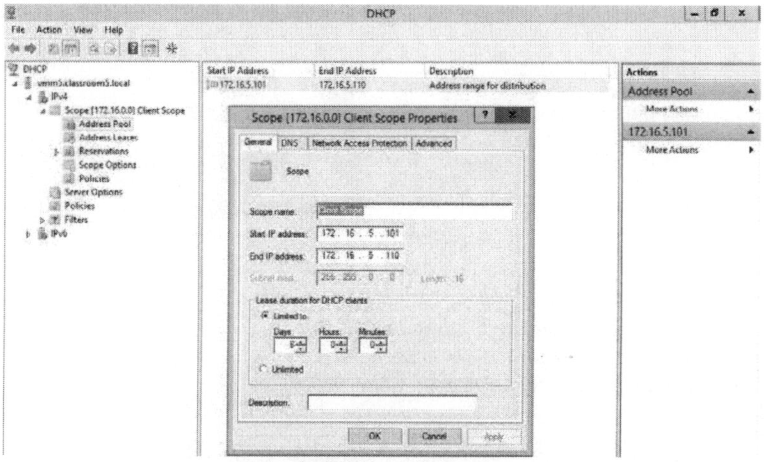

Configuring DHCP on Windows Server

The server maintains a 1-to-1 mapping of scopes to subnets. That is, no scope can cover more than one subnet and no subnet can contain more than one scope. This is because in situations where a server provides IP configuration for multiple subnets, it must choose the scope to service each request based on the subnet from which the request originated.

There is no mechanism for a client to choose between multiple servers. Therefore, if multiple DHCP servers are deployed (for fault tolerance for instance) they must be configured with non-overlapping scopes. DHCP for multiple subnets is usually handled by configuring relay agents to forward requests to a central DHCP server.

DHCP Leases

Along with the scope, you also need to define a **lease period**. A long lease period means the client does not have to renew the lease as frequently but the DHCP server's pool of IP addresses is not replenished. Where IP addresses are in short supply, a short lease period provides a means of utilizing addresses from computers that are not in use.

The client can **renew** the lease when at least half the lease period has elapsed (T1 timer) so that it keeps the same IP addressing information.

If the original DHCP server does not respond to the request to renew the lease, the client attempts to **rebind** the same lease configuration with any available DHCP server. By default, this happens after 87.5% of the lease duration is up (T2 timer). If this fails, the client reinitializes and continues to broadcast to discover a server.

A Windows client can be forced to release a lease using the command `ipconfig` *with the appropriate switches. In Linux, you can usually use the* `dhclient` *command.*

DHCP Options

When the DHCP server provides IP settings to a client, it must supply at a minimum an IP address and subnet mask. Depending on the configuration of the network, it may also provide other IP-related settings, known as DHCP options. Each option is identified by a tag byte or decimal value between 0 and 255 (though neither 0 nor 255 cannot be used as option values). Some widely used options include:

- The default gateway (IP address of the router).
- The IP address(es) of DNS servers.
- The DNS suffix (domain name) to be used by the client.
- Other useful server options, such as time synchronization (NTP), file transfer (TFTP), or VoIP proxy.

A set of **default (global)** options can be configured on a server-wide basis. Default options can be overridden by setting **scope-specific** options. It is also possible to set user-specific options based on a **class ID**. Different options can also be set for **reserved** IP addresses.

DHCP Reservations

While DHCP provides central management of IP configuration, a disadvantage is that the standard **dynamic allocation** method does not guarantee that any given client will retain the same IP address over time. In most cases this is not a problem; for example, as long as a desktop PC has a valid IP address for its subnet, it does not generally matter what that IP address actually is. However, there are some cases where it would be advantageous for certain hosts, such as network printers or wireless access points, to retain their IP addresses.

One solution is to configure these devices statically, using IP addresses outside the DHCP scope. While this solution works, it loses the advantages of central configuration. An alternative approach is to create a **DHCP reservation**. This is a mapping of a MAC address to a specific IP address. When the DHCP server receives a request from the given MAC address, it always provides the same IP address. This is also referred to as **static** or **fixed** address assignment.

Automatic allocation refers to an address that is leased permanently to a client. This is distinct from static allocation as the administrator does not pre-determine which particular IP address will be leased.

DHCP Relay and IP Helper

Normally routers do not forward broadcast traffic. This would mean that to contact a DHCP server, each broadcast domain (such as a switch or VLAN) must be served by its own DHCP server. On a large network, this would mean provisioning and configuring a large number of DHCP servers. To avoid this scenario, a **DHCP relay agent** can be configured to provide forwarding of DHCP traffic between subnets. Routers that can provide this type of forwarding are described as RFC 1542 compliant.

The DHCP relay intercepts any broadcast BOOTP / DHCP frames, applies a unicast address for the appropriate DHCP server, and forwards them on the interface for the subnet containing the server. It also performs the reverse process of directing responses from the server to the appropriate client subnet.

NTP Server

Many applications on networks these days are time dependent and time critical (such as authentication and security mechanisms, scheduling applications, or backup software). The **Network Time Protocol (NTP)** provides a transport over which to synchronize these time dependent applications. NTP works over UDP on port 123.

Top-level NTP servers (stratum 1) obtain the Coordinated Universal Time (UTC) from a highly accurate source, such as an atomic clock. Lower tier servers then obtain the UTC from multiple stratum 1 servers and sample the results to obtain an authoritative time. Most organizations will use one of these stratum 2 servers to obtain the time for use on the local network.

Servers at lower tiers may then perform the same sort of sampling operation, adjust for the delay involved in propagating the signal, and provide the time to clients. Clients themselves usually obtain the time using a modified form of the protocol (Simple NTP).

Review Questions / Module 2 / Unit 4 / Network Services

Answer these questions to test what you have learned in this unit.

1) What configuration parameter must be entered to enable a client to use DNS?
2) How could you determine that a name resolution service is not running?
3) What is the MX record on a DNS server for?
4) What type of DNS server might you install on a network that does not host any domain records?
5) True or false? nslookup can only be used with host names.
6) What information is required to configure a DHCP server?
7) What function is performed by an "NTP" server?

Module 2 / Unit 5

Virtualization Services

Objectives

On completion of this unit, you will be able to:

- Describe different technologies that can be used to deliver virtualization services.
- Understand the range of tasks performed by virtualization services.
- Describe the advantages and disadvantages of virtual platforms.

Virtualization Basics

For most of the history of the microcomputer, a single computer has been able to run a single operating system at any one time. This makes multiple applications available on that computer (whether it be a workstation or server) but the applications must all share a common environment.

Virtualization means that multiple operating systems can be installed and run simultaneously on a single computer. There are many different ways of implementing this and many different reasons for doing it.

A virtual platform requires at least three components:

- Computer(s) - the platform (or "host") that will host the virtual environment. Optionally, there may be multiple computers networked together.
- Hypervisor (or Virtual Machine Monitor [VMM]) - manages the virtual machine environment and facilitates interaction with the host hardware and network.
- Guest operating systems (or Virtual Machines [VM]) - operating systems installed under the virtual environment. The number of operating systems is generally only restricted by hardware capacity.

The presence of other guest OSs can be completely transparent to any single OS. Each OS "thinks" it is working with a normal CPU, memory, hard disk, and network link. The guest OSs can be networked together or they may be able to share data directly through the hypervisor (though this is not commonly done for security reasons).

Hypervisors

Some of the main functions of the hypervisor are as follows:

- Emulation - each guest OS expects exclusive access to resources such as the CPU, system memory, storage devices, and peripherals. The hypervisor emulates these resources and facilitates access to them to avoid conflicts between the guest OSs. The guest OSs must be provided with drivers for the emulated hardware components.

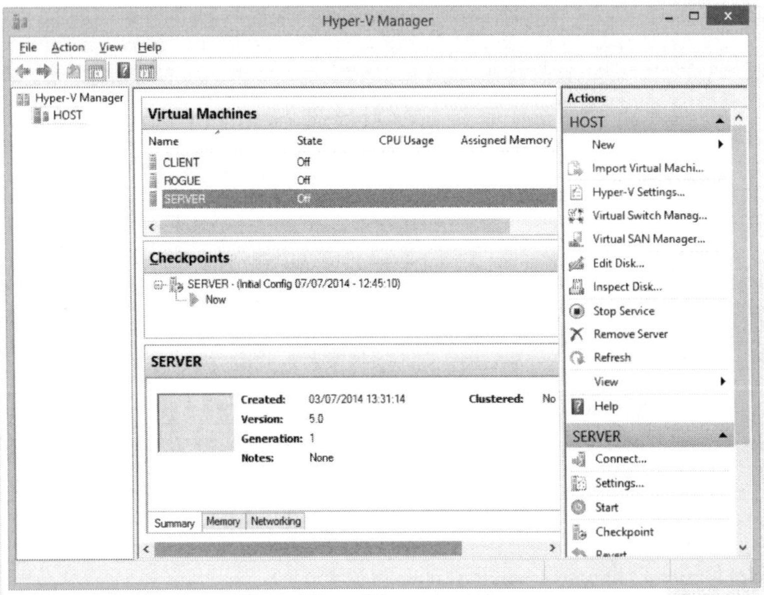

Microsoft Hyper-V hypervisor software

- Guest OS support - the hypervisor may be limited by the different types of guest operating system it can support. Virtualization is often used as a means of installing old OSs (such as MS-DOS and Windows 9x) as well as modern versions of Windows and Linux.

- Assign resources to each guest OS - each guest OS requires sufficient CPU, memory, and storage resources to operate (see below).

- Configure networking - a hypervisor will be able to create a virtual network environment through which all the guest OSs can communicate. It will also be able to create a network shared by the host and by guest OSs on the same host and on other hosts. Enterprise virtual platforms allow the configuration of virtual switches and routers.

- Security - ensures that guest OSs are "contained" and cannot access other guest OSs or the host except through authorized mechanisms. This is important to prevent data "leaking" from one VM to another, to prevent one compromised VM from compromising others, and to prevent malware from spreading between VMs or from a VM to the host.

Management Interface

All virtualization products provide a local management console for configuring the guests installed on one server.

In a complex network, a management server may be deployed, running management software such as VMware vCenter Server or vSphere. This sort of software manages VMs across the whole network, in the same way that systems management software can manage physical servers. Quite often, new versions of systems management software allow for the management of virtual infrastructure too. There can be complexities in mixing products from different vendors however. It is difficult not to become locked into a proprietary solution.

The management server will be able to perform the following sorts of tasks:

- Receive any alerts or alarms generated by the VMs or hypervisors.
- Allow the configuration and starting or stopping of VMs remotely.
- Provide tools for managing the virtual network.
- Deploy new VM images or move VMs between physical servers.

  A VM image can be loaded into the management server as a **virtualization template**. The VM image would contain the OS plus any applications and configurations required to make the server perform in its designated role. When a new instance of the VM is required, the template file is copied to a virtual server and then sysprepped or configured with unique machine settings (host name and network configuration for instance).

- Deploy security patches and updates to hypervisors and VMs.
- Set up disaster recovery plans and failover / redundant services and resources.
- Monitor and optimize performance.

Resource Allocation

An important function of the hypervisor is to allocate resources to each guest OS whilst reserving sufficient resources for the host.

- CPU - most virtualization hosts will have multiple CPU instances, whether physically separate chips, multi-core processors, virtual HyperThreading processors, or a combination of the above. Each guest can be allocated one or more virtual CPUs.
- System memory - similarly, each guest can be allocated a portion of system RAM. You might make a fixed allocation or a dynamic allocation, depending on the type of hypervisor and the type of guest virtualization.

- Storage - each guest can have one or more local "disks", implemented as virtual disk image files. These are set to a maximum amount when the guest is created and can either be configured to immediately claim that amount of space for the virtual disk file or be allowed to grow to that size dynamically. It is usually possible to expand the virtual disk beyond its initial allocation though this will may involve detaching the image from the guest.
- Video - graphics capabilities are often overlooked in designing virtualization products. Many uses of virtualization do not require advanced graphics. However as virtualization starts to penetrate industries such as design and creative media, the need for graphics processing such as 3D or texture effects becomes apparent. Some hypervisors can address this need by fully emulating the functionality of dedicated graphics adapters and sharing them between guests. It is also possible to install multiple adapters to better support more guests.

Host versus Bare Metal Hypervisors

One basic distinction that can be made between virtual platforms is between host and bare metal methods of interacting with the hardware platform.

In a **guest OS (or host-based)** system, the hypervisor application (known as a **Type 2** hypervisor) is itself installed onto a **host operating system**. Examples of host-based hypervisors include VMware Workstation, Oracle Virtual Box, and Parallels Workstation. The hypervisor software must support the host OS.

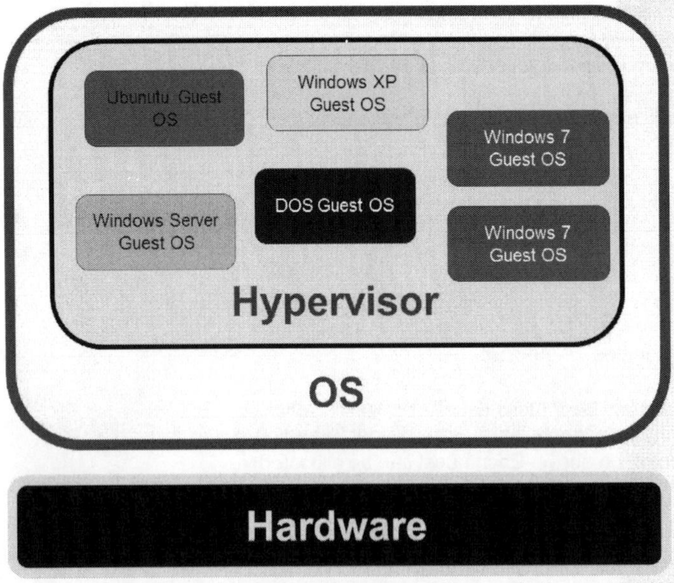

Guest OS virtualization (Type 2 Hypervisor) - the hypervisor is an application running within a native OS and guest OS are installed within the hypervisor

A **bare metal** virtual platform means that the hypervisor (**Type 1** hypervisor) is installed directly onto the computer and manages access to the hardware platform without going through a host OS. A normally installed operating system (working as a "supervisor") uses code that can work at one of four privilege levels or "rings". Ring 0 is accessible exclusively to the kernel; rings 1 and 2 are used by device drivers while most application code works in ring 3. A CPU with hypervisor extensions (AMD-V or Intel VT) creates a ring -1 below ring 0 to allow a type 1 hypervisor to allow a guest OS to access ring 0 natively with no adverse impacts on other guest OSs.

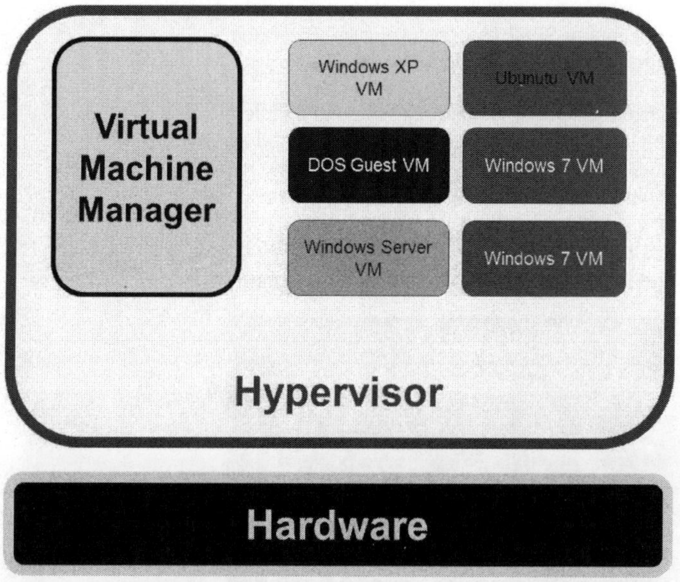

Type 1 "bare metal" hypervisor - the hypervisor is installed directly on the host hardware along with a management application then VMs are installed within the hypervisor

Examples of type 1 hypervisors include VMware ESX Server, Microsoft's Hyper-V, and Citrix's XEN Server. The hardware need only support the base system requirements for the hypervisor plus resources for the type and number of guest OSs that will be installed.

Hyper-V is often described as a hybrid of a type 1 and type 2 hypervisor. The Hyper-V role is installed from within the host OS but as part of that installation, Hyper-V is installed to the "bare metal" while the host OS becomes a sort of more privileged guest OS located in a parent partition.

If the hypervisor is running in a 64-bit environment, 32-bit guest OSs can still be installed (providing the hypervisor supports them). 32-bit hypervisors will not support 64-bit guest OSs however.

Resource Requirements

CPU Compatibility Support

As virtualization solutions have become more popular, CPU vendors have built special instruction sets to facilitate running virtualization. The Intel technology for this is called VT (Virtualization Technology) while AMD call it AMD-V. Most virtualization products also benefit from a processor feature called Second Level Address Translations (SLAT), which improves the performance of guest OSs' use of virtual memory. Intel implement SLAT as a feature called Extended Page Table (EPT) and AMD call it Rapid Virtualization Indexing (RVI).

Some virtualization software *requires* a CPU with virtualization support enabled and performance of the VMs will be impaired if virtualization is not supported in hardware. Some cheaper CPU models ship without the feature. If specifying a server that will be used for virtualization, check the CPU specification carefully to confirm that it supports Intel VT or AMD-V and SLAT if necessary. Also verify that the computer's BIOS or UEFI firmware is compatible and that virtualization extensions have not been disabled via the system setup program:

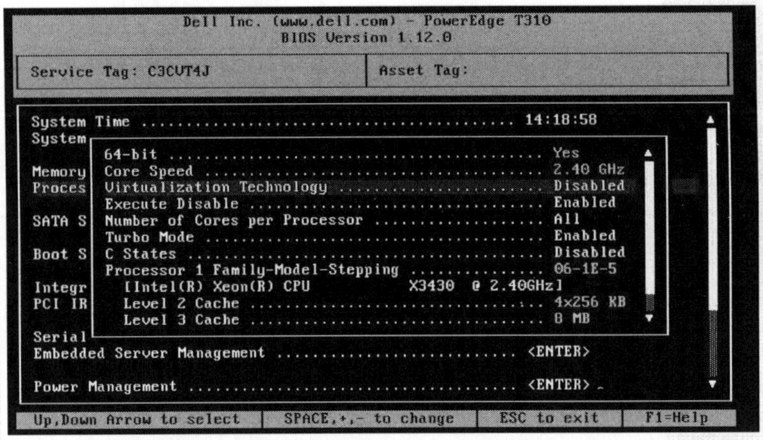

Check that virtualization technology has not been disabled via system setup

Multiple CPU resources - whether through Symmetric Multiprocessing (SMP or multiple physical processors), multi-core, or HyperThreading - will greatly benefit performance, especially if more than one guest OS is run concurrently.

System RAM

As mentioned above, each guest OS requires sufficient system memory over and above what is required by the host. For example, it is recommended that Windows 7 be installed on a computer with at least 1 GB memory. This means that the host must have at least 2 GB and possibly more. As you can see, if you want to run multiple guest operating systems concurrently the resource demands can quickly add up. If the VMs are only used for development and testing then performance might not be critical and you may be able to specify less memory.

Disk Space

Each guest OS also takes up a substantial amount of disk space. The VM's "hard disk" is stored as an image file on the host. Most hypervisors use a "dynamically expanding" image format that only takes up space on the host as files are added to the guest OS. Even so, a typical Windows installation might require 20 GB. More space is required if you want to preserve snapshots. A snapshot is the state of a disk at a particular point-in-time. This is useful if you want to be able to roll back changes you make to the VM during a session.

Most hypervisors also allow guest VMs to use the host's adapters (sound card for instance) and peripherals (input devices, printers, and USB devices for instance).

Virtual Networks

Where multiple virtual machines are running on a single platform, virtualization provides a means for these VMs to communicate with each other and with other computers on the network (both physical and virtual) using standard networking protocols.

The guest operating system running in each virtual machine is presented with an emulation of a standard hardware platform and for the most part is unaware that it is *not* running on an actual physical machine. Among the hardware devices emulated will be one or more network adapters. The number of adapters and their connectivity can typically be configured within the hypervisor.

Within the virtual machine, the virtual adapter will look exactly like an ordinary NIC and will be configurable in exactly the same way. For example, protocols and services can be bound to it and it can be assigned an IP address.

Typically, a hypervisor will implement network connectivity by means of one or more **virtual switches** (or vSwitch using VMware's terminology). These perform exactly the same function as Ethernet switches, except that they are implemented in software rather than hardware. Connectivity between the virtual network adapters in the guest VMs and the virtual switches is configured via the hypervisor. This is analogous to connecting patch cables between real computers and real switches. Multiple virtual machines may be connected to the same virtual switch or to separate switches. The number of virtual switches supported varies from one hypervisor to another.

In this networking model, the virtual machines and the virtual switch can all be contained within a single hardware platform, so no actual network traffic is generated; instead, data is moved from buffers in one virtual machine to another.

It is also possible to configure connectivity between the host computer's physical NIC and the virtual switches. This provides a bridge between the virtual switches within the host platform and the physical switches on the network, allowing frames to pass between physical and virtual machines and between the virtual machines and the host.

For example, in Microsoft's Hyper-V virtualization platform, three types of virtual switch can be created:

- External - binds to the host's NIC to allow the VM to communicate on the physical network.
- Internal - creates a switch that is usable only by VMs on the host and the host itself.
- Private - creates a switch that is usable only by the VMs. They cannot use the switch to communicate with the host.

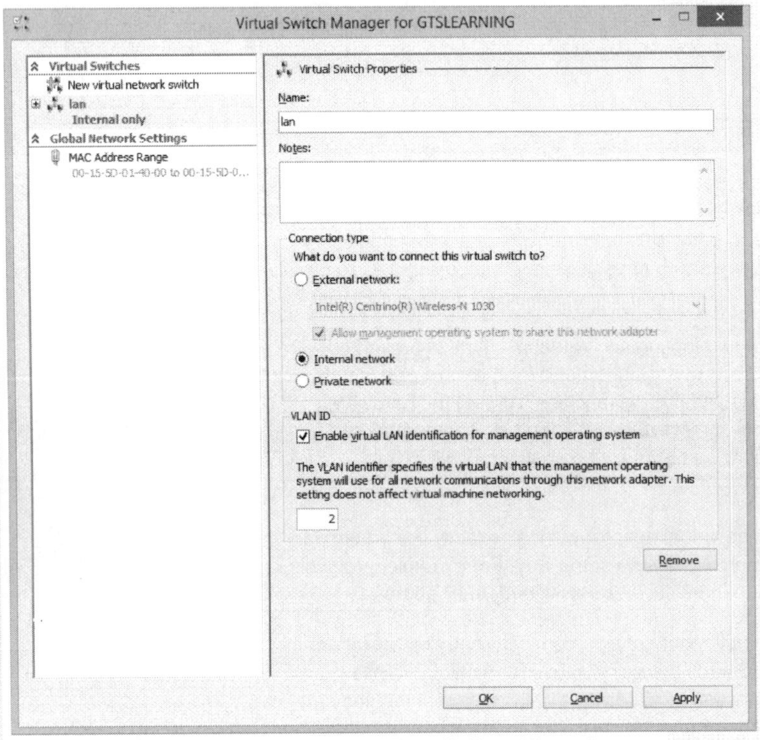

Configuring a virtual switch in Microsoft's Hyper-V hypervisor

When the VMs are allowed to interact with a "real" network, the host must support a high bandwidth, high availability network link. Any failure of the physical link will affect multiple VMs.

Virtual switches can be as simple or complex as the hypervisor software makes them. As you can see from the screenshot above, they can be used to implement VLANs. They can often be configured as a DHCP server or use Network Address Translation (NAT) to provide a valid IP configuration to VMs connecting to the network. In a more advanced network such as VMware's vSphere, you could also have virtual switches that can connect guests running on multiple hosts and configure advanced switching, such as QoS and traffic shaping.

Virtual Routers and Firewalls

Any guest Linux or Windows Server VM can be configured as a router for a VM network. Similarly, either OS (or third-party software installed under the guest VM) could be used to implement a firewall. The VMs have exactly the same functionality as software installed on "real" computers.

Purposes of Virtual Machines

In principle, any type of OS can be virtualized. This includes client OSs and server OSs. Note that some hypervisors have limited support for certain operating systems. For example, Hyper-V only provides support for particular distributions of Linux, such as Ubuntu, though the situation is improving as the Hyper-V Linux Integration Services (LIS) drivers get added to the kernel of more Linux distributions. There are also many different purposes for deploying a virtual platform.

Guest OS Virtual Platforms

Desktop virtual platforms, based on some sort of guest OS hypervisor, are unlikely to provide good performance. They are typically used for testing and development:

- Virtual labs - create a research lab to analyze viruses, worms, and Trojans. As the malware is contained within the guest OS, it cannot infect the researcher's computer or network.
- Support legacy software applications - if the host computers have been upgraded, software may not work well with the new operating system. In this scenario, the old OS can be installed as a VM and the application software accessed using the VM.
- Development environment - test software applications under different OSs and resource constraints.
- Training - lab environments can be set up so that students can practice using a live operating system and software without impacting the production environment. At the end of the lab, changes to the VM can be discarded so the original environment is available again for the next student to use.

Server Consolidation

Bare metal platforms can fill the same functions as guest OS virtual platforms but their main use is better **hardware utilization** through **server consolidation**. A typical hardware server may have resource utilization of about 10%. This implies that you could pack the server computer with another 8 or 9 server software instances and obtain the same performance.

Virtual Desktop Infrastructure (VDI)

To date, use of virtual platforms has mostly focused on test environments and consolidating server software. **Virtual Desktop Infrastructure (VDI)** refers to using a VM as the "main" environment for corporate desktops.

In a typical VDI, desktop computers are replaced by low-spec, low-power **thin client** computers. When the thin client starts, it boots a minimal OS allowing the user to log on to a VM stored on the company server infrastructure. The user makes a connection to the VM using some sort of remote desktop protocol (Microsoft Remote Desktop or Citrix ICA for instance). The thin client has to find the correct image and use an appropriate authentication mechanism. There may be a 1:1 mapping based on machine name or IP address or the process of finding an image may be handled by a connection broker. All application processing and data storage is performed by the server. The thin client computer only has to be powerful enough to display the screen image, play audio, and transfer mouse / key commands and video / audio information over the network.

All data is stored on the server so it is easier to back up. The desktop VMs are easier to support and troubleshoot. They are better "locked" against unsecure user practices because any changes to the VM can easily be overwritten from the template image. With VDI, it is also easier for a company to completely off-load their IT infrastructure to a third-party services company.

The main disadvantage is that in the event of a failure in the server or network infrastructure, users have no local processing ability so downtime events may be more costly in terms of lost productivity.

Application Virtualization

Application virtualization is a more limited type of VDI. Rather than run the whole client desktop as a virtual platform, the client either accesses a particular application **hosted** on a server or **streams** the application from the server to the client for local processing.

Most application virtualization solutions are based on Citrix XenApp (formerly MetaFrame / Presentation Server) though Microsoft has developed a RemoteApp product with its Server 2008 range and VMware have their ThinApp product.

Terminal Services

Terminal Services is the "old", pre-virtual platform way of providing hosted applications. A terminal server can host multiple connections from clients to one or more published applications running on the server. Clients can either be ordinary desktops or thin clients. Terminal services architecture is also referred to as **Server Based Computing (SBC)**.

Storage Virtualization

Another element in a virtual platform is **storage virtualization**. In a virtual storage platform, a software layer is inserted between client operating systems and applications and the physical storage medium (a **Storage Area Network [SAN]**). This abstraction makes it easier to expand or shrink storage capacity allocated to any particular client without having to reconfigure the client. It can also simplify operations such as backup, replication, and migration by consolidating data storage in one physical location.

One of the problems in data storage is data duplication. This refers to the way a single data file may get duplicated in multiple locations, through user file copy actions, attaching the file to email, and making backups. **Data de-duplication** refers to techniques to consolidate multiple copies of the same file in a single location, making more efficient use of the resources available. Data de-duplication is greatly facilitated by storage virtualization, as each user reference to a file can point to the same physical file location (without the user having to track where this might be).

Storage virtualization also assists the implementation of tiered storage hierarchies. The principle here is of where to store archived information. An **offline** storage medium might require physical interaction to access the data (such as putting a tape into a drive). **Nearline** storage refers to technology such as tape loaders or "slow" hard disk media that can operate in low-power states.

This sort of hard disk architecture is referred to as **MAID (Massive Array of Idle Disks)** or **power-managed RAID**. The storage virtualization software can create storage pools for different data access requirements (transactional, online, nearline, or offline) and optimize the capacity required in any one pool with energy efficiency criteria.

Virtualization Best Practices and Risks

Secure and efficient use of virtual platforms is an evolving discipline. Some of the pros and cons and best practices and risks are presented below.

Pros and Cons

As described above, some of the "pros" of server virtualization are better **hardware utilization** and **reduced infrastructure**. Fewer physical servers means less space required to house them, less electricity to run and cool them, and less waste when they are decommissioned. Desktop virtualization allows companies to deploy much lower power **thin clients**, with much lower running costs and environmental impact (though a substantial investment cost).

Virtualization also allows more **centralized administrative control** over IT infrastructure, which should reduce downtime and troubleshooting incidents. It also makes the enforcement of security policies simpler.

Locating the entire IT infrastructure within a single physical "space" can also make **disaster recovery** easier. Providing the VM images have been backed up at an appropriate point and there is no underlying hardware problem, system state can be restored simply by re-applying the backed up image.

One of the advantages of using virtual platforms for research, development, and training is the reduced cost of deploying new applications. Conversely, switching to a virtual desktop infrastructure or complex virtualized server environment may involve substantial investment costs, in terms of hardware, software, and training.

The other cons of deploying virtual machines mostly affect performance and security.

Performance and Host Elasticity

Virtualization only offers more efficient performance if the hardware server platform was *underutilized* in the first place. The use of a hypervisor and running an application within a virtual environment will always compare unfavorably to running the application on physical hardware. VMs tend to be used for a single, simple applications, such as web servers, rather than trying to run multiple web servers, messaging servers, and database applications within each guest OS.

If the shared hardware resources on the host are underspecified, because you have multiple servers or desktops contending for the same resources, performance problems will be multiplied across many more servers and desktops than would be the case in a physical network infrastructure. In project management terms, there is less "slack" or "elasticity" available to cope with unforeseen events.

As well as the resources of the server computer, also consider the resources available to the network. Network links, switches, and routers that were previously managing traffic for one server may suddenly have to cope with ten.

As mentioned above, the whole network infrastructure connecting guest OSs can also be virtualized, but this still requires substantial processing power and creates an even more vulnerable single point of failure if all this infrastructure is running within a single physical server.

Host Security and Availability

Another key security vulnerability in a virtual platform is that if the host is compromised, then *nn* guest servers have also been compromised. Host availability represents a **single point of failure**. For example if the CPU on the host crashes, *nn* guest OSs will suddenly go offline.

Another point is that running the host at a constantly high level of utilization could decrease the **Mean Time Between Failure (MTBF)** of its components. The MTBF is the number of hours the manufacturer expects that a component will run before experiencing some sort of hardware problem. If hardware is subjected to greater than expected loads, it may fail more often than expected.

A successful **Denial of Service (DoS)** attack on a host machine, host OS, or hypervisor will cause far more damage to the server infrastructure than a DoS on a single web server. As an example, the undo disks feature of some hypervisors (allowing the user to revert to the saved image after making changes) can be misused to perform DoS (by causing the undo file to grow to the point where it consumes all the available disk space on the host).

These sorts of vulnerability can be mitigated by duplicating the guest OS on a redundant physical server that can be used as a fail-over. This is costly however and keeping the redundant server up-to-date and ready to be deployed can be complex.

Another solution to the problem of host availability and elasticity is to use a cloud computing environment to provide the virtualization services.

Review Questions / Module 2 / Unit 5 / Virtualization Services

Answer these questions to test what you have learned in this unit.

1) What "type" designation is given to a "bare metal" hypervisor?

2) What would be the main limitation of running a 32-bit hypervisor?

3) What type of resource allocation might a virtualization service need to offer other than CPU, memory, disk, and networking?

4) What feature would reduce the initial disk storage requirements of guest operating systems?

5) You are reconfiguring a server to host virtual machines but the hypervisor setup software reports that the CPU is not compatible. The vendor documentation indicates that the CPU model should support AMD-V. What should you do?

6) What term is used to describe a computing architecture where thin clients are used to access images of client operating systems stored on a server?

7) What is server consolidation?

Module 2 / Summary
Server Networking

You learned how to configure network connectivity and settings for servers and how to configure routers and firewalls. You also learned about servers that provide basic network services, such as DNS and DHCP, and about virtualization services.

Module 2 / Unit 1 / Ethernet

- You should know the characteristics of copper and fiber cable and connector types and their support for Ethernet standards.
- Make sure you know the tools and procedures used to install network cable.
- Server-class network adapters can be configured with aggregated links, using adapter teaming or port bonding.
- Network troubleshooting involves similar principles to server troubleshooting. Be aware of the OSI model layers and how to take a top-to-bottom or bottom-to-top approach.

Module 2 / Unit 2 / Internet Protocol

- You should be able to configure an adapter with an appropriate IPv4 address, subnet mask, default gateway, and client DNS / WINS settings.
- Make sure you can identify the IP address ranges associated with a subnet mask or network prefix and know the private address ranges.
- You can use ipconfig / ifconfig to report the IP configuration of an adapter and use the ping tool to perform a basic connectivity test.
- You should know the format of an IPv6 address and network prefix and distinguish between global and link-local addressing schemes.

Module 2 / Unit 3 / Routers and Firewalls

- You should understand the basic concepts of routing and how to configure a NAT service.
- Use the route command to investigate the local routing table and the tracert / traceroute utility to identify routing issues in an internetwork.
- Understand the different uses of TCP and UDP and make sure you can identify the well known ports listed by the CompTIA exam blueprint.
- You can use netstat to investigate open ports on a host.
- Subnets and firewalls can be used to create different security zones, such as a DMZ. Make sure you understand the usage of terms such as intranet and extranet.

- You should be able to describe different types of firewall and the basics of configuring network and host firewalls.
- Understand the use of VLANs to isolate broadcast domains and understand the effect of VLANs when configuring services such as DHCP and DNS.

Module 2 / Unit 4 / Network Services

- DNS is a critical network service and you should understand the structure of FQDNs, the process of name resolution, and the types of record that can be configured on a DNS server.
- You can use nslookup and the HOSTS file to troubleshoot DNS configuration. Be aware that legacy Windows networks might use the WINS service and LMHOSTS file for name resolution and that the netstat tool can be used to troubleshoot these services.
- The DHCP service can be used to automate the provision of IP address information to clients. Note that DHCP is not usually used to configure critical network servers or appliances.
- Many network services depend on hosts being synchronized to the same date and time and the NTP service can be used to obtain this information.

Module 2 / Unit 5 / Virtualization Services

- Understand the different technologies that can be used to implement virtual platforms and be aware of the distinction between Type I and Type II hypervisors.
- Understand the options for networking guest machines and for configuring networking between the guest and host / physical network.
- Understand the uses of virtualized applications and best practice and security issues.

Module 3 / Server Applications

The following table lists the CompTIA Server+ domain objectives and content examples covered in the units in this module:

Refer To	Domain Objectives/Examples
Unit 3.1 / Configuring Server Roles	**2.1 Install and configure server operating systems** *Enable services • Install features / roles / applications*
	2.2 Compare and contrast server roles and requirements for each *Web server • Application server • Database server • Messaging server • Mail server*
	7.4 Given a scenario, effectively diagnose network problems, selecting the appropriate tools and methods *Common problems (User unable to logon, Email failure, Resource unavailable)*
Unit 3.2 / Storage Services	**3.1 Given a scenario, install and deploy primary storage devices based on given specifications and interfaces** *Interfaces (Fibre Channel)*
	3.3 Summarize hardware and features of various storage technologies *DAS • NAS (iSCSI, FCoE) • SAN (Fibre Channel, LUN & LUN masking, HBAs and fabric switches) • JBOD • Tape (Drive, Libraries) • Optical drive • Flash, Compact Flash and USB drive*
	3.4 Given a scenario, calculate appropriate storage capacity and plan for future growth *Base10 vs. Base2 disk size calculation (1000 vs. 1024) • Disk quotas • Compression • Capacity planning considerations (Operating system growth [Patches, Service packs, Log files], Temporary directories, Databases, Application servers, File servers, Archival)*
Unit 3.3 / Volume Management	**7.3 Given a scenario, effectively troubleshoot software problems, selecting the appropriate tools and methods** *Common problems (OS boot failure, Cannot mount drive) • Cause of common problems (Corrupted files, Lack of hard drive space, Fragmentation) • Software tools (Defragmentation tools, Disk property tools [Usage, Free space])*
	7.5 Given a scenario, effectively troubleshoot storage problems, selecting the appropriate tools and methods *Common problems (Slow file access, OS not found, Data not available, Error lights, Unable to mount the device, Drive not available, Cannot access logical drive, Data corruption, Slow I/O performance, Cache failure, Multiple drive failure) • Causes of common problems (Media failure, Drive failure, Controller failure, HBA failure, Loose connectors, Cable problems, Mis-configuration, Improper termination, Corrupt boot sector, Corrupt file system table, Array rebuild, Improper disk partition, Bad sectors, Cache battery failure, Cache turned off, Insufficient space, Improper RAID configuration, Mis-matched drives, Backplane failure) • Storage tools (Partitioning tools, Disk management, RAID array management, Array management, System logs, Monitoring tools)*

Refer To	Domain Objectives/Examples
Unit 3.4 / Directory Services	**2.1 Install and configure server operating systems** *Join domain / directory*
	2.2 Compare and contrast server roles and requirements for each *Directory server*
	4.3 Explain basic network security systems and protocols *Authentication protocols (LDAP)*
	4.4 Implement logical access control methods based on company policy *Access control lists (Users, Groups, Roles, Resources [Administrative rights, Distribution lists]) • Permissions (Superuser)*
	7.3 Given a scenario, effectively troubleshoot software problems, selecting the appropriate tools and methods *Cause of common problems (User Account Control [UAC / sudo])*
Unit 3.5 / File and Print Services	**2.2 Compare and contrast server roles and requirements for each** *File server • Print server*
	4.4 Implement logical access control methods based on company policy *Access control lists (Resources [File system, Network ACLs, Peripheral devices]) • Permissions (Read, Write / Modify, Execute, Delete, Full control, File vs. share)*
	7.3 Given a scenario, effectively troubleshoot software problems, selecting the appropriate tools and methods *Common problems (User cannot access resources, Users cannot print) • Cause of common problems (Print server drivers / services, Print spooler) • Software tools (Disk property tools [Volume or drive mapping])*
	7.4 Given a scenario, effectively diagnose network problems, selecting the appropriate tools and methods *Networking tools (net use / mount)*
	7.5 Given a scenario, effectively troubleshoot storage problems, selecting the appropriate tools and methods *Storage tools (net use / mount command)*
Unit 3.6 / Troubleshooting Software	**2.1 Install and configure server operating systems** *Performance baseline (Server optimization)*
	2.4 Given a scenario, perform proper server maintenance techniques *Performance monitoring (CPU utilization, Memory utilization, Network utilization, Disk utilization [Disk IOPS, Storage capacity], Comparison against performance baseline, Processes and services monitoring, Log monitoring)*
	7.3 Given a scenario, effectively troubleshoot software problems, selecting the appropriate tools and methods *Common problems (Memory leak, BSOD / stop, Driver issues, Runaway process, Cannot write to system log, Slow OS performance, Patch update failure, Service failure, Hangs no shut down) • Cause of common problems (Lack of system resources, Virtual memory [misconfigured, corrupt]) • Software tools (System logs, Monitoring tools [Resource Monitor, Performance Monitor])*

Module 3 / Unit 1

Configuring Server Roles

Objectives

On completion of this unit, you will be able to:

- Use Windows and Linux tools to configure roles and install applications and services.
- Configure web and FTP servers.
- Understand how application and database servers are structured.
- Understand the services provided by messaging servers.

Installing Roles and Applications

In order to configure a server in a particular role, you are likely to need to install (or at least enable) a server application. The server application may be installed from its own setup files or it may be a component of the NOS.

Installing Windows Components

Windows Server 2008 provides a **Configure My Server** wizard to assist with the configuration of server roles supported directly by the NOS (DHCP, DNS, Active Directory, web / email, and so on). You can install Windows components manually using the **Add or Remove Windows Components** tool (from **Control Panel > Add or Remove Programs / Programs and Features**).

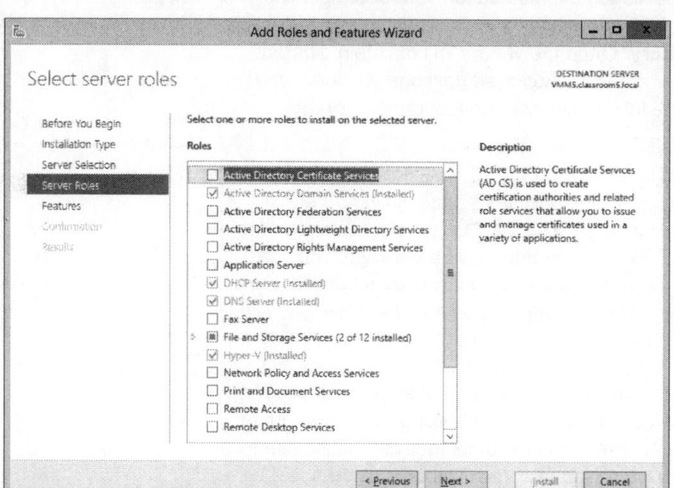

Add Roles and Features Wizard - configuring roles

In Windows Server 2012, roles and features are configured via the expanded **Roles and Features Wizard**, accessed via **Server Manager**. When you select a role, the wizard takes you through the process of installing any additional files that are required and setting the initial configuration options.

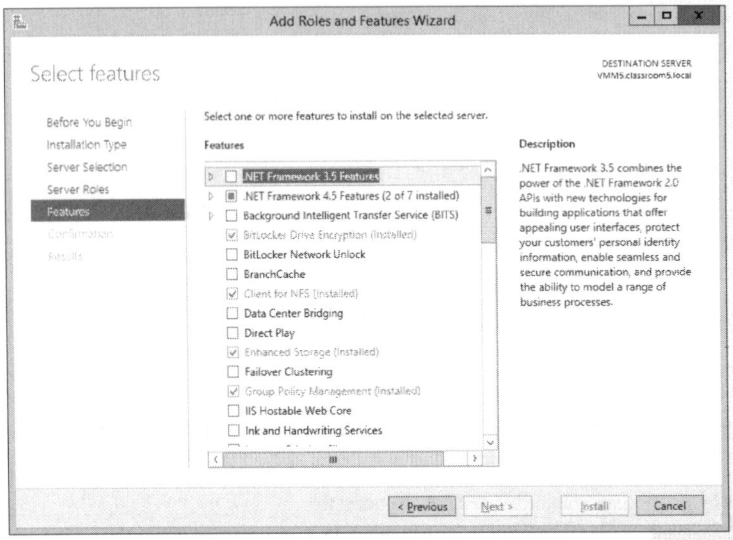

Add Roles and Features Wizard - configuring features

Most Windows components are configured via a management console snap-in added to the **Administrative Tools** folder or **Control Panel**. In Server 2012, these consoles can be accessed from the **Tools** menu in Server Manager.

Installing Linux Components

Linux is very much based on distributions. A distribution contains the Linux kernel plus any other software packages the distribution vendor or sponsor considers appropriate. Copies of these packages (including any updates) will be posted to a **software repository**. Often the vendor will maintain different repositories (for example, one for officially supported package versions, one for beta / untested versions, and one for "at own risk" unsupported packages).

The integrity of a package is usually tested by making an MD5 hash of the compiled package. The MD5 value is published on the package vendor's site. When you download a package, you can run **`md5sum`** *on the package file and compare the output with the published value. If they do not match, you should not proceed with the installation.*

Linux software is made available both as source code and as pre-compiled applications. A source code package needs to be run through the appropriate compiler with the preferred options. Pre-compiled packages can be installed using various tools, such as **rpm** (Red Hat), **apt-get** (Debian), or **yum** (Fedora). Many distributions also provide GUI package manager front-ends to these command-line tools.

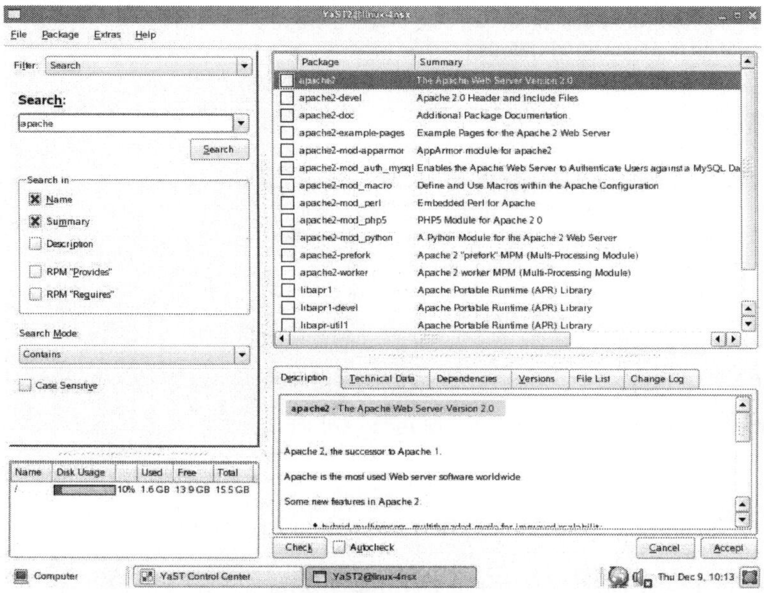

YaST package manager in SUSE

The package manager needs to be configured with the web address of the software repository (or repositories) that you want to use. It can then be used to install, uninstall, or update the software.

Most Linux software is configured by editing one or more text files with the required parameters, though again, some software may provide a GUI front-end.

Database and Application Servers

Typical server applications include email, groupware (calendaring and scheduling), databases, accounting, and web development. As applications can be demanding to run, they are often located on dedicated application servers.

Databases are demanding applications that require substantial processing and storage capacity. Major database server products include Oracle, Microsoft SQL Server, IBM's DB2 and Informix, and Sybase. Many databases are operated using Structured Query Language (SQL, pronounced "sequel"). The freeware MySQL database is a popular choice to provide database functionality on websites.

In **client/server** software, a server application runs constantly (barring periods in which it is shut down for configuration or security) waiting for **requests** from clients. The client application can be opened or closed as needed without affecting the server, allowing the user to control resources running on the local workstation. When the server application gets a request, it performs the task requested and returns the data or confirmation that the client was expecting.

Client/server applications can be **stateful**, which means that the server stores information about the client and its requests, or **stateless**.

Application Server Models

In client/server software, the amount of processing can be balanced between the server and the client, depending on the capabilities of each. A **thin** client is one that performs very little processing, leaving all the work to the server. A **fat** client may be used to reduce the load on the server, but requires higher specification client machines. A server computer can (and commonly does) run more than one server application. Part of the server planning process is deciding whether applications require dedicated hardware to run on; which applications should run on which servers?

Various application server models have been proposed and utilized to extract the best performance from the underlying server hardware.

Dedicated Application Server

This term refers to server hardware that runs one application only. The advantage of this model is that the application gets reliable performance from the server hardware. The disadvantages are higher costs in terms of providing dedicated equipment and, if the application is not used constantly, there will be periods where the server hardware is inactive, wasting capacity.

Distributed Application

The application is provided by more than one physical server on the network. Data can be distributed around these servers. This distribution is not apparent to the client application, which thinks it is accessing a single server. This model provides robustness. Services are not generally interrupted because of the failure of individual services. It can also improve performance by distributing load between different machines.

Related to distributed applications is the concept of tiered applications. A client/server application is 2-tiered (interface processed by the client and back-end processing by the server). In a multi-tiered model, a middle tier (or tiers) operates between the client interface (front-end) and database back-end. The middle tier provides features such as transaction processing and queuing. This architecture can improve performance and simplify application development.

There are two main frameworks for multi-tier enterprise application development:

- **J2EE (Java 2 Platform Enterprise Edition)** - developed by Sun Microsystems. Clients run a **Java Virtual Machine (VM)** to support applications. The platform is freely available and supports many different OSs.
- **.NET** - developed by Microsoft as a platform for integrated web and Windows development. Clients need to run the **.NET Framework** to support applications (currently only available on Windows).

Peer-to-Peer Application (P2P)

A precise definition of P2P would be somewhat controversial, as the term means different things to different people. Roughly speaking, as with a peer-to-peer network, each instance of the application can act as both client and server to other instances. The applications are said to be **decentralized**, which means that no one instance is in overall control or can demand more resources than another instance. Another key feature of P2P applications is that they are capable of utilizing spare capacity from all nodes to improve performance.

Web Servers

A server connected to the Internet can function as a web application server, providing services such as marketing and e-commerce. As these are customer-driven sites, availability, performance, and reliability are critical.

A web server responds to browser requests by processing the request and returning the results. By default, it listens to TCP port 80, although an alternate port may be configured for additional security. Servers may hold static and dynamic pages of HTML and may also sustain active processes.

Web services also have a role to play on internal networks (intranets), with internal web servers hosting databases and web portals, for business intelligence and document sharing.

Establishing a Website

Most organizations have an online presence, represented by a website. In order to run a website, it must be hosted on an HTTP server connected to the Internet. Typically, an organization will lease a server or space on a server from an ISP (web hosting). Larger organizations or SMEs with good technical skills and a high bandwidth Internet connection may host websites themselves. When using an ISP, the degree to which the server may be customized, responsibility for security, and amount of technical support will all vary according to the contract terms. Greater flexibility may mean greater responsibility for securing the server and monitoring availability and performance.

As with any third-party service, analyze the Service Level Agreement (SLA) to confirm what the ISP is contracted to do and satisfy yourself that these obligations are being met (for example, demand reports of backup operations, security patch management, effective account management, and so on).

Running your own website gives complete control over the configuration of the server but also complete responsibility for performance and security. The main web server platforms are:

- **Apache** - open source software and powerful, robust features combine to make this server the most popular. It is available for UNIX, Linux, Mac OS X, and Windows but is most widely deployed on Linux. Apache accounts for about 50% of the most active websites.
- **Microsoft Internet Information Server (IIS)** - bundled with Windows Servers (and client versions of Windows). IIS accounts for about 12% of busy sites.
- **nginx** - an open source web server and load balancer specially designed to cope with very high traffic. nginx ("Engine X") accounts for about 17% of the active sites.

HTTP Secure (HTTPS)

HTTPS allows for a secure dialog between the client and server. This security is provided using a server-side certificate. Traffic between the client and server is encrypted and sent over TCP port 443 rather than the open and unencrypted port 80. A web browser will open a secure session to a server providing this service using a URI starting with HTTPS://.

A certificate is a digital proof of identity. When a client connects to a server to perform an online transaction involving, for example, credit card numbers, the user would want to be sure that the server they are connected to is who it claims to be. The certificate, issued by a digital Certificate Authority, provides this assurance.

Web Server Configuration

Web servers are one of the most popular targets for attackers and so must be very carefully configured.

An Internet-facing web server should be placed in a DMZ and run only web services (running other services exposes the server to more attacks).

Access Control

Most web servers have to allow access to guests (that is, unauthenticated users). The guest account must be secured so that it cannot be used to modify any data on the server (that it has read-only or browse permissions only). The guest account on IIS is called IUSER; an account named httpd or apache is typically configured for guest access to Apache. The guest account should have no permissions outside the directory set up for browsing. Similarly, passwords to administrative accounts must be strong, securely stored, and changed periodically. Do not re-use passwords used for private network administrative accounts on a publicly accessible machine.

Where confidential information needs to be exchanged, the web server should be configured to use a secure method, such as HTTPS. Where a web server is leased, a secure means of uploading files and configuration changes needs to be used (SSH for example). Remember that ordinary FTP connections are **not** secure (critically, authentication information is transmitted in plaintext).

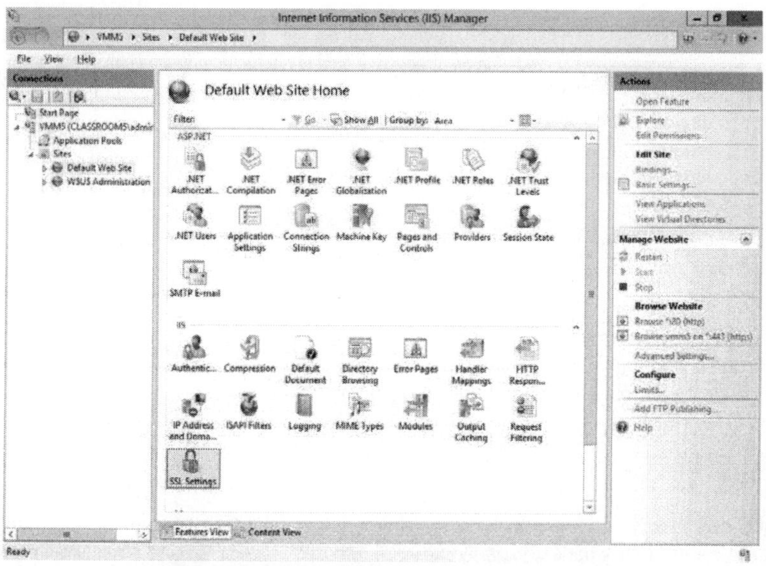

IIS Manager web server management tool for Server 2012

Root Directory

The **root directory** specifies the starting point for the web server. This is the directory that has been configured to hold all the content and sub-directories for access through the WWW service. For example, **c:\inetpub\wwwroot** is the default root directory on an IIS server, and **/var/www/** is the default on Apache.

You should not attempt to allow access to other parts of the server's file system to web users - place everything served by the web server within the server root.

Forms and Interactivity

HTTP also features a forms mechanism (POST) whereby a user can submit data from the client to the server. HTTP is a **stateless protocol**; this means that the server preserves no information about the client during a session. However, the basic functionality of HTTP servers is also often extended by support for scripting (JavaScript) to control functions of the web client and programmable features on the server. Technologies such as Java, ASP, and integration with databases (PHP and XML) create fully-featured **web applications**.

Most web servers provide a **CGI-bin** folder which is configured to hold scripts and binary applications. This folder is configured with Execute Only permissions. Read permissions are disabled to prevent access to the source code.

Index Files

Often a URL points to a directory rather than a specific file; for example: www.isp.net. When a server receives this type of request, it displays a specific index file (typically called **index.HTML**) instead of the directory contents. Some web servers use alternative names for this file such as **default.htm**.

Directory Browsing

Enabling directory browsing displays a list of all files and folders in the published directory, in the form of hyperlinks. Files can be displayed and folders opened by clicking on the appropriate hyperlink. This has the advantage that pages are readily available and quick to set up. There are also disadvantages; users must understand filenames, directory browsing is unattractive in appearance, and allowing file names and folders to be visible raises security issues.

Sample Files

Web servers are typically installed with sample pages (and even scripts) plus help documentation. These samples often contain vulnerabilities and should be removed from a production server.

Error Pages

HTTP also has a system of codes that provide feedback on the status of the request made by the client. There are many codes, broadly grouped into the following ranges:

- 2xx - request successful.
- 3xx - redirect to another URI.
- 4xx - client error (notably 403 - Forbidden and 404 - Not Found).
- 5xx - server error (the request was properly formatted but the server experienced an error in trying to process it, usually because it has crashed, is overloaded, or does not support the functionality requested).

If a user attempts to access a page that does not exist, for which he or she does not have permission, or a directory that is not viewable from the web, a default error page is displayed with the error code. These pages can be customized to present something more in keeping with the rest of the site.

Throttling

Throttling is used to limit the number of simultaneous connections that are allowed. It can be performed on a site-by-site basis (especially if one site generates all the traffic).

Hardening

There are various software utilities available to scan a web server to detect unpatched software exploits or configuration errors. You should use these periodically.

Logging

Servers provide facilities to log the web server activity. **Logging** provides the web administrator with valuable information regarding the use of the website.

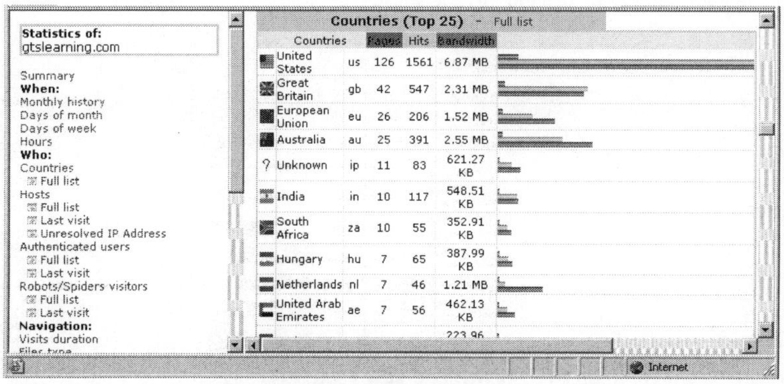

Viewing logged information through awstats Linux utility

Web Server Performance Issues

The performance of a web server may be affected by the following:

- The **bandwidth** available on the connection to the Internet. This is typically the most important issue.
- **Server hardware** - processor(s), memory, and performance of the disk sub-system. Multiple servers are often used as a method of improving performance.
- **Server caching** can improve the performance of the web server by holding recently used data in memory. Server response is significantly faster when the page is cached in memory, rather than obtaining the page from a slower storage device.
- **Reverse-proxying** - this process can be used to reduce the load on the web server(s). The proxy listens to requests from the Internet and then forwards them to the appropriate web server. These requests may be cached at the proxy server to reduce load.

File Transfer Services (FTP)

The **File Transfer Protocol (FTP)** was one of the earliest protocols used on TCP/IP networks and the Internet. It is a connection-oriented protocol utilizing TCP that is especially useful for transferring files between hosts (especially when the hosts run different operating systems). While HTTP-based web services and web applications can now offer simpler file transfer services to *end users*, FTP is still often used to perform *administrative* upload of files to and from servers and appliances. For these uses, it is important to secure the FTP session.

FTP Clients

The FTP client may take a number of forms:

- Most installations of TCP/IP include a command line client interface. The commands PUT and GET are used to upload and download files respectively.
- Dedicated GUI clients allow you to connect to servers, browse directories and upload and download files.
- Internet browsers allow you to connect to an FTP service and download files. You use a **Uniform Resource Locator (URL)** to connect to an FTP server; for example, **ftp://ftp.microsoft.com/**.

Active Versus Passive FTP

A client connects to TCP port 21 on an FTP server and opens a chosen dynamic client port number (N). The TCP port 21 **control port** is used to transfer commands and status information, but not for data transfer. Data transfer can operate in one of two modes: active or passive.

In active mode, the client sends a PORT command specifying its chosen **data connection** port number (typically N+1) and the *server* opens the data connection between the chosen client port and TCP port 20 on the server.

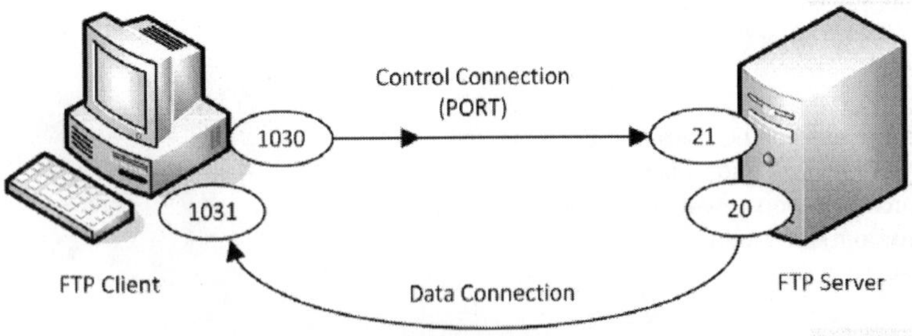

FTP in active mode

In passive mode, the *client* opens a data port (again, typically N+1) and sends the PASV command to the server's control port. The server then opens a random high port number and sends it to the client using the PORT command. The *client* then initiates the connection between the two ports.

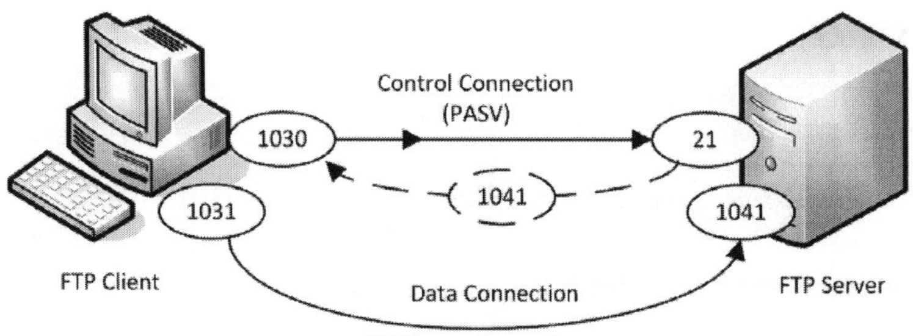

FTP in passive mode

Active FTP poses a configuration problem for some firewalls, as the server is initiating the inbound connection but there is no way of predicting which port number will be utilized. However, not all FTP servers and clients can operate in passive mode. If this is the case, check that firewalls installed between the client and server can support active FTP (stateful inspection firewalls).

Another problem is that the control connection can remain idle when the data connection is in use, meaning that the connection can be "timed out" by the firewall (or other routing device).

*You should check that users do not install unauthorized servers on their PCs (a **rogue server**). For example, a version of IIS that includes HTTP, FTP, and SMTP servers is shipped with client versions of Windows, though it is not installed by default.*

SFTP and FTP/S

FTP is an unsecure protocol. All transmissions are in plain text so someone with access to the network traffic could intercept passwords or change information in the files being downloaded. There are two ways of using FTP securely:

- SFTP - this refers to establishing an SSH (Secure Shell) connection over TCP port 22 then tunneling FTP traffic (control information and data) through the SSH port.
- FTP/S - this refers to using the SSL / TLS protocol to authenticate the hosts and establish a secure connection. With FTP/S there are two main modes of operation. A client can establish an implicit FTP/S connection over port 990. Port 989 is used for the secure data channel, by default. Alternatively, the client can initiate an implicit connection over port 21 in conjunction with sending an AUTH SSL command to start the secure session negotiation. It is possible for a client to request that only the connection channel be secured and to leave the data channel (port 20 or the defined passive port range) unsecure.

Configuring an FTP Server

A FTP service is provided with all web server packages. It represents the standard way to upload files to a web server, though the basic protocol should be protected by a security mechanism such as SSL or SSH or it is vulnerable to packet sniffing. Most FTP server packages allow you to configure a number of parameters. For example:

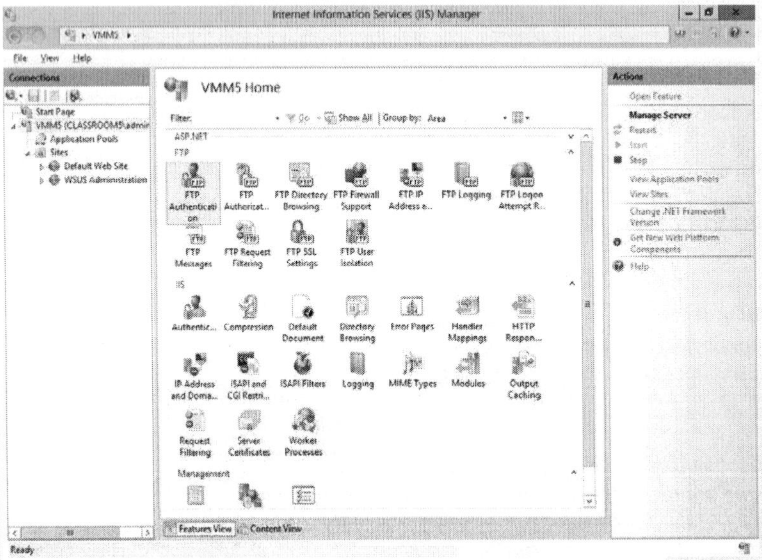

Managing the FTP server component of IIS

Connections

The number of simultaneous connections allowed (**throttling**). FTP servers are generally configured for a lower number of connections than a web server, since the average FTP session is longer and also transfers much more data. This value should be reduced if FTP client requests are placing an excessive load on the server.

Permissions

FTP directories may be configured to support **Read** and/or **Write** access. Read permission allows users to list files and copy them from the server to the client. Write permissions allow users to upload files to the server.

It is recommended practice to provide a dedicated directory for uploading files to ensure that users are not able to inadvertently overwrite files with the same name.

Logging

FTP servers support logging. The level of detail may be configured for security and audit purposes.

Email (SMTP / POP / IMAP)

Electronic mail enables a person to compose a message and send it to another user on their own network (intranet) or anywhere in the world via the Internet.

SMTP Protocol

The **Simple Mail Transfer Protocol (SMTP)** specifies how mail is delivered from one system to another. It is a relatively straightforward protocol that makes the connection from the sender's server to that of the recipient and then transfers the message. The SMTP server of the sender discovers the IP address of the recipient SMTP server using the domain name part of the email address. The SMTP server for the domain is registered on the DNS using a **Mail Exchanger (MX)** record. SMTP servers are configured to listen on TCP port 25.

SMTP is not used for transferring the message from the recipient's SMTP server to its email client because it requires that both source and destination are online to make a connection. The SMTP server retries at regular intervals before timing out and returning a **Non-Delivery Report (NDR)** to the sender.

Post Office Protocol (POP)

SMTP is only useful to deliver mail to hosts that are permanently available. Mail users require the convenience of receiving and reading their mail when they choose. The **Post Office Protocol (POP)** is designed to allow mail to be downloaded to the recipient's email client at his/her convenience.

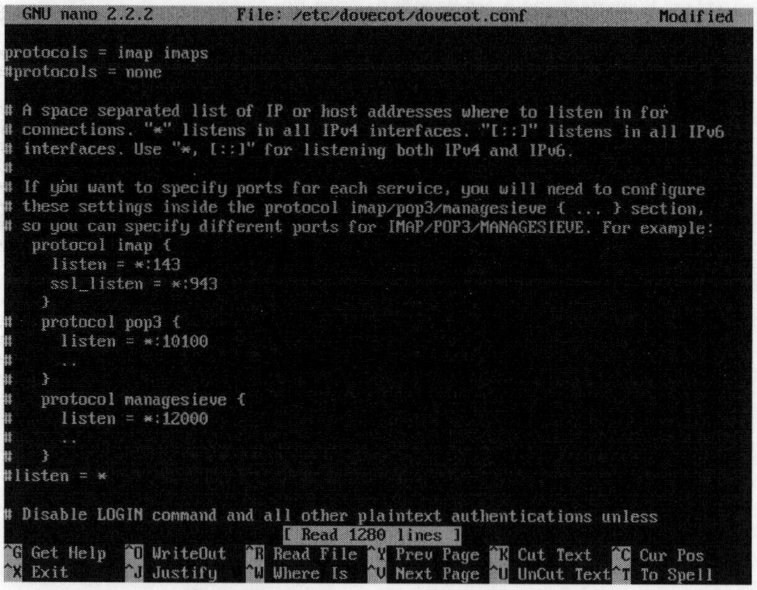
```
  GNU nano 2.2.2          File: /etc/dovecot/dovecot.conf                Modified

protocols = imap imaps
#protocols = none

# A space separated list of IP or host addresses where to listen in for
# connections. "*" listens in all IPv4 interfaces. "[::]" listens in all IPv6
# interfaces. Use "*, [::]" for listening both IPv4 and IPv6.
#
# If you want to specify ports for each service, you will need to configure
# these settings inside the protocol imap/pop3/managesieve { ... } section,
# so you can specify different ports for IMAP/POP3/MANAGESIEVE. For example:
  protocol imap {
    listen = *:143
    ssl_listen = *:943
   }
#   protocol pop3 {
#     listen = *:10100
#     ..
#   }
#   protocol managesieve {
#     listen = *:12000
#     ..
#   }
#listen = *

# Disable LOGIN command and all other plaintext authentications unless
                              [ Read 1280 lines ]
^G Get Help  ^O WriteOut  ^R Read File ^Y Prev Page ^K Cut Text  ^C Cur Pos
^X Exit      ^J Justify   ^W Where Is  ^V Next Page ^U UnCut Text^T To Spell
```

Configuring mailbox access protocols on a server

POP is often referred to as POP3 as the active version of the protocol is version 3.

A POP client application (such as Microsoft Outlook or Mozilla Thunderbird) establishes a TCP connection on TCP port 110 to the POP server. This is generally a different *service* running on the *same machine* as the SMTP server. The user is authenticated (by user name and password) and the contents of his or her mailbox are downloaded for processing on the local PC. Generally speaking, the messages are deleted from the server when they are downloaded, though some clients have the option to leave messages on the server.

Like other TCP application protocols, unless an encryption service is configured, POP transfers all information as cleartext. This means anyone able to monitor the session would be able to obtain the user's credentials. POP can be secured using SSL/TLS. The default TCP port for secure POP is port 995.

Internet Message Access Protocol (IMAP)

While POP is widely used, it does have limitations, some of which are addressed by the **Internet Message Access Protocol (IMAP)**. Clients connect over TCP port 143 (993 for SSL). They authenticate themselves then retrieve messages from the designated folders. SMTP is still needed to support mail delivery. Like POP, IMAP is a mail retrieval protocol only.

There are however a number of differences between POP and IMAP. POP is primarily designed for dial-up access; the client contacts the server to download its messages then disconnects. IMAP supports permanent connections to a server and connecting multiple clients to the same mailbox simultaneously. It also allows a client to manage the mailbox on the server (to organize messages in folders and control when they are deleted for instance) and to create multiple mailboxes.

Messaging Servers

"Messaging" can mean several different technologies:

- Email - hosting mailboxes for an organization's users and facilitating transfer of email messages within the organization and over the Internet.
- Instant Messaging - supporting text messaging and file transfer between users on a local network and / or over the Internet.
- VoIP / PBX - providing voice communications between users and possibly linking to the telephone network.
- Online conferencing - allowing virtual meetings that may incorporate several different communications methods (voice, video, texting, and desktop sharing for instance).

- Fax - enabling users to send and receive fax communications.
- Groupware - in addition to communications, messaging servers often provide calendar and task-sharing functions, enabling users to schedule meetings and appointments and manage project tasks.

Any one messaging server may be provisioned to support one or a mix of these different technologies. Some technologies may require a mix of servers (for example, back-end email servers hosting mailboxes and front-end email servers providing Internet transport). A server supporting all these different communication methods is referred to as a **Unified Communications** server.

Messaging is typically a demanding application in terms of hardware (especially storage) and network resources. It is also demanding in terms of securing the service against attack and abuse (email is a vector for viruses and worms and junk mail [spam]).

Some well-known messaging server applications include Microsoft's Exchange, Communications Server, and Lync Server products, Lotus Notes, and Novell GroupWise.

Troubleshooting Services

When you get to the upper layers of the OSI model (or the "Application" layer of the TCP/IP stack), troubleshooting issues become quite specific to the application server. For example:

- A HTTP server might report that a resource is unavailable because the server is down, because a link is misconfigured, or because the client is not supported.
- An email server might fail to process mail for any number of reasons: bad email address, mailbox quota exceeded, spam filtering, DNS problems, or some sort of software problem with the server application itself.
- A directory services server may not accept logons or resource access requests because the user does not have sufficient permissions or supplies the wrong password or because of some sort of link connectivity, name resolution, or firewall problem between the server and the client.

When troubleshooting services and applications, you should examine the log to see if there are any events related to the problem. One basic test that can be applied to pretty much all applications is to verify that the application port is open or in a listening state (ready to receive connections).

Tools such as protocol analyzers can be deployed to troubleshoot application protocol issues in more detail by capturing and interpreting the packets exchanged between client and server.

Review Questions / Module 3 / Unit 1 / Configuring Server Roles

Answer these questions to test what you have learned in this unit.

1) What security precautions should you take when installing applications on a Linux server?
2) What does it mean if a server is stateless?
3) What is the name of Sun's multi-tier enterprise development platform?
4) What two web server platforms are popularly used on Linux?
5) What is throttling?
6) What sort of information gets logged by a web server?
7) A firewall filters applications based on their port number. If you want to configure a firewall to allow a PC to download email messages from a server, which port(s) might you have to open?

Module 3 / Unit 2

Storage Services

Objectives

On completion of this unit, you will be able to:

- Understand the use of NAS and SAN to provide network storage solutions.
- Identify the principal components of Fibre Channel.
- Understand the principles of storage capacity planning.

DAS, NAS, and SAN

Traditional server-based (or direct attached) storage means that the data a server hosts is stored on its internal hard drives or on a USB or eSATA external device connected only to that server.

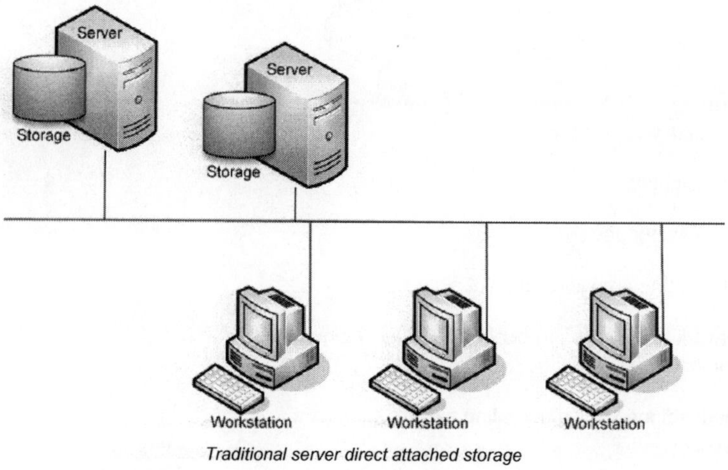

Traditional server direct attached storage

Such **direct attached storage** creates certain problems:

- It is resource inefficient because while some servers have space free, other may be running low on storage capacity.
- Traditional storage creates unplanned redundancy, because multiple instances of files may exist on multiple servers.
- There is little cross-platform sharing of data (for example, Apple Mac and Windows) because the file system may only be accessible to one type of client.

Vendors have been coming up with methods for attaching storage devices to the network for shared use by servers and clients. These are usually divided into **Network Attached Storage (NAS)** solutions and **Storage Area Networks (SAN)** solutions.

Network Attached Storage

For a **Network Attached Storage (NAS)** solution, the vendor supplies a box, which essentially plugs into the network like any other device, but you won't need to attach it via a PC file server.

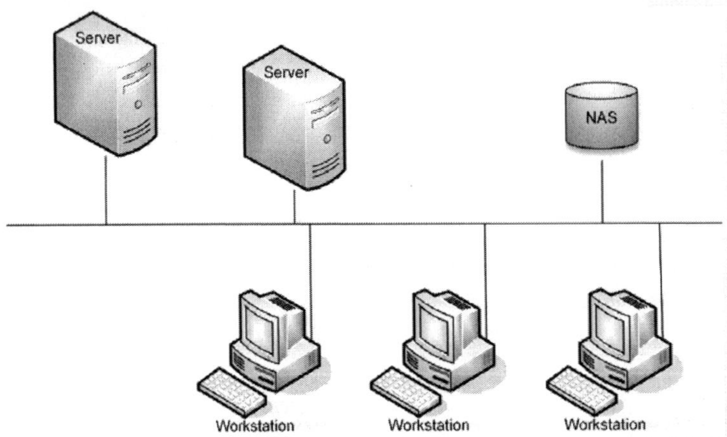

Network Attached Storage

NAS devices share these characteristics:

- They are usually IP-based network devices.
- Clients attach directly to them (they provide file-level access).
- They support multiple network file access protocols (NFS [Unix / Linux] and SMB / CIFS [Windows] for instance).
- They contain an embedded, stripped down operating system such as a Linux kernel and file processor.
- Configuration is via a web browser interface.
- They are generally cheaper than PC file servers.
- Most support RAID 1 and some will support RAID 5 or 6 or nested RAID plus hot pluggable drives.

Storage Area Network

NAS provides a cheap storage solution and is very easy to set up. NAS is typified as providing access to clients at **file level** (via the file name [File I/O]). In a **Storage Area Network (SAN)**, access is provided at **block level** (that is, the actual location of data on the media [Block I/O]). This is much more efficient for database applications, as it does not mean copying the whole file across the network to access a single record.

A SAN can integrate different types of storage technology - RAID arrays and tape libraries for instance. It can contain a mixture of high-speed and low cost devices, allowing for tiered storage to support different types of file access requirements without having to use high-cost, fast drives unnecessarily.

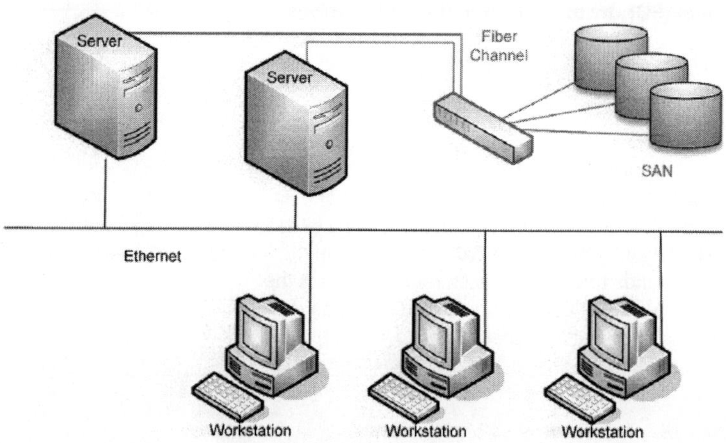

Storage Area Network

A SAN can integrate different types of storage technology - RAID arrays and tape libraries for instance. It can contain a mixture of high-speed and low cost devices, allowing for tiered storage to support different types of file access requirements without having to overprovision high-cost, fast drives.

A SAN can provide robust and extensible storage solutions for local networks and for remote storage but at greater cost than NAS. Consequently, SANs are typically deployed in enterprise networks and data centers while NAS is more of a small office or workgroup solution.

The SAN is isolated from the main network. It is only accessed by servers, not by client workstations. A SAN can be implemented using a variety of technologies, but the most popular are high bandwidth Fibre Channel and iSCSI fiber optic networks.

Fibre Channel

Fibre Channel is defined in the T11 ANSI standard. The spelling "fibre" is deliberately used to distinguish the standard from fiber optic cabling, which it often uses but on which it does not rely. The standard transfer rates are 1GFC (1 Gbps), 2GFC, 4GFC, 8GFC, and 16GFC. Two other rates (10GFC and 20GFC) use different encoding and are incompatible with devices supporting only the standard rates.

Fibre Channel Hardware

A SAN based on a **Fibre Channel (FC) Switched Fabric (FC-SW)** involves three main types of component:

- Initiator - this is a Host Bus Adapter (HBA) installed in the file or database server.
- Target - the network port for a storage device. Typical devices include single drives, RAID drive arrays, tape drives, and tape libraries. Space on the storage devices is divided into logical disks, each identified by a 64-bit **Logical Unit Number (LUN)**. The initiator will use SCSI, SAS (Serial Attached SCSI), or SATA commands to operate the storage devices in the network, depending on which interface they support. Most devices have multiple ports for load balancing and fault tolerance.

  A LUN can span multiple physical devices and a volume (as managed by the OS) can comprise multiple LUNs.

  The initiators and targets are identified by 64-bit **World Wide Names (WWN)**; similar to network adapter MAC addresses. Collectively, initiators and targets are referred to as **nodes**. Nodes can be allocated their own WWN, referred to as a WWNN (WorldWide Node Name). Also, each port on a node can have its own WorldWide Port Name (WWPN).

- FC switch / fabric switch - this provides the interconnections between initiators and targets. The switch topology and interconnections would be designed to provide multiple paths between initiators and targets, allowing for fault tolerance and load balancing. High performance FC switches are often referred to as directors.

Using fiber optic cabling, an FC fabric can be up to 10 km (6 miles) in length using single mode cable or 500m (1640ft) using multimode cable.

Fibre Channel over IP (FCIP)

Fibre Channel over IP is a tunneling protocol allowing the transfer of frames of FC data over any IP-based network, such as the Internet. This is a cost-effective way to link SANs in different geographic locations.

iSCSI

Internet SCSI (iSCSI) is also an IP tunneling protocol and enables the transfer of SCSI data over an IP-based network. Unlike FC, iSCSI works with ordinary Ethernet network adapters and switches. It could be deployed with bonded Gigabit links or with Ethernet 10G adapters and switches.

iSCSI can be used to link SANs (as per FCIP) but is also seen as an alternative to Fibre Channel itself, as it does not require FC-specific switches or adapters.

iSCSI can also be used to drive NAS appliances, which can lead to better performance in some scenarios. You might use iSCSI where a single server needs to use a storage device. Using iSCSI means that the storage (referred to as the target) is attached over the network but to the server (called the initiator) it appears to be a locally attached drive.

To implement iSCSI using normal Ethernet adapters you just need to bind iSCSI initiator client software to the adapter. For better performance, you may specify a dedicated iSCSI HBA or a Converged Network Adapter (CNA). The main advantage of a dedicated adapter is the presence of a chipset that offloads processing of iSCSI traffic from the host CPU.

Fibre Channel over Ethernet (FCoE)

Provisioning separate Fibre Channel adapters and cabling is expensive. As its name suggests, **Fibre Channel over Ethernet (FCoE)** is a means of delivering Fibre Channel packets over 10G Ethernet cabling, NIC/HBAs (referred to as Converged Network Adapters [CNA]), and switches. FCoE uses a special frametype, identified by the EtherType value 0x8096. The protocol maps WWNs onto MAC addresses.

FCoE does not quite run on standard Ethernet. It requires quality of service mechanisms to ensure flow control and guaranteed delivery. FCoE compliant products are referred to as lossless Ethernet, Data Center Ethernet, or Converged Enhanced Ethernet.

Jumbo Frames

Ordinarily, an Ethernet frame can carry a data payload or Maximum Transmission Unit (MTU) of up to 1500 bytes. When you are transferring data around a SAN with a 10 Gbps switching fabric, a 1500 byte limit means using a lot of frames. A **jumbo frame** is one that supports a data payload of up to around 9000 bytes (often 9216 bytes). This reduces the number of frames that need to be transmitted, which can reduce the amount of processing that switches and routers need to do. It also reduces the bandwidth requirement somewhat as fewer frame headers are being transmitted. The benefits of jumbo frames are somewhat disputed however.

When implementing jumbo frames, it is critical that all hosts and appliances (switches and routers) along the communication path be able and configured to support them. It is also vital to ensure that each device supports the same maximum MTU. Also, it can be complex to calculate the maximum MTU if any additional headers are used (for IPsec for instance).

Fibre Channel Security Issues

As with IP, all FC frames are transferred unencrypted, meaning that an attacker with access to the switch fabric could easily perform eavesdropping or Man-in-the-Middle modification attacks.

LUN Masking

One basic FC security technique is to use **LUN masking**. This could be configured on the HBA but is more typically implemented on the storage device. LUN masking means that the device is configured with an access control list of valid WWNs (or WWPNs). A server without a matching WWN will not be able to access the storage device.

It is possible to spoof a WWN (in a similar way to spoofing a MAC address). Consequently it is important to secure the management interfaces of HBAs and switches to prevent unauthorized changes or the attachment of rogue devices.

Zoning

Another option is to configure zoning. When implemented using an FC switch (hard zoning), a zone is somewhat similar to a VLAN. Each device is placed in a zone based on the switch port it is connected to and the switch determines whether they are allowed to communicate.

Fibre Channel Security Protocols (FC-SP)

Legacy FC security depends on the physical security of the network and the servers used to access it. A security protocol (FC-SP) was standardized in 2004. FC-SP allows for the use of encryption for authentication and confidentiality:

- **Diffie-Hellman Challenge Handshake Authentication Protocol (DH-CHAP)** - this allows initiators and targets to authenticate by configuring the same shared secret on each device or by configuring a RADIUS server to hold device authentication information.
- **Fibre Channel Authentication Protocol (FCAP)** - provides authentication through digital certificates installed on the devices.
- **Encapsulating Security Protocol (ESP)** - this provides message confidentiality and integrity (in the same sort of way as IPsec).

When used over IP (FCIP or iSCSI) native IP security mechanisms such as IPsec can be used directly.

Tape Drives

Magnetic tape drives provide a low cost per byte method of creating security backups and archiving data. They may be internal or external units, supplied with SATA, SAS, USB, or Firewire interfaces (or ATA/EIDE or SCSI in the case of legacy drives).

Tape Drive Types

Some of the more popular formats are summarized below:

- Quarter-Inch Cartridge (QIC) - this is the oldest tape drive format still in use. Tapes can store up to 4 GB. All tape types have a range of standards associated with them. Typically, a tape drive will be incompatible with later standards. In some cases, a drive may also not be compatible with earlier standards (or may have read-only compatibility).

Compression increases tape capacity but also makes backup jobs slower to complete.

- Travan - the Travan backup format (now owned by Imation) is a development of the QIC system. Tapes can store up to 10 GB uncompressed data.
- Digital Audio Tape (DAT) - this uses a digital format with two magnetic heads: one to read and one to write. DAT backup systems conform to a standard called **Digital Data Storage (DDS)** and support up to 36 GB uncompressed capacity.
- 8mm Tape Systems - offers high-capacity (up to 200 GB) data storage in a cartridge that appears identical to 8 mm (1/4") video tapes, although it uses a much higher quality magnetic media. The 8 mm standard is mainly being developed by the **Advanced Intelligent Tape (AIT)** forum, sponsored notably by Sony.

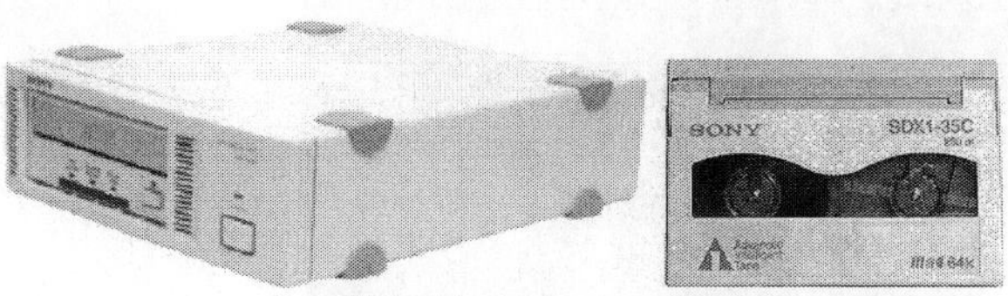

Sony AIT-3 drive and tape cartridge

- Digital Linear Tape (DLT) - This tape technology was developed for high-speed, LAN-based backup systems. DLT is a popular format for mini-computers and large servers and is much faster than other tape backup formats.

  DLT was originally developed by DEC but the standard is now maintained by Quantum, Fujitsu, Hitachi, and Imation. The standard has **VS (Value Series)** and **Super-DLT** variants, with capacity up to 300 GB. Another DLT format, **Linear Tape-Open (LTO)**, was set up by HP and IBM. LTO-based products go under the brand name Ultrium. Tapes have up to 2.5 TB uncompressed capacity while the tape drives have a transfer rate of up to 160 MBps.

Ultrium data cartridge

Tape Libraries

A **tape library** is a high-end backup solution in which an **AutoLoader** is pre-loaded with tapes, which it then auto-changes, allowing for fully-unattended backups. This minimizes the chance of human error (forgetting to change the tape or inserting the wrong tape for instance). It also allows for much larger capacities (unless a backup operator is on-hand to change the tape, the capacity of a stand-alone system is limited to the capacity of a single tape).

The other advantage is that a greater number of restore points are available online (that is, a technician does not have to locate and load the cartridge on which the required data are stored).

StorageTek manufactures autoloaders offering capacity from 2 TB (20 cartridges) to 26.4 PB (it can employ up to 132,000 cartridges).

HP StorageWorks tape library

Maintaining Tape Drives

When installing or upgrading a tape drive, it is important to use the manufacturer's latest drivers, to ensure that the full set of features is supported. Tape drives needs periodic cleaning, notably the drive heads. Most newer drives feature built-in head cleaners. Most media come pre-formatted and should only be erased using the supplied software. From time-to-time, the tape may need re-tensioning to ensure reliability; again this can be done via the supplied software.

Other Storage Media

While disks and tape account for a good deal of the storage technologies used by server networks, there are some other media types that you should be aware of.

Optical and WORM Media

Optical discs - CD, DVD, and Blu-ray (BD) - are mostly used for distributing software and for file transfer and archiving or possibly occasional backups. They are not suitable for use as part of a scheduled backup (often they do not have sufficient capacity, recording speeds are too slow, and the discs are not designed for continual overwriting). Most optical formats are now rewritable but older types may be **Write Once Read Many (WORM)**, meaning that once the disc is written, it cannot be deleted or overwritten. Rewritable media can also be "closed" to this state. This is useful when the media is designed for archiving.

There are several main recordable formats:

Disc	Type	Capacity
CD-R	WORM	700 MB
CD-RW	Rewritable	700 MB
DVD±R	WORM	4.7 GB single layer 8.5 GB dual layer / single sided 9.4 GB single layer / double sided 17.1 GB dual layer / double sided
DVD±RW	Rewritable	4.7 GB single layer 8.5 GB dual layer
BD-R	WORM	25 GB
BD-R XL	WORM	100 GB triple layer 128 GB quad layer
BD-RE	Rewritable	25 GB

Drives of a newer generation almost always support recording and playback of older discs.

Optical discs are generally more robust than many other media types, making them a good choice for archiving. Despite manufacturers' claims they tend not to be completely scratch-proof however, and so must still be stored and handled carefully.

Optical Jukebox

An **optical jukebox** is an autoloader for recordable and rewritable optical media, such as CD-R or DVD-RW. HP also produced an "Optical Jukebox" StorageWorks product designed for Magneto-Optical discs, which never became a mainstream storage technology.

Flash Media

There are many flash media devices, from USB thumb drives, through memory cards, to SSD hard drive replacements. Portable devices generally support capacities of up to 256 GB. Larger SSDs are available but only at enormous cost.

Flash media is probably too expensive for any sort of large-scale backup use (though costs should come down quite rapidly over the next few years) but it is highly portable and fast and so a good choice for making offsite backups. There are also used for specialist purposes, such as storing encryption keys, and are becoming increasingly popular as a home backup solution.

Just a Bunch of Disks (JBOD)

Just a Bunch of Disks (JBOD) refers to a hard disk storage array or storage pool that is configured as a single volume but without any RAID functionality such as striping, parity, or mirroring. The pool is, as the name suggests, just a bunch of disks. As with RAID 0, there is no redundancy in the volume and a single device failure will cause the volume to fail and in all likelihood data to be lost. With JBOD, you do not get the performance benefit of striping either. The only advantage is that you can mix disks of different sizes and utilize their full capacity in the volume. Like RAID 0, JBOD has only niche uses, such as for testing or development.

Storage Capacity Planning

Storage capacity planning is the business of working out how much storage your servers or network will require over short and medium terms. Storage capacity planning is a discipline in itself with many complex issues to consider and tools to assist with decisions. However to simplify things, there are a few principal areas to consider:

- Server / appliance OS growth - a server, network appliance, or desktop PC needs a certain amount of local disk space to install the OS and applications files. The amount of space required for these is generally predictable but you do need to account for potential growth. This might come from patches and service packs, from upgrades, or from new applications or a changed service role. Adding direct attached storage to a device is usually relatively problematic so it is worth allowing plenty of headroom when specifying the server requirements in the first place.

A complication with this is that the highest capacity devices tend not to be the best performing ones. Smaller HDDs are usually a bit faster than larger ones and SSDs are much faster still but will cost much more per gigabyte.

- Application - software applications generate a certain amount of data either as a results of processing (in databases and records for instance) or as a result of users creating files with the application. It is usually prudent to separate the "content" part of the application, such as its database, from the "processing" part. If the content part is stored on some sort of shared storage, it will be easier to add capacity later.
- File server - these allow users to take over management of files that they create. Working out the capacity requirements of users can be quite challenging but again, if a scalable storage solution is used, adding capacity is usually straightforward, unless you haven't been monitoring usage carefully enough!
- Temporary files - software is also often associated with the generation of temporary files. These are files that do not usually need to be retained but in some cases it may be difficult just to delete them periodically.
- Logs - you also have to consider log files. These could be generated by both the OS and by applications software. It is possible to set logs to overwrite automatically but this might not be allowed in respect of security or regulatory policies. If logs have to be retained, it will usually be best to save them remotely to a storage pool that can be expanded easily.
- Backup / archive - having generated all this data, you also have to make copies of it as a security backup. One way to reduce the volume of data that has to be backed up (and stored on "live" systems) is to transition some of it into archival media.

Backup procedures are discussed in *Unit 5.6*.

Disk Size Calculation

One issue to take account of when provisioning disk storage is the value of units used in the calculations. File sizes are measured in bits or multiples of 8 bits called bytes. It is when you start using multiples of bytes that things get complicated. Most file systems show file size values in base 2. When calculated in base 2 (binary), a unit such as "kilo" means 2^10 (2 to the power of 10) or 1024; in base 10 (decimal), kilo means 10^3 or 1000. All storage vendors advertise capacity in base 10, so 300 GB means 300,000,000,000 bytes. In binary units, those 300,000,000,000 bytes are "only" 279.397 "GB".

```
300,000,000,000 / 1024 / 1024 = 279.3967724
```

Technically speaking, binary multiples should use SI (International System of Units) designations, such as KiB (kibibyte), MiB (mebibyte), GiB (gibibyte), and TiB (tebibyte). Many operating systems - notably Windows - report file sizes using base 2 but with decimal unit designations. Ubuntu Linux and some other distributions have switched to using SI units. Versions of OS X 10.6 and up report decimal file sizes and media capacity.

When working out capacity requirements, make sure you are using units consistently and converting where necessary.

You should also be comfortable working out percentages. For example, if a 300 GB disk has 25% utilization, that means that it contains 75 GB of data already (300 * 0.25).

In the exam you will be provided with an on-screen calculator tool so you do not need to perform these calculations in your head.

Disk Quotas

One means of keeping within the capacity requirements that you have forecast is to impose **disk quotas** on users. A disk quota is a limit to the amount of space any one user can take up on a volume.

In Windows for example, quotas are enabled or disabled on each volume using the drive's property dialog.

Quota limits can be hard (deny more disk space to users exceeding their limit) or soft (log the event and warn the user only). You can set a default quota limit for new users or you can use the **Quota Entries** button to set limits on a per-user or per-group basis. Alternatively you can use group policy to set default quota limits for different OUs.

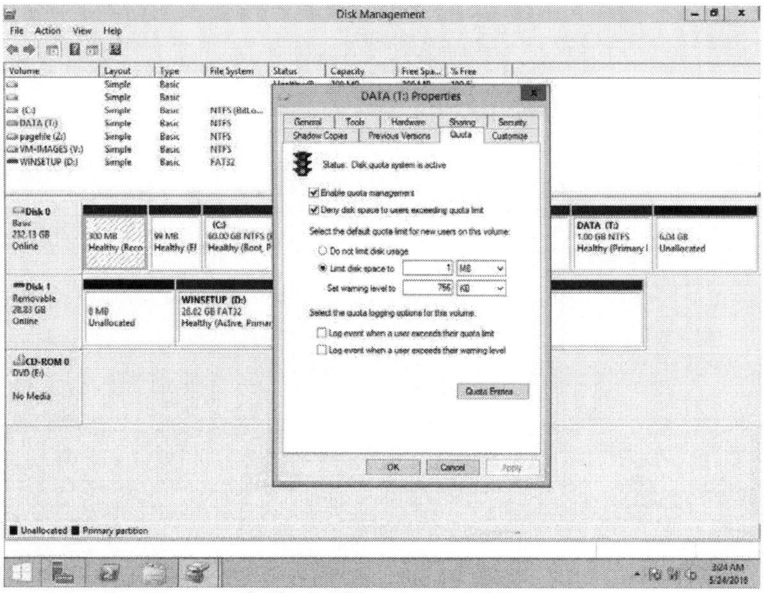

Configuring disk quotas on a volume

Most other modern file systems support the imposition of quotas, including ext2, ext3, ext4, ZFS, and UFS.

Compression

Another means of reducing storage requirements is to apply file compression to reduce the space a file takes up on disk. Files can be compressed manually using zip-type software or compression can be applied universally to all files in a folder or on a volume using the file system (transparent compression). File system compression is supported by NTFS and ZFS but not ext. Most tape hardware also supports compression when backing up. The downside is that compression can reduce performance. Also, many file types (images and video files for instance) are already heavily compressed and their file size will not be affected by another layer of compression.

Review Questions / Module 3 / Unit 2 / Storage Services

Answer these questions to test what you have learned in this unit.

1) What basic distinction could you make between NAS and SAN solutions?
2) What ID is given to logical disks in a Fibre Channel fabric?
3) What is the main distinction between Fibre Channel and iSCSI?
4) What type of values are used to configure an ACL when implementing LUN masking?
5) What type of tape format is likely to be selected for a new backup solution?
6) True or false? A hard disk advertised using base 10 units will have much lower capacity, as measured in bytes, when installed and formatted by a Windows OS.

Module 3 / Unit 3

Volume Management

Objectives

On completion of this unit, you will be able to:

- Use disk management tools to mount volumes and maintain the file system.
- Troubleshoot storage and volume availability problems.

Disk Management Tool

Windows provides a GUI **Disk Management** console snap-in to format disks and manage partitions. The Disk Management utility displays a summary of any fixed and removable drives attached to the system. The top pane lists drives (or volumes) with information about the file system, capacity, and free space available. The bottom pane lists disks, showing information about the partitions created on each disk plus any **unpartitioned** space.

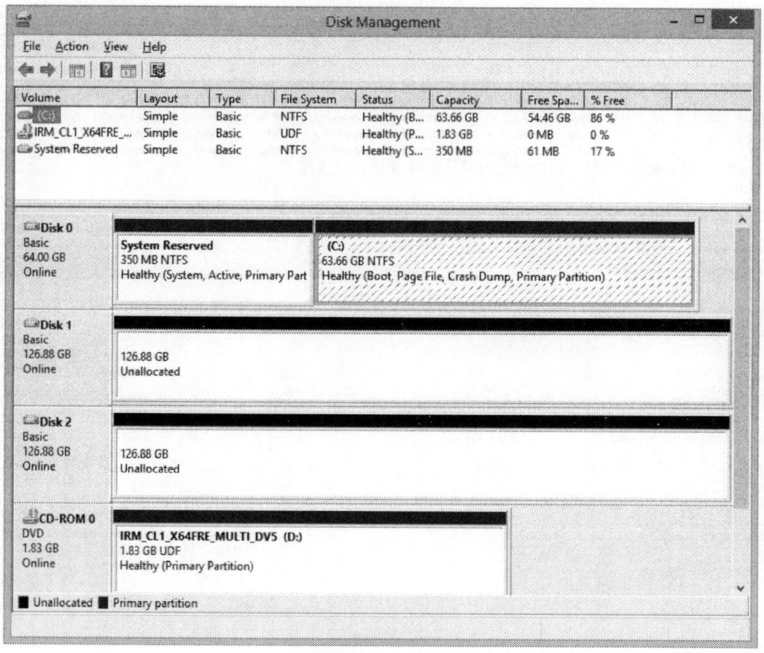

Disk Management utility

Initializing Disks, Adding Drives, and Assigning Drive Letters

You can create a new partition if there is unpartitioned space on the disk. If you add a hard disk to the system, you will be prompted to initialize it when you start Disk Management. You can choose whether to use the MBR or GPT partition style for the new disk. When a disk has been initialized, you can create partitions on it.

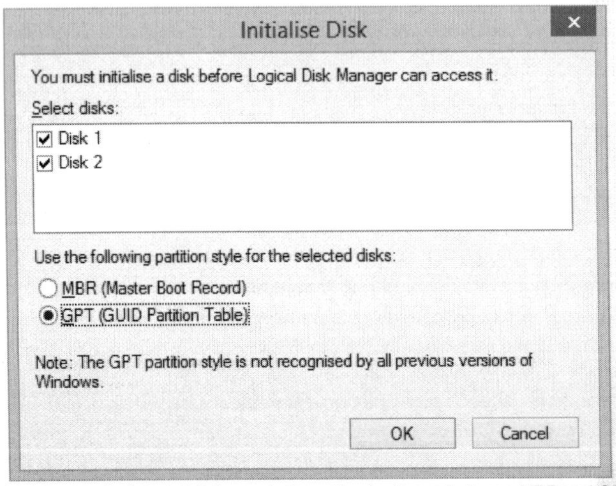

Initializing newly detected disks - note the option to choose between MBR and GPT

To create a new partition, right-click an area of unallocated space and select **New Simple Volume**. Complete the wizard to select:

- Amount of disk space to use (in megabytes - recall that 1024 MB is 1 GB).
- Assign a drive letter or a mount point. You can also choose not to assign a drive or mount point, in which case the volume will be inaccessible via Explorer.

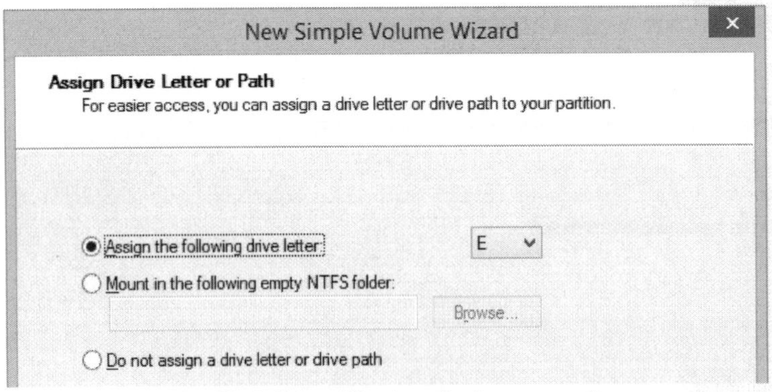

New Simple Volume Wizard - configuring access path

- Choose the file system - you can make the following choices:

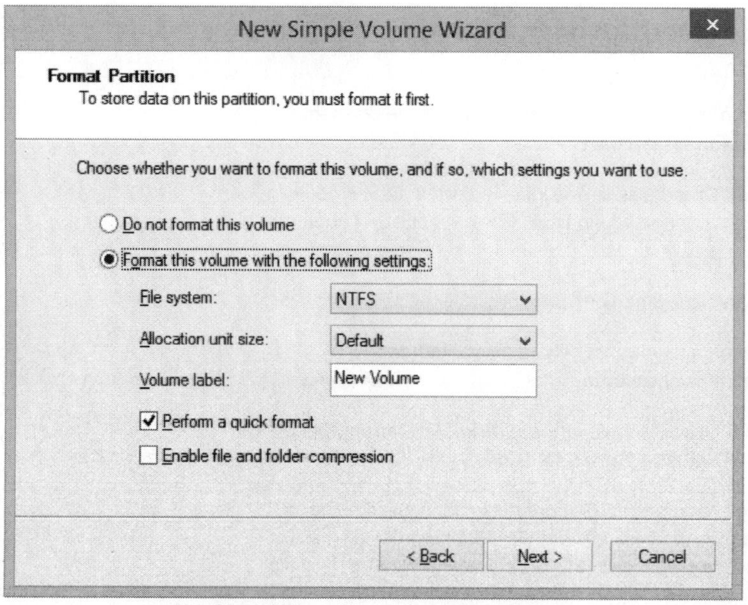

New Simple Volume Wizard - formatting the volume

- NTFS or FAT for the file system.
- Allocation unit size - default settings are usually best (selects a size based on the volume size). As a rule of thumb, a small allocation unit size is efficient if the disk stores mainly small files or vice versa.
- Volume label - shown in Explorer along with the drive letter.
- Quick format - a full format checks the disk for bad sectors; selecting the quick format option skips this check. Both types of format remove references to existing files in the volume boot record but the actual sectors are not "scrubbed" or zeroed. Existing files will be overwritten as new files are added to the volume but in principle data can be recovered from a formatted disk (using third-party tools). A secure format utility prevents this by overwriting each sector with a zero value, sometimes using multiple passes.

Having setup the disk structure, if you want to change it in the future then partitions can be managed using the shortcut menu, which contains options to mark a partition as active, re-format or delete it, or change its drive letter. You can also access the volume properties sheet, which contains options for the disk performance tools and access permissions and quota management (on NTFS volumes).

You cannot format or delete system or boot partitions.

Adding Arrays (Dynamic Storage)

Dynamic storage allows the creation of volumes spanning multiple disks that can be shrunk and expanded (an **array**).

Only fixed disks can be used. A fixed disk is one installed within the computer and connected by SATA. Disks connected via USB, Firewire, or eSATA cannot be converted to dynamic.

Dynamic volumes can be in the following configurations:

- **Simple** - occupies space on a single disk. There is little difference in practice between this and a basic volume.
- **Spanned** - a volume using space on two or more disks. This arrangement is also referred to as **JBOD (Just a Bunch Of Disks)**.
- **Striped** - a volume using space on two or more disks configured using RAID 0 to improve performance. Basically data is written across all disks whereas spanned just uses up space on the volume using the standard file access pattern.

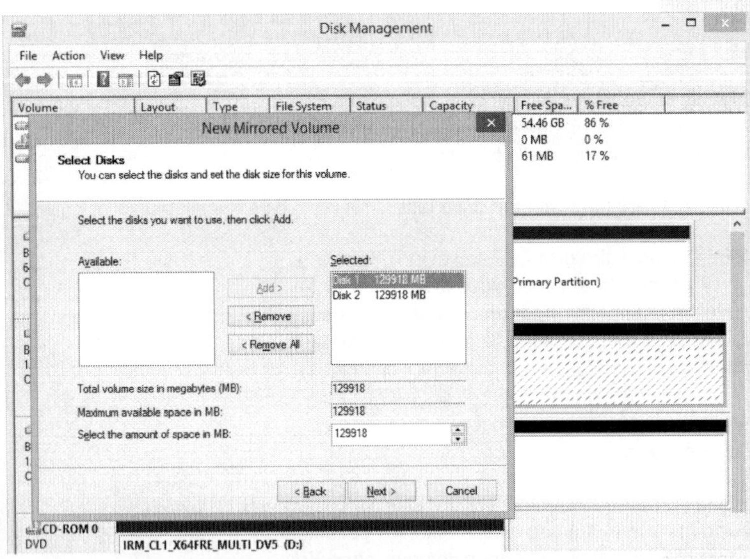

Creating a mirrored volume dynamic disk array

- **Mirrored** - a volume where one disk stores a copy (mirror) of the other disk. This provides redundancy (RAID 1).
- **RAID 5** - a volume where data is spread across three or more disks. The system writes parity information alongside the data. If one of the disks is damaged, the remaining data can be combined with the remaining parity information to keep the volume functioning.

When a mirrored volume has been setup, you have two options for converting the mirror set back to a simple volume:

- Breaking the mirror leaves the data in the volumes on both disks intact. You would also use this option to replace one of the disks in the mirror set (install the physical disk then use the **Add Mirror** command on the existing volume).

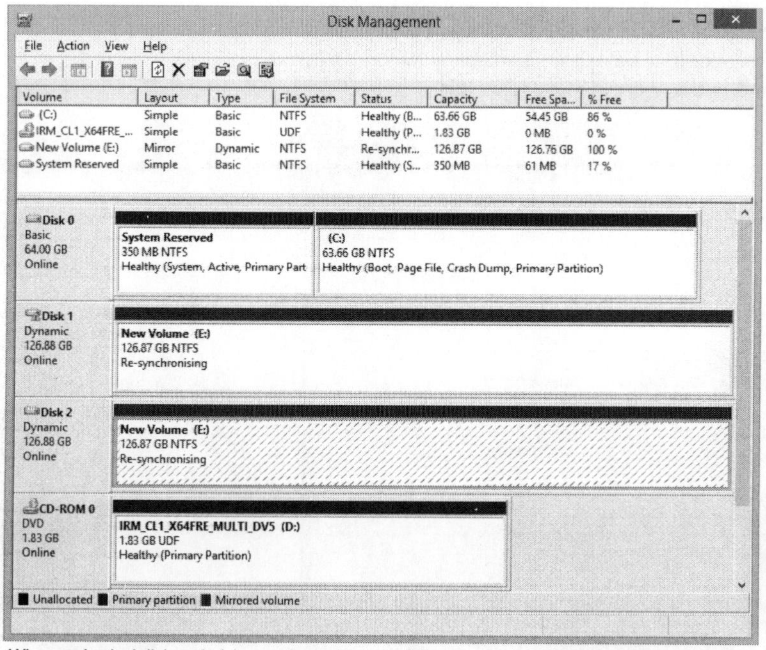

When a physical disk underlying a mirrored volume fails, you can install another disk and add it to the mirror - a resynching process will start to copy data from the first disk to the second

- Removing a mirror deletes the volume (and any files it contains) from that disk, leaving the volume on the other disk as a simple volume.

Spanned and striped volumes offer flexibility, but if any of *the disks in the array fails,* all *data on the volume will be lost. Only mirroring and RAID-5 provide redundancy.*

A dynamic disk can be converted back to basic, but the volumes (and any data on them) must be deleted first. As with basic partitions, volumes must be formatted (NTFS or FAT / FAT32) before they can be available to the OS.

Mount Points

A **mount point** means that rather than allocating a drive letter to a volume, it is accessed from a designated folder in the file system. The host file system must be NTFS but the volume mounted can be formatted with any type of file system. For example, you might partition and format a removable hard disk then mount it as a DATA volume within a user's Documents folder. To assign a volume to a mount point, first create a folder at the point in the file system you want to mount the drive. This folder must be empty. Next, either run the **New Partition/Volume Wizard** or unassign the drive letter from an existing partition and mount it (use the **Change Drive Letter and Paths** shortcut menu to do this).

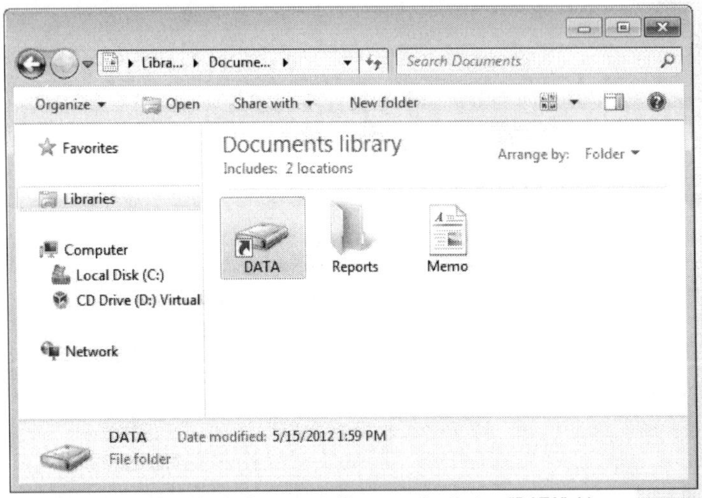

DATA volume mounted within the Documents library - notice that no "DATA" drive appears under any of the drive letters

Drive Status and Disk Tools

Each disk and drive displays status indicators in the Disk Management program. Disks can have the following status indicators:

- **Online** - the disk is OK.
- **Not Initialized** - when you add a new unpartitioned disk, a wizard runs prompting you to initialize, partition, and format the disk. If you cancel the wizard the disk will appear as Not Initialized - right-click to start the wizard again.
- **Unreadable** - the disk is damaged. This message can be transitory so try right-clicking the **Disk Management** tool and selecting **Rescan Disks**. If the disk is still shown as unreadable, you would have to use third-party tools to try to recover data from it.
- **Foreign** - if you configure a disk as dynamic on one computer, then install the disk in another computer, it will be marked as foreign. Right-click the disk and select **Import Foreign Disk** to make it accessible to the system.

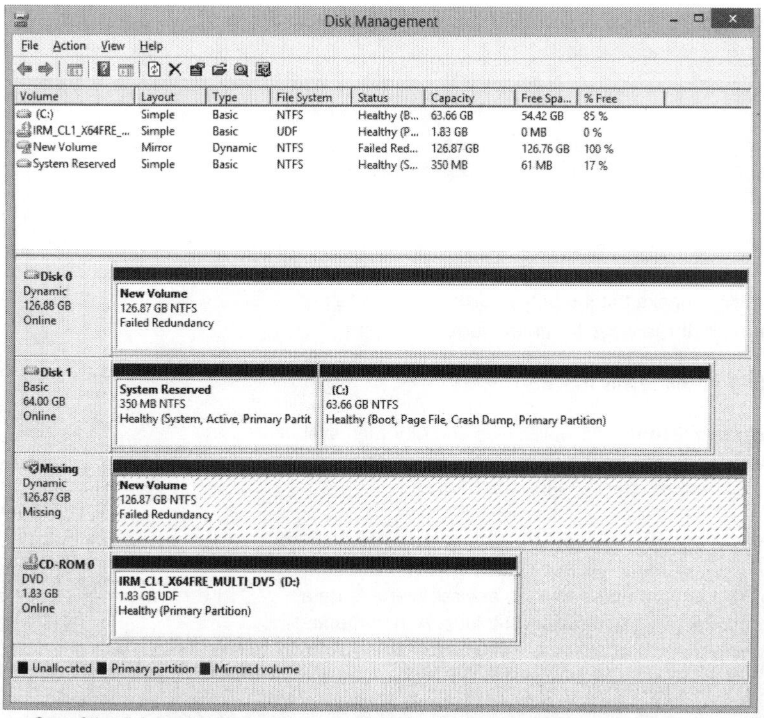

One of the disks underlying the mirrored volume is missing and consequently the volume is marked as failed

- **Offline / Missing** - a disk configured as dynamic cannot be read. This could be a transitory error but is more likely to indicate that the drive or I/O to the drive is damaged, a cable is unplugged, the disk has been switched off, and so on. There are two options:

    - If the disk can be restored, use the **Reactivate Disk** option to add it back to the array

    - If the disk cannot be restored, use the **Remove Disk** option

Volumes (or partitions) can have the following status indicators:

- **Healthy** - the volume is formatted and ready to read and write data. **Healthy (System)** indicates that the volume contains the boot loader while **Healthy (Active)** represents the system volume used to boot. **Healthy (Boot)** represents a volume containing an OS while **Healthy (Page File)** shows one storing a pagefile. A drive may also display as **Healthy (At Risk)**, which means that a number of I/O errors are occurring - a good sign that the disk or controller is failing.

- **Failed** - this either indicates a damaged disk (basic) or a dynamic volume where the supporting disk drives are not available. You need to check the status of the devices (if cabling and power are OK the disk[s] or controller may have been damaged).

- **Formatting** - a user-initiated format is in progress. Wait for the format to complete before trying to access the volume.

If you prefer working at the command line, you can perform disk management tasks using the `diskpart` *utility.*

Check Disk

The **Check Disk** (`chkdsk`) utility checks the integrity of disks and can repair any problems detected. There are three ways to run the tool:

- **No option selected** - runs in Read-Only mode.
- **Automatically fix file system errors** - corrupted files and other file system errors are caused by crashes, power loss, and the like. At a command-line, use **chkdsk** ***volume*****: /f**, where *volume* is the drive letter.
- **Scan for and attempt recovery of bad sectors** - bad sectors are damage to the actual drive. If a drive has many bad sectors, it is probably nearing the end of its useful life. You are prompted to save any recoverable data, which is copied to the root directory as **file*nnnn*.chk** files. At a command-line, use **chkdsk** ***volume*****: /r**, where *volume* is the drive letter.

`chkdsk` *can take a* ***long*** *time to scan and fix errors on a large disk. You cannot cancel once started. Run a Read-Only scan first.*

Check Disk cannot fix open files, so you may be prompted to schedule the scan for the next system restart. A version of Check Disk (**autochk**) will also run automatically if the system detects file system errors. The other main parameters and switches for the command-line version are as follows:

Switch	Use
Path	Specify a path (and optionally file name) to check.
/x	Force the volume to dismount. This will cause file errors for users with files open on the volume. If the volume is in use and you use the **/f** or **/r** switches without **/x**, you are prompted to schedule **chkdsk** for the next system restart.
/i /c	On NTFS volumes only, skips parts of the checking process.

Disk Defragmenter

The **Disk Defragmenter** (**defrag**) reorganizes a drive to store information relating to each file in contiguous sectors of the disk. This improves performance by reducing the time required to load a file. The Disk Defragmenter can also move data to the start of the disk, leaving a single free area of disk for use by new files.

Although it is possible to run this utility in the background, it will slow the server and prevent defragmentation of open files. It is usually better to run defragment when the server is not being used. It may also be necessary to disable applications that run in the background, such as anti-virus software.

The Defragmenter requires above 15% of free disk space to work effectively. If insufficient free disk space is available, some files may not be defragmented.

At a command prompt, the basic syntax is **`defrag volume`**, where *volume* is a drive letter or volume name. The main switches are as follows:

Switch	Use
`/a`	Analyze the volume and display a report.
`/f`	Force the volume to be defragmented.
`/v`	Display complete analysis and defragmentation reports.
`/c`	Defragment all volumes.
`/e`	Defragment all volumes *except* those specified.
`/h`	Run the tool at normal (rather than low) priority.
`/m`	Perform defrag of multiple volumes in parallel.
`/x`	Consolidate free space (try to make all empty sectors contiguous). This option is useful if you want to try to shrink a volume.

Managing Disks in Linux

In Linux, the directory structure is defined as a **File System Hierarchy**. Unlike Windows, drive letters like C: or D: are not used. The file system starts at the **root**, represented by `/`. Directories and subdirectories can be created from the root to store files.

Note that Linux uses the forward slash (/) to delimit directory names while Windows uses a back slash (\).

It is important to realize that *everything* available to the Linux OS is represented as a file in the file system, including devices. This is referred to as the **unified file system**. For example, a single hard drive attached to a SATA port would normally be represented in the file system by **/dev/sda**. A second storage device - perhaps one attached to a USB port - would be represented as **/dev/sdb**.

When Linux boots, a system kernel and virtual file system are loaded to a RAM drive. The virtual file system identifies the location of the persistent root partition from the appropriate storage device and loads the file system stored on the disk.

Mounting Partitions

A file system configured on a partition on a particular storage device is attached to a particular directory (**mount point**) within the unified file system using the `mount` command. For example:

```
mount /dev/sda1 /mnt/diskC
```

...mounts partition 1 on the mass storage device **sda** to the directory **/mnt/diskC**. Mountable file systems are listed in the **/etc/fstab** file. The `umount` command can be used to dis-mount a volume.

Think of the root file system representing everything on the computer as "THE" file system and a file system for a particular partition as just "A" file system.

Disk Maintenance Tools

Most Linux distributions use some version of the **ext** file system to format partitions on mass storage devices. **ext3** is a 64-bit file system with support for journaling, which means that the file system tracks changes, giving better reliability and less chance of file corruption in the event of crashes or power outages. Support for journaling is the main difference between ext3 and its predecessor (ext2). **ext4** delivers significantly better performance than ext3 and would usually represent the best choice for new systems.

Most Linux distributions would also provide GUI tools for managing disks and quotas, but the following represent the main commands:

- `fdisk` - used to manage partitions on a hard disk. For disks over 2 TB or for GPT-style partitioning, you can use `parted` or `gdisk`.
- `mdadm` or **Logical Volume Manager (LVM)** - used to create and manage RAID volumes.
- `mkfs` - used to format a partition with a particular file system (for example `mkfs -t ext3 /dev/sda2` formats partition 2 on disk "sda" with the ext3 file system).
- `fsck` - check a partition for errors.

Linux file systems do not require defragmenting. Linux leaves gaps between each file, allowing the files to grow or shrink within their own "space", avoiding the worst effects of fragmentation. Most Linux distributions will be set to clean out temp directories automatically.

Troubleshooting Storage

Hard drives are most likely to fail due to mechanical problems either in the *first few months* of operation or after a *few years*, when they begin to reach the end of their useful life. Sudden loss of power can also damage a disk, especially if it is in the middle of a read/write operation. A hard drive that is failing will display the following symptoms:

- Bad sectors - diagnostic utilities can test the surface of the hard disk. If more bad sectors are located each time the test is run, it is a sure sign that the disk is about to fail.
- Data corruption - if multiple files become unreadable it is usually because one or more of the sectors it is stored on has been corrupted. A single corrupt file could be the result of a problem with a single save operation or some sort of bug in an application. It is only if multiple files are being corrupted that you should consider a problem with the disk itself. If the boot sector is corrupted, the server will become unbootable. Boot sector corruption can also be caused by malware or clumsy use of partition managers.

There are utilities to recover data from damaged hard disks but the only completely reliable solution is to have an up-to-date backup.

- Cannot mount drive / access logical drive - if a mount point or drive letter is no longer working, the disk behind that volume will have failed. In Windows, removable drives can sometimes be mounted with a different drive letter than was used previously. This can cause "data not available" or "file not found" errors in applications. You can reserve the drive letter assigned to a particular removable drive using the Disk Management console.

If the drive is a removable drive (a DVD or tape drive for instance), consider that the media in the drive might have failed. Try substituting with a "known good" disc or tape.

- Constant LED activity.
- Noise - a healthy hard disk makes a certain low-level noise when accessing the platters. A loud or grinding noise or any sort of clicking is a sign of a problem.

Hard Disk Not Accessible

If a hard drive is not detected at boot, first check that it is powering up. Drive activity is usually indicated by an LED on the front panel of the system unit case. A server is likely to have an error light if it has detected any sort of disk failure. If the LEDs are inactive, check that the drive has a power connector attached.

If there are multiple drives and none of them are powering up, you would have to suspect some sort of failure in the drive controller, host bus adapter, or backplane. Try to boot the server to its diagnostic utility and run checks to try to isolate the problem.

If you can isolate the problem to a single drive rather than its controller or backplane, try the following...

Configuration

- If the system is not booting correctly from the hard drive, check that the boot sequence is set correctly in system setup and that there are no removable disks in floppy or optical drives.
- Check the data cables are not damaged and that they are correctly connected to the drive and motherboard. Try substituting a cable with a "known good" one.
- For a SCSI drive, check that the host adapter driver is working and that ID numbers and terminators are set correctly.
- If the drives are connected to a motherboard controller, check that it has not been disabled by a jumper or system firmware setting.

File System Structure

If you cannot boot from the hard disk, try booting from recovery media and accessing the system partition from the command line. If this produces the error message **Invalid media type**, the disk has no valid file system structure on it. This is likely to be because the sector containing the file system information has been damaged. If you type **C:** at the prompt and this produces the error message **Invalid drive specification**, the drive may have an improper partition structure. You can check the drive's partition structure with **`diskpart`** (Windows) or **`fdisk`** (Linux).

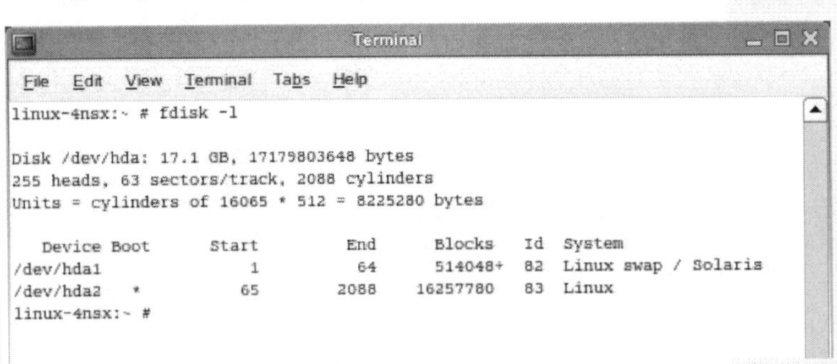

fdisk program showing a hard disk partition structure

If the utility reports that the hard disk has no partitions, the partition table may have become corrupted by a virus or by a drive failure. You may be able to resolve this by partitioning and formatting the drive but if the drive is failing the problem will only reoccur - replace the disk.

Troubleshooting RAID

When troubleshooting RAID, proceed with the same approach as with any other disk related problem. Typically, you will have received a notification that a disk has failed - probably by an alert and a message logged into the system log. As the system will continue to operate, which is the point of RAID, you need not replace the offending disk immediately and have time to investigate the cause of the problem. However, it should be noted that performance can be degraded when a disk has become orphaned during a failover. Some RAID levels provide better performance when degraded than others.

However, it is an obvious but worthwhile point that disks are comparatively cheap, while data is expensive - so simply replacing a suspect disk ASAP is an acceptable solution; provided that solves the problem being experienced. Bear in mind that disks manufactured at the same time, with the same load and usage, might fail at a similar moment. Therefore, since RAID supports the failure of one disk in the array (generally) then order in another - just in case!

Failures in Hardware Arrays

The precise process for managing a disk failure with a hardware array will be dependent on the vendor that supplied the array and the configuration being supported. All array controllers will be capable of generating an event to the NOS system log and perhaps of generating an alert message for the administrator.

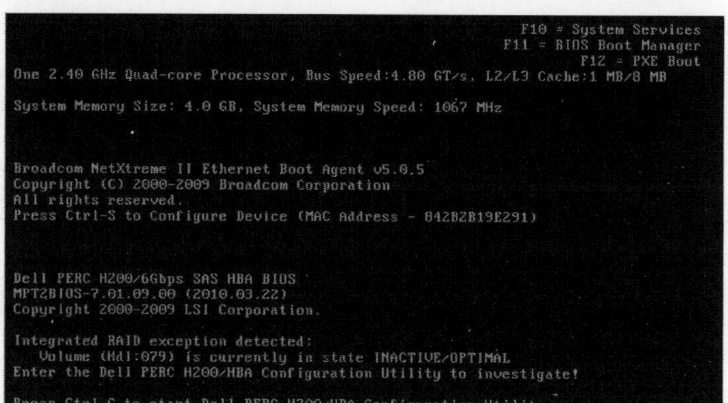

Boot message indicating a problem with the RAID volume - press Ctrl+C to start the utility and troubleshoot

If the array supports hot swapping, then the new disk can simply be inserted into the chassis of the computer or disk chassis. The RAID controller should recognize this fact and start to resynchronize the disks.

When hot-swapping a faulty disk out, take extreme caution not to remove a healthy disk from the array as making a mistake could cause the array to fail, depending on the configuration. Disk failure is normally indicated by a red LED. Always make a backup beforehand.

By way of example, as with software RAID 5, with hardware-based RAID 5, you can still only lose one disk in the array. The basic rules don't change. However, if you are implementing a more complex configuration, which supports enterprise-level features, then the disk need not be replaced. You may choose to reconfigure the array on the fly to support an alternate configuration. For example, if you currently implement 3-way mirroring and a disk fails, you could simply reconfigure for 2-way mirroring. Alternatively, there could be a hot spare configured to cut-in when a disk in the set fails.

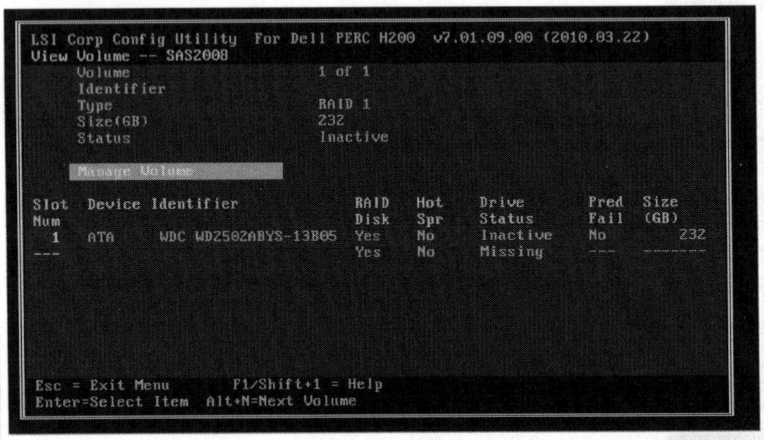

Diagnosing RAID errors using the configuration utility - this volume is missing one of its disks

Rebuilding the array can place a lot of stress on the remaining disks, making a failure in one of them more likely. It is a good idea to ensure that there is a current backup before starting the rebuild process.

If a volume is not available, either more than the tolerated number of disks has failed or the controller or SAN Host Bus Adapter (HBA) has failed. If the boot volume is affected then the OS will not start. If too many disks have failed, you will have to turn to the latest backup or try to use file recovery solutions. If the issue is controller failure, then data on the volume should be recoverable, though there may be file corruption if a write operation was interrupted by the failure. Either install a new controller or import the disks into another system.

Cache and Cache Battery Failure

All modern hard drives come equipped with onboard RAM providing a high speed buffer or cache between the physical drive and system RAM. In addition to individual hard drive RAM buffers or cache, RAID arrays and NAS / SAN units also typically have RAM caches of their own. These can have battery backups for use when write caching is implemented (data to be written to disk is stored in RAM before the disk to even out bursts of disk writes). These batteries ensure that if mains power is lost unsaved disk writes in cache RAM can be successfully written.

A failure of any of these cache components typically results in slower performance at least, although a cache failure is often a symptom of a fault on the drive controller board itself which may make the drive completely unresponsive. If the battery fails, this can cause file corruptions. Ideally, the controller should detect that the battery has failed and disable the cache until it is replaced, but this does not always happen.

If the cache has failed for any reason, some controllers will disable the array completely. Otherwise, the array may continue to work (in "write-through" mode) but performance will be reduced. You are likely to have to replace the controller. Troubleshooting failures in these devices typically means using manufacturer specific tools and diagnostics. For example, on a Dell Server fitted with a RAID controller, `F10` is used at boot time to enter the **Lifecycle Controller** and then use the **Hardware Configuration Wizard** which allows the RAID controller and disks to be checked and diagnosed for faults. On an HP Proliant server the `F8` key is used at boot time to enter the equivalent RAID tool.

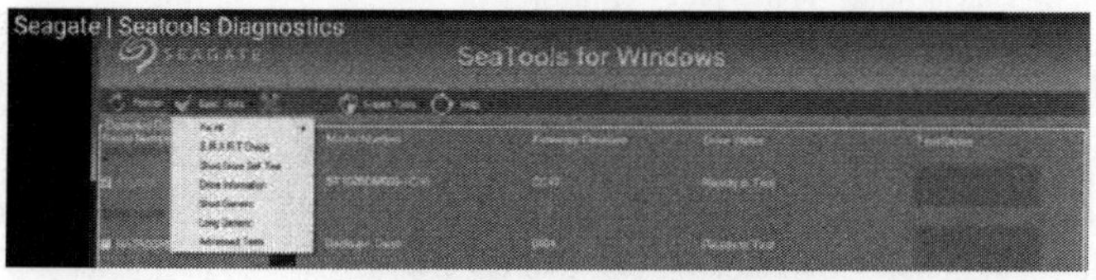

Seagate's SeaTools for Windows

Mismatched Drives

Some RAID systems (especially hardware solutions) insist on having all drives in an array matching (type and size). If a mismatched disk is inserted the controller will not use the drive. It will normally alert support staff, but only if the correct management software has been installed on the OS. Otherwise an administrator may think they have disk redundancy when in fact they are only one disk failure away from disaster! Occasionally a system will recognize an incorrectly sized drive and incorporate it into a RAID array. This may work at first but as the array fills may cause the array to report as being full or having **insufficient space** prematurely. This could cause an OS to crash if the problem was on a system partition.

Backplane Failure

Probably the most damaging failure to occur in a redundant storage environment is a RAID controller backplane failure. The backplane connects all the individual, hot swappable drives into the controller electronics. In most cases, the fault will be on a single drive connector (often caused by rough handling or a damaged drive connector being inserted). On most systems, all drive connectors are universal and, at least in the short term, the drive can be inserted into a different slot until the entire controller is repaired or replaced. As the drives have individual IDs, the controller will piece the RAID array components together correctly.

Using the manufacturer's RAID controller management software, diagnostic tests can be performed to see which drives (and backplane connectors) are visible and working.

Troubleshooting Disk Performance

If file access or I/O performance is slow, you will need to use a tool such as Performance Monitor to discover which counters are varying from the baseline and diagnose the cause. Some typical causes of slow file access are:

- Most file access takes place over a network so check that it is not network performance that is slowing things down.
- If a RAID array is rebuilding, performance will be slower than usual. Try to schedule rebuilds outside peak work hours.
- If a background process such as backup software or anti-virus software is running, it could slow down file access. Try to schedule these processes to run outside peak work hours. Make sure that anti-virus software is configured to exclude the files recommended by the NOS vendor. For example, scanning Windows Update or file replication databases can cause serious performance problems in Windows.
- Check that the RAID cache is enabled and properly tuned. You can balance cache between read and write - if server access patterns have changed you may need to retune the cache to reflect this (for example, if read performance is good but write performance is poor, cache allocation could be the cause of the problem).

Windows offers a feature which allows the OS to use solely the disk hardware write cache (by turning off the Windows Write Buffer cache flushing). This can increase performance but should only be used when the hard drive or storage array in the server has a battery backed write cache of its own. Without this major data corruption could occur in the event of any power failure or interruption.

- If there is insufficient space on a disk (if it is over about 80% full) or if files on the volume are highly fragmented, performance will suffer.
- There may be a fault in the file sharing protocol or client software - check NOS advisories for any known problems affecting particular clients and servers. There may be a patch or hotfix to resolve the problem.
- Check whether there is a firmware update for the drives or the drive controller.
- If the file share is on the same disk as the pagefile, excessive paging could be reducing performance. Try to move the pagefile to a different disk or add more system memory.
- Check whether a single process is performing excessive disk writes - there could be a virus problem or a faulty application.

Review Questions / Module 3 / Unit 3 / Volume Management

Answer these questions to test what you have learned in this unit.

1) What two options does Windows have for making a volume available?
2) A user reports that they cannot access a shared volume mounted on a Windows server. What should you do?
3) True or false? The Disk Management tool lets you see which volumes are low on free space.
4) What Windows utility would you use to identify bad sectors?
5) If you have created a partition on a removable drive in Linux, what command would you use to make it available as a volume?
6) With what type of disk or interface would "Improper termination" be an issue?
7) What command could you use to verify the partition structure of a disk in Linux?
8) What are the two main risks from cache failure on a RAID controller?

Module 3 / Unit 4

Directory Services

Objectives

On completion of this unit, you will be able to:

- Understand the structure of an X.500 directory and the use of LDAP and Active Directory.
- Manage user and group accounts on Windows and Linux servers.
- Use group policy to assign system privileges.

Configuring Directory Services

Directory services are the principal means of providing privilege management and authorization on an enterprise network. Depending on the sort of access control model used, the **owner** or **systems administrator** can share resources (folders, printers and other resources) to make them available for network users. The resources can then be protected with a security system based around the **authentication credentials** provided by each user at logon to gain access to a system-defined **account**. Windows and UNIX / Linux systems all provide versions of this type of security.

When logging on to the network, the user *must* supply logon credentials. This username and password (or other authentication data) are compared with the server's **security database**, and if both match, the user is authenticated. The server security service generates an **access key** for the user. This contains the username and **group memberships** of the authenticated user.

All resources on server-based systems have an **Access Control List (ACL)** that is used to control access to the resource. The access list contains entries for all users and groups that have **permission** to use the resource. It also records the *level* of access available for each entry. For example, an access list may allow a user named **user1** to view the *name* of a file in a folder but not read the file *contents*. Whenever the user *attempts* to access a resource, his or her access key is provided as identification. The server's security service matches username and group memberships from the access key with entries in the access list, and from this, it calculates the user's access privileges.

All this information is stored in a directory. Most directories are based on the LDAP standard. As well as enterprise networking directories, LDAP also provides a model for Internet directory access, such as providing contact lists for IM (Instant Messaging) applications.

Lightweight Directory Access Protocol

A directory is like a database, where an **object** is like a record and things that you know about the object (**attributes**) are like fields. In order for products from different vendors to be interoperable, most directories are based on the same standard.

The main directory standard is the **X.500** series of standards, developed by the **International Telecommunications Union (ITU)** in the 1980s. As this standard is complex, most directory services are implementations of the **Lightweight Directory Access Protocol (LDAP)**. LDAP is not a directory standard but a protocol used to query and update an X.500 directory or any type of directory that can present itself as an X.500 directory. LDAP is widely supported in current directory products (Windows Active Directory, Novell eDirectory, Apple OpenDirectory, or the open source OpenLDAP for instance).

The fact that different products are based on the same standard does not necessarily make them easily interoperable. A vendor's implementation of a standard may not be completely compliant.

LDAP uses TCP and UDP port 389 by default. LDAP can also be used over an encrypted SSL/TLS connection (LDAPS), in which case the default port used is 636.

Under Active Directory, searches can be targeted against an entire forest rather than the local domain controller. A server supporting this type of query is called a Global Catalog server. Using port 3268 rather than 389 initiates a global catalog query.

X.500 Distinguished Names

A **Distinguished Name** is a unique identifier for any given resource within the directory. A distinguished name is made up of *attribute=value* pairs, separated by commas. The most specific attribute is listed first and successive attributes become progressively broader. This most specific attribute is also referred to as the **Relative Distinguished Name**, as it uniquely identifies the object within the context of successive (parent) attribute values.

The types of attributes, what information they contain, and the way object types are defined through attributes (some of which may be required and some optional) is described by the directory **schema**. Some of the attributes commonly used are as follows:

Attribute	Field	Usage
CN	Common Name	Identifies the person or object.
OU	Organizational Unit	A unit or department within the organization.
O	Organization	The name of the organization.
L	Locality	Usually a city or area.
ST	State	A state, province, or county within a country.
C	Country	The country's 2-character ISO code (such as c=US or c=UK).
DC	Domain Component	Components of the object's domain.

For example, the Distinguished Name of a web server operated by Widget in London might be:

```
CN=WIDGETWEB, OU=Marketing, O=Widget, L=London,
ST=London, C=UK, DC=widget, DC=com
```

Directory Information Tree

X.500 directories are hierarchical (a **Directory Information Tree**). Each directory starts at the root and passes through a number of levels of **container** objects, such as country (optional), organization, and organizational units (also optional). Actual network resources, such as users, computers, printers, folders, or files, are referred to as **leaf** objects.

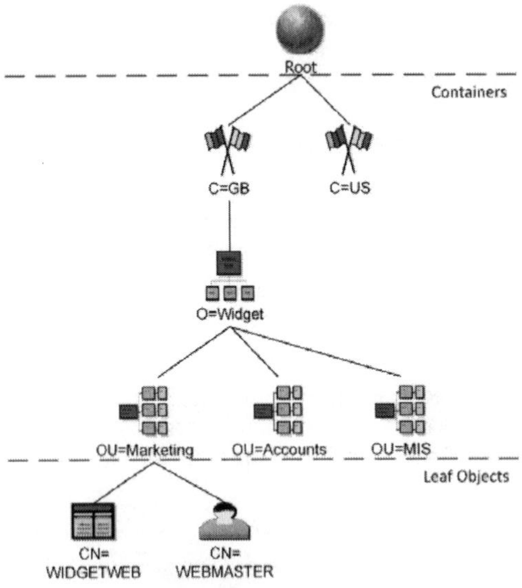

LDAP Directory Information Tree

Active Directory

In server-based Windows networks, the directory service is provided by **Active Directory**. The following notes discuss some of the organizational and administrative principles of planning an AD network. The same principles can apply to networks based around other directory products however.

Domain Controllers

The Active Directory is implemented as a database stored on one or more servers called **Domain Controllers (DC)**. Each server configured with AD maintains a copy of the domain database. The database is multi-master, which means that updates can be made to any copy and replicated to the other servers.

Domain Controllers provide a critical service. Without them, users are not able to log on to the network. The network design should ensure that these services are highly available.

Domains

In legacy Windows networks, **domains** provided the primary grouping of users, groups, and computers. The simplest AD design is a single domain, representing the entire organization. Some organizations may require a more complex structure however.

Trees and Forests

In enterprise networks, multiple domains can be linked in a hierarchy, called a **tree**. For example, the widget.com parent domain (the root of the tree) could contain child domains (sales.widget.com, mis.widget.com, partners.widget.com, and so on). These domains have **two-way transitive trusts**, meaning that (for example) a user account in one domain in the tree could access resources (an application or file server for instance) in another domain.

Using fewer domains (one if possible) simplifies management. It is also cheaper; each domain must be supported by at least one domain controller server. Multiple domains might have been used in earlier Windows networks to provide different security boundaries and policies, delegate administrative control within very large organizations, or reduce replication traffic. In an Active Directory network these goals are generally better met by implementing Organizational Units (OU) or multiple forests (see below) to manage administrative and security boundaries and sites to manage replication traffic.

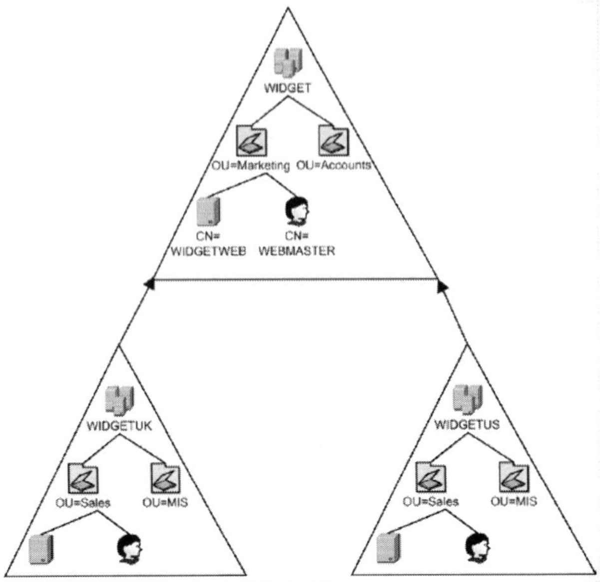

Windows tree

It is possible to configure multiple trees. For example, you might use two different public IDs within your organization. You might have a global ID (widget.com) and national subsidiaries (widget.co.uk and widget.de for instance). These different trees can be linked within the same **forest**. The domains within trees within the same forest also automatically have two-way transitive trusts so (for example) users configured within widget.co.uk could access resources configured within widget.com.

Finally, an enterprise might decide to use *multiple* forests across its network. Creating multiple forests incurs a substantial administrative overhead. The principal reason for doing so would be to create different security boundaries between parts of the organization. For example, a healthcare company might want to completely separate confidential patient data from sales and marketing functions. A user authenticated to the "sales" forest would not be able to access data stored in the "patient" forest. Administrative control is also separated.

The decision to use multiple forests is likely to focus on business needs. For example, there may be legal or regulatory reasons to have separate administrative control over some business functions.

Forests can also have different schemas. For example, installing the Microsoft Exchange communications server makes substantial changes to the AD schema. When testing the rollout of such a product, it may be preferable to install it to a different forest to avoid the complexity of rolling back changes to the production environment should the deployment be cancelled.

Organizational Units

Organizational Units (OU) provide a way of dividing a domain up into different administrative realms. For example, you might create OUs to delegate responsibility for administering different company departments or locations. For example, a "Sales" department manager could be delegated control with rights to add, delete, and modify user accounts but no rights to change account policies, such as requiring complex passwords, or manage users in the "Accounts" OU.

Generally speaking, defining OUs instead of multiple domains will simplify administration.

Sites

When you have networks based at separate geographic locations, you have to consider the effect of replication traffic on the network link. Replication between locations can be managed by configuring **sites**. Within a site (intrasite), replication occurs whenever there is a change or every 7 minutes. Between sites connected by a slow link (intersite) replication can be scheduled to particular times (when it will not impact other network operations) and the replication traffic can be compressed.

It is critical to carefully place domain controllers and DNS servers so that these services remain fully available at each site. If the services fail, users will not be able to access the network.

Member Servers

Member servers are any server-based systems that have been configured into the domain, but do not maintain a copy of the Active Directory database and are therefore unable to provide logon services. Because the user validation process consumes resources, most servers are configured as member servers rather than domain controllers. They will provide file and print and application server services (such as Exchange for email or SQL Server for database or line-of-business applications).

A member server would normally be joined to a domain using an answer file or script as part of an automated install. To add a server to a domain manually, first ensure the server is configured with an appropriate IP address and the address of a suitably configured DNS server. The domain's DNS server uses SVR records to advertise service availability. Use Server Manager to enter the domain name (optionally you can change the host name too) then enter the credentials of an account with permission to join the domain. This would usually be a domain administrator account.

Managing Users

The purpose of a **user account** is to identify the individual as he or she logs on to the computer network. The user's identity is used to determine his or her access to network resources. It is also used for accounting, as actions performed by the user on system settings and resources can be logged and audited. It can also be linked to a **profile** and a **logon script** that define user settings for the workstation.

In Active Directory, users and groups are uniquely identified by a Security Identifier (SID) rather than the user or group name. This means that if the object is deleted and recreated with the same name, it will not inherit permissions granted to the deleted object.

Administrative Accounts

All server-based network operating systems provide an **administrative account**, which has access to all services and resources on a server. In Windows, this account is called **Administrator**; in Linux, it is called **root**.

It is best practice only to use these accounts to install the OS. Subsequently they should be disabled. One or more accounts with administrative privileges are then created for named system admins (so that their actions can be audited). This makes it harder for attackers to identify and compromise an administrative account. This can be referred to as **generic account prohibition**.

It is a good idea to restrict the number of administrative accounts as far as possible (the more accounts there are, the more likely it is that one of them will be compromised). On the other hand, you do not want administrators to share accounts as this compromises accountability.

As well as the administrator account, Windows also has a built-in Guest account. This account has limited privileges but can still logon to the desktop or shut down the machine. The Guest account is disabled by default on all recent versions of Windows.

An administrative account must be used when performing any security or configuration task on the server; for example, changing the system time, adding a user, or providing access to a resource. The latest versions of Windows use User Account Control (UAC) to prevent administrative privileges from being invoked without specific authorization. In older versions administrators can use the Run As shortcut menu or command line option to access administrative privileges for a particular program.

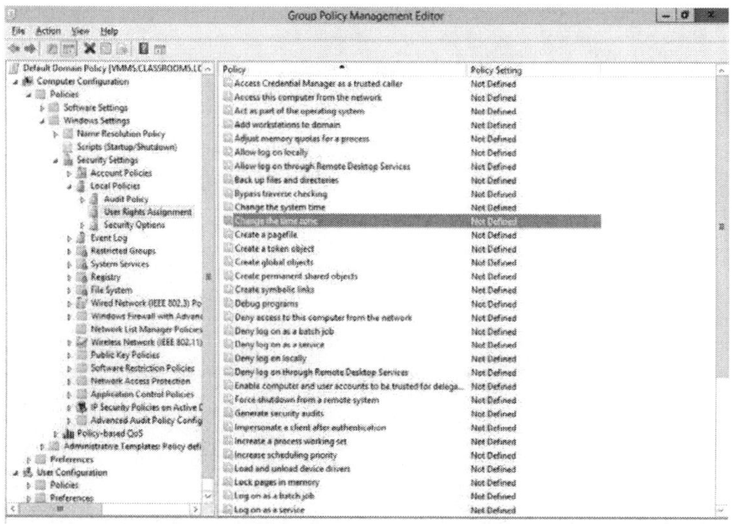

Actions that require administrative privileges are set as defaults in Windows but can also be configured differently if necessary

User Account Management in Windows

In a **Windows Active Directory Domain** environment, before you can manage accounts, you must log in as a user with membership of the **Domain Admins** or **Account Operators** groups. Changes to the domain security database can be *made* from any machine, but a domain controller must be available to accept the updates. A new user account is created by selecting the **New User** option from the context menu in **Active Directory Users and Computers**. If appropriate, a new user may be copied from an existing user or template account.

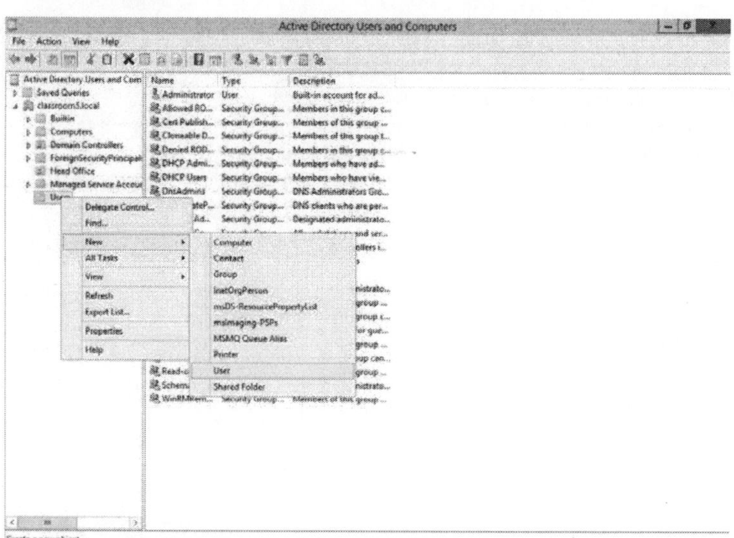

Active Directory Users and Computers console

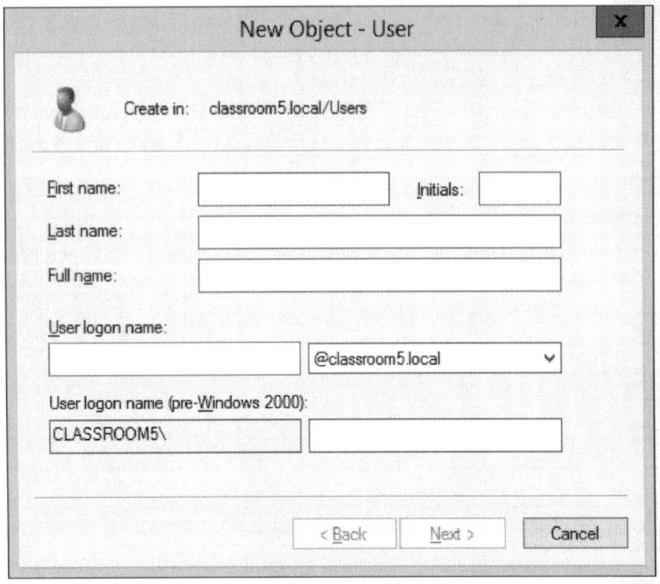

Adding a user account

There is also an option to disable an account rather than deleting it completely. A disabled account cannot be used to logon.

There are also local users and groups stored in the computer's Security Accounts Manager (SAM), which is part of the Registry. These accounts are managed using the **Local Users and Groups** tool. Local accounts can only be granted permissions on resources located on the same computer. User properties can be updated or user objects removed from the same folders.

Creating and Managing Linux User Accounts

Linux, like most operating systems, supports multiple users. These user accounts are linked to a primary group which determines many aspects of security in Linux. User and group settings are stored in the **/etc/passwd** and **/etc/group** files. The user password is typically stored as an encrypted hash in the **/etc/shadow** file, along with other password settings, such as age and expiration date. The command-line utilities `useradd`, `usrmod`, and `userdel` can be used to add, modify, and delete user information.

Many distros have GUI based utilities that allow user and group management. YaST is an example of one of these.

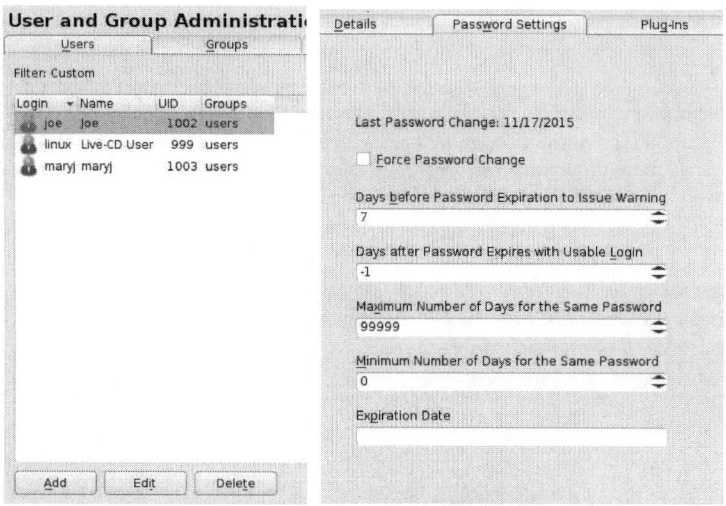

User and group Administration tool in YaST

The open source software **OpenLDAP** is usually used to provide network directory services. As it is based on LDAP, this can be made interoperable with Active Directory.

su (Superuser)

The **su** command allows a normal Linux user to become **superuser** (or **root**). The command will prompt the user for the root user's password. Additionally it is possible to put a different user name after the **su** command and become that user, assuming the password is known.

sudo (Superuser Do)

The **sudo** command allows a normal user to run specified commands with superuser privilege level. The superuser first has to edit the **/etc/sudoers** file listing the commands and users that are allowed to run them. The user enters the **sudo** command followed by the path of the command they wish to run.

passwd (Password Utility)

The **passwd** command allows a user to change their own password or superuser (root) to change or reset someone else's. When a user runs the command, Linux will prompt first for the existing password then the new one, twice. Superuser can reset another user's password by typing the username after the command. The existing password is not required in this case.

```
passwd fredb
```

Managing Group Accounts

System administration can be simplified through the use of **group accounts**. Groups allow you to set **permissions** (or **rights**) for several users at the same time. Users are given membership of the group and then the group is given access to the resource or allowed to perform the action.

Avoid assigning permissions to user accounts directly. This makes permissions very difficult to audit (the process of checking that only valid users have access to given resources).

A user can be a member of multiple groups and can, therefore, receive rights and permissions from several sources.

Domain Local, Global, and Universal Groups

Windows distinguishes between three scopes of group: **domain local**, **global**, and **universal**. The scope of a group refers both to who can be members of the group and where it can be used to determine access permissions.

- **Domain Local** groups can be used to assign rights to resources within the same domain only. Accounts or universal and global groups from any trusted domain can be a member of a domain local group.
- **Global** groups can contain only user and global or universal group accounts from the same domain but can be used to assign rights to resources in any trusted domain (essentially, the opposite of domain local scope).
- **Universal Groups** can contain accounts from any trusted domain and can also be used to grant permissions on any object in any trusted domain.

Microsoft's **AGDLP (Accounts go into Global groups, which go into Domain Local groups, which get Permissions)** system recommends putting user accounts into one or more global groups based on their role(s) within the company. The global groups are then assigned to domain local groups, which are assigned permissions over local resources, such as file shares and printers. This model provides scalability (in case additional domains are added later) and security (it is simpler to audit rights for users based on the role they have within the company).

Smaller organizations, especially those that know they will never have to support multiple domains, may find it simpler just to use global groups and assign both users and permissions to them. AGDLP is useful where the administrative function of assigning users to roles is separate from the administrative function of providing resources for each role.

Don't confuse "Domain Local" groups with "Local groups". "Local" groups can be configured on servers and workstations but only apply to that same computer.

Security and Distribution Groups

One use for groups is to assign permissions to access resources, as described above. This is referred to as a **security group**. You can also configure **distribution groups** or **distribution lists**, used to send messages to lists of recipients. Distribution groups cannot be configured with access permissions.

Built-in and Special Group Accounts

Windows and Active Directory include a number of default groups. These groups are already assigned sets of rights and permissions and can be used to simplify network management. In addition to the built-in groups, Windows includes other groups that have special functions.

Everyone

The **Everyone** group includes all users from all domains. It cannot be deleted. It is often used to provide the default share permission for resources; that is, **Full Control** for all users in the group. To better secure the resource, NTFS permissions are assigned to other groups.

Guest (Anonymous) Users

Windows allows users to attach to the domain without providing a valid username and password. In most cases however the guest account is disabled.

*The users with guest access to the domain **ARE** members of the **Everyone** group, so it is essential that permissions assigned to Everyone are carefully restricted.*

System Groups

System groups are used internally by Windows and they cannot be assigned permissions. System groups include the following:

- **Interactive** – any local user of the computer.
- **Network** – any user connected over the network.
- **System** – the Windows operating system.
- **Creator/owner** – the user who created the directory or print job.

Creating Group Accounts

Groups can be created using either the **Active Directory Users and Computers** tool or **Local Users and Groups**.

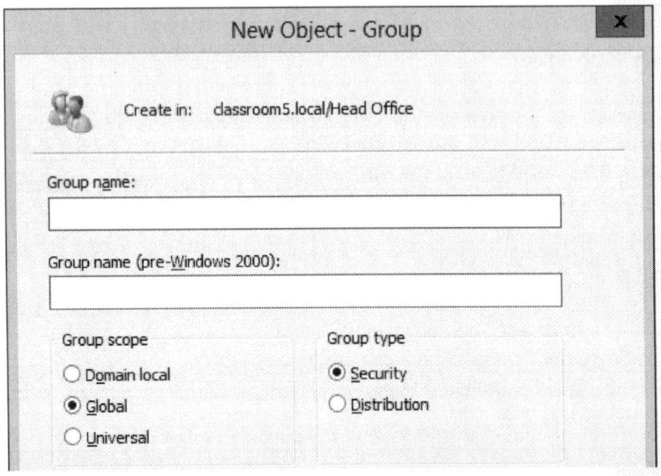

Creating a group in Active Directory

Groups can be created using either the **Active Directory Users and Computers** tool or **Local Users and Groups**. A user's group memberships can also be viewed and modified by selecting the **Member Of** tab on the **User Properties** dialog.

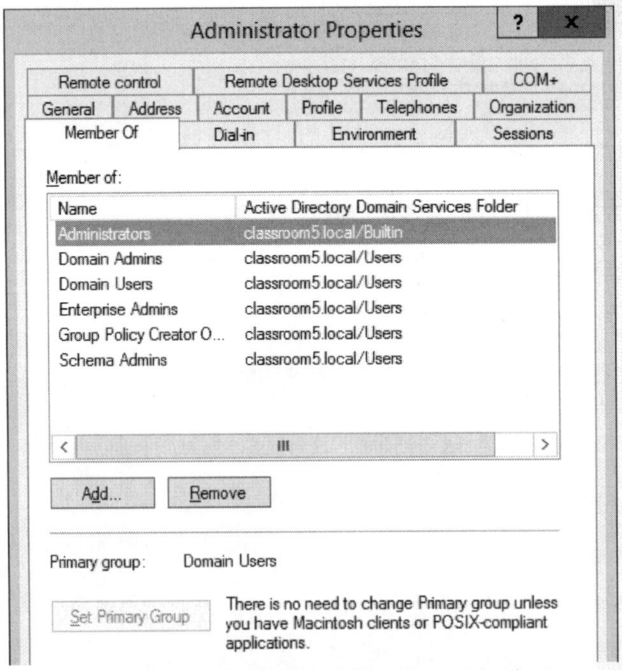

Configuring group memberships via the user properties sheet

It is wise to develop a naming scheme to structure groups and keep them organized. Microsoft recommend distinguishing security and distribution groups and recording the scope of the group within the label. For example, **`DIST-DLG-sales`** would refer to a distribution list for sales used at the domain level; **`SEC-GLO-accounts`** would refer to a global security group for accounts staff.

For local and domain local groups, which should be used to assign permissions to resources, use the server name, file share, and permissions granted. For example, **`SEC-DLG-CX0001-data-read`** would represent a domain local group granted read permissions on a Data folder shared on a server named CX0001.

Linux Group Accounts

In Linux, the **`groupadd`**, **`groupmod`**, and **`groupdel`** commands can be used to manage groups. The **`group`** command lists the groups that a user belongs to.

A user can belong to many groups but can only have one *effective* group ID at any one time. The effective group ID is listed for the user account in **etc/passwd**. A user has to change the "focus" to a different group with the **`newgrp`** command to use that group's permissions.

Account Policy Enforcement

Under Windows, the security configuration of the local machine and what a user is allowed to do are controlled via security policies.

Group Policy

Under Windows Server, policies can be configured for domain objects via **Group Policy Objects (GPO)**.

GPOs are a means of applying security settings (as well as other administrative settings) across a range of computers and users. GPOs are linked to network administrative boundaries in Active Directory, such as sites, domains, and Organizational Units (OU).

GPOs can be used to configure software deployment, Windows settings, and (through the use of **Administrative Templates**) custom Registry settings. Settings can also be configured on a per-user or per-computer basis.

A system of inheritance determines the **Resultant Set of Policies (RSoP)** that apply to a particular computer or user. GPOs can be set to override or block policy inheritance where necessary.

Windows ships with a number of default **security templates** to provide the basis for GPOs (**configuration baselines**). These can be modified using the Group Policy Editor or Group Policy Management Console. GPOs can be linked to objects in Active Directory using the object's property sheet.

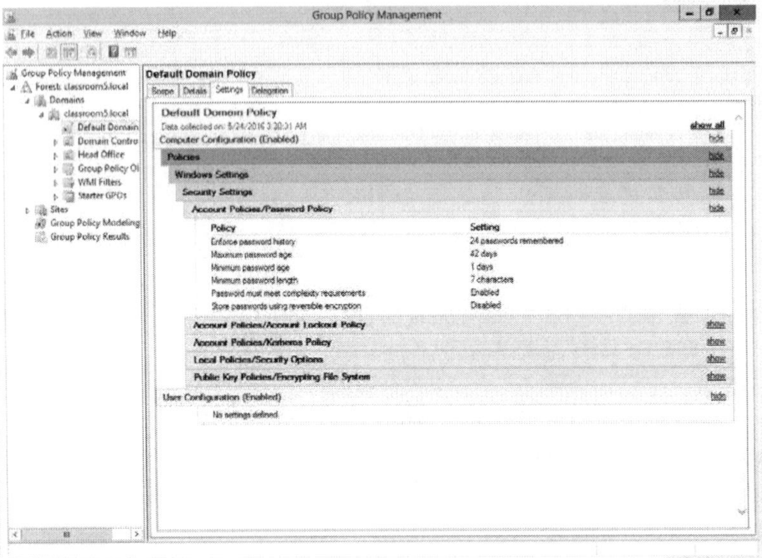

Group Policy Management console

Logon Script

A **logon script** can be linked to a user account. The script runs after the user authenticates. A script can be used to set up the user's profile or configure rights or permissions (if something like group policy is not supported). You can also create log off scripts (to run a backup program for instance).

In Windows logon scripts were historically written using **VBScript**, though they could use a simple batch file populated with command-line instructions. A scripting language provides more support for programming features such as conditional statements and object variables. On modern versions of Windows, the **PowerShell** scripting environment is preferred.

In Linux, the shell is the equivalent of the Windows command prompt. The **bash** shell script supports both simple batch commands and similar functions to VBScript. Other popular choices include **perl** and **Python**.

To run a script in Windows you enter the path to the script in the user's property sheet (**Profile** tab). In Linux, the script is called from **.bash_login** in the user's home directory.

When using a script, you must ensure that the relevant interpreter is installed locally (wscript.exe or cscript.exe for VBScript for instance). You also need to remember that the script will usually run with the privileges of the logged in user.

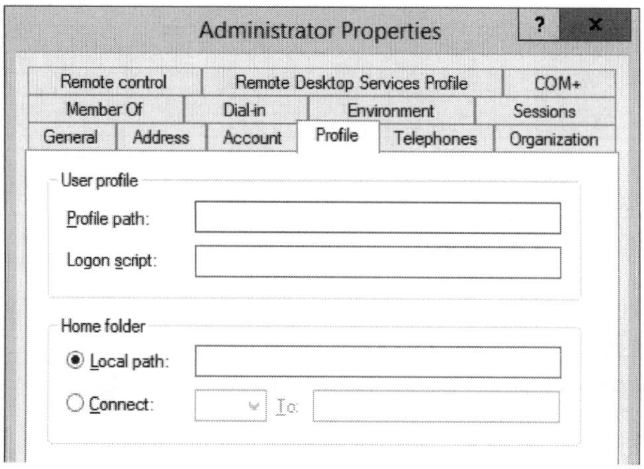

Profile properties for a user

It may be possible to run the script with elevated permissions but you need to find a method of doing that that doesn't involve coding the administrator password in the script, as that is unsecure.

Role-based Access Control

Role-based Access Control (RBAC) adds an extra degree of administrative control to the Discretionary Access Control (DAC) model represented by group accounts. Under RBAC, a set of organizational roles are defined and users allocated to those roles. Under this system, the right to modify roles is reserved to administrative accounts. Therefore the system is non-discretionary, as each user has no right to modify the ACL of a resource, even though they may be able to change the resource in other ways. Users are said to gain rights *implicitly* (through being assigned to a role) rather than *explicitly* (being assigned the right directly).

Ideally, the rights of a role are set at design time and not changed under normal operating conditions. This means that administrators can focus on membership of different role groups, rather than what the roles can do. It also makes it harder for an attacker to "escalate" permissions gained through a hacked user account.

RBAC can be *partially* implemented in Windows through the concept of group accounts. To fully implement RBAC, you also need to define what tasks users can perform in a given application. Object-based ACLs are not flexible enough to do this. You also need to "turn off" the discretionary aspect of the underlying OS - not something that is currently supported by Windows.

Review Questions / Module 3 / Unit 4 / Directory Services

Answer these questions to test what you have learned in this unit.

1) What protocol allows for interoperability between different directory standards, such as Active Directory and eDirectory?
2) What is the lowest level container for leaf objects in an X.500 directory?
3) True or false? Any Windows server participating in a domain must be joined to the domain as a Domain Controller.
4) In Windows, the account named "administrator" is rarely used and often disabled after installation. What security policy describes this?
5) When configuring Linux, what is the significance of the "root" user?
6) In Linux, what file stores user accounts?
7) What command should a Linux user run to perform a task requiring administrator privileges?
8) What is the meaning of AGDLP?
9) In Linux, which command sets a user's current group membership?
10) What tool can be used to configure computer settings automatically on logon in a Windows network?

Module 3 / Unit 5
File and Print Services

Objectives

On completion of this unit, you will be able to:

- Configure shares and NTFS permissions on Windows and permissions on a Linux file system.
- Configure and troubleshoot print services.

Configuring File Shares

File and Print services are two of the core functions of Network Operating Systems. Security is enforced by **Access Control Lists (ACL)**, that is, each resource is configured with a list of authorized users and their permissions.

Sharing Folders in Windows

In Windows, sharing a folder makes it available over the network. Sharing is configured through the folder properties (on the **Sharing** tab) by giving the share a name and (optionally) limiting the number of users able to access the share at the same time.

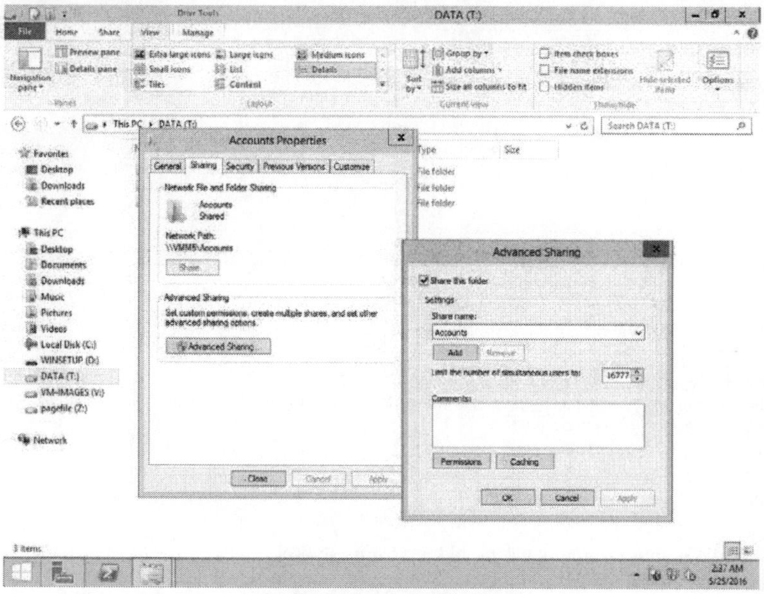

Configuring a share in Windows

Share permissions can be defined to determine which users will have access over the network. Windows provides three levels of share permissions:

- **Full Control** - allows users to read, edit, create, and delete files and subdirectories, and to assign permissions to other users and groups.
- **Change** - this is similar to full control but does not allow the user to set permissions for others.
- **Read** - users are permitted to connect to the resource, run programs, and view files. They are not allowed to edit, delete, or create files.

Each permission may be either **allowed** or **denied** for each user or group object. Users are *implicitly* denied access unless they have been granted an allow permission. *Explicitly* denying a share permission always overrides an allowed permission. For example, if the Everyone group is allowed Full Control, but the Users group is denied Full Control, members of the Users group will be denied full control. In most cases, shares are established by giving the Everyone group Full Control. Specific user or group permissions are then configured using the more secure and flexible system of NTFS permissions (see below).

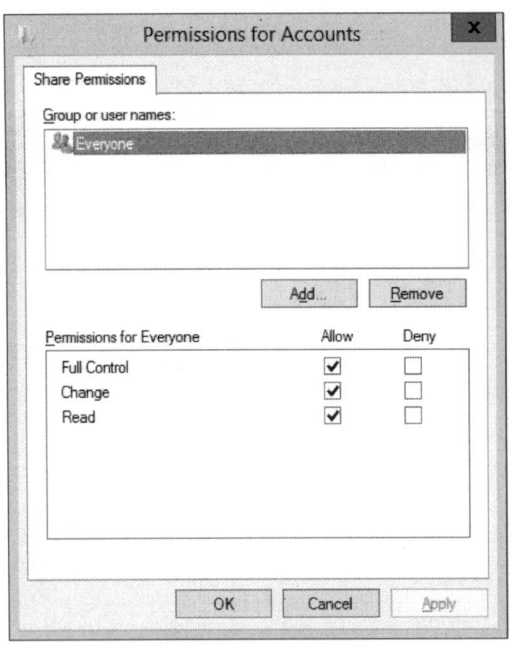

Configuring share permissions - add user or group accounts to the share then configure allow or deny permissions for each account

Administrative Shares

If you add a $ sign at the end of the share name, it will be hidden from general browsing but can still be accessed via the command-line or by mapping a drive to the share name. Windows automatically creates a number of hidden **administrative** shares, including the root drive (C$) and the system folder (ADMIN$).

net Commands

There are a number of **net** command utilities that can be used to view and configure shared file and print resources. We will only consider a few of the commands here, but you can view the full list by entering `net /?` You can view help on a specific command by (for example) entering `net use /?`

- `net use` ***`DeviceName`*** `\\`***`ComputerName`***`\`***`ShareName`*** - connect to a network resource, such as a folder or printer. For example, to map the DATA folder on MYSERVER to the M: drive, you would enter

  `net use M: \\MYSERVER\DATA /persistent:yes`

  To redirect print output sent to LPT2 to a printer shared as "OfficePrinter" from MYSERVER, you would enter:

  `net use LPT2: \\MYSERVER\OfficePrinter /persistent:yes`
- `net use` ***`DeviceName`*** `/delete` - remove a connection (`net use * /delete` removes all connections).
- `net use` - view connections on the local computer; use `net use \\`***`ComputerName`*** to view connections on another computer.
- `net stop` ***`Service`*** - stops the named service. For example, to stop the printer service, you would enter: `net stop spooler`.
- `net start` ***`Service`*** - starts the named service.
- `net print \\`***`ComputerName`***`\`***`QueueName`*** - shows the named print queue.

The **netsh** commands are also enormously useful for configuring Windows network services and clients via the command line.

Linux File Shares

Linux can use a number of file sharing protocols. The Network File System (NFS) allows sharing between Linux machines (and with UNIX); Samba allows for file sharing with Windows (the Server Message Block [SMB] protocol). To share using NFS for example, the directory needs to be added to the **/etc/export** file on the server computer and the relevant permissions configured (see below).

On the client computer, the share is mounted to a particular directory (**mount point**) using the `mount` command. For example:

```
mount 192.168.1.1:/share /mnt/nfs/lamp
```

...mounts the directory "share" located on the host with IP 192.168.1.1 to the directory "/mnt/nfs/lamp" on the local file system.

Windows can be installed with the NFS Server role to facilitate file sharing with UNIX-like OSs. NFS Client software is also available.

NTFS File and Folder Permissions

The share permissions described above ensure that the resource is protected when users connect over the network. Unfortunately, share permissions have a number of limitations:

- The resource is only protected when a user connects over the network. Someone gaining access to the local machine would not have the same restrictions.
- The permissions set apply from the root of the share and all subdirectories and files within the share assume the same permissions.

Volumes formatted with the FAT file system are only able to support share permissions but with NTFS it is possible to implement a much more comprehensive and flexible system of permissions. NTFS security protects the resource even when it is accessed locally and has a configurable system of propagation and inheritance.

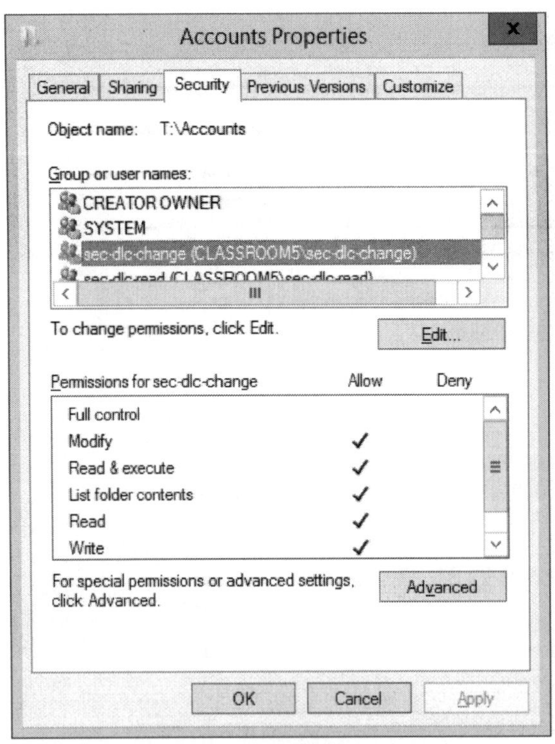

Security tab for a folder (NTFS permissions)

Windows enforces local security on an NTFS volume by holding an **Access Control List (ACL)** as part of the record for each file and folder stored in the volume's **Master File Table (MFT)**. When a user attempts to access a file or directory, the security system checks which users and groups are listed in the **ACL**. A list of permissions is then obtained for that user.

Security can be applied to individual files or (more commonly) to folders. When folders are secured, the matter of **inheritance** needs to be considered.

Configuring NTFS Permissions

To configure the NTFS security settings of a file or folder, select the **Security** tab of the object's **Properties** dialog. To set local file and directory permissions, you must either be the **owner** of the object or have the **P** (**Change Permissions**) permission to the file. The **Advanced options** button allows for a change of ownership. Members of the **Administrators** and **Server Operators** groups can always set NTFS permissions. Each permission may be either allowed or explicitly denied for each user or group object. If no explicit permission exists, an implicit deny prevents access. Permissions that may be applied to folders differ from those that apply to files.

Folder Permissions

Permission	Allows
Read	View files and subfolders including their attributes, permissions, and ownership.
Write	Create new folders and files, change attributes, view permissions, and ownership.
List	View the names of files and subfolders.
Read & Execute	Pass-through folders for which no permissions are assigned, plus read and list permissions.
Modify	Includes Read / Execute and Write permissions, as well as the ability to rename and delete the folder.
Full Control	All the above, plus changing permissions, taking ownership and deleting subfolders and files.

File Permissions

Permission	Allows
Read	Read the contents of the file and view attributes, ownership, and permissions.
Write	Overwrite the file and view attributes, ownership, and permissions.
Read & Execute	Read permissions, plus the ability to run applications.
Modify	Includes Read / Execute and Write permissions, as well as the ability to rename and delete the file.
Full Control	All the above, plus changing permissions and taking ownership.

These are available via the basic interface. There are in fact twelve individual permissions that could be applied to a file or folder (click Advanced), but the combinations listed are usually sufficient.

Effective Permissions and Allow Versus Deny

Generally speaking, permissions are usually applied at one of three levels:

- For application folders, the read / execute permission is granted to the appropriate group.
- For data areas, the modify or read permission is assigned as appropriate.
- To home directories (personal storage areas on a network), full control is assigned to the relevant user.

A user may obtain multiple permissions from membership of different groups (or by having permissions allocated directly to his or her account). As with share permissions, an explicit "Deny" overrides anything else (in most cases) but otherwise the user obtains the most effective "allow" permissions. For example, if one group gives the user "Read" permission and another group gives the user "Modify" permission, the user will have "Modify" permission.

Permission Propagation and Inheritance

NTFS permissions that are assigned to a folder are automatically **inherited** by the files and subfolders created under the folder. To prevent this from happening, open the **Security** page and click **Advanced**.

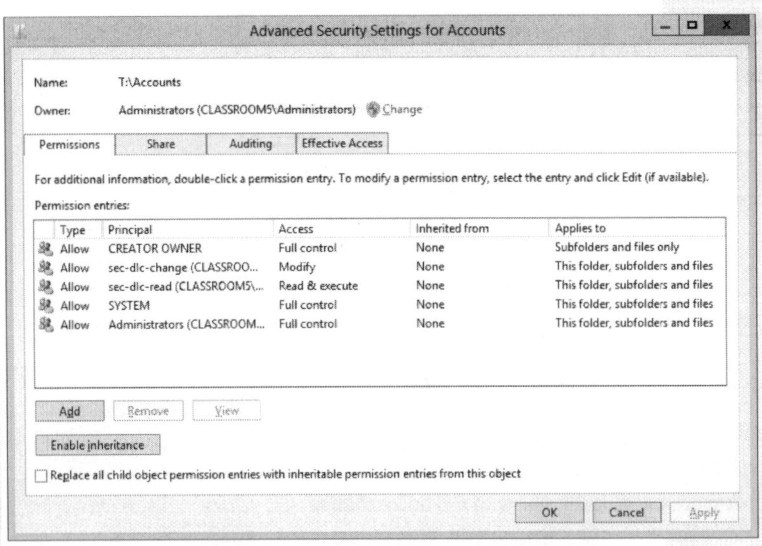

Configuring permissions inheritance on a folder

Click the **Disable inheritance** button or uncheck the **Include inheritable permissions** box (on earlier versions). Then choose whether to **Convert inheritable permissions into explicit permissions** (alternatively the **Copy** option) or **Remove** inherited permission. You can then modify the permissions on this folder independently of its parent.

To apply security settings for the current folder to all child objects (permission propagation), check the **Replace all child object permissions with inheritable permissions** box.

Directly assigned permissions (explicit permissions) always override inherited permissions, including "deny" inherited permissions. For example, if a parent folder specifies deny write permissions but an account is granted allow write permissions directly on a child file object, the effective permission will be to allow write access on the file object.

Ownership

The **owner** of a resource can manage that resource in terms of permissions and other attributes. Generally speaking, if a user *creates* a file they will *own* the file.

Administrators can assign ownership to some other user (or group). This might be done because the current owner of a resource has been deleted from the user accounts database.

When a folder's ownership details are modified, the administrator can choose to propagate the changes down the tree to subfolders and their contents.

Moving and Copying NTFS Files and Folders

The behavior of NTFS permissions when moving and copying files under Windows is summarized in the table below:

Action	Effect
Moving files and folders on the same NTFS volume	Write permission is required for the destination folder and Modify for the source folder. NTFS permissions are retained.
Moving files and folders to a different NTFS volume	Write permission is required for the destination folder and Modify for the source folder. NTFS permissions are inherited from the destination folder and the user becomes the Creator/Owner.
Copying files and folders on the same NTFS volume or different NTFS volumes	Write permission is required for the destination folder and Read for the source folder. NTFS permissions are inherited from the destination folder and the user becomes the Creator/Owner.
Moving files and folders to a FAT or FAT32 partition	Modify permission is required for the source folder. All permissions and NTFS attributes (such as encryption) are lost, as FAT does not support permissions or special attributes.

Combining NTFS and Share Permissions

It is possible to use a combination of share and NTFS permissions to secure resources. The factors to consider are as follows:

- Share permissions only protect the resource when it is accessed across the network.
- NTFS permissions are used to protect the resource from unauthorized local access.
- Disk partitions using the FAT file system can only be protected using share permissions.
- Share permissions are set at the root of the share and all files and subdirectories inherit the same permissions.
- NTFS permissions are used in combination with the share permissions to provide greater flexibility; for example, to place more restrictive permissions at lower levels in the directory structure.
- If both share and NTFS permissions are applied to the same resource, the *most restrictive* applies (when the file or folder is accessed over the network). For example, if the group "Everyone" has **Read** permission to a share and the "Users" group is given **Modify** permission through NTFS permissions, the effective permissions for a member of the "Users" group will be **Read**.

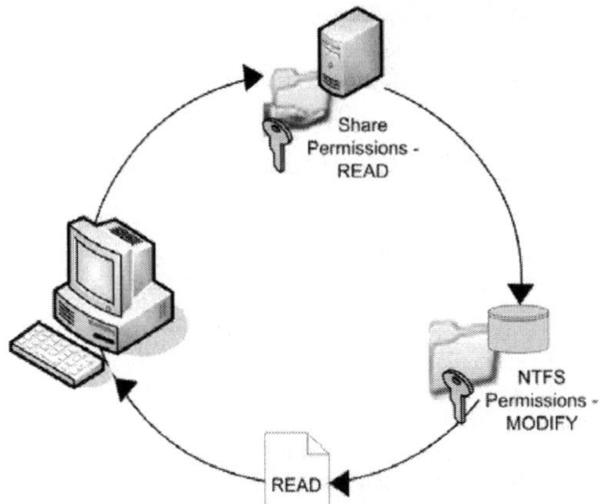

Effective Permissions through a Shared Folder

If you do not have sufficient permissions to access or modify a resource, you will see an "Access denied" error message.

Securing a Linux File System

The Linux file system has a relatively simple security system compared to Windows NTFS. There are just three different rights as shown in the table below:

Access Right	Grants
Read (r)	View the contents of a file or directory.
Write (w)	Modify or delete the object (in the case of directories, allows adding, deleting, or renaming files within the directory).
Execute (x)	Run an executable file or script. For directories, execute allows the user to do things like change the focus to the directory and access or search items within it.

For each object, these permissions are set for the **owner**, the **group** the owner belongs to, and for **other** users ("the world"). Using symbolic notation, each permission is allowed (**r** or **w** or **x**) or denied (**-**). If you run `ls -l` to obtain a directory listing, directory or file object permissions will be shown as follows:

```
drwxr-xr-x 2 administrator administrator Desktop
-rw-rw-r-- 1 administrator administrator MEMO.txt
```

The leading character designates the file type. For example, `-` represents a regular file and `d` indicates a directory. The permissions for the "Desktop" directory show that the owner (administrator) has full (rwx) permissions while the group (also administrator) and "other" have read and execute (r-x). For the "MEMO.txt" file, the user and group have read/write (rw-) permissions while "other" has read permissions only (r--).

Permissions can also be expressed numerically, using the octal value format shown below. An octal value can represent up to eight digits (0-7):

Digit	Permission	Binary Value	Rights
0	- - -	0000	Deny all
1	- - x	0001	Execute
2	- w -	0010	Write
3	- w x	0011	Write and execute
4	r - -	0100	Read-only
5	r – x	0101	Read and execute
6	r w -	0110	Read and write
7	r w x	0111	Allow all

So, for example, a file with numeric permission **0775** (the leading zero is identifies the value as an octal, but can often be omitted) grants all rights to the owner and the owner's group and Read / Execute rights to everyone else.

Alternatively, remember that Execute=1, Write=2, and Read=4 - add those values together to get a particular combination of permissions.

From the shell, the **chmod** command can be used to secure files and folders, using either symbolic or octal notation. Only the owner can change permissions. The command **chown** allows the superuser to change the owner of a file or directory while **chgrp** can be used to change the group.

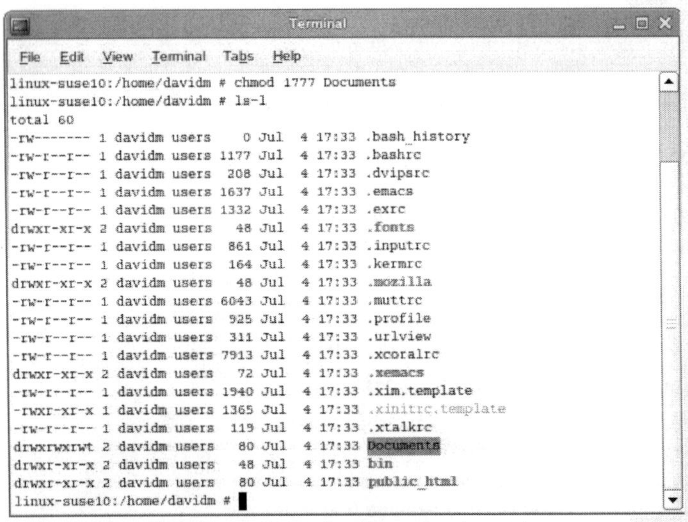

Setting permissions from the command prompt

As with Windows, what can be achieved at the command prompt can more easily be achieved using the GUI. In SUSE Linux, one of a number of GUI shells can be used to configure permissions.

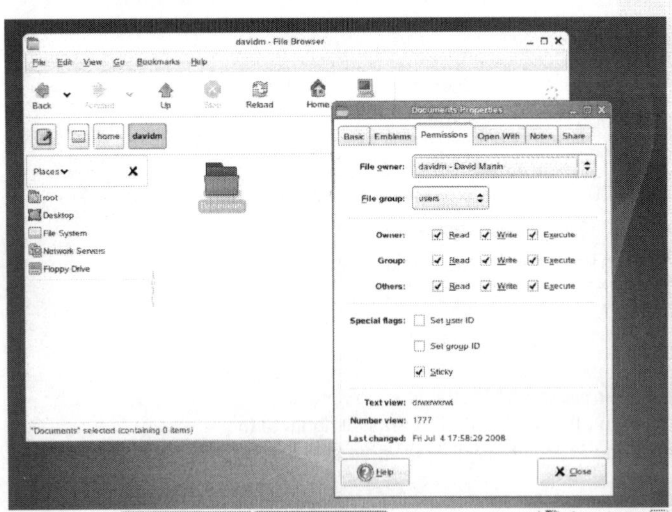

Setting permissions from the GUI

Print Servers

As well as hosting disk resources (sharing folders and files) another basic server task is acting as a **print server**. There are two main options for sharing a printer on the network: Windows printer sharing and hardware print server sharing.

Integrated Hardware Print Servers / NAS

Some printers come with integrated or embedded print server hardware and firmware, allowing client computers to connect to them over the network without having to go via a server computer. You can also purchase print servers or use a solution such as a Network Attached Storage (NAS) device that supports print sharing. Many wireless Internet routers can be configured to work as a NAS / print server solution. The manufacturer's management software (such as HP Jetadmin) can be used to detect, configure, and share the device.

You can also purchase external print servers, such as HP's Jetdirect, that connect to a USB or parallel port on the printer and to the network via a standard port.

HP print server (Image © 2014 Hewlett-Packard Development Company)

In place of a standard network card, a printer could be fitted with a Wi-Fi wireless adapter to make it available in a wireless network.

A network printer needs to be configured so that it has a valid address. On a TCP/IP network, you might set the printer to obtain an address automatically via a DHCP server or configure it with a static IP address and subnet mask. The printer will need to communicate with computers over one or more Transmission Control Protocol (TCP) or User Datagram Protocol (UDP) network ports. If a network connection cannot be established, verify that these ports are not being blocked by a firewall or other security software.

Most printers provide a mechanism for locally configuring the printer. Usually, this is by means of a menu system which you navigate by using an LCD display and adjacent buttons or a touchscreen on the front of the printer.

Configuring the IP address via the printer's front panel

This method is suitable for small office environments where you have few printers to manage. It is also useful in troubleshooting situations when the printer is inaccessible from the network. However, the printer vendor will usually supply a web-based utility to discover and manage their printers while more advanced management suites are available for enterprise networks.

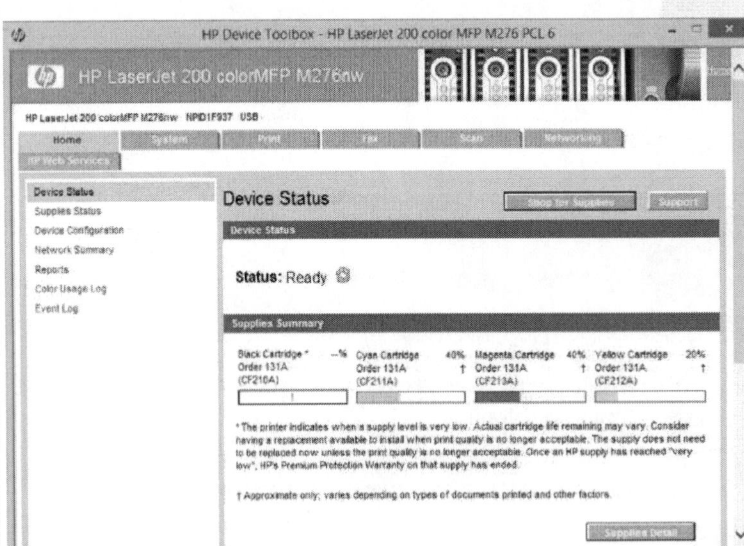

Managing an HP printer using a browser

Windows Print Server

An administrator can share any locally installed printer via its **Sharing** tab in the **Properties** dialog. Locally installed means that Windows communicates with the print device directly over the relevant port. It does not matter whether the port is wired (USB, serial, or Ethernet) or wireless (Bluetooth or Wi-Fi).

Note that when configuring sharing, only one Windows server should be designated as the server for any one print device. If multiple machines try to act as the server for the same print device, the result will be confusion. Drivers for different operating systems can also be installed locally so that clients can obtain the appropriate driver when connecting to the print share.

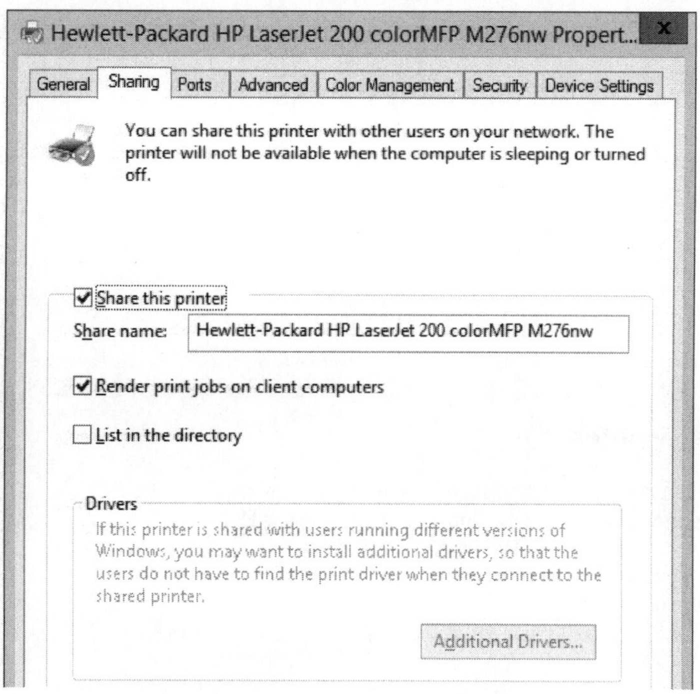

Sharing a printer via the Printer Properties dialog

If the network has clients running a mix of different operating systems, you need to consider how to make a printer driver available for each supported client. If the printer supports a "Type 3" driver, you need only add x86 (32-bit Windows) and / or x64 (64-bit Windows) support. For earlier "Type 2" drivers, each specific Windows version requires its own driver.

Windows Server 2012 adds support for Type 4 drivers. These are designed to move towards a print class driver framework, where a single driver will work with multiple devices. Where a specific print device driver is required, the client obtains it from Windows Update rather than the print server.

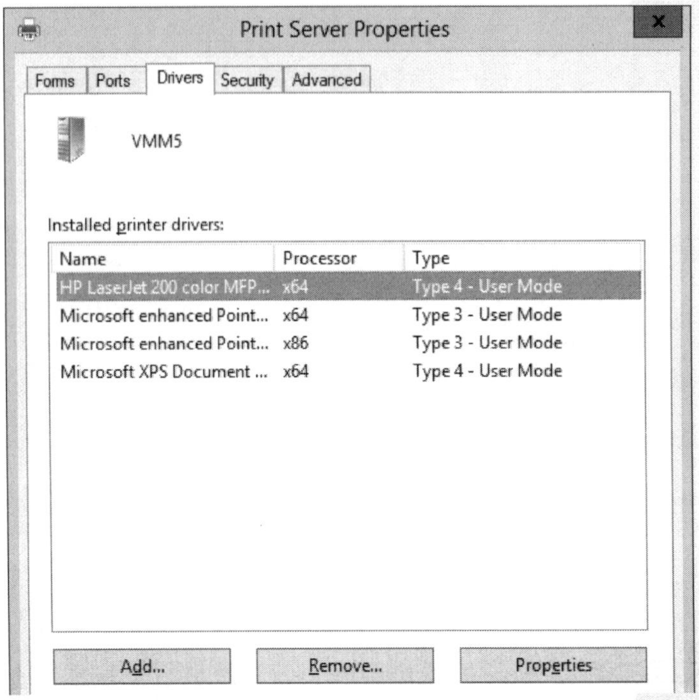

Configuring a Windows print server to install drivers for operating systems other than the host

Connecting to a Shared Printer

An ordinary user can connect to a network printer (assuming that the printer administrator has given them permissions to use it). One way of doing this is to browse through the network resources using the **Network** object in File Explorer. Open the server computer hosting the printer then right-click the required printer and select **Connect**.

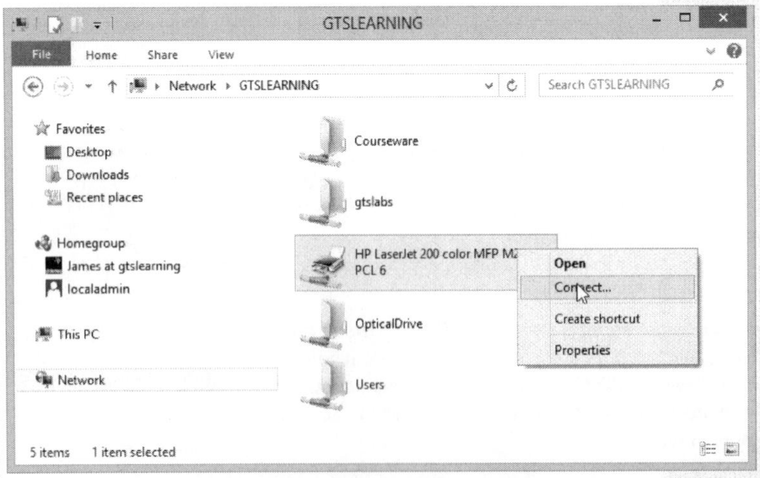

Connecting to a network printer via File Explorer

Alternatively, you can use the **Device Setup** wizard. If the printer is not auto-discovered, you can select how you want to locate the printer.

Print Device Permissions

Printer permissions are used to determine which users are allowed to send jobs to a printer or configure it. Windows provides four printer permissions:

- **Print** - use the printer to print documents.
- **Manage Printers** - print documents, adjust printer settings, change sharing status, pause and restart the printer, change spooler settings, and so on.
- **Manage Documents** - control the print queue.
- **Deny** - overrides all other permissions.

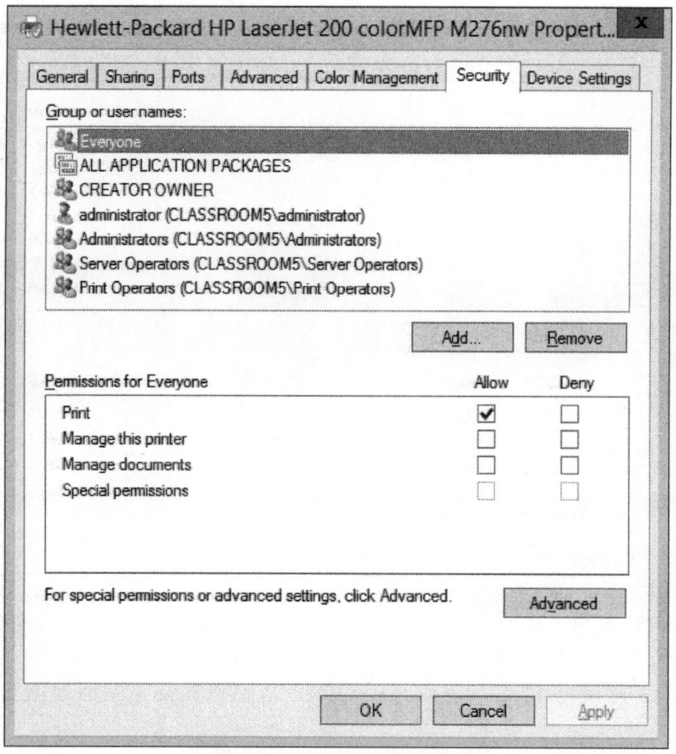

Security tab for Printer Properties

Print Problems

If users cannot print, first verify that the print device is online and working (print a test page at the device then print a test page from the server). If you cannot print a test page from the server, check the network link or printer cable. If these are fine, try clearing the print queue and restarting the print spooler service.

If there is no problem between the server and the printer, and only a single user (or specific group of users) is experiencing a problem, the most likely cause is that the server is not making the correct driver available for the client's workstation (perhaps the workstation is 64-bit and the server only has 32-bit drivers installed or vice versa). You should also check that the user has permission to use the printer. After that, you would have to investigate whether the application has some particular problem with the print driver.

If a particular job will not print, double-click the printer to open its print queue. Try restarting the job (right-click the document name). You need permission to "Manage Documents" on the printer object to restart or cancel jobs. If that does not work, delete it and try printing again. Many problems, including "Low memory" or "Out of memory" errors, can also be solved by cycling the power on the printer and clearing a backed up print queue.

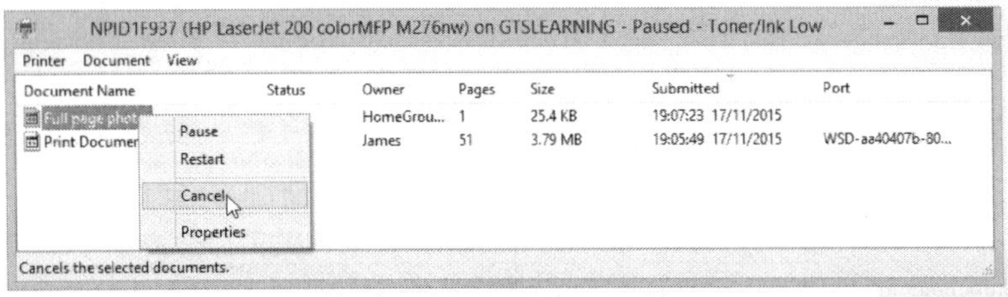

Use the print queue to manage jobs

If you cannot delete a job (if the print queue is stalled), you will need to stop the **Print Spooler** service. Open the **Services** snap-in.

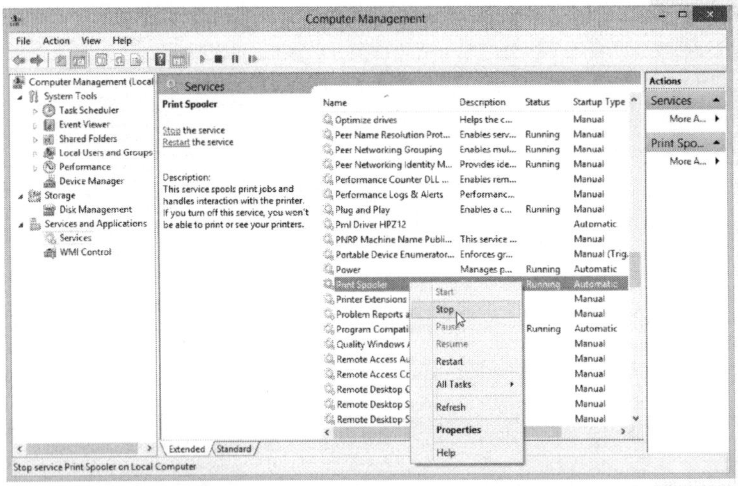

Managing the spooler service using the Computer Management console

Right-click the **Print Spooler** service and select **Stop**. Use Windows Explorer to delete the spooled file from **%SystemRoot%\System32\Spool\Printers**. There will be a *.SPL file (the print job) and possibly a *.SHD file (status information) too. Start the Print Spooler service again.

Alternatively you can use "net" commands to manage the spooler service. Enter the commands **`net stop spooler`** and **`net start spooler`** at the **Run** dialog or command prompt.

Review Questions / Module 3 / Unit 5 / File and Print Services

Answer these questions to test what you have learned in this unit.

1) How would you connect to a network share TOOLS located on a server named BIGJOBS using the T drive letter for the current session only?
2) What permission allows users to modify permissions in Windows?
3) True or false? Both local and network permissions can be enforced on FAT32 partitions.
4) What file permissions can be set under Linux?
5) What would the command 'chmod 644 index.htm' accomplish?
6) If a printer is connected directly to the network anyway, what are the advantages of hosting it via a Windows server?

Module 3 / Unit 6

Troubleshooting Software

Objectives

On completion of this unit, you will be able to:

- Use monitoring tools for Windows and Linux.
- Access system logs for Windows and Linux servers.
- Troubleshoot problems with server operating systems and applications.

Server Monitoring

With monitoring tools, you will usually have the option of choosing between vendor tools and the utilities provided with the server OS.

Health Monitoring

Tools can be used to alert administrators to (and provide early warning of) problems such as device temperature, fan speeds, voltage fluctuations, disk failure, chassis intrusion, component failure, and so on.

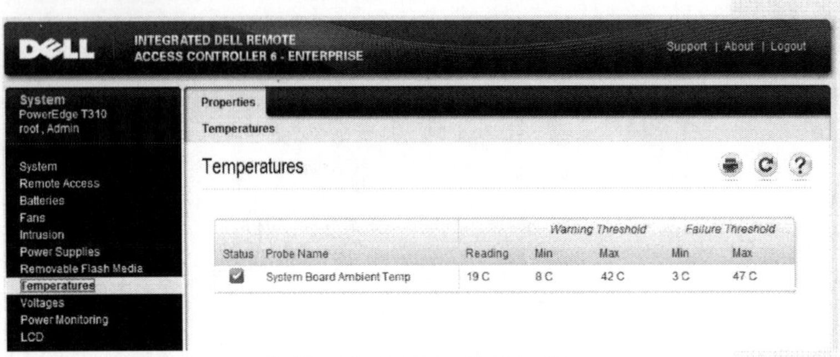

Dell remote access monitoring utility

Server vendors normally ship monitoring and diagnostic tools with all server models (though enterprise software for managing tens or hundreds of servers may have to be purchased). These tools provide "Lights Out Management" and do not depend on the OS running.

Performance Monitoring

When you install a network server for a given purpose, you will have tried to anticipate user demand for the service you wish to provide, and will have installed a server with the appropriate hardware resources. As time goes by, users' demands on the system will increase, making additional demands on the server's resources until a point is reached where service availability and/or throughput is compromised to such an extent that users begin to experience problems. You then add resources to the server and the cycle begins again. Performance Monitoring allows you to determine that resources are being stretched before the point is reached where service function is impaired.

Establishing a Baseline

From time-to-time, you may have experienced a situation where a network suddenly stops performing well. Perhaps it takes an age to access a website or a document that previously took a few moments to copy down from a file server now takes several minutes. This is (informal) performance monitoring, with comparison to a baseline. In this case, the baseline is your personal experience of the responsiveness of the network under a given load.

An administrator needs to establish a more accurate baseline for comparison, in order to measure system responsiveness at a later date. A good time to do baselining is prior to the system going live. Build your network, choose the appropriate resource configuration, and then place a simulated load on the network (for which third-party and vendor specific tools exist). Then collect statistics for resource usage and network performance for future analysis. Changes to the system require a new baseline to be taken. Some examples of when this should be done are:

- Hardware or software upgrade.
- Installation of new devices / services.
- Changed user access volume or patterns.
- Changed server role.

Establishing Thresholds

Thresholds are points of reduced or poor performance that generate an administrative alert. Examples include packet loss, link bandwidth drops, number of sessions established, low disk space, and so on. Setting thresholds is a matter of balance. On the one hand you do not want performance to deteriorate to the point that it affects user activity; on the other you do not want to be overwhelmed by performance alerts.

Key Server Resources

A server has four key resources: Memory, Disk, Processor, and Network. These are the resources that determine a server's throughput in a given situation. Which of these is the most important is dependent upon several factors. What the optimum configuration is for each is also variable.

Memory Utilization

The memory in a server is the working area, and generally speaking, the more memory you have, and the faster it is, the better the server will perform. This is especially true for file servers, which need to service requests from network clients and pass these through to the disk sub-system as fast as possible.

In most operating systems, if you have more memory than you need to run programs, then the excess is allocated to file cache. File cache comes in different forms:

- Read caching, in which data read is stored in memory in case it is needed again.
- Read-ahead caching in which the operating system makes assumptions on what data will be requested next, and retrieves that data, storing it in memory in case it is needed.
- Lazy writing (or write-behind caching) in where requests being written to the disk are deferred (held in memory), allowing the user to proceed without the need to wait for the disk write to complete.

File servers need plenty of fast memory

Servers which function as file servers need plenty of high speed memory. In addition, application servers, which process requests from clients in the local processor (such as SQL Server or messaging systems like GroupWise) need plenty of memory as working space. This is to service programs, rather than disk access.

Disk Utilization

As we have seen, a file server will make requests of the disk sub-system - either read or write requests, which can be measured in terms of Input/Output Operations per Second (IOPS). Having plenty of memory will enable caching, which allows a degree of optimization even in a poorly configured disk system. However, that is not enough on its own. With an optimized disk sub-system, a file server will perform far better.

File servers also need a super-fast disk sub-system

It is also worth noting than most operating systems support swap files (also known as virtual memory). This an area on disk set aside for the situation when the operating system has insufficient memory available to satisfy a memory request, perhaps for application program needs. Pages of memory are moved to the swap file, freeing physical RAM to service the request. Clearly, this imposes an additional load on the disk. As such, a server with insufficient memory will impose more load on the disk sub-system.

The final point to note is capacity. You need to ensure that storage capacity is sufficient as running out of space on a volume can cause critical errors and degrade performance.

CPU Utilization

A file server doesn't do much processing; it merely handles disk requests for client machines. However, an application server, such as a database platform like MySQL, will need a high-end processor configuration because it is performing processing on behalf of client machines. If insufficient processor resource is available, client requests will be handled slowly.

Optimize the processor for application servers

Network Utilization

Any kind of server will be receiving requests from the network from many client machines. The client only needs to communicate with one, or perhaps several, servers. However, a server supports connections from perhaps hundreds of users.

Good network configuration for network services

The network infrastructure becomes crucial for servers but more so for servers of a specific type. File and media servers need an optimized network, so that the end-to-end delay for saving or retrieving a file is as low as possible. If the memory and disk are optimized, then delay can still be introduced through poor network configuration.

Any server providing network services such as DNS or DHCP will need to support high volumes of traffic at particular times of the day. The network external to the server can be optimized in terms of cabling choice, speed of network (Gigabit Ethernet versus older networks), use of switches, and so on. This throughput and performance can be measured using third-party tools and network analyzers.

Measuring Performance in Windows

Windows comes with a number of tools to help to evaluate and measure system performance.

Task Manager and Resource Monitor

The **Task Manager** utility allows an administrator to see a quick snapshot of system performance (CPU and network utilization for instance). In recent versions of Windows Server, Task Manager is supplemented by **Resource Monitor**.

Like Task Manager, Resource Monitor is also used to view performance data in real time but there is far more information available to display.

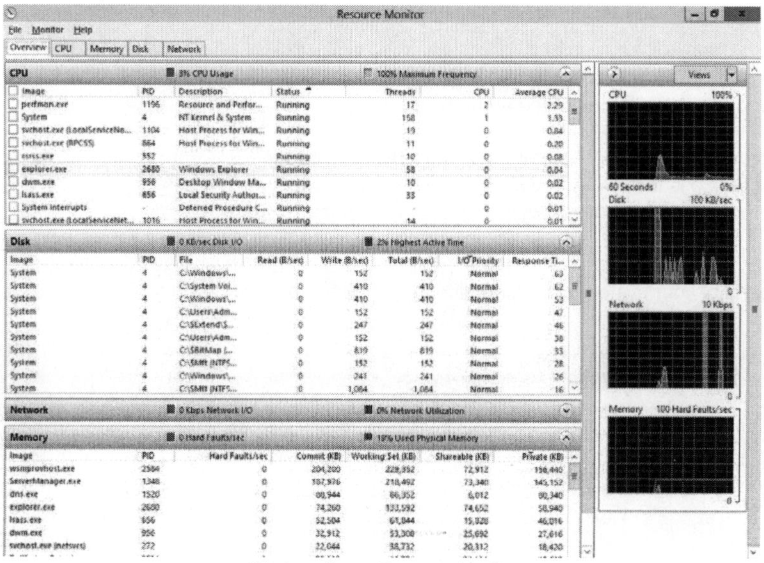

Windows Server Resource Monitor

Performance Monitor

Performance Monitor is available in all versions of Windows Server. It can be used to provide real-time charts of system resources but its real use is to log information to a file for viewing at a later date.

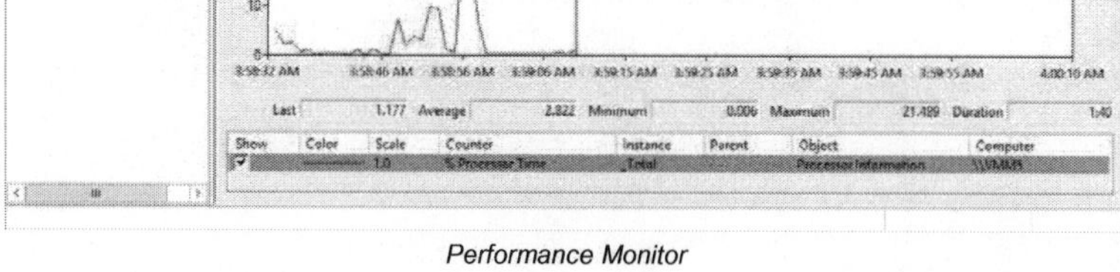

Performance Monitor

By monitoring different resources at different times of the day, an administrator can detect bottlenecks in a system that are causing problems. These problems can then be rectified.

Objects and Counters

Resources, such as memory and disk, are collected into **objects**. Objects have **counters** and there can be multiple **instances** of the same type of object.

For example, the disk performance can be measured using the Physical Disk Object and the best counter to use is the Average Queue Length. If there are two disks, three instances of this object can be viewed: disk 0, disk 1, and disks Total.

You can monitor different parts of your system by adding different counters to your monitor chart.

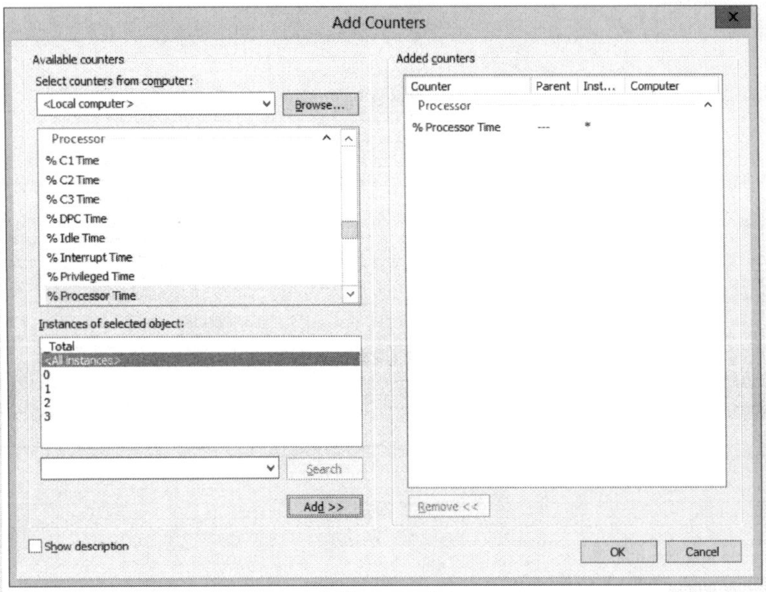

Adding a counter

Some of the most commonly used counters are listed in the table below.

In addition to these key system resource counters, applications and services add their own counters to help monitor their specific performance.

Notice that it is not always immediately apparent which component is causing a problem. Many counters are interrelated and must be viewed with other counters in mind. For instance, if you lack RAM, then the disk will likely be slow because of excessive paging.

Object	Counter	Description
Processor	% Processor Time	The percentage of time that the processor is executing a non-idle thread. In general terms this should be low. If it is greater than 85% for a measured period, then you may have a processor bottleneck.
System	Processor Queue Length	Threads waiting to be processed across all CPUs. Should be between 1-2x the CPU count.
LogicalDisk	% Free Space	As a general guideline, there should be at least 25% free space on a disk.
Physical Disk	% Disk Time	The percentage of elapsed time that the selected disk drive is busy servicing read or write requests. This is a good overall indicator of how busy the disk is. Again, if the average exceeds 85% for a measured time period, you may have a disk problem.
	Current Disk Queue Length	The number of requests outstanding on the disk at the time the performance data are collected. Taken with the preceding counter, this gives a better indicator of disk problems.
Memory	Pages / sec	The number of pages read from or written to disk to resolve hard page faults. This means your system is using the paging file. An excessive amount (above 1000) can indicate a memory leak, where the process consumes memory without ever releasing it. This (and excessive CPU utilization) can be caused by poor application design but can also be an indicator of malware infection. The Private Bytes and Handle Count counters of the Process object can help to confirm whether it is causing the problem. You can also investigate via the Processes tab in Task Manager.
	% Committed Bytes	This indicates virtual memory usage. If over 80%, more physical memory should be installed.
	Available / Committed Bytes	Observe these counters when you close programs - if the values don't change then it's possible a process is not releasing memory.
	Pool Paged / Nonpaged Bytes	If these values steadily increase there could be a memory leak.
Paging File	% Usage	The amount of the pagefile instance in use. If your paging file is currently 2 GB on the disk and this figure averages fifty percent, then it means you might benefit from adding memory (about 1 GB in fact). Don't forget that if your system pages excessively, then disk performance will suffer - paging is disk intensive.
Network Interface	Bytes Total / sec	The amount of data sent and received (both can also be measured separately). If consistently high (utilization over 70%) you may need to add bandwidth. If there are spikes, look for events occurring at the same time to pinpoint the cause.
	Output Queue Length	A value of 2 or more indicates a bottleneck or malfunction.
	Packets	Various counters to monitor packets sent, received, discarded, with errors, and so on.

Using Counter Log Files

Counter logs allow you to collect statistics about resources, such as memory, disk and processor. These can be used to determine system health and performance. In Server 2012, a counter log can be created as a particular type of user-defined **Data Collector Set**:

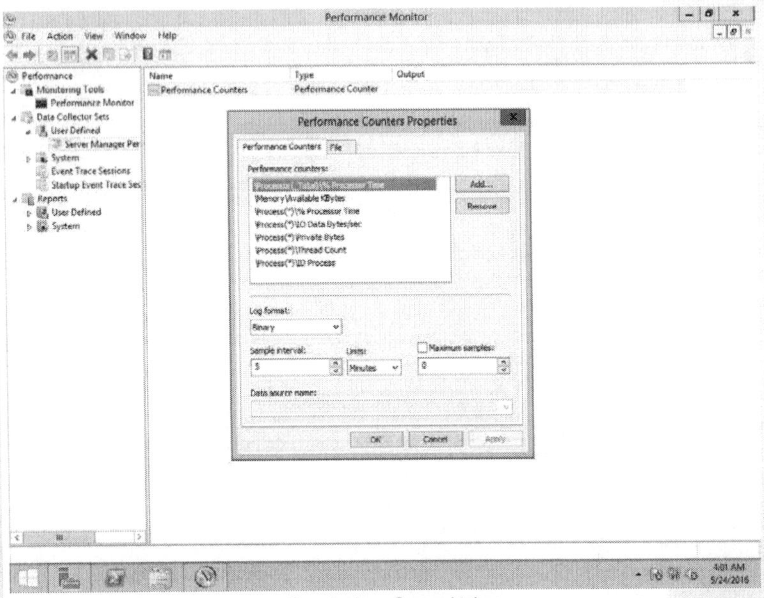

Counter log - General tab

You can add the counters you wish to be logged and set the logging interval. Be aware than you can't expect the system to collect vast amounts of data on many objects every half second. Therefore, set a suitable logging interval.

Also ensure that you measure over a suitable period. For example, there is not much point logging disk activity for a computer when the users are at lunch - it is not representative of typical usage.

You can force the log to start or stop by alt-clicking it.

Once a log file has been created you can load the logged data into Performance Monitor. Once the log file is loaded, you can add the counters stored in the log to the chart to view the static data.

Using Trace Logs

Trace logs can collect statistics about services, providing you with detailed reports about resource behavior. In essence, trace logs provide extensions to the Event Viewer, logging data that would otherwise be inaccessible.

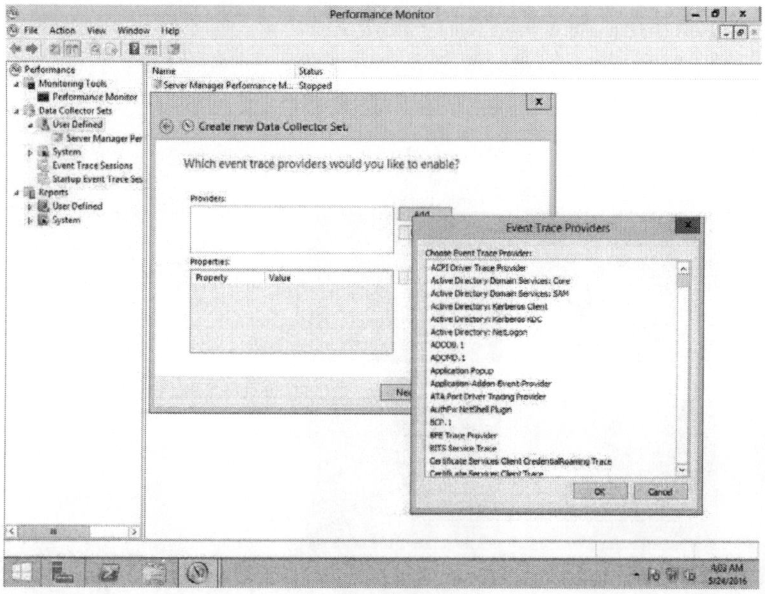

Creating a trace log

Measuring Performance in Linux

Linux distributions are all different, so the tools available vary. However, using SUSE, the following tools prove useful for performance monitoring purposes.

A graphical tool called **KDE System Guard** allows the administrator to view the same sort of objects and statistics as with Windows Performance Monitor.

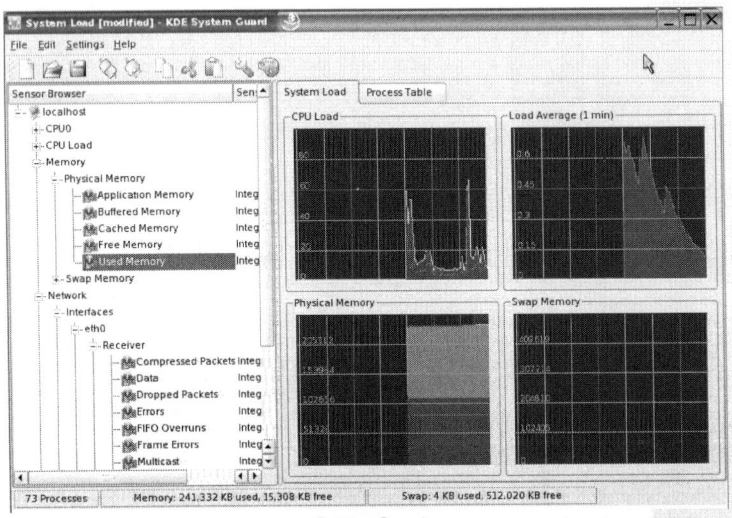

System Guard

A range of statistics related to the four key resources can be viewed easily.

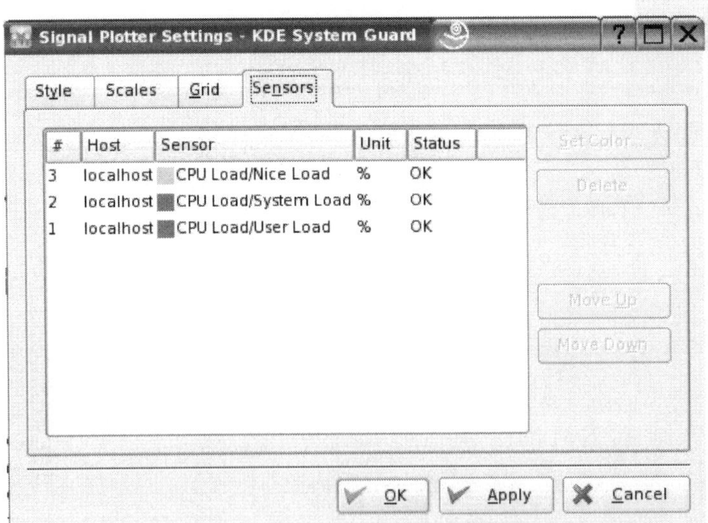

Configuring objects for monitoring

Aside from this tool, administrators can also access some elements within the **KDE Info Centre**, which can report, as shown, on memory consumption.

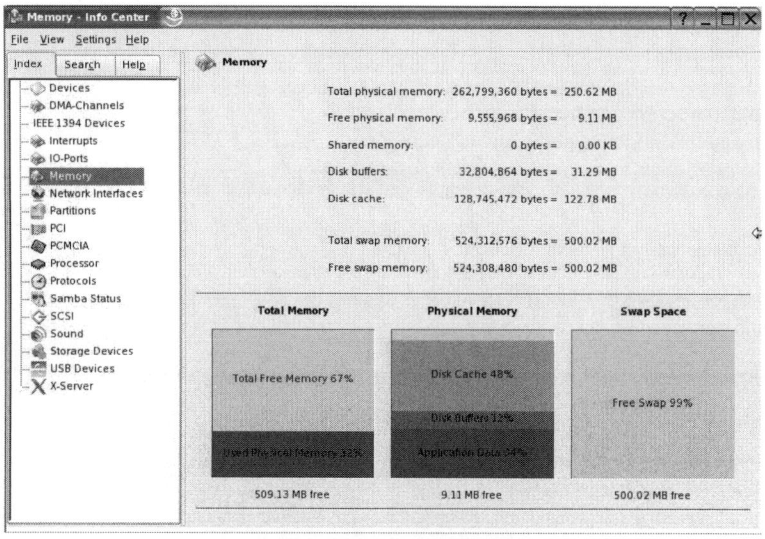

Viewing memory with Info Center

As well as graphical utilities, many command-line programs can be used to extract useful information about the server's performance. These include:

Program	Function
vmstat	Provides data on memory usage, CPU and interrupts.
ps	Lists the running processes.
df	Lists available and consumed disk space on attached devices.
top	Shows resources being consumed by running processes.

The following is the output from **top**, executed on SUSE Linux.

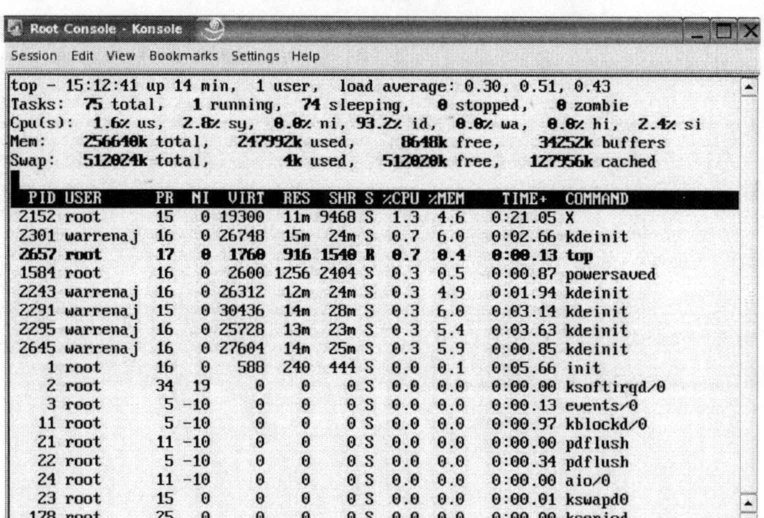

top output from SUSE

System Logs

Logs are one of the most valuable sources of performance, troubleshooting, and security (auditing) information. A single logged event will comprise metadata, such as the date and time, category, and event ID, plus a description and possibly contents of error output.

Logs can be categorized into the following sorts of function:

- **System** logs record events generated by the kernel and other system or driver-level processes and services.
- **Application** (or **General**) logs record user-mode or application-initiated incidents.
- **History** (or **Security** or **Audit**) logs record user activity.

Audit logs typically associate an action with a particular user. This is one of the reasons that it is critical that users not share log on details. If a user account is compromised, there is no means of tying events in the log to the actual attacker.

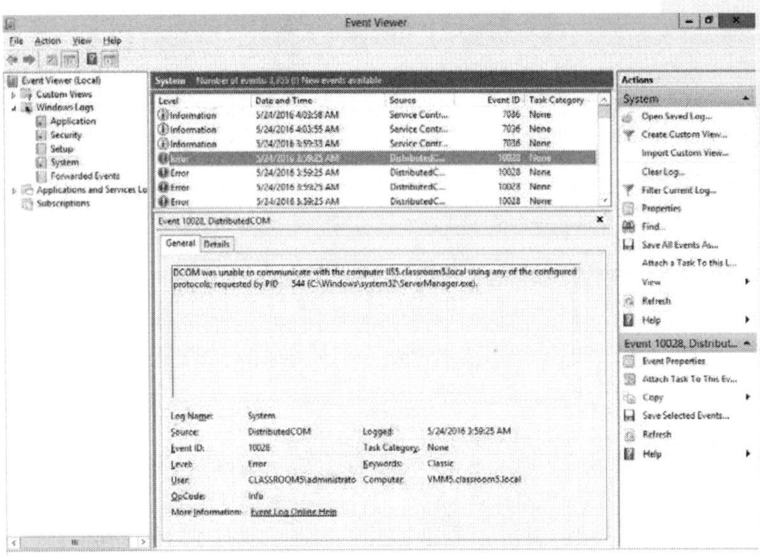

Viewing Windows logs in Event Viewer

- **Performance** logs record defined metrics over a period of time.

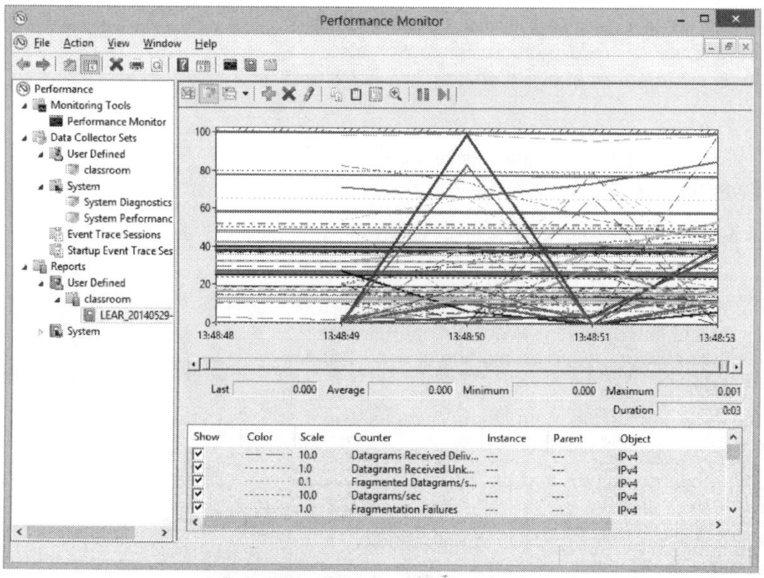

Data retrieved from a performance log file

A network logging system may be able to aggregate the logs from numerous devices into a central control panel, using a protocol such as SNMP. Alternatively, the logs from appliances such as switches and routers can typically be transferred using FTP, TFTP, or SSH.

Windows operating systems store system logs internally and these logs can be viewed through Event Viewer. The standard logs (System, Application, and Security) may be supplemented by other software-specific logs, as additional services and applications are installed.

Windows Event Viewer

The **Event Viewer** collects statistics and messages related to system behavior. If your system has generated a fault, then there are quite likely to be events listed in the log files.

Event Viewer can be used to view the three main Windows log files:

Log	Contents
System Log (SysEvent.evt)	Contains information about service load failures, hardware conflicts, driver load failures, and so on.
Security Log (SecEvent.evt)	This log holds the audit data for the system.
Application Log (AppEvent.evt)	Contains application or user-related events.

Installing Windows services and other applications will make other log files available (DNS events for instance). Some applications do not write logs to Event Viewer. Check the application's documentation to get the location of the log file.

The log file size for each of the three logs is set to 16 MB but this can be changed from the **Log Settings** option of the **Log** menu. This option also allows the overwrite option to be set to never, after a predetermined time, or whenever necessary.

You can also change the location of a log file (the default is **%SystemRoot%\System32\config**.

Event Viewer classes each event as a defined type. The types of events are:

Event	Contents
Information	Significant events that describe successful operations, such as a driver starting or service starting or a document printing.
Warning	Events that may indicate future problems, such as when the system runs low on disk space.
Error	Significant problems, such as service failures and device conflicts.
Critical	An unrecoverable error that made the application or Windows close unexpectedly.
Successful Audit	Security access attempts that were successful.
Failure Audit	Security access attempts that were unsuccessful. This may indicate a possible security breach or a mistyped password.

More information for each event can be displayed by double-clicking the event in question. This will display a screen that contains:

- An event ID, plus the date and time of the event.
- The user and computer names associated with an event.
- Event Source - which application or object within the system that generated the event; for example, The Directory Service, the Spooler, and so on.
- Category - will depend upon which event source has been selected, but might include (for the Directory Service) logon events and so forth.
- A description of the event plus data in bytes and words.

Typically you are going to be interested in a particular event or events and some logs contain a *lot* of events. The utility allows you to filter the displayed events by the event information listed above (category, user, date/time, and so on).

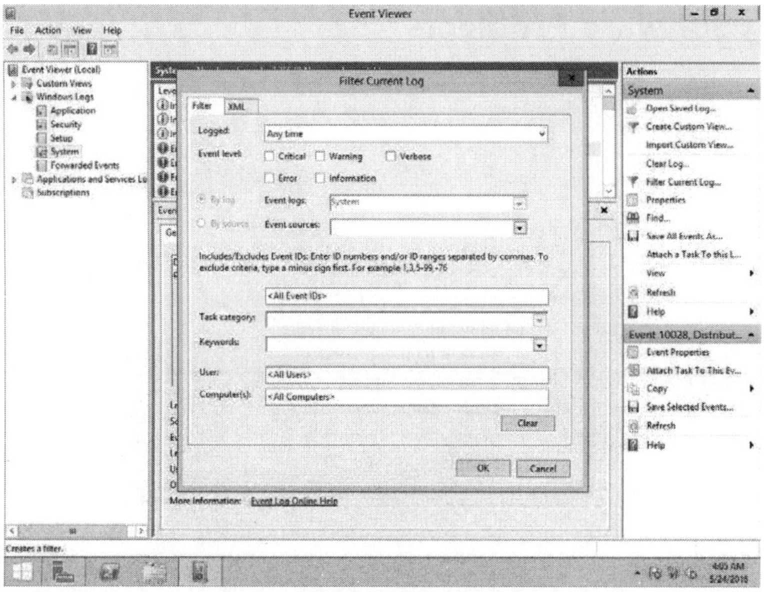

Applying a filter to the Windows event logs

Linux Logs

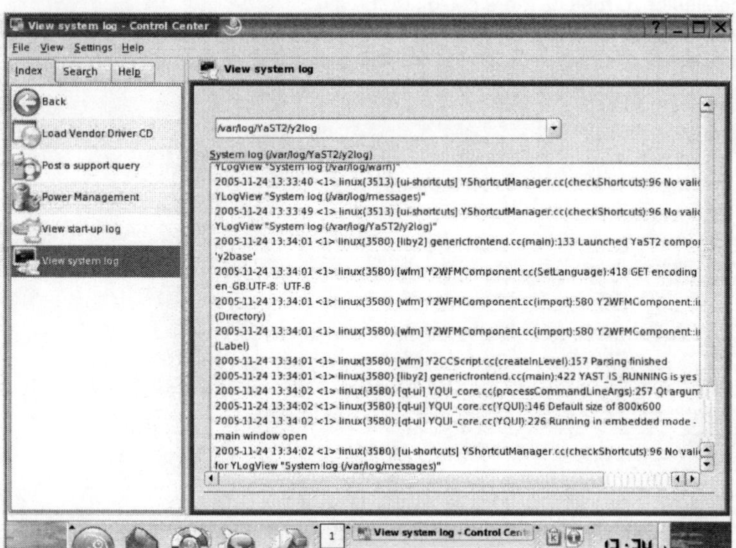

Viewing the system log via YaST

Linux also records events to logs, which can be viewed with a text editor. These are stored in the **/var/log** folder, generally speaking.

SUSE Linux provides a graphical way (via YaST) to view the logs. Viewing logs requires **root** privilege.

Troubleshooting Software Problems

The errors encountered in troubleshooting Windows software typically fall into one of the following categories:

Drivers

Problems with device drivers may manifest as performance problems, as a memory leak or Blue Screen of Death (BSOD), or as some sort of compatibility problem. The typical approach is to check for an updated version of the driver or, if updating the driver has caused the problem, rolling back to the previous version. Hardware conflicts rather than driver problems can also cause boot problems, so check Device Manager to ensure there are no conflicting addresses set. Also bear in mind that safe mode, or in worst case scenarios, the recovery console could be used to boot the system, after which the offending driver or service could be replaced.

Services

The system will display a message if a service fails to start. Check system logs to find out which one has failed. A service may fail following the installation of some other software because of a compatibility problem or because a system or application file has been deleted or corrupted. There could also be a problem with permissions preventing the service from running. Remember that some services have dependencies on other services, so the problem may take a little tracking down.

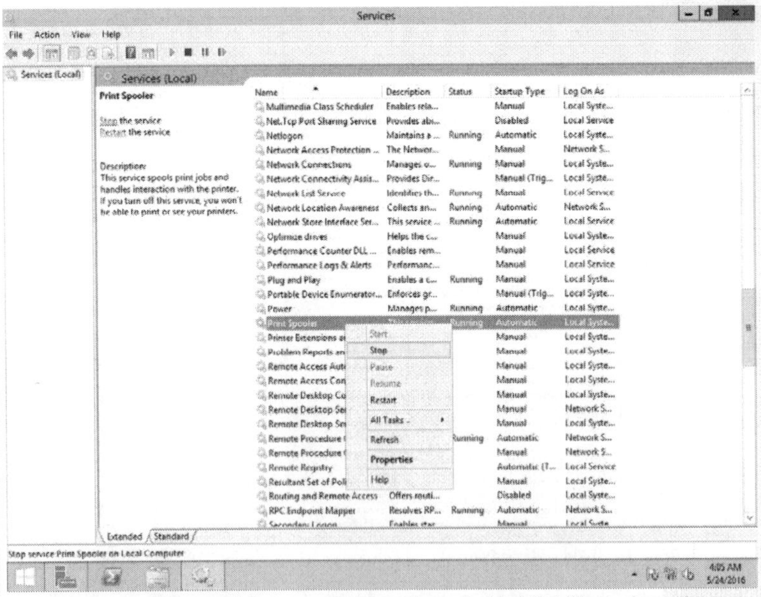

Managing services - check that a service has not been disabled, that it is running under an account with sufficient permissions, and that a dependency on another service is not preventing it from running

If you cannot identify the cause, try reinstalling the application that installed the service or restoring the whole system back to a point when the service worked.

Blue Screens

Blue Screens (of Death or BSOD) during installation or following the addition of hardware usually indicate a hardware / driver problem. If Last Known Good or System Restore does not solve the problem, make a note of the stop error code (which will be in the form: **Stop: 0x0...**) and use the Microsoft Knowledge Base to troubleshoot.

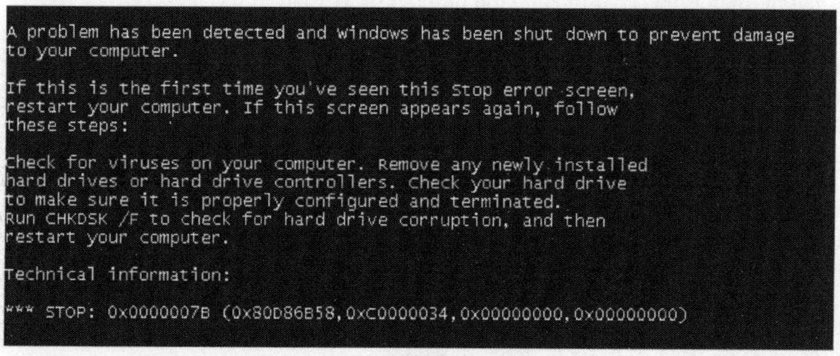

BSOD

Bluescreens at other times can be caused by file system errors, a corrupt pagefile, corrupt registry data, or faulty memory chips.

Runaway Processes and Memory Leaks

A **runaway process** is typically a task that enters an infinite loop running forever. The result of these processes on a system is excessive CPU usage (on one or more processors or cores) and often memory usage. A runaway process will normal starve others of resources causing them to slow down, or perform erratically. A **memory leak** is a process that consumes bytes of system memory without ever releasing them.

It is normally relatively easy to spot processes that are in a runaway state using Windows Task Manager or the `top` command in Linux. By sorting based on CPU usage, these processes can be identified and killed using Task Manager or the `kill` command.

Typically, a faulty process will slow the system down and eventually crash it completely. When the system is restarted, it may work normally for a short time before the process starts to use up all the system resources again. As a runaway process is often the result of faulty coding or bugs it is worth continuing to monitor the system and try to identify the organization responsible for the program (using the process properties option in Task Manager) and enquire about possible known issues.

If a valid application or driver misbehaves like this, you need to contact the vendor to obtain a hotfix or driver update. If you cannot identify the process, you should suspect a malware infection or that someone has installed unauthorized software. Use anti-virus tools to remove the malware and try to use the system logs to discover the culprit. Make sure that administrative accounts are secured to prevent users from installing applications.

Slow OS Performance

Slow OS performance will generally indicate some sort of underlying hardware problem - usually a lack of system resources. Try reducing the number of applications installed on the server or throttling user access. If this resolves the problem, the server is underpowered for the roles you are trying to load on it. You could try upgrading the CPU, memory, and disks, but is likely to be more cost-effective to provision a second server to run some of the applications.

If reducing the load on the server doesn't fix the performance problem, you'll need to start investigating each subsystem. Check that virtual memory is properly configured for instance. Verify that the NOS and applications have had the latest updates and service packs applied.

Individual NOS versions and applications can experience any number of performance-related problems and you will just have to use the vendor troubleshooting tools to try to identify which is affecting your system.

Shut Down

If a server hangs at shut down, the typical cause is a driver, service, or program not responding to the shut down command to close. This could be because a user has a file open or an application is waiting for user input or it could be because the process is faulty. The former problem should only occur intermittently while the latter would occur each time the server is shut down. To troubleshoot, observe the process monitor while the server shuts down to see which processes remain.

A corrupt pagefile or boot volume with no free space could also cause shut down to hang.

Virtual Memory Configuration and Corruption

Virtual memory is often considered an antiquated feature on modern server based computers with 32 or 64 GB of RAM or more. This is often enough to run all the applications and processes executing on the server. However, most operating systems still create and expect disk space to be reserved as a pagefile or swapfile. This is primarily for application compatibility.

Corruption of the virtual memory space can occur for many reasons including:

- Physical disk space corruption.
- Excessive disk I/O causing buffer overflows.

- Bugs in the OS, memory managers, or application environments.

Typically once memory corruption has occurred there is little that can be done other than to kill the application or process, or in the case of shared virtual memory usage a good old fashioned reboot might be needed. Using the system log files it may be possible to identify if the fault is caused by a particular application or process or is more hardware / system related.

Most operating systems allow the virtual memory space to be located on any disk media. As a general rule try to place the pagefile / swapfile on a fast, underutilized disk. This can be achieved on Windows using the **Advanced System Properties** or using the `mkswap` and `swapon` commands in Linux.

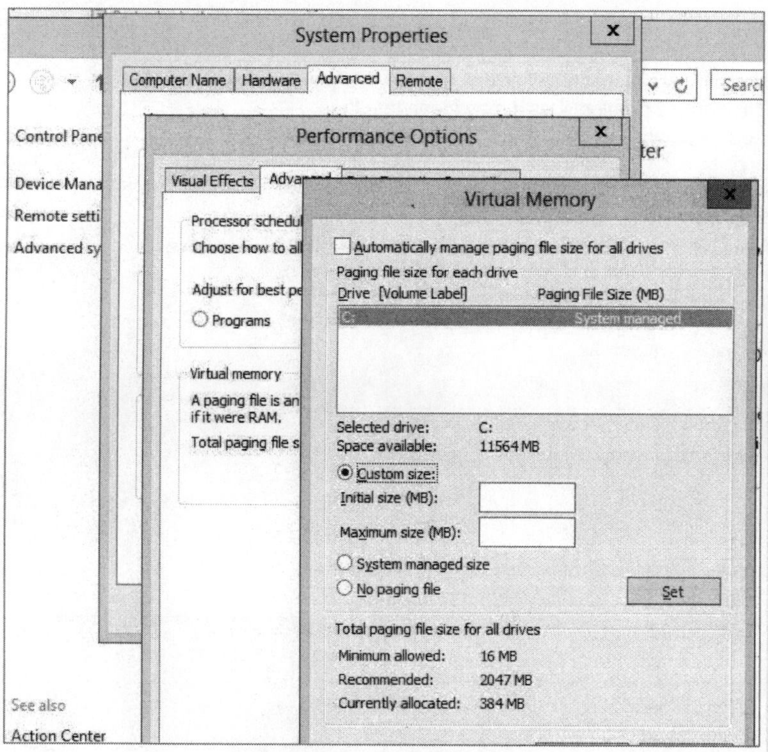

Configuring virtual memory in Windows

Also as a general rule, avoid placing virtual memory space on an SSD drive as although they are quicker than traditional drives, they have a much lower number of disk accesses before failure and virtual memory will be constantly swapping between RAM and disk.

System Log

By default, system logs are set with a maximum log size and are configured to overwrite older events when the log reaches its maximum size. If a log is configured to preserve older events and reaches its maximum size, the system will not be able to write to the log. If you need to preserve all logged events, it is best to set the system to archive logs automatically.

You do need to keep an eye on log sizes however, especially if there is limited disk space on the volume housing the logs. Set up a system to move archived logs onto an archive storage medium.

Patch Update Failure

Patching the NOS and applications is a fact of technical support life. If a patch update fails, it can cause considerable problems, as it may mean that the system cannot obtain subsequent patches (it gets "stuck" trying to apply the failed patch).

To troubleshoot a patch issue, you need to investigate the appropriate log. In Windows, this is the windowsupdate.log file stored in the system root. The log file should contain an installation error code and you can look that up on the vendor's support site to obtain troubleshooting information.

Review Questions / Module 3 / Unit 6 / Troubleshooting Software

Answer these questions to test what you have learned in this unit.

1) What are the four main factors impacting server performance?
2) If pagefile usage is intensive, should you add more memory or use faster disks?
3) What two tools can you use in Windows to view system performance metrics in real time?
4) What command can you use to check free disk capacity in Linux?
5) What types of Windows events represent urgent problems?
6) What command in Linux might you use to diagnose a problem with a runaway process?
7) Users are complaining of slow file performance. The problem lasts for about 2 hours and always occurs at the same time each day. What would you suspect was the cause?
8) Apart from bad sectors and application bugs, what is the other major cause of pagefile corruption?

This page left blank intentionally.

Module 3 / Summary
Server Applications

You learned about different server roles and how they might be combined and deployed in terms of hardware and network configuration.

Module 3 / Unit 1 / Configuring Server Roles

- Know the Windows and Linux tools used to install applications and configure roles.
- Understand how application and database servers are structured.
- Understand the use of web services and some of the options that can be configured on a web server, including connection security (HTTPS).
- FTP provides a basic file transfer service. Connection security can be enforced using SSH (SFTP) or SSL (FTP/S).
- Email services use SMTP to transfer messages between servers and POP3 or IMAP to allow clients to access a server mailbox. Make sure you know the ports associated with these protocols.

Module 3 / Unit 2 / Storage Services

- A server can use Direct Attached Storage (DAS) but a shared storage solution, such as Network Attached Storage (NAS) or a Storage Area Network (SAN) is usually more efficient. NAS provides file-level access while a SAN provides block-level access.
- A SAN is often implemented using Fibre Channel HBAs, switches, and cabling. Make sure you know the basic configuration settings and also about means of running FC over other types of network, such as iSCSI, FCIP, and FCoE.
- Storage solutions are not just based on use of hard disks. Tape media and optical / WORM media are also used, especially for backup and archiving.
- Be aware of the factors affecting capacity planning and some of the tools used to restrict storage requirements, such as quotas and compression.

Module 3 / Unit 3 / Volume Management

- When disk storage is provisioned, it has to be partitioned and formatted to make it available to users. In Windows, these operations are accomplished using Disk Management. You can create RAID volumes using this tool too.
- Make sure you understand the meaning of disk and volume status messages and the function of Windows disk management tools such as chkdsk and defrag plus the functions of disk management tools in Linux.

- You should be able to identify common causes of storage and RAID problems from typical symptoms and select the best tool to use to troubleshoot.

Module 3 / Unit 4 / Directory Services

- Information about network objects is stored in a database, often following the X.500 schema. LDAP can be used to query and update this type of directory. In Windows, the network directory is Active Directory.
- Make sure you know the tools for managing users and groups in Windows and Linux and the distinction between standard users and administrator / root.
- In Windows, group policy can be used to enforce system policies and restrict privileges. Ensure you are familiar with the concept of Role Based Access Control (RBAC) to assign privileges.

Module 3 / Unit 5 / File and Print Services

- Windows can use a combination of share and NTFS permissions to control access to folders and files. Make sure you understand the permissions that can be set and how they interact.
- Learn the commands to use to configure file sharing in Linux and how to set symbolic or numeric permissions on a file or directory.
- Printers can be attached directly to a network but often they are hosted by a print server. Make sure you know the options for configuring drivers and about the settings that affect troubleshooting.

Module 3 / Unit 6 / Troubleshooting Software

- A health monitoring tool reports on the status of the server's hardware components, such as temperature and fan speed.
- Performance monitoring tools can be used to establish baseline utilization of key resources, such as CPU, memory, disk, and network. The baseline provides a point of comparison for future tests, which will drive upgrade or troubleshooting strategy if performance reduces.
- Logs are one of the most important resources available to troubleshoot software and security (and some hardware) problems.
- Make sure you can diagnose common software problems from typical symptoms and select the appropriate tool to use to investigate or resolve the issue.

Module 4 / Server Maintenance

CompTIA Server+ SK0-004 Domain Areas	Weighting
1.0 Server Architecture	12%
2.0 Server Administration	24%
3.0 Storage	12%
4.0 Security	13%
5.0 Networking	10%
6.0 Disaster Recovery	9%
7.0 Troubleshooting	20%

The following table lists the CompTIA Server+ domain objectives and content examples covered in the units in this module:

Refer To	Domain Objectives/Examples
Unit 4.1 / Server Hardware	**1.2 Given a scenario, install, configure and maintain server components** *CPU* (*Multiprocessor vs. multicore, Socket type, Cache levels: L1, L2, L3, Speeds* [*Core, Bus, Multiplier*], *CPU stepping, Architecture* [*x86, x64, ARM*]) • *RAM* (*ECC vs. non-ECC, DDR2, DDR3, Number of pins, Static vs. dynamic, Module placement, CAS latency, Timing , Memory pairing*) • *Bus types, bus channels and expansion slots* (*Height differences and bit rate differences, PCI, PCIe, PCI-X*) • *NICs* • *Hard drives* • *Riser cards* • *RAID controllers* • *USB interface / port* • *Hot-swap vs. non-hot-swap components*
Unit 4.2 / Environment and Maintenance	**1.3 Compare and contrast power and cooling components** *Cooling* (*Airflow, Thermal dissipation, Baffles / shrouds, Fans, Liquid cooling*)
	2.4 Given a scenario, perform proper server maintenance techniques *Hardware maintenance* (*Check system health indicators* [*LEDs, Error codes, Beep codes, LCD messages*], *Preventive maintenance* [*Clearing dust, Check proper airflow*], *Proper shut down procedures*)
	4.6 Given a scenario, implement proper environmental controls and techniques *HVAC* (*Room and rack temperature and humidity* [*Monitoring and alert notifications*], *Airflow* [*Rack filler / baffle / blanking panels*], *Hot aisle and cold aisle*)
	7.2 Given a scenario, effectively troubleshoot hardware problems, selecting the appropriate tools and methods *Environmental issues* (*Dust, Humidity, Temperature*) • *Hardware tools* (*Compressed air*)
Unit 4.3 / Power Distribution	**1.3 Compare and contrast power and cooling components** *Power* (*Voltage* [*110v vs. 220v vs. -48v, 208v vs. 440v / 460v / 480v*], *Wattage, Consumption, Redundancy, 1-phase vs. 3-phase power, Plug types* [*NEMA, Edison, Twist lock*])

Refer To	Domain Objectives/Examples
Unit 4.3 / Power Distribution	**4.6 Given a scenario, implement proper environmental controls and techniques** *Power concepts and best practices* (*UPS* [*Run time vs. capacity, Automated graceful shutdown of attached devices, Periodic testing of batteries, Maximum load, Bypass procedures, Remote management*], *PDU* [*Connect redundant rack PDUs to separate circuits*], *Capacity planning* [*PDU ratings, UPS ratings, Total potential power draw*], *Multiple circuits* [*Connect redundant power supplies to separate PDUs*])
	7.2 Given a scenario, effectively troubleshoot hardware problems, selecting the appropriate tools and methods *Environmental issues* (*Power surge / failure*)
Unit 4.4 / Server Hardware Troubleshooting	**2.4 Given a scenario, perform proper server maintenance techniques** *Hardware maintenance* (*Replace failed components* [*Fans, Hard drives, RAM, Backplanes, Batteries*])
	4.6 Given a scenario, implement proper environmental controls and techniques *Safety* (*ESD Procedures*)
	7.2 Given a scenario, effectively troubleshoot hardware problems, selecting the appropriate tools and methods *Common problems* (*Failed POST, Overheating, Memory failure, Onboard component failure, Processor failure, Incorrect boot sequence, Expansion card failure, Operating system not found, Drive failure, Power supply failure, I/O failure*) • *Causes of common problems* (*Third party components or incompatible components, Incompatible or incorrect BIOS, Cooling failure, Mismatched components, Backplane failure*) • *Hardware tools* (*Power supply tester / multimeter, Hardware diagnostics, ESD equipment*)
Unit 4.5 / Server Management	**2.3 Given a scenario, use access and control methods to administer a server** *Local hardware administration* (*KVM, Serial, Virtual Administration console*) • *Network-based hardware administration* (*KVM over IP, ILO, iDRAC*) • *Network-based operating system administration* (*RDP, SSH, VNC, Command line / shell*)
Unit 4.6 / Configuration Management	**2.4 Given a scenario, perform proper server maintenance techniques** *Change management* • *Outages & Service Level Agreements* (*Scheduled downtime, Unscheduled downtime, Impact analysis, Client notification, MTTR*)
	2.5 Explain the importance of asset management and documentation *Asset management* (*Licensing, Labeling, Warranty, Lifecycle management* [*Procurement, Usage, End of life, Disposal / recycling*], *Inventory* [*Make, Model, Serial number, Asset tag*]) • *Documentation* (*Service manuals, Network diagrams, Architecture diagrams, Dataflow diagrams, Recovery documentation, Baseline documentation, Change management policies, Service Level Agreement, Server configuration*) • *Secure storage of sensitive documentation*

Module 4 / Unit 1

Server Hardware

Objectives

On completion of this unit, you will be able to:

- Identify components of the server chassis and motherboard.
- Describe server-class features of CPUs, memory, and expansion cards and perform upgrades.

Motherboard Components

The **motherboard** (or **main board** or **system board**) is a **Printed Circuit Board (PCB)** containing chips, circuitry, connectors, and power regulators. The motherboard provides a connection point for the other upgradable components of the server. The motherboard form factor means its size and shape and the location of components on it.

Intel Xeon CPU-based motherboard with (1) PCI-X expansion slots, (2) PCI expansion slots, (3) AGP port, (4) SATA connectors, (5) Floppy drive connector, (6) ATA/IDE connectors, (7) DIMM memory slots, (8) CPU sockets, (9) Power connector, (10) Network ports, (11) Parallel, serial, and video ports, (12), Keyboard and mouse (PS/2) ports, (13) USB ports

The main components of the motherboard are as follows:

- Integrated I/O (Input / Output) ports, such as USB, serial, parallel, and PS/2, provide a point for peripheral devices to be connected to the computer. They are positioned in a standard layout on the motherboard so as to match up to slots or holes in the chassis.
- Memory slots (DIMMs) provide connection points for system memory. The number and type of slots determines the type and maximum amount of memory that can be installed.
- The processor socket provides a connection point for a supported CPU. There are several different socket designs. Many server boards have multiple CPU sockets (2, 4, or even 8).
- The chipset provides interfaces between the CPU and the components on the motherboard. It may also provide "onboard" or "integrated" expansion features, such as basic video and network (NIC) adapters.
- Expansion bus - an expansion bus provides the means to install adapter (or expansion) cards to add functionality to the computer. The motherboard will contain a number of expansion slots, possibly of different bus types.
- Drive controllers - drive controllers provide connection points for different types of storage device. A server motherboard may also feature a RAID controller.

The type of motherboard must be matched to a suitable case (or chassis) and power supply.

- Tower servers are typically based on a standard PC motherboard form factor (ATX) and can use "off-the-shelf" power supplies.
- Servers designed for rack mounting are more likely to use a proprietary form factor and power supply, especially if they are low profile (1 or 2U).
- Blade servers use separate expansion, cooling, and power systems by plugging into an enclosure.

Servers designed to be rack mounted or housed in an enclosure (blade servers) typically have a much more compact layout. There is often limited scope for adding expansion cards and slots are often presented using a riser architecture (installed at a right-angle to the main board).

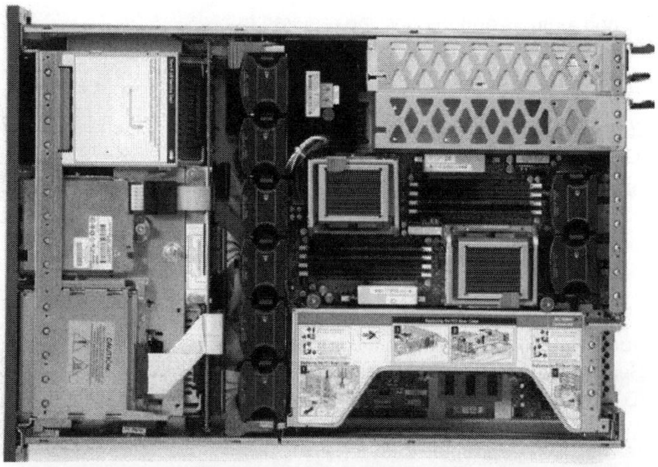

HP Proliant rack-mounted server - note the riser cages for installing adapters

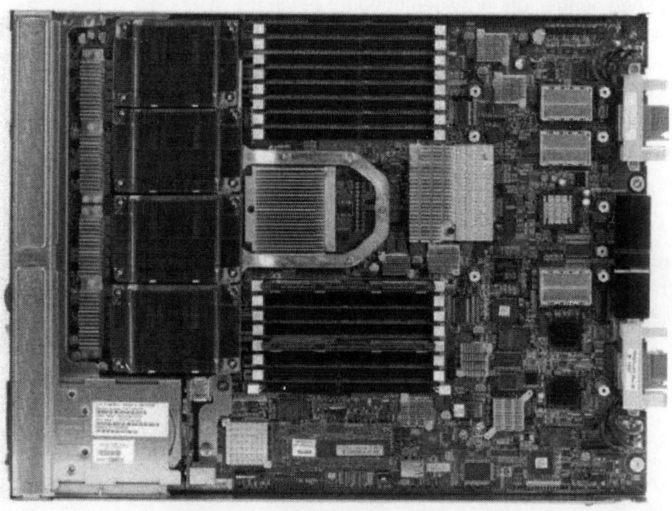

HP blade server - note that there are no standard expansion slots but adapters for "mezzanine" cards that install parallel to the mainboard

DIP Switches, Jumpers, and Diagnostic LEDs

DIP (Dual Inline Package) switches and **jumpers** are means of configuring settings on the motherboard (or other components such as hard drives and RAID controllers). A DIP switch is moved between on and off positions (there are "slide" and "rocker" types). A jumper is enabled by sliding a block over two pins (or disabled by removing the block) - the block contains a metal strip that makes an electrical circuit between the two pins.

Not many motherboards make serious use of "hard" configuration techniques. Most of the settings you can configure are controlled via the system setup program or a remote management application. One typical example of a "hard" switch is a firmware reset jumper (enabling the system to be recovered from a failed firmware update or lost management password for instance).

The default position of DIP switches and jumpers and the position required to achieve a particular configuration may be printed on the component or will otherwise be recorded in the system documentation or maintenance guide.

A server motherboard will also feature a number of **diagnostic LEDs**. These would typically indicate whether the power supply and fans are working. There may also be warning LEDs for temperature and component (CPU and memory) failure.

Drive and RAID Support

The motherboard will have connectors for various disk drives. On a tower system, there will be a number of Serial ATA (SATA) connectors, which can be used to attach hard drives, CD/DVD drives, or tape units.

A legacy server system may feature a **SCSI** host adapter, allowing the connection of SCSI-compatible drives and other devices. Newer motherboards will have **Serial Attached SCSI (SAS)** connectors provided onboard or via a host bus adapter. In most cases the drive adapter will also function as a RAID controller. Rack-mounted and blade systems (and some towers) use backplanes for connecting drives rather than cabling.

See Unit 1.2 for more information about storage connectors and backplanes.

The drive units are fitted into expansion bays. The bays for the hard drives are typically located on the front of the server for easy access. The drives are typically attached to a caddy which slides into the enclosure and is locked into place using a lever.

CPU Features

While overall performance requires a careful balance of components and consideration of the server role, the CPU is still the most expensive component of most servers and the most important factor in determining how powerful the server is.

Typical installation and upgrade activities involving the CPU will include replacing a faulty chip, upgrading a single chip to a higher specified version, and adding CPUs to a multiprocessor system.

Like desktops, CPUs for PC-type servers are produced by Intel and AMD. Each company produces enterprise server-class CPUs: Intel's range being the Xeon and AMD's the Opteron. Generally speaking, these will be very similar to the desktop product but come with support for multiprocessing (installing more than one physical CPU) and more cache. Entry-level servers may well use ordinary desktop CPUs.

The following are the major features that differentiate CPUs.

This information is far from being exhaustive and there is no room to present details of the various processor generations or models. For more information about CPUs, use the web. Useful resources include intel.com, amd.com, wikipedia.org, and tomshardware.com.

Processor Architecture

Historically, CPU architectures have either been based on **Reduced** or **Complex Instruction Set Computing (RISC / CISC)**. A RISC architecture uses few instructions; in theory leading to simpler design and faster processing. CISC makes more instructions available; in theory this makes programming simpler and requires less memory.

Intel's Pentium and subsequent chips use a combination of these approaches where the CPU divides instructions into smaller microcode operations and runs them in parallel (superpipelining).

The instruction set used by IBM PC compatible CPUs is called **x86-32** or **IA-32** (Intel Architecture).

This has been extended with SIMD instructions (such as MMX) and the way the instructions are processed internally has been modified and optimized by various different CPU architectures, but otherwise the same platform has been in use for the last 30 years (IA-32 updated the 16-bit x86 instruction set, first launched in 1978).

Up until a few years ago, CPUs were designed to run 32-bit code. This means that each instruction can be up to 32-bits in length. A 32-bit CPU's **General Purpose (GP)** registers are also 32-bits wide. However, since 2005, all server CPUs released to the market have been capable of running 64-bit code.

Intel first developed a 64-bit instruction set for its Itanium server CPU platform in 2001. This platform (**IA-64**) has never gained acceptance in the PC server market however. AMD's 64-bit instruction set (**AMD64**) has proved more popular and was adopted by Intel for its 64-bit. Intel refers to it as **EM64T** or **Intel 64**. The same instruction set is also called **x86-64** or **x64**.

Most server NOS and applications have been ported to 64-bit code. For example, Windows Server 2008 is 32-bit or 64-bit but the R2 update and Server 2012 are 64-bit only. Exchange moved to 64-bit with the 2007 version and SQL Server has been available for 64-bit since 2000. Similarly all the major Linux distributions and applications have been available as 64-bit for years (and some are now exclusively so). Some client software is still 32-bit however and that can cause compatibility problems, especially when hardware drivers are called upon to interact with the server software.

ARM

While Intel's CPU platform currently dominates the server CPU market, there may be competition from the **Advanced RISC Machine (ARM)** platform in the future. As a 32-bit platform, ARM CPUs have been very widely used in mobile devices such as smartphones and tablets. Some of these mobile devices are now moving to a 64-bit ARM architecture and it is possible that this architecture will be used as a server and network appliance (switch and router) platform in data centers.

ARM does not manufacture CPUs itself but licenses the architecture to vendors who mostly use the design to create a System on a Chip (SoC), that is an entire computer "product" based on a single integrated circuit.

HyperThreading

One way to make instruction execution more efficient is to improve the way the pipeline works. The basic approach is to do the most amount of work possible in a single clock cycle (multitasking). There are various ways to achieve this goal though.

CPUs process multiple instructions at the same time (for example, while one instruction is fetched, another is being decoded, another is being executed, and another is being written back to memory). This is referred to as a superscalar architecture, as multiple execution units are required. Superscalar architectures also feature longer pipelines with multiple stages but shorter actions (micro-ops) at each stage, referred to as superpipelining.

The original Pentium had a 5-stage pipeline; by contrast, the Pentium 4 had up to *31* stages (NetBurst architecture). NetBurst actually proved relatively inefficient in terms of power and thermal performance, so Intel reverted to a modified form of the P6 architecture it used in Pentium IIs and IIIs for its current Core and Xeon CPUs (with around 14 stages).

Another approach to maximizing the efficiency of a single physical CPU is Simultaneous Multithreading (SMT), called **HyperThreading** by Intel.

A thread is a stream of instructions generated by a software application. Most applications run a single process in a single thread; software that runs multiple parallel threads within a process is said to be multithreaded. SMT allows the threads to run through the CPU at the same time. It duplicates many of the registers of the CPU. This reduces the amount of "idle time" the CPU spends waiting for new instructions to process. To the OS, it *seems* as though there are two CPUs installed.

SMT works best with multithreaded software. As multithreaded server application design has improved, HyperThreading has witnessed something of a comeback. HyperThreading was implemented on premium models in the Pentium 4 range but was not used on the first models in the Core range. It has been reintroduced as a feature of Core and Xeon CPUs. AMD CPUs do not support SMT (at the time of writing).

Multiprocessing and Multi-core

Another approach to making a computer system faster is to use two or more physical CPUs, referred to as **Symmetric Multiprocessing (SMP)**. An SMP-aware OS can then make efficient use of the processing resources available to run application processes on whichever CPU is "available". This approach is not so dependent on software *applications* being multithreaded to deliver performance benefits. Traditionally, SMP was provided by physically installing two or more CPUs in a multi-socket motherboard. Obviously, this adds significantly to the cost and so is only implemented on servers and high-end workstations.

However, improvements in CPU manufacturing techniques have led to another solution: dual-core CPUs (or **Chip Level Multiprocessing [CMP]**). A dual-core CPU is essentially two processors combined on the same die. The market has quickly moved beyond dual-core CPUs to **multi-core** packages with 3, 4, or 8 processors. All modern server CPUs, such as Intel's Xeon range and AMD's Opteron range, are multi-core CPUs.

Speed and Clock

The "headline" or "core" speed of a CPU is the clock rate at which its internal registers work, rated in gigahertz. Modern server CPUs work at between 2 and 4 gigahertz.

The internal clock speed is not the only factor governing performance however. The CPU is supported by a chipset to allow it to communicate with system memory (the "northbridge" chip) and (through what was originally called the "southbridge") the expansion bus (PCIe and PCI-X) and hard drives (SAS or SATA interface).

While the expansion bus chipset remains, the trend is now for CPUs to incorporate the memory controller as part of the CPU. This was started by AMD with their Opteron CPUs and has now been adopted by Intel. While the system memory bus speed is still slower than the internal CPU speed, the integrated memory controller reduces latency.

The **system clock** synchronizes the operation of all parts of the server and provides the basic timing signal for the CPU. Clock speeds are measured in Megahertz (MHz) or Gigahertz (GHz). The clock consists of a **clock generator** that sets up a timing signal and **clock multipliers** that take the timing signal produced by the generator and apply a multiplication factor to produce different timing signals for different types of bus. This means that one type of bus can work at a different speed to another type of bus.

Cache

Because the CPU can work 3-4x faster than any of the other main components, **cache** is used to smooth out the discrepancy and keep the CPU as occupied as possible. Cache is used to store instructions and data that the CPU is using most often (meaning that it does not have to spend time fetching them from system memory). When the CPU successfully retrieves something from the cache, it is called a cache hit; when it looks at the cache and doesn't find the instruction or data it needed, that is a cache miss. If a cache is well designed, hits should strongly outweigh misses.

Cache is typically provided in three levels. A multi-level cache design has to balance exclusivity and inclusivity (whether data is available in different cache levels), cache size (larger caches can store more but take longer to access, increasing latency), and associativity (making the mapping between RAM and cache entries more flexible - n-way associativity allows data to persist in the cache for longer but also increases latency).

- L1 - small (64 KB) cache usually exclusive to a CPU (or core) with low associativity.
- L2 - larger (from 512 KB up to 8 MB) cache. In a multi-core CPU, this cache may be shared between the cores or it might be divided with specific allocations to each core. The earliest CPUs used cache RAM installed on the motherboard and accessed it at lower speed (the "backside" bus) but these days it is part of the processor package and accessed at full speed.
- L3 - a third cache level is a feature of server- or workstation-class CPUs. It usually delivers the best performance benefit in a multiprocessor or multi-core system when all the CPUs are processing the same threads in parallel.

Apart from clock speed, the amount of L2 and L3 cache provided is one of the main differentiators between CPU models within a particular family.

Virtualization Support

Virtualization software allows a single computer to run multiple operating systems (or Virtual Machines [VM]). Intel's **Virtualization Technology (VT)** and AMD's **AMD-V** provides processor extensions to support virtualization. This makes the VMs run much more quickly. These extensions are usually features of premium models in a given processor range but almost all server-class CPUs will support them.

CPU Packaging and Sockets

CPU packaging refers to the CPU's form factor and how it is connected to the motherboard.

When AMD started producing CPUs to compete with Intel, the chips could be fitted to a standard socket (7) and chipset. That situation changed quickly and now the vendors use incompatible processor sockets and slots and chipsets. Also, a new CPU model quite often involves a change of socket form factor or new chipset, so new CPU models from the same vendor may no longer be compatible with a particular motherboard. Consequently, upgrading CPUs is now a relatively rare occurrence - it is often more practical just to buy a new server.

Pin Grid Array (PGA)

The most popular type of CPU package has been the **Pin Grid Array (PGA)** chip, designed to fit in a **Zero Insertion Force (ZIF)** socket on the motherboard.

Many AMD Opteron sockets are still based on the PGA form factor.

As the name suggests, a PGA chip has a number of pins on the underside of the processor. These plug into corresponding holes in the socket. Care must be taken to orient the CPU correctly with the socket and to insert it so as not to bend or break any of the pins.

This socket has a **ZIF (Zero Insertion Force)** lever at one side. When you release this lever, you can lift the processor out of the socket by hand with very little force. To avoid bending the pins on the chip, ensure that you lift the processor straight out of the socket.

Flip Chip Pin Grid Array (FC-PGA)

Some socket designs use a slightly modified type of PGA called **Flip Chip PGA (FC-PGA)**. This reverses the orientation of the CPU die to make better contact with the heatsink. FC-PGA2 also added a heat spreader to the package.

Land Grid Array (LGA)

The socket type used most by Intel, **Land Grid Array (LGA)**, saw the pins move from the CPU to the socket, reducing the likelihood of damage to the CPU but increasing the chance of damaging the motherboard. AMD have started to use this form factor in some of their socket designs.

To remove the chip, lift the lever then pull up the metal cover and take the chip out, taking care to handle it by its edges only.

Voltage Regulator Modules (VRM)

Another feature of processor sockets are the voltage regulators. These step down the power supplied to the processor (typically 12V) to the core voltage used within the CPU (around 1-2V). Voltage regulators are the barrel-like components positioned around the socket. They automatically detect the required voltage using a Voltage ID (VID) code from the CPU.

Early socket designs featured replaceable Voltage Regulator Modules (VRM) and replaceable modules can be found on many boards designed for server systems. Otherwise, Voltage Regulator Downs (VRD) are soldered to the board.

CPU Upgrades

Make sure you take ESD precautions before handling a CPU. If retaining the CPU, make sure that it is placed in suitable packaging immediately, to prevent damage to the pins or from ESD.

Removing the Fan and Heatsink

Before you can remove the processor it is usually necessary to remove the fan and heatsink. Most heatsinks and fans are designed to be removed without the use of tools. Usually there will be a metal clip that can be squeezed to release the heatsink or fan (this may require some force or the use of screwdriver, but be aware that a slip could prove expensive). Note that the fan assembly will have a power connector.

Upgrading a Single CPU

As with any upgrade, you should check that the motherboard and firmware support the new processor, either by referring to the motherboard's documentation or by confirming with the vendor. A firmware update (applied before installing the new CPU) is often required to recognize the new chip correctly. To check that an upgrade has been recognized, view the startup messages when rebooting the server or use a system diagnostics program.

Upgrading to SMP

An SMP-capable motherboard may have slots or sockets for 2 or 4 CPUs (referred to as 2-way or 4-way). 6-way or higher systems are likely to be implemented using multiple system boards.

In an SMP system, the CPUs must be identical in terms of clock speed, cache, and internal architecture. The same brand of CPU (such as Pentium Core and Xeon) will feature many different models, with different clock speeds and cache sizes. Different models cannot be mixed in an SMP system.

Furthermore, vendors release update versions of CPU models under different **steppings**, consisting of a letter and number, starting with A-0. When a minor update is made, the number is incremented (for example, A-1). When a major update is made, the next letter is used (for example, B-0).

You can use a system summary tool such as CPU-Z or a vendor-supplied tool to identify the processor stepping in a running system. A 5-character code in the serial number printed on the chip also identifies the stepping, though you need to use Intel's or AMD's website to decode the identifier (using processorfinder.intel.com for instance).

Generally speaking, you need to use CPUs with identical stepping, though the vendor's website should have information about compatibility between steppings.

Upgrading an SMP system (for example, to use faster CPUs) involves changing all the processors. As with a single processor upgrade, the motherboard firmware may need to be flashed first.

This type of upgrade is not often performed as it is usually simpler to purchase a new server.

Most NOSs support SMP but you may need to upgrade to support more than 2- or 4-way systems. For example, Windows Server 2003 Standard edition supports 2-way and 4-way, the Enterprise edition also supports 8-way, and the DataCenter edition supports 8-way, 32-way, and 64-way SMP. Conversely, the current Linux kernel supports up to 64 CPUs without restriction.

When you upgrade a single processor system to SMP, you may need to update the computer's configuration manually (after installing the CPUs), as the OS may not recognize the change. For example, to update the computer specification in Windows, complete the following steps:

1) Open **Device Manager** and expand the **Computer** icon.

2) Alt-click the current PC device and choose **Update Driver**.

3) Choose the options to locate a driver manually and select the appropriate multiprocessor option (for example, **ACPI Multiprocessor PC**).

In Linux, you would set the appropriate parameters in the boot configuration file.

Upgrading the Heatsink and Fan

If you upgrade a processor, you may also need to upgrade the cooling system. If a CPU runs faster, it may also run hotter and will require a more powerful fan. Upgrade chips are sold either "bare" (without a cooling system) or "boxed" (with a heatsink and fan). If cooling is a problem in a particular server, you can purchase more powerful third-party heatsinks and fans.

System Memory

Memory is an often-performed upgrade, as it is one of the cheapest ways of improving system performance. You will either replace existing chips or add extra chips into spare slots.

There are different types of memory and ways of implementing system memory on the motherboard.

Static versus Dynamic RAM

The RAM type used for system memory in computers and servers is **Dynamic RAM (DRAM)**. DRAM stores each data bit as an electrical charge within a single **bit cell**. A bit cell consists of a **capacitor** to hold a charge (the cell represents 1 if there is a charge and 0 if there is not) and a **transistor** to read the contents of the capacitor. The electrical charge gradually dissipates, causing the memory cell to lose its information. In order to preserve the information, dynamic memory has to be refreshed periodically by accessing each bit cell at regular intervals. The refresh cycles slow down the operation of DRAM but it supports high densities (more MB per memory module) and is relatively low cost.

This differs from the **Static RAM (SRAM)** used for as cache for components such as the CPU.

Memory Type and Speed

Before fitting any new RAM, you must check the correct type and speed of memory at which the motherboard operates. Going back to the 1990s, there have been four main types of system memory:

- SDRAM - runs at the same speed as the system bus and uses a 64-bit data bus. "Plain" SDRAM is obsolete.
- DDR SDRAM - runs at the same speed as the system bus but performs transfers twice per clock cycle. This is expressed in units called megatransfers per second (MT/s). The original DDR specification is also obsolete.
- DDR2 SDRAM - as per DDR except that the bus speed is twice that of the internal memory circuitry. This produces scalable speed improvements without making the chips too unreliable or hot. The drawback is increased latency, as data takes longer to access on each chip. Thermal performance is also improved by working at lower voltages - SDRAM works at 3.3V, DDR at 2.5V, DDR2 at 1.8V, and DDR3 at 1.5V.
- DDR3 SDRAM - as for DDR2 except that the bus speed is trebled compared to the chip speed.

Within the DDR2 and DDR3 standards, the following speeds are supported:

Type	Memory Clock	Bus Clock	Data Rate	Transfer Rate
DDR2-400 / PC2-3200	100 MHz	200 MHz	400 MT/s	3.2 GBps
DDR2-533 / PC2-4200	133 MHz	267 MHz	533 MT/s	4.266 GBps
DDR2-667 / PC2-5300	167 MHz	333 MHz	667 MT/s	5.333 GBps
DDR2-800 / PC2-6400	200 MHz	400 MHz	800 MT/s	6.4 GBps
DDR2-1066 / PC2-8500	266 MHz	533 MHz	1066 MT/s	8.533 GBps
DDR3-1066 / PC3-8500	133 MHz	533 MHz	1066 MT/s	8.533 GBps
DDR3-1333 / PC3-10600	166 MHz	666 MHz	1333 MT/s	10.66 GBps
DDR3-1600 / PC3-12800	200 MHz	800 MHz	1600 MT/s	12.8 GBps
DDR3-1866 / PC3-14900	233 MHz	933 MHz	1866 MT/s	14.933 Gbps
DDR3-2133 / PC3-17000	266 MHz	1066 MHz	2133 MT/s	17.066 Gbps

While not included on the syllabus, DDR4 SDRAM is also available. This runs at higher clock speeds and lower voltages but at the time of writing carries a price premium. DDR4 may also see the growth of Non-Volatile DIMM (NVDIMM) technology (essentially DDR with a flash memory cache and an optional backup power source).

More information on SDRAM standards can be obtained from www.jedec.org.

Memory Packaging

System memory is packaged as **Dual In-line Memory Modules (DIMMs)**, though there are a number of different pin formats and form factors.

- DDR SDRAM - 184 pins

Corsair ValueSelect DDR SDRAM in 184-pin DIMM

- DDR2 / DDR3 SDRAM - 240 pins (keyed differently)

Corsair ValueSelect DDR2 SDRAM in 240-pin DIMM

Corsair XMS DDR3 SDRAM in 240-pin DIMM - note the different pin position and heatsink

Remember that the motherboard will only support a particular type of memory (that is, DDR SDRAM cannot be used with DDR2 slots).

DIMMs have pins on both edges of the board. Memory chips (DRAMs or devices) can be located on one or both sides of the board.

Standard DIMMs are either 43mm (1.7") or 38mm (1.5") in height. Low Profile LP-DIMMs, designed for use in 1U servers, are about 30mm (1.2"); Very Low Profile VLP-DIMMs, designed for use in blade servers, are 18mm (0.72"). Some low profile chassis have angled connectors that can accept taller form factor modules.

Most memory slots are placed on the motherboard. Some servers may support additional memory installed via a riser card, though this type of configuration is not common.

Chips

The capacity of an SDRAM memory module is determined by the number of chips (**devices** or **DRAMs**) and the size of each chip. Most SDRAM and DDR RAM modules are configured with 8 or 16 chips, though server-class modules more typically feature 18 or 36 devices. Each DRAM chip typically has a size (or density) of either 64 MB or 32 MB.

The way a chip stores data is expressed as the depth of the chip by its width. For example, 64Mx8 means the storage locations in the chip are organized into 64 rows and 8 columns with a total capacity of 512 mega*bits*. If there were 8 such chips on a module, the module would be (64Mx8)*8 and have a capacity of 512 MB (mega*bytes*).

x4 chips are cheaper than x8 or x16 chips but can cause problems with some motherboards, especially in high capacity modules (1 GB and over). There are also **high density** chips (128M, 256M, 512M, and higher) but these usually need to be registered DIMMs (see below).

Typical total capacities for server-class memory modules are between 1 and 4 GB. DDR supports up to 1 GB while DDR2 allows up to 4 GB (with 2 gigabit chips). DDR3 allows for higher density chips still (up to 8 gigabits) and therefore much larger modules (up to 16 GB, though no modules larger than 8 GB are available at the time of writing and even these carry a very hefty price premium over 4 GB modules).

The number and layout of chips on a memory board does not generally affect system performance, except when **interleaving** is enabled or a dual channel motherboard is used (see below). That said, for optimum stability, use the same density (and brand) of memory in all sockets, if available.

Latency

Within each brand of DDR, you can find modules at different price points supporting different timings.

Memory latency is referred to as **Column Address Strobe (CAS) Latency (CL)**. There are actually four timing statistics (such as 9-9-9-24), but the CAS value (the first number) is the most important and is sometimes the only figure quoted (CL9 for instance). It represents the number of clock cycles it takes for the controller to look up a memory location. Lower (or "tighter") values represent better performance than higher (or "looser") ones. Memory modules with "loose" CL timings will be marketed as budget RAM while modules with "tight" timings will be marketed as high performance RAM.

CL timings are not directly comparably between different types of SDRAM. To compare SDRAM types, you need to work out the access time in nanoseconds from the latency timings and memory speed. This sort of calculation is relevant whenever a faster type of RAM comes onto the market, as you may need to work out whether it is more cost effective to purchase higher clocked modules with loose timings than it is to purchase lower clocked modules with tight timings.

For optimum performance, install modules with the same CAS timings.

Memory Banks

When memory is installed, it must fill a **bank**, which (in this context) is defined as the amount of data the memory controller expects to fetch. Standard SDRAM (and its DDR variants) uses a 64-bit data bus. ECC (see below) SDRAM uses a 72-bit data bus (with an extra 8 bits for the error correction code).

This usually means that a single DIMM in a single slot will fill a bank. However, as explained in a bit more detail below, there are also dual- and triple-channel memory controllers that access two banks at a time (128-bit [standard] or 144-bit [ECC] data paths).

Also, in multiprocessor systems, each processor has its own memory banks. When installing memory for multiprocessor systems, the memory must usually be **balanced**. This means that the same size memory module should be installed in each CPU bank (that is, the memory configuration for one CPU should be a mirror image of that of the other CPU). Unbalanced configurations may work but are unlikely to be supported by the server vendor.

If a server has two CPU sockets but only one CPU is installed, don't put the memory modules into the missing CPU's banks!

Dual-channel Motherboards

The increasing speed and architectural improvements of CPU technologies have led to memory becoming a bottleneck to system performance. To address this, Intel and AMD developed a dual-channel memory architecture for DDR and DDR2 RAM. Dual-channel is very commonly found on server-level hardware.

With a dual-channel memory controller on the motherboard, there can effectively be two pathways through the system bus, meaning that 128 bits of data can be transferred per "transaction" rather than 64 bits. Ordinary RAM modules are used (that is, there are no "dual channel" memory modules).

A dual-channel motherboard will have at least four DIMM slots arranged in color-coded pairs. Each pair represents one **channel**; each slot represents one of the two **sockets** in each channel. The memory modules installed must be identical in terms of speed and capacity and chip number, density, and location (**memory pairing**). If only two slots are used, the modules must be installed in socket 1 of each channel (that is, slot 1 and slot 3 in most motherboard layouts). Unfortunately there is no standardized color-coding. As well as using different colors, some motherboard manufacturers use the same color for the same channel; others use the same color for the same socket. Check the documentation carefully.

Adding an odd number of modules or adding mismatched DIMMs will cause the system to operate in single-channel mode. Dual channel mode may also need to be enabled via system setup.

Some of Intel's CPUs and supporting chipsets have triple or quadruple channel memory controllers. AMD are starting to release quadruple channel controllers. In these architectures, if the full complement of modules is not installed, the system will revert to dual- or single-channel operation.

There are plenty of more advanced server memory configurations, utilizing multiple controllers, separate memory boards, mirrored memory, online spare modules, and so on. These can be designed to provide better performance and / or reliability (fault tolerance and redundancy).

Other Memory Features

Dual-rank Memory

Data is transferred to and from the memory controller and data bus in 64-bit chunks called words (though motherboards supporting ECC memory use an extra 8 bits for parity calculations). **Single *rank*** memory is a module where all the chips are used simultaneously to read or write a single word; that is, the CPU can access all of the DRAMs on the module(s) at the same time.

Dual *rank* memory divides the memory chips on a single module into two groups. The controller can access one rank or the other using a Chip Select (CS) command, but not both simultaneously. This makes the memory higher *density* (equivalent to stuffing two modules into one slot) but degrades *performance* slightly. There are also **quad-rank** modules, found on some server-level hardware.

The physical location of chips on one or both sides of a memory module is usually, but not always, an indicator of whether the module is single- or dual-rank. Single-sided modules are always single-rank; double-sided unbuffered (see below) modules are always dual-rank. Double-sided, registered DIMMs can be single-, dual- or quad-rank. On some modules, two "layers" of DRAMs are "stacked" on top of one another.

The memory controller on the motherboard will only be able to support a given number of ranks across all available slots (each rank constitutes a separate **electrical load**). Consequently, DIMM slots may not always support dual rank modules or may only support one dual rank module (typically this must be installed in the first slot) - check the motherboard documentation or vendor memory configuration tool carefully.

In some cases, support for dual or quad rank memory may be enabled through a firmware update. There may also be the option to enable or disable support through System Setup.

ECC

Motherboards used to use a simple error detection method called **parity checking**. Each byte of data in memory is accompanied by a ninth bit. This bit is set to 1 or 0 to make the total number of bits set to 1 in the byte an odd or even number, depending on the type of parity checking being performed.

When the byte is read, its parity is checked to ensure that the parity value is still odd (or even). If this is not the case, a bit must have become corrupted.

System memory for most desktops is **non-parity**; that is, it does not perform error checking (except for the startup memory count). For systems that require a high level of reliability (such as workstations and servers), **Error Checking and Correcting (ECC)** memory is available.

ECC memory is enhanced parity circuitry that can detect internal data errors and make corrections. ECC will detect and correct single-bit errors and allow the system to continue functioning normally. It will also detect errors of 2, 3 or 4 bits but will not correct them; instead, it will generate an error message and halt the system.

ECC memory has an extra chip and a 72-bit data bus rather than 64-bit. The motherboard must support the use of ECC memory modules (and the option to use them must typically be enabled in system setup). ECC memory cannot be mixed with non-ECC modules.

HP DDR ECC Registered memory module

An ECC DIMM will have an odd number of memory chips while non-parity DIMMs will have an even number of memory chips.

ECC memory is often identified with an "E" tag on the product brand. For example, ECC-type DDR3 memory for an 800 MHz system bus would be listed as **PC3-12800E**.

Registered and Buffered Memory

The larger a RAM module is, the greater the electrical load placed on it by the memory controller. A buffered module is one with a register between the DRAM devices and the memory controller. The buffer regulates the electrical load that can be placed on the module at the expense of slowing access down slightly.

Registered modules are memory in which address and control lines are buffered, but data lines are not. **Fully buffered modules** are where data and address and control lines are all buffered. Registered memory is connected to the controller via a "stub bus"; a single electrical path with branches to each module (wired in parallel). FBDIMMs have a point-to-point connection with the controller (wired in series). This allows the board to support more slots and consequently use lower density modules, which perform better. It also reduces signal problems that affect a parallel bus.

Most (but not all) ECC memory is registered or fully buffered. Most memory for desktop PCs is **unbuffered**; that is, the chipset connects directly to the memory chips. Memory for servers, if not ECC, then tends to be at least registered or fully buffered because of the amount of RAM installed.

As with ECC, registered memory must be supported by the motherboard and cannot be mixed with other types. Often the motherboard will support **only** registered memory or requires registered memory if more than a set amount of RAM is installed.

Registered memory is packaged in **RDIMMs**; fully buffered memory is packaged in **FBDIMMs**. The modules are differently keyed to prevent them being used in the wrong type of slot. You may find "ordinary" unbuffered DIMMs listed as **UDIMMs** on some vendors' sales sites.

To identify whether memory is ECC or registered, look at the chips on the card. An ECC module will have 9 similar-size chips rather than 8; a registered or fully buffered module will have an extra smaller chip.

Expansion Cards

A server motherboard will contain basic display, networking, storage and peripheral adapters and ports. Additional functionality can be provided by installing an expansion card into a suitable slot.

Expansion Buses and Slots

An expansion card must be matched to a free slot of the appropriate bus. Slots and cards feature a number of pins and pin configurations to prevent the insertion of an incompatible card.

Depending on its age, a server may support a number of bus types. Depending on its size, a server may support a number of slots. 1U and 2U rack servers typically have very little expansion potential. These servers may only support low-profile cards or use riser cards (so that the expansion card is inserted at a right-angle to the motherboard). The main expansion bus types are as follows:

- PCI (Peripheral Component Interconnect) - support for this 32-bit parallel bus is still quite common. The bus runs at 33 MHz allowing for 133 MBps bandwidth shared between all connected adapters (up to 5 are allowed). A 64-bit version of PCI was released as a standard but servers are more likely to support PCI-X.
- PCI eXtended (PCI-X) - this is a server version of PCI. PCI-X is a 64-bit parallel interface running at 133 MHz (with a bandwidth of about 1 GBps). PCI-X revision 2 defined faster bus speeds of 266 MHz and 533 MHz. PCI-X slots can usually accept PCI cards, but this slows down the whole bus to PCI speeds.

A PCI or PCI-X bus will only work at the speed of the slowest component. There are also 3.3V, 5V, and universal versions. 3.3V and 5V are not compatible. Key positions on the cards and slots prevent insertion of a 5V card in a 3.3V slot, and vice versa.

- PCI Express (PCIe) - this is the current bus standard. It uses serial, point-to-point links between devices, meaning that there is no bandwidth sharing. A link can use a number of lanes. PCIe slots are different sizes depending on the number of lanes they support (x1, x2, x4, x8, x16, or x32). A PCIe switch negotiates the maximum possible number of lanes to use (for example, x8 and x16 devices would use 8 lanes). Version 1 PCIe lanes support 250 MBps each way while version 2 doubles that (to 500 MBps), version 3 doubles it again (to 1 GBps), and version 4 allows 2 GBps per lane. A card will fit in any connector with an equal or greater number of lanes. For example, a x8 card will fit in a x8 or x16 socket, but *not* in a x1 or x4 socket.

  PCIe is software-compatible with PCI, meaning that PCI connectors can be included on a motherboard (to support legacy adapter cards) but PCI cards *cannot* be fitted into PCIe sockets.

  PCIe can supply up to 75W to a device via the motherboard slot and an additional 75W via an auxiliary power connector. PCIe 2 increases power to 150W from the slot and auxiliary connector. PCIe also features power management functions and support for hot-pluggable adapters.

Don't confuse PCI-X with PCIe (Express). PCI-X is an older, parallel interface; PCIe is a newer, serial interface.

Types of Expansion Cards

- NIC (Network Interface Card) - most motherboards will support at least one network adapter. Add-in cards provide more ports or support for different media types (a fiber optic link for instance). Wi-Fi cards enable the server to communicate via a wireless network, though such links are usually too low bandwidth to support server traffic.

See Unit 2.1 for more information about features of server-class NICs.

- HBA (Host Bus Adapter) - this provides an expansion bus not supported on the motherboard. On a server, this is most likely to be a SAS host adapter or a card providing advanced RAID functionality or SAN connectivity.

An adapter that can function as both an Ethernet adapter and fibre channel adapter is referred to as a Converged Network Adapter (CNA).

- Port expansion card - this is an HBA for external interfaces. You may need to install one to support unusual interfaces, such as Firewire (IEEE 1394) or eSATA, to provide extra USB ports, or to support legacy interfaces that would no longer be supported on a server motherboard, such as a parallel or serial port. The following table lists key features of the main port types:

Technology	Max Transfer Rate	Cabling / Range	Connectors	Other Features
PS/2		~10m	6-pin	Mouse and keyboard only
Serial	~115 Kbps	~15m	9-pin or 25-pin	
Parallel (SPP)	~150 KBps	~5m	25-pin at host; 36-pin at device	Unidirectional
Parallel (ECP/EPP)	~2 MBps	~10m	25-pin at host; 36-pin at device	Bidirectional
USB 1.1	12 Mbps	5m	Type A at host; Type B or Mini/Micro-B at device	Up to 127 devices; supports hot swapping; up to 2.5W power
USB 2.0	480 Mbps	5m	As above	As above
USB 3.0 / 3.1	5 Gbps / 10 Gbps	~3m	As above	As above but up to 4.5W power
Firewire (IEEE 1394)	400 Mbps	4.5m	6-pin or 4-pin (unpowered)	Up to 63 devices; supports hot swapping; up to 15W power
Firewire (IEEE 1394b)	800 Mbps	4.5m	9-pin	As above but up to 45W power plus support for network media
SCSI	Up to 320 MBps	12m (for LVD)	Usually 68-pin	Up to 16 devices (wide bus)

USB 3 connectors are 9-pin but USB 3 Type A connectors and ports are compatible with older versions. Type B connectors and ports are not compatible between USB 3 and USB 1+2. SuperSpeed-capable cables do not have an official maximum length but up to about 3m is recommended.

- Video - the adapter provided in the chipset will usually be adequate. Servers do not generally need advanced graphics capabilities.

That said, there are now opportunities for virtualizing workstations used for CAD and other graphics tasks. These use specialist graphics adapters, designed for use with virtualization.

- Audio - server chipsets are unlikely to support audio (speakers and microphone) beyond diagnostic beeps. If this functionality is required for some reason you could install an audio expansion card.

Installing an Expansion Card

Unless the card is hot-swappable, you must power down the server before adding or removing an adapter. If changing a hot-swappable card, use the card's driver to disable it first (or there may be a switch on the card itself). Insert the card into the appropriate type of expansion slot and ensure that it is fully inserted. Some force will be required to push the card all the way into the expansion slot. Do not use excessive or sudden force and ensure that the adapter card does not bend. Secure the adapter card to the system case with a screw. Cover any unused slots with banking plates, securing them with a screw. Low profile and blade servers are likely to feature a riser cage or mezzanine board layout where cards are installed parallel with the main board.

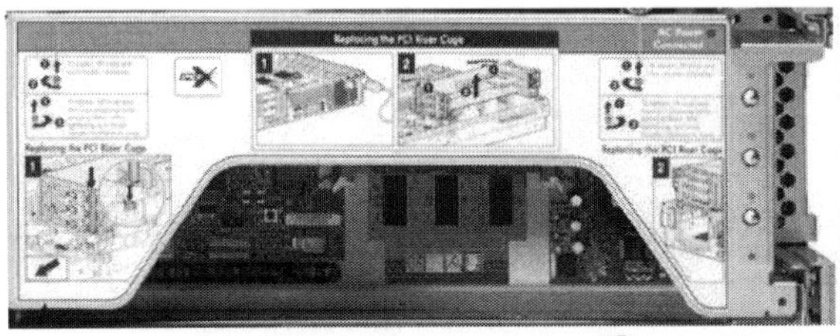

Riser cage on an HP Proliant server (Image © 2014 HP)

In a blade server, mezzanine card ports are normally lettered A, B, and so on. When installing interconnect adapters (such as Ethernet or Fibre Channel), each blade must use the same type of adapter in a given mezzanine port. For example, you could not install a Fibre Channel card in port A of blade 1 and an Ethernet adapter in port A of blade 2; the Ethernet adapter would have to go in port B. Additionally, each mezzanine port must be matched to an appropriate interconnect module / switch. For example, the Fibre Channel cards in port A of blades 1 and 2 would be wired to an FC module installed in the enclosure's second or third interconnect bay. The midplane determines which interconnect bays map to which mezzanine ports - refer to the enclosure's installation guide for this information.

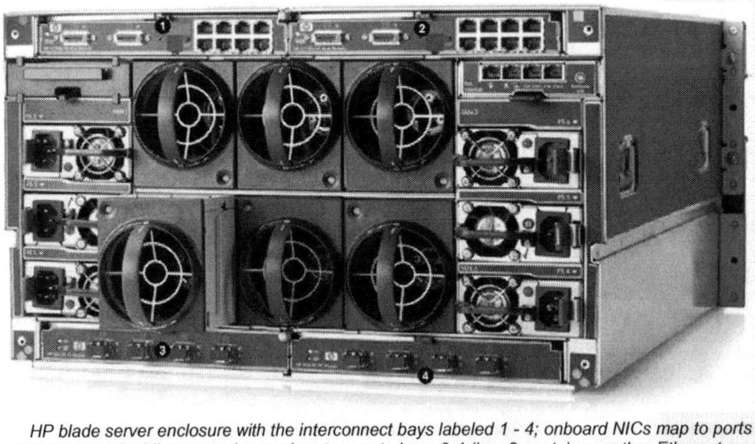

HP blade server enclosure with the interconnect bays labeled 1 - 4; onboard NICs map to ports in interconnect 1 while mezzanine card ports map to bays 2-4 (bay 2 contains another Ethernet module while bays 3 and 4 contain FC modules (Image © 2014 HP)

There are also low-profile form factor expansion cards.

Review Questions / Module 4 / Unit 1 / Server Hardware

Answer these questions to test what you have learned in this unit.

1) What is stepping and why is it important?
2) True or false? HyperThreading exposes multiple logical processors to the operating system.
3) What step do you need to take when adding a CPU to a single-CPU system?
4) Is it true that DDR SDRAM chips of different speeds can be installed on the same motherboard?
5) You are planning a memory upgrade and have some space 4 GB UDIMM modules. Can you mix UDIMMs and FBDIMMs on the same motherboard?
6) You need to improve reliability in a critical database server. Can you update the motherboard firmware to support ECC RAM?
7) If using dual- or quad-rank memory modules, why might you not be able to fill all the available slots on a motherboard?
8) What is the difference between PCI Express and PCI?
9) Why might you have to install expansion cards into a riser card?
10) You need to install a Host Bus Adapter into a PCI slot on a server with a low-profile server chassis. The only low-profile HBA card you have is a PCIe one. Can you proceed with the installation?

Module 4 / Unit 2

Environment and Maintenance

Objectives

On completion of this unit, you will be able to:

- List the environmental factors that should be considered when placing and maintaining server equipment.
- Describe the components of server and rack cooling systems.
- Understand the requirements for specifying and installing HVAC systems.

Developing a Server Management Plan

A management plan is as important as installation or upgrade plans. The management plan should indicate what tasks are to be performed, when, and by whom. Tasks would include monitoring performance and hardware status, performing backups, resolving and recording errors, cleaning and environmental checks, identifying security threats and measures, detecting and resolving security breaches and intrusions, and so on.

It is essential that the plan sets out clear responsibilities and procedures for auditing action items (that is, ensuring that tasks are carried out properly and securely). Technicians responsible for maintenance may have different levels of access to the system. For example, administrators may have access to all configuration options on a server but backup operators can only access backup software and media.

The results of management activities would be reported back and fed into development plans, to identify upgrade requirements. In the event that a problem is discovered during routine maintenance, a proper change management procedure should be followed to ensure that the solution is tested and verified without further impacting performance, reliability, or security.

Preventive Maintenance

Preventive Maintenance (PM) involves identifying and resolving environmental factors that contribute to system failure.

It is important to establish a preventive maintenance schedule, identifying the key cleaning and inspection tasks. The frequency at which tasks should be performed will depend on the environmental factors, but consider the following guidelines:

- Physical Inspection 1-2x week (check warning lights, cables, temperature / humidity monitors, air intakes and outlets, inspect for damage, pay attention to unusual noises or smells).

- Software Inspection 1-2x week (review monitoring software and logs; review vendor's websites for security updates and other news).
- Physical Service 1-2x year (clean chassis and replace air filters; inspect internal cables and connections).

Maintenance activity should be recorded in a log.

Server Chassis Features

Much server management is done remotely but there are still instances where you need to work with the physical server unit and you should understand the external components of the server chassis.

Power and Reset Buttons

One of the key distinctions between a desktop PC and a server is that you never turn a server off without a very good reason and a lot of planning!

Consequently, the **power button** on a server will often be protected by some sort of locking mechanism. Even if there is no lock, it is usually the case that you need to hold down the power button for a few seconds for anything to happen.

Often the power button may not completely power down the server but put it into standby mode instead (allowing it to be woken by remote management software) and you may need to remove the AC cord to completely power off the server.

Some servers may also feature a **reset button**, which will shut down then reboot the server. This is usually only a feature of older server models though.

The precise operation of server-level hardware is very often vendor- or model-specific. Check the user or maintenance guide carefully if you are at all unfamiliar with the server model.

Diagnostic LEDs

Servers can be managed remotely, with alerts and event information being sent to a management station. Sometimes however, there is no substitute to patrolling the data center floor looking for problems. Server vendors make this sort of frontline troubleshooting and maintenance easier by providing a number of status and diagnostic LEDs on the front and back of the chassis.

For example, the HP DL 165 server provides the following diagnostics:

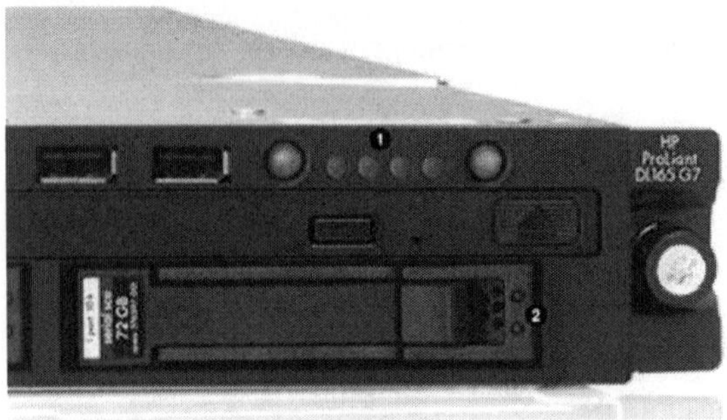

HP DL 165 rack-mounted server with 1) UID, power, health, and NIC activity LEDs and 2) Drive LEDs

- Power - the LED is green for on and amber for standby.
- System health - this shows red when the server is shutting down or in a critical state, amber when it is powering up or in a degraded state, and green otherwise.
- UID (Unique ID) - this blue LED can be activated remotely and helps a technician locate the server in the rack. It flashes when there is a remote management connection. Remember to switch the UID off when you have finished whatever work you needed to do.
- NIC(s) - steady green represents a network link and flickers represent activity on a network card.
- Hard drive online - this LED can be set to blue using management software (to ID the drive) or shows orange if the drive has failed.
- Hard drive activity - flashes to show disk activity.
- Optical disc - flashes to show disc activity.

The rear of the chassis has a rear UID indicator and NIC LEDs to show the link status, speed, and activity.

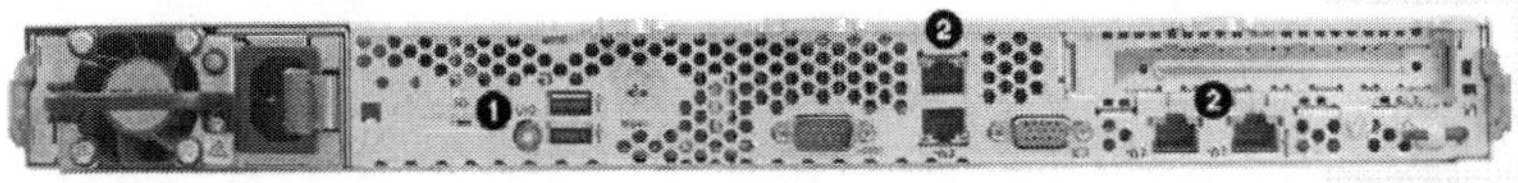

HP DL 165 rack-mounted server with 1) Rear UID indicator and 2) NIC speed and activity LEDs

Some servers may come with small LCDs to display status messages (such as "Power supply failed") on the front panel.

Performing Shut Down

It is important that when an administrator shuts down a server, the proper procedure is followed. This ensures that users are not disrupted, data is not damaged or lost, and applications can close in an orderly manner.

All operating systems provide mechanisms for system restart or shut down and many log the event.

Shutting Down Windows

Only authorized users can perform a system shut down. On servers, that means members of the built-in group **Administrators** (and **Server Operators** in domain environments). The shut down server permission can also be assigned using group policy security settings to any user or group.

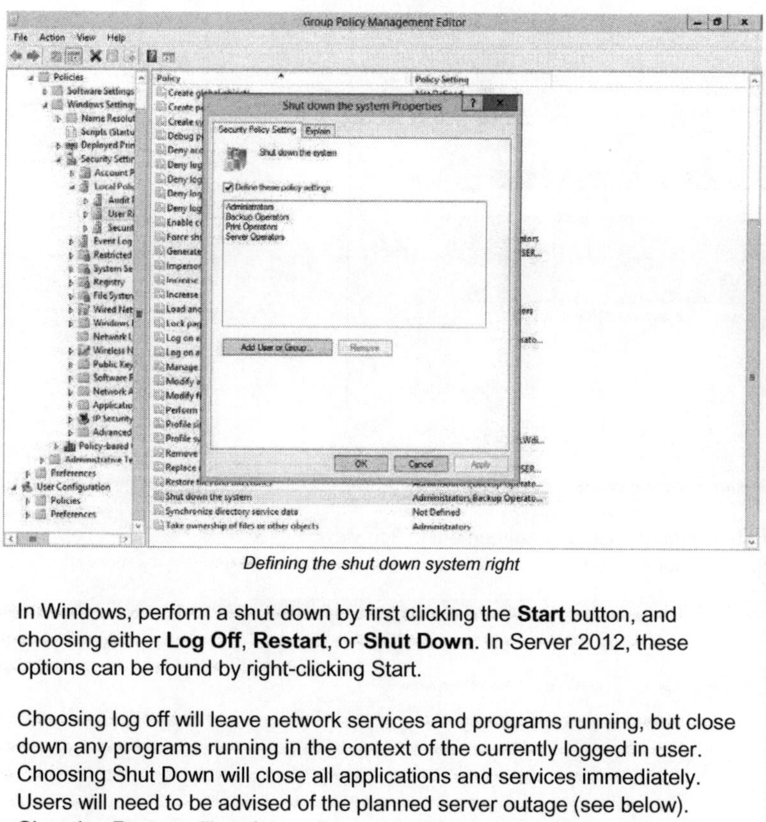

Defining the shut down system right

In Windows, perform a shut down by first clicking the **Start** button, and choosing either **Log Off**, **Restart**, or **Shut Down**. In Server 2012, these options can be found by right-clicking Start.

Choosing log off will leave network services and programs running, but close down any programs running in the context of the currently logged in user. Choosing Shut Down will close all applications and services immediately. Users will need to be advised of the planned server outage (see below). Choosing Restart will perform a "warm boot" (the server will shut down then boot again immediately).

An alternative method for gaining access to shut down is to press **`Ctrl+Alt+Del`** and choose the appropriate option. If a user lacks the rights to shut down the system, the option is grayed out.

The administrator must describe the reason for a shut down or restart event, which shows up in the log, though in Server 2012 no comment needs to be entered.

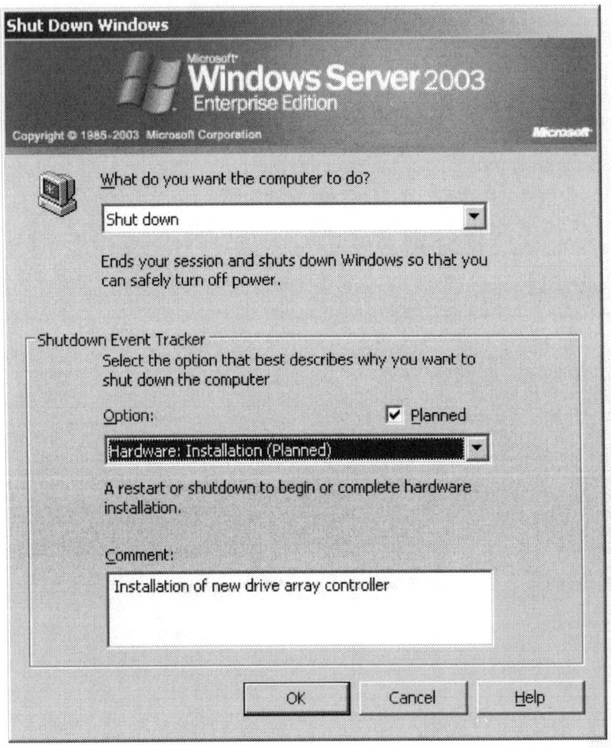

Shut down event tracker in Windows Server 2003

Before a shut down or restart, use the computer management tool to view open sessions (connected workstations)...

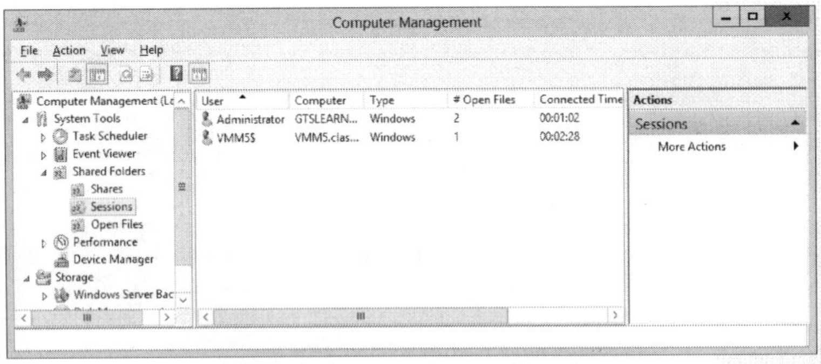

Monitoring sessions using Computer Management

...or open files. You can then send a message to the user to save and disconnect from the server.

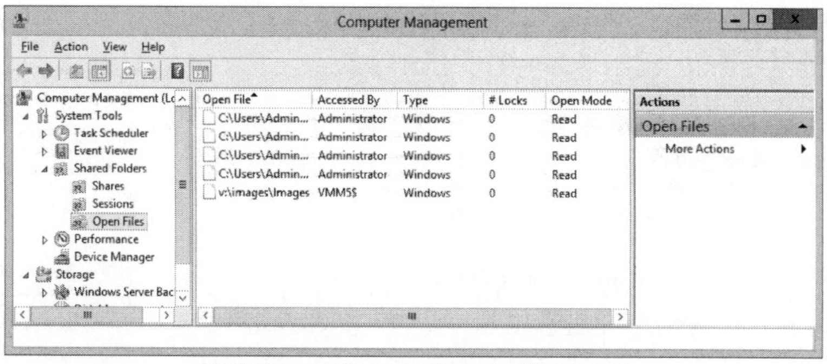

Monitoring open files using Computer Management

shutdown.exe can also be run from a command line with a number of switches, allowing shut down of a remote computer:

```
shutdown \\computername /switches
```

The following switches are available:

Switch	Usage
`/l`	Shut down the local computer.
`/r`	Restart.
`/t:xx`	Specify a timeout (in seconds); the default if omitted is 20 seconds.
`/y`	Answer "Yes" to any prompts.
`/c`	Force applications to quit without saving data.
`/a`	Quit a shut down if entered within the timeout period.

Shutting Down Linux

One of the key "selling points" of Linux is that unlike Windows it almost never needs to be shut down or restarted. Nonetheless, like Windows, if the need to shut down or restart a Linux server does arise, it should be done so "cleanly", giving users time to log off, processes time to terminate, and disk writes time to complete.

On server distributions, the root user, or those users delegated with the authority (as defined in the **sudoers** file in the **/etc** directory), can perform a shut down or restart task. This is to ensure only proper and appropriate server shut downs can occur.

To perform the shut down, open a console (command prompt) in super user mode, and enter the command `shutdown`.

The command's usage is:

```
shutdown -Switches Time Warning
```

Time can be the keyword **`now`**, which means immediately, an absolute time (***`hh:mm`***), or a number of minutes in the future (**`+m`**).

There are a number of other switches which enable different modes of shut down, shown in the table below.

Switch	Purpose
`-a`	Used when the logged in user may not have the permissions to shut down. The entries in the file **/etc/sudoers** will determine who can perform the shut down.
`-k`	Don't really shut down, but warn of shut down.
`-r`	Reboot after shut down (warm boot).
`-h`	Halt after shut down.
`-z`	Shut down with software suspend.
`-f`	Skip disk check on restart.
`-F`	Force disk check on restart.
`-n`	Don't shut down cleanly using init, but shut down instantly.
`-c`	Cancel a shut down which is already running.
`-t`	Number of seconds between statement being issued and being executed.

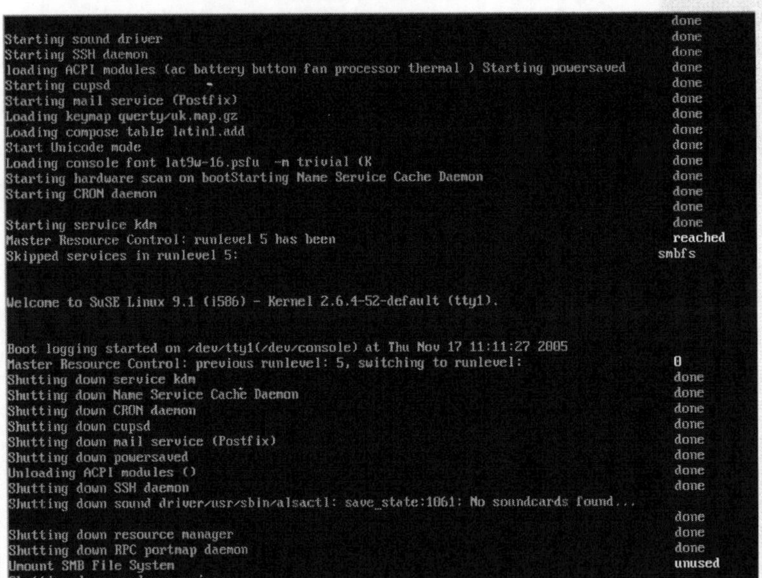

Linux shut down in progress

Server Startup Sequence

If you have to shut down a number of servers, there is likely to be an optimum order in which to restart the servers. While every environment is different, the following general order should minimize problems with dependencies between different servers:

1) Network services (DHCP, DNS, Domain Controllers).
2) Shared data storage.
3) Back-end databases and middleware.
4) Front-end application servers.

If a server has attached devices, you should normally power those up before starting the server.

Server Cooling

When a component draws power, only a portion of the power is turned into useful work (computer processing). A substantial amount of the power is lost as heat. This heat needs to be removed from the computer system as excessive heat within the case will cause the components to malfunction.

Cooling and Thermal Design Power

Thermal Design Power (TDP) is a measure of how much cooling a component requires. For example, a CPU with a TDP of 65 W requires a cooling system rated for a TDP of 65 W. TDP is calculated as the demand under average use; peak demand may be higher and power consumption when idle may be lower.

Cooling within the server chassis is achieved by a number of factors...

Passive Cooling

A **heatsink** is a large block of metal with one flat side and one side broken up into "fins". The fins expose a greater surface area to the surrounding air and are therefore cooled more easily (thermal dissipation). The flat side is placed close to the processor and conducts heat away from it to the relatively cooler fins by the process of conduction and from the fins to the air. The warmth in the air surrounding the heat sink is gradually taken away to other parts of the case (and out of the case via any exhaust vents) by the process of convection.

Active Cooling

A heatsink will only work so long as the air around it is cool enough. Modern CPUs generate more heat than passive cooling can cope with so a system of **fans** is required to draw cool air from outside the computer across the heatsink and out of an exhaust vent.

In a tower server, a fan mounted on top of the heatsink draws air across it. Another larger fan is provided in the power supply to suck warm air out of the case. Servers often feature multiple additional case fans, which would either blow cool air in (if the fan is mounted on the front of the case) or suck warm air out (if the fan is mounted on the back, next to the PSU fan). PSUs are based on the ATX standard. The original ATX 1.0 standard specified that the PSU fan should blow air into the case. This standard was used in the time when CPUs only needed a passively cooled heatsink. The ATX standard was subsequently revised to make the PSU fan suck warm air out. You are extremely unlikely to come across any ATX 1.0 systems.

In a 1U or 2U rack-mounted server or blade, there is more likely to be a row of system fans located within the case, as there is not enough room to put the fans on top of the component's heatsink.

Most chassis designs incorporate a system of plastic shrouds, baffles, and/or ducts to channel the flow of cool air over components and take warm air to the rear exhaust vents.

Plastic shroud (1) covering the CPU and channeling the air to the fan exhaust (2) on an HP PC system

Hot air rises so, on a tower case, a fan that blows air in should be located low down and one that sucks warm air out should be located high up.

As mentioned above, fans are rated at a particular TDP level. The basic measure of performance for a fan is the amount of air it can shift, measured in Cubic Feet per Minute (CFM). This is largely determined by the speed at which the fan spins (measured in revolutions per minute [rpm]) and its size. Fans are also rated for their noise level, measured in decibels (dB).

The main problem with active cooling is that it requires electricity to run the fans and therefore means the system is consuming more energy (just to cope with the amount of energy it is consuming!) Most fans support variable speeds, allowing software to slow the fan down when it is not needed, reducing energy consumption. Internal monitors record the temperature at the location of each fan.

When installing or replacing a fan, remember to connect the power cable to the appropriate port on the motherboard.

Redundant Cooling

Enterprise-class servers will provide two or more redundant cooling fans. This means that if one fan fails, the other should still be able to cool the chassis adequately until the failed unit can be replaced.

Redundant fans may also be hot-swappable so that they can be swapped over without shutting down the server.

Liquid Cooled Servers

Water or liquid cooling refers to a system of pumping water or other coolant around the chassis. Liquids are a much more effective coolant than air convection and a good pump can run more quietly than numerous fans. Dual circuit systems with redundancy (in case one pump fails) are available.

Liquid cooling has its advocates but it is usually more costly and makes maintenance and upgrades more difficult. Many administrators are also nervous about allowing liquid in such close proximity to server circuits. Consequently it is not used as a chassis cooling method by any of the major server vendors.

Water cooling units for racks are available though. One solution is a water-cooled heat exchanger at the back of the rack to absorb the warmth from the air blown out of the server exhausts.

Ventilation and Airflow

Cooler air around the server makes it easier to reduce the temperature within the case. Obviously, there is a limit to what the computer user will put up with but for unoccupied computer rooms and data centers this is the most efficient way to achieve cooling.

Heating, Ventilation, Air Conditioning (HVAC)

A **Heating, Ventilation, Air Conditioning (HVAC)** system ensures adequate cooling and humidity and dust control within a room or other enclosed space. All airflow into and out of the room is run through ducts, fans, and filters and warmed or cooled to the correct temperature and humidity.

You might also see the term Computer Room Air Conditioner (CRAC) for units specifically designed for computer facilities and data centers.

Temperature and Humidity

It is highly beneficial to install servers and network equipment in a dedicated room or area. This can be isolated from the rest of the premises for security and also helps to control the environmental conditions around the server equipment. Servers and other networking equipment are often housed in a purpose-built facility (a data center).

An environment that is too warm will raise the chances of system components overheating and failing. An environment that is too cold can cause stress on components with moving parts (such as hard drives and fans) and is more susceptible to static damage (ESD).

Also, the temperature in the server room should not be allowed to *vary* by too much. Temperature variations could cause condensation and, if extreme enough, cause components to expand or contract. Over time, connectors can work free from their sockets (chip creep) and cause errors.

A humid environment runs the risk of condensation forming on components, which can lead to short circuits or corrosion. A low humidity environment greatly increases the chance of ESD.

Environmental Monitoring

Spaces housing data equipment and cabling should be kept at an ambient temperature of between 18-24°C (64-75F) and at a relative humidity of 30-55%.

Some data centers (notably those operated by Google) are allowing higher temperatures (up to around 26ºC / 80ºF). This can achieve significant energy cost savings and modern electronics is proving reliable at this temperature.

This would normally be maintained by the building **HVAC** system with **environmental monitors** to measure temperature and relative humidity in each space. **Network-enabled** monitors can be connected to switches or connected to a PC via USB and integrated with network management software to provide an alert if environmental conditions change. Monitors connected to **rack controllers** can provide feedback on the conditions within a single rack.

When using an air conditioning system, ensure that it is inspected and maintained periodically. Systems may be fitted with alarms to alert staff to problems. Highly mission-critical systems may require a backup air conditioning system.

HP Dynamic Smart Cooling sensors integrate with the air conditioning system to target cooling to a particular rack (Image © 2011 Hewlett-Packard Development Company, L.P)

Use a portable monitor to verify that the HVAC's temperature and humidity sensors are returning the correct readings.

Device Placement and Airflow

The room should also provide decent airflow around the network equipment. Airflow is provided by ensuring enough space (at least 3 feet or 1 meter) around the server or rack. Obviously, air conditioning vents should not be blocked by racks or equipment. If cool air circulates via space under a raised floor with perforated tiles to draw it over the server equipment, these should not be blocked. Where possible, the space should not be exposed to direct sunlight.

If multiple racks are used, install equipment so that servers are placed back-to-back not front-to-back, so that the warm exhaust from one bank of servers is not forming the air intake for another bank. This is referred to as a **hot aisle / cold aisle** arrangement.

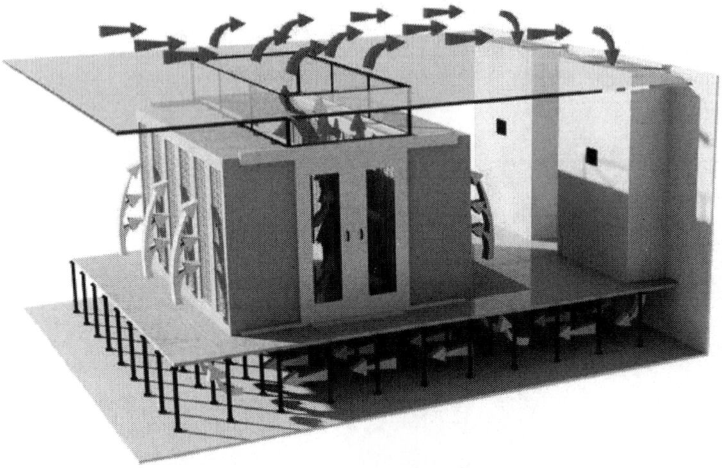

Hot aisle containment design by www.keyzone.com - cold air circulates from the air conditioner under the floor and around the rack while hot air is drawn from between the racks through the ceiling space (plenum) to a heat exchanger; in this design it is very important that hot air does not leak from the ceiling or from the floor space between the racks

In order to prevent **air leaks** from the hot aisle to the cold aisle, ensure that any gaps in racks are filled by appropriate measures:

- **Blanking / filler panels** box the rack in so that there are no gaps in the front where positions in the rack are not filled by devices. This helps to maintain the pressure differential between the front and back of the rack created by the rack fans. Blanking panels are available in different U heights (typically 1U, 2U, and 4U panels). There are flat and vented versions. Another option is a brush panel that allows cables to pass through.
- **Baffles** can be positioned at an angle at the top of the rack to channel the warm air exhaust away from cooled areas.
- **Strip curtains or excluders** cover any spaces above or between racks.

An equipment room should not be used as storage space. Do not leave boxes or unused equipment in it. Also, do not install unnecessary devices that generate a lot of heat, such as printers.

The heat generated by equipment per hour is measured in British Thermal Units (BTU) or KiloWatts (KW). 1 KW is 3412 BTU. To calculate the cooling requirement for an air conditioning system, multiply the wattage of all equipment in the room (including lighting) by 3.41 to get the BTU/hour. If the server room is occupied (unlikely in most cases), add 400 BTU/person. The air conditioner's BTU-rating must exceed this total value.

Low-end air conditioning systems are usually rated between 5,000 and 10,000 BTU. Larger units may be rated by tonnage. One ton of load is 12,000 BTU/hour.

Fans can also be installed on the server racks themselves to provide adequate airflow and cooling within the rack. Additional sensors may also be provided to direct cooling where it is most needed, reducing energy costs (air conditioning and high speed fans use a lot of power).

It is also essential to insulate the room properly and to stop any potential air leaks. Allowing cold air to leak will cause the HVAC system to have to work harder to maintain the correct climate, using more energy. Air leaks may be caused by obvious things like open doors or windows or by missing wall or floor tiles or holes punched for cabling.

Dust

Dust can damage computer components with moving parts or openings, such as floppy drives, tape drives, and fans. If a layer of dust builds up on components, it can contribute to overheating.

Dust can be controlled by periodic cleaning but this will involve switching the server off. Fans and vents can be fitted with filters to remove dust, but these require periodic cleaning or replacement. A costlier solution is to provide for air filters as part of the air conditioning system.

As with any computer system, ensure that any unused adapter slots or drive bays on the server case are covered by banking plates. It is also best not to carpet the floor in the server room, as this generates more dust and can increase the risk of ESD damage.

Review Questions / Module 4 / Unit 2 / Environment and Maintenance

Answer these questions to test what you have learned in this unit.

1) What might be the significance of a blue LED on the back of a server chassis?
2) Write the command to reboot a Linux server immediately:
3) Why might pressing the power button on a server have no effect?
4) What metric can be used to specify appropriate an cooling product for a CPU?
5) What arrangement of racks makes optimum use of HVAC cooling?
6) You are installing multiple racks in a server room. What layout guidelines should you try to follow?

Module 4 / Unit 3
Power Distribution

Objectives

On completion of this unit, you will be able to:

- Implement server-class power supplies and UPS.
- Describe features of data center power distribution.

Power

To understand power distribution to servers and problems that can arise, you should understand some basic concepts about electrical power supplies. Electricity is the flow of electrons through a conductor. The characteristics of the electricity supply are measured as volts, current (amperage), resistance, and power.

- **Voltage** - the potential difference between two points (often likened to pressure in a water pipe) measured in Volts (V).
- **Current** - the actual flow of electrons, measured in Amps (I). A current flows in a **circuit**, which is made when conductors form a continuous path between the positive and negative terminals of a power source. The size of the current is determined by the conductivity of the circuit (for example, a higher current can flow in a thicker wire than can in a thinner one).
- **Resistance** - the conductivity of the media, measured in Ohms (Ω or R).
- **Power** - the rate at which electricity is drawn from the supply by the device using it, measured in Watts. Power is equal to the Voltage multiplied by the Current (W=V*I).
- **Energy** - the amount of power consumed by a device over time. This is measured in Watt-hours (or more typically Kilowatt-hours [kWh]).

In a Direct Current (DC) circuit, the charge flows in one direction from the positive to negative terminals of the power source at a constant voltage. DC is used for electronic circuits, which require stable voltages.

Mains electricity is supplied as Alternating Current (AC), which means that the current flows in both directions around the circuit and the voltage alternates between a peak and neutral (often 0). In the UK, consumer mains power is supplied at a peak value of 220-240 VAC ("high-line") while in the US it is 110-120 VAC ("low-line"). Power supplied to commercial and industrial properties is usually higher still (440 / 460 / 480 VAC). AC is a cheap way to distribute electrical power over long distances but is incompatible with electronics. A transformer in the computer's power supply is used to convert AC to DC voltages.

Fuses

A **fuse** is a circuit breaker designed to protect the device and users of the device from faulty wiring or supply of power (**overcurrent protection**). Faults could damage device components, cause fires, or expose the user to electric shock.

A fuse contains a wire that can support a specified amount of current; if excess current flows then the wire melts and breaks the circuit. A fuse is normally used in the outlet plug and needs to be replaced if it "blows". There may also be internal fuses at points within the device where electrical current flows over any sort of wiring.

Grounding

A connection to **ground** (or **earth**) provides a return path for electrical current. This is usually a safety feature; if an electrical connection short circuits into the metal chassis, a ground wire ensures that the current flows to ground rather than electrocuting someone handling the faulty device.

Some power circuits contain a ground wire. If the circuit does not contain a ground wire, any electrical devices with metal cases (or any metal objects that could come into contact with electrical wires) must be bonded to the building's earth system.

Surges

The AC power supply is fairly clean (almost a pure sine wave) when it leaves the power station but it can become corrupted by electrical noise, or interference, from the devices connected to it.

A **spike** (or **surge**) is an abrupt, but very brief, change in the value of the voltage. It can last from a few billionths of a second (a transient) to a few thousandths of a second. It can be caused by a light being turned off or a nearby lightning storm.

Many spikes are very small and of too short a duration to cause problems, but some can take the supply several hundred volts over its normal value and cause sufficient interference to a computer's power supply to crash, reboot, or even damage it. An instance of a large power spike is shown below.

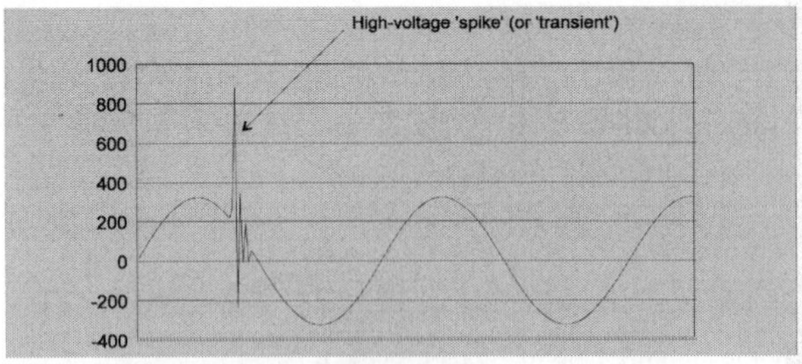

Power Spike

Sags

Some electrically powered devices require very high starting, or inrush, current. These include items with large motors (for example, lifts, washing machines, power tools), PC power supplies, transformers, and industrial power tools.

When this kind of device is turned on, the large current surge into the device may cause the available voltage within the locality to dip for a brief period of time, causing a **sag.** Sags may also be caused by the switching of power distribution circuits by the generating companies. A power sag may only last for a few milliseconds but sags of longer than about 10 to 20 milliseconds can cause computer equipment to malfunction.

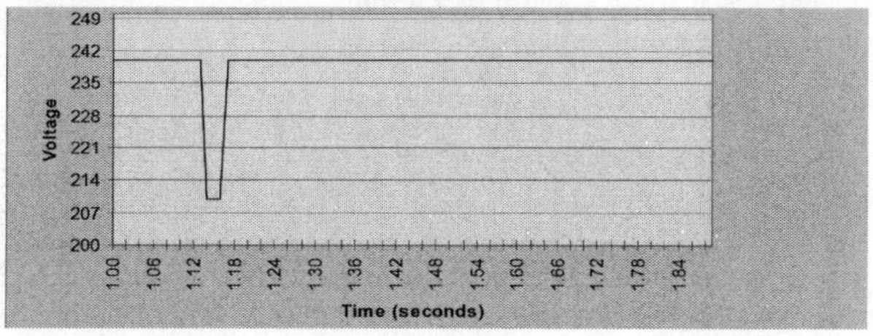

Sag

Brownouts

If a sag lasts for longer than a second, it is often called a **brownout**. Overloaded or faulty mains distribution circuits sometimes cause brownouts.

Brownouts make up the vast majority of computer power problems.

Blackouts

A complete power failure is called a **blackout**. A blackout may be caused by a disruption to the power distribution grid (an equipment failure or the accidental cutting of a cable during construction work, for example), or may simply happen because a fuse has blown or a circuit breaker has tripped.

Electromagnetic Interference

ElectroMagnetic Interference (EMI or **electromagnetic radiation**) is emitted by a variety of sources including fluorescent lights, air conditioning, and power cables. It can corrupt signals in cables with noise and cause errors.

Power Supply Unit

As on a desktop computer, a server **Power Supply Unit (PSU)** converts the incoming AC supply to 3V, 5V, and 12VDC to power the server components (though these days only the 12V supply if of much significance).

The power supply form factor determines its compatibility with both the motherboard (in terms of power connectors) and the system case (in terms of available room plus screw and fan locations). Most PSUs are based on the ATX form factor.

An ATX PSU should be 150mm wide by 86mm high by 140mm deep. The "server-class" EPS12V specification allows PSUs to be 180mm or 230mm deep. The Flex ATX form factor (81x40x150mm) is often used in 1U server designs.

Wattage and Power Rating

A PSU must be able to supply adequate power to all the server's components. The maximum power output (**power rating**) available from a PC power supply is measured in **watts**, calculated as voltage multiplied by current (V*I). The power *output* is not the same as the power the PSU *draws* from the mains (or **power consumption**). If a PSU works at around 75% efficiency, a 300W supply would draw 400W from the outlet. The extra energy is lost mainly as heat.

The PSU found in a standard desktop PC is typically rated at around 200-300W. Servers tend to require more power than desktops though, with PSUs starting at 400W and going up to 700 or 1000W models.

Rack-mounted and Blade PSUs

2U and larger rack-mounted servers normally take standard ATX PSUs (unless the vendor uses a proprietary design anyway). 1U servers use proprietary PSU designs. In a blade server, the PSUs are installed in the enclosure rather than in each server.

Redundant Power (Hot Plug PSUs)

An enterprise-class server or blade enclosure is likely to feature two or more PSUs, providing load balancing and redundancy. A hot plug PSU can be replaced (in the event of failure) without powering down the system. Hot plug PSUs do not have their own ATX and SATA / SAS connectors. They plug into a distribution board (backplane), which houses the connectors.

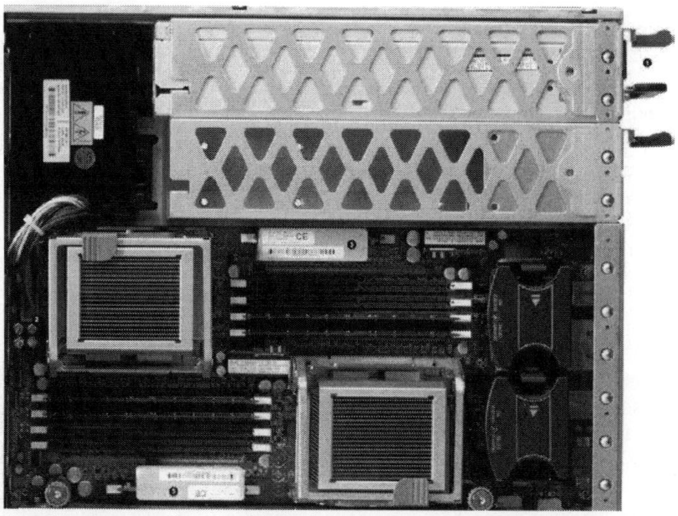

Hot-pluggable power supplies on an HP Proliant server released using the locking levers (1) - the backplane connector is to the top-left with the ATX connector below it (2); also note the VRMs next to each CPU (3)

System software will allow you to disable the PSU prior to removing it. A power supply LED should indicate when the PSU is safe to remove. The PSU will have a lever to use to remove it. Installing the replacement is simply a case of sliding the unit into the bay until it clicks into place. The PSUs must all be rated for the same power output (you could not mix one 400W and one 700W PSU for instance).

Unused PSU or fan bays should be filled with blanks to maintain the correct airflow and cooling within the chassis.

Standalone PSUs

To upgrade a standalone PSU you must power down the system. Remove all the connectors from the old PSU then unscrew it from the case.

Insert the new PSU, screw it to the case, then re-connect the cables. The connectors are all keyed and cannot be inserted the wrong way round.

Under no circumstances should you attempt any further disassembly of the PSU.

Connector Types and Voltages

The power connectors supply various combinations of 3.3V, 5V, and 12V positive and negative current. Not all components use power at precisely these voltages. **Voltage regulators** on the motherboard are used to correct the voltage supplied from the PSU to the voltage required by the component.

The ATX PSU standard has gone through a number of revisions, specifying different connector types.

P1 Connector

In the original ATX specification, the **20-pin P1** (2x10) connector (also called the main connector) supplies power to the motherboard. Note that black wires are ground, yellow wires are +12V, red wires are +5V, and orange wires are +3.3V.

Most systems are now based on the ATX12V version 2 specification. This defines a **24-pin** (2x12) P1 connector to replace the 20-pin one. This is sometimes implemented as 20+4-pin P1 cable for compatibility with older ATX motherboards that have 20-pin connectors.

ATX PSU with various power connectors (1) 20-pin P1 motherboard; (2) +4-pin P1 connector; (3) P4 CPU connector; (4) 4-pin Molex device connector; (5) 15-pin SATA device connector; (6) 4-pin floppy (Berg)

Molex and SATA Connectors

4-pin (1x4) **Molex** connectors and 15-pin (1x15) **SATA (Serial ATA)** connectors supply +12V and +5V power for peripheral devices housed within the system case. The number of connectors determines the number of devices (such as hard drives and optical drives) that can be supported.

Modular *PSUs have cables that are detachable from the PSU unit, allowing only the connectors actually required to be used. This reduces clutter within the chassis, improving airflow and cooling.*

PCIe Connectors

A 6-pin (2x3) connector is used to supply an extra 75W power (+12V) to PCIe graphics cards. This was updated to an 8-pin (2x4) connector delivering 150W in the ATX12V v2.2 specification. Some adapters or dual-card systems will require the use of multiple PCIe auxiliary power connectors.

EPS12V

The **Entry-level Power Supply (EPS)** specification was developed initially for server-class hardware. Many of its features were incorporated in ATX12V. EPS12V defines an 8-pin +12V ("P4") connector to support the operation of the CPU. This is normally implemented as 2x4-pin connectors so that an EPS12V PSU can be connected to an ATX motherboard with a 4-pin +12V port.

Power Problems and UPS

Power problems can have disastrous effects on computer equipment. A range of power protection devices is available to either reduce the symptoms of the power problem or to eliminate it altogether.

So-called **passive protection devices** can be used to filter out the effects of spikes and surges. The simplest devices (**surge suppressors**) come in the form of adapters, trailing sockets, or filter plugs, with the protection circuitry built into the unit. These devices offer low-cost protection to one or two pieces of equipment.

The maximum current that can be carried by a filter unit varies. You must always make sure that the device is of the correct rating and will not be overloaded in use.

Larger industrial power filter units (**line conditioners**) can be used to protect entire power circuits from the effects of surges or brownouts, but they are unable to remove or reduce the effects of blackouts. However, line conditioners are generally built into **Uninterruptible Power Supplies (UPS)**, which do eliminate the effects of complete power failure.

Very few devices will provide complete protection from lightning strikes. The only option is to provide adequate lightning protection measures on the building.

A UPS will provide a temporary power source in the event of power loss (this may range from a few minutes for a desktop-rated model to hours for an enterprise system). The time allowed by a UPS is sufficient for an alternative power source to kick in (such as a standby generator) or at least to allow the administrator to shut down the server properly (users can save files and the operating system can complete the proper shut down routines). Most UPS are also able to mitigate the effects of **power surges** and **spikes**.

In its simplest form, a UPS comprises the following:

- A bank of **batteries**.
- A **charging circuit** for the batteries.
- A **DC-to-AC converter** (**inverter**) to generate AC voltage from the batteries.

The UPS typically also contains a degree of processing capability, enabling it to alert the computer to which it is attached in the event of an outage. This alerts the administrator to the problem, who can then take action.

Most UPS fall into one of the following topologies.

Online

An **online** UPS (or **double-conversion online** UPS) first converts the mains supply to DC (using a component called the rectifier). It uses the DC current to charge the battery and to feed an inverter, which converts the flow back to AC to power the server(s). There is also a backup path (bypass) from the power supply in case the battery and/or inverter fail. The AC power is therefore converted to DC and back to AC, hence the name "double-conversion".

The power signal from an online UPS is very "clean" but the complexity of the circuitry and energy efficiency design mean that online UPS perform best at high load (5 kVA and upward). APC market a "Delta-conversion" online UPS that provides better efficiency than the double-conversion online type. The Delta circuit provides some of the output power under normal conditions, reducing power loss from converting from AC to DC and back again.

The AC mains supply can be subject to "noise" and spikes that could interfere with the smooth running of electronic equipment. This is especially likely when mains power fails and a backup generator starts. The line conditioning circuitry in a UPS cleans up the signal.

Line Interactive

In a **line interactive** type of UPS, the incoming AC supply is always passed through the inverter, providing a "clean" power signal, while the charging circuit recharges the battery. If the mains supply fails, a switch cuts the battery supply in. Most mid-size UPS (between 1 and 5kVA) are of the line-interactive type as it provides a good balance between cost and efficiency at these loads (online units tend to be bulkier and heavier). Line-interactive units work less efficiently than online units if the mains supply is unstable.

Offline

An **offline** (or **standby**) UPS keeps the batteries charged all the time but does not operate the inverter until the power fails.

Offline UPS are cheaper to build and do not dissipate as much heat as the online or line interactive varieties but they are less efficient at high power loads (over about 1kVA). This technology is used for "personal" UPS (home-office solutions protecting a workstation or laptop or even a workgroup server).

Ride-through Capability

When a line interactive or standby UPS goes online or offline, there is a momentary interruption to the power supply during the transition. A server-class power supply unit should support a ride-through capability (or holdup time) of 10-20 ms, meaning that it will continue to work for that time. The UPS has to switch well within the holdup time (within about 5 ms).

UPS Sizing

APC desktop Smart-UPS with (1) Diagnostic LEDs; (2) Serial monitoring port; (3) Modem protection ports; (4) Power receptacles for connecting to PSUs (Image © 2016 Schneider Electric)

Different UPS models support different power outputs, and form factors - from desktop to rack mounted depending upon your needs.

APC rack mounted Smart-UPS (Image © 2016 Schneider Electric)

UPS sizing refers to matching the maximum load supported by the UPS to the requirements of the server or rack. Load can be calculated either in Watts or in Volt-Amps (VA). With some equipment, the differences in these values can cause sizing problems. The Watt value represents the **actual power** drawn by an appliance; the VA value represents **apparent power**. Apparent power arises from AC supplies because some of the current may flow in and out of the load without delivering energy. The difference between actual and apparent power is called the **power factor**.

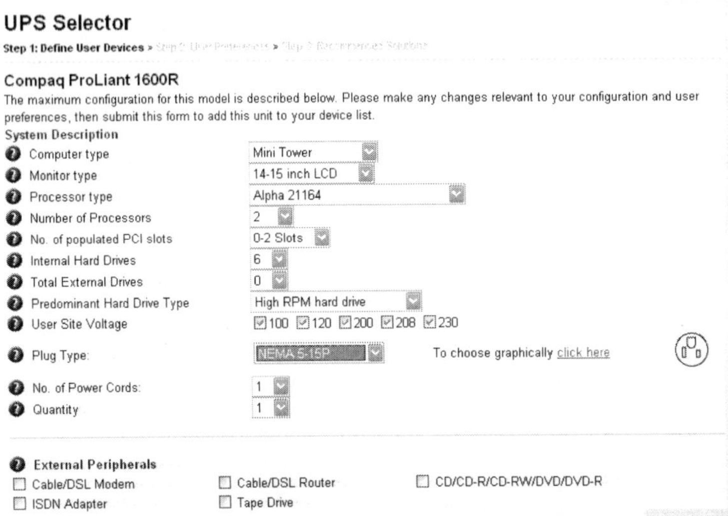

Choosing the UPS - defining the server and peripherals

In older computer power supplies, the power factor was often assumed to be 0.6. For example, a PSU with a VA of 110V * 5 amps and a power factor of 0.6 outputs 330W rather than 550W. Modern PSUs for servers, switches, and routers are **Power Factor Corrected (PFC)** however and have a power factor close to 1.0.

If you are uncertain whether a power supply is PFC or not, always ensure that the Watt rating *of the* UPS *is equal to or greater than the* VA rating *of the* load. *The UPS must be able to match the VA rating of the load.*

Your server vendor should be able to supply the Watt and VA ratings. If not, some UPS vendor websites have a configuration wizard, which you can complete to determine what the power output you require is, and what UPS models would suit. Remember that you should add an extra margin both for reliability and for future expansion. This would allow you to add devices to the rack without having to replace or expand the UPS.

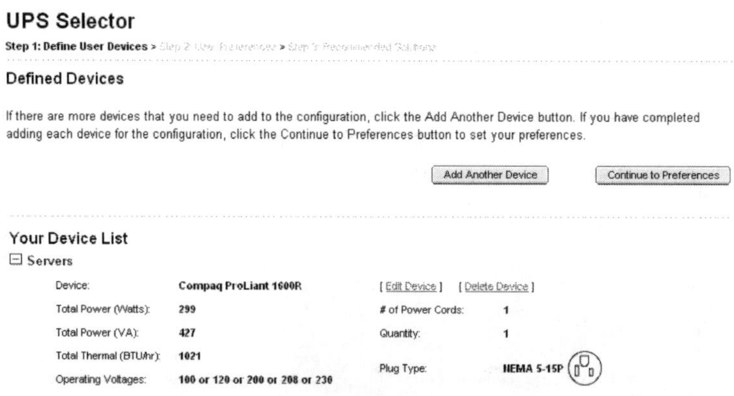

Your chosen server

As you can see, you also specify the **run time**; the maximum duration of battery power (10 minutes for instance) which enables you to determine how much charge the unit must be able to hold to supply your needs.

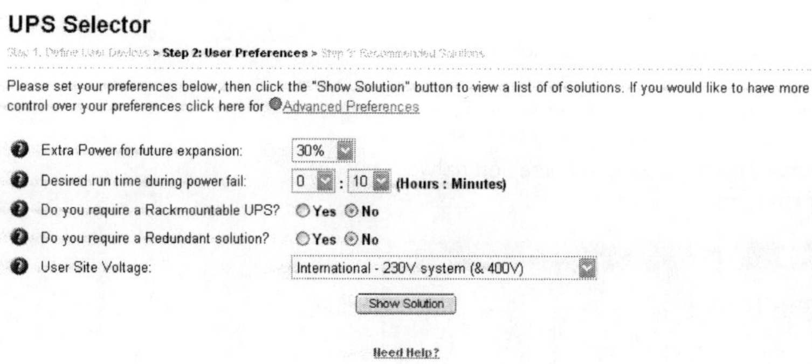

Defining the power requirements

Run Time versus Capacity

As noted above, as well the capacity (or maximum load) of the UPS, you also need to consider for how *long* that capacity can be served. The number of batteries within the UPS determines the amount of time for which it can store and supply power (the **run time**). As a cell discharges, the voltage it can sustain reduces. The UPS will cut off when the voltage reduces below a certain point (the Final Value). Run time before the Final Value is reached can be expressed in amp-hours (Ah). 1 Ah means that the batteries can supply 1 amp for 1 hour. If the load current is 6A, then a 1 Ah UPS can supply that for 10 minutes.

Most vital computer systems require UPS power for at least ten minutes. This gives the time needed either to bring a standby power generator online or for "graceful" shut down in the event of a complete power failure.

UPS in the Data Center

In terms of data center capacity planning, calculating the total potential power draw for a rack is a question of scaling up the requirements for each device. In the data center, you are likely to be using different types of power distribution circuits too (see below). Check the type of UPS is suitable for the equipment to be protected and line conditions or phase type of the AC mains supply.

Rear view of APC rack mounted Smart-UPS with (1) Network management card featuring USB and network ports; (2) Serial and USB monitoring ports; (3) Power receptacles for connecting to PSUs (Image © 2016 Schneider Electric)

UPS Monitoring

Proper monitoring of a UPS is vital to ensure that it is doing the job it is supposed to. If the power fails it will be a bit late to discover that your UPS also has a flat battery! The UPS is connected to the server via a monitoring port - traditionally over a serial port, but more recently over USB. With a rack installation, the UPS will normally be connected to some sort network-based monitoring and management system.

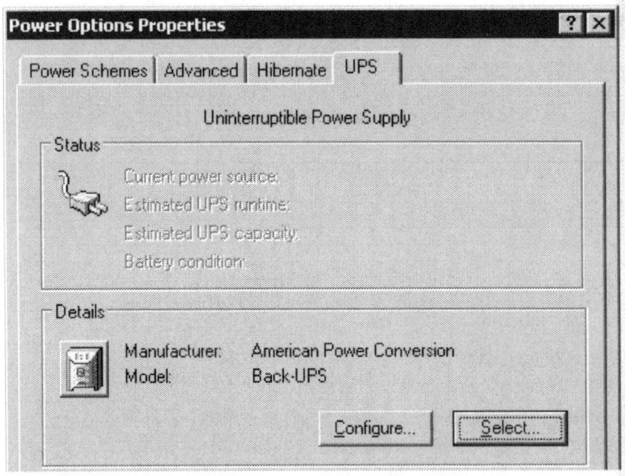

Selecting your UPS in Windows

See Unit 4.5 for more information about remote management tools.

The complexity of this connection and the software provided to monitor it varies depending on the make and model of UPS specified, and the user's needs. The monitoring software should be able to report the load attached to the UPS and record any events, such as power failures or low battery states.

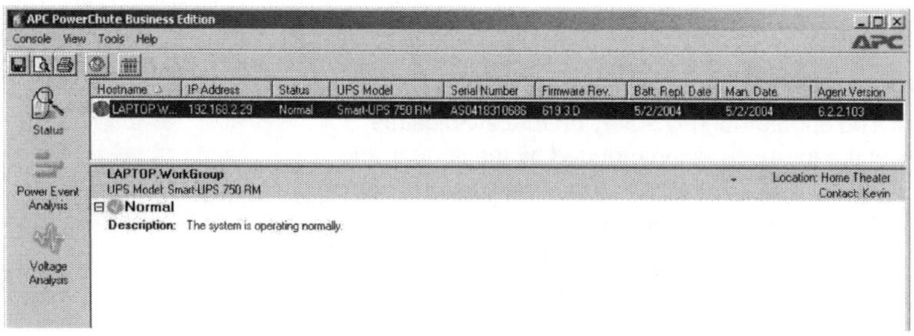

Monitoring software - events

As the UPS can only provide power for a short period, there will come a point when the UPS battery is exhausted, and the server will still not shut down cleanly. To avoid this, the administrator can configure the shut down behavior, so that if power is still not available after a defined period, then the UPS monitor will close down all active files cleanly and perform a "graceful" shut down of the server (or other attached appliances such as switches).

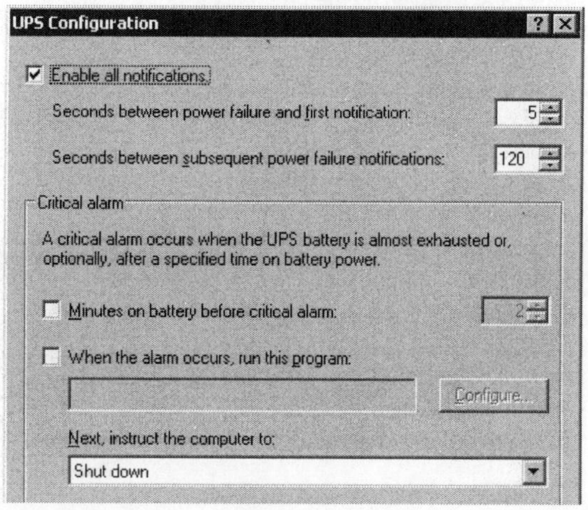

Configuring the UPS

In any case, the software must record events, such as a switch to battery power, and back again, because the administrator will not always be around to observe this. Hence, UPS monitoring software will write events to the OS log files. Some UPS can communicate with monitoring software such as SNMP (Simple Network Management Protocol) via a network connection.

Size and weight

All UPS are heavy and generate heat; very high power UPS are particularly large and heavy and may need extra consideration when placing them on site (especially as regards floor strength and cooling).

Battery Replacement

As well as monitoring software, a UPS should have LED indicators to show the load level and battery health. You should not rely solely on these indicators however. *Always* test a UPS at the intervals recommended by the vendor and record the result in a service log. To test a small UPS (one that supports one or two servers only), first disconnect users from the server and close any database-type applications (and make sure data is backed up). Cut the power and measure that the UPS run time is acceptable. If it is not, obtain a new battery (or a new UPS). Vendors' trade-in programs often make buying a new UPS more economical than buying new batteries.

An enterprise-level UPS will require more careful testing. Scheduling downtime for the testing to take place is obviously more complex when the UPS is supporting tens of servers. This sort of maintenance work is usually undertaken by specialist teams.

Some more advanced UPS systems support features such as online battery replacements. A battery has a limited lifetime, and if replacing the battery means turning off the UPS, then that also means turning off the server - which is not always possible in larger, mission critical environments. Battery hot swapping (using the UPS's **bypass mode**) negates this requirement, allowing the administrator to perform the swap out without interrupting users. Online UPS also support a static bypass mode so that if the UPS circuitry (the inverter) fails, mains power to the server is sustained. If the UPS does not support maintenance bypass mode, a "wraparound" device can be purchased.

Ensure that used batteries are disposed of correctly, either by shipping the used battery back to the UPS vendor or by taking it to an appropriate recycling center (note that not all recycling facilities will accept batteries). It is usually illegal to discard batteries as general waste, as they can cause severe environmental damage when they degrade.

PDUs and Power Circuits

The first requirement for the server room is that the circuits supplying mains power are sufficient to meet the load capacity of all the installed equipment (plus room for growth). Consequently, circuits to a server room will typically be higher capacity than domestic or office circuits (30 or 60 amp as opposed to 13 amp for instance). The circuit is also likely to be higher voltage than normal. These circuits may be run through a **Power Distribution Unit (PDU)**. This allows greater management of the power supply, circuitry to "clean" the power signal, and integration with UPS devices.

Each PDU will support a defined maximum load. For example, a 30-amp PDU working at 208 VAC can nominally support a load of up to 6240 watts (30 amps multiplied by 208 V). To account for conversions and inefficiency you would normally need to allow at least 20% overhead. This means not exceeding a total potential load of around 5000 W from devices in that rack.

The server PSU is connected to the PDU using an IEC C13 / 14 (10 amp) or C19 / 20 (16 amp) cord. C13 and C19 are the female connectors and C14 and C20 are male. C13 / 14 adapters have beveled edges while C19 / 20 are rectangular. Lockable versions of these connectors, using a spring catch, are also available.

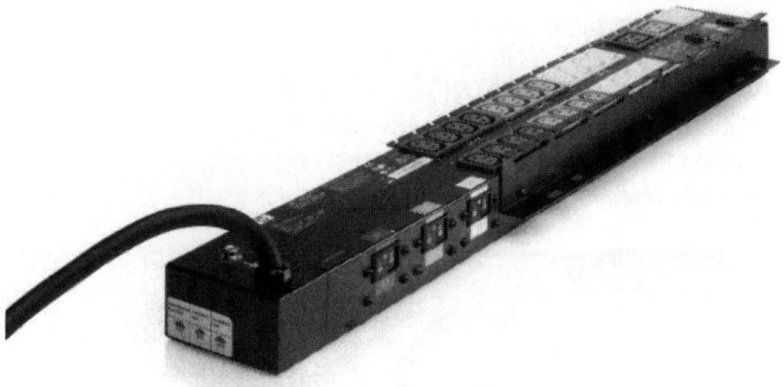

HP rack-mounted PDU with monitoring functionality (Image © 2014 HP Ltd)

On a smaller scale, PDUs are also available as "strip" sockets that can take a higher load than a typical 13 amp rated strip. Such sockets are rack mounted and can be oriented horizontally or vertically to allow for different cabling and layout options. These devices also often support remote management functions, such as reporting load and status, switching power to a particular socket on and off, or switching sockets on in a particular sequence.

Servers connect to ordinary strip or wall AC sockets using the country-specific plug. Example include a grounded NEMA 5-15P or NEMA 5-30P or "Edison connector" in North America or BS-1363 in the UK. With NEMA, the first number indicates the plug type (such as with or without ground pin and voltage input) while the second value is the maximum amperage (so 5-15P is up to 15 amps for instance).

APC power cord with C19 device connector (left) and NEMA 5-15P plug (right) (Image © 2016 Schneider Electric)

NEMA Type	Maximum Voltage
NEMA 5	125V
NEMA 6	250V
NEMA 7	277V

Receptacles are identified by an "R" designation (5-15R for example).

Twist Lock Plugs

Cabling in the power distribution system in a high voltage environment will typically use more secure plug types than the standard NEMA or country-specific outlets mentioned above. There is a series of **twist lock** NEMA plug types designed for this purpose, such as NEMA L5 (125V), NEMA L6 (250V), NEMA L7 (277V), or NEMA L8 (480V). As with regular NEMA connectors, each is also rated to a given amperage. For example, a NEMA L5-30 is rated for 30 amps of current while a NEMA L5-50 is rated for 50A. NEMA twist lock plugs are sometimes referred to as Hubbell connectors after their inventor. To insert, orient the plug and receptacle using the "L-shaped" pin then insert and turn counterclockwise; to release, turn clockwise.

APC power cord with C19 device connector (left) and NEMA L6-20P twist lock plug (right) (Image © 2016 Schneider Electric)

Power Circuits

A server or UPS installed in a typical office environment will probably be using a standard mains supply AC voltage of either around 110V or 220V, depending on the country. Where servers are installed together in a data center or large server room, the incoming mains circuits will be designed to cope with a higher power load by supplying power at higher voltages (440V, 460V, or 480V depending on the country and power company).

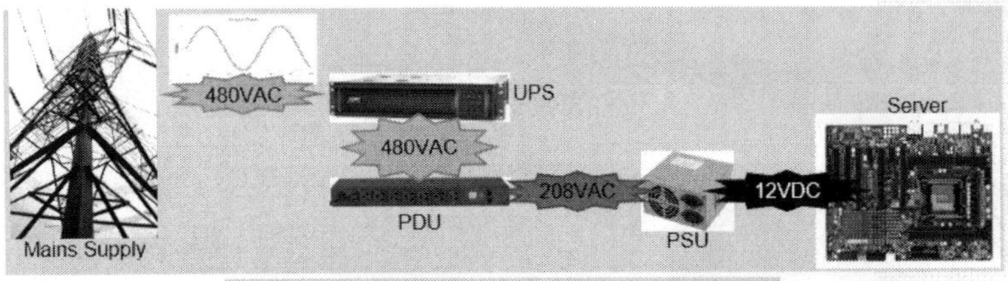

Typical single phase power distribution (North America)

The following conversions then take place:

- These high voltages are delivered to the UPS, which will either output the same voltage to the PDU or use a 3-phase scheme (see below) to output 480 / 277 VAC or 415 / 240 VAC to the PDU.
- The PDU converts the high voltage AC mains supply to a "regular" AC voltage (usually one of 208 VAC, 277 VAC, or 240 VAC) for the PSUs.
- The PSUs then perform their power conversion to deliver 12VDC to the server components or blade enclosure.

3-phase Power Supply

A **3-phase** supply is a means of serving multi-kilowatt power requirements more efficiently. A single phase power supply has one live wire and one neutral wire, with the voltage alternating between peak and zero.

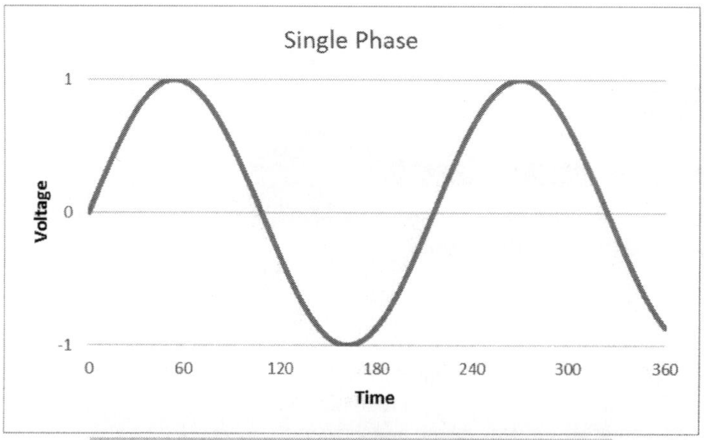

Single phase power - note that the voltage drops to zero periodically

A 3-phase supply has 3 live (or "hot") wires (plus neutral, if the distribution is "wye" rather than "delta", and possibly also ground).

The three live wires are cycled at 120 degrees out of phase with one another. This means that current is delivered at a more stable voltage. A 3-phase supply delivers about 1.73 times more power than a single phase supply, reducing the number of circuits that need to be provisioned.

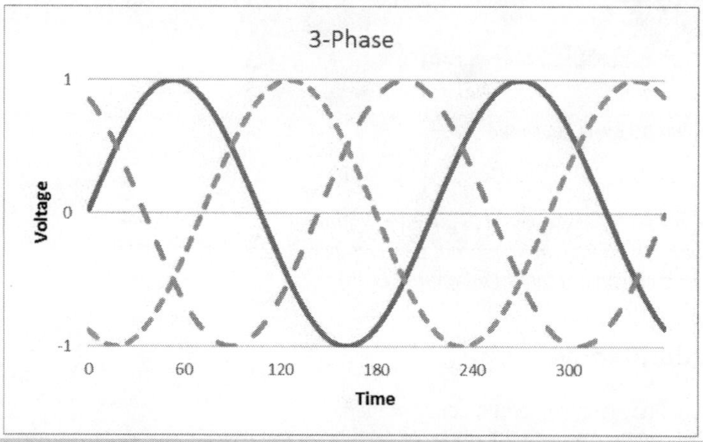

3-phase power - because each wire is out-of-phase relative to the others, the voltage never drops to zero

3-phase power is usually delivered either at the UPS level or at the rack level (to a 3-phase PDU) or both. A server with a universal PSU will be able to connect to a 3-phase PDU. Older servers with fixed-input voltage PSUs may require special configuration of the supply. Some blade server enclosures can connect directly to a 3-phase supply. 3-phase supplies usually use IEC 309 connectors.

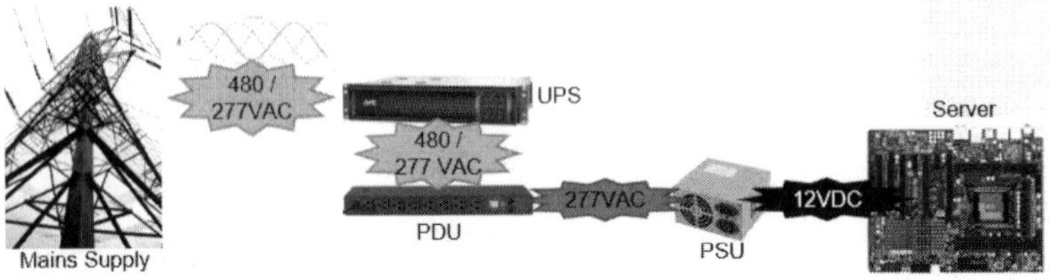

Typical 3-phase power distribution (North America)

DC Power Circuits

As you can see, the AC mains supply schema introduces multiple conversions between AC and DC to finally step down to the 12VDC supply required by the computer components. Some data center power designs are switching to use -48VDC distribution. This means that a special type of **row-based DC UPS** outputs -48VDC to the PDU and the PDU outputs -48VDC to each PSU in the rack. The PSUs then step down the voltage to the 12VDC expected by the server / blade circuit boards. This requires -48VDC input compatible components at each stage in the process (UPS, PDU, and PSUs).

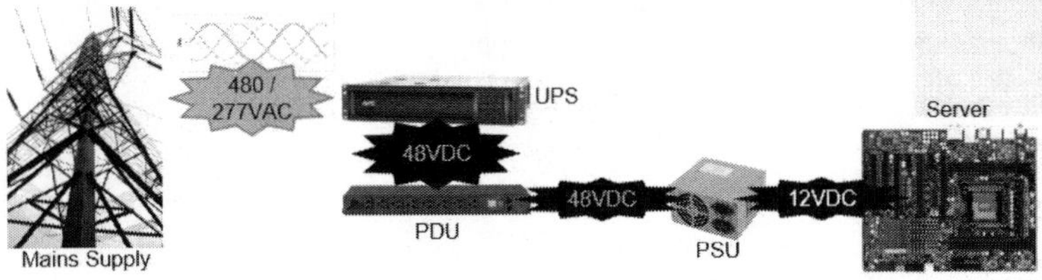

Typical 48VDC power distribution

-48VDC supplies are also often deployed in telephone Central Offices (CO) / exchanges, though in a different configuration (they use modular components rather than an integrated UPS).

Power Circuits and Redundancy

As well as supply voltage, redundancy is an important consideration in designing power circuits. A PDU can be connected to multiple circuits so that if one fails there will be no interruption to the power supply. You could also connect multiple circuits to multiple PDUs and then connect the PSUs to different PDUs within the same rack.

Review Questions / Module 4 / Unit 3 / Power Distribution

Answer these questions to test what you have learned in this unit.

1) Given a device's VA rating, how do you calculate its load in Watts?
2) What type of power problem is mitigated by a UPS?
3) What ports are available for connecting a UPS?
4) With what types of UPS may PSU holdup time be an issue?
5) What is the benefit of provisioning a 3-phase mains power?
6) What designation represents a twist locking electrical plug designed for 208V input and up to 30 amps?

Module 4 / Unit 4

Server Hardware Troubleshooting

Objectives

On completion of this unit, you will be able to:

- Follow installation and upgrade best practice and know how to minimize the risk of damaging components.
- Diagnose problems relating to hardware components and the boot process.

Adding and Removing Components

Unless you are building something to order, it is not often (if ever) that you will put together a server system from scratch. Most systems are specified using an online tool then purchased pre-built from the vendor. Most work you will do on the hardware side will involve adding and/or replacing components. Before you start to work on hardware you should consider doing the following:

- Check that components have been supplied intact and complete. Gather any information related to the installation (FAQs, support site, ReadMe file, and so on).
- Do not take a server offline without first identifying potential impacts and notifying stakeholders. Schedule the downtime to minimize impact on services.
- Take a backup of important data and ensure there is a rollback plan (to get the old system back online if an upgrade fails).
- Create a clean work environment with plenty of working space and suitable anti-static precautions.
- Gather all necessary tools and equipment. A notepad and pen may be useful for making diagrams and notes. Work methodically to a pre-prepared checklist of actions.
- Make sure that all devices are powered off and disconnected from the mains before removing them (except in the case of hot-pluggable devices). Make sure users are informed of downtime and that it is scheduled with due sensitivity to other business processes.
- Always take time and care. Test that the installation or upgrade has succeeded (switch on the server and check that any new hardware is recognized during the power-on sequence) before bringing the system back online.
- Place static-sensitive equipment such as processors and memory in anti-static bags.

- Update server documentation or maintenance logs to record what was done, when it was done, and who did it. Make sure that other technicians are aware of the changes. Update users on any new working practices.
- Get baseline performance figures for the new system so that performance can be monitored on an on-going basis.

Accessing the Case

Read the vendor's documentation carefully to determine how to remove access panels and bezels covering the chassis interior. These are retained either by screws or clips. New server designs invariably allow tool-free access to the chassis but there may be a chassis lock that can only be operated with a specific key.

Some servers may have chassis intrusion sensors that trip when the case is opened. This may sound an audible alarm or generate numerous administrative alerts. You need to use the firmware's system setup program (see later) to reset the alarm (or turn off chassis intrusion alerting completely).

Also be aware of the location and fitting of heat shrouds / baffles covering heat sensitive components, such as the CPU and memory. These are often critical to maintaining proper airflow and cooling and so must be replaced correctly when maintenance work is done. Take note of any special or proprietary power connections, cabling, or wiring between components and the chassis. If you need to disconnect any of these, make a diagram of how to reconnect them correctly.

ElectroStatic Discharge (ESD) Procedures

An **ElectroStatic Discharge (ESD)** occurs when a surface with low potential difference is brought near a surface with high potential difference. This can cause a spark to leap between the two surfaces. The spark is not dangerous to human health (it is high voltage but low current) but can cause serious damage to electronic circuits, such as CPUs and system memory modules.

Where possible, handle vulnerable components by holding the edges of the plastic mounting card and avoid touching the surfaces of the chips themselves. Using an **anti-ESD wrist strap** can dissipate static charges more effectively. The wrist band should fit snugly around your wrist to maximize contact with the skin. Do not wear it over clothing. The wrist strap ground is made either using a grounding plug that plugs into a wall socket or a crocodile clip that attaches to a grounded point or an unpainted part of the computer's metal chassis. An anti-ESD service mat is also useful. Sensitive components can be placed on the mat safely.

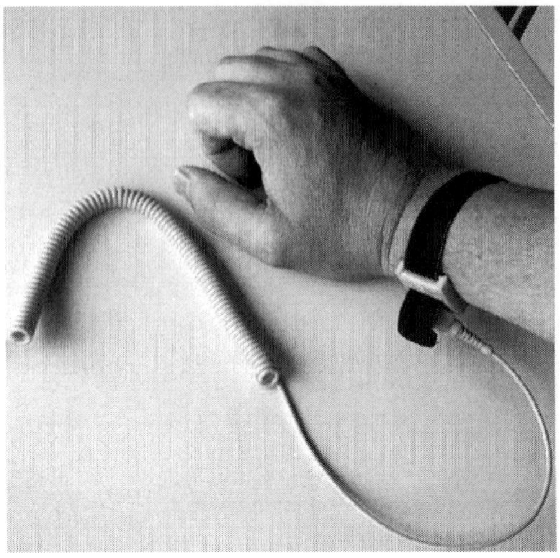

Anti-ESD wrist strap and grounding cord

An anti-ESD service mat is also useful. Sensitive components can be placed on the mat safely.

Troubleshooting Power and POST Problems

If mains power fails, and the server is connected to a UPS, depending on the environment you will either switch to an alternative power source (a backup generator) or use the grace period provided by the UPS to shut down the servers gracefully and wait for mains power to be restored.

It could also be the case that the Power Supply Unit (PSU) in a server fails however.

The PSU converts the AC mains supply to DC voltages. DC voltage is used to power the internal drives and motherboard components. When the PSU is sure that it is providing a stable supply, it sends a power good signal to the processor.

Symptoms of power problems are that LEDs on the front panel do not light up and that the fans and drives do not spin up.

Assuming there is not a blackout and the power cabling is good, you can test the power supply using a multimeter. Bear in mind that in most cases the inbuilt server monitors will detect and report a power supply failure and that simply swapping out the PSU with a new one will be faster and more economical.

Another possibility is that the power supply is insufficient for the number of devices connected to the system. This could also be a cause of intermittent faults (lockups or unexpected shut downs).

Multimeters

A multi-purpose meter can be used to measure voltage, current, and resistance; these are known as **multimeters** or **VOMs (Volt-Ohm-Milli-ammeters)**.

Most modern meters are digital and have an LED or LCD readout. Digital meters are more robust and are generally easier to read than analog types. They often have additional built-in testing functions; for example, a transistor tester, conductance, temperature, diode status, or an audio Wattmeter.

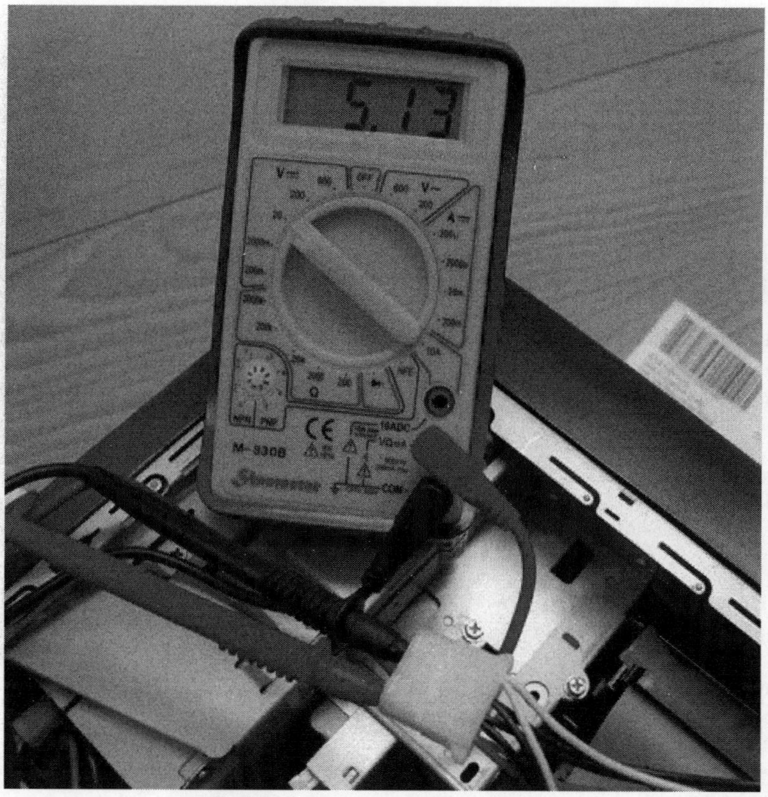

Testing a Molex connector with a multimeter

Power Supply Tester

A **Power Supply Tester** is a device designed (unsurprisingly) with the sole purpose of testing PSUs. It is much simpler to use than a multimeter as you do not have to test each pin in turn.

Typical models come with ports for the 20/24-pin P1, Molex, SATA, plus 8-pin, 6-pin, and 4-pin connectors found on different models of PSU. Usually each pin on each port has an LED to indicate whether the voltage supplied is good.

Casebuy EZ Power Supply Tester (www.casebuy.com.tw)

Troubleshooting POST

Once the CPU has been given the power-good signal, the firmware performs the **Power-On Self Test (POST)**. The POST is a built-in diagnostic program that checks the hardware to ensure the components required to boot the server are present and functioning correctly. If POST is not running correctly, there will be no beeps from the onboard speaker and the screen may be blank. To troubleshoot, try the following tests and solutions:

- Ask what has changed - if the firmware has been flashed and the server has not booted since, the firmware update may have failed.
- Check cabling and connections, especially if maintenance work has just been performed on the server. An incorrectly oriented drive cable or a badly seated or faulty expansion card can stop the POST from running. Correct any errors, reset adapter cards, and then reboot the server.
- Check for faulty interfaces and devices - it is possible that a faulty expansion card or device is halting the POST. Try removing one device at a time to see if this solves the problem (or remove all non-essential devices then add them back one-by-one).
- Check for a faulty CPU. If possible, replace the CPU chip with a known good one.
- If none of the above reveals a problem, the issue could lie with a faulty onboard component (perhaps there has been ESD damage). POST test adapter cards and system board testers can interpret the debug codes given by the firmware. The card displays the codes, so that you can check where the POST stopped executing.
- Some motherboards have jumpers to configure modes (such as firmware recovery) or processor settings. If the jumpers are set incorrectly it could cause the computer not to boot. If a computer will not work after being serviced, check that the jumpers have not been changed.

Remember to ask "What has changed" when troubleshooting. For example, it is best practice to check that a system works properly after performing any sort of servicing work (such as updating the firmware) but not all technicians are so diligent.

If the CMOS battery is losing power, settings stored in CMOS will be lost or corrupted. If this happens, the computer is likely to display the message **CMOS Checksum Error** during the boot process. CMOS errors can also be caused by viruses or a faulty motherboard or power supply.

POST Errors

If POST runs but detects a problem, it generates an error message. As the error may prevent the computer from displaying anything on-screen, the error is often indicated by a series of beeps.

Each firmware vendor uses different beeps and error codes to indicate problems. The meaning of beep and error codes can be obtained from the firmware manufacturer's website.

To resolve beep code errors, decode the pattern of beeps and take the appropriate action.

Error messages on the screen are usually descriptive of the problem. For example:

- Hard disk drive controller failure.
- Memory configuration error.
- CMOS battery low.
- Keyboard stuck or not present.

Operating System Search

Once the POST tests are complete, the firmware searches the drives as specified in the boot sequence. If the first drive in the sequence is not found, it then moves on to the next; for example, if drive A: contains no disk, the boot sequence goes to drive C:. If no boot device is found, the system displays an error message and halts the boot process. Check system setup to verify that the boot sequence is configured correctly.

The code from the boot sector on the selected device is loaded into the memory and takes over from the firmware. The boot sector code loads the rest of the operating system files into RAM. Error messages such as "Operating system not found" or "[*System File*] Missing or Corrupt" are generally caused because the bootloader files have been deleted or become unreadable. This could be caused by sudden loss of power or it could be a sign that a hard drive is failing. It could also indicate a virus infection.

You can try replacing the boot files or repairing the boot sector blocks using the recovery tools provided with the OS. If these tools do not work, you will need to replace the drive and restore the system from backup.

Troubleshooting Processor, Memory, and I/O Failure

Any component (or **Field Replaceable Unit [FRU]**) in the server may fail. Most hardware problems can be diagnosed to a particular component by analyzing and understanding the symptoms. If the cause of a problem is not obvious (for example, if the system experiences lockups or spontaneous reboots that are intermittent), you can use a diagnostic utility to run tests on hardware components. All the major server vendors ship utilities with their systems. These utilities can often either be used "online" when the server is running (by installing the utility as an application) or "offline", by installing to a utility partition (selectable during the boot process) or diagnostic boot disk.

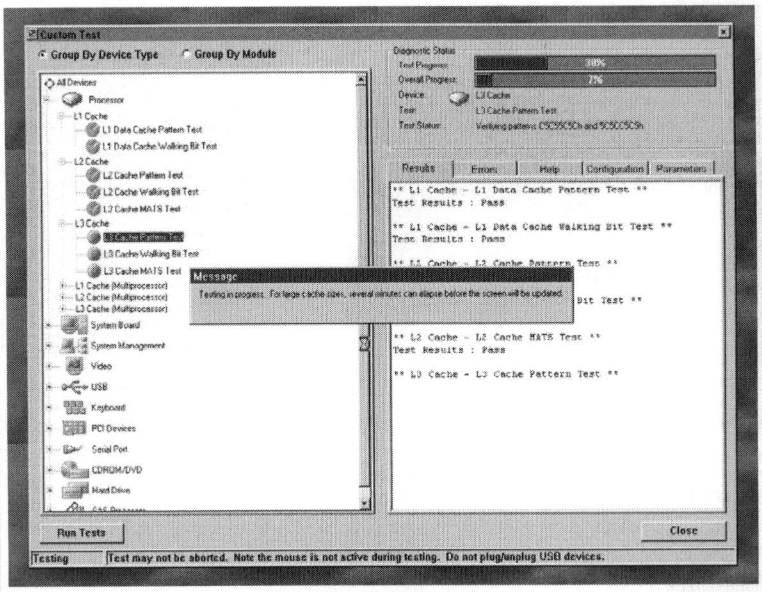

Dell Online Diagnostics utility

These tests should help to isolate the problem to the processor, cache, system memory, or I/O device. Some tests may take quite a long time to complete (up to a few hours) and may need to be run multiple times to identify transitory faults.

Overheating

Insufficient cooling is the main cause of processor problems. Thermal faults are normally cyclic: a system works for some time, crashes, and then works again later. Powering down allows the processor to cool.

A server environment should have numerous monitors that will detect the failure of cooling devices such as system fans or HVAC systems. The main cause of overheating is therefore likely to be an air leak in the data center (causing warm air to contaminate the cold air) or a build-up of dust within the server chassis, clogging fans and exhaust vents. You can clean the dust using a PC vacuum or compressed air blower but you should investigate the cause of the dust build-up too - servers should be installed in a controlled environment designed to prevent this sort of problem occurring.

CPUs and other system components heat up while running. Take care not to burn yourself when handling internal components.

Thermal protection circuitry in the CPU may throttle it (slow it down) if it becomes too hot.

ECC / Parity Memory Errors

If an error occurs at boot-time, check the system settings to ensure that ECC has not been enabled with non-ECC memory cards installed. If the error always occurs at the same address, there is likely to be a hardware fault with the memory. You can check this by booting several times to ensure that the error is always at the same address. If so, you should replace the memory modules. If an error occurs during use and does not re-occur after reboot, it is likely to be a transient error. If the error persists, you should run diagnostic tests or replace the memory modules.

Troubleshooting Incompatible Components

Issues with incompatible components should be obvious immediately after performing the upgrade, so long as you test system functionality after performing the upgrade!

Most compatibility issues will arise from memory and CPU upgrades. You should also be aware that server vendors may offer only limited support for third-party components. Even something as simple as a hard disk may cause compatibility problems with an OEM RAID controller card.

Processor Appears Not To Work

If a new processor (or an upgrade) has just been installed, you should perform these simple diagnostic checks:

- **Compatibility** - check that the processor is supported by the motherboard and firmware. In an SMP-system, check that the CPUs are identical models and versions (stepping).
- **Orientation** - make sure the processor has been inserted correctly into its socket.

- **Voltage** - double-check the voltage settings for the board or through System Setup. If the voltage has been set incorrectly, try correcting it and seeing if the CPU still works.
- **Configuration** - double-check the system settings or motherboard jumpers to make sure they are correct.
- **Swap** - test by substitution: if the old processor works then the new one may be faulty.

New Memory Not Recognized

After performing a memory upgrade, rebooting, and then checking the memory count, the memory may not be recognized. You should first check that the modules have been installed correctly in their sockets. If this does not solve the problem, check the following:

- Memory type
    - Does the motherboard support the memory card capacity that you have installed?
    - Does the motherboard chipset support the memory technology you have installed (for example, ECC)?
- Configuration
    - Are the memory banks complete?
    - Have the memory banks been filled in the correct sequence?
    - Is the motherboard operating in dual-channel mode?

In both cases, refer to the motherboard guide for guidance.

Performing a Memory Upgrade

When upgrading memory, bear the following guidelines in mind:

- Check the motherboard documentation to confirm that the memory is compatible (memory type and speed, ECC and/or non-ECC) and check the maximum amount of RAM that your motherboard and OS will recognize.
- On a server-system, it is considered good practice to use the server vendor specific memory RAM (or to use RAM from the same manufacturer [same brand]). This gives the best reliability and least trouble if you have to contact them for technical support.
- It is *possible* to mix different SDRAM speeds (for example, PC3-12800 with PC3-17000) but this is *not* a good idea on a server and the memory will work at the lower speed.

- You *cannot* mix different types (for instance, ECC RAM with non-ECC RAM, DDR2 with DDR3 SDRAM, registered with unbuffered, and so on).
- When installing dual- or triple-channel memory, use **memory kits** (that is, two or three boards supplied together). Kits will generally be more reliable than trying to match up individual modules.
- Try to purchase the highest capacity modules you can afford, to maximize future upgrade potential (using higher capacity modules leaves more banks free for future upgrades).

Memory Configuration Example

As you can see, the issues involved in planning and specifying a memory configuration that will be supported by the motherboard and chipset are complex!

To illustrate these issues with an example: consider that a server in a dual channel configuration might have 6 physical memory slots comprising 3 *banks* of 2 *slots* each and furthermore support up to 8 *ranks*. If dual-rank memory is installed in the first two banks (slots 1-4), the third bank (slots 5 and 6) must remain empty, as the maximum number of ranks are occupied. An alternate configuration might be to use dual-rank memory in bank 1 (4 ranks) and single rank memory in banks 2-3 (another 4 ranks).

Installing and Removing Modules

In order to remove DIMMs, you must release the plastic or metal catches at either end. Once you have released the catches, you can remove the memory module by hand. Handle the module by the edges - avoid touching the chips.

DIMM catches

Most memory sockets are numbered on the motherboard. This numbering may start at 0 or 1. Some motherboards allow these slots to be filled in any order, but most require that you fill the slots from the lowest numbered slot upwards. Refer to the motherboard documentation for any specific requirements.

1) Line up the memory card. There are notches at the bottom edge of a memory card to ensure that the card is inserted correctly and that the card is compatible with the slot.

2) Insert the memory card. DIMMs are pushed straight down into the socket, and the retaining clips at either end are moved towards the center until they lock into the notches cut at the side of the DIMM.

3) Reboot the server and check that the memory chips have been recognized (during POST there is normally a memory test and summary display or you can use a system summary utility once the OS has loaded).

If you are using a riser card, install the modules on the riser card before *installing the riser card in the server. You must usually populate the lowest numbered banks on the card first.*

Review Questions / Module 4 / Unit 4 / Server Hardware Troubleshooting

Answer these questions to test what you have learned in this unit.

1) What is the purpose of an anti-static wrist strap?

2) You have backed up data and created a clean work area with all the tools and components you need to perform an upgrade without the risk of ESD damage. What other resource should you make available?

3) What would be your first step in troubleshooting a server where the POST does not run?

4) What is the best way of identifying a suspected fault in a system component?

5) How would you solve an error message such as "Operating System Not Found"?

Module 4 / Unit 5

Server Management

Objectives

On completion of this unit, you will be able to:

- Understand local and remote access management methods.
- Configure and use local, network, and OS-based administration tools.

Server Management Methods

There are two ways of managing a server: locally and remotely. *Some* tasks can *only* be performed locally, with direct access to the server itself (such as cleaning or upgrading hardware). *Most* tasks can be performed locally *if necessary*, by logging on to the server at the console. However, most software tasks can be performed *remotely* more efficiently.

Remote management has significant advantages in terms of saving time and personnel. The advantages for managing geographically separate locations should be obvious, but even within a building, remote management can simplify administration and if correctly configured, can enhance security (by restricting personnel needing to access the server room). Proper configuration and security measures are essential however, if the network is not to be made vulnerable to attack via abuse of the remote management interface.

Remote management tools are available in two different classes:

- In-band tools use the ordinary network connection to manage the server. These are the tools commonly-used for basic management tasks.

  With in-band tools, a careful consideration needs to be made on the security implications. Thought also needs to be given on the impact on the network of running the remote management software.

- Out-of-band tools access the server via an alternative connection (such as a dedicated LAN management port or a dial-up modem or serial port). This is also often referred to as "Lights Out Management (LOM)" (highlighting the fact that the server can be powered on remotely). These are used when the network is not available or when the server is not available to ordinary software tools (such as during power off and on, in the early stages of OS setup routines, or if the server has crashed).

  As with in-band management, the connection must be properly secured to prevent unauthorized access.

Some network management systems are proprietary while others use standard protocols.

Desktop Management Interface

DMI was an early standard for tracking the components installed in PC-based systems. It was defined by the Desktop Management Task Force, a committee comprised of many of the leading players in the computer market, including Intel, 3Com, Sun, HP, Novell, and Microsoft.

Software agents on each PC (known as the service layer) respond to requests for information from the management console by sending data in a **Management Information File (MIF)**.

Products such as Novell ZENworks and HP OpenView support DMI. DMI-compatible products can also be incorporated within SNMP.

Intelligent Platform Management Interface (IPMI)

IPMI is a framework for interoperable server systems monitoring and alerting. IPMI allows for out-of-band management (when the OS is not available) of server equipment as well as in-band management.

An embedded chip on the motherboard, the **Baseboard Management Controller (BMC)**, runs the system management tasks. The controller has its own battery power and can work independently of other components.

IPMI 1.5 defines a serial interface for the client software. IPMI 2.0 addresses security concerns with this interface by specifying support for Serial Over LAN (SOL), authentication (SHA-1), and encryption (AES).

For more information, visit www.intel.com/design/servers/ipmi.

Web Based Enterprise Management (WBEM)

Web Based Enterprise Management (WBEM) was developed from the Desktop Management Interface (DMI) standard. It is maintained by the **Distributed Management Task Force (DMTF [**www.dmtf.org**])**, which is a consortium of most of the major network and server hardware and software vendors. It is not a protocol but a set of specifications that runs on web protocols (HTTP for transport, SSL for security, and XML as a data format).

The basis of the specification is the **Common Information Model (CIM)**, which is a schema for recording and reporting information about the configuration or performance of a hardware device or software application. CIM is an object-based model. There are default **classes** for things such as routers, switches, servers, or network adapters and each class has distinct **attributes**. A particular server or network card is an **instance** of its class. Custom classes can be created to represent vendor-specific hardware or software. The description of a particular class or instance is called a **Managed Object Format (MOF)**; this is the equivalent of an MIB in SNMP or a MIF in DMI.

WBEM information is stored in a server called a repository. The server can be queried using HTTP and XML or through a variety of other methods. Likewise, the repository can be populated via a number of methods, including querying SNMP agents and MIBs.

Windows Management Instrumentation (WMI)

Windows Management Instrumentation (WMI) is Microsoft's implementation of WBEM for its operating system and application server products. WMI supports both monitoring of the software and (via a scripting language) remote configuration.

WMI uses the **Distributed Component Object Model** (**DCOM**) and consequently the **Remote Procedure Call (RPC)** port 135 may need to be open to accept DCOM connections, though implementations on later server and application products can run over HTTP. You also usually need to use Group Policy to enable the **Allow remote administration exception** in the Windows Firewall.

There are any number of developer tools and resources associated with WMI. One you should be aware of is **WBEMTest.exe**, a graphical tool for querying WMI providers on a local or remote host.

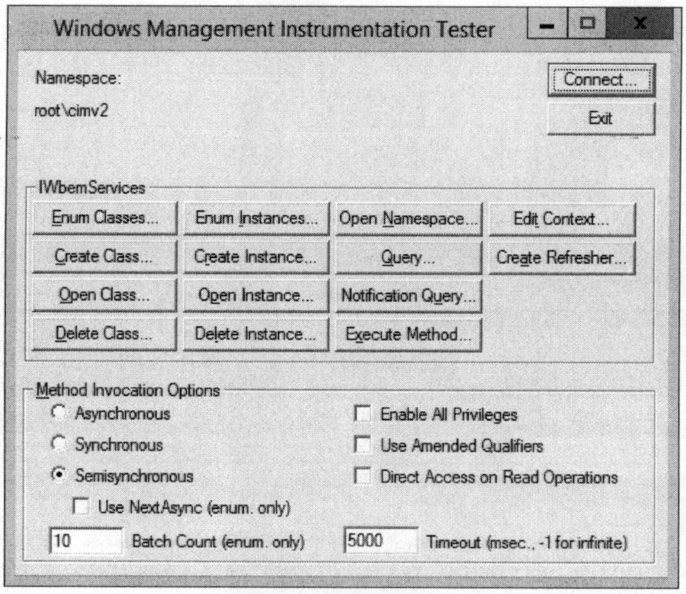

WBEMTest WMI query tool

Local Hardware Administration

The major server vendors have their own software for managing and monitoring multiple servers (and desktops). If you do not have access to this kind of software, you can also use features of the OS.

KVM (Keyboard, Video, Mouse)

Few servers are equipped with a dedicated keyboard, mouse, and monitor; servers without input / output devices are described as "headless". Most of the time local access is via a **Keyboard, Video, Mouse (KVM) switch**. KVM switches range from simple 2-port devices to those capable of managing up to 32 servers.

HP rack with KVM

Rack mounted KVM usually consists of a drawer with LCD screen, keyboard, and touchpad. KVM units allow the control of multiple servers with a single set of input / output devices. KVMs have a number of ports corresponding to the number of servers they can control. A physical switch or keyboard combination is used to switch between servers.

KVM are cabled using standard connectors (PS/2 or USB for the mouse and keyboard and VGA, DVI, or HDMI for the video signal). Some KVM also support remote or dial-up access (KVM over IP).

8-port and higher KVM switches are often IP-based and can be operated remotely. Each port on the switch is linked to an IP address and the input and output signals are compressed and packetized then carried over a short segment of Ethernet cable. At the server end, a console adapter provides the video and mouse / keyboard connectors (PS/2 or USB) to plug into the server and an RJ-45 port for the cable back to the KVM switch. This reduces the amount of cable required and makes connections into the KVM device much simpler.

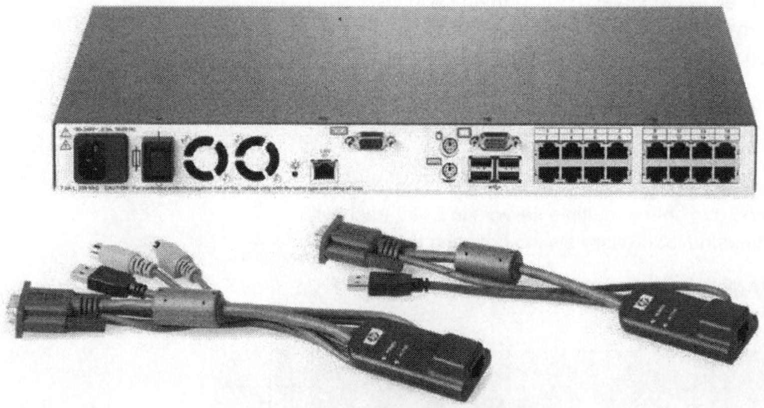

HP KVM IP console switch and adapters

Another means of using KVM over IP is to install a management card in the server (see "Console Redirection" below).

Console Port

The functions of a managed switch or router can be accessed via one of the appliance's management interfaces. A network appliance may support the following interfaces:

- **Console port** - this requires connecting a terminal (a laptop for instance) to the appliance via a physical serial interface using a special console (or rollover) cable. The terminal can then be used to start a Command Line Interface (CLI).
- **Management port / virtual terminal** - this means configuring a virtual network interface and IP address on the switch to use for management functions and connecting to it via one of the normal Ethernet ports. The port has to be enabled for this function (or some switches come with a dedicated management port). Most switches support a browser-based interface (HTTP/HTTPS) as well as a CLI using Telnet or Secure Shell (SSH). Using a CLI remotely in this way is referred to as a **virtual administration console**.

OS Administration Tools

Windows allows for the administration, configuration, and monitoring of a server using three main protocols: RDP, WMI, and Telnet.

Remote Desktop Protocol (RDP)

The **Remote Desktop Protocol (RDP)** allows client software running on a remote workstation to connect to server software over an IP network. The server can share a single application, or, as in the Remote Desktop admin utility, its whole desktop. This allows the user to perform any Windows configuration task, view the event logs, run an application stored on the server, configure file sharing, and so on.

RDP runs on TCP port 3389. The Remote Desktop server must be enabled and permitted users configured from system properties on the server.

Rather than create a remote desktop for each server, Microsoft provide the Remote Desktop snap-in. You can define multiple servers in a list, each with different connection properties and then easily switch between them.

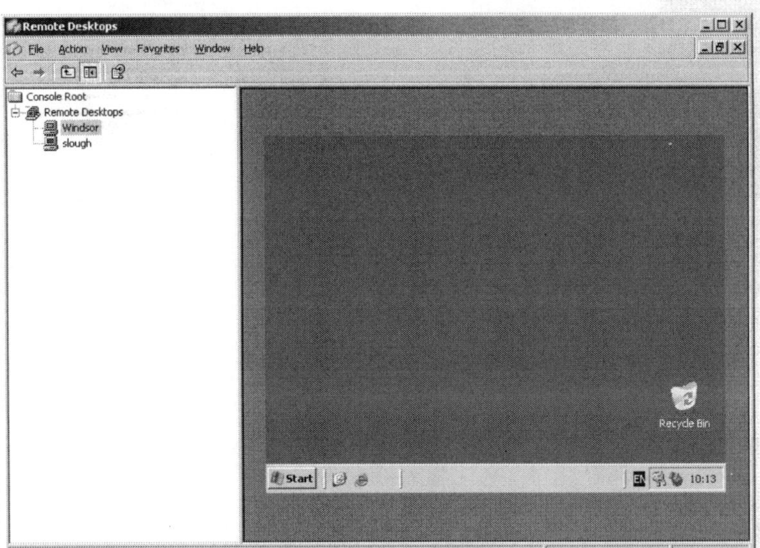

Using the Remote Desktop snap-in management console

Windows Management Instrumentation (WMI)

As described above, **Windows Management Instrumentation (WMI)** is Microsoft's implantation of WBEM. You can use scripts to configure a server but you can also use the **Administrative Tools** in most client and server versions of Windows to connect to a remote server.

For example, if you open **Computer Management**, you can select **Connect to another computer** from the **Action** menu. Enter the host name or IP address of the remote server then connect with the appropriate credentials. You can now access management consoles on the remote server (Event Viewer, Task Scheduler, Disk Management, Services, Performance Monitor, and so on).

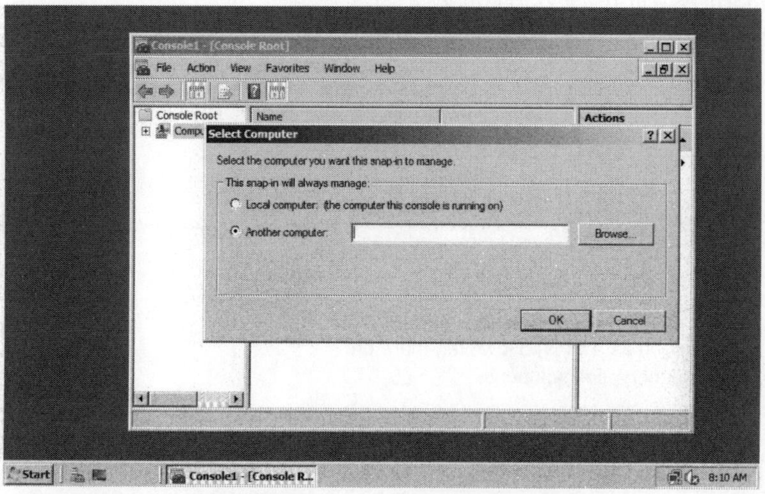

Using WMI to manage another computer remotely

The **Remote Server Administration Tools (RSAT)** are designed to provide remote access to all the Windows Server configuration utilities. For example, RSAT allows you to access the Configure My Server or Hyper-V Server Manager consoles remotely. You need to ensure that Windows Firewall is configured to allow remote administration and that the correct user privileges have been configured. WMI can either be facilitated via RPC (port 135) or using WinRM (see below), which works over HTTP.

Telnet Server Administration

Microsoft also provide a Telnet server administration program. Provided the administrator is equipped with a Telnet client (and that the Telnet daemon has been configured on the server), he or she can gain access to a server at the command prompt only. This allows for some degree of remote management, but obviously doesn't allow for the use of graphical tools. Also, Telnet is unsecure.

Windows Server 2008 and 2012 support an improved remote command line utility. The server runs a service called **WinRM (Windows Remote Management)**. The client executes a utility called **WinRS (Remote Shell)**. This provides better security than Telnet (it is the equivalent of the SSH tool often used to configure Linux servers remotely).

Remote Management with UNIX/Linux

Telnet was first developed for UNIX and remains available as a means of connecting to Linux servers remotely. It is not secure however and consequently should not be used for management tasks. Telnet has been replaced by **Secure Shell (SSH)**. As with Telnet, SSH involves a server component (the daemon) and a client. The difference from Telnet is that communications between the client and server can be encrypted, to prevent eavesdropping, replay, and modification attacks.

Virtual Network Computing (VNC)

Virtual Network Computing (VNC) is a freeware product with similar functionality to RDP. There are versions for Windows, Linux, and Mac OS. It works over TCP port 5900.

Freeware versions of VNC provide no connection security and so should only be used over a secure connection (such as a VPN). However, there are commercial products packaged with encryption solutions.

Network Hardware Administration Tools

In certain situations, such as when an administrator has branch offices to manage, servers may not be physically accessible during the troubleshooting process. While the remote desktop and terminal emulation technologies outlined above are useful in these situations, they require the operating system to be running. Remote Desktop, for example, is of no use in troubleshooting the boot process, accessing the recovery tools, or using a RAID configuration utility or startup diagnostic tools. In these more critical situations, something like **console redirection** may be appropriate. A console redirection solution such as **KVM over IP** has the ability to redirect GUI input and output over a network port. A KVM over IP device may be installed as an adapter card in a single server or as a rack-mount appliance.

ILO and iDRAC

There are also Baseboard Management Controller (BMC) implementations integrated directly on the motherboard. These provide a dedicated network management port to connect to a remote control server. Two popular implementations are offered on server solutions from HP and Dell:

- HP Integrated Lights Out (ILO).
- Integrated Dell Remote Access Controller (iDRAC).

With console redirection it is possible to power the server on and off, view the POST sequence, access low-level system firmware configuration and adapter firmware utilities, access system logs, and so on. The management and monitoring tool is typically accessed via a browser.

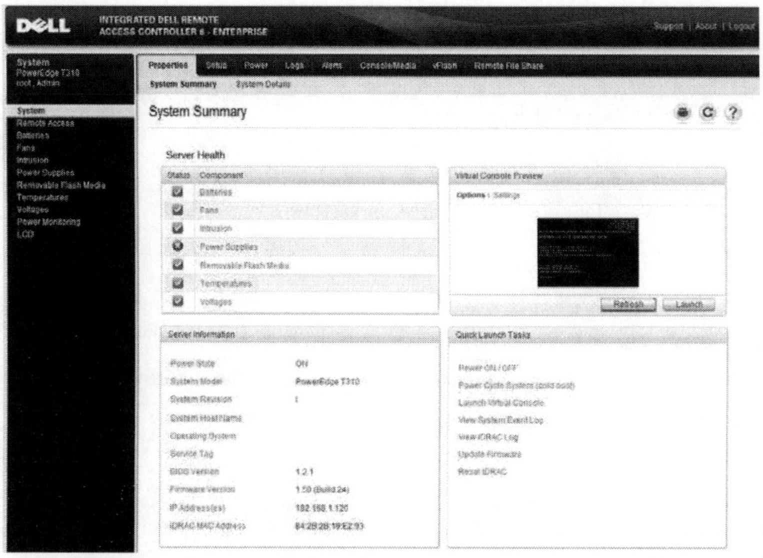

The iDRAC management controller in this Dell server enables low-level boot settings to be monitored and configured from a remote console - access can be via a dedicated management port, the regular network ports, or via a serial port

Software Deployment

Another feature of console redirection is the ability to install software on a server remotely. Not only can you configure the RAID array and partition the disk, you can launch the vendor's software deployment tool to connect to the setup files. Another feature is that installation options can be scripted so that the process can be fully automated.

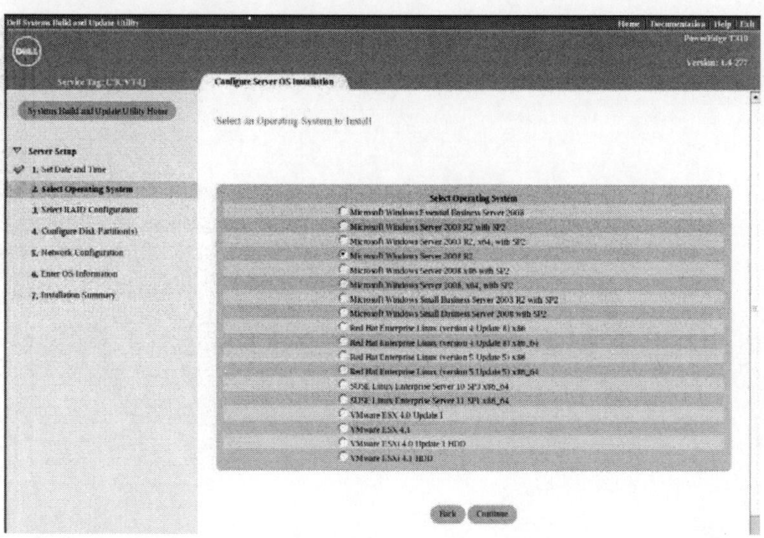

Dell System Build utility

Review Questions / Module 4 / Unit 5 / Server Management

Answer these questions to test what you have learned in this unit.

1) What are the protocols and frameworks for network and server monitoring products?

2) What protocol defines an out-of-band management interface for a server?

3) True or false? An IP-based KVM is connected to an RJ-45 port on the server.

4) What in-band GUI console redirection tool can be used to log on to a Windows Server remotely?

5) You provide managed services for a company that prefers HP servers and appliances. What hardware-level network console redirection technology would you expect to be using?

6) You are installing a Linux server at a remote office. You need to establish a means of connecting to a secure command line from your main office. What system administration tool is best suited to this task?

Module 4 / Unit 6
Configuration Management

Objectives

On completion of this unit, you will be able to:

- Understand the role of configuration and asset management policies, procedures, and documentation in server administration.
- Understand the use of change management procedures.
- Compare and update server and rack schematics, diagrams, and job logs.

Change and Configuration Management

Configuration Management means identifying all components of ICT infrastructure (hardware, software, and procedures) and their properties. **Change management** means putting policies in place to reduce the risk that changes to these components could mean service disruption (network downtime).

ITIL Configuration Management Model

ITIL® (IT Infrastructure Library) is a popular documentation of *good and best practice* activities and processes for delivering IT services. Under ITIL, configuration management is implemented using the following elements:

- **Service assets** are things, processes, or people that contribute to the delivery of an IT service.
- A **Configuration Item (CI)** is an asset that requires specific management procedures for it to be used to deliver the service. Each CI must be identified by some sort of label. CIs are defined by their **attributes**, which are stored in a **Configuration Management Database (CMDB)**.
- **Baseline** - a fundamental concept in configuration management is the baseline. The baseline represents "the way it was". A baseline can be a **configuration baseline** (the ACL applied to a firewall for instance) or a **performance baseline** (such as the throughput achieved by a server).
- A **Configuration Management System (CMS)** is the tools and databases that collect, store, manage, update, and present information about CIs.

One of the goals of the CMS is to understand the *relationships* between CIs. Another is to track *changes* to CI attributes (and therefore variance from the baseline) over time.

Implementing Configuration Procedures

The main difficulty in implementing a workable configuration management system is in determining the level of *detail* that must be preserved. This is not only evident in capturing the asset database and configuration baseline in the first place but also in managing **Moves, Adds, and Changes (MACs)** within the network infrastructure. In terms of network tasks, a CMS will require that configuration changes be made *only* when there is a valid job ticket authorizing the change. This means that the activity of all network personnel, whether it be installing new devices or troubleshooting, is recorded in **job logs**. Consequently, configuration management involves drafting and enforcing **policies** and **procedures** (Standard Operating Procedures or SOPs) to govern all levels of network configuration and troubleshooting activity.

Requesting Changes

In order to reduce the risk that changes to configuration items will cause service disruption, a documented change management process can be used to implement changes in a planned and controlled way. The need to change is often described either as **reactive**, where the change is forced on the organization, or as **proactive**, where the need for change is initiated internally. Changes can also be categorized according to their **potential impact** and level or risk (major, significant, minor, or normal for instance).

In a formal change management process, the need or reasons for change and the procedure for implementing the change is captured in a **Request for Change (RFC)** document and submitted for approval. The RFC will then be considered at the appropriate level and affected stakeholders will be **notified**. This might be a supervisor or department manager if the change is normal or minor. Major or significant changes might be managed as a separate project and require approval through a **Change Advisory Board (CAB)**.

Implementing Changes

Regardless of whether an organization is large enough to require formal change management procedures and staff, the implementation of changes should be carefully planned, with consideration for how the change will affect dependent components. For most significant or major changes, organizations should attempt to trial the change first. Every change should be accompanied by a **rollback** (or remediation) plan, so that the change can be reversed if it has harmful or unforeseen consequences.

Changes should also be scheduled sensitively if they are likely to cause system downtime or other negative impact on the workflow of the business units that depend on the IT system that is to be modified. Most networks have a scheduled **maintenance window** period for **authorized downtime**.

When the change has been implemented, its impact should be assessed and the process reviewed and documented to identify any outcomes that could help future change management projects.

Implementing a CMS, CMDB, and Job Logs

The implementation of the administration system could be paper-based but computer records are much easier to search and update. The following tools could be used for a configuration management system:

- Spreadsheet - something like Microsoft Excel can quite comfortably store baseline CIs on a small network though it is less suitable for tracking jobs and changes to the configuration.

- Custom database - there are a number of dedicated applications for implementing a CMS. While they are correspondingly expensive and difficult to configure, these provide the best means of preserving accurate information and controlling procedures through job ticketing.

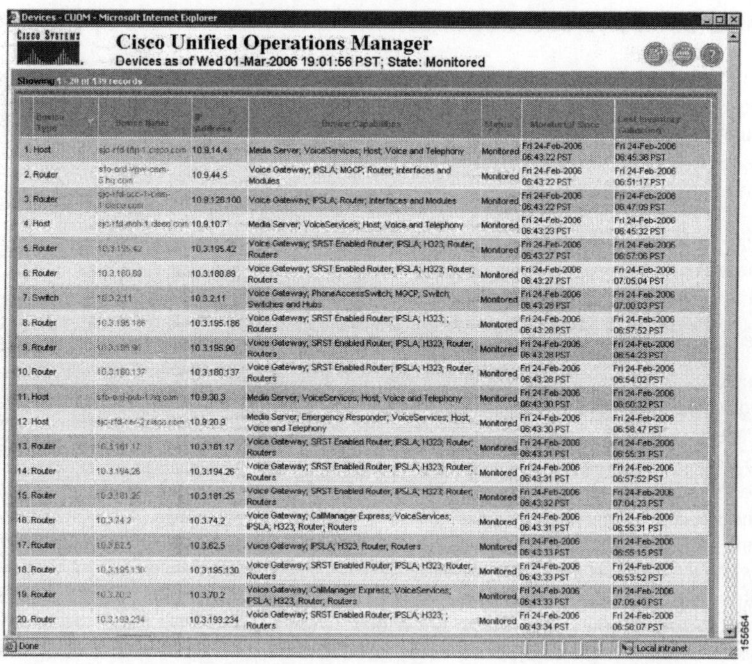

- Diagrams - Microsoft Visio is widely used to prepare network schematics. Detailed blueprints would require a Computer Aided Design (CAD) application.

As with any communications, job tickets should be completed professionally, with due regard for spelling, grammar, and clarity. Remember that other people may need to take action using just the information in the ticket and that analysis of tickets will take place as part of quality assurance procedures. It is also possible that tickets will be forwarded to customers as a record of the jobs performed.

Documentation

The purpose of **documentation** in terms of change and configuration management is as follows:

- Identify each component (CI) and label it.
- Capture each CI and its (relevant) attributes in a CMDB.
- Capture relationships between CIs - this is best done using diagrams.
- Capture changes to a CI as a job log and update the CMDB.

Asset Management and Vendor Documentation

It is crucial for an organization to have a well-documented inventory of its tangible and intangible assets and resources. In terms of network management, these will include network appliances (routers, switches, threat management devices, access points), servers, workstations, and passive network infrastructure (cabling and interconnects).

There are many software suites and associated hardware solutions available for tracking and managing assets (or **inventory**). An asset management database can be configured to store as much or as little information as is deemed necessary, though typical data would be type, make, model, serial number, asset ID, location, user(s), value, and service information. Tangible assets can be identified using a barcode label or RFID tag attached to the device (or more simply using an identification number). RFID stands for Radio Frequency ID. An RFID tag is a chip programmed with asset data. When in range of a scanner, the chip powers up and signals the scanner. The scanner alerts management software to update the device's location. As well as asset tracking, this allows the management software to track the location of the device, making theft more difficult.

Intangible assets can be harder to track but one critical piece of documentation will be a database of software licenses identifying on which physical or virtual servers each OS or application license is installed and ensuring that sufficient licenses have been purchased.

For each asset record there should also be a copy of or link to the appropriate **vendor documentation**. This would include both an invoice and warranty / support contract and support and troubleshooting guidance.

Network Diagrams

Diagrams are the best way to capture the complex relationships between network elements. They are also the most effective means of locating particular items within the network. Diagrams can be used to model **physical** and **logical** relationships at different levels of scale and detail.

Blueprint

A **blueprint** is a detailed diagram of cable runs and wall outlet positions. Blueprints will generally require the assistance of an architect to draw with any accuracy. Building blueprints will also show the architecture of the building along with other services, such as power wiring and plumbing. These may be difficult even to *interpret* without the help of an architect or electrician!

Network Architecture / Schematic / Block Diagram

A **schematic** is a simplified representation of the overall architecture of a system. In terms of the physical network topology, it can show the general placement of equipment and telecommunications rooms plus device and port IDs without trying to capture the exact position or relative size of any one element.

Schematics can also be used to represent the logical structure of the network, in terms of zones and subnets. In this sense, schematics can use either representative icons or pictures or drawings of actual product models. Another possibility is to identify traffic flows to show where bandwidth on the network or to a particular server is restricted.

Schematics can either be drawn manually using a tool such as Microsoft Visio or compiled automatically from network mapping software.

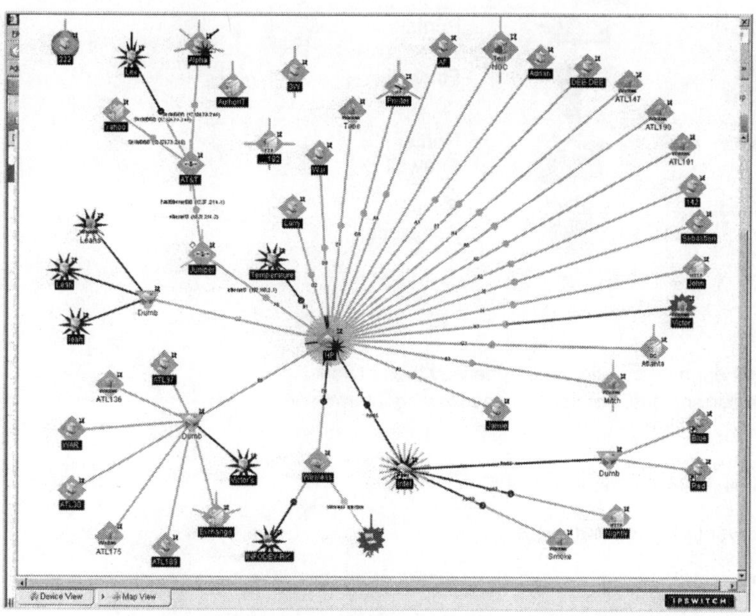

Ipswitch WhatsUpGold network mapping software (www.whatsupgold.com)

As far as icons go, the ones created by Cisco are recognized as standards. Some of the more commonly used devices are shown below:

Icon	Device	Icon	Device
	Hub		Branch Office
	Access Point		End Office
	Bridge		Cloud
	Workgroup Switch		File Server
	Layer 3 Switch		PC
	Multilayer Switch		Laptop
	Content Switch		Phone
	Router		Cellular Phone
	Wireless Router		IP phone
	Modem		Fax
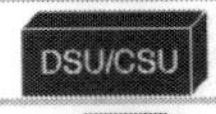	CSU / DSU		Printer
	PBX		Firewall
	Broadband Router		Router / Firewall
	Cable Modem		Security Appliance

Network Mappers

Network mapping means gathering information about the way the network is built and configured and the current status of hosts. The following information is all of use:

- Protocols, services, and applications running on the network.
- Host workstation and server OS types and patch status.
- Network addresses / IP address utilization and host names.
- Network interconnect device types and status.
- Network security appliances and software.
- User accounts and groups (especially administrative / root accounts) and passwords.

This sort of information may be gathered by network management software, such as CiscoWorks, Microsoft's System Center, HP's OpenView, or numerous other third-party products. There are also tools such as Nmap that can perform the same sort of function but are often associated more with attempts to penetrate the network than to maintain it.

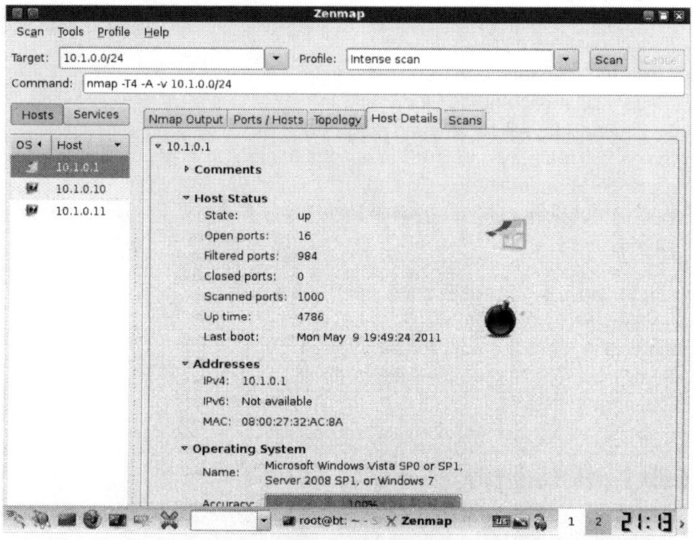

A tool such as Nmap can discover hosts connected to the network and report on their configuration

Service Documentation

The following **service documentation** should be created and maintained for each server commissioned to perform lifecycle management:

- Procurement / installation log - installer and date of installation, vendor specification and warranty details (plus location of documentation, technical support contacts, service tag, and so on), NOS and applications software, intended server role, and responsible administrator(s).
- Configuration log - RAID configuration, custom configuration for any applications, details of services available (plus startup type - manual or automatic), network configuration, and performance baseline.
- Usage / service log - details of update testing and patches applied, any hardware or software upgrades or repairs performed, updated performance baselines, plus additional useful troubleshooting information. If a patch is released and not applied because it causes problems with an application or hardware, it is very important to record why the patch has not been applied and what security or performance issues this could raise.
- End-of-life / decommissioning log - verify software license removal and data disposal or archiving and identify the option used to dispose of the physical hardware, whether by sale, donation, or waste / recycling service.

You need to keep the same sort of logs for each virtual server too.

If the server gains a new role, you should add that information to the relevant log. If the server is repurposed in a completely different role, it is probably best to start a new set of logs.

Vendor-specific Documentation

As well as installation and service logs, you should keep vendor documentation available to assist with maintenance and troubleshooting. Always familiarize yourself with the user or service guide before starting on hardware maintenance or upgrade. The vendor will have listed supported upgrades and configurations for things like memory and RAID. You should also be able to find "best practice" information about maintenance and troubleshooting. Many vendors supply troubleshooting diagnostic tools or checklists specific to a model of server.

Use the vendor's support website to obtain copies of user guides plus drivers and troubleshooting information. Make sure invoice and warranty support information is available so that technicians know the appropriate support channels available (phone, email, text chat for instance) and the terms of warranty work (onsite or back-to-base for instance).

Systems Architecture and Dataflow Diagrams

As well as the layout of network components, it is also important to model the processing of information by software applications running on the server infrastructure. A **dataflow diagram** shows where information is processed and stored as it passes through the system. For example, a customer order might be received by a front-end web server and passed to a middle tier application, which would generate processes for the invoicing and fulfilment functions of the system. A dataflow diagram helps to identify dependencies between different systems, which assists troubleshooting. Dataflow diagrams might also be important for compliance reasons; to demonstrate that personal or confidential data is processed in a secure way.

Secure Documentation

The information contained in the configuration management documentation would be extremely useful to anyone seeking to attack the network. Any details of system configuration or errors that have been experienced would help an attacker to penetrate the security systems set up to defend the network or individual servers. Consequently, the configuration management documentation should be secured against snooping. Printed documents could be stored in a secure room or safe while electronic documents should be encrypted and protected by file access control permissions.

Another point to be made is about storage of passwords for administrator-level accounts. Generally speaking, administrative privileges should be delegated to personal accounts and the account holder be made responsible for the security of the account (that is, making sure that only the account holder knows his or her password). This means, among other things, that the password should never be written down or stored in any sort of computer file.

Some network devices, support websites, or web hosting packages do not support personal accounts however so it is often necessary to use shared administrator accounts and to make the same password known to several different technicians. Shared admin passwords should be avoided where possible but if they are absolutely necessary, it is best to store them using password manager software. The password manager encrypts the file and restricts access to authorized users. Each technician would need to access the password manager using their personal authentication credentials and the security system should log access attempts.

Passwords should *not* be recorded in routine systems documentation.

Do not reuse admin passwords for different sites. For example, if you have a support account with a server vendor, you should never use a password on that account that is also used on your own network. It might seem tempting to reduce the number of admin passwords that have to be remembered, but repeating a password somewhere else means that your security will then only be as good as the remote site's security.

Don't forget that if a technician leaves the company, you need to change any shared passwords that the technician may have known.

Procedures and Standards

As a vital component of a company's IT infrastructure, employees must understand how to use ICT securely and safely and be aware of their *responsibilities*. To support this, an organization needs to create proper documentation, to help staff to understand and fulfill their responsibilities and follow proper procedures.

The value of a comprehensive policy is that it removes any *uncertainty* that employees may have about what to do in a given situation. For example, if you work for a large company and meet someone you do not recognize in your work area, should you smile and say hello or smile, say hello, ask them where they want to be, and then escort them to that place? If there is a company policy saying that visitors to the workplace **must** be escorted at all times, it will be much easier for employees to take it upon themselves to "police" this sort of circumstance.

Standards and Guidelines

Policy is an overall statement of intent. In order to establish the correct working practices, three different mechanisms can be put in place:

- Standard - a standard is a measure by which to evaluate compliance with the policy.

- Procedure - a procedure (often referred to as a SOP [Standard Operating Procedure] or an Internal Operating Procedure [IOP]) is an inflexible, step-by-step listing of the actions that must be completed for any given task. Most critical tasks should be governed by SOPs.
- Guidance - guidelines exist for areas of policy where there are no procedures, either because the situation has not been fully assessed or because the decision-making process is too complex and subject to variables to be able to capture it in a procedure. Guidance may also describe circumstances where it is appropriate to deviate from a specified procedure.

Developing a Management Plan

In a network environment, standards, procedures, and guidelines need to be established for the installation, maintenance, and troubleshooting of network equipment. A **management plan** for all network servers, devices, and workstations is the central plank in ensuring a secure, efficient, and well-documented network. A management plan should indicate what tasks are to be performed, when, and by whom.

Tasks would include monitoring performance and hardware status, performing backups, resolving and recording errors, cleaning and environmental checks, identifying security threats and countermeasures, detecting and resolving security breaches and intrusions, and so on.

It is essential that the plan sets out clear responsibilities and procedures for auditing action items (that is, ensuring that tasks are carried out properly and securely). Technicians responsible for maintenance may have different levels of access to the system. For example, administrators may have access to all configuration options on a server but backup operators can only access backup software and media. The results of management activities should be reported back and fed into development plans, to identify upgrade requirements. In the event that a problem is discovered during routine maintenance, a proper change management procedure should be followed to ensure that the solution is tested and verified without further impacting performance, reliability, or security.

Standard Business Documents

It is important to remember that although one can outsource virtually any service or activity to a third party, one cannot outsource legal accountability for these services or actions. You are ultimately responsible for the services and actions that these third parties take. This is why it is so important that you vet them thoroughly. Do you trust their hiring practices? Their training practices? Their access controls? If they have any access to your data or systems, any security breach in their organization (for example unauthorized data sharing) is effectively a breach in yours. Issues of security risk awareness, shared duties, and contractual responsibilities can be set out in a formal legal agreement.

The following types of agreement are common:

- Memorandum of Understanding (MOU) - usually a preliminary or exploratory agreement to express an intent to work together. MOUs are intended to be relatively informal and not to act as binding contracts. MOUs almost always have clauses stating that the parties shall respect confidentiality however.
- Statement of Work (SOW) - a contractual agreement setting out the detailed terms under which a one-off service or project is provided. An SOW might be used when a contractor is hired to install or upgrade a network for example. The SOW would show in detail what requirements the project will meet, the actions and equipment that will be provided and their costs, timescales for completing the project, plus acceptance criteria for the customer to approve the successful completion of the project.
- Service Level Agreement (SLA) - a contractual agreement setting out the detailed terms under which an ongoing service is provided. Metrics for SLAs are discussed in more detail below.
- Master Service Agreement (MSA) - a master contract governing sub-contracts (often written as SOWs). The MSA will set out standard terms applicable to multiple contracts, such as payment terms, confidentiality agreements, and dispute resolution mechanisms.

A legal agreement is all very well, but it is still up to you to make sure that your suppliers, vendors, and contractors can live up to them. If they can't, you may successfully sue them, but if they go out of business, you are still accountable for their actions or failure to act.

Conversely, you need to ensure that you can comply with the requirements and performance standards of any agreements that you enter into as a service provider.

Key Performance Indicators

Any time that an organization's staff spend in the workplace without access to the computer system (an **outage**) is likely to be time wasted and therefore a significant cost. Similarly, time that customers cannot access a sales site or make enquiries because a system is down represents costs in terms of lost sales opportunities and reputation. If you can quantify these costs, you can provide a cost-based justification for upgrading the network infrastructure to improve reliability.

Key Performance Indicators (KPI) are metrics used in quality and performance management and are also likely to be quoted in an SLA. Some of the main KPIs relating to service availability are as follows.

- **Availability** (or **uptime**) can be calculated as the percentage of time that the network is available and working, measured over a defined period (typically one year). The corollary of availability is downtime (that is, the percentage or amount of time during which the system is unavailable). Full availability is usually loosely described as 24x7 (24 hours per day, 7 days per week) or 24x365 (24 hours per day, 365 days per year). For a critical system, availability will be described as "two-nines" (99%) up to five- or six-nines (99.9999%):

Availability	Annual Downtime	Approximately
99.9999%	00:00:32	30 seconds
99.999%	00:05:15	5 minutes
99.99%	00:52:34	1 hour
99.9%	08:45:36	½ day
99.0%	87:36:00	3-4 days

Availability is not restricted to catastrophic crashes or complete system failures. A system that is slow is also costing time (and probably contributing to stress and low morale in the workplace). Systems also need to be taken offline occasionally for new installs, upgrades, service, and troubleshooting. Downtime can be calculated from the sum of *scheduled* service intervals plus *unplanned outages* over the period.

Downtime may or may not be defined to include agreed scheduled service time. It is important to verify this point when drawing up Service Level Agreements (SLA).

- **Response time** is a measure of the mean time taken to acknowledge a support request (but not necessarily to fix the problem).
- **Mean Time to Failure (MTTF)** and **Mean Time Between Failures (MTBF)** represent the expected lifetime of a product or system. MTTF should be used for non-repairable systems. For example, a hard drive may be described with an MTTF while a server (which could be repaired by replacing the hard drive) would be described with an MTBF. You will often see MTBF used indiscriminately however. For most devices, failure is more likely early and late in life, producing the so-called "bathtub curve".
- **Mean Time to Repair (MTTR)** is a measure of the time taken to correct a fault so that the system is restored to full operation. This can also be described as mean time to "replace" or "recover".
- **Mean Time Between Service Incidents (MTBSI)** represents the time between the point of failure of a system and its next point of failure (that is, MTBF + MTTR).

Review Questions / Module 4 / Unit 6 / Configuration Management

Answer these questions to test what you have learned in this unit.

1) Why would a MAC require a job ticket?
2) What inventory information should an asset management database capture?
3) Users have reported poor performance from an application server. What type of documentation would assist in identifying whether the problem was caused by network bandwidth?
4) How might SLAs affect server upgrade plans?
5) True or false? The local administrator or root user password should be recorded in the system installation log to ensure the password is never lost, which would permanently deny access to the system.
6) You are assessing whether a service provider's SLA meets your stated Recovery Time Objective (RTO) of 6 hours. Which SLA metric(s) should you identify?
7) A client's web server is at severe risk of exploitation unless a patch is installed. There is no time or resource to set up a test system, There is no particular reason to suspect any compatibility issues but installing the patch will require a restart and disruption to the web service. How should you proceed?

This page left blank intentionally.

Module 4 / Summary
Server Maintenance

You learned how to install, upgrade, and troubleshoot hardware components and about environmental and power requirements for computer rooms and data centers. You learned about different methods and tools to use to administer and monitor servers remotely and about maintaining proper asset and services documentation.

Module 4 / Unit 1 / Server Hardware

- Make sure you can identify components of the server chassis and motherboard.

- You need to be able to select compatible components to use in an upgrade and be familiar with the features of CPUs, memory, and expansion cards and perform upgrades.

Module 4 / Unit 2 / Environment and Maintenance

- You can observe a server's status indicators to determine whether there is a problem. Make sure you know the procedures for shutting down a server cleanly.

- Know about the environmental factors that should be considered when placing and maintaining server equipment.

- You should be able to describe the components of server and rack cooling systems and understand the requirements for specifying and installing HVAC systems.

Module 4 / Unit 3 / Power Distribution

- You should understand the characteristics of electrical circuits and the problems that can affect computer equipment.

- Server Power Supply Units (PSU) must be specified to handle the load imposed by the components installed. Many servers and blade enclosures can be configured with multiple hot-swappable PSUs for redundancy.

- You should know how to specify and configure an appropriate UPS for a given server system or rack.

- Make sure you know the features of the electrical mains circuits and the means of connecting them to rack and server equipment safely.

Module 4 / Unit 4 / Server Hardware Troubleshooting

- When upgrading or troubleshooting server hardware, follow installation and upgrade best practice and know how to minimize the risk of damaging components.
- Make sure you can diagnose problems relating to hardware components and the boot process from typical symptoms and select an appropriate tool to use to identify or correct the problem.

Module 4 / Unit 5 / Server Management

- You should be able to distinguish between local and remote administration tools and identify the features of common tools.

Module 4 / Unit 6 / Configuration Management

- Make sure that you understand the role of configuration management policies, procedures, and documentation in server administration.
- You should be able to compare and update server and rack schematics, diagrams, and job logs.

Module 5 / Server Security

CompTIA Server+ SK0-004 Domain Areas	Weighting
1.0 Server Architecture	12%
2.0 Server Administration	24%
3.0 Storage	12%
4.0 Security	13%
5.0 Networking	10%
6.0 Disaster Recovery	9%
7.0 Troubleshooting	20%

The following table lists the CompTIA Server+ domain objectives and content examples covered in the units in this module:

Refer To	Domain Objectives/Examples
Unit 5.1 / Site Security	**4.1 Compare and contrast physical security methods and concepts** *Multifactor Authentication (Something you have, Something you know, Something you are) • Security concepts (Mantrap, RFID chip, ID card, Biometric, Keypad, Access list, Security guard, Security camera, Keys & Locks [Cabinet, Rack mount, Server], Safe)*
	4.5 Implement data security methods and secure storage disposal techniques *Storage encryption (File level encryption, Disk encryption, Tape encryption) • Storage media (Soft wipe [File deletion], Hard wipe [Zero out all sectors], Physical destruction, Remote wipe)*
	4.6 Given a scenario, implement proper environmental controls and techniques *Safety (Fire suppression)*
Unit 5.2 / Remote Access Services	**2.2 Compare and contrast server roles and requirements for each** *Routing and remote access server*
	4.3 Explain basic network security systems and protocols *Authentication protocols (RADIUS, TACACS, TACACS+) • PKI (Private key, Public key, Certificate authority, SSL / TLS) • VPN • IPsec*
Unit 5.3 / Server Hardening	**2.1 Install and configure server operating systems** *Address security concerns (Patching, OS hardening, Compliance to company procedures / standards)*
	2.4 Given a scenario, perform proper server maintenance techniques *Patch management (Operating System updates, Application updates, Security software updates, Firmware updates, Device drivers updates, Compatibility lists [Operating systems, Hardware, Applications], Testing and validation)*

Refer To	Domain Objectives/Examples
Unit 5.3 / Server Hardening	**4.2 Given a scenario, apply server hardening techniques** *OS hardening (Stopping unneeded services / closing unneeded ports, Install only required software, Install latest operating system patches) • Application hardening (Install latest patches, Disabling unneeded services / roles / features) • Endpoint security (HIDS, Anti-malware) • Remediate security issues based on a vulnerability scan • Hardware hardening (Disabling unneeded hardware and physical ports / devices, BIOS password, Disable WOL [Wake on LAN], Setup boot order, Chassis locks / intrusion detection)*
Unit 5.4 / Security Software	**4.2 Given a scenario, apply server hardening techniques** *Endpoint security (HIDS, Anti-malware) • Remediate security issues based on a vulnerability scan*
	4.3 Explain basic network security systems and protocols *Port security / 802.1x / NAC • NIDS*
	7.6 Given a scenario, effectively diagnose security issues, selecting the appropriate tools and methods *Common problems (File integrity issue, Privilege escalation, Applications will not load, Can't access network file / shares, Unable to open files, Excessive access, Excessive memory utilization) • Causes of common problems (Open ports, Active services, Inactive services, Intrusion detection configurations, Anti-malware configurations, Local / group policies, Firewall rules, Misconfigured permissions, Virus infection, Rogue processes / services) • Security tools (Port scanners, Sniffers, Cipher, Checksums, Telnet client, Anti-malware)*
Unit 5.5 / Disaster Recovery	**2.4 Given a scenario, perform proper server maintenance techniques** *Fault tolerance and high availability techniques (Clustering [Active / active, Active / passive], Load balancing [Round robin, Heartbeat])*
	6.1 Explain the importance of disaster recovery principles *Site types (Hot site, Cold site, Warm site) • Replication methods (Disk to disk, Server to server, Site to site) • Continuity of Operations (Disaster recovery plan, Business continuity plan, Business impact analysis [Who is affected, What is affected, Severity of impact])*
Unit 5.6 / Backup	**6.2 Given a scenario, implement appropriate backup techniques** *Methodology (Full / Normal [Copy], Incremental, Differential, Snapshot, Selective, Bare metal, Open file, Data vs. OS restore) • Backup media (Linear access [Tape], Random Access [Disk, Removable media, Optical media]) • Media and restore best practices (Labeling, Integrity verification, Test restorability, Tape rotation and retention) • Media storage location (Offsite, Onsite, Security considerations, Environmental considerations)*
	7.5 Given a scenario, effectively troubleshoot storage problems, selecting the appropriate tools and methods *Common problems (Restore failure, Unsuccessful backup)*

Module 5 / Unit 1
Site Security

Objectives

On completion of this unit, you will be able to:

- Describe the use of zones, barriers, gateways, and surveillance in planning and implementing site security.
- Use encryption and media disposal techniques to protect data.
- Understand what to do in an emergency situation and the basics of fire prevention and suppression systems.

Authentication

Assuming that an account has been created securely (the identity of the account holder has been verified), **authentication** verifies that only the account holder is able to use the account (and that the system may only be used by account holders). Authentication is performed when the account holder supplies the appropriate **credentials** to the system. These are compared to the credentials stored on the system. If they match, the account is authenticated.

There are many different technologies for defining credentials. They can be categorized as the following factors:

- Something you **know** (such as a password).
- Something you **have** (such as a smart card).
- Something you **are** (such as a fingerprint).

Each has advantages and drawbacks.

Something You Know Authentication

The typical "something you know" technology is the log on: this comprises a **username** and a **password**. The username is typically not a secret (though it doesn't do to go round publishing it) but the password must be known only to the account holder. A **passphrase** is a longer password comprising a number of words. This has the advantages of being more secure and easier to remember. A **Personal Identification Number (PIN)** is another example of something you know.

Windows logon dialog

Another important concept in authentication based on facts that a person knows is **Personally Identifiable Information (PII)**. PII includes things such as full name, birth date, address, social security number, and so on. Some bits of information (such as a social security number) may be unique; others uniquely identify an individual in combination (for example, full name with birth date and street address).

PII is often used for password reset mechanisms and to confirm identity over the telephone. For example, PII may be defined as responses to challenge questions, such as "What is your favorite color / pet / movie?"

Disclosing PII inadvertently can lead to identity theft (where someone usurps a legally valid identity to conceal their illegal activities). PII can often be relatively easy to obtain so caution needs to be exercised when depending on this information for authentication.

Something You Have Authentication

There are various ways to authenticate a user based on something they have. Examples include a smart card, USB token, or key fob that contains a chip with authentication data, such as a **digital certificate**.

Digital certificates are an encryption technology. See Unit 5.2 for more information about cryptography.

The card must be presented to a card reader before the user can be authenticated. A USB token can be plugged into a normal USB port.

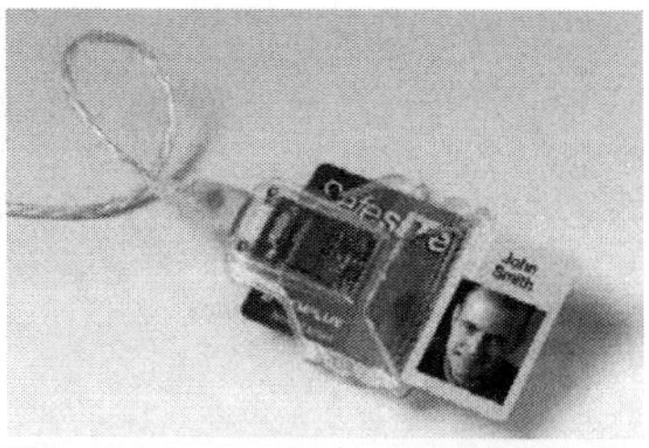

GemPlus USB smart card reader (courtesy GemPlus image library)

When the card is read, the card software prompts the user for a **Personal Identification Number (PIN)** or password, which mitigates the risk of the card being lost or stolen. Another option is a hardware token that generates a **one-time password**. The token displays a number that changes periodically; the number and frequency of changes is mathematically linked to an algorithm on the authenticating server, so inputting the correct code proves possession of the token.

The main concerns with "something you have" technologies are loss and theft and the chance that the device can be counterfeited. There are also hardware and maintenance costs.

Something You Are Authentication

"Something you are" means employing some sort of **biometric** recognition system. Many types of biometric information can be recorded, including fingerprint patterns, signature recognition, iris or retina recognition, or facial recognition. The chosen biometric information (the **template**) is scanned and recorded in a database. When the user wants to access a resource, s/he is re-scanned and the scan compared to the template. If they match to within a defined degree of tolerance, access is granted.

Multifactor Authentication

An authentication technology is considered "strong" if it combines the use of more than one type of technology (**multifactor**). Single factor authentication systems can quite easily be compromised: a password could be written down or shared, a smart card could be lost or stolen, and a biometric system could be subject to high error rates.

Two-factor authentication combines something like a smart card or biometric mechanism with "something you know", such as a password or PIN. Three-factor authentication combines all three technologies. An example of this would be a smart card with integrated thumb- or fingerprint reader. This means that to authenticate, the user must possess the card, the user's fingerprint must match the template stored on the card, and the user must input a PIN.

Multifactor authentication requires a combination *of* different *technologies. For example, requiring a PIN along with Date of Birth may be stronger than entering a PIN alone, but it is not multifactor.*

Designing a Secure Site

Physical access controls depend on the same security triad as network or operating system security:

- Authorization - create barriers around a resource so that access can be controlled through defined access points.
- Authentication - create access lists and identification mechanisms to allow approved persons through the barriers.
- Accounting - keep a record of when access points are used and detect security breaches.

Reasons for Physical Controls

The most obvious need to provide physical security is to prevent valuable server and network equipment being stolen, by intruders or by staff!

As well as protecting the value of the asset however, physical intrusion into a company's premises risks data loss and hacking. An intruder with access to computer systems may be able to copy data onto a portable drive, observe logins (shoulder surfing) and capture authentication details, get information about the models of computers and routers used in the network, and so on.

Defense in Depth

One of the key principles in designing a security system is to provide **defense in depth**. Any one security countermeasure may be relatively easy to overcome but defeating a series of countermeasures gets harder the more layers you add.

For example, you could protect a server by putting it in a room with a key-operated locked door. But this single layer of defense is vulnerable to a variety of attacks; an attacker could force the door, steal the key, or find it left open by accident. In response, the door could be made self-closing and operated using a fingerprint reader, it could be monitored by CCTV, a motion-sensing alarm could be used in the room, a security guard could be patrolling the corridor...

The only downside to defense in depth is that physical security mechanisms are expensive. The cost of controls needs to be balanced against risk.

Security Zones

Physical site security can be thought of in terms of **zones**. Each zone should be separated by its own **barrier(s)**. **Access points** through the barriers need to be controlled by one or more security mechanisms. Progression through each zone should be progressively more restricted.

The number of zones will depend on the size of the site and the type of operations that take place there, but you could categorize the following general areas:

- External - the areas outside the premises. It may be difficult to control these areas, with security mechanisms limited to surveillance.
- Perimeter - for a single site, this will be the walls of the building itself. A large site with many buildings will have an outer perimeter (fencing) and then inner perimeters for each building. Many businesses will share premises with other companies, in which case access to the building and monitoring of common parts is likely to be the responsibility of the landlord or building management company. A critical point in the perimeter is any location where voice and data cabling enter.
- Public - these are areas of the building where guests are invited, deliveries accepted, and so on. Public zones are typically high traffic (that is, people move through them frequently).
- Restricted - these are areas where most employees work. Guests may be invited into these zones, if they are subject to the proper controls. Depending on the level of security, it may or may not be appropriate to control the movement of employees between restricted zones.
- Secure - these are areas where access is strictly limited because they contain critical systems or confidential data. A typical example would be a network closet or equipment room housing servers and switch and router appliances.

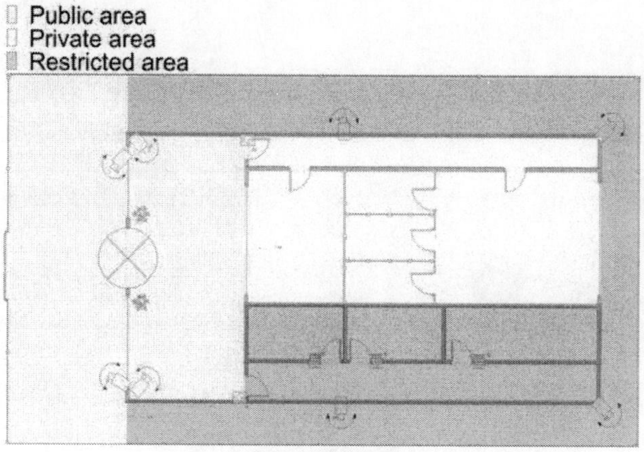

Defining security zones

Site Security Controls

Given a site design, a number of specific controls can be used to implement security.

Door Access Controls

A **barricade** is something that prevents access. As with any security system, no barricade is completely effective; a wall may be climbed or a lock may be picked, for instance. The purpose of barricades is to channel people through defined **access points**. Each access point should have an **authentication** mechanism (or **door access control**) so that only authorized persons are allowed through.

Most door access controls depend on some type of lock mechanism. Locks can be categorized as follows:

- Conventional - a conventional lock prevents the door handle from being operated without the use of a key. More expensive types offer greater resistance against lock picking.
- Deadbolt - this is a bolt on the frame of the door, separate to the handle mechanism.
- Electronic - rather than a key, the lock is operated by entering a PIN on an electronic keypad. This type of lock is also referred to as cipher, combination, or keyless.

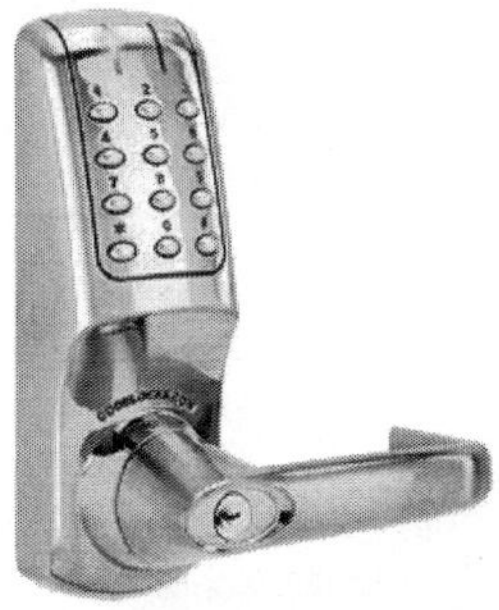

CodeLock combination digital lock

- Token-based - a smart lock may be opened using a magnetic swipe card or feature a proximity reader to detect the presence of a wireless key fob or one-time password generator (physical tokens) or smart card.
- Biometric - a lock may be integrated with a biometric scanner.
- Multifactor - a lock may combine different methods (for example, smart card with PIN).

A secure gateway will normally be self-closing and self-locking, rather than depending on the user to close and lock it.

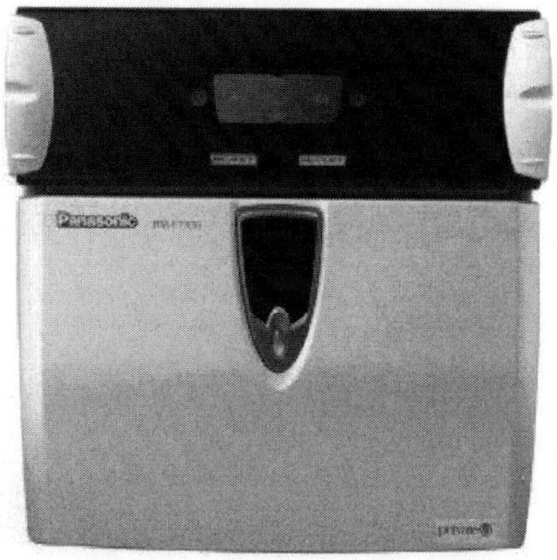

Panasonic Iris Recognition Camera System

ID Cards and Badges

A photographic **ID badge** showing name and (perhaps) access details is one of the cornerstones of building security. Anyone moving through secure areas of a building should be wearing an ID badge; anyone without an ID badge should be challenged.

An **entry control roster** held at each secure gateway records who is allowed to enter. This might be enforced by a security guard. Alternatively, **Radio Frequency ID (RFID) badges** can be used with proximity readers to monitor the location of the subject. When the RFID badge passes a reader (with a range up to about 5m), it registers a signal and transmits its ID to the management software.

As well as using RFID for wireless use, **smart card** badges and **key fobs** can be programmed with **biometric** authentication or with some sort of **token-generating** or **certificate-based** authentication. This type of badge could be used to open smart locks, as described above.

Turnstiles and Mantraps

Apart from being vulnerable to lock picking, the main problem with a simple door or gate as an entry mechanism is that it cannot accurately record who has entered or left an area. Multiple people may pass through the gateway at the same time; a user may hold a door open for the next person; an unauthorized user may "tailgate" behind an authorized user.

This risk may be mitigated by installing a **turnstile** (a type of gateway that only allows one person through at a time). Where security is critical and cost is no object, a **mantrap** could be deployed. A mantrap is where one gateway leads to an enclosed space protected by another barrier. Mantraps can operate in a number of modes:

- All doors normally unlocked - opening one door causes the other to lock.

- All doors normally locked - unlocking one door prevents the other from being unlocked.
- One door locked / other unlocked - when one door is open the other cannot be unlocked.

Security Guards

Surveillance is typically a second layer of security designed to improve the resilience of perimeter gateways. Effective surveillance mechanisms ensure that attempts to penetrate a barricade by other means are detected. Surveillance may be focused on perimeter areas or within security zones themselves.

The visible presence of guards is a very effective intrusion detection and deterrence mechanism, but is correspondingly expensive. It may also not be possible to place security guards within certain zones because they cannot be granted an appropriate security clearance. Training and screening of security guards is imperative.

Video Monitoring and CCTV

Video monitoring is a cheaper means of providing surveillance than maintaining separate guards at each gateway or zone, though still not cheap to set up if the infrastructure is not already in place in the premises. It is also quite an effective deterrent.

Panasonic mini-dome CCTV

The other big advantage is that movement and access can be recorded. The main drawback is that response times are longer and security may be compromised if not enough staff are in place to monitor the camera feeds.

A camera is either fixed or can be operated using Pan-Tilt-Zoom (PTZ) controls. Different cameras suit different purposes. If you want to record the image of every person entering through a door, a fixed, narrow focal length camera positioned on the doorway will be perfectly adequate. If you want to survey a large room and pick out individual faces, a camera with PTZ is required.

The cameras in a **CCTV (Closed Circuit Television)** network are typically connected to a multiplexer using coaxial cabling. The multiplexer can then display images from the cameras on one or more screens, allow the operator to control camera functions, and record the images to tape or hard drive. Newer camera systems may be linked in an IP network, using regular data cabling. Small **IP cameras** can use Power Over Ethernet (PoE), avoiding the need to provision a separate power circuit.

Physical Access Logs / Lists

The principle of "least privilege" dictates that as few people as possible should be granted the right to enter restricted areas, such as the server room or data center floor. Access to a building or area in a building may also be subject to limited hours access (for example, most staff would not be permitted to remain in the building after work hours). On the other hand, the fewer staff you have in a building at any one time, the more reliant you are on the integrity of those members of staff.

You may also want to time-limit technicians' access to server equipment, though this can be difficult to enforce. The principle here is to suspect anyone spending an unusual amount of time down in the server room. There could be any number of legitimate reasons for this of course - a security policy always has to strike the right balance between ensuring integrity and confidentiality and maintaining legitimate access.

An electronic lock may be able to log access attempts or a security guard can manually log movement. At the lowest end, a sign-in and sign-out sheet can be used to record authorized access.

Staff

The cheapest form of surveillance is to leverage ordinary employees to provide it. Security policies should explain staff responsibilities and define reporting mechanisms. One of the most important parts of surveillance is the **challenge** policy. This sets out what type of response is appropriate in given situations and helps to defeat **social engineering** attacks. This must be communicated to and understood by staff. Challenges represent a whole range of different contact situations. For example:

- Challenging visitors who do not have ID badges or are moving about unaccompanied.
- Insisting that proper authentication is completed at gateways, even if this means inconveniencing staff members (no matter how senior!)
- Intruders and/or security guards may be armed. The safety of staff and compliance with local laws has to be balanced against the imperative to protect the company's other resources.

It is much easier for employees to use secure behavior in these situations if they know that their actions are conforming to a standard of behavior that has been agreed and is expected of them.

Hardware Security

As well as access to the site, physical security can be used for network appliances and cabling.

Cable Locks and Locking Cabinets

The most vulnerable point of the network infrastructure will be the communications room. This should be subject to the most stringent access and surveillance controls that can be afforded.

Another layer of security can be provided by installing equipment within **lockable rack cabinets**. These can be supplied with key-operated or electronic locks.

At the appliance level, a **server chassis** can also be protected by a locking mechanism to prevent unauthorized access.

If installing equipment within a cabinet is not an option, it is also possible to obtain **cable hardware locks** for use with portable devices such as laptops.

HP rack cabinet with key-operated lock

Kensington cable lock installed on an HP laptop docking station

Safes

Portable devices and media (backup tapes or USB media storing encryption keys for instance) may be stored in a **safe**. Safes can feature key-operated or combination locks but are more likely to come with electronic locking mechanisms. Safes can be rated to a particular cash value for the contents against various international grading schemes. There are also fire safes that give a certain level of protection against exposure to smoke and flame and to water penetration (from fire extinguishing efforts).

Protected Distribution

As well as the switches, routers, and servers housed in equipment cabinets, thought needs to be given to cabling. A physically secure cabled network is referred to as a **Protected Distribution System (PDS)**. There are two principal risks:

- An intruder could attach eavesdropping equipment to the cable (a **tap**).
- An intruder could cut the cable (Denial of Service).

A hardened PDS is one where all cabling is routed through sealed metal conduit and subject to periodic visual inspection. Lower grade options are to use different materials for the conduit (plastic for instance). Another option is to install an alarm system within the cable conduit, so that intrusions can be detected automatically.

Data Encryption

When data is hosted on a file system, it can be protected by the operating system's security model. Each file or folder can be configured with an Access Control List (ACL), describing the permissions that different users (or user groups) have on the file. Files often have to be stored outside of the OS's file system and there is also the chance that a disk could be physically removed. With an NTFS volume, if the disk is attached to another computer, the local administrator can take ownership of all the files on the volume and change the original access control lists. To protect data at-rest against these risks, the information stored on a disk can be **encrypted**. If the files are encrypted, only the key holder can decrypt the files and the key will not be stored with the encrypted data (unless the key holder has been extremely foolish!)

File / Folder Encryption

One approach to encrypting data at-rest is to apply encryption to individual files or folders. The **Encrypting File System (EFS)** under NTFS supports file and folder encryption under professional and server versions of Windows. Without strong authentication, encrypted data is only as secure as the user account. If the password can be compromised then so can the data. Note also that the files are decrypted when moved to a different file system or accessed over a network share.

There are also many third-party encryption products. For Linux, the ext4 and ZFS file systems support transparent encryption.

Full Disk Encryption

Another option is to use a **Full Disk Encryption (FDE)** product. The BitLocker FDE product is built into Windows Server and the Enterprise client editions. OS X has a FileVault FDE product. It can also be enabled using a third-party product, such as TrueCrypt (now discontinued) or Symantec Drive Encryption.

Disk encryption carries a processing overhead but modern PCs usually have processing capacity to spare. It is particular useful for mobile devices, such as laptops, and removable drives. The main advantage is that it does not depend on the user to remember to encrypt data so mitigates the risk of data loss in the case of the theft or loss of the device. Disk encryption also encrypts the swap file, print queues, temporary files, and so on.

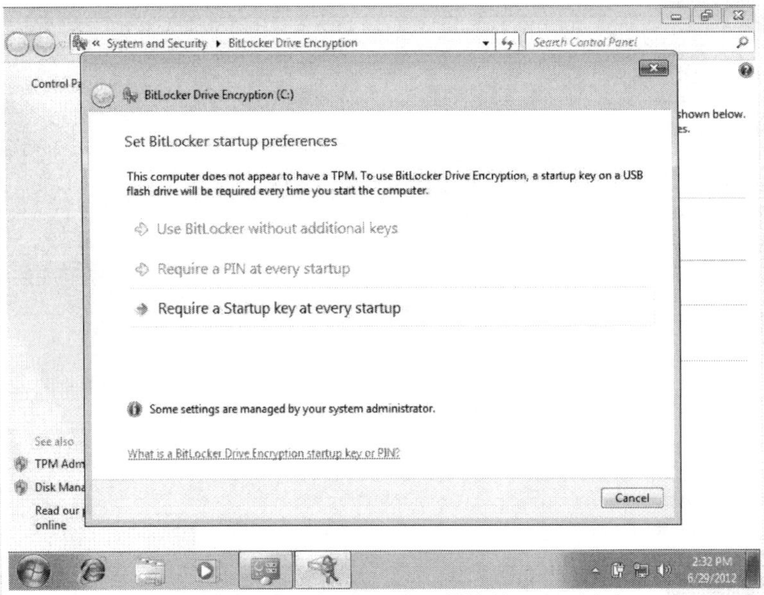

Configuring BitLocker in Windows 7 - rather than using a TPM this system is being configured with a startup key; a USB stick that must be present at boot-time

Hardware-based Encryption Devices

Some disk encryption products, including BitLocker and PGP, can make use of a **Trusted Platform Module (TPM)** chip in the computer to tie use of a hard disk to a particular motherboard. The TPM is used as a secure means of storing the encryption key and to ensure the integrity of the OS used to boot the machine. Alternatively the key could be stored on a USB stick or smart card.

Hardware-based FDE products are also being marketed by Seagate and Hitachi. The drives perform encryption at the controller level, removing the load from the CPU. These products depend on the presence of a secure boot password or **Pre-boot Authentication** environment.

Database Encryption

For most end-user software, encryption at the disk or file level is usually sufficient. Encrypting client / server databases is more complex as the data must usually be accessible from multiple client devices. Encryption can also cause significant performance overheads. Consequently database security tends to focus more on access control than on encryption per se.

A multi-user database would not usually be encrypted using the sort of file or disk encryption products provided with the OS (though these could be used on backup copies of the database or on copies made to removable media). Instead, the **Database Management System (DBMS)** would come with its own encryption technology or you may select a specialist third-party product for use with a particular database technology.

Encryption is generally applied at the column (or field) level. For example, a customer's name and address might be stored in plaintext but their credit card number would be encrypted. This type of encryption is primarily deployed against malicious insider threats (database administrators who would normally be able to access any information in the database). The primary key of a table (the column used to uniquely identify each record) should never be encrypted.

Tape Encryption

The need for backup media to be encrypted needs to be carefully considered too. If the data has already been encrypted (via EFS for instance) backup solutions will preserve the encryption attributes. In this scenario, you need to have a separate backup of users' encryption keys in order to restore the data.

It is also possible to use tape drive hardware that supports encryption, though this can have an impact on performance. Many LTO generation 4+ drives support hardware-level encryption. As with any other encryption technology, it is vitally important to keep the encryption keys secure or it will be impossible to restore the backed up data. The encryption key must be kept separately from the encrypted media; keeping them together is just like leaving your key in the front door!

Troubleshooting Encryption

With encryption, there is always the risk that the key will be lost or damaged, making the encrypted data permanently unavailable. If the boot volume is encrypted and the key is not available to the system at boot time, the OS will not be bootable. It is usually possible to configure a recovery account to provide a secondary means of decrypting the data if the original key is lost.

Data Wiping and Disposal

A wiping / disposing policy refers to the procedures that the organization has in place for disposing of obsolete information and equipment.

Hard drive sanitation refers to fully erasing hard disks. More generally, **remnant removal** refers to decommissioning various media, including flash drives, tape media, CD and DVD ROMs, and so on. The problem has become particularly prominent as organizations recycle their old computers, either by donating them to charities or by sending them to a recycling company, who may recover and sell on parts. The problem also applies to network printers, which often have installable hard disks to use to cache print jobs.

There are at least three reasons that make remnant removal critical:

- An organization's own confidential data could be compromised.
- Third-party data that the organization processes could be compromised, leaving it liable under Data Protection legislation (in addition to any contracts or Service Level Agreements signed).
- Software licensing could be compromised.

The main issue is understanding the degree to which data on different media types may be recoverable. Data "deleted" from a magnetic-type disk (such as a hard disk) is not erased. Rather, the sectors are marked as available for writing and the data they contain will only be removed as new files are added. This can also be referred to as a **soft wipe**. Similarly, using the standard Windows format tool will only remove references to files and mark all sectors as useable. In the right circumstances and with the proper tools, any deleted information from a drive could be recoverable.

There are several approaches to the problem of data remnants on disks:

- Overwriting / hard wiping - hard wiping ensures that old data is destroyed by writing to each location on the media, either using zeroes or in a random pattern. This is suitable for all but the most confidential data, but is time consuming and may require special software.

  The `cipher` *tool can be used to overwrite free disk space and erase deleted data (*`cipher /w:`***`FolderName`****).*

- Remote wipe - this means that a device initiates a hard wipe or factory reset when issued with a "kill" command over a network. This functionality is usually used in conjunction with mobile devices, such as smartphones and tablets.

- Low Level Format - most disk vendors supply tools to reset a disk to its factory condition. These are often described as low level format tools and will have the same sort of effect as disk wiping software. Technically speaking a low level format creates cylinders and sectors on the disk. This can generally only be done at the factory. The disk utilities just clean data from each sector; they don't re-create the sector layout.

Active KillDisk data wiping software

- Physical destruction - a magnetic disk can be mechanically shredded or degaussed (exposing the disk to a powerful electromagnet disrupts the magnetic pattern that stores the data on the disk surface) in specialist machinery. Obviously, this sort of machinery is costly and will usually render the disk unusable, so it cannot be reused.

  A less expensive method is to destroy the disk with a drill or hammer - do be sure to wear protective goggles. This method is not appropriate for the most highly confidential data as it will leave fragments that could be analyzed using specialist tools.

- Disk encryption - as discussed above, this method encrypts *all* the information in a volume, so that any remnants could not be read without possession of the encryption key.

Optical media cannot be reformatted. Discs should be destroyed before discarding them. Shredders are available for destroying CD and DVD media.

Fire Prevention and Suppression

Fire can be catastrophic to a business, not to mention the danger it poses to people.

Fire Prevention

The essential point about fire prevention is that flammable materials should be kept away from sources of ignition. Office spaces should be kept clear of flammable materials, such as boxes or polystyrene, and ignition sources (no smoking!). Most countries require businesses to commission a fire inspection annually, during which an inspector will advise of any risks and check safety procedures and equipment. It is also wise to carry out your own checks monthly, to ensure that fire detectors and alarms work.

Building Layout and Emergency Alert Systems

Health and safety legislation dictates what mechanisms an organization must put in place to detect and suppress fires. At the very least each building must have well-marked fire exits and a fire escape plan that is tested and practiced regularly. **Building layout** in larger premises needs to be designed in such a way that fire cannot be allowed to spread quickly, by separating different areas with fire-resistant walls and doors (which must be kept shut).

Buildings also need to be fitted with automatic smoke or fire detection **emergency alert systems**, as well as alarms that can be operated manually. There are several types of detector:

- Photoelectric smoke detector - measures the integrity of an internal beam of light. The alarm will sound if the beam degrades (for example, if it is obscured by smoke).
- Ionization smoke detector - a radioactive source creates a regular movement of ionized particles, which can be disrupted by smoke.
- Heat detector - these alarms sound if heat rises to a certain point or if the rate of temperature increase exceeds the defined limit.
- Flame detector - these use infrared sensors to detect flames, and are the most effective (and expensive) type.

Escape Plans, Routes, and Drills

Every building requires a **fire escape plan** (or **evacuation plan**) for use in emergency. The plan instructs staff on how to leave the building safely and assemble at a designated marshal point outside. The plan assigns the persons responsible for ensuring that the building has been cleared and that everyone (staff and visitors) has been accounted for.

Safety/emergency exits from the building must be clearly signed and keep unobstructed. The plan should also set out the procedure to follow should an escape route be blocked; usually this will be to find an opening window and close the doors to the room.

The escape plan should be tested by performing an evacuation **drill** periodically. This ensures that all staff are familiar with the plan and with escape routes and marshal points.

Fire Suppression Systems

Fire suppression systems work on the basis of the Fire Triangle. The Fire Triangle works on the assumption that a fire requires heat, oxygen, and fuel to ignite and burn. Removing any one of those elements provides fire suppression (and prevention).

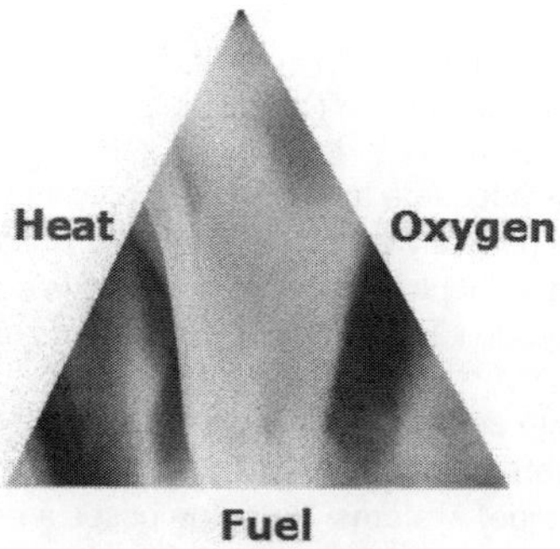

Fire triangle

The fire triangle has been updated in most firefighting literature to the fire tetrahedron (or pyramid). This is because some fires involving chemicals can be sustained by the chain reaction of the chemicals involved and cannot safely be extinguished by normal means.

In the US (and most other countries), fires are divided by class under the NFPA (National Fire Protection Association) system, according to the combustible material that fuels the fire. Fire extinguishers come in several different types; each type being designed for fighting a particular class of fire. Using the wrong type of extinguisher on a fire can have catastrophic effects.

Class	Color	Symbol	Pictogram	Usage
A	Silver	Green Triangle		Ordinary combustible materials such as paper, wood, cardboard, and most plastics.
B	Red	Red Square		Flammable or combustible liquids, solids (notably oils, paints, alcohol), and gases.
C	Red	Blue Circle	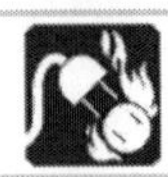	Electrical equipment.
D	Yellow	Yellow Star		Combustible metals, such as those found in a laboratory.
K	Silver	Black Hexagon		Highly flammable materials, such as cooking oils or fats.

Under the European classification system, "electrical" fires are Class E and cooking oil fires are Class F.

Firefighting equipment requires adequate training to use properly. In an office workspace, this equipment will normally consist of a number of fire extinguishers. A fire extinguisher should only be used to tackle a small fire. The first consideration should be to identify a clear route to an emergency exit.

Premises may also be fitted with an overhead **sprinkler** system. Most sprinklers work automatically, are triggered by heat, and discharge water. These are referred to as "wet-pipe" systems. Wet-pipe poses a problem for areas containing sensitive equipment or materials, such as network communications rooms and library or museum archives. Wet-pipe systems constantly hold water at high pressure, so there is some risk of burst pipes and accidental triggering, as well as the damage that would be caused in the event of an actual fire. There are a number of alternatives to wet-pipe systems that can minimize the damage that may be caused by water flooding the room.

- Dry-pipe - these are used in areas where freezing is possible; water only enters this part of the system if sprinklers elsewhere are triggered.
- Pre-action - a pre-action system only fills with water when an alarm is triggered; it will then spray when the heat rises. This gives protection against accidental discharges and burst pipes and gives some time to contain the fire manually before the sprinkler operates.
- Halon / clean agent - gas-based systems have the advantage of not short circuiting electrical systems and leaving no residue. Up until a few years ago, most systems used Halon 1301. The use of Halon has been banned in most countries as it is ozone depleting. Alternatives to Halon are referred to as "clean agent". Examples include INERGEN (a mixture of CO_2, Argon, and Nitrogen), FM-200 / HFC-227, and FE-13.

Review Questions / Module 5 / Unit 1 / Site Security

Answer these questions to test what you have learned in this unit.

1) What might physical security controls add to software controls, such as encryption or ACLs?
2) True or false? Anyone targeting computer equipment will be attempting to steal data.
3) What type of gateway protects against "tailgating"?
4) True or false? Rack doors cannot be protected by sophisticated security mechanisms, such as fingerprint scanners, because they are too bulky.
5) What type of device might be able to detect the removal of an appliance from company premises?
6) What two types of fire extinguisher could be used around server equipment?

Module 5 / Unit 2

Remote Access Services

Objectives

On completion of this unit, you will be able to:

- Understand the use of encryption and hashing technologies and PKI.
- Identify the use of protocols to configure a remote access server or VPN.

Digital Security

Encryption is an ancient technique for hiding information. A reader cannot understand encrypted information unless s/he possesses a **key**. The use of encryption allows sensitive data to travel across a public network (such as the Internet), and remain private. If the data packets were intercepted and examined, the content would be unreadable.

The use of encryption and other digital security techniques provides users with two important security facilities on computer networks: **privacy** and **authentication**. Cryptographic hashing, symmetric encryption, and asymmetric encryption are very important to digital security. Often two or more of these three different types are used together in the same product or technology.

Symmetric Encryption

In symmetric encryption, a single **secret key** is used to both encrypt and decrypt data. Alternatively, there may be two keys but one is easy to determine from possession of the other.

Symmetric encryption is also referred to as single-key or private-key. Note that "private key" is also used to refer to part of the PKI process (see below), so take care not to confuse the two uses.

The secret key is so-called because it must be kept secret. If the key is lost or stolen, the security is breached. The main problem with symmetric encryption is secure distribution and storage of the key. This problem becomes exponentially greater the more widespread the key's distribution needs to be. The main advantage is speed, as symmetric key encryption is less processor intensive than asymmetric encryption.

Symmetric encryption is used to encode data for storage or transmission over a network. Some of the principal symmetric encryption technologies (or ciphers) are 3DES, AES, RC (Rivest Cipher), IDEA, Blowfish/Twofish, and CAST.

One of the principal measures of the security of an encryption cipher is the size of the key. Early ciphers used between 32- and 64-bit keys. Currently, 1024-bit keys would be selected for general use, with larger keys required for highly sensitive data. The larger the key however, the more processing is required to perform encryption and decryption.

Asymmetric Encryption

In asymmetric encryption (or Public Key Cryptography as it is more commonly called), a secret private key is used to *decrypt* data. A mathematically related **public key** is used to *encrypt* data. This public key can be widely and safely distributed to anyone with whom the host wants to communicate, because the private key *cannot* be derived from the public key.

Most asymmetric encryption depends on the difficulty of finding the prime factors of very large integers.

Asymmetric encryption is mostly used for authentication (digital certificates and signatures) and key exchange (that is, exchange of symmetric encryption keys, which are used to exchange data in the current "session"). Asymmetric encryption is more complex, taking longer for a computer to process, and so typically only used on small amounts of data.

Public Key Infrastructure (PKI)

Asymmetric encryption is an important part of **Public Key Infrastructure (PKI)**. PKI is a solution to the problem of authenticating unknown users on public networks.

Under PKI, users or server computers (subjects) are validated by a Certificate Authority (CA), which issues the server with a digital certificate. The digital certificate contains a public key associated with the subject embedded in it. The certificate has also been signed by the CA, guaranteeing its validity. Therefore, if a client trusts the signing CA, they can also trust the subject. The user can validate the CA's signature, because the CA's **root certificate** is installed on the computer.

The client can then send the server (Amazon.com for example) data (their credit card details for example) encrypted using the public key, safe in the knowledge that only that particular server will be able to decrypt it (using its secret private key).

Root certificates have to be trusted implicitly so it would obviously be highly beneficial if a malicious user could install a bogus root certificate and become a trusted root CA. Installing a trusted root certificate usually requires administrative privileges. In a Windows environment, most root certificate updates are performed as part of Windows Update or installed by domain controllers or administrators as part of running Active Directory

Public / private key pairs can also be used the other way round to **sign** messages. The user uses his or her private key to *encrypt* a message signature then distributes the linked public key wrapped in a digital certificate to the message recipient. The fact that the certificate can decrypt the signature proves that the sender signed it. Digital certificates are also used for secure authentication to computer networks.

Cryptographic Hashes

A **hash** is a short representation of data; a **cryptographic hash** makes it impossible to recover the original data from the hash. This technique can be used to prove that a message has not been tampered with and for secure storage of data where the original meaning does not have to be recovered (passwords for instance).

Two of the most commonly used cryptographic hash algorithms are SHA-1 and SHA-2 (Secure Hash Algorithm) and MD5 (Message Digest). A typical use of a cryptographic hash is to secure passwords securely. They are also often used in conjunction with symmetric and asymmetric encryption to create different security products.

Remote Access Server

Remote access describes a situation where access to the network does not depend on the user being physically present. Typically, use is made of a public WAN (the Internet) or leased lines. Some of the uses of remote access are:

- Connectivity between different sites, such as between two offices or between a home worker (or "telecommuter") and the office.
- Mobile access to corporate data, such as email, calendaring, and databases.
- Sharing data with customers and suppliers (an extranet).
- Remote administration of servers and workstations.

Providing remote connectivity is referred to as **Remote Access Services (RAS)**. The components of RAS are the network media, RAS protocols, and client and server applications implementing those protocols. Most WAN communication links use serial communications (such as PSTN, ISDN, or leased line). The remote server and client must agree a data link protocol to use to organize serial information into the frames required by the network.

Virtual Private Networks

Providing secure leased lines is difficult and expensive. A more practical solution is to use Internet infrastructure and set up a *secure* tunnel for private communications through it. This is called a **Virtual Private Network (VPN)**. Most business and domestic sites have Internet connectivity, so this solution is very efficient in terms of cost. VPNs can also be deployed in other topologies to suit the type of network access required.

Host-to-Site VPN

In a **host-to-site** or **remote access** topology, hosts connect to a VPN gateway (a VPN-enabled router) on the local network. This is the "telecommuter" model, allowing home-workers and employees working in the field to connect to the corporate network. The VPN clients will connect over the Internet.

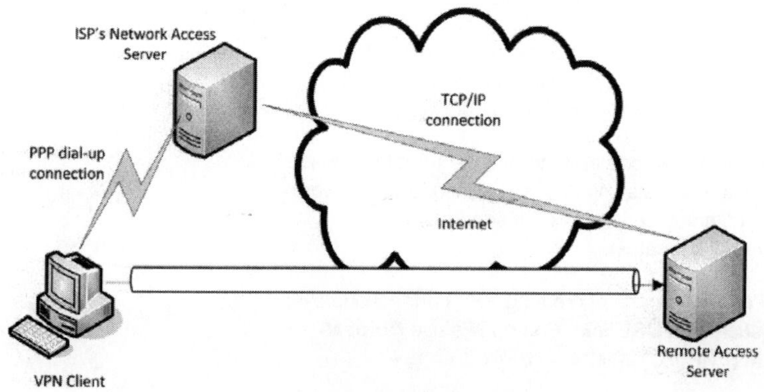

Remote access VPN

Site-to-Site VPN

The **site-to-site** model connects two or more local networks, each of which runs a VPN gateway (or router). Historically, this type of connection might have been made by ISDN or a leased line. Using a VPN brings significant cost-savings, especially over long distances.

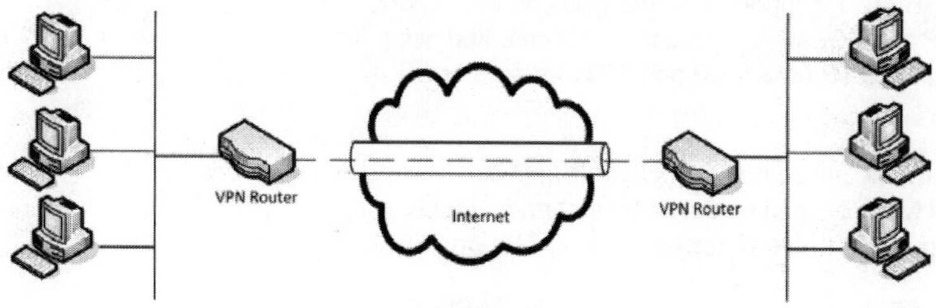

Site-to-site VPN

Host-to-Host VPN

A **host-to-host** VPN is similar to a site-to-site VPN but rather than connecting two or more subnets, the link is between two hosts only. There might be special security reasons for configuring a secure tunnel between two hosts. It may also be the case that a single host on each network acts as a proxy for other network client computers.

While VPNs are being covered here as part of remote access, note that they can be just as usefully deployed on local networks. For example, the department for product development might need to provide secure communications with the marketing department.

Remote Access Protocols

Most WAN communication links use serial communications (such as leased lines). The remote server and client must agree a data link protocol to use to organize serial information into the frames required by the network.

- **Point-to-Point Protocol (PPP)** - the cornerstone of most remote access methods. Its basic function is as a data link (layer 2) transport for network protocols over a variety of communications links. It supports user authentication and dynamic IP allocation.
- **PPP over Ethernet (PPPoE)** - a means of creating PPP connections over an Ethernet connection (such as a DSL link). Some ISPs use **Point-to-Point Protocol over ATM (PPPoA)** rather than PPPoE
- **Point-to-Point Tunneling Protocol (PPTP)** - runs on top of PPP to provide encryption, creating a secure VPN. A control link is established over TCP port 1723 on the server to negotiate connection parameters. The client and server exchange data securely by re-packaging the data using the Generic Routing Encapsulation Protocol (GRE). This payload can be encrypted using Microsoft Point-to-Point Encryption (MPPE).
- **Layer 2 Tunneling Protocol (L2TP)** - the main advantage of L2TP over PPTP is interoperability. There is support for frame types and transport protocols other than PPP and TCP/IP. Encryption is implemented using the IPsec layer 3 protocol suite. L2TP uses UDP port 1701 for data and connection control.
- **IPsec** - a layer 3 protocol suite providing security for IP packets. IPsec can provide both confidentiality (by encrypting data packets) and integrity/anti-replay (by signing each packet). IPsec works over TCP/UDP port 1293.
- **Secure Sockets Layer (SSL) / Transport Layer Security (TLS)** - provides transmission encryption and (through digital certificates and PKI) authentication for application level TCP/IP services such as HTTP.

Where authentication is integrated with the network user database, this can be thought of as a sort of VPN. Two advantages of an SSL VPN compared to L2TP/IPsec are that no special client software is required and that configuration is much simpler. Another is that access is restricted to defined services rather than the whole network, protecting the network in the event that remote access clients are compromised. The main disadvantage of SSL VPNs is just that they do not extend the network to the remote user, which can make management of the remote client more complex and preventing direct access to software that cannot be deployed as a web application.

OpenVPN is an open-source SSL VPN solution that does provide a VPN solution for all layers of the network stack. OpenVPN creates an authenticated and encrypted tunnel (over UDP port 1194 by default, though any UDP or TCP port can be used) using SSL then multiplexes network traffic through the tunnel.

Remote Access Server

Most NOSs support remote access. In Windows, the service is called **Routing and Remote Access**.

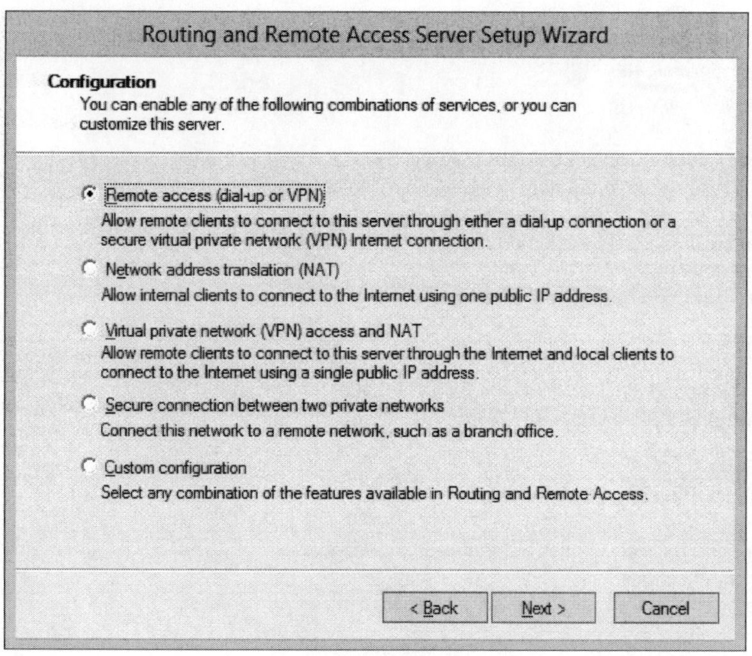

Installing RRAS

Remote servers can be configured to allow access to the entire network or just to the server itself. In the first case, the remote server forwards requests to other servers on the network.

Enterprise Remote Access Authentication

Enterprise networks and ISPs potentially need to support hundreds or thousands of users and numerous different remote and wireless access technologies and devices. The problem arises that each remote access device needs to be configured with authentication information and this information needs to be synchronized between them. A scalable authentication architecture can be developed using the **RADIUS (Remote Authentication Dial-In User Service)** protocol. Within RADIUS, Authentication, Authorization, and Accounting is performed by a separate server (the AAA server). Remote access devices (such as routers, wireless access points, or network servers) function as client devices of the AAA server. Rather than storing authentication information, they pass this data between the AAA server and the remote user.

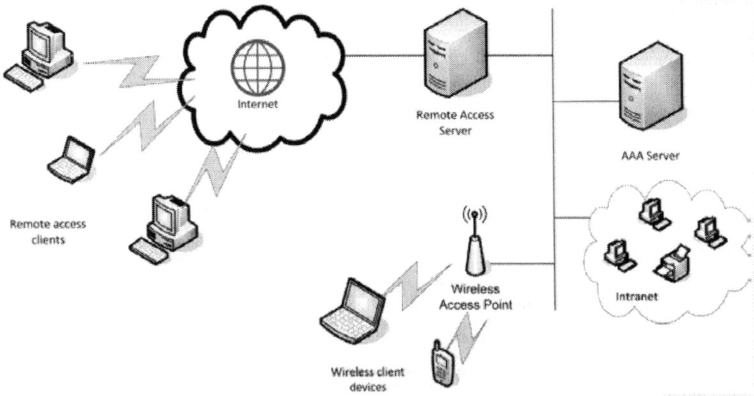

RADIUS

Terminal Access Controller Access Control System (TACACS+) is a similar protocol to RADIUS but designed to be more flexible and reliable. TACACS+ was developed by Cisco but is also supported on many of the other third-party and open source RADIUS server implementations. Where RADIUS is often used in VPN implementations, TACACS+ is often used in authenticating administrative access to routers and switches.

TACACS+ was developed by Cisco from the older TACACS standard. The two are not interoperable.

Remote Authentication Protocols

A number of protocols have been devised to pass authentication credentials over remote access network connections.

PAP

The **Password Authentication Protocol (PAP)** is unsophisticated authentication method developed as part of the **Point-to-Point Protocol (PPP)**, used to transfer TCP/IP data over serial or dial-up connections. It relies on cleartext password exchange and is therefore obsolete for the purposes of any sort of secure connection.

CHAP

The **Challenge Handshake Authentication Protocol (CHAP)** was also developed as part of PPP as a means of authenticating users over a remote link. CHAP relies on an encrypted challenge in a system called a **three-way handshake**.

1) **Challenge** - the server challenges the client, sending a randomly generated challenge message.

2) **Response** - the client responds with an encrypted hash, computed from the challenge message and the client's password.

> *In theory, the password cannot be recovered from the response because the hash function is one-way. Hashes of weak passwords (those that are short and non-complex) are vulnerable to dictionary and brute-force password cracking tools. The hash function used is MD5.*

3) The server performs its own hash using the challenge and the password hash stored for the client. If it matches the response then access is granted; otherwise the connection is dropped.

4) The Challenge-Response is repeated with a *different* challenge message periodically during the connection (though transparently to the user). This guards against replay attacks (where a previous session could be captured and reused to gain access).

MS-CHAP is Microsoft's first implementation of CHAP, supported by older clients, such as Windows 95. An enhanced version (MS-CHAPv2) was developed for recent Windows clients (Windows 2000 and later).

EAP

The **Extensible Authentication Protocol (EAP)** is intended to replace CHAP. The protocol is designed to support different types of authentication; it defines a *framework* for negotiating authentication mechanisms rather than the details of the mechanisms themselves. EAP is often implemented as part of the IEEE 802.1X standard. 802.1X defines the **EAP over LANs (EAPoL)** protocol to encapsulate EAP messages as they are moved over Ethernet and Wi-Fi networks. EAP / 802.1X involves three components:

- **Supplicant** - this is the client requesting authentication.
- **Authenticator** - this is the device that receives the authentication request (such as a remote access server or wireless access point). The authenticator establishes a channel for the supplicant and authentication server to exchange credentials using the EAP over LAN (EAPoL) protocol. It blocks any other traffic until authentication is granted.
- **Authentication Server** - the server that performs the authentication (typically an AAA RADIUS or TACACS server).

Widely adopted now, vendors can write extensions to the protocol to support third-party security devices. EAP authentication mechanisms can include smart cards, one-time passwords, biometric scanning, or simpler user name and password combinations. Some of the most popular implementations of EAP are described below:

EAP-TLS

EAP-TLS is currently considered the strongest type of authentication and is very widely supported. An encrypted Transport Layer Security (TLS) tunnel is established between the supplicant and authentication server using public key certificates on the authentication server *and* supplicant.

As *both* supplicant and server are configured with certificates, this provides mutual authentication. The supplicant will typically provide a certificate using a smart card or a certificate could be installed on the client PC, possibly in a Trusted Platform Module (TPM).

Protected Extensible Authentication Protocol (PEAP)

In **Protected Extensible Authentication Protocol (PEAP)**, as with EAP-TLS, an encrypted tunnel is established between the supplicant and authentication server but PEAP only requires a server-side public key certificate. The supplicant does not require a certificate. With the server authenticated to the supplicant, user authentication can then take place through the secure tunnel with protection against sniffing, password-guessing/dictionary, and Man-in-the-Middle attacks. There are two versions of PEAP, each specifying a different user authentication method (also referred to as the "inner" method):

- PEAPv0 (EAP-MSCHAPv2) - uses MS-CHAPv2 for authentication. This is by far the most popular implementation.
- PEAPv1 (EAP-GTC [Generic Token Card]) - Cisco's implementation.

PEAP is supported by Microsoft as an alternative to EAP-TLS. It is simpler and cheaper to deploy than EAP-TLS because you only need a certificate for the authentication server.

EAP-TTLS

EAP-Tunneled TLS (EAP-TTLS) is similar to PEAP. It uses a server-side certificate to establish a protected tunnel through which the user's authentication credentials can be transmitted to the authentication server. The main distinction with PEAP is that EAP-TTLS can use any inner authentication protocol (PAP or CHAP for instance) while PEAP must use EAP-MSCHAP or EAP-GTC).

Review Questions / Module 5 / Unit 2 / Remote Access Services

Answer these questions to test what you have learned in this unit.

1) What is the third party that establishes trust between a client and server in PKI?
2) True or false? A cryptographic hash function operates as one-way only so the original value is not recoverable from the hash value.
3) What three main topologies are used to establish VPNs?
4) Which protocol is most likely to be used to establish a secure connection between two hosts on the same local network?
5) What type of VPN protocol would allow the user to access network resources and applications via web browser client software?

Module 5 / Unit 3

Server Hardening

Objectives

On completion of this unit, you will be able to:

- Understand the concepts of hardening, baseline configurations, and host management.
- Apply operating system and application software patches and firmware updates.

Hardening Techniques

The process of securing a PC, operating system, or application for use is called **hardening**. For an OS functioning in any given role, there will usually be a fairly standard series of steps to follow to configure it to perform securely in that role.

It is also important to establish a maintenance cycle for each device and keep up-to-date with new security threats and responses for the particular software products that you are running.

Baseline Operating System Security and Settings

A **baseline** is a snapshot of the typical activity on your network or on any given host. Baseline counters are most useful for performance monitoring (you cannot tell whether performance has improved or degraded unless you know the starting point).

Another use of "baseline" is to mean a system in the minimum working configuration that is also secure. This can also be described as **host software baselining**. The essential principle is that a system should run only the protocols and services required by legitimate users and no more. This reduces the potential **attack surface**. If a particular configuration deviates from the baseline set, that can be taken as suspicious and the variations investigated.

- **Interfaces** provide a connection to the network. Some machines may have more than one interface. For example, there may be wired and wireless interfaces or a modem interface. Some machines may come with a management network interface card. If any of these interfaces are not required, they should be explicitly disabled rather than simply left unused.
- **Services** provide a library of functions for different types of application. Some services support local features of the OS and installed applications. Other services support remote connections from clients to server applications. Unused services should be disabled.

- **Application service ports** allow client software to connect to the application. Again, these should be closed if remote access is not required. Also consider that an application may use multiple ports. For example, there may be a "standard" user port and another port for management functions. Finally, be aware that a server might be configured with a non-standard port. For example, an HTTP server might be configured to use 8080 rather than 80.

Any service, interface, or port that is enabled through the default installation and left unconfigured should be considered a vulnerability.

In the last few years, vendors have started shipping devices and software in secure configurations. This means that the default installation is (theoretically) secure but minimal. Any options or services must explicitly be enabled by the installer. This is not the case for older devices and software though; these would often be shipped with all the "Bells and Whistles" activated to make set up easier.

Host Software Baselining Security Checklist

The following checklist shows the sort of steps that are required to harden the OS of a workstation PC:

1) Remove (or disable) devices that have no authorized function. These could include a legacy modem or floppy disk or standard optical disk drives, USB ports, and so on.
2) Install OS and application patches and driver / firmware updates (when they have been tested for network compatibility) according to a regular maintenance schedule. Patches for critical security vulnerabilities may need to be installed outside the regular schedule
3) Uninstall all but the necessary network protocols.
4) Uninstall or disable services that are not necessary (such as local web server or file and print sharing) and remove or secure any shared folders.
5) Enforce Access Control Lists on resources, such as local system files and folders, shared files and folders, and printers.
6) Restrict user accounts so that they have "least privilege" over the workstation (especially in terms of installing software or devices).
7) Secure the local administrator or root account by renaming it and applying a strong password.
8) Disable default user and group accounts (such as the Guest account in Windows) and verify the permissions of system accounts and groups (removing the Everyone group from a folder's ACL for instance).

9) Install anti-virus software (or malware protection software) and configure it to receive virus definition updates regularly. Anti-virus software should also be configured so that the user cannot disable it and so that it automatically scans files on removable drives, that have been downloaded from the Internet, or received as email/IM file attachments.

Server and Application Hardening

Much the same procedure applies to servers and web applications, only "more so". Obviously a server will host more shares and services than a client, but the same principle of running only services (or application features) that are required applies.

The other side of running services and protocols is availability. You may need to consider the likelihood of Denial of Service (DoS) attacks against a particular service and provide alternative means for clients to access it. This could mean providing multiple network links, redundant servers, configuring separate physical servers for different server applications, and so on.

Firmware Security

Different firmware (BIOS or UEFI) will provide different support for system passwords. There are usually at least two passwords, though some systems may allow for more:

- **Supervisor / Administrator** - protect access to the system setup program. Amongst other things, this prevents a malicious user from changing the enabled boot device options or boot device priority. Once the OS is installed, any other boot option should normally be disabled, to prevent a malicious attacker with local access from booting the server using USB media or similar.

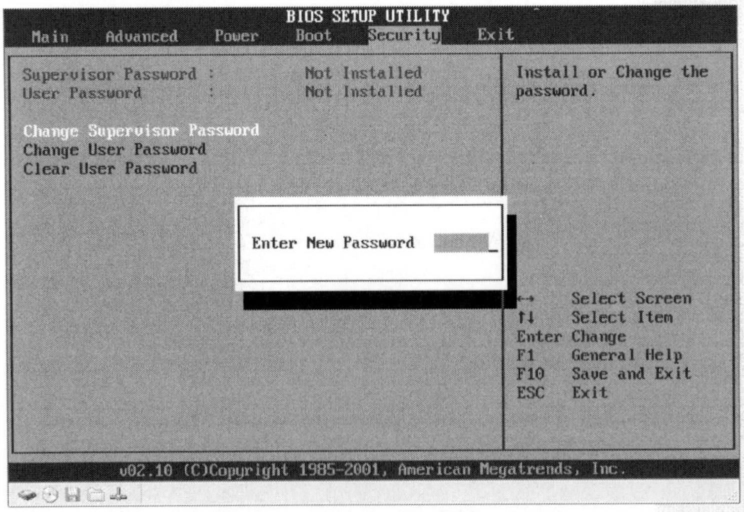

Configuring a supervisor or user BIOS password

- **User** - lock access to the whole computer. This is nominally a very secure way of protecting the computer as nothing can be done until the POST has taken place. The problem is that the password has to be shared between multiple users, unless some sort of pre-boot authentication software is used.

In most cases there is some sort of recovery mechanism. This might involve the BIOS supervisor password or a password recovery disk.

Disable Wake on LAN (WoL) and Hardware

As well as locking down the boot device, the firmware system setup program also offers the opportunity to disable any ports, adapters, or features not required by the server's application role. You will typically want to ensure that legacy serial or parallel ports are turned off; you may also want to disable external USB ports or wireless adapters such as Bluetooth.

Wake on LAN allows the computer to be switched on remotely via a network "magic packet". You may want to disable this feature to prevent unauthorized activation of a server.

Intrusion Detection

A computer chassis can be installed with sensors to report intrusion detection (if the chassis or lockable faceplate is opened) to management software or display an alert at boot time. Some system firmware can lock the server automatically if an intrusion is detected, requiring a supervisor to log on with the relevant password to unlock it again.

Patch Management

Software updates resolve issues that a vendor has identified in the initial release of their product, based on additional testing or customer feedback. Many updates address security vulnerabilities. In this sense, patching tools are a type of security control used to improve **availability**.

There are two approaches to applying updates:

- Apply all the latest patches to ensure the system is as secure as possible against attacks against flaws in the software.
- Only apply a patch if it solves a particular problem being experienced.

The second approach obviously requires more work, as the administrator needs to keep up-to-date with security bulletins. However, it is well recognized that updates (particularly service releases) can cause problems, especially with software application compatibility, and so the second approach is wisest.

Some applications may require *the operating system to be patched to a certain level.*

It makes sense to test and validate an update, especially a service release, on a lab system to try to discover whether it will cause any problems. Approach the update like a software installation or upgrade (make a backup and a rollback plan). Read the documentation accompanying the update carefully. Updates may need to be applied in a particular order and there may be known compatibility issues or problems listed in the ReadMe.

The results of patch testing can be published as a separate **compatibility list** for a given operating system, hardware configuration, and application. These lists can guide separate departments in a large organization where responsibility for installing patches might be devolved. Vendors might also perform their own compatibility testing and publish the results along with the patch download file. Testing application compatibility is usually the most complex task. An OS patch might cause a problem with a particular application; conversely an application patch might not work on a particular OS version or under a particular hardware configuration.

Windows Update

Microsoft make the following distinctions between different types of software patch:

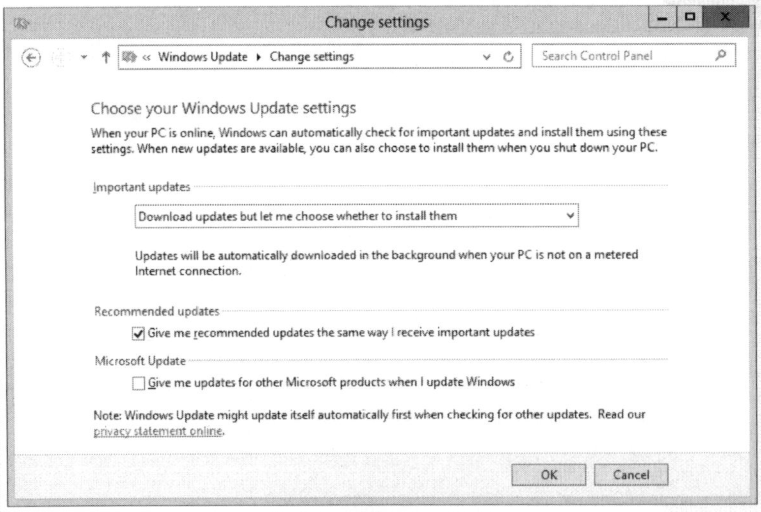

Configuring Windows Update

- **Updates** are widely released fixes for bugs. **Critical** updates address performance problems while **security** updates address vulnerabilities and can be rated by severity (critical, important, moderate, or low). There are also **definition** updates for software such as malware scanners and junk mail filters and **driver** updates for hardware devices.
- **Hotfixes** are patches supplied in response to specific customer troubleshooting requests. With additional testing these may later be developed into public release updates.
- **Feature packs** add new functionality to the software.
- **Service packs** and **update rollups** form a tested collection of updates and hotfixes that can be applied in one package.

Patches, driver updates, and service packs for Windows (and other Microsoft software) can be installed using the **Windows Update** client. This client can be configured to obtain and install updates automatically. The settings used for automatic updates are often configured in Group Policy.

Windows Server Update Services (WSUS)

Connecting each client directly to the Windows Update website to download patches can waste a lot of bandwidth. On a network with a lot of computers, it can make more sense to deploy an **update server**. The update server for Windows networks is called **Windows Server Update Services (WSUS)**.

Another benefit of using a local update server is that some versions of Windows have been vulnerable to attack if allowed to connect to the Internet unpatched. Using a local server mitigates that risk.

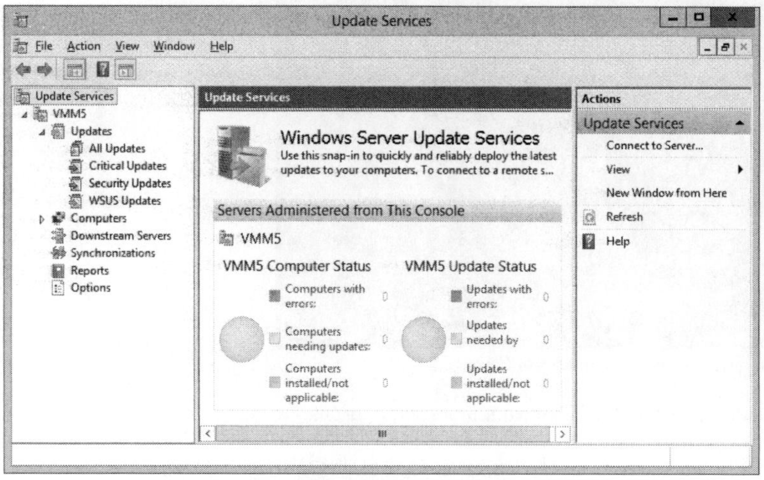

Management interface for WSUS

The WSUS server works as a proxy. It scans the network to identify clients and determines what updates they require. An administrator can review the list of required updates and choose whether to apply or decline them. The server then downloads the updates from Microsoft's website and clients connect to it to obtain the patches. Computers can be placed into pools, each with different update settings. For example, you could have a pool of test clients and servers and a pool of production computers. Updates could be applied to the test pool and then only applied to the production pool if the update is shown not to cause compatibility issues.

Linux Patch Management

A Linux distribution contains the kernel plus any other software packages the distribution vendor or sponsor considers appropriate. Copies of these packages (including any updates) will be posted to a **software repository**. With commercial Linux distributions, access to the repository is usually a subscription service.

To run updates, the package manager needs to be configured with the web address of the software repository (or repositories) that you want to use. It can then be used to install, uninstall, or update the software.

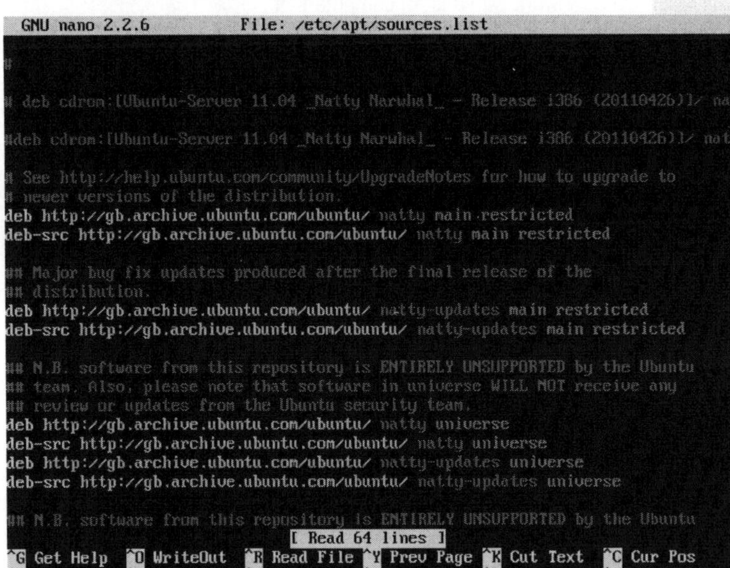

Configuring package manager sources in Ubuntu

Updates to the Linux kernel and a distribution's software tools and applications can be obtained via the package manager.

For example, you can edit a configuration file in the unattended-packages package to allow apt to obtain different types of updates. In the example below, only security updates are being obtained - the other types are commented out.

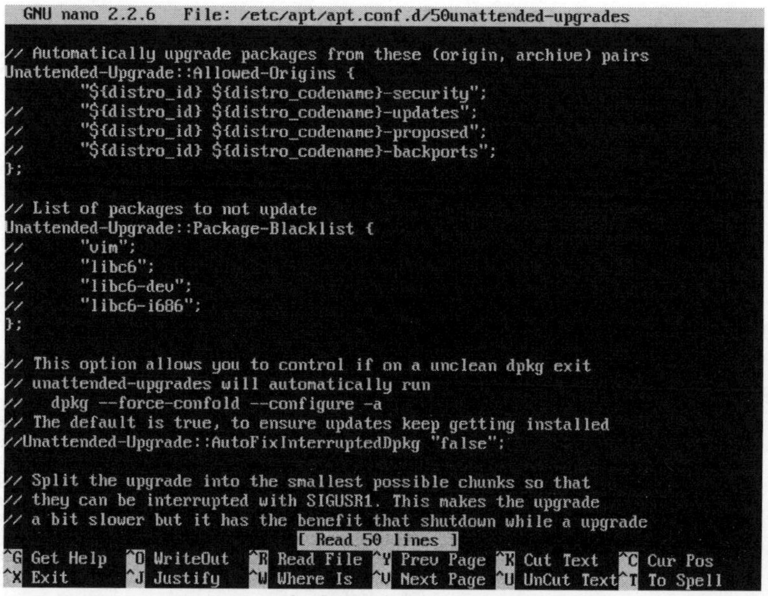

Configuring update types

Having configured automatic updates, another configuration file sets options for the frequency of updates, cleaning out temporary files, and so on. Finally, you would use an executable update task for scheduling by the **cron** tool.

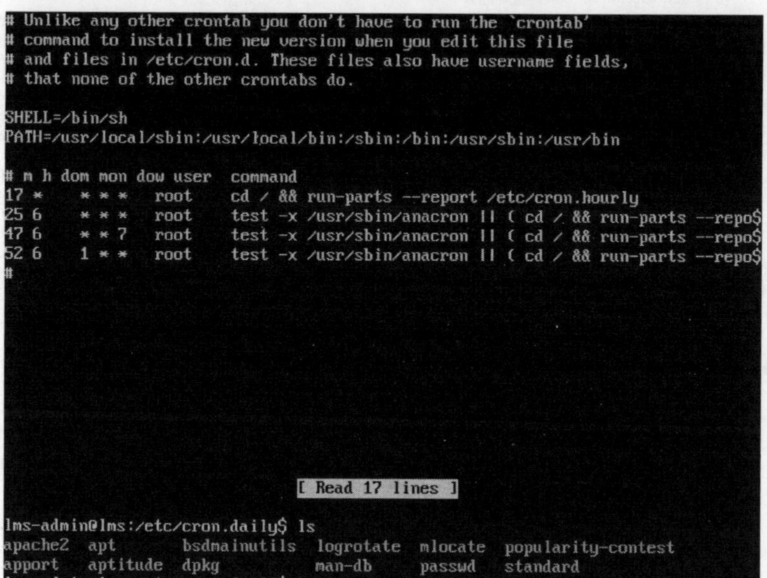

The apt script runs as a daily task to install updates as per the configuration files

You could set up a local update server along the lines of WSUS to conserve Internet bandwidth.

Application Patch Management

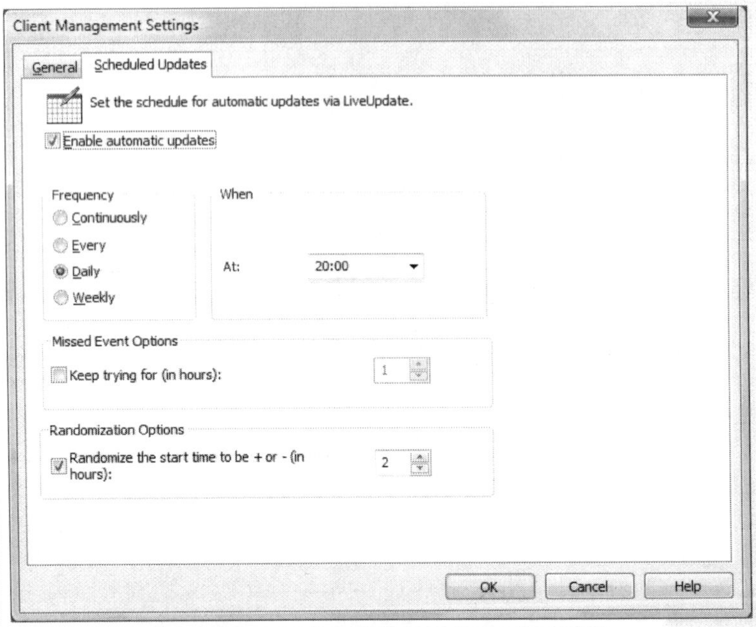

Scheduling regular virus definition and scan engine updates

As with operating system updates, applications should be kept current in terms of fixes and security patches. Most also support an automatic mechanism, as shown above for the Symantec LiveUpdate client updater for anti-virus and intrusion protection definitions.

Firmware Updates

As well as software updates, it is also important to keep hardware up-to-date with the latest patches. There are two main types of updates for hardware devices:

- Driver - this is software that provides an interface between the operating system and the device.
- Firmware - this is software instructions stored on a ROM chip or (more usually) flash memory. This type of chip does not require a power supply so the data does not have to be moved in and out of disk storage.

The firmware on a device such as a router / firewall may be a very sophisticated piece of software. It is quite common for such software to have known vulnerabilities, so it is vital to use a secure version.

Updating firmware is known as "flashing" the chip. This is generally done via a vendor-supplied setup program. It is important to make a backup of the system configuration (especially for a firewall) before performing a firmware update or upgrade.

Review Questions / Module 5 / Unit 3 / Server Hardening

Answer these questions to test what you have learned in this unit.

1) What general procedures are involved in server hardening?
2) In a security context, what would disabling WoL achieve?
3) What is WSUS?
4) Name three Linux package managers that can be configured to install application updates.
5) Following an update cycle, multiple servers in your company are experiencing high packet loss due to checksum errors. What type of update rollback is most likely to fix this type of problem?
6) What type of update is most likely to require frequent installation and least likely to require extensive testing?

Module 5 / Unit 4

Security Software

Objectives

On completion of this unit, you will be able to:

- Understand the role of security software such as anti-malware, IDS, and NAC.
- Diagnose and troubleshoot security issues.

Anti-malware Software

Firewalls restrict traffic based on network policies (rules). Anti-malware software and Intrusion Detection Systems (IDS) on the other hand are designed to prevent malicious software code and attempts to perform packet or protocol abuse from reaching the network or a particular host on the network.

Privilege Escalation

An application or process must have privileges to read and write data and execute functions. Depending on how the software is written, a process may run using a system account, the account of the logged on user, or a nominated account. If a software exploit works, the attacker may be able to execute their own process (a worm or Trojan for instance) with the same privilege level as the exploited process.

Malware Symptoms

The following are examples of the symptoms that may indicate a virus infection:

- The computer fails to boot or experiences lock ups.
- The file system or individual files are corrupted or deleted.
- Date stamps and file sizes of infected files change.
- Permissions attributes of files change, resulting in "Access Denied" errors.
- New executable files (EXEs and DLLS) appear in system folders. They may have file names that are very close to valid programs (notpad.exe).
- Strange messages or graphics appear on the screen.

- Security applications or services (anti-virus, firewall, Windows Update) stop working.
- Applications or Windows tools (Notepad for instance) stop working or crash frequently.
- Performance at startup or generally is very slow. There might be excessive use of CPU and memory resources by suspicious processes.
- Network performance is slow or Internet connections are disrupted.

Any sort of activity or configuration change that was not initiated by the user is a good reason to suspect malware infection. The best response will generally be to use anti-malware software to scan the infected host.

Anti-virus / Anti-malware Software

Anti-virus (A-V) software uses a database of known virus patterns (**definitions**) plus **heuristic** (meaning to learn from experience) malware identification techniques to try to identify infected files and prevent viruses from spreading. Typically the software is configured to run automatically when a user or system process accesses a file, but can also be initiated by the user (an on-demand scan). The anti-virus software scans the file and blocks access if it detects anything suspicious. The user can then decide either to try to **disinfect** the file, **quarantine** it (block further access), or **delete** it. The software might be configured with a default action to take that the user can override. The latest anti-virus software usually includes anti-Trojan software, as well as spam, adware, and spyware blockers. Consequently the term anti-virus software is now generally interchangeable with **anti-malware software**.

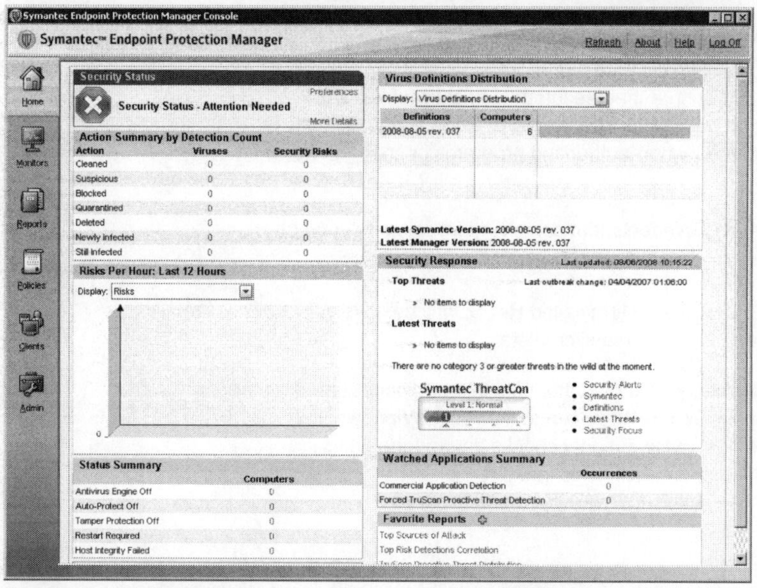

Symantec Endpoint Protection Manager enables centralized monitoring and oversight of anti-virus, anti-spyware, IDS, firewall, and application / device control

Anti-malware software tends to come as either personal security suites, designed to protect a **single host**, or network security suites, designed to be centrally managed from a server console. A **server-based** option means that each client runs a lightweight scanning agent. This agent relies on the server for definition updates and policies. The centralized server allows network administrators to initiate remote scans and updates as well as monitor events such as infection outbreaks. A **cloud-based** solution offers the same sort of options but means that rather than installing the management server on the local network, it is located on the service provider's servers and accessed over the Internet.

Most anti-virus software is designed for Windows PCs and networks, as these are the systems targeted by most virus writers, but software is available for Linux and Apple Mac OS as well.

Some of the major vendors are Symantec (including the Norton brand), McAfee, Computer Associates (CA), Trend Micro, Kaspersky, and BitDefender.

Another option is for malware scanning to be incorporated on a network appliance that combines the functions of firewall and anti-malware. This type of **Unified Threat Management (UTM)** solution is discussed below.

To work effectively, the virus definitions and scan engine must be kept up-to-date. Such software is typically configured to update every day (or every few hours) automatically from the vendor website or company server.

File Integrity Issues

System and application files are always a target for virus and malicious software writers, who seek to subtly infiltrate a corporate data center. Servers should be regularly checked to ensure that the integrity of critical files is maintained. This goes beyond basic virus checking and extends to validating that files have not been updated by non-authorized programs or changed from their original format.

Whilst some operating systems have tools that can check file integrity (`sfc` on Windows for instance), most automated tools are provided by third parties.

Windows Server 2012 has a new file system called ReFS, which natively supports file integrity checking via Powershell cmdlets

Tripwire, amongst others, provide well known products that originally started out as an open source offering. **SecureCheq** is a tool for both Windows and Linux that performs a whole host of file integrity checks and reports on its findings. **AIDE** is another open source Linux file integrity tool.

Another file integrity issue is that of verifying executable files downloaded from the Internet. Windows operates a code-signing policy that warns the user if an application has not been signed by certificate guaranteed by a trusted Certificate Authority. Alternatively, when using public Internet repositories, the author will usually compute a checksum for the uploaded package to derive an SHA or MD5 hash value. You can perform the same checksum on the package after downloading it to ensure that it matches.

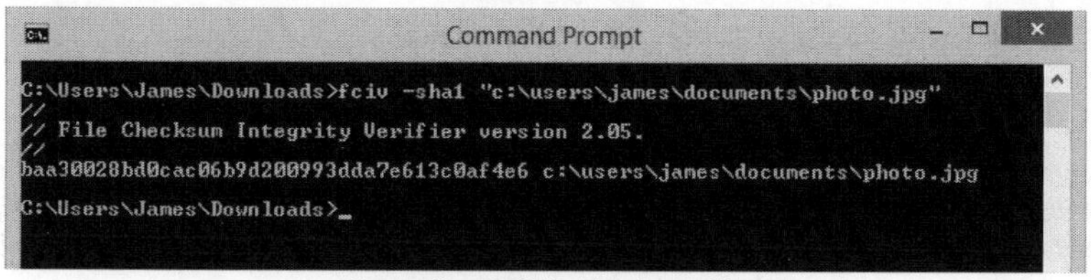

Computing an SHA value from a file

Preventive Measures

If a host is infected with malware, as well as cleaning the infection you should investigate how the malware was able to execute. You should check that the anti-malware solution is up-to-date and any relevant software vulnerabilities are patched or mitigated.

You might also need to investigate whether there are misconfigured permissions assigning excessive access to a particular user account. All server operating systems have their own method of securing files and folders / directories. Some like Windows are complicated and come with their own inbuilt tools for showing what permissions an individual or group will have. The **Effective Access** tab under Advanced Security settings allows an administrator to see this.

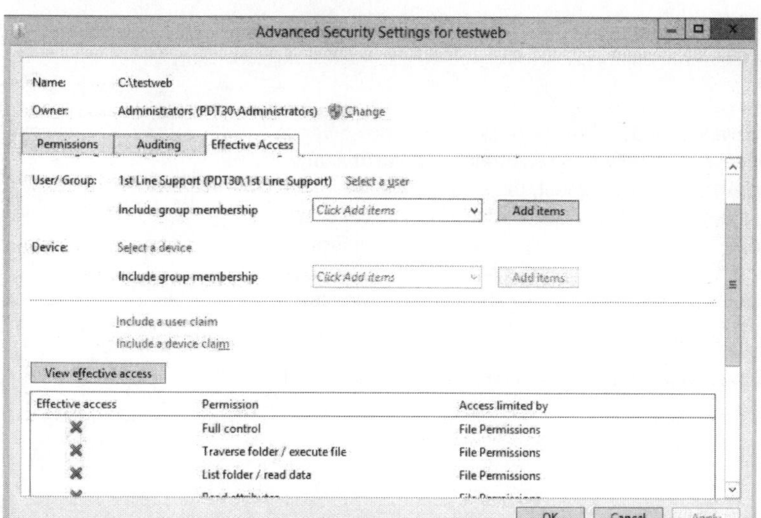

Checking effective access

Operating systems will also typically have auditing services that can be used to check who has accessed files or folders with a certain permission level. These audit services are not normally enabled by default as they use CPU resources. If audit records show that users are exercising system privileges they should not have, check local or group security policies to ensure that the principle of least privilege is being applied to rights assignment.

There are Windows third party tools available (such as Sysinternals Suite) which can check the entire file system looking for excessive permissions or Powershell scripts that can be downloaded.

Conversely, users might experience problems accessing files and shares because their permissions are insufficient. Refer back to *Unit 3.4* *for notes on group policy and* *Unit 3.5* *for file system security.*

Linux in contrast has a much simpler file permission structure and the use of the `ls -l` command is normally sufficient to see who has (or is going to have) access.

Intrusion Detection Systems (IDS)

An **Intrusion Detection System (IDS)** is a means of using software tools to provide *real-time* analysis of either network traffic or system and application logs. Intrusion detection is similar to anti-virus software but protects against a broader range of threats.

Network-based Intrusion Detection Systems

A **Network IDS (NIDS)** is basically a packet sniffer (referred to as a **sensor**) with an **analysis engine** to identify malicious traffic and a **console** to allow configuration of the system.

Typically, NIDS sensors are placed inside a firewall or close to some server of particular importance (the idea is to identify malicious traffic that has managed to get *past* the firewall). In a switched environment, the sensor must be connected to a mirrored port on the switch in order to monitor traffic passing through the switch on other ports. If the switch does not support port mirroring, another option is to install a tap. This is a device that connects directly to the network media. There are also wireless IDS, typically installed as a wireless controller.

The sensor does not slow down traffic and is undetectable by the attacker (it is not connected to the same logical network).

The basic functionality of NIDS is to provide **passive detection**; that is, to log intrusion incidents (and to display an alert at the management interface or to email the administrator account). A NIDS will be able to identify and log hosts and applications, detect buffer overflow attacks, password guessing attempts, port scans, worms, backdoor applications, malformed packets or sessions, and policy violations (ports or IP addresses that are not permitted for instance).

Some NIDS have prevention capabilities however. These are classified as **active detection** (or **reactive** detection). One typical preventive measure is to close the TCP connection (sending a TCP reset packet to the attacking host). This will not always succeed in preventing an attack however. Another option is for the sensor to apply a temporary filter on the firewall to block the attacker's IP address (shunning). Finally, the sensor may be able to run a script or third-party program to perform some other action not supported by the IDS software itself.

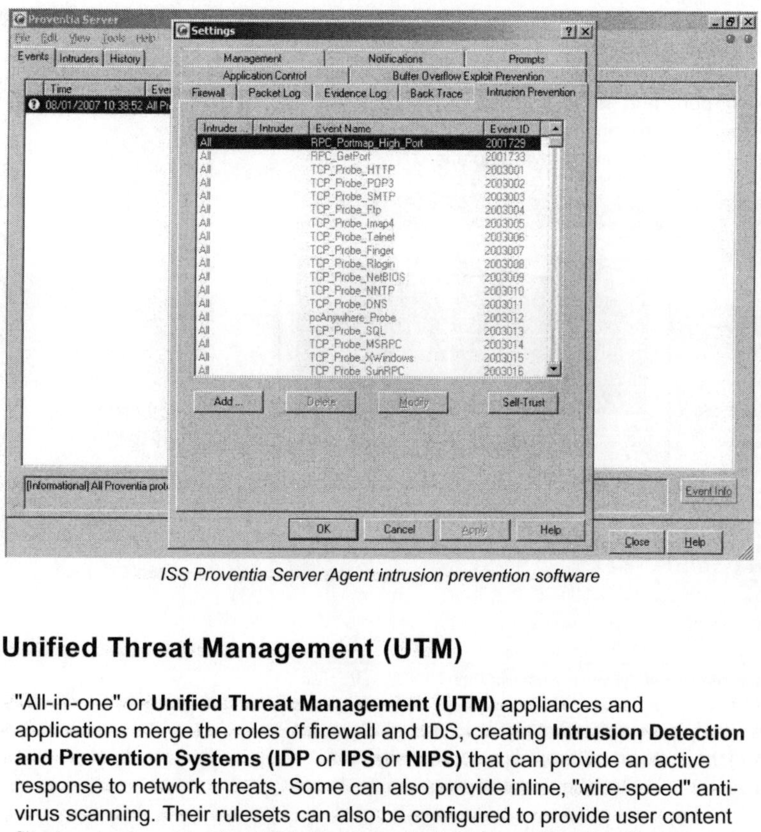

ISS Proventia Server Agent intrusion prevention software

Unified Threat Management (UTM)

"All-in-one" or **Unified Threat Management (UTM)** appliances and applications merge the roles of firewall and IDS, creating **Intrusion Detection and Prevention Systems (IDP** or **IPS** or **NIPS)** that can provide an active response to network threats. Some can also provide inline, "wire-speed" anti-virus scanning. Their rulesets can also be configured to provide user content filtering, such as blocking URLs, applying keyword-sensitive blacklists or whitelists, or applying time-based access restrictions.

UTM appliances are positioned like firewalls at the border between two network zones. As with proxy servers, the appliances are "inline" with the network, meaning that all traffic passes through them (also making them a single point-of-failure if there is no fault tolerance mechanism). This obviously means that they need to be able to cope with high bandwidths and process each packet very quickly to avoid slowing the network down.

IDP software is capable of advanced measures, including throttling bandwidth to attacking hosts, applying complex firewall filters, and even modifying suspect packets to render them harmless.

Host-based IDS (HIDS)

A **Host-based IDS (HIDS)** captures information from a single host (a server, router, or client computer for instance).

HIDS come in many different forms with different capabilities. The core ability is to capture and analyze log files, but more sophisticated systems can also monitor OS kernel files, monitor ports and network interfaces, and process data and logs generated by specific applications (such as HTTP or FTP). Very often it will be combined with an anti-malware software solution.

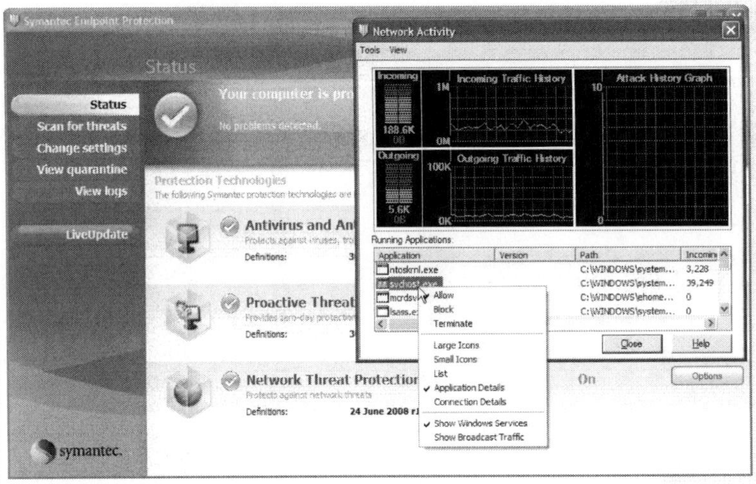

Monitoring services and intrusion attempts in Symantec Endpoint Protection security suite

Installing host-based IDS is simply a case of choosing which hosts to protect then installing and configuring the software. There will also normally be a reporting and management server to control the agent software on the hosts.

Host-based active response can act to preserve the system in its intended state. This means that the software can prevent system files from being modified or deleted, prevent services from being stopped, log off unauthorized users, and filter network traffic.

IDS Analysis Engine

In both network and host intrusion detection, the **analysis engine** is the component that scans and interprets the traffic captured by the sensor or agent with the purpose of identifying suspicious traffic. The analysis engine determines whether any given event should be classed as an **incident** (or violation of the security policy or standard). There methods of doing this include signature-based, behavior-based, and anomaly-based detection.

Signature-based Detection

Signature-based detection (or pattern-matching) means that the engine is loaded with a database of attack patterns or signatures. If traffic matches a pattern then the engine generates an incident.

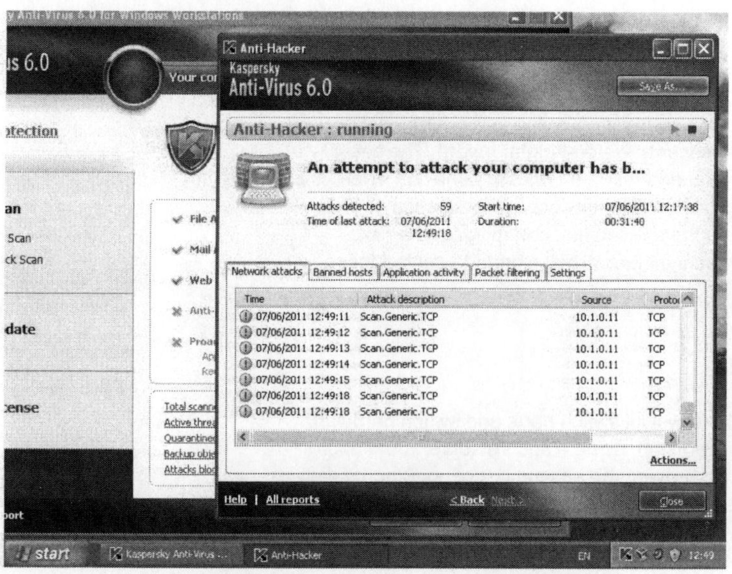

Detecting a network scanning attack with Kaspersky Anti-Virus

Behavior-based Detection

Behavior-based detection (or statistical- or profile-based detection) means that the engine is trained to recognize baseline "normal" traffic or events. Anything that deviates from this baseline (outside a defined level of tolerance) generates an incident. The idea is that the software will be able to identify "zero-day" attacks (those for which the exploit has not been detected or published).

The engine does not keep a record of everything that has happened and then try to match new traffic to a precise record of what has gone before. It uses heuristics to generate a statistical model of what the baseline looks like (it may develop several profiles to model network use at different times of the day). This means that the system generates false positive and false negatives until it has had time to improve its statistical model of what is "normal".

Anomaly-based Detection

Often behavior- and anomaly-based detection are taken to mean the same thing (in the sense that the engine detects anomalous behavior). Anomaly-based detection can also be taken to mean specifically to look for irregularities in the use of protocols. For example, the engine may check packet headers or the exchange of packets in a session against RFC standards and generate an alert if they deviate from strict RFC compliance.

Endpoint Security

Endpoint security is a set of security procedures and technologies designed to restrict network access at a device level. Endpoint security contrasts with the focus on perimeter security established by topologies such as DMZ and technologies such as firewalls. Endpoint security does not replace these but adds **defense in depth**.

The portability of devices such as removable storage, wireless access points, VoIP phones, cell phones, smartphones, and laptop computers, makes penetrating network perimeter security more straightforward. The security of these devices is often heavily dependent on good user behavior. There is also the circumstance of providing guests with network facilities, such as web access and email. While training and education can mitigate the risks somewhat, endpoint security technologies are designed to control these threats.

Physical Port Security

With wired ports, access to the physical switch ports and switch hardware should be restricted to authorized staff, using a secure server room and/or lockable hardware cabinets. To prevent the attachment of unauthorized client devices, a switch port can be disabled using the management software or the patch cable can be physically removed from the port. Completely disabling ports in this way can introduce a lot of administrative overhead and scope for error. Also, it doesn't provide complete protection as an attacker could unplug a device from an enabled port and connect their own PC. Consequently, more sophisticated methods of ensuring port security have been developed.

MAC Limiting and Filtering

MAC filtering means specifying which MAC addresses are allowed to connect to a particular port. This can be done by specifying a list of valid MAC addresses but this "static" method is difficult to keep up-to-date and relatively error-prone. Some switch models allow you to specify a **limit** to the number of permitted addresses and automatically learn a set number of valid MAC addresses. For example, if port security is enabled with a maximum of two MAC addresses, the switch will record the first two MACs to connect to that port but then drop any traffic from machines with different network adapter IDs that try to connect.

802.1X

The **IEEE 802.1X** standard defines a **Port-based Network Access Control (PNAC)** mechanism. PNAC means that the switch (or router) performs some sort of authentication of the attached device before activating the port.

Under 802.1X, the device requesting access is the **supplicant**. The switch, referred to as the **authenticator**, enables the **Extensible Authentication Protocol over LAN (EAPoL)** protocol only and waits for the device to supply authentication data. Using EAP, this data could be a simple username / password (EAP-MD5) or could involve using a digital certificate or token.

The authenticator passes this data to an **authenticating server**, typically a RADIUS server, which checks the credentials and grants or denies access. If access is granted, the switch will configure the port to use the appropriate VLAN and enable it for ordinary network traffic. Unauthenticated hosts may also be placed in a "guest" VLAN with only limited access to the rest of the network.

Network Access Control

As well as authenticating users, **Network Access Control (NAC)** allows administrators to devise policies or profiles describing a minimum security configuration that devices must meet to be granted network access. This is called a **health policy**. Typical policies check things such as malware infection, firmware and OS patch level, personal firewall status, and presence of up-to-date virus definitions. A solution may also be able to scan the registry or perform file signature verification. Some of the key features of NAC solutions are:

- Gathering data - information can be collected from a device either by installing an agent or by polling the device.
- Remediation - this refers to what happens if the device does not meet the security profile. A non-compliant device may be refused connection completely or put in a quarantined area (VLAN) or captive portal (a web application), from which there is the option to install the required patches or malware definitions.
- Management - the system for defining policies and reporting and logging.
- Pre- and post-admission control - most NAC solutions work on the basis of pre-admission control (that is, the device must meet the policy to gain access). Post-admission control involves subsequently polling the device to check that it remains compliant. Some solutions only perform post-admission control; some do both.
- Integration - many agent-based solutions are integrated with other client software, such as anti-virus and intrusion detection.

Vulnerability Assessments

A **vulnerability assessment** is the process of scanning a network (or application) for known vulnerabilities. A vulnerability is a weakness that could be triggered accidentally or exploited maliciously to cause a security breach. An unpatched software application, a host with no anti-virus software, and an administrator account with a weak password are examples of vulnerabilities.

Vulnerability assessments generally use **passive** techniques. A vulnerability scanner would probe the network or application to try to discover issues but would not attempt to exploit any vulnerabilities found. An assessment would also look at the configuration of security controls and try to identify whether there is a lack of controls that might be considered necessary or whether there is any misconfiguration of the system that would make the controls less effective or ineffective.

Port Scanners and Vulnerability Scanners

Numerous tools are available to perform vulnerability scanning. Port scanners such as **Nmap** (and to some extent tools that facilitate attacks such as spoofing and password cracking) are of the "dual-use" kind that make them useful to both attackers and defenders.

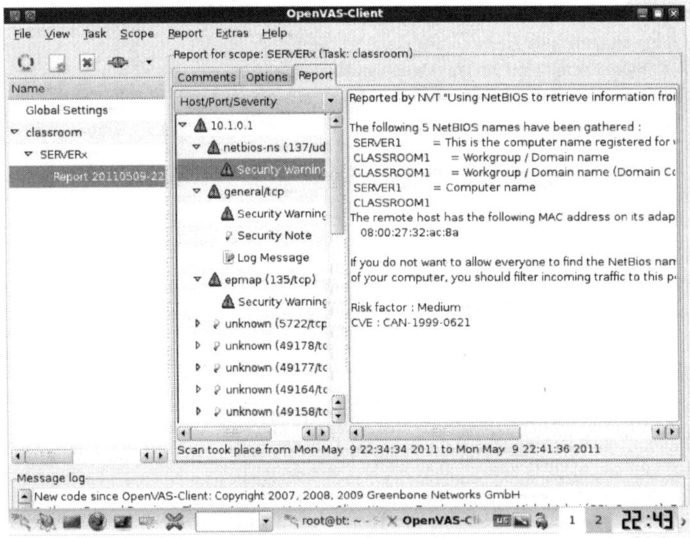

OpenVAS vulnerability scanner

A **vulnerability scanner** is a type of network mapper that aims to detect whether the network is exposed to any threats. To that end, as well as mapping the network for hosts and detecting running services, they scan for things such as patch level, security configuration and policies, network shares, unused accounts, weak passwords, rogue access points and servers, anti-virus configuration, and so on. The tool then compiles a report and classifies each detected vulnerability with an impact warning. Most tools also suggest current and ongoing remediation techniques.

Active detection scanners work by bouncing packets at a host and examining the replies. A **passive** scanner works in a way similar to Network Intrusion Detection Systems. The scanner sniffs network traffic to detect packets that would reveal vulnerabilities. This incurs less performance overhead and is not disruptive to the network, as some active scans can be, but careful placement of the scanner is required to ensure that it is monitoring relevant traffic.

A scanner can be implemented purely as software or as a security appliance, connected to the network. One of the best known software scanners is **Tenable Nessus**. As a previously open source program, Nessus also provides the source code for many other scanners. Some other products include SAINT, eEye Retina, and Rapid7 NeXpose.

As with anti-malware software, a vulnerability scanner needs to be kept up-to-date with information about known vulnerabilities.

In the absence of more sophisticated tools, even something as simple as a Telnet client can be used to probe open ports (`telnet 192.168.1.1 80` for instance). Not all services will respond with a prompt but anything other than a "Connect failed" message, even a blank screen, indicates that the port is open.

Packet Sniffers

Sniffing refers to capturing and reading data packets as they move over the network. A malicious user might do this to try to steal information (such as unencrypted account credentials) but packet sniffers are also useful security tools. You can use a sniffer to identify suspicious traffic and services or rogue hosts.

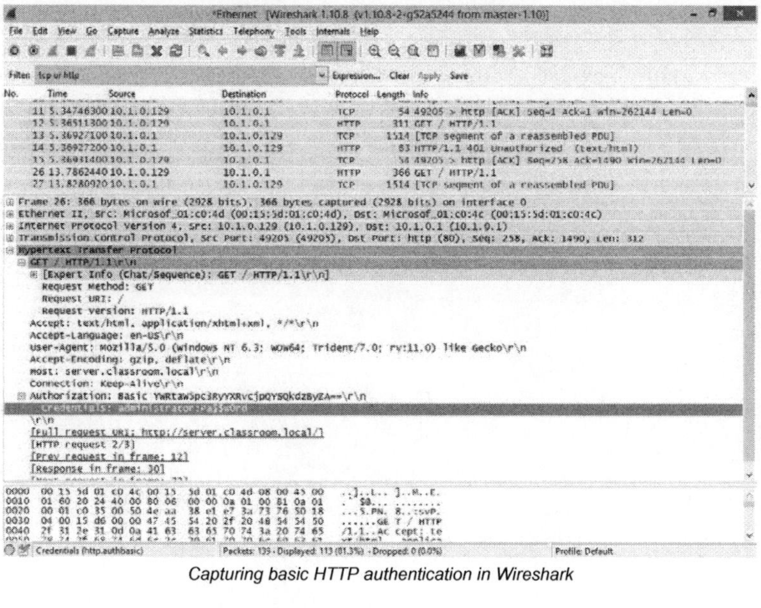

Capturing basic HTTP authentication in Wireshark

Review Questions / Module 5 / Unit 4 / Security Software

Answer these questions to test what you have learned in this unit.

1) What term describes exploiting a software bug to obtain access to system functions that would not normally be permitted?
2) Why might Task Manager be a useful tool in diagnosing the presence of malware?
3) Why might SHA-1 be used to verify file integrity (if at all)?
4) What policies help to make malware protection software more effective?
5) What class of security software attempts to identify suspicious network traffic?
6) What class of security product prevents devices from accessing the network unless they conform to a health policy?

Module 5 / Unit 5

Disaster Recovery

Objectives

On completion of this unit, you will be able to:

- Develop effective Business Continuity Plans (BCP) and Disaster Recovery Plans (DRP).
- Understand the importance of fault tolerance and identify the main components that require redundancy.
- Understand the use of clusters, load balancing, and replication methods to maintain hot, cold, and warm sites.

Business Continuity Concepts

Business continuity means planning and testing systems and operations so that they are as little affected by incidents as possible and so that the resources are available to recover from them.

NIST have published a guide to IT contingency planning (SP800-34). There are also BSI and ISO standards associated with business continuity planning.

Organizations other than businesses need continuity plans so sometimes the terms "Continuity of Operations (COOP)" or "Continuity of Government (COG)" are used.

Business Impact Analysis

When setting up a security system (or reviewing an existing one), one of the first steps is to set up a team responsible for **risk management**. Risk management starts with an initial risk investigation or analysis, often called a **Business Impact Analysis (BIA)**. This has four main components:

- Identify the critical functions or processes of the business or organization.
- Identify the assets and resources on which the functions depend.
- Identify threats to the organization's functions and assets.
- Assess the risk to each function or asset, given the threats.

The results of the BIA are then used to create business continuity plans. The cornerstone of business continuity plans will be selecting countermeasures (or security controls) to mitigate the risks identified in the BIA.

Identification of Critical Systems

In order to design a security plan, you must know what you want to make secure. It is crucial for an organization to perform the **identification of critical systems**. This means compiling an inventory of its business processes and its tangible and intangible assets and resources. These could include:

- People (employees, visitors, and suppliers).
- Tangible assets (buildings, furniture, equipment and machinery (plant), ICT equipment, electronic data files, and paper documents).
- Intangible assets (ideas, commercial reputation, brand, and so on).
- Procedures (supply chains, critical procedures, standard operating procedures).

Within the inventory of assets and business processes it is important to assess their relative importance. Which business functions are critical and which are only necessary? In the event of a disaster that requires that recovery processes take place over an extended period, critical systems must be prioritized over merely necessary ones.

For most businesses, the most critical systems will be those that enable customers to find them and for the business to interact with them. In practical terms, this means telecoms and web presence. Following that is probably the capability to fulfil products and services. Back-office functions such as accounting, HR, and marketing are probably necessary rather than critical.

This is all subject to circumstance. If the disaster strikes the day before the CEO is due to present to the company's most important customers, ensuring that the presentation goes ahead smoothly might be expected to take precedence. If the customers are all going to be there in that room, getting the web server back is not going to be as high a priority.

Threat Identification

Threat identification means compiling a prioritized list of probable and possible threats. Some of these can be derived from the list of assets (that is, threats that are specific to your organization); others may be non-specific to your particular organization.

- Natural disaster (flood, earthquake)
- Theft, vandalism, conflict
- Espionage

- Fire (accidental or malicious)

It's important to note that threats could be created by something that the organization is *not* doing or an asset that it does *not* own as much as they can from things that it *is* doing or *does* own. Consider (for instance) the impact on business processes of the following:

- Public infrastructure (transport, utilities, law and order).
- Supplier contracts (security of supply chain).
- Customer's security (the sudden failure of an important customer due to their own security vulnerabilities can be as damaging as an attack on your own organization).
- Epidemic disease.

As well as understanding the range of threats, it is important to be up-to-date with best practice and standards relevant to the type of business or organization. This can help to identify procedures or standards that are not currently being implemented but should be. Make sure that the asset identification process captures systems architecture as well as individual assets (that is, understand and document the way assets are deployed and used and how they work together).

Diagrams are the most useful way to show how systems interconnect or how processes and procedures work. There are a number of tools for doing this, notably Microsoft Visio.

Risk Calculation

For each resource and each threat, you must quantify the degree of risk that exists. Calculating risk is complex but the basic formula depends on evaluation of likelihood and impact:

- **Likelihood** is the chances of the threat being realized.
- **Impact** may be determined by factors such as the value of the asset or the cost of disruption if the asset is compromised.

It is important to realize that the value of an asset does not refer solely to its material value. The two principal additional considerations are direct knock-on costs associated with the asset being compromised (downtime) and cost to intangible assets, such as the company's reputation. For example, a server may have a material cost of a few hundred dollars. If the server were stolen, the costs incurred from not being able to do business until it can be recovered or replaced could run to thousands. In addition, that period of interruption where orders cannot be taken or go unfulfilled leads customers to look at alternative suppliers, resulting in perhaps more thousands of lost sales and goodwill.

There are two methods of risk assessment: quantitative and qualitative.

Quantitative Risk Assessment

Quantitative risk assessment aims to assign concrete values to each risk factor.

- Single Loss Expectancy (SLE) - the amount that would be lost in a single occurrence of the risk factor. This is determined by multiplying the value of the asset by an Exposure Factor (EF). EF is the percentage of the asset's value that would be lost.
- Annual Loss Expectancy (ALE) - the amount that would be lost over the course of a year. This is determined by multiplying the SLE by the Annual Rate of Occurrence (ARO).

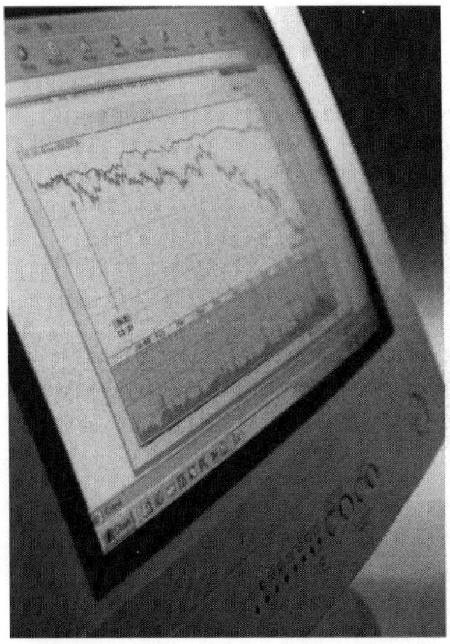

Quantitative risk assessment aims to assign concrete values to each risk factor

The problem with quantitative risk assessment is that the process of determining and assigning these values is extremely complex and time consuming. The accuracy of the values assigned is also very difficult to determine without historical data (often, it has to be based on subjective guesswork). However, over time and with experience this approach can yield a detailed and sophisticated description of assets and risks and provide a sound basis for justifying and prioritizing security expenditure.

Qualitative Risk Assessment

Qualitative risk assessment avoids the complexity of the quantitative approach and is focused on identifying significant risk factors. The qualitative approach seeks out people's opinions of which risk factors are significant. Assets and risks may be placed in simple categories. For example assets could be categorized as Irreplaceable, High Value, Medium Value, and Low Value; risks could be categorized as one-off or recurring and as Critical, High, Medium, and Low probability.

Another simple approach is the "Traffic Light" impact grid. For each risk, a simple Red, Amber, or Green indicator can be put into each column to represent the severity of the risk, its likelihood, cost of controls, and so on. This approach is simplistic but does give an immediate impression of where efforts should be concentrated to improve security.

Risk Factor	Impact	ARO	Cost of Controls	Overall Risk
Legacy Windows clients	!	X	!	X
Untrained staff	OK	!	OK	!
No anti-virus software	!	X	!	X

Traffic light impact grid

Disaster Recovery Planning

Business continuity means planning systems and operations so that they are as little affected by incidents as possible and so that the resources are available to recover from them.

Disaster recovery plans describe the procedures to follow in the event of severe incidents. When planning a network, the administrator must consider the impact of data loss and service unavailability on the organization. If a local plumber loses his email connection for a day, then the chances are he or she will lose little business because of it and he will still be able to function in his primary role of plumber (conversely, losing a cell phone could be catastrophic!). Therefore little consideration would be needed to plan for disasters. Conversely, if a major bank lost its trading floor link to its partners, even for an hour, since the organization's primary function (trading) would be impossible, huge losses may result. Significant thought is required to ensure that a disaster does not cause this kind of loss to what are termed **mission critical systems**.

A disaster could be anything from a fairly trivial loss of power, or failure of a minor component, through to man-made or natural disasters, such as fires, earthquakes, or acts of terrorism.

Creating Disaster Recovery Plans

An organization sensitive to these risks will develop an effective, documented **Disaster Recovery Plan (DRP)**. This should accomplish the following:

- Identify scenarios for natural and non-natural disaster and options for protecting systems. Plans need to take account of **risk** (a combination of the likelihood the disaster will occur and the possible impact on the organization) and **cost**.

  There is no point implementing disaster recovery plans that financially cripple the organization. The business case is made by comparing the cost of recovery measures against the cost of downtime. Downtime cost is calculated from lost revenues and ongoing costs (principally salary). The recovery plan should not generally exceed the downtime cost. Of course, downtime will include indefinable costs, such as loss of customer goodwill, restitution for not meeting service contracts, and so on.

  For each disaster scenario, a **Business Impact Analysis (BIA)** is made, identifying risks and vulnerabilities and advising on appropriate countermeasures.

- Identify tasks, resources, and responsibilities for responding to a disaster.
  - Who is responsible for doing what? How can they be contacted? What happens if they are not available?
  - Which functions are most critical? Where should effort be concentrated first?
  - What resources are available? Should they be pre-purchased and held as stock? Will the disaster affect availability of supplies?
  - What are the timescales for resumption of normal operations?
- Train staff in the disaster planning procedures and how to react well to change.

Secure Recovery

When a disaster has occurred, then the recovery plan will swing into action to get the failed part of the network operational as soon as possible. If a disk has failed, swap it out. If a node in a cluster has failed, remove and replace or repair the node to provide for high reliability as soon as possible. If data becomes corrupted or lost, utilize your restore plan to recover the data.

With the pressure to get systems running again though, it is important not to overlook the process of re-securing the system against intrusion. The system needs to be restored to its baseline **secure** configuration.

Another issue is that creating a duplicate of anything doubles the complexity of securing that resource properly. The same security procedures must apply to redundant sites, spare systems, and backup data as applies to the main copy.

IT Contingency Planning

Computer systems require protection from hardware failure, software failure, and system failure (failure of network connectivity devices for instance).

When implementing a network, the goal will always be to minimize **single points of failure** and to allow ongoing service provision despite a disaster. To perform **IT Contingency Planning (ITCP)**, think of all the things that could fail, determine whether the result would be critical loss of service, and whether this is unacceptable. Then work out how to make the service fault tolerant.

Fault Tolerance

A system that can experience failures and continue to provide the same (or nearly the same) level of service is said to be **fault tolerant**. Fault tolerance is often achieved by provisioning **redundant** components. A redundant component is one that is not essential to the normal function of a system but that allows the system to recover from the failure of another component.

Examples of devices and solutions that provide fault tolerance and high availability include the following:

- Redundant components (power supplies, network cards, drives (RAID), and cooling fans) provide protection against hardware failures. Hot swappable components allow for easy replacement (without having to shut down the server).
- Uninterruptible Power Supplies (UPS) and Standby Power Supplies.
- Backup strategies - provide protection for data.
- Cluster services are an (expensive) way of ensuring that the total failure of a server does not disrupt services generally.

While these computer systems are important, thought also needs to be given about how to make a business "fault tolerant" in terms of staffing, utilities (heat, power, communications, transport), customers, and suppliers.

The following components are often provided with redundancy on server systems.

Load Balancing Network Links

Without a network connection, a server is not of much use! As network cards are cheap, it is commonplace for a server to have multiple cards (adapter fault tolerance).

Multiple adapters can be configured to work together (adapter teaming). This provides fault tolerance (if one adapter fails, the network connection will not be lost) and can also provide **load balancing** (connections can be spread between the cards).

Note that adapter teaming does have a functional benefit (higher bandwidth). If one of the adapters fails, that benefit would be lost. For the system to be fault tolerant, the higher bandwidth must not be critical to the function.

Network cabling should be designed to allow for **multiple paths** between the various servers, so that during a failure of one part of the network, the rest remains operational (**redundant connections**). Routers are great fault tolerant devices, because they can communicate system failures and IP packets can be routed via an alternate device.

Multiple switching paths require use of Spanning Tree Protocol (STP) to prevent loops. Also note that routers can only be fault tolerant if there are multiple routes to choose from!

Power Supply

Power supplies are one of the components more likely to break down than others. They are cheap, but they do take up a lot of space. A second power supply can be configured to take over from the first if it fails.

A redundant power supply unit does not protect against problems with the supply of power itself. For this you need a Universal Power Supply (UPS) and/or backup generator.

A **UPS** is always required to provide against any interruption to computer services. A backup generator cannot be brought online fast enough to respond to a power failure. The drawback of a UPS is that it is battery-based and therefore only able to provide power for a limited time; this could range from a few minutes to a few hours depending on the size of the battery bank and the server load. The UPS also obviously only provides power to critical server components, not lighting, HVAC, mains distribution, or other features of buildings power.

A **backup generator** can provide power to the whole building, often for several days. Most generators use diesel, propane, or natural gas as a fuel source. With diesel and propane, the main drawback is safe storage (diesel also has a shelf-life of between 18 months and 2 years); with natural gas, the issue is the reliability of the gas supply in the event of a natural disaster.

Cooling Fans

Because servers contain many heat generating components (notably processors, hard drives, and power supplies), efficient cooling systems are particularly important. As a mechanical component, fans are more likely to fail than many other computer components. Each component that "runs hot" will have its own cooling fan. Obviously it is not practical to provide redundant versions of these, but the system may have "general" fans to cool the interior of the case and monitoring in-place to warn of failures.

Hardware and Spare Parts

Subject to budget and storage facilities, companies may keep an inventory of spare parts.

The simplest (but most expensive) approach is to keep fully functioning hardware such as spare servers and workstations so that faulty units can simply be swapped out and the fault investigated offline. This provides the least downtime.

Alternatively, spares of CPUs, memory, network cards, hard disks, and so on can be kept. The main issue here is maintaining an inventory that is compatible with the various technologies deployed on the network.

Given the swift turnover of technology, obsolescence makes spare part storage an expensive business. One solution is to use older equipment for emergency failovers, but there will be a substantial decrease in performance.

Hard Disks

The hard disks store the most valuable component of any computer system: data. Data can be protected by making backups, but only very expensive backup solutions can make up-to-the minute copies of data.

Multiple disks on a server, NAS device, or SAN are typically configured as RAID arrays. Depending on the RAID type, this can provide for fault tolerance (if one disk fails, the data is not lost and the server can keep functioning) and/or improved performance.

See the topics on RAID in Unit 1.3 for more information.

Clusters and Sites

As well as providing redundancy at a device level, whole servers or even sites can be provisioned.

Clusters

A **cluster** is a group of servers, each of which is referred to as a node. A cluster provides fault tolerance for critical applications. They do this by being in a position to take over the processing of a failed node in the cluster should a problem occur. There are essentially two types of clustering: Active / Active and Active / Passive.

Active / Active (A/A) Clustering

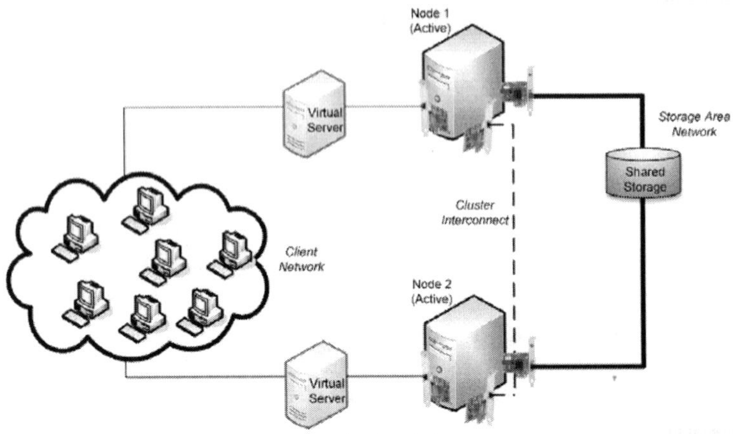

Active/Active cluster

Active / Active configurations consist of *n* nodes, all of which are processing concurrently. This allows the administrator to use the maximum capacity from the available hardware while all nodes are functional. In the event of a failover (the term used to describe the situation where a node has failed) the workload of the failed node is immediately (and transparently) shifted onto the remaining node(s). At this time, the workload on the remaining nodes is higher and performance is degraded during failover - a significant disadvantage.

Active / Passive (A/P) Clustering

Active / Passive configurations use a redundant node to failover. In other words, in an 8-node Active / Passive cluster, the eighth node doesn't do anything and supports no services (other than those needed to support the cluster itself) until a failover occurs. It then assumes responsibility for the failed node's services. The major advantage of Active / Passive configurations is that performance is not adversely affected during failover. However, the hardware and operating system costs are higher because of the unused capacity.

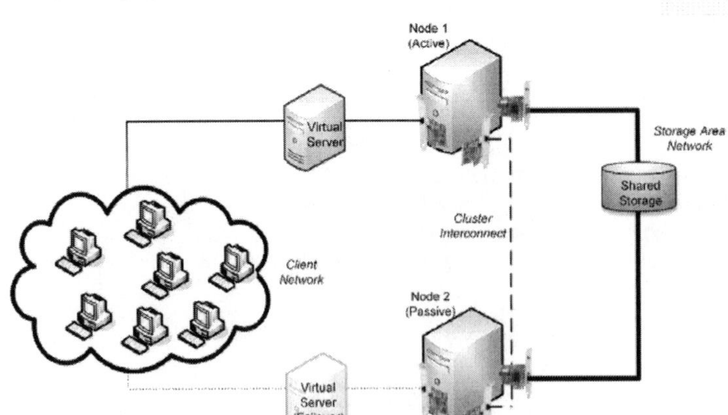

Active/Passive Cluster

Some applications and services will not function in a clustered environment and some sub-components of cluster aware applications cannot run on a cluster. You will need to be aware of these restrictions when planning the cluster implementation.

Uses for Clustering

Clustering is generally used to provide a high level of fault tolerance for **back-end** applications. For example, if you wanted to provide a resilient online purchasing system based around SQL Server, you might install a clustering solution to support the actual SQL databases.

At the **front-end**, a network load balancing solution for the web servers might be more suitable than a cluster. This is because the web servers don't contain data that changes; they merely handle client requests to such data. The SQL Servers do contain data which will change (stateful data).

Most implementations of clustering work on the principle of linking the nodes together using a private network, which does not support client connections (another network is provided for this). A heartbeat message is sent periodically between the nodes to demonstrate that a node is healthy and available. Absence of this message from a node would cause a failover.

To allow for the quick shift of services from one node to another, most vendors support a shared disk technology. As well as their own private storage, nodes share access to a disk array (usually a Storage Area Network), which contains the data that will be switched in during failover.

Round Robin DNS

There are other techniques that can be employed to avoid the need for load balancing hardware. One example is **Round Robin DNS (RRDNS)**, which is where a client enters a web server name in a browser and the DNS server responsible for resolving that name to an IP address for client connectivity will return one of several configured addresses, in turn, from amongst a group configured for the purpose. This can be cost-effective but load balancing appliances provide better fault tolerance and more efficient algorithms for distribution of requests than RRDNS.

Hot, Warm, and Cold Spares

In the absence of configuring clusters, many administrators have standby servers set aside (spares), which are not on the live network, in readiness for recovery situations. Standby servers can be classified as cold, warm, or hot:

- **Cold server** - the server is configured with the OS and then left turned off.
- **Warm server** - the server is updated periodically with backup data.
- **Hot server** - the server is updated regularly and is ready to take over in the event of a failure.

Hot, Warm, and Cold Sites

Providing redundant devices and spares allows the spare devices to be swapped in if existing systems fail. Enterprise-level networks often also provide for spare **sites**. A site is another location that can provide the same (or similar) level of service. Operations are swapped over to the new site until the previous site can be brought back online.

Sites are also referred to as being **hot**, **warm**, or **cold**. A hot site can be brought into operation almost immediately (within hours for example). It generally means that the spare or site is already within the organization's ownership and is ready to deploy. A cold site takes longer to set up (more than 1 day for instance).

For example, a hot site could consist of a building with operational computer equipment that is kept updated with a mirrored data set. A warm site could be similar, but with the requirement that the latest data set will need to be loaded. A cold site may be an empty building with a lease agreement in place to install whatever equipment is required when necessary.

Clearly, providing redundancy on this scale can be very expensive. Sites are often leased from service providers, such as Comdisco or IBM (a **subscription service**). However, in the event of a nationwide emergency, demand for the services is likely to outstrip supply!

Another option is for businesses to enter into **reciprocal arrangements** to provide mutual support. This is cost effective but complex to plan and set up.

Replication

Replication is the process of duplicating data between different servers or sites. RAID mirroring and server clustering are examples of disk-to-disk and server-to-server replication.

Replication can either be **synchronous** or **asynchronous**. Synchronous replication means that the data must be written at both sites before it can be considered committed. Asynchronous replication means that data is mirrored from a primary site to a secondary site.

Disk-to-disk and server-to-server replication are relatively simple to accomplish as they can use direct access RAID or local network technologies. Site-to-site replication is considerably harder and more expensive as it relies on Wide Area Network technologies. Determining the optimum distance between two replicating sites depends on evaluating two competing factors:

- If the sites are too close together (within about 500km), they could *both* be affected by the same disaster.
- The farther apart the sites are, the more costly replication will be. Synchronous replication is particularly sensitive to distance as the longer the communications pathway, the greater the latency of the link. Latency can be mitigated by provisioning fiber optic links.

Review Questions / Module 5 / Unit 5 / Disaster Recovery

Answer these questions to test what you have learned in this unit.

1) What is a BIA?
2) What are the main factors in a calculation of risk?
3) Why are disaster recovery exercises an important part of creating a disaster recovery plan?
4) In which types of disaster recovery site(s) would you expect to have to install computer equipment as part of the recovery process?
5) What sorts of solutions provide fault tolerance for network services?
6) How is a cluster topology with a fully redundant node usually described?
7) What is the disadvantage of locating a backup site near to the main site to make data replication cheaper?

Module 5 / Unit 6

Backup

Objectives

On completion of this unit, you will be able to:

- Implement data and security backup and archive strategies and technologies.

Backup Plans and Policies

One of the most important operations in ensuring data security is the creation of a secure backup. The execution and frequency of backups must be carefully planned and guided by policies.

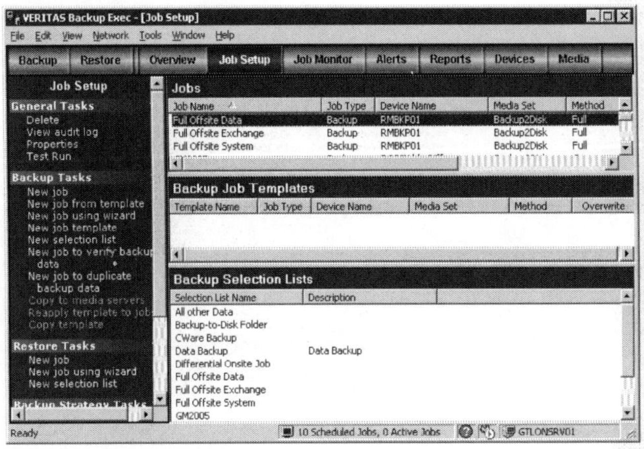

Performing a backup using Veritas BackupExec

Archiving and Backups

You should be aware of a distinction between **archiving** and **backup**:

- A backup is made for security - it is a second (or third or fourth) copy of data made with the intention of being able to restore the original should it be lost or damaged.
- Archive material is data that has passed its immediate usefulness and does not need to be accessed "live" but cannot be deleted. It may need to be retained for historical, regulatory, or legal reasons. Generally this means that it is moved from an immediately available storage area, such as a file server, to tape or optical media. An archive therefore is not a *copy*. It is likely to be important to continue to maintain additional security copies of archive material however, that is, to back up the archive.

Roughly speaking, a backup is a copy operation and archiving is a move operation.

Backup Types

When considering a backup made against an original copy of data, the backup can usually be performed using one of three main types: Full, Incremental, and Differential.

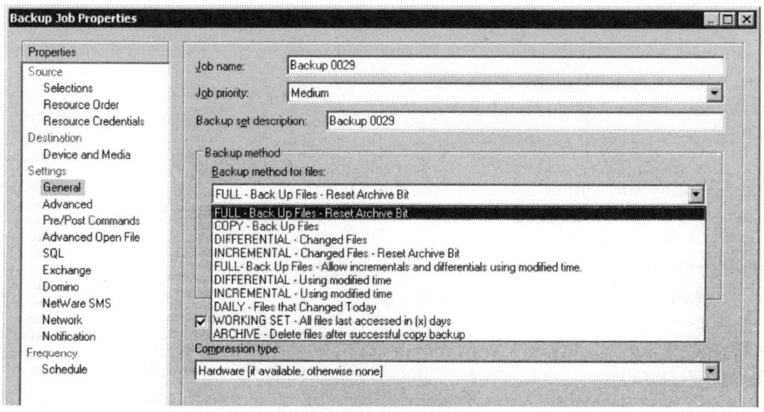

Choosing the backup type

In Windows, a **full** backup includes all selected files and directories while **incremental** and **differential** backups check the status of the **archive attribute** before including a file. The archive attribute is **set** whenever a file is modified. This allows backup software to determine which files have been changed and therefore need to be copied.

Linux doesn't support a file archive attribute. Instead, a date stamp is used to determine whether the file has changed.

The following table summarizes the three different backup types:

Type	Data Selection	Backup / Restore Time	Archive Attribute
Full	All selected data regardless of when it has previously been backed up	High / low (one tape set)	Cleared
Incremental	New files and files modified since the last backup	Low / high (multiple tape sets)	Cleared
Differential	All data modified since the last full backup	Moderate / moderate (no more than 2 sets)	Not Cleared

The criteria for determining which method to use is based on the time it takes to **restore** versus the time it takes to **back up**. Assuming a backup is performed every working day, an incremental backup only includes files changed during that day, while a differential backup includes all files changed since the last full backup.

Incremental backups save backup time but can be more time-consuming when the system must be restored. The system must be restored from the last full backup set and then from each incremental backup that has subsequently occurred. A differential backup system only involves two tape sets when restore is required.

Doing a full backup on a large network every day takes a long time. A typical strategy for a complex network would be a **full weekly backup** followed by an **incremental** or **differential** backup at the **end of each day**.

- The advantage of using a **full daily backup** is that one tape set is only required to restore the system.
- The advantage of an **incremental backup** is that it takes less time to back up but several tape sets may need to be restored before the system is operational.
- The advantage of a **differential backup** is the balance of time for both restoring and backing up.

Do not combine differential and incremental backups.
Use full backups interspersed with differential backups, or full backups interspersed with incremental backups.

Normal and Selective Backups

Most software also has the capability to do **normal** or **copy** backups. These are made outside the tape rotation system (ad hoc) and do not affect the archive attribute. Similarly, a **selective** backup may be used to backup a subset of data on a server (perhaps a user's home folder) and would not affect the archive or backup timestamp.

Retention Policy

Data retention needs to be considered in the short and long term:

- In the short term, files that change frequently might need retaining for version control. Short term retention is also important in recovering from virus infection. Consider the scenario where a backup is made on Monday, a file is infected with a virus on Tuesday, and when that file is backed up later on Tuesday, the copy made on Monday is overwritten. This means that there is no good means of restoring the uninfected file.

  Short term retention is determined by how often the youngest media sets are overwritten.

- In the long term, data may need to be stored to meet legal requirements or to comply with company policies or industry standards. Any data that must be retained in a particular version past the oldest sets should be moved to archive storage.

For these reasons, backups are kept back to certain points in time. As backups take up a lot of space, and there is never limitless storage capacity, this introduces the need for storage management routines and techniques to reduce the amount of data occupying backup storage media while giving adequate coverage of the required **recovery window**. The recovery window is determined by the **Recovery Point Objective (RPO)**, which is determined through business continuity planning.

A retention policy can either be based on redundancy (the number of copies of each file that should be retained) or on a recovery window (the number of days into the past that should be retained). Advanced backup software can prevent media sets from being overwritten in line with the specified retention policy.

Database and System Backups

Database Backups

If the data that you're considering backing up is part of a database, such as SQL data or a messaging system, such as Exchange, then the data is probably being used all the time. Often copy-based mechanisms will be unable to backup open files. Short of closing the files, and so the database, a copy-based system will not work. To get round this, most databases support two useful features: replication and online backups.

Most modern RDBMS (Relational Database Management Systems) support **transactional** updates, and in most situations, the transactions can be posted to multiple replicas of the database, providing redundancy.

This doesn't protect you from accidentally deleting a record, however, because it is a valid transaction which will be propagated amongst all the replicas at the next scheduled replication interval. Therefore you should also provide **online** backups of database systems.

The problem with backing up at the database level is that to restore a record (or in Exchange terms, a message or perhaps a mailbox) is tricky. In fact, you generally have to restore the entire database. For example, the recovery scenario for Exchange typically involves a non-production server being used to restore the data and then the required messages/mailboxes being copied into the production system.

Some backup software allows for the backup of a database in a more targeted way. Staying with our Exchange scenario, both the third-party systems mentioned above support backup and restore at different *granular* levels - server, database, mailbox, or message.

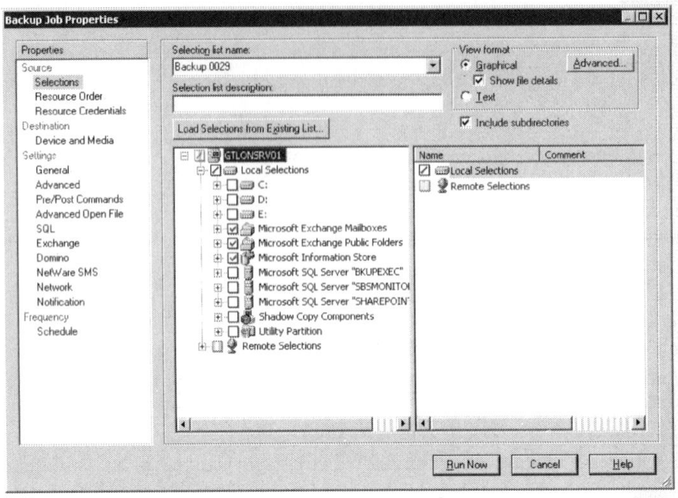

Online backups with Exchange Server

The disadvantage with backing up at the mailbox level is that it is more time consuming. However, in the event of a problem, the system is more readily recoverable to the desired state.

Snapshots

Snapshots are another means of getting round the problem of open files. A snapshot is a point-in-time copy of data. A backup program can use the snapshot rather than the live data to perform the backup. In Windows, snapshots are provided for on NTFS volumes by the **Volume Shadow Copy Service (VSS)**. They are also supported on Sun's ZFS file system, and under some enterprise distributions of Linux. Virtual system managers can also usually take snapshot copies of VMs.

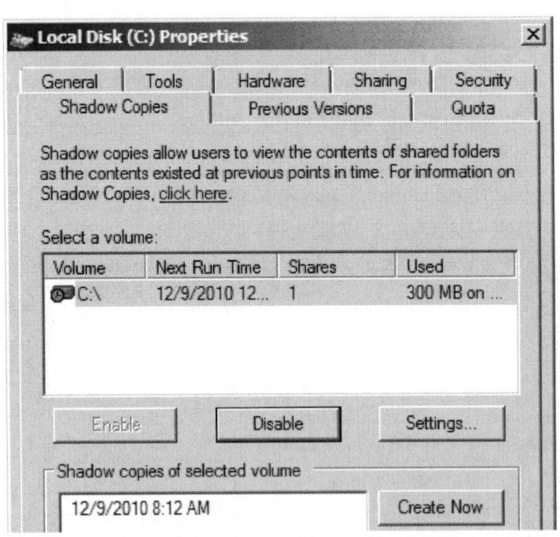

Configuring Shadow Copies through disk properties on Windows Server

System Backups

A system backup makes a copy of the OS and installed applications so that a server can be recovered without having to manually reinstall software and reconfigure settings.

Older methods of system backup could involve lengthy recovery procedures. Typically the operating system would have to be reinstalled then the backup applied to the new OS to recover the old configuration.

A **bare metal** backup is one that can be applied directly to a partitioned drive without the separate step of reinstalling the OS. Bare metal backups typically work by making an **image**. The backup software provides a recovery boot disk which enables the system to connect to the recovery media (an external hard drive or network drive for instance).

The only drawback of this method is that system images typically require multi-gigabyte storage media. A system image can also be quite time-consuming to create, so this method works best if the system configuration is kept fairly static and user data is stored separately from the OS volume. There may also be issues applying the image to a machine with a different hardware specification.

Virtual machines can be backed up and restored in the same way (in fact, most VMs are deployed using images in the first place).

Backout Contingency Plan

Another reason for making a backup is to support a **backout contingency plan**. Backout plans are most closely associated with rolling back OS updates (in the event that they cause some sort of problem with legacy hardware or software). A backout plan should be formulated for any sort of software or hardware upgrade though.

A backout plan allows the system to be restored to the state it was in prior to applying the patch or upgrade. As a *scheduled* backup may not be able to reverse *only the specific change* made during the upgrade, it may be necessary to perform a *specific* backup before performing the upgrade.

Backup Execution and Frequency

A backup is executed by selecting the files and folders for backup and setting the schedule (frequency) and the backup media.

There is no "best" media type for backups and archiving. Different media have different characteristics that make them more or less suitable for different storage tasks. Technologies and costs also change over time. The nature of storage means there is as much "looking back" to support older technologies as there is looking forward to opportunities that new or cheaper technologies may bring.

Linear Access (Tape)

Historically, tape has been used for most large-scale backup operations. Tape is extremely reliable and can offer a cost-effective solution. The main problem with tape is that backup and especially restore operations can be very slow, due to the limitations of the linear access method.

See Unit 3.2 for a discussion of different tape formats.

Hard Disk and SANs

Random access or "disk-to-disk" backup now predominates much of the storage and backup market. Hard disks support very large and (with RAID) easily extensible capacity at quite low cost. The disks do not need to be high performance so cheap 5K rpm units can be specified. Even low-speed drives are far faster than tape solutions, especially when it comes to restoring data. A set of removable hard disks could be used to backup most small business servers and allow for onsite and offsite storage.

A NAS (Network Attached Storage) device or SAN (Storage Area Network) could be used as a backup or archive solution for larger networks. The main drawback of a networked-disk solution is that there is no offsite storage (unless the backup takes place over a WAN). Consequently, many enterprise storage architectures use a tiered solution:

- "Online" storage is provided by a high-performance server RAID array (15K SAS drives or SSDs for instance).
- "Nearline" storage and security backup is provided by a SAN, probably using cheaper and slower RAID components (5K SATA drives for instance).
- "Offline" and offsite storage and archiving is provided by tape or optical media.

Data is transitioned through the storage system (disk-to-disk-to-tape) according to data retention policies.

Media (Tape) Rotation

Once a suitable backup method and media type has been determined, a **tape rotation** method must be established to minimize the number of tapes required for maintaining an adequate history of the backup jobs.

"Tape" could really be any media set - you could rotate a set of portable hard drives for instance.

A commonly used tape rotation method is known as **Grandfather-Father-Son**. This method uses **three sets** of media in which **monthly**, **weekly**, and **daily** tapes correspond to the generations. Before starting the system, a **full backup** of all media should be made. The system then proceeds as follows:

1) Daily backups, which may be incremental *or* differential, use the **son** tapes. These are **reused** each week and remain the youngest in the rotation.

2) Weekly full backups are written to the **father** tapes. A father tape set is required for each week of the month except the last.

3) The **final weekly** backup is written to the monthly grandfather tape set.

Assuming a network is operational five days per week, the following tape sets are required:

Type	Frequency	Number of Sets
Son	Daily	4 sets
Father	Weekly	4 sets (plus one to be held off site)
Grandfather	Monthly	12 sets

In any sort of tape rotation scheme, labeling the tapes and using the correct tape at the correct time is critical.

Storage Issues

Backed up and archived data needs to be stored as securely as "live" data. It is likely to have the same confidentiality considerations. One critical problem is planning for events that might compromise both the live data *and* the backup set. Natural disasters such as fire, earthquake, flood plus theft could leave an organization without a data backup, unless they have kept a copy **offsite**. Offsite storage is obviously difficult to keep up-to-date. Without a network that can support the required bandwidth, the offsite media must be physically brought onsite (and if there is no second set of offsite media, data is at substantial risk at this time), the latest backup performed, and then removed to offsite storage again. Quite apart from the difficulty and expense of doing this, there are data confidentiality and security issues in transporting the data.

As Internet bandwidth improves, remote offline backup becomes less dependent on leased lines. There are more and more "cloud"-based remote backup solutions, principally targeted at small and medium size enterprises.

Backup media is typically physically secured against theft or snooping by keeping it in a restricted part of the building, with other server and network equipment. Many backup solutions also use encryption to ensure data confidentiality should the media be stolen.

Restoring Data and Verifying Backups

It is *critical* to test that backup operations work properly. There can be no worse feeling in IT support than turning to the backup media you have been happily writing to and rotating for the last 8 months only to discover that a critical data folder has never been included in the job!

- **Compatibility** - a tape backup is useless without a drive capable of reading the media. Most drives can read from tape formats from the previous generation (or more). If a legacy drive fails and there is no replacement available, there is a very real risk to the security of the organization's data.
- **Error detection / integrity verification** - problems with the tape or configuration can cause backup jobs to fail. Depending on the error, the whole job may be cancelled or some data may not get backed up. Backup software usually has the facility to verify a backup (obviously this makes the backup operation longer though), report errors to a log, and send alerts by email.

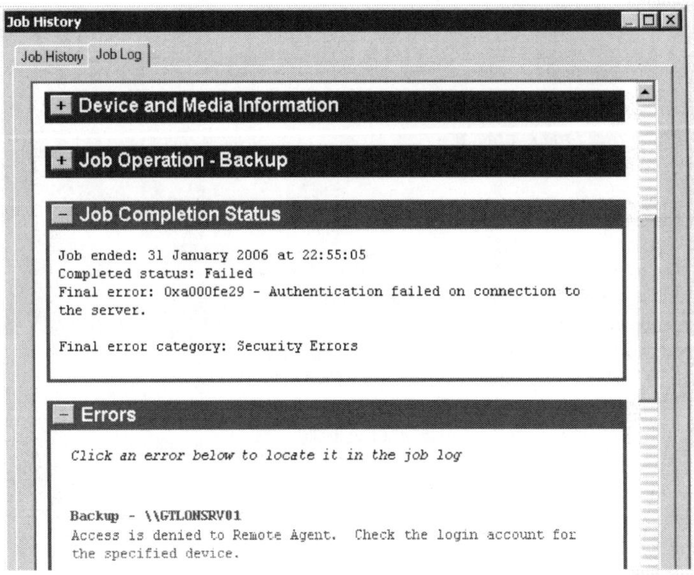

Viewing failed backup job log under Veritas BackupExec

- **Configuration** - when setting up a new job (and periodically thereafter), it is wise to check the media catalog to ensure that all the expected data has been backed up.
- **Test restore** - another option is to test that a restore operation can be performed successfully. This is important when using new backup software, to test old tapes, to check a new job, and to carry out random spot checks. When you do a test restore, you **redirect** the data to a different folder, to avoid overwriting live data.

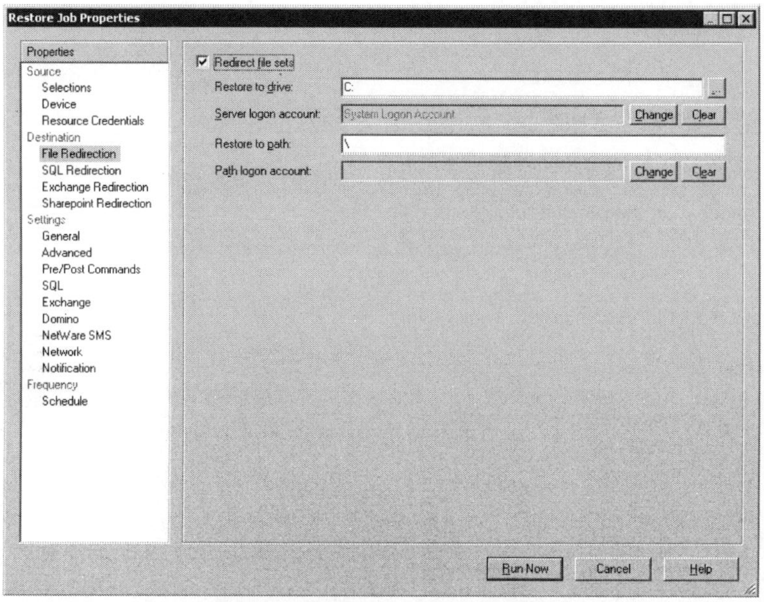

Redirecting file output for a restore operation

A **restore failure** could occur for a number of reasons::

- The required files were not included in the backup schedule - a configuration error such as this is difficult to recover from but check whether different backup jobs might have included the files. Also check other media across the network (you might find a copy on a client PC somewhere) and the host's Recycle Bin / Trash folder to see if a copy can be located elsewhere. At the last resort, file recovery tools might be able to restore the data from the original media.

- Security / overwrite issues - the original file might be locked or the backup operator's permissions might not be sufficient to restore the files to the original location. Close open files (or mailbox / database sessions) or reconfigure the permissions or account used to perform the restore.

Restoring data to databases and email mailboxes is usually complex. Make sure the correct commands have been sent to the restore utility.

- Media issues - if the media is faulty or has run out of space, the backup files might have been corrupted. Always test the integrity of backups at the time they are made. Also check that the correct media have been selected for the restore operation. If a file cannot be located, the media catalog may be corrupt or someone might have mislabeled a backup tape. Try re-cataloging the media to find the file.

If there is a general failure to restore anything from backup, check that the required services are running and view the event logs to look for problems.

Review Questions / Module 5 / Unit 6 / Backup

Answer these questions to test what you have learned in this unit.

1) Which backup types do not change the archive attribute or date stamp?
2) What is an RPO?
3) What is the benefit of a file system that can create snapshots?
4) What is a bare metal backup?
5) What is the benefit of a backup media rotation system like GFS?

Module 5 / Summary
Server Security

In this module, you learned about site and server security technologies and best practices and how to configure security software to protect against viruses and other threats. You also learned about disaster recovery plans and how to provide for fault tolerant services.

Module 5 / Unit 1 / Site Security

- Authentication technologies require users to supply the correct credentials to access an account or other resource. Authentication factors can be something you know, have, or are; multifactor authentication is considered much stronger than single factor.
- Be aware of the reasons for provisioning physical security controls and defense in depth.
- You should be able to describe the use of zones, barriers, gateways, and surveillance in planning and implementing site security and the use of locks and cabinets to secure hardware.
- Data removed from its access control system might be vulnerable as an attacker can easily change permissions and become its owner. This risk can be mitigated by encrypting the data, either file-by-file or on the whole disk. There are also encryption schemes for databases and tape media.
- Be aware of the need to and methods of removing data from media before it is disposed of.
- Emergency and fire safety procedures are vital for any workspace.

Module 5 / Unit 2 / Remote Access Services

- Cryptographic technologies include symmetric encryption, asymmetric encryption, and cryptographic hashes. Make sure you know the basic principles behind PKI and digital certificates.
- You should understand the different remote access / VPN topologies and the protocols that can be used to implement them. Also be aware of the functions and relative merits of authentication protocols used over remote networks.

Module 5 / Unit 3 / Server Hardening

- You should be aware of the policies for deploying hardened servers with the minimum possible configuration to reduce the potential attack surface. Do not overlook the requirement to secure system firmware too.
- Hardened servers must also be kept up-to-date with OS, application, device driver, and firmware updates.

Module 5 / Unit 4 / Security Software

- You should be able to diagnose malware and other security issues from typical symptoms and select appropriate tools to restore a server to a secure configuration.
- IDS / IPS works to detect or prevent security threats beyond malware.
- A NAC solution can prevent network access if a host does not meet a defined health policy.

Module 5 / Unit 5 / Disaster Recovery

- Be aware of the use of Business Impact Analysis (BIA) and Disaster Recovery Plans (DRP).
- You should understand the importance of fault tolerance and be able to identify the main components that require redundancy.
- Understand recovery procedures and the use of replication methods to maintain hot, cold, and warm servers and sites.

Module 5 / Unit 6 / Backup

- Backup is essential to effective data security. You should be able to distinguish between the different backup methodologies.
- You should be able to identify appropriate media for different types of backup and understand the use of rotation methods to maximize capacity and retention.
- Be aware that backups must be tested for integrity and to eliminate configuration errors.

Taking the Exams

When you think you have learned and practiced the material sufficiently, you can book a time to take the test.

Preparing for the Exam

We've tried to balance this course to reflect the percentages in the exam so that you have learned the appropriate level of detail about each topic to comfortably answer the exam questions. Read the following notes to find out what you need to do to register for the exam and get some tips on what to expect during the exam and how to prepare for it.

Questions in the exam are weighted by domain area as follows:

CompTIA Server+ SK0-004 Domain Areas	Weighting
1.0 Server Architecture	12%
2.0 Server Administration	24%
3.0 Storage	12%
4.0 Security	13%
5.0 Networking	10%
6.0 Disaster Recovery	9%
7.0 Troubleshooting	20%

The objectives and content examples are covered in units in the course as listed in the table below. You can also use the index at the back of the book to look up specific content examples:

Domain Objectives/Examples	Refer To
1.1 Explain the purpose and function of server form factors *Rack mount (Dimensions [1U, 2U, 4U], Cable management arms, Rail kits) • Tower • Blade technology (Blade enclosure [Backplane / Midplane, Power supply sockets, Network modules / switches, Management modules], Blade server)*	Unit 1.1 / Servers and Racks
1.2 Given a scenario, install, configure and maintain server components *BIOS / UEFI (CMOS battery) • Firmware*	Unit 1.4 / System Setup
CPU (Multiprocessor vs. multicore, Socket type, Cache levels: L1, L2, L3, Speeds [Core, Bus, Multiplier], CPU stepping, Architecture [x86, x64, ARM]) • RAM (ECC vs. non-ECC, DDR2, DDR3, Number of pins, Static vs. dynamic, Module placement, CAS latency, Timing , Memory pairing) • Bus types, bus channels and expansion slots (Height differences and bit rate differences, PCI, PCIe, PCI-X) • NICs • Hard drives • Riser cards • RAID controllers • USB interface / port • Hot-swap vs. non-hot-swap components	Unit 4.1 / Server Hardware

Domain Objectives/Examples	Refer To
1.3 Compare and contrast power and cooling components *Cooling (Airflow, Thermal dissipation, Baffles / shrouds, Fans, Liquid cooling)*	Unit 4.2 / Environment and Maintenance
Power (Voltage [110v vs. 220v vs. -48v, 208v vs. 440v / 460v / 480v], Wattage, Consumption, Redundancy, 1-phase vs. 3-phase power, Plug types [NEMA, Edison, Twist lock])	Unit 4.3 / Power Distribution
2.1 Install and configure server operating systems *Update firmware • BIOS / UEFI configuration (Boot order) • Disk preparation (RAID setup, Partitioning, Formatting, File system type [ext 2, 3, 4, NTFS, FAT32, ReiserFS, UFS, VMFS, ZFS], Swap)*	Unit 1.4 / System Setup
Determine server role / purpose • Configure host name • Local account setup • Connect to network • Install drivers • Performance baseline (Swap or pagefile optimization) • Unattended / remote installations (Deploying images and cloning, Scripted installs [PXE boot, TFTP])	Unit 1.5 / Server Operating Systems
Enable services • Install features / roles / applications	Unit 3.1 / Configuring Server Roles
Join domain / directory	Unit 3.4 / Directory Services
Performance baseline (Server optimization)	Unit 3.6 / Troubleshooting Software
Address security concerns (Patching, OS hardening, Compliance to company procedures / standards)	Unit 5.3 / Server Hardening
2.2 Compare and contrast server roles and requirements for each *Network services server (DHCP, DNS / WINS, NTP)*	Unit 2.4 / Network Services
Web server • Application server • Database server • Messaging server • Mail server	Unit 3.1 / Configuring Server Roles
Directory server	Unit 3.4 / Directory Services
File server • Print server	Unit 3.5 / File and Print Services
Routing and remote access server	Unit 5.2 / Remote Access Services
2.3 Given a scenario, use access and control methods to administer a server *Local hardware administration (KVM, Serial, Virtual Administration console) • Network-based hardware administration (KVM over IP, ILO, iDRAC) • Network-based operating system administration (RDP, SSH, VNC, Command line / shell)*	Unit 4.5 / Server Management
2.4 Given a scenario, perform proper server maintenance techniques *Performance monitoring (CPU utilization, Memory utilization, Network utilization, Disk utilization [Disk IOPS, Storage capacity], Comparison against performance baseline, Processes and services monitoring, Log monitoring)*	Unit 3.6 / Troubleshooting Software
Hardware maintenance (Check system health indicators [LEDs, Error codes, Beep codes, LCD messages], Preventive maintenance [Clearing dust, Check proper airflow], Proper shut down procedures)	Unit 4.2 / Environment and Maintenance
Hardware maintenance (Replace failed components [Fans, Hard drives, RAM, Backplanes, Batteries])	Unit 4.4 / Server Hardware Troubleshooting

Domain Objectives/Examples	Refer To
2.4 Given a scenario, perform proper server maintenance techniques *Change management • Outages & Service Level Agreements (Scheduled downtime, Unscheduled downtime, Impact analysis, Client notification, MTTR)*	Unit 4.6 / Configuration Management
Patch management (Operating System updates, Application updates, Security software updates, Firmware updates, Device drivers updates, Compatibility lists [Operating systems, Hardware, Applications], Testing and validation)	Unit 5.3 / Server Hardening
Fault tolerance and high availability techniques (Clustering [Active / active, Active / passive], Load balancing [Round robin, Heartbeat])	Unit 5.5 / Disaster Recovery
2.5 Explain the importance of asset management and documentation *Asset management (Licensing, Labeling, Warranty, Lifecycle management [Procurement, Usage, End of life, Disposal / recycling], Inventory [Make, Model, Serial number, Asset tag]) • Documentation (Service manuals, Network diagrams, Architecture diagrams, Dataflow diagrams, Recovery documentation, Baseline documentation, Change management policies, Service Level Agreement, Server configuration) • Secure storage of sensitive documentation*	Unit 4.6 / Configuration Management
2.6 Explain the purpose and operation of virtualization components *Hosts and guests • Management interface for virtual machines • Hypervisor (Type I, Type II, Hybrid) • Hardware compatibility list (BIOS / UEFI compatibility and support, CPU compatibility support, AMD-V / Intel VT) • Resource allocation between Guest and Host (CPU, Storage, Memory, Network connectivity [Direct Access (Bridging) vs. NAT, Virtual NICs, Virtual switches], Video)*	Unit 2.5 / Virtualization Services
3.1 Given a scenario, install and deploy primary storage devices based on given specifications and interfaces *Disk specifications (RPM, Dimensions / form factor, Capacity, Bus width, IOPS, Seek time and latency, Hot-swap vs. non-hot-swap components) • Interfaces (SAS, SATA, SCSI, USB) • Hard drive vs. SSD*	Unit 1.2 / Storage Devices
Interfaces (Fibre Channel)	Unit 3.2 / Storage Services
3.2 Given a scenario, configure RAID using best practices *RAID levels and performance considerations (0, 1, 5, 6, 10) • Software vs. hardware RAID (Performance considerations) • Configuration specifications (Capacity, Bus types, Drive RPM) • Hot-swap support and ramifications • Hot spare vs. cold spare • Array controller (Memory, Battery backed cache, Redundant controller)*	Unit 1.3 / RAID
3.3 Summarize hardware and features of various storage technologies *DAS • NAS (iSCSI, FCoE) • SAN (Fibre Channel, LUN & LUN masking, HBAs and fabric switches) • JBOD • Tape (Drive, Libraries) • Optical drive • Flash, Compact Flash and USB drive*	Unit 3.2 / Storage Services

Domain Objectives/Examples	Refer To
3.4 Given a scenario, calculate appropriate storage capacity and plan for future growth *Base10 vs. Base2 disk size calculation (1000 vs. 1024) • Disk quotas • Compression • Capacity planning considerations (Operating system growth [Patches, Service packs, Log files], Temporary directories, Databases, Application servers, File servers, Archival)*	Unit 3.2 / Storage Services
4.1 Compare and contrast physical security methods and concepts *Multifactor Authentication (Something you have, Something you know, Something you are) • Security concepts (Mantrap, RFID chip, ID card, Biometric, Keypad, Access list, Security guard, Security camera, Keys & Locks [Cabinet, Rack mount, Server], Safe)*	Unit 5.1 / Site Security
4.2 Given a scenario, apply server hardening techniques *OS hardening (Stopping unneeded services / closing unneeded ports, Install only required software, Install latest operating system patches) • Application hardening (Install latest patches, Disabling unneeded services / roles / features) • Endpoint security (HIDS, Anti-malware) • Remediate security issues based on a vulnerability scan • Hardware hardening (Disabling unneeded hardware and physical ports / devices, BIOS password, Disable WOL [Wake on LAN], Setup boot order, Chassis locks / intrusion detection)*	Unit 5.3 / Server Hardening
Endpoint security (HIDS, Anti-malware) • Remediate security issues based on a vulnerability scan	Unit 5.4 / Security Software
4.3 Explain basic network security systems and protocols *Firewall (Network-based, Host-based) • Router access list • VLAN • Security zones (DMZ, Public and private, Intranet and extranet)*	Unit 2.3 / Routers and Firewalls
Authentication protocols (LDAP)	Unit 3.4 / Directory Services
Authentication protocols (RADIUS, TACACS, TACACS+) • PKI (Private key, Public key, Certificate authority, SSL / TLS) • VPN • IPsec	Unit 5.2 / Remote Access Services
Port security / 802.1x / NAC • NIDS	Unit 5.4 / Security Software
4.4 Implement logical access control methods based on company policy *Access control lists (Users, Groups, Roles, Resources [Administrative rights, Distribution lists]) • Permissions (Superuser)*	Unit 3.4 / Directory Services
Access control lists (Resources [File system, Network ACLs, Peripheral devices]) • Permissions (Read, Write / Modify, Execute, Delete, Full control, File vs. share)	Unit 3.5 / File and Print Services
4.5 Implement data security methods and secure storage disposal techniques *Storage encryption (File level encryption, Disk encryption, Tape encryption) • Storage media (Soft wipe [File deletion], Hard wipe [Zero out all sectors], Physical destruction, Remote wipe)*	Unit 5.1 / Site Security
4.6 Given a scenario, implement proper environmental controls and techniques *Safety (Proper lifting techniques, Rack stability, Floor load limitations, Sharp edges and pinch points)*	Unit 1.1 / Servers and Racks

Domain Objectives/Examples	Refer To
4.6 Given a scenario, implement proper environmental controls and techniques *HVAC (Room and rack temperature and humidity [Monitoring and alert notifications], Airflow [Rack filler / baffle / blanking panels], Hot aisle and cold aisle)*	Unit 4.2 / Environment and Maintenance
Power concepts and best practices (UPS [Run time vs. capacity, Automated graceful shutdown of attached devices, Periodic testing of batteries, Maximum load, Bypass procedures, Remote management], PDU [Connect redundant rack PDUs to separate circuits], Capacity planning [PDU ratings, UPS ratings, Total potential power draw], Multiple circuits [Connect redundant power supplies to separate PDUs])	Unit 4.3 / Power Distribution
Safety (ESD Procedures)	Unit 4.4 / Server Hardware Troubleshooting
Safety (Fire suppression)	Unit 5.1 / Site Security
5.1 Given a scenario, configure servers to use IP addressing and network infrastructure services *MAC addresses • Network Interface Card configuration (NIC teaming, Duplexing [Full, Half, Auto], Speeds [10 / 100 / 1000 Mbps, 10 Gbps])*	Unit 2.1 / Ethernet
IPv4 vs. IPv6 • Default gateway • CIDR notation and subnetting • Public and private IP addressing • Static IP assignment vs. DHCP	Unit 2.2 / Internet Protocol
NAT / PAT	Unit 2.3 / Routers and Firewalls
DNS (FQDN, Default domain suffix / search domain) • WINS • NetBIOS	Unit 2.4 / Network Services
5.2 Compare and contrast various ports and protocols *TCP vs. UDP • SNMP - 161 • SMTP - 25 • FTP - 20 / 21 • SFTP - 22 • SSH - 22 • SCP - 22 • NTP - 123 • HTTP - 80 • HTTPS - 443 • TELNET - 23 • IMAP - 143 • POP3 - 110 • RDP - 3389 • FTPS - 989 / 990 • LDAP - 389/3268 • DNS - 53 • DHCP – 68*	Unit 2.3 / Routers and Firewalls
5.3 Given a scenario, install cables and implement proper cable management procedures *Copper (Patch cables [Crossover, Straight through, Rollover], CAT5, CAT5e, CAT6) • Fiber (Single-mode, Multi-mode) • Connectors (ST, LC, SC, SFP, RJ-45, RJ-11) • Cable placement and routing (Cable channels, Cable management trays [Vertical, Horizontal]) • Labeling • Bend radius • Cable ties*	Unit 2.1 / Ethernet
6.1 Explain the importance of disaster recovery principles *Site types (Hot site, Cold site, Warm site) • Replication methods (Disk to disk, Server to server, Site to site) • Continuity of Operations (Disaster recovery plan, Business continuity plan, Business impact analysis [Who is affected, What is affected, Severity of impact])*	Unit 5.5 / Disaster Recovery
6.2 Given a scenario, implement appropriate backup techniques *Methodology (Full / Normal [Copy], Incremental, Differential, Snapshot, Selective, Bare metal, Open file, Data vs. OS restore) • Backup media (Linear access [Tape], Random Access [Disk, Removable media, Optical media]) • Media and restore best practices (Labeling, Integrity verification, Test restorability, Tape rotation and retention) • Media storage location (Offsite, Onsite, Security considerations, Environmental considerations)*	Unit 5.6 / Backup

Domain Objectives/Examples	Refer To
7.1 Explain troubleshooting theory and methodologies *Identify the problem and determine the scope* (*Question users / stakeholders and identify changes to the server / environment, Collect additional documentation / logs, If possible, replicate the problem as appropriate, If possible, perform backups before making changes*) • *Establish a theory of probable cause / question the obvious* (*Determine whether there is a common element of symptom causing multiple problems*) • *Test the theory to determine cause* (*Once theory is confirmed, determine next steps to resolve problem, If theory is not confirmed, establish new theory or escalate*) • *Establish a plan of action to resolve the problem and notify impacted users* • *Implement the solution or escalate as appropriate* (*Make one change at a time and test / confirm the change has resolved the problem, If the problem is not resolved, reverse the change if appropriate and implement new change*) • *Verify full system functionality and if applicable implement preventive measures* • *Perform a root cause analysis* • *Document findings, actions and outcomes throughout the process*	Unit 1.6 / Troubleshooting Procedures
7.2 Given a scenario, effectively troubleshoot hardware problems, selecting the appropriate tools and methods *Environmental issues* (*Dust, Humidity, Temperature*) • *Hardware tools* (*Compressed air*)	Unit 4.2 / Environment and Maintenance
Environmental issues (*Power surge / failure*)	Unit 4.3 / Power Distribution
Common problems (*Failed POST, Overheating, Memory failure, Onboard component failure, Processor failure, Incorrect boot sequence, Expansion card failure, Operating system not found, Drive failure, Power supply failure, I/O failure*) • *Causes of common problems* (*Third party components or incompatible components, Incompatible or incorrect BIOS, Cooling failure, Mismatched components, Backplane failure*) • *Hardware tools* (*Power supply tester / multimeter, Hardware diagnostics, ESD equipment*)	Unit 4.4 / Server Hardware Troubleshooting
7.3 Given a scenario, effectively troubleshoot software problems, selecting the appropriate tools and methods *Common problems* (*OS boot failure, Cannot mount drive*) • *Cause of common problems* (*Corrupted files, Lack of hard drive space, Fragmentation*) • *Software tools* (*Defragmentation tools, Disk property tools* [*Usage, Free space*])	Unit 3.3 / Volume Management
7.3 Given a scenario, effectively troubleshoot software problems, selecting the appropriate tools and methods *Cause of common problems* (*User Account Control* [*UAC / sudo*])	Unit 3.4 / Directory Services
Common problems (*User cannot access resources, Users cannot print*) • *Cause of common problems* (*Print server drivers / services, Print spooler*) • *Software tools* (*Disk property tools* [*Volume or drive mapping*])	Unit 3.5 / File and Print Services
Common problems (*Memory leak, BSOD / stop, Driver issues, Runaway process, Cannot write to system log, Slow OS performance, Patch update failure, Service failure, Hangs no shut down*) • *Cause of common problems* (*Lack of system resources, Virtual memory* [*misconfigured, corrupt*]) • *Software tools* (*System logs, Monitoring tools* [*Resource Monitor, Performance Monitor*])	Unit 3.6 / Troubleshooting Software

Domain Objectives/Examples	Refer To
7.4 Given a scenario, effectively diagnose network problems, selecting the appropriate tools and methods *Causes of common problems (Component failure, Bad cables, Mis-configured NIC)*	Unit 2.1 / Ethernet
Common problems (DHCP server mis-configured, non-functional or unreachable, Destination host unreachable) • Causes of common problems (Improper IP configuration, IPv4 vs. IPv6 misconfigurations) • Networking tools (ping, ipconfig / ifconfig)	Unit 2.2 / Internet Protocol
Common problems (Internet connectivity failure, Default gateway mis-configured, Failure of service provider) • Causes of common problems (Improper IP configuration, VLAN configuration, Port security, Improper subnetting, Incorrect OS route tables, Firewall [mis-configuration, hardware failure, software failure], Routing / switch issues) • Networking tools (ping, tracert / traceroute, route, netstat)	Unit 2.3 / Routers and Firewalls
Common problems (Unknown host, Cannot reach by host name / FQDN) • Causes of common problems (DNS and/or DHCP failure, Mis-configured hosts file) • Networking tools (nslookup, nbtstat, netstat)	Unit 2.4 / Network Services
Common problems (User unable to logon, Email failure, Resource unavailable)	Unit 3.1 / Configuring Server Roles
Networking tools (net use / mount)	Unit 3.5 / File and Print Services
7.5 Given a scenario, effectively troubleshoot storage problems, selecting the appropriate tools and methods *Common problems (Slow file access, OS not found, Data not available, Error lights, Unable to mount the device, Drive not available, Cannot access logical drive, Data corruption, Slow I/O performance, Cache failure, Multiple drive failure) • Causes of common problems (Media failure, Drive failure, Controller failure, HBA failure, Loose connectors, Cable problems, Mis-configuration, Improper termination, Corrupt boot sector, Corrupt file system table, Array rebuild, Improper disk partition, Bad sectors, Cache battery failure, Cache turned off, Insufficient space, Improper RAID configuration, Mis-matched drives, Backplane failure) • Storage tools (Partitioning tools, Disk management, RAID array management, Array management, System logs, Monitoring tools)*	Unit 3.3 / Volume Management
7.5 Given a scenario, effectively troubleshoot storage problems, selecting the appropriate tools and methods *Storage tools (net use / mount command)*	Unit 3.5 / File and Print Services
Common problems (Restore failure, Unsuccessful backup)	Unit 5.6 / Backup
7.6 Given a scenario, effectively diagnose security issues, selecting the appropriate tools and methods *Common problems (File integrity issue, Privilege escalation, Applications will not load, Can't access network file / shares, Unable to open files, Excessive access, Excessive memory utilization) • Causes of common problems (Open ports, Active services, Inactive services, Intrusion detection configurations, Anti-malware configurations, Local / group policies, Firewall rules, Misconfigured permissions, Virus infection, Rogue processes / services) • Security tools (Port scanners, Sniffers, Cipher, Checksums, Telnet client, Anti-malware)*	Unit 5.4 / Security Software

Registering for the Exam

CompTIA Certification exams are delivered exclusively by Pearson VUE.

- Log on to VUE (www.pearsonvue.com/comptia) and register your details to create an account.
- To book a test, log in using your account credentials then click the link to schedule an appointment.
- The testing program is CompTIA and the exam code is SK0-004.
- Use the search tool to locate the test center nearest you then book an appointment.
- If you have purchased a voucher or been supplied with one already, enter the voucher number to pay for the exam. Otherwise, you can pay with a credit card.
- When you have confirmed payment, an email will be sent to the account used to register confirming the appointment and directions to the venue. Print a copy and bring it with you when you go to take your test.

Arriving for the Exam

- Arrive at the test center at least 15 minutes before the test is scheduled.
- You must have two forms of ID; one with picture, one preferably with your private address, and both with signature. View CompTIA's website for more information on CompTIA's candidate ID policy and examples of acceptable forms of ID.
- Books, calculators, laptops, cellphones, smartphones, tablets, or other reference materials are not allowed in the exam room.
- You will be given a pad and marker to make notes but you must not attempt to write down questions or remove anything from the exam room.
- It is CompTIA's policy to make reasonable accommodations for individuals with disabilities.
- The test center administrator will demonstrate how to use the computer-based test system and wish you good luck. Check that your name is displayed, read the introductory note, and then click the button to start the exam.

Taking the Exam

CompTIA has prepared a Candidate Experience video (https://www.youtube.com/embed/kyTdN2GZiZ8). Watch this to help to familiarize yourself with the exam format and types of questions.

- There are up to 100 multiple-choice questions and performance-based items, which must be answered in 90 minutes. The passing score is 750 on a scale of 100-900.
- Read each question and its option answers carefully. Don't rush through the exam as you'll probably have more time at the end than you expect.
- At the other end of the scale, don't get "stuck" on a question and start to panic. You can mark questions for review and come back to them.
- As the exam tests your ability to recall facts and to apply them sensibly in a troubleshooting scenario, there will be questions where you cannot recall the correct answer from memory. Adopt the following strategy for dealing with these questions:
    - Narrow your choices down by eliminating obviously wrong answers.
    - Don't guess too soon! You must select not only a *correct* answer, but the *best* answer. It is therefore important that you read all of the options and not stop when you find an option that is correct. It may be impractical compared to another answer.
    - Utilize information and insights that you've acquired in working through the entire test to go back and answer earlier items that you weren't sure of.
    - Think your answer is wrong - should change it? Studies indicate that when students change their answers they usually change them to the wrong answer. If you were fairly certain you were correct the first time, leave the answer as it is.
- Don't leave any questions unanswered! If you really don't know the answer, just guess.
- The exam may contain "unscored" questions, which may even be outside the exam objectives. These questions do not count towards your score. Do not allow them to distract or worry you.
- The exam questions come from a regularly updated pool to deter cheating. Do not be surprised if the questions you get are quite different to someone else's experience.

Good Luck!

Do not discuss the contents of the exam or attempt to reveal specific exam questions to anyone else. By taking the exam, you are bound by CompTIA's confidentiality agreement.

After the Exam

- A score report will be generated and a copy printed for you by the test administrator.

- The score report will show whether you have passed or failed and your score in each section. Make sure you retain the report!
- 5 days after passing the exam, go to www.comptia.org/careerid and create an account (or log on to an existing account) using the information in your score report. You can use this site to order your certificate and ID card.
- If 6 weeks have passed after taking your exam and you haven't received a copy of your certificate, contact questions@comptia.org.
- You can use your Career ID to track your certification progress on CompTIA's website order duplicate certificates, and download certification logos in various image file formats.

Retaking the Test

If you do fail the certification test at the first attempt, then you can retake it at your convenience. However, should you fail the test at the second, third, or subsequent try, you will not be able to retake the exam for at least 30 days after your last attempt. Study your score report to see which areas of the exam you were weak on.

CompTIA Continuing Education Program

When you achieve your certification, it will remain valid for 3 years. The certification can either be renewed by taking the next exam iteration or by joining the **CompTIA Continuing Education Program** and earning the relevant credits. For more information, visit https://certification.comptia.org/continuing-education.

Answers for Review Questions / Module 1 / Unit 1 / Servers and Racks

1) Load balancing - distributing requests between multiple components.
2) Better density (fitting more servers into the same space).
3) The midplane.
4) 1U (1.75").
5) Check cables will run between devices that need to be connected. Position heavier devices lower in the rack. Check pull-out trays do not cause tipping and add ballast if necessary. Put servers controlled by KVM in a logical order.
6) Place the object where it will not topple and watch out for pinch points where you might hurt your fingers.

Answers for Review Questions / Module 1 / Unit 2 / Storage Devices

1) False - they are different hard drive form factors (3.5" versus 2.5"). SSDs (Solid State Drives) are the alternative to HDDs.
2) Seek time and rotational latency. These are reduced by spinning the disks faster (rpm).
3) Through a backplane (the drive "mates" to a port on the backplane without requiring cabling).
4) SAS. Ultra320 is a type of parallel SCSI and is no longer used for hard disks (legacy servers may use it though and it is still an option for provisioning tape drives).
5) Ensure all devices use a compatible SCSI standard and signaling type, set termination correctly, and configure each device with a unique SCSI ID.
6) True, though an SAS device cannot be connected to an SATA port.
7) Each write operation degrades the memory circuitry slightly. This is mitigated by wear leveling routines to avoid over-using any single location.
8) SSDs should offer the best performance.

Answers for Review Questions / Module 1 / Unit 3 / RAID

1) Read versus write operations and sequential versus transactional access patterns.
2) RAID 1 (and often RAID 10 too). Remember that RAID 0 is not fault tolerant.
3) One that has suffered disk failure that has not broken the redundancy of the volume (typically a single disk failure).
4) Battery-backed cache.
5) Just a Bunch of Disks spans multiple disks but doesn't use striping, mirroring, or parity to improve performance or provide fault tolerance.
6) 600 GB - (7-2)*120.

Answers for Review Questions / Module 1 / Unit 4 / System Setup

1) Basic Input Output System (BIOS) and Unified Extensible Firmware Interface (UEFI)
2) Configure BIOS compatibility mode (and disable Secure Boot).
3) Using the server's System Setup firmware (Boot Device Order).
4) Ensure that the server is connected to a working Uninterruptible Power Supply (UPS) to mitigate against the risk of power loss during the upgrade.
5) A server with UEFI firmware rather than BIOS. UEFI supports a new partition table format (GPT) allowing for partitions larger than the 2.2 TB limit in MBR.
6) GRUB or LILO.
7) ZFS (VMFS also supports snapshots but is proprietary to VMware and not generally available for use as a generic *nix file system).

Answers for Review Questions / Module 1 / Unit 5 / Server Operating Systems

1) Specify server hardware and software, identify how it will be integrated into the network, and make a management plan.
2) A test program to ensure that a new server (or server upgrade) can be made operational without risking damage or disruption to network services or data.
3) A command-line operated Server Core installation option and a stand-alone Hyper-V Server virtualization platform.
4) A Linux server running web (Apache), database (MySQL), and application (PHP) environments.
5) That the hardware vendor has met the software vendor's standards (in terms of performance, stability, driver compatibility, and so on).
6) Some sort of network boot mechanism (PXE for instance) to connect to the installation files on a network share plus an answer file or script to configure installation settings.
7) A Windows image needs to be sysprepped to set a unique SID (and configure other unique settings from an answer file). A Linux image might just need a script to configure a unique host name and network settings.
8) False - you can obtain a performance benefit by hosting the pagefile on a different drive or drive controller to the OS. Putting multiple pagefiles in different partitions on the same disk will not improve performance (it may even reduce performance).

Answers for Review Questions / Module 1 / Unit 6 / Troubleshooting Procedures

1) Performing root cause analysis.
2) Questioning users and stakeholders, identifying what might have changed, collecting information from documentation and logs, attempting to replicate the problem, and performing a backup.
3) Take the system "back to base" by reducing it to a minimal configuration and adding components back until the problem is revealed.
4) To detect the underlying cause of a problem and prevent its recurrence.

Answers for Review Questions / Module 2 / Unit 1 / Ethernet

1) Gigabit Ethernet over twisted pair copper wire.
2) True.
3) RJ-45 is designed for the 4-pair cable used in data networks. RJ-11 is for 2-pair cable used in voice / modem cabling.
4) It suffers less attenuation (and therefore longer range) and is immune to EMI and eavesdropping.
5) Media Access Control is a unique identifier coded into every network adapter.
6) That it supports the correct speed (for example, Fast or Gigabit) and connector (for example, RJ-45 or fiber optic).
7) Use bonded Gigabit NICs.
8) Substitute with a known good cable.

Answers for Review Questions / Module 2 / Unit 2 / Internet Protocol

1) An IP address is a 32-bit number expressed as four octets (bytes). A byte can be expressed as the decimal values 0 - 255 and these are used to represent the IP address, with dots between each decimal number. This scheme is easier for people to read than a binary number and reduces configuration errors.
2) Class C. Note that this is an informal designation and does not mean a classful addressing scheme is in place.
3) It is a private address and cannot be reached directly over the Internet. The host must use a router with address translation or a proxy service to communicate on the Internet.
4) False - the router must be on the local network for the host to be able to reach it. It is the router's job to send packets on to remote networks.
5) Automatically allocates a TCP/IP configuration (IP address, subnet mask, default gateway, and DNS servers) to hosts when they join the network.
6) False.
7) ipconfig /renew
8) ifconfig.
9) You could test the server's IP configuration, specifically the default gateway or name resolution or you could check that the cable is good.
10) A failure message (typically "Request timed out").

Answers for Review Questions / Module 2 / Unit 3 / Routers and Firewalls

1) A list of known routes to other hosts and networks.
2) Network Address Translation - a router can map private network IP addresses onto a public IP address. Private addressing keeps the local network more secure and reduces the demand for unique IP addresses.
3) tracert.
4) The source host knows the route to the destination but the target is not online or not able to route back to the source.
5) True.
6) Transmission Control Protocol (TCP).
7) True - UDP carries less overhead so is better suited to playing media files where small glitches due to lost packets are less of a problem than the whole video freezing.
8) 21 (TCP).
9) Either using two firewalls (external and internal) as a screened subnet or using a triple-homed firewall (one with three network interfaces).
10) The servers are in different VLANs.
11) A VLAN that is not routable to the rest of the network. This might be used to prevent the attachment of unauthorized devices to unused ports.

Answers for Review Questions / Module 2 / Unit 4 / Network Services

1) The IP address of a DNS server on the local network or network reachable by the client.
2) Add a static IP:name mapping to the local server's HOSTS file.
3) Mail eXchanger - the address of a mail server for the domain.
4) A cache-only or forwarding server.
5) False.
6) Scope (range of IP addresses), subnet mask, lease period, other optional information (such as default gateway or DNS).
7) Network Time Protocol - synchronize systems to the same date and time. This is critical for many functions, especially authentication and directory services.

Answers for Review Questions / Module 2 / Unit 5 / Virtualization Services

1) Type 1.
2) You could not install 64-bit guest OS's.
3) Video / graphics adapter processsing.
4) Configure the virtual disks as dynamically expanding.
5) Check the System Setup program to ensure that AMD-V is enabled.
6) Virtual Desktop Infrastructure.
7) Taking servers that are currently running on multiple physical server computers and installing them as virtual servers on a single machine.

Answers for Review Questions / Module 3 / Unit 1 / Configuring Server Roles

1) Make sure that the repositories configured in the package manager are trustworthy. You can also verify file integrity using MD5 checksums.
2) The server does not store any information about a client or its requests.
3) Java 2 Platform Enterprise Edition (J2EE).
4) Apache and nginx.
5) Limiting the number of simultaneous connections allowed to a web or FTP server.
6) All sorts! The main areas of interest are records of site traffic (numbers, regions, browser types, and so on), search engine requests (keywords that bring people to your site), and error records (such as broken links).
7) Either TCP port 110 or TCP port 143 depending on whether the mail access protocol in use was POP or IMAP. Note that port 25 (SMTP) is used to send mail between servers, not to access messages stored on a server.

Answers for Review Questions / Module 3 / Unit 2 / Storage Devices

1) NAS servers provide file-level access to storage using file sharing protocols (such as CIFS / Samba or NFS) while SANs provide block-level access to storage devices using some form of the SCSI command set (Fiber Channel or iSCSI).
2) Logical Unit Number (LUN).
3) iSCSI can use ordinary Ethernet NICs and switches while FC requires dedicated hardware.
4) The World Wide Names (WWN) or WorldWide Port Names (WWPN) of the nodes permitted to access the LUN. A WWN identifies a host bus adapter while a WWPN identifies a particular port on the HBA.
5) Linear Tape-Open (LTO) / Ultrium.
6) False - the number of bytes available stays the same (with a little adjustment for formatting overheads). It is only the multiples (mega, giga, and so on) that cause calculation problems.

Answers for Review Questions / Module 3 / Unit 3 / Volume Management

1) Mapping to a drive letter or mounting the volume within a folder.
2) Use the Disk Management utility to investigate the status of the volume.
3) True - free space and utilization is shown in the top panel.
4) Check Disk (chkdsk /r)
5) The mount command.
6) Parallel SCSI.
7) fdisk.
8) Slow performance and data corruption.

Answers for Review Questions / Module 3 / Unit 4 / Directory Services

1) Lightweight Directory Access Protocol (LDAP).
2) Organizational Unit (OU).
3) False - an application server can be joined to the domain as a member server.
4) Generic account prohibition.
5) This is the system administrator account.
6) /etc/passwd.
7) sudo (the user must be included in etc/sudoers).
8) Accounts go into Global groups, which go into Domain Local groups, which get Permissions - a means of designing a robust role-based permissions system using Active Directory security groups.
9) newgrp.
10) Group Policy Objects (GPO).

Commented [AB5]: Both these are appearing as Question #7 in the excel file, but in this file, under review section, they appear as 7 and 8

Answers for Review Questions / Module 3 / Unit 5 / File and Print Services

1) net use t: \\BIGJOBS\TOOLS /persistent:no
2) Full Control (or specifically the "Change Permissions" permission, which is included in Full Control).
3) False - NTFS is required to apply local permissions.
4) Read allows the user to view the contents of a file or directory. Write allows modifying or deleting an object. Execute enables a user to run an application or script.
5) Causes the file 'index.htm' to be read only for everyone except the owner, who has read/write access.
6) The server can be used to assign usage permissions and set defaults for printer properties and preferences.

Answers for Review Questions / Module 3 / Unit 6 / Troubleshooting Software

1) CPU, memory, disk, and network.
2) Add more memory.
3) Task Manager and Resource Monitor.
4) df.
5) Critical and Error type events.
6) top.
7) A background process running at that time, such as backup or virus scan.
8) Excessive disk I/O causing buffer overflows.

Answers for Review Questions / Module 4 / Unit 1 / Server Hardware

1) Stepping is the manufacturing build of a CPU. Processors in a multiprocessor system must be identical, so CPUs of the same stepping are required (unless the vendor's documentation indicates otherwise).
2) True - for example, an NOS would identify a dual-core HT chip as four separate CPUs.
3) Update the OS to recognize that the system is now multiprocessor.
4) This is true (so long as the RAM speed is equal to or greater than the system clock speed). However, it can cause system instability, so is not the best upgrade decision for a mission-critical system.
5) No.
6) No - the motherboard would need replacing.
7) The memory controller will have a maximum possible electrical load, equating to a maximum number of supported ranks. If quad- or dual-rank memory is used the limit might be reached before the slots are filled.
8) PCI uses parallel communications on a shared bus. PCI Express implements point-to-point, serial links between two devices or a device and the controller.
9) In a low-profile system the case may not be large enough for the expansion card to be installed vertically. A riser card means it can be installed horizontally.
10) No, PCIe cards are not physically compatible with PCI slots.

Answers for Review Questions / Module 4 / Unit 2 / Environment and Maintenance

1) This is most likely to be a UID to help identify the server picked for some maintenance task out of the others in the rack.
2) shutdown -r now
3) The button may be locked through hardware or software to prevent unauthorized shutdowns.
4) Thermal Design Power (TDP).
5) Hot aisle / cold aisle (avoiding the contamination of HVAC-cooled air by the air warmed in the servers).
6) Allow a 3 foot service gap behind each rack (for access and cooling). Install racks back-to-back not back-to-front for optimum cooling.

Answers for Review Questions / Module 4 / Unit 3 / Power Distribution

1) Multiply by the power factor.
2) The primary function of a UPS is to provide battery power to replace the loss of mains power (brownout or blackout). However, most UPS also have line conditioner circuits to mitigate against surges and spikes too. A UPS can only provide temporary power during a blackout (often only a few minutes).
3) Traditionally, a UPS uses a serial port but most units can now use USB too.
4) Line interactive or standby UPS.
5) Provides more power than single phase, so long as there is sufficient load (under light load, 3-phase can be less efficient). This means less cabling to deliver the same amount of power.
6) NEMA L6-30R.

Answers for Review Questions / Module 4 / Unit 4 / Server Hardware Troubleshooting

1) Minimize the risk of ElectroStatic Discharge (EDS) when handling electronic components by minimizing the potential difference between the technician and component.
2) System documentation - unless you are very familiar with the server model you need the documentation to explain how to open the chassis, locate and undo components such as drive cages, baffles, and so on.
3) Check that connectors and plug-in cards are properly seated.
4) Run the server's diagnostic test program.
5) Verify that the server is booting from the hard drive. If so, try using a recovery tool to restore the boot files or repair the drive's boot blocks.

Answers for Review Questions / Module 4 / Unit 5 / Server Management

1) Desktop Management Interface (DMI), Web Based Enterprise Management (WBEM), and Intelligent Platform Management Interface (IPMI).
2) IPMI (Intelligent Platform Management Interface).
3) False - connections are made to the VGA and PS/2 or USB ports on the server; the ports on the KVM and console adapter are RJ-45.
4) Remote Desktop.
5) Integrated Lights Out (ILO).
6) Secure Shell (SSH).

Answers for Review Questions / Module 4 / Unit 6 / Configuration Management

1) In the context of configuration management, a Move, Add, or Change (MAC) should be properly authorized and documented.
2) Type, make, model, serial number, asset ID or tag, location, user(s), value, and service information.
3) Dataflow diagram.
4) A Service Level Agreement is a commitment to provide a certain level of service to customers. The upgrade work needs to be planned carefully to ensure it does not breach SLAs.
5) False - passwords should not generally be written down. If they must be shared it should be through a secure password management system.
6) Response time and Mean Time to Repair (MTTR).
7) As the patch must be installed the best option is to notify the client and perform an impact analysis to identify the best time to schedule maintenance.

Answers for Review Questions / Module 5 / Unit 1 / Site Security

1) Defense in depth - layers of different countermeasures delay attacks and mitigate against failures or misconfiguration of one particular control.
2) False - computer equipment may be stolen for its commercial value. The thief may not even realize the value of data stored on a device. You need to consider different motivations to design effective security systems.
3) A turnstile or mantrap.
4) False - the only object is cost.
5) An RFID tag.
6) ABC Dry Powder or Carbon Dioxide can both be used against fires where there may be live electrical systems but CO2 is much less likely to damage computers. Portable "clean agent" extinguishers are also available, though at much higher cost.

Answers for Review Questions / Module 5 / Unit 2 / Remote Access Services

1) Certificate Authority (CA).
2) True.
3) Host-to-site, site-to-site, and host-to-host.
4) IPsec (IP Security).
5) Secure Sockets Layer (SSL) / Transport Layer Security (TLS).

Answers for Review Questions / Module 5 / Unit 3 / Server Hardening

1) Establish a configuration baseline identifying the necessary services and ports that should be open and running and software that should be installed and disable or uninstall everything else. Make sure that OS and application patches and drivers are kept up-to-date. Configure security software and access permissions / privileges appropriately.
2) Prevent a server from being turned on over the network without authorization.
3) Windows Server Update Services is a Windows service for managing product update deployment.
4) rpm (RedHat), apt-get (Debian), and yum (Fedora).
5) Most likely to be a driver issue.
6) Security software (anti-malware) updates are often issued frequently and should have the least impact on system reliability, though problems can occur.

Answers for Review Questions / Module 5 / Unit 4 / Security Software

1) Privilege escalation.
2) Firstly, to identify unknown processes and secondly, to identify excessive resource utilization.
3) SHA-1 (Secure Hash Algorithm) can be used to generate a file checksum. If a downloaded file does not match the checksum of the source file, its integrity should be suspected.
4) Configure the software to update with the latest definitions and scan engines automatically, configure it to scan on-access, prevent users from disabling it, and only use administrative accounts for designated management tasks (not for general browsing etc).
5) Intrusion Detection System (IDS). You might also mention Unified Threat Management (UTM) and some types of firewall perform IDS-type functions.
6) Network Access Control (NAC).

Answers for Review Questions / Module 5 / Unit 5 / Disaster Recovery

1) A Business Impact Analysis / Assessment identifies critical functions and assets and threats and the level of risk to which the business is exposed.
2) Likelihood and impact.
3) Full-scale exercises can identify mistakes in the plan that might not be apparent when drafting procedures. It also helps to familiarize staff with the plan.
4) While definitions vary, this is typically true of cold sites only. Warm sites have existing processing capability but not the latest data set, as hot sites would have.
5) Multiple cable paths, NIC teaming, and routers provide fault tolerance for the network infrastructure. Server clusters provide fault tolerant services.
6) Active / Passive.
7) The backup site could be affected by the same disaster as the main site.

Answers for Review Questions / Module 5 / Unit 6 / Backup

1) Normal / copy and selective backups.
2) Recovery Point Objective - the maximum permissible time in which data can be lost (a day, an hour, 15 minutes, and so on).
3) Backup software can work on a copy of an open file or database, avoiding file locking problems. Snapshots also allow for multiple versions of a file to be made available to users.
4) A backup that can be applied directly to computer hardware. For example, the restore operation would not require an OS to be installed first.
5) It preserves backup copies at different points in time.

This page left blank intentionally.

Glossary

10/100/1000BASE-T
Specifications for Ethernet running over twisted pair cable at 10/100/1000 Mbps.

32-bit versus 64-bit
Processing modes referring to the size of each instruction processed by the CPU. 32-bit CPUs replaced earlier 16-bit CPUs and were used through the 1990s to the present day, though most CPUs now work in 64-bit mode. The main 64-bit platform is called AMD64 or EM64T (by Intel). This platform is supported by 64-bit versions of Windows as well as various Linux distributions. Software can be compiled as 32-bit or 64-bit. 64-bit CPUs can run most 32-bit software but a 32-bit CPU cannot execute 64-bit software.

802.1X
802.1X (or EAP [Extensible Authentication Protocol]) is an authentication standard, developed to allow remote, wireless, and wired authentication to be centrally managed. A client device such as an access point passes authentication information to a RADIUS server on the wired network for validation. The authentication information could be a user name and password or could employ smart cards or tokens.

8mm Tape Backup
8mm (¼") data tape storage systems appear similar to the tape cartridges used by many video cameras, although the media is higher quality.

AAA
Authentication, Authorization, and Accounting - the principal stages of security control. A resource should be protected by all three types of control.

AC (Alternating Current)
When electricity is produced by a generator at the power station, the rotational movement of the magnetic coils causes the current produced to oscillate like a sine wave (it is said to alternate). Computers require direct current (at a constant voltage). A transformer is used to convert AC from the power outlet into the 3.3, 5, and 12VDC supply required by the computer.

Access Control
Creating one or more barriers around a resource such that only authenticated users can gain access. Each resource has an Access Control List (ACL) specifying what users can do. Resources often have different access levels (for example, being able to read a file or being able to read and edit it).

Access Time
Access time is the speed at which memory or a disk drive can be addressed and utilized (opened, read from, or written to).

Account Policies
A set of rules governing user security information, such as password expiration and uniqueness, which can be set globally.

Active Directory
The database that contains the users, groups, and computer accounts in a Windows Server domain.

Active Partition
The primary partition marked as active; there is only one per system. This becomes the bootable partition. In Microsoft terminology, the partition that the computer boots from is referred to as the system partition.

Adapter Card
Circuit board providing additional functionality to the computer system (video, sound, networking, modem, and so on). An adapter card fits a slot on the PC's expansion bus and often provides ports through slots cut into the back of the PC case. Different cards are designed for different slots (PCI or PCIe).

Adapter Teaming
Adapter teaming allows two or more NICs to function as one logical interface, providing load balancing and fault tolerance

Addressing (Network)
In order to communicate on a network, each host must have an address. Different protocols use different methods of addressing. For example, IPv4 uses a 32-bit binary number, typically expressed as a 4-part decimal number (dotted decimal notation) while IPv6 uses a 128-bit binary number expressed in hexadecimal. A routable addressing scheme such as IP also provides identification for distinct networks as well as hosts.

AMD (Advanced Micro Devices)
CPU manufacturer providing healthy competition for Intel. AMD chips such as the K6, Athlon 64, and Opteron have been very popular with computer manufacturers and have often out-performed their Intel equivalents.

Anti-virus
Software capable of detecting and removing virus infections and (in most cases) other types of malware, such as worms, Trojans, rootkits, adware, spyware, password crackers, network mappers, DoS tools, and so on. Anti-virus software works on the basis of both identifying malware code (signatures) and detecting suspicious behavior (heuristics). Anti-virus software must be kept up-to-date with the latest malware definitions and protect itself against tampering.

APIPA (Automatic Private IP Addressing)
A computer with TCP/IP installed will usually be configured to attempt to locate an IP address from a DHCP server. If no server responds, the computer may use APIPA to choose an IP address in the range 169.254.x.y.

Application Server
Any server making a software application available to clients. Applications are developed on different models (dedicated, distributed, and peer-to-peer). There are various frameworks for application development, notably Sun's J2EE (Java) and Microsoft's .NET platform

ARP (Address Resolution Protocol)
When two systems communicate using TCP/IP, an IP address is used to identify the destination machine. The IP address must be mapped to a device (the network adapter's MAC address). ARP performs the task of resolving an IP address to a hardware address.

Auditing
Windows and other operating systems provide the ability to track system and file access and usage and report this activity to a log file. The administrator can use this trail to track appropriate (or inappropriate) access of resources.

Authentication
A means for a user to prove their identity to a computer system. Authentication is implemented as either something you know (a user name and password), something you have (a smart card or key fob), or something you are (biometric information). Often, more than one method is employed (2-factor authentication).

Backplane
In a backplane, rather than using cabled connectors, the drives plug (or "mate") into a combined data and power connector on the enclosure. This means that drives can be easily added and removed from the front of the case without having to open the chassis. On some blade enclosures, two circuit boards are used, with the backplane hosting power circuitry and the midplane data interconnections.

Backup
Recovery of data can be provided through the use of a backup system. Most backup systems provide support for tape devices. This provides a reasonably reliable and quick mechanism for copying critical data. Different backup types (full, incremental, or differential) balance media capacity, time required to backup, and time required to restore.

Bandwidth
Generally used to refer to the amount of data that can be transferred through a connection over a given period. Bandwidth more properly means the range of frequencies supported by transmission media, measured in Hertz.

Basic Storage
Any disk that has not been converted to dynamic storage is referred to as a basic disk.

BCD (Boot Configuration Data)
Windows stores information about operating systems installed on the computer in a boot configuration data store, located in \boot\bcd on the system partition. The BCD can be modified using the bcedit command-line tool or msconfig.

Beep Codes
During the series of Power-On Self-Test (POST) diagnostics that are performed during startup, errors in hardware or the ROM data can be brought to the attention of the user by beep noises. Each beep code is able to draw attention to a particular fault with the hardware. It was once customary for a computer to beep once to indicate that POST has been successful, though most modern computers boot silently.

Biometric
Identifying features stored as digital data can be used to authenticate a user. Typical features used include facial pattern, iris, retina, or fingerprint pattern, and signature recognition. This requires the relevant scanning device, such as a fingerprint reader, and a database of biometric information (template).

BIOS (Basic Input / Output System)
The BIOS is firmware that contains programs and information relating to the basic operation of PC components such as drives, keyboard, video display, and ports. It also contains specific routines to allow set-up configuration to be viewed and edited and it contains the self-diagnostic Power-On Self-Test (POST) program used to detect fundamental faults in PC components. BIOS can also be used to secure components not protected by the OS by specifying a supervisor password (to prevent tampering with BIOS settings) and a user password (to boot the PC).

BitLocker
Feature of Windows allowing for encryption of disks and partitions. The encryption key can be stored in a TPM chip on the computer or on a USB drive.

Blade Server
A thin server form factor designed to optimize density (the amount of space taken up in a rack). Blades are connected in an enclosure, which provides a common power, cooling, and interconnect solution

Blue Screen (or Blue Screen of Death [BSoD])
This indicates an error from which a Windows system cannot recover (also called a stop error). Blue screens are usually caused by bad driver software or hardware faults (memory or disk).

Boot Partition
In Microsoft terminology, the partition that contains the operating system (that is, the \WINDOWS folder) is referred to as the boot partition. This is typically a different partition to the system partition (the partition containing the boot files).

bootrec
Windows command in Windows allowing for the repair (or attempted repair) of the boot manager and boot loader.

Bridge
A bridge can be used to divide an overloaded network into separate segments. Intrasegment traffic (traffic between devices on the same segment) remains within this segment and cannot affect the other segments. Segments on either side of a bridge are in separate collision domains but the same broadcast domain. The function of Ethernet bridges is now typically performed by switches.

Brownout
A brownout occurs when the power that is supplied by the electrical wall socket is insufficient to allow the computer to function correctly. Brownouts are long sags in power output that are often caused by overloaded or faulty mains distribution circuits or by a failure in the supply route from electrical power station to a building.

BTU (British Thermal Unit)
A measure of heat energy generated by equipment. 1 watt is 3.41 BTU.

Bus
Buses are the connections between components on the motherboard and peripheral devices attached to the computer. Buses are available in industry standard formats, each with its own advantages and disadvantages. The standard functions of a bus are to provide data sharing, memory addressing, power supply, and timing. Common bus types include PCI, PCI Express, ExpressCard, and USB.

Cache
Caching is a technique used for maintaining consistent performance during file access and data processing. It generally works where components are mismatched in terms of the speed at which they can operate. Caching allows a slow component to store data it cannot process at that moment (a disk drive storing up write instructions for instance) or a fast component to pre-fetch data that it might need soon (a CPU storing instructions from system memory for re-use for example).

Cat Cable Standards
Twisted pair cabling is rated by the ANSI/TIA/EIA "cat" standards for different Ethernet applications. Cat3 is rated for 10 Mbps applications at up to 100m, Cat5 for 100 Mbps and Cat5e and Cat6 for 1 Gbps. Cat6 and Cat6a are also rated for 10 Gbps at 55m and 100m respectively.

CHAP (Challenge Handshake Authentication Protocol)
Authentication scheme developed for dial-up networks that uses an encrypted three-way handshake to authenticate the client to the server. The challenge-response is repeated throughout the connection (though transparently to the user) to guard against replay attacks.

chkdsk
A program that verifies the integrity of a disk's file system.

CIA
Confidentiality, Integrity, and Availability - the goals for providing a secure information management system.

CIDR (Classless Interdomain Routing)
Using network prefixes for network identification ("supernetting"). This replaced the old method of assigning class-based IP addresses based on the network size.

Classful Addressing
In the early days of IP addressing, the network ID was determined automatically from the first octet of the address. When subnet masks were introduced, the "default" masks (255.0.0.0, 255.0.0, and 255.255.255.0) that corresponded to treating the first octet as classful were commonly described as "class A", "class B", and "class C" masks. The Internet no longer uses classful addressing but many LANs use the private IP address ranges and the default masks.

Cluster (Allocation Unit)
As reading and writing data directly to 512 byte sectors is inefficient, they are grouped in clusters of 2, 4, 6, 8... The drawback is that if a file does not completely fill a cluster (if a cluster is equivalent to 4 KB and the file is 512 bytes for instance), some of the cluster is wasted. Thus, the smaller the cluster size, the lower the data overhead in terms of wasted space but larger clusters may deliver better performance.

Compression
Reducing the amount of space that a file takes up on disk using various algorithms to describe it more efficiently. File storage compression uses lossless techniques. NTFS-formatted drives can compress files automatically while ZIP compression adds files to a compressed archive. Lossy compression, such as that used by JPEG and MPEG image and video formats, discards some information in the file more or less aggressively, allowing for a trade-off between picture quality and file size.

Cooling Device
A CPU generates a large amount of heat that must be dissipated to prevent damage to the chip. Generally, a CPU will be fitted with a heatsink (a metal block with fins) and fan. Thermal compound is used at the contact point between the chip and the heatsink to ensure good heat transfer. The PSU also incorporates a fan to expel warm air from the system. Modern motherboards have temperature sensors that provide warning of overheating before damage can occur. Very high performance or overclocked systems or systems designed for quiet operation may require more sophisticated cooling systems, such as liquid cooling. Cooling systems that work without electricity are described as passive; those requiring a power source are classed as active.

CPU (Central Processing Unit)
The principal microprocessor in a computer or smartphone responsible for running operating system and applications software.

CRU (Customer Replaceable Unit)
A system component that a systems vendor may require the customer to self-install (or charge for installation, depending on the terms of the warranty contract).

DAT (Digital Audio Tape)
Digital audio tapes can be used as a high-capacity storage medium for PC data storage. DAT data tapes are similar in appearance and size to the DAT audio tapes produced by Sony. Data tapes all conform to Digital Data Storage standards and can support up to 36 GB (uncompressed), although the different formats are occasionally incompatible.

Database Server
Databases are demanding applications that require large processing and storage capacity. Major database server products include Oracle, Microsoft SQL Server, IBM's DB2 and Informix, and Sybase. Many databases are operated using Structured Query Language (SQL, pronounced "sequel"). The freeware MySQL database is a popular choice to provide database functionality on websites.

Daughter Board
A circuit board that connects to the motherboard to provide extra expansion slots or connectors. Typically these are used in slimline case designs so that adapter cards can be installed parallel to the motherboard, reducing the height of the case.

DC (Direct Current)
PCs and most computer components function by using power supplied in the form of direct current. This is normally at low voltage and is produced by stepping down the voltage from the mains supply. Direct current, unlike alternating current, does not oscillate between positive and negative states.

DDR SDRAM (Double Data Rate SDRAM)
Standard for SDRAM where data is transferred twice per clock cycle (making the maximum data rate 64x the bus speed in bps). DDR2/DDR3 SDRAM uses lower voltage chips and higher bus speeds.

Default Gateway
The default gateway is a TCP/IP address parameter that identifies the location of a router on the local subnet that the host can use to contact other networks.

Defragment
Fragmentation occurs when a data file is not saved to contiguous sectors on a disk. This decreases performance by making the disk read/write heads move between fragments. Defragmentation is a software routine that compacts files back into contiguous areas of the disk.

Device Driver
A small piece of code that is loaded during the boot sequence of an operating system. This code, usually provided by the hardware vendor, provides access to a device, or hardware, from the OS kernel. Under Windows, a signing system is in place for drivers to ensure that they do not make the OS unstable.

DFS (Distributed File System)
Windows Server technology allowing shares located on different computers to be accessible to users from a single "virtual" file system.

DHCP (Dynamic Host Configuration Protocol) Server
A service that provides dynamic allocation of IP addresses to appropriately configured clients.

Digital Certificate
An X.509 digital certificate is issued by a Certificate Authority (CA) as a guarantee that a public key it has issued to an organization to encrypt messages sent to it genuinely belongs to that organization. Both parties must trust the CA. The public key can be used to encrypt messages but not to decrypt them. A message can only be decrypted by the private key, which is mathematically linked to the public key but not derivable from it. This is referred to as asymmetric encryption. Part of the CA's responsibility is ensuring that this private key is known only to the organization owning the certificate. This arrangement is referred to a Public Key Infrastructure (PKI).

DIMM (Dual Inline Memory Module)
Dual in-line memory modules are the standard packaging for system memory. There are different pin configurations for different RAM types (SDRAM [168], DDR SDRAM [184], and DDR2/3 SDRAM [240]).

Directory
A file system object used to organize files. Directories can be created on any drive (the directory for the drive itself is called the root) and within other directories (subdirectory). Different file systems put limits on the number of files or directories that can be created on the root or the number of subdirectory levels. In Windows, directories are usually referred to as folders.

Disaster Recovery
Contingency planning to provide for speedy resumption of services and data after a critical event (business continuity). Disaster recovery also aims to prevent services from being affected in the first place by providing for fault tolerance/redundancy. Elements of a disaster recovery plan will include backup systems, spares (redundant components and devices that can be switched over to operation), and sites (a different location to which business activities can be switched over). Spares and sites can be maintained at different levels of readiness (referred to as hot, warm, and cold).

diskpart
Command-line utility used to configure disk partitions.

DLT (Digital Linear Tape)
DLT is a high-end backup system used for both mini-computers and large servers. DLT systems are very fast and have high data transfer rates and capacity. A similar format is Ultrium-brand cartridges, using the Linear Tape Open (LTO) standard.

DMZ (Demilitarized Zone)
An enterprise DMZ is an Internet-facing zone that is not trusted by hosts on the private network. An enterprise DMZ is implemented using either two firewalls (screened subnet) or a single three-legged firewall (one with three network ports). In some SOHO router documentation, a DMZ is used to mean hosts or ports not protected by the firewall (completely open to other Internet hosts).

DNS (Domain Name System)
This industry standard name resolution system provides name to IP address mapping services on the Internet and large intranets.

Domain
A group of computers which share a common accounts database, referred to as the directory.

Domain Controller
Any Windows-based server that provides domain authentication services (logon services) is referred to as a domain controller (DC). Domain controllers maintain a master copy of the database of network resources.

DoS (Denial of Service)
A network attack that aims to disrupt a service, usually by overloading it. A Distributed DoS (DDoS) attack uses multiple compromised computers (a "botnet" of "zombies") to launch the attack.

DRAM (Dynamic RAM)
Dynamic RAM is a type of volatile memory that stores data in the form of electronic charges within transistors. Due to the effects of leakage and the subsequent loss of electrical charge, DRAM has to be refreshed at regular intervals and requires a constant power source. Standard DRAM is the lowest common denominator of the DRAM types. Modern PCs use a Synchronous DRAM (SDRAM) derivative to store data (currently DDR2/3 SDRAM).

Dynamic Storage
Business / professional versions of Windows and Windows Server allow disks to be configured as dynamic. Volumes on dynamic disks can be configured to span multiple disks and can be shrunk and expanded, unlike partitions on basic disks (though the boot and system volumes cannot be modified).

EAP (Extensible Authentication Protocol)
Designed to support different types of authentication. EAP defines a framework for negotiating authentication mechanisms rather than the details of the mechanisms themselves. EAP implementations can include smart cards, one-time passwords, biometric scanning, or simpler user name and password combinations.

ECC (Error Checking and Correcting [or Error Correcting Code])
System memory (RAM) with built-in error correction security. It is more expensive than normal memory and requires motherboard support. It is typically only used in servers.

EFS (Encrypting File System)
Under NTFS, files and folders can be encrypted to ensure privacy of the data. Only the user who encrypted the file can subsequently open it.

Email
An electronic store and forward messaging system. Email supports text messages and binary file attachments. For Internet email, an SMTP (Simple Mail Transfer Protocol) server is used to forward mail to a host. A mail client then uses either POP3 (Post Office Protocol) or IMAP (Internet Mail Access Protocol) to access the mailbox on the server and download messages.

Encryption
Scrambling the characters used in a message so that the message can be seen but not understood or modified unless it can be deciphered. Encryption provides for a secure means of transmitting data and authenticating users. It is also used to store data securely. Encryption systems allow for different levels of security (128-bit encryption is currently considered secure).

ESD (Electrostatic Discharge)
Metal and plastic objects can become charged if they are in close proximity to electrical sources or if they are brushed against. When this happens, a charge builds up on the surface. This can discharge if a potential difference is formed between the charged object and an oppositely charged conductive object. This electrical discharge, which often occurs at pointed regions of the object, can damage silicon chips and computer components if they are exposed to it. Care should be taken when working on exposed computer components so that they do not become damaged, or that you do not experience static shocks.

Ethernet
Popular Local Area Networking technology defining media access and signaling methods. Ethernet has been developed for use with coax (thicknet [10BASE-5] and thinnet [10BASE-T]), UTP cable (10BASE-TX, 100BASE-TX, 1000BASE-T, and 1000BASE-TX), and fiber optic (10BASE-F, 100BASE-FX, 1000BASE-X, and 10G standards). Wireless devices can also connect to Ethernet networks via a Wireless Access Point.

Extranet
A network that provides distributed, authenticated access to resources. Generally, this refers to allowing secure access to a private network from outside the network or connecting several private networks securely

FAT (File Allocation Table)
When a disk is formatted using the FAT or FAT32 file system a File Allocation Table (FAT) is written in a particular track or sector. The FAT contains information relating to the position of file data chunks on the disk; data is not always written to one area of the disk but may be spread over several tracks. The original 16-bit version (FAT16, but often simply called FAT) was replaced by a 32-bit version that is almost universally supported by different operating systems and devices. A 64-bit version (exFAT) was introduced with Windows 7 and is also supported by XP SP3 and Vista SP1 and some versions of Linux and OS X.

Fault Tolerance (Redundancy)
Protection against system failure by providing extra (redundant) capacity. Generally, fault tolerant systems identify and eliminate single points of failure. For example, data can be made fault tolerant by implementing redundant disks (RAID); a UPS provides for emergency power.

FCIP (Fibre Channel over IP)
Fibre Channel over IP is a tunneling protocol allowing the transfer of frames of FC data over any IP-based network, such as the Internet. This is a cost-effective way to link SANs in different geographic locations.

Fiber Optic Cable
Fiber optic cable employs light signals as the basis for data transmission as opposed to the electrical signals that are used by the other main cable types. The light pulses travel down the glass core of the fiber (known as the waveguide). The cladding that surrounds this core reflects light back to ensure transmission efficiency. Two main categories of fiber are available; multi-mode, which uses cheaper, shorter wavelength LEDs or VCSEL diodes, or single-mode, which uses more expensive longer wavelength laser diodes. At the receiving end of the cable, light-sensitive diodes re-convert the light pulse into an electrical signal.

Fibre Channel Hardware
A combination of networking technology and the SCSI command set as an implementation of a Storage Area Network (SAN). Depending on the media used, an FC bus can be up to 6 miles (10K) long and support 1, 2, 4, or 10 Gbps maximum data rates. The bus can be implemented in point-to-point, loop, or switched topologies.

File Server
In file server based networks, a central machine(s) provides dedicated file and print services to workstations. Benefits of server-based networks include ease of administration through centralization.

File System
When data is stored on a disk, it is located on that medium in a particular, standardized format. This allows the drive and the computer to be able to extract the information from the disk using similar functions and thus data can be accessed in a predictable manner. Examples of file systems include FAT16, FAT32, and NTFS (all used for hard disks), the ext and ReiserFS systems used with Linux, the UFS system used with UNIX, and CDFS (ISO 9660) and UDF (Universal Disk Format), used for optical media such as CD, DVD, and Blu-ray.

Firewall
Hardware or software that filters traffic passing into or out of a network (for example, between a private network and the Internet). A basic packet-filtering firewall works at Layers 3 and 4 (Network and Transport) of the OSI model. Packets can be filtered depending on several criteria (inbound or outbound, IP address, and port number). More advanced firewalls (proxy and stateful inspection) can examine higher layer information, to provide enhanced security.

Firewire (IEEE 1394 Standard)
Firewire is the brand name for the IEEE standard 1394. This serial SCSI bus standard supports high data rates (up to 400 Mbps) and this in turn, makes it attractive for applications requiring intensive data transfer (such as video cameras, satellite receivers, and digital media players).

Firmware
This refers to software instructions stored semi-permanently (embedded) on a hardware device (BIOS instructions stored in a ROM chip on the motherboard for instance).

Foreign Drive
A disk configured as dynamic that has been inserted into a PC under a different Windows installation.

Form Factor
The size and shape of a component, determining its compatibility. Form factor is most closely associated with PC motherboard, case, and power supply designs.

format
Command-line utility for creating a file system on a partition.

FQDN (Fully Qualified Domain Name)
A name in DNS specifying a particular host within a subdomain within a top-level domain.

FRU (Field Replaceable Unit)
An adapter or other component that can be replaced by a technician on-site. Most PC and laptop components are FRUs while the components of smartphones are not.

FTP (File Transfer Protocol)
A protocol used to transfer files across the Internet. Variants include S(ecure)FTP and T(rivial)FTP. FTP utilizes ports 20 and 21.

Full-duplex
Two-way communications taking place simultaneously.

Fuse
A circuit breaker designed to protect the device and users of the device from faulty wiring or supply of power (overcurrent protection).

Gateway
A gateway is a computer or other device that acts as a translator between two completely dissimilar computer systems. For example, a connection from a PC LAN to an IBM mainframe would require a gateway. Gateways tend to be slower than bridges or routers. The term "default gateway" is also used to denote a router on an IP network, though this is not a gateway in the sense described above.

GPT (GUID Partition Table)
Modern disk partitioning system allowing large numbers of partitions and very large partition sizes.

gpupdate / gpresult
Command-line tools to apply and analyze group policies. Group policies are a means of configuring registry settings.

Ground
An equipment ground provides a safe path for electrical current to flow away in the event that a device or cable is faulty. Self-grounding removes any static potential difference between a technician's clothes and body and a device they are handling, reducing the risk of damaging the component through Electrostatic Discharge (ESD).

Group Account
A group account is a collection of user accounts. These are useful when establishing file permissions and user rights because when many individuals need the same level of access, a group could be established containing all the relevant users. The group could then be assigned the necessary rights.

HAL (Hardware Abstraction Layer)
An OS driver that allows the operating system to run on different microprocessor architectures.

Half-duplex
Two-way communications not taking place simultaneously.

HAV (Hardware Assisted Virtualization)
Instruction set extensions (Intel VT and AMD-V) that facilitate the operation of virtual machines.

Hazard
As part of health and safety, employers must identify and mitigate workplace hazards. Employees must not cause hazards and report any hazards they detect. PC maintenance can expose a technician to a number of hazards, notably electric shock, laser light, and thermal (burns). Hazards such as heat, dust, EMI, or ESD can also affect PC operation

HBA (Host Bus Adapter)
A component allowing storage devices to exchange data with a computer system using a particular interface (PATA, SATA, SCSI, and so on). Motherboards will come with built-in host adapters and more can be added as expansion cards if necessary.

HCL (Hardware Compatibility List)
Before installing an OS, it is vital to check that all the PC components have been tested for compatibility with the OS (that they are on the Hardware Compatibility List [HCL] or Windows Logo'd Product List). Incompatible hardware may not work or may even prevent the installation from completing successfully.

HDD (Hard Disk Drive)
High capacity units typically providing persistent mass storage for a PC (saving data when the computer is turned off). Data is stored using platters with a magnetic coating that are spun under disk heads that can read and write to locations on each platter (sectors). A HDD installed within a PC is referred to as the fixed disks. HDDs are often used with enclosures as portable storage or as Network Attached Storage (NAS).

High Availability
A system that minimizes the amount of downtime experienced. Downtime can be measured as a percentage of time through the year where the system is not available because of planned or unexpected outages (conversely, uptime is the percentage of time the system is available). High availability is achieved through good quality components and providing redundant links and appliances.

Hot Swappable
A device that can be added or removed without having to restart the operating system.

HTTP (HyperText Transfer Protocol)
The protocol (HyperText Transfer Protocol) used to provide web content to browsers. HTTP uses port 80. HTTPS provides for encrypted transfers, using SSL and port 443.

Hub
An OSI layer 1 (Physical) network device used to implement a star network topology. All hosts on the network have a cabled connection to the hub, which enables communications between all connected devices.

HVAC (Heating, Ventilation, Air Conditioning)
Building control systems maintain an optimum working environment for different parts of the building. The acronym HVAC (Heating, Ventilation, Air Conditioning) is often used to describe these services. For general office areas, this basically means heating and cooling; for other areas different aspects of climate control, such as humidity may be important.

HyperThreading
Intel CPU architecture. HT exposes two or more logical processors to the OS, delivering performance benefits similar to SMP.

ICMP (Internet Control Message Protocol)
Operates at layer 3 (Network) to report errors about the delivery of TCP/IP packets.

IDS (Intrusion Detection System)
Software or security appliance designed to monitor network traffic (NIDS) or configuration files and logs on a host (HIDS) to record and detect unusual activity. Many systems can automatically take preventive action (Intrusion Prevention System [IPS]). Detection is either signature-based or anomaly-based (or both). IDS software typically requires a lengthy period of configuration and "training" to recognize baseline "normal" activity.

IEEE (Institute of Electrical and Electronics Engineers)
The Institute of Electrical and Electronics Engineers was formed as a professional body to oversee the development and registration of electronic standards. Examples of IEEE standards include the 802 protocols that describe the function and architecture of different network technologies.

IIS (Internet Information Services)
Web server product shipped with Windows.

Image
A duplicate of an operating system installation (including installed software, settings, and user data) stored on removable media. Windows makes use of image-based backups and they are also used for deploying Windows to multiple PCs rapidly.

IMAP4 (Internet Message Access Protocol)
TCP/IP application protocol providing a means for a client to access email messages stored in a mailbox on a remote server. Unlike POP3, messages persist on the server after the client has downloaded them. IMAP also supports mailbox management functions, such as creating subfolders and access to the same mailbox by more than one client at the same time. IMAP4 utilizes TCP port number 143.

Intel
Intel processors were used in the first IBM PCs and the company's CPUs and chipsets continue to dominate the PC, laptop, and server markets.

Intranet
An intranet uses the same technologies as the Internet, such as web sites, and email, but is only accessible from within a single local network.

IP Address
Each IP host must have a unique IP address. This can be manually assigned or dynamically allocated (using a DHCP server). In IPv4, the 32-bit binary address is expressed in the standard four byte, dotted decimal notation: 10.0.5.1. In IPv6, addresses are 128-bit expressed as hexadecimal (for example, 2001:db8::0bcd:abcd:ef12:1234). IPv6 provides a much larger address space, stateless autoconfiguration (greatly simplifying network administration), and replaces inefficient broadcast transmissions with multicast ones.

ipconfig
Command-line utility providing information about the IP configuration of a workstation.

IPsec
Mechanism to provide encryption between devices using TCP/IP. Can be used in local as well as remote network environments.

iSCSI
iSCSI is a tunneling protocol allowing the transfer of frames of SCSI data over any IP-based network, such as the Internet. This is a cost-effective way to implement Storage Area Networks (SAN).

JBOD (Just a Bunch Of Disks)
Configuring a spanned volume across a number of disks without any sort of RAID striping functionality.

Jumper
Jumpers were a common configuration method in the early years of the IBM PC compatible. A jumper is a conductor used to connect two pins in a particular configuration. Most devices are now jumperless.

Kerberos
Named after the mythical multi-headed guard-dog of the underworld, Kerberos is an authentication standard and protocol. Windows networks use this protocol for client and server authentication.

Kernel
All operating systems have a kernel, which is a low-level piece of code responsible for controlling the rest of the operating system. Windows uses a multiprocessor aware, pre-emptive multitasking kernel.

Key (Encryption)
An encryption cipher scrambles a message (plaintext) using an algorithm. The algorithm is given a key so that someone intercepting the message could not just reverse the algorithm to unscramble the message; they must also know the key. In symmetric encryption, the same key is used for encryption and decryption. In asymmetric encryption, different keys are used (one key is linked to but not derivable from the other key).

KVM (Keyboard Video Mouse)
KVM is a box attached to a keyboard, display, and mouse (or other pointing device). The KVM box has multiple ports (between 2 and 32) for connecting to different servers. This saves the expense and space requirements of providing separate input and output devices for each server.

L2TP (Layer 2 Tunneling Protocol)
An alternative to PPTP, providing support for VPNs. L2TP works at Layer 2 (Data Link).

LC (Lucent Connector)
Small form factor connector used with fiber optic cable.

LDAP (Lightweight Directory Access Protocol)
Used to query and update directory services, such as network objects or email address books.

Linux
An open-source operating system supported by a wide range of hardware and software vendors.

Load Balancing
A type of switch or router that distributes client requests between different resources, such as communications links or similarly-configured servers. This provides fault tolerance and improves throughput.

Logical Partition
A partition created within an extended partition to divide the disk space between logical drives, each of which can be allocated a drive letter.

Loopback Test
A loopback test is used to verify the integrity of a port. To perform the test, a signal is generated by test software and sent to a loopback plug, connected to the port. The signal passes around the bus, network, or circuit and returns back to the plug. The plug compares what was sent to what was received, to evaluate whether the signal has degraded.

LPD / LPR (Line Printer Daemon / Line Printer Remote)
Remote printing protocol and software based on RFC 1179. The print server runs the LPD (Line Printer Daemon) software. Client software uses the LPR suite of programs to send print jobs and manage the print queue.

LUN (Logical Unit Number)
A means of identifying a logical device (as distinct from the hardware device ID) when using SCSI.

MAC (Media Access Control) Address
A MAC is a unique hardware address that is hard-coded into a network card by the manufacturer. This is required for directing data frames across a network and for allowing the network card to compare destination addresses (coded into the data frame) and its own unique MAC address. A MAC address is 48 bits long with the first half representing the manufacturer's Organizationally Unique Identifier (OUI).

Mailbox
Part of a message store designed to receive emails for a particular recipient. A mailbox may be associated with more than one email address by creating aliases for the recipient.

MAPI (Message Application Programming Interface)
Windows messaging interface used primarily by the email client software Outlook to communicate with an Exchange mail server and for Exchange servers to communicate with one another.

Mapping
The term used to describe the process of establishing a connection with a file resource on a remote server - for example, mapping a network drive.

MBR (Master Boot Record)
Sector on a hard disk storing information about partitions configured on the disk.

Member Server
Any Windows-based server computer configured into a domain but not maintaining the Active Directory database (authenticating users) is referred to as a member server. Servers in a workgroup are referred to as standalone servers.

Microsoft
The world's foremost supplier of operating system and Office productivity software. Microsoft has dominated the PC market since the development of the first IBM compatible PCs running MS-DOS.

MIME (Multi-purpose Internet Mail Extensions)
A protocol that handles Internet mail format and attachments.

Mount Point
A partition or volume mapped to a folder in another file system rather than allocated a drive letter.

MSTSC (Microsoft Terminal Services Client)
The client software for Remote Desktop.

Multimeter
An electrical meter capable of measuring voltage, resistance, and current. Voltage readings can be used to determine whether, for example, a power supply unit is functioning correctly. Resistance readings can be used to determine whether a fuse or network cable is functioning correctly. Most multimeters are digital devices, capable of displaying discrete readings.

Multiprocessing
A motherboard supporting two or more CPUs. This can allow operations to be shared thereby increasing performance. Most server OSs support Symmetric Multiprocessing (SMP) though there can be licence restrictions on the number of CPUs supported.

NAS (Network Attached Storage)
NAS is a storage device with an embedded OS that supports typical network file access protocols (FTP and SMB for instance).

NAT (Network Address Translation)
Where hosts on a private network need Internet access, it is no longer practical or secure to allocate each host a unique IP address. Instead, hosts on the private network use private addressing. A router or proxy server provides Network Address Translation to map the private address to one or more publicly accessible IP addresses. As well as being easier to configure, this hides the private network addressing scheme from Internet users.

nbtstat
Utility to show NetBIOS information (when NetBIOS is running over TCP/IP).

net
Family of commands allowing configuration tasks to be performed on Windows networks. net use maps a network resource to a local drive path.

NetBEUI (NetBIOS Extended User Interface)
Simple to use protocol for early Windows networks. NetBEUI is not a routable protocol. Windows networks have used TCP/IP as the default protocol since version 2000.

NetBIOS (Network Basic Input / Output System)
A session management protocol used to provide name registration and resolution services on older Microsoft networks. WINS provides NetBIOS name resolution.

netstat
Utility to show network information on a machine running TCP/IP, notably active connections and the routing table.

Network Adapter (NIC [Network Interface Card])
The network adapter allows a physical connection between the host and the transmission media. A NIC can address other cards and can recognize data that is destined for it, using a unique address known as the Media Access Control (MAC) address. The card also performs error checking. Network cards are designed for specific types of networks and do not work on different network products. Different adapters may also support different connection speeds and connector types.

NFS (Network File System)
Remote file access protocol used principally on UNIX and Linux networks.

NOS (Network Operating System)
An operating system designed to support simultaneous access by tens, hundreds, or thousands of users. An NOS may also be bundled with servers to support common network functions, such as routing, remote access, DNS, and DHCP.

nslookup
TCP/IP utility allowing for DNS troubleshooting.

NTFS (New Technology Filing System)
The NT File System supports a 64-bit address space and is able to provide features such as file-by-file compression and RAID support as well as advanced file attribute management tools, encryption, and disk quotas.

NTP (Network Time Protocol)
TCP/IP application protocol allowing machines to synchronize to the same time clock. NTP runs over UDP port 123.

OSI (Open Systems Interconnection) Reference Model
This reference model was developed in 1977 by the ISO to aid the understanding of how a network system functions in terms of both software and hardware components. The OSI divides the actions of hardware and software into seven separate sub-tasks: Physical, Data Link, Network, Transport, Session, Presentation, and Application. The OSI model serves as a functional reference for network communication. It does not represent any individual standard although many protocols do comply with its guidelines.

OU (Organizational Unit)
A container in an LDAP-based directory schema. Might contain users, groups, or computer objects.

Packet Sniffer
Most original TCP/IP application protocols transmit data in plaintext. Ethernet-based networks can run in promiscuous mode, meaning that a host can receive all data packets, even if they are not intended for it (though this is made more difficult over switched Ethernet). Packet sniffing software exploits these two facts and means that it is simple to capture information about the network and data that is being transmitted (including passwords) unless encryption is used.

Parity
Parity provides a simple error checking system for data transmission and storage by sending a bit indicating whether the sum of other bits should be odd or even. Most systems now use more advanced error checking, such as Cyclic Redundancy Check (CRC) or Error Correcting Code (ECC).

Partition
A discrete are of storage defined on a hard disk using either the Master Boot Record (MBR) scheme or the GUID Partition Table (GPT) scheme. Each partition can be formatted with a different file system and a partition can be marked as active (made bootable).

Patch Panel
A type of wiring cross-connect with IDCs to terminate fixed cabling on one side and modular jacks to make cross-connections to other equipment on the other. Patch panels simplify Moves, Adds, and Changes (MACs) in network administration.

PCI (Peripheral Component Interconnect) Bus
The PCI bus was introduced in 1995 with the Pentium processor. It connects the CPU, memory, and peripherals to a 32-bit bus working at 33 MHz. PCI supports bus mastering, IRQ steering, and Plug-and-Play. Later versions defined 64-bit operation and 66 MHz clock but were not widely adopted on desktop PCs.

PCI Express
PCI Express (PCIe) is the latest expansion bus standard. PCI Express is serial with point-to-point connections. Each device on the bus can create a point-to-point link with the I/O controller or another device. The link comprises one or more lanes (x1, x2, x4, x8, x12, x16, or x32). Each lane supports a full-duplex transfer rate of 250 MBps (v1.0), 500 MBps (v2.0), or 1 GBps (v3.0). The standard is software compatible with PCI, allowing for motherboards with both types of connector.

PCI-X
PCI-X (PCI-eXtended) is an update of PCI to use a 64-bit bus and higher clock speeds (66, 133, 266, and 533 MHz). It is backward compatible with PCI (using the same connectors).

Performance Monitor
Tool for viewing CPU, memory, and pagefile utilization, accessible through the Performance and Reliability Monitor. You can also view statistics on the Performance tab in Task Manager.

Permissions
To access files and folders on a volume, the administrator of the computer will need to grant file permissions to the user (or a group to which the user belongs). File permissions are supported by NTFS-based Windows systems.

PGA (Pin Grid Array)
CPU socket form factor where pins are located on the bottom of the processor to fit in the matching holes in the motherboard socket. PGA-type sockets are still used by AMD but Intel have switched to Land Grid Array (LGA), where the pins are located on the socket rather than the chip.

Phase
Residential and office electricity is supplied single phase, where the voltage alternates between two values. 3-phase power supplies live current over three wires where the voltages are out-of-phase with one another, delivering a stable overall voltage. This is more efficient than single phase (depending on the load) and therefore allows for less cabling.

ping
Command-line utility for testing TCP/IP configuration.

Plenum Cable
Electrical cable (including coaxial or twisted pair) laid in plenum spaces (a void in a building designed to carry Heating, Ventilation, and Air Conditioning (HVAC) systems) must comply with stringent fire safety regulations. Plenum cable is fire-resistant, Teflon coated, and produces minimal smoke if burned.

PoE (Power over Ethernet)
Supplying power to a small device such as a VoIP handset, access point, or thin client over Ethernet cabling.

POP3 (Post Office Protocol)
TCP/IP application protocol providing a means for a client to access email messages stored in a mailbox on a remote server. The server usually deletes messages once the client has downloaded them. POP3 utilizes TCP port 110.

Port
In TCP and UDP applications, a port is a unique number assigned to a particular server application protocol (such as HTTP or SMTP) and the number assigned by a client to keep track of a session. The port numbers (with the IP address) form a socket between client and server. For security, it is important to allow only the ports required to be open (ports can be blocked using a firewall).

POST (Power-On Self-Test)
The POST procedure is a hardware checking routine built into the PC firmware. This test sequentially monitors the state of the memory chips, the processor, system clock, display, and firmware itself. Errors that occur within vital components are signified by beep codes emitted by the internal speaker of the computer. Further tests are then performed and any errors displayed as on-screen error codes and messages. Additional interpreter boards can be purchased that can supply information concerning boot failure.

PPP (Point to Point Protocol)
Dial-up protocol working at Layer 2 (Data Link) used to connect devices remotely to networks. Often used to connect to an ISP's routers and out to the Internet. PPPoE (PPP over Ethernet) or PPPoA (PPP over ATM) are used to provide broadband connections (over DSL or cable Internet for instance).

PPTP (Point to Point Tunneling Protocol)
PPTP provides the mechanisms for creating a secure PPP channel as a virtual private network. The security of PPTP contains exploitable weaknesses however. PPTP works at Layer 2 (Data Link).

Primary Partition
A partition that is primary can be marked as active, and hence made bootable.

Print Server
Windows-based machine sharing its printer with other computers. Standalone print servers (such as HP Jetdirect) are also available.

Protocol
A set of rules enabling systems to communicate (exchange data). A single network will involve the use of many different protocols. In general terms a protocol defines header fields to describe each packet, a maximum length for the payload, and methods of processing information from the headers.

PSU (Power Supply Unit)
Transformer that converts AC mains power into 3.3V, 5V, and 12VDC to power components on the motherboard. The type of PSU must match the case and motherboard form factor.

PXE (Preboot Execution Environment)
A feature of a network adapter that allows the computer to boot by contacting a suitably configured server over the network (rather than using a local hard disk).

QIC (Quarter Inch Cartridge)
This type of storage media has been available for many years. Tape storage systems are generally a popular form of backup strategy as they are available at a low cost per byte price. Capacities range up to 4 GB (without compression).

Quota Management
Quota management provides an administrator with the ability to restrict disk storage on a per user basis. Windows supports quota management on NTFS partitions.

Rack
A storage solution for server and network equipment. Racks are designed to a standard width and height (measured in multiples of 1U or 1.75"). Racks offer better density, cooling, and security than ordinary office furniture.

RADIUS (Remote Authentication Dial-in User Service)
RADIUS is used by ISPs to authenticate and audit Internet access by account holders. RADIUS is now also widely used to manage remote and wireless authentication infrastructure. Users supply authentication information to RADIUS client devices, such as wireless access points. The client device then passes the authentication data to the RADIUS server, working as an AAA (Authentication, Authorization, and Accounting) server, which processes the request.

RAID (Redundant Array of Independent / Inexpensive Disks / Devices)
Using RAID technology, multiple hard disks can be configured to provide improved performance and/or protection for data (fault tolerance). Several levels of backup are suggested by this system, ranging from level 0 to level 6, each level representing a particular type of fault tolerance. Note that RAID 0 provides no fault tolerance.

RAS (Remote Access Service)
A server configured to process remote connections. Historically, this meant dial-up connections. These days, remote connections are more likely to be created via a VPN. Remote access policies define how users are able to connect to the server (media, protocols, authentication method, time of day restrictions, and so on) and rights and accessibility of resources over the connection.

Remote Desktop
A Windows remote control feature allowing specified users to log onto the Windows computer over the network and work remotely. Remote Desktop uses the RDP protocol over TCP port 3389.

Replication
The process of duplicating data held in multiple locations. Replication methods are typically either synchronous, meaning that writes must be committed to both locations at the same time using acknowledgements to confirm each transaction, or asynchronous, where one site is primary and the other secondary and writes to the secondary site are delayed.

RFID (Radio Frequency IDentification)
A chip allowing data to be read wirelessly. RFID tags are used in barcodes and smart cards.

Riser Card
A space-saving feature of some motherboards, a riser card puts the PC's expansion slots on a separate board installed at right-angles to the main board. This allows the system components to fit within a slimline case.

RJ (Registered Jack) Connector
Connector used for twisted pair cabling. 4-pair network cabling uses the larger RJ-45 connector. Modem / telephone cabling uses the RJ-11 connector.

Router
A router works at Layer 3 (Network) of the OSI model to move traffic between different logical networks (around an internetwork). Routers form the basic connections of the Internet. They allow data to take multiple paths to reach a destination (reducing the likelihood of transmission failure) based upon the parameters of speed, traffic loads, and cost. Routers are able to link networks using different transmission media. IP routers on a LAN can also be used to divide the network into logical subnets.

Sag
A sag can occur when the power supply entering a computer's components dips briefly below that which is required. Sags are commonly caused when certain types of device are turned on - especially those that require a large initial voltage - thus draining the local supply of power.

SAN (Storage Area Network)
A network of storage devices providing a flexible and high-capacity shared storage medium for servers.

SAS (Serial Attached SCSI)
Developed from parallel SCSI, SAS represents the highest performing disk technology available.

SATA (Serial ATA)
Legacy IDE/ATA uses parallel data transmission. Serial ATA allows for faster transfer rates and longer, more compact cabling (it features a 7-pin data connector). There are three SATA standards specifying bandwidths of 1.5 Gbps, 3 Gbps, and 6 Gbps respectively. SATA drives also use a new 15-pin power connector, though adapters for the old style 4-pin Molex connectors are available. External drives are also supported via the eSATA interface.

SCSI (Small Computer Systems Interface)
Legacy expansion bus standard allowing for the connection of internal and external devices. SCSI 1 defines the original 8-bit bus with a transfer rate of 5 MBps. SCSI 2 features a 16-bit data bus implementation (Wide SCSI) and a faster transfer rate (Fast SCSI) while maintaining backward compatibility with most of the original devices. SCSI 3 introduces further data rate enhancements (Ultra SCSI) and a serial SCSI standard (Firewire). Each device on a SCSI bus must be allocated a unique ID. The bus must also be terminated at both ends.

SDRAM (Synchronous DRAM)
Synchronous DRAM is a variant on the DRAM chip designed to run at the speed of the system clock thus accelerating the periodic refresh cycle times. SDRAM can run at much higher clock speeds than previous types of DRAM. Basic SDRAM is now obsolete and has been replaced by DDR/DDR2/3 SDRAM.

Sector
A sector is the term given to the regularly sized subdivision of a drive track. During low-level formatting, the size and position of the sectors is written to the disk so that the data can be placed into uniform spots that the drive head can easily access.

Service
A service (or daemon) is a non-interactive (typically) process that runs in the background to support an OS or application function, such as Plug-and-Play, the print spooler, DHCP, and so on. In Windows, services can be viewed, configured, and started/stopped via the Services console. You can also configure which services run at startup using msconfig. You can view background services (as well as applications) using the Processes tab in Task Manager.

Share
Any resource, such as a folder or printer device, which needs to be made available on a network must first be shared. Windows supports shares via File and Print Sharing. Linux can use a number of protocols, including NFS (Network File System) and SMB (Server Message Block, the protocol underpinning Windows file sharing).

Share Permissions
When a resource is shared over a network, it can be assigned Read, Change, Full Control, or Deny permissions on the share. Windows supports user level security; users have permissions depending upon who they are. Share permissions only protect the resource from access over the network. Local access can be secured by NTFS permissions.

SID Security Identifier)
A unique string identifying a user, group, or computer account on a Windows computer or domain network.

Simple Volume
Any partition on a dynamic disk formatted and ready to contain data is referred to as a simple volume.

SMB (Server Message Block)
The application protocol underpinning file and printer sharing on Windows networks. SMB is also sometimes referred to as the Common Internet File System (CIFS).

SMTP (Simple Mail Transfer Protocol)
The protocol used to send mail between hosts on the Internet. Messages are sent over TCP port 25.

SNMP (Simple Network Management Protocol)
TCP/IP application protocol used for monitoring and managing network devices. A management system collates data sent by agents running on each device. The agents maintain a Management Information Base of configuration and usage data. An agent can also generate a trap, alerting the management system of some notable event (such as a printer being out of paper). SNMP works over UDP ports 161 and 162 by default.

Spike
A spike can occur when electrical devices are turned off or when electrical storms are happening. Normally, spikes and surges are not sufficient to cause problems but occasionally big fluctuations may lead to the system crashing or hanging.

Spool
A generic term describing how a print output stream is passed from a client application and stored temporarily at a print server until the print monitor can route the job to the print device.

SSH (Secure Shell)
A remote administration and file copy program with connection security that is flexible enough to support VPNs too (using port forwarding). SSH runs on TCP port 22.

SSL (Secure Sockets Layer)
SSL was developed by Netscape to provide privacy and authentication over the Internet. It is application independent (working at Layer 5 [Session]) and can be used with a variety of TCP-based protocols, such as HTTP or FTP. The protocol is now being developed as Transport Layer Security (TLS).

ST (Straight Tip) Connector
Bayonet-style twist-and-lock connector for fiber optic cabling.

Straight-through Cable
Ethernet cables and connectors carry data over Transmit (Tx) and Receive (Rx) pairs. Normally, a host would be linked to a connectivity device such as a hub or a switch using straight-through (or standard) cabling and connectors. The hub receives the Tx signal from the host on its Tx pair, performs a crossover, and broadcasts it to the destination host on the Rx pair.

Striped Volume
A disk array access pattern where data is written in stripes to two or more disks sequentially, improving performance. Note that a RAID 0 striped volume provides no redundancy, and if any of the physical disks in the set fails, the whole volume will be lost.

Subnet Mask
An IP address is divided into a network ID and a host ID. In classful addressing, these portions are fixed (the default Class A mask is 255.0.0.0 or 8 network ID bits; Class B is 255.255.0.0 or 16 bits; Class C is 255.255.255.0 or 24 bits). A network can be divided into subnets by using host bits as a subnet ID. For example, if you have a Class B address and use 4 bits for subnetting, the mask will be 255.255.240.0 (20 bits for the network ID including subnet and 12 bits for host IDs). This can also be expressed in slash or classless notation as the network IP address and network prefix length in bits; for example 172.16.0.0/20. IPv6 does not use masks as the network ID and host ID are always 64 bits each. The network ID portion is hierarchical however, with different size prefixes defining larger and smaller network boundaries when routing. For example, Internet routers might only process the first 48 bits of the IPv6 address (a /48 prefix) while a /64 prefix would be used by LAN routers for subnetting.

Surge Suppressor
A simple device intended to protect electrical devices against the damaging effects of a power spike.

Switch
A network appliance capable of creating temporary virtual circuits between two Ethernet interfaces to reduce contention on the network. Switches have replaced hubs on most Ethernet networks. Most switches work at Layer 2 (Data Link) but more advanced models work at Layer 3 (Network), functioning much like a router.

System Partition
In Microsoft terminology, the system partition is the bootable partition on the hard disk. This is now usually separate to the boot partition, which contains the operating system.

Tape Drive
Tape drives are a popular form of data backup. They provide robust, high-speed, high-capacity storage systems. These drives are available for various PC ports (such as parallel or USB) and can be connected to the SCSI, ATAPI, or SATA buses.

TCP (Transmission Control Protocol)
Protocol in the TCP/IP suite providing connection-oriented, guaranteed delivery of packets.

Telnet
Basic terminal emulation software supporting a connection to the command interface of a remote computer. Telnet works over TCP port 23. Telnet communications are not secured.

Tower Server
A server mounted in standard PC-like tower case. Server cases are normally larger than ordinary PCs, with better cooling designs.

TPM (Trusted Platform Module)
A specification for hardware-based storage of digital certificates, keys, hashed passwords, and other user and platform identification information. Essentially it functions as an embedded smart card.

tracert
This TCP/IP utility is used to trace the route taken by a packet as it "hops" to the destination host on a remote network.

Troubleshooting
Troubleshooting requires a methodical approach. Having ensured that any data has been backed up, the first step is to gather information (from the user, error messages, diagnostic tools, or inspection). The next is to analyze the problem, again consulting documentation, web resources, or manufacturer's help resources if necessary. When analyzing a problem, it helps to categorize it (for example, between hardware and software). The next step is to choose and apply the most suitable solution. Having applied a solution, the next step is to test the system and related systems to verify functionality. The last step is to document the problem, steps taken, and the outcome. If the problem cannot be solved, it may be necessary to escalate it to another technician or manager.

Twisted Pair Cable
Twisted pair is two insulated copper wires twisted about each other; a cable is made up of a number of pairs (usually four in data networking). The twisting of the wires acts to reduce interference and crosstalk. Each pair of wires is twisted at a different rate to ensure that the pairs do not interfere with each other. Drawbacks of twisted pair cabling are its sensitivity to EMI and eavesdropping and its attenuation (it cannot be used for long-distance transmission). Cabling is categorized according to EIA/TIA standards; Cat3 cable was specified for 10 Mbps Ethernet and Cat5 for 100 Mbps (Fast Ethernet). Cabling is now either Cat5e or Cat6, both of which support Gigabit Ethernet. Most cabling is unshielded (UTP) though in continental Europe, foil screened cabling is commonly used (Foil Twisted Pair [FTP] or Screened Twisted Pair [ScTP]). Screened cable is less susceptible to EMI and eavesdropping but is more complex to install and consequently more expensive.

UDF (Universal Disk Format)
File system used for optical media, replacing CDFS (ISO 9660).

UDP (User Datagram Protocol)
Protocol in the TCP/IP suite operating at the transport layer to provide connectionless, non-guaranteed communication with no sequencing or flow control. Faster than TCP, but does not provide reliability.

UEFI (Unified Extensible Firmware Interface)
A type of system firmware providing support for 64-bit CPU operation at boot, full GUI and mouse operation at boot, and better boot security.

UNC (Universal Naming Convention)
Microsoft standard naming convention for local network resources, in the format \\server\share\file, where server is the name of a remote machine, share is the name of a folder on that machine, and file is the file you wish to access.

UNIX Systems
UNIX was originally developed by the telecommunications company AT&T during the late 1960s and early 1970s. UNIX is now a family of more than 20 related operating systems that are produced by various companies. It has become the operating system of choice for many high powered workstations. It is capable of supporting parallel processing and can run on a wide variety of platforms. UNIX offers a multitude of file systems in addition to its native system.

UPS (Uninterruptible Power Supplies)
Uninterruptible power supplies provide an alternative AC power supply in the event of power failure. A UPS requires an array of batteries, a charging circuit, an inverter to convert DC to AC current, a circuit to allow the system to take over from a failing power supply, and some degree of spike, surge, or brownout protection (possibly including a line conditioner).

UTM (Unified Threat Management)
All-in-one security appliances and technologies that combine the functions of a firewall, malware scanner, intrusion detection, vulnerability scanner, and so on.

Virtual Memory
Virtual memory (also known as swapping or paging) is an area on the hard disk allocated to contain pages of memory. When the operating system doesn't have sufficient physical memory (RAM) to perform a task (such as load a program) pages of memory are moved to the paging file (also known as a swap file). This frees physical RAM to enable the task to be completed. When the paged RAM is needed again, it is read back into memory. Understanding and configuring virtual memory settings is critical to optimizing the performance of the operating system.

Virtualization Technology
Software allowing a single computer (the host) to run multiple "guest" operating systems (or Virtual Machines [VM]). The VMs are configured via a hypervisor or VM Monitor (VMM). VMs can be connected using virtual networks (vSwitch) or leverage the host's network interface(s). It is also possible for the VMs to share data with the host (via shared folders or the clipboard for instance). VT is now used as major infrastructure in data centers as well as for testing and training.

Virus
A malicious software program that attempts to replicate by infecting the boot sector of disks or inserting itself in program code (for example, in application files or macro-enabled files).

VM (Virtual Machine)
In hardware virtualization, a partition in which a guest operating system can run on an emulated platform. A process-based VM is an application that runs within an OS to provide a platform-independent environment for software to run, with some degree of isolation from the host OS.

VMFS (Virtual Machine File System)
Disk file system developed by VMware for use with its virtualization products to store system images.

Voltage
The potential difference between two points (often likened to pressure in a water pipe) measured in Volts (V). In the UK, mains power is supplied at 220-240VAC. In the US, mains power is 110-120VAC.

Volume
A storage area formatted with the same file system. A volume might be mapped to a single hard disk partition or it could span multiple disks or represent a storage media that cannot be partitioned (such as an optical disc).

VPN (Virtual Private Network)
VPNs are created over public networks such as the Internet. Two networks may be connected end-to-end through a public network or a remote host may connect to a LAN via the public network. Encryption software is used to ensure privacy of data as messages transit through the public network. Protocols such as PPTP, L2TP, or SSL are utilized to provide the encryption.

WINS (Windows Internet Name Service)
In TCP/IP based networks, when computers attempt to access other computers using a name, the name must be converted into an IP address. This process is known as name resolution and is usually managed by DNS. Some Microsoft Windows networks use the WINS service to provide dynamic name resolution to legacy Windows clients (NT and 9x).

WMI (Windows Management Instrumentation)
Microsoft's implementation of WBEM (Web Based Enterprise Management) for its operating system and application server products. WBEM is a set of specifications for recording network device and software configuration and performance information and reporting it to a monitoring server. WBEM uses the Common Information Model (CIM). WMI supports both monitoring of the software and (via a scripting language) remote configuration.

WORM (Write Once, Read Many) Drive
A WORM drive is able to write data to a recordable CD disc only once, although the data can be read many times.

X.500
A widely supported and industry recognized directory standard. Handles directory access and editing. Too cumbersome for most vendors to implement - opting instead for LDAP based schemes.

Index

Where a term or phrase is abbreviated, the acronym is the form listed in the index. Note that index references are made to the nearest main heading for the topic in which the term appears.

E

F

G

H